Renault Scénic
Service & Repair Manual

R M Jex

Models covered

(4297 - 368)

Renault Scénic and Grand Scénic, including special/limited editions

Petrol engines: 1.4 litre (1390cc) & 1.6 litre (1598cc)
Turbo-Diesel engines: 1.5 litre (1461cc) & 1.9 litre (1870cc) dCi

Does NOT cover models with 2.0 litre petrol engines

© Haynes Publishing 2006

ABCDE
FGHIJ
K

A book in the **Haynes Service and Repair Manual Series**

ISBN 978 0 85733 894 5

British Library Cataloguing in Publication Data
A catalogue record for this book is available from the British Library.

Printed in the USA

Haynes Publishing
Sparkford, Yeovil, Somerset BA22 7JJ, England

Haynes North America, Inc
861 Lawrence Drive, Newbury Park, California 91320, USA

Haynes Publishing Nordiska AB
Box 1504, 751 45 UPPSALA, Sverige

Printed using 33-lb Resolute Book 65 4.0 from Resolute Forest Products Calhoun, TN mill. Resolute is a member of World Wildlife Fund's Climate Savers programme committed to significantly reducing GHG emissions. This paper uses 50% less wood fibre than traditional offset. The Calhoun Mill is certified to the following sustainable forest management and chain of custody standards: SFI, PEFC and FSC Controlled Wood.

Contents

LIVING WITH YOUR RENAULT SCÉNIC

MAINTENANCE

Routine maintenance and servicing

Contents

REPAIRS AND OVERHAUL

Engine and associated systems

Transmission

Brakes and suspension

Body equipment

Wiring diagrams

REFERENCE

Index

Advanced driving

Many people see the words 'advanced driving' and believe that it won't interest them or that it is a style of driving beyond their own abilities. Nothing could be further from the truth. Advanced driving is straightforward safe, sensible driving - the sort of driving we should all do every time we get behind the wheel.

An average of 10 people are killed every day on UK roads and 870 more are injured, some seriously. Lives are ruined daily, usually because somebody did something stupid. Something like 95% of all accidents are due to human error, mostly driver failure. Sometimes we make genuine mistakes - everyone does. Sometimes we have lapses of concentration. Sometimes we deliberately take risks.

For many people, the process of 'learning to drive' doesn't go much further than learning how to pass the driving test because of a common belief that good drivers are made by 'experience'.

Learning to drive by 'experience' teaches three driving skills:

☐ Quick reactions. (Whoops, that was close!)
☐ Good handling skills. (Horn, swerve, brake, horn).
☐ Reliance on vehicle technology. (Great stuff this ABS, stop in no distance even in the wet...)

Drivers whose skills are 'experience based' generally have a lot of near misses and the odd accident. The results can be seen every day in our courts and our hospital casualty departments.

Advanced drivers have learnt to control the risks by controlling the position and speed of their vehicle. They avoid accidents and near misses, even if the drivers around them make mistakes.

The key skills of advanced driving are **concentration,** effective all-round **observation, anticipation** and **planning.** When **good vehicle handling** is added to these skills, all driving situations can be approached and negotiated in a safe, methodical way, leaving nothing to chance.

Concentration means applying your mind to safe driving, completely excluding anything that's not relevant. Driving is usually the most dangerous activity that most of us undertake in our daily routines. It deserves our full attention.

Observation means not just looking, but seeing and seeking out the information found in the driving environment.

Anticipation means asking yourself what is happening, what you can reasonably expect to happen and what could happen unexpectedly. (One of the commonest words used in compiling accident reports is 'suddenly'.)

Planning is the link between seeing something and taking the appropriate action. For many drivers, planning is the missing link.

If you want to become a safer and more skilful driver and you want to enjoy your driving more, contact the Institute of Advanced Motorists at www.iam.org.uk, phone 0208 996 9600, or write to IAM House, 510 Chiswick High Road, London W4 5RG for an information pack.

Working on your car can be dangerous. This page shows just some of the potential risks and hazards, with the aim of creating a safety-conscious attitude.

General hazards

Scalding

• Don't remove the radiator or expansion tank cap while the engine is hot.
• Engine oil, automatic transmission fluid or power steering fluid may also be dangerously hot if the engine has recently been running.

Burning

• Beware of burns from the exhaust system and from any part of the engine. Brake discs and drums can also be extremely hot immediately after use.

Crushing

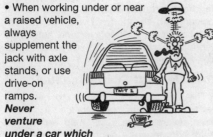

• When working under or near a raised vehicle, always supplement the jack with axle stands, or use drive-on ramps. *Never venture under a car which is only supported by a jack.*
• Take care if loosening or tightening high-torque nuts when the vehicle is on stands. Initial loosening and final tightening should be done with the wheels on the ground.

Fire

• Fuel is highly flammable; fuel vapour is explosive.
• Don't let fuel spill onto a hot engine.
• Do not smoke or allow naked lights (including pilot lights) anywhere near a vehicle being worked on. Also beware of creating sparks (electrically or by use of tools).
• Fuel vapour is heavier than air, so don't work on the fuel system with the vehicle over an inspection pit.
• Another cause of fire is an electrical overload or short-circuit. Take care when repairing or modifying the vehicle wiring.
• Keep a fire extinguisher handy, of a type suitable for use on fuel and electrical fires.

Electric shock

• Ignition HT voltage can be dangerous, especially to people with heart problems or a pacemaker. Don't work on or near the ignition system with the engine running or the ignition switched on.

• Mains voltage is also dangerous. Make sure that any mains-operated equipment is correctly earthed. Mains power points should be protected by a residual current device (RCD) circuit breaker.

Fume or gas intoxication

• Exhaust fumes are poisonous; they often contain carbon monoxide, which is rapidly fatal if inhaled. Never run the engine in a confined space such as a garage with the doors shut.
• Fuel vapour is also poisonous, as are the vapours from some cleaning solvents and paint thinners.

Poisonous or irritant substances

• Avoid skin contact with battery acid and with any fuel, fluid or lubricant, especially antifreeze, brake hydraulic fluid and Diesel fuel. Don't syphon them by mouth. If such a substance is swallowed or gets into the eyes, seek medical advice.
• Prolonged contact with used engine oil can cause skin cancer. Wear gloves or use a barrier cream if necessary. Change out of oil-soaked clothes and do not keep oily rags in your pocket.
• Air conditioning refrigerant forms a poisonous gas if exposed to a naked flame (including a cigarette). It can also cause skin burns on contact.

Asbestos

• Asbestos dust can cause cancer if inhaled or swallowed. Asbestos may be found in gaskets and in brake and clutch linings. When dealing with such components it is safest to assume that they contain asbestos.

Special hazards

Hydrofluoric acid

• This extremely corrosive acid is formed when certain types of synthetic rubber, found in some O-rings, oil seals, fuel hoses etc, are exposed to temperatures above 400ºC. The rubber changes into a charred or sticky substance containing the acid. *Once formed, the acid remains dangerous for years. If it gets onto the skin, it may be necessary to amputate the limb concerned.*
• When dealing with a vehicle which has suffered a fire, or with components salvaged from such a vehicle, wear protective gloves and discard them after use.

The battery

• Batteries contain sulphuric acid, which attacks clothing, eyes and skin. Take care when topping-up or carrying the battery.
• The hydrogen gas given off by the battery is highly explosive. Never cause a spark or allow a naked light nearby. Be careful when connecting and disconnecting battery chargers or jump leads.

Air bags

• Air bags can cause injury if they go off accidentally. Take care when removing the steering wheel and/or facia. Special storage instructions may apply.

Diesel injection equipment

• Diesel injection pumps supply fuel at very high pressure. Take care when working on the fuel injectors and fuel pipes.

⚠ *Warning: Never expose the hands, face or any other part of the body to injector spray; the fuel can penetrate the skin with potentially fatal results.*

Remember...

DO

• Do use eye protection when using power tools, and when working under the vehicle.

• Do wear gloves or use barrier cream to protect your hands when necessary.

• Do get someone to check periodically that all is well when working alone on the vehicle.

• Do keep loose clothing and long hair well out of the way of moving mechanical parts.

• Do remove rings, wristwatch etc, before working on the vehicle – especially the electrical system.

• Do ensure that any lifting or jacking equipment has a safe working load rating adequate for the job.

DON'T

• Don't attempt to lift a heavy component which may be beyond your capability – get assistance.

• Don't rush to finish a job, or take unverified short cuts.

• Don't use ill-fitting tools which may slip and cause injury.

• Don't leave tools or parts lying around where someone can trip over them. Mop up oil and fuel spills at once.

• Don't allow children or pets to play in or near a vehicle being worked on.

Renault Scénic

The Renault Scénic II was introduced into the UK in September 2003, replacing the previous successful Scénic MPV range. The new model takes its styling cues from its sister car, the controversially-styled Mégane. Design innovations include a keyless card entry system, automatic headlights and wipers, and an assortment of handy storage compartments being offered.

The engine range is essentially carried over from the previous Scénic, but all units feature upgrades to boost engine power, while reducing fuel consumption and emissions. In the new car, the petrol engines are 16-valve double overhead camshaft designs, with the 1.6 litre unit having variable valve timing (VVT).

New to the range of direct-injection common-rail diesel engines is a 1.5 litre unit, first seen in the Clio.

In common with the rest of the modern Renault range, the new Scénic offers class-leading levels of passenger safety, scoring a full five stars in the Euro NCAP safety tests. To an impact-absorbing bodyshell and highly-rigid cabin are added adaptive front airbags, side and curtain airbags, side impact bars, and seat belt tensioners with load limiters. With all-wheel disc brakes, ABS, EBD and Brake Assist on every model, it's clear that Renault have made a big commitment to active as well as passive safety with the new car.

The Scénic is only available as a 5-door Hatchback, but in February 2004, the longer-wheelbase 7-seater Grand Scénic arrived, offering an alternative to the standard 5-seater model.

All models have front-wheel-drive, with a choice of five- or six-speed manual transmissions (or an optional four-speed automatic on some models, offering sequential shifting). The front suspension is of conventional MacPherson strut type, incorporating lower arms, and an anti-roll bar; at the rear, a semi-independent beam axle is combined with compact under-floor springs and inclined shock absorbers to maximise the load/passenger area.

The car has a high equipment level, even at the lower end of the model range. Besides the valuable safety equipment already mentioned, all feature variable power steering, trip computer, engine immobiliser, rear seat headrests, radio/cassette, remote central locking, and electric front windows/mirrors. Air conditioning, CD player and automatic handbrake are among the equipment fitted higher up the range.

Your Renault Scénic manual

The aim of this manual is to help you get the best value from your car. It can do so in several ways. It can help you decide what work must be done (even should you choose to get it done by a garage). It will also provide information on routine maintenance and servicing, and give a logical course of action and diagnosis when random faults occur. However, it is hoped that you will use the manual by tackling the work yourself. On simpler jobs it may even be quicker than booking the car into a garage and going there twice, to leave and collect it. Perhaps most important, a lot of money can be saved by avoiding the costs a garage must charge to cover its labour and overheads.

The manual has drawings and descriptions to show the function of the various components so that their layout can be understood. Tasks are described and photographed in a clear step-by-step sequence.

References to the 'left' and 'right' of the car are in the sense of a person in the driver's seat, facing forwards.

Acknowledgements

Thanks are due to Draper tools Limited, who provided some of the workshop tools, and to all those people at Sparkford who helped in the production of this manual.

We take great pride in the accuracy of information given in this manual, but car manufacturers make alterations and design changes during the production run of a particular car of which they do not inform us. No liability can be accepted by the authors or publishers for loss, damage or injury caused by any errors in, or omissions from, the information given.

Renault Grand Scénic

The following pages are intended to help in dealing with common roadside emergencies and breakdowns. You will find more detailed fault finding information at the back of the manual, and repair information in the main chapters.

If your car won't start and the starter motor doesn't turn

☐ Open the bonnet and make sure that the battery terminals are clean and tight.

☐ Switch on the headlights and try to start the engine. If the headlights go very dim when you're trying to start, the battery is probably flat. Get out of trouble by jump starting (see next page) using another car.

If your car won't start even though the starter motor turns as normal

☐ Is there fuel in the tank?

☐ Has the engine immobiliser been deactivated? This should happen automatically, or when the keycard is inserted into the facia slot. However, if a faulty card causes the card reader slot to flash rapidly, consult a Renault dealer for advice.

☐ On manual transmission models, if the car is in gear, the clutch must be depressed; otherwise, the footbrake must be applied.

☐ If it's a model with automatic transmission, the footbrake must be applied, and the selector must be in N or P.

☐ Is there moisture on electrical components under the bonnet? With the ignition off, wipe off any obvious dampness with a dry cloth. Spray a water-repellent aerosol product (WD-40 or equivalent) on ignition and fuel system electrical connectors like those shown in the photos. Pay special attention to the ignition coil wiring connectors.

A Check the condition and security of the battery connections.

B With the ignition off, check that the wiring connectors are securely connected to the four ignition coils (petrol models).

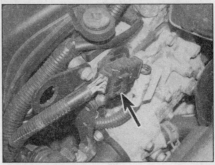

C Check that the camshaft position sensor wiring plug is securely connected.

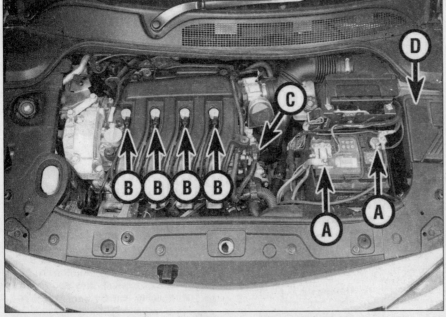

Check that electrical connections are secure (with the ignition switched off) and spray them with a water-dispersant spray like WD-40 if you suspect a problem due to damp

D With the ignition off, check the fuses and relays in the engine compartment fusebox.

Jump starting

When jump-starting a car using a booster battery, observe the following precautions:

✔ Before connecting the booster battery, remove the key card from the facia slot.

✔ Ensure that all electrical equipment (lights, heater, wipers, etc) is switched off.

✔ Make sure that the booster battery is the same voltage as the discharged one in the vehicle.

✔ Take note of any special precautions printed on the battery case.

✔ If the battery is being jump-started from the battery in another vehicle, the two vehicles MUST NOT TOUCH each other.

✔ Make sure that the transmission is in neutral, and press the footbrake.

✔ Once the booster battery has been connected, insert the key card into the facia slot.

 HAYNES HiNT Jump starting will get you out of trouble, but you must correct whatever made the battery go flat in the first place. There are three possibilities:

1 The battery has been drained by repeated attempts to start, or by leaving the lights on.

2 The charging system is not working properly (alternator drivebelt slack or broken, alternator wiring fault or alternator itself faulty).

3 The battery itself is at fault (electrolyte low, or battery worn out).

1 Connect one end of the red jump lead to the positive (+) terminal of the flat battery

2 Connect the other end of the red lead to the positive (+) terminal of the booster battery.

3 Connect one end of the black jump lead to the negative (-) terminal of the booster battery

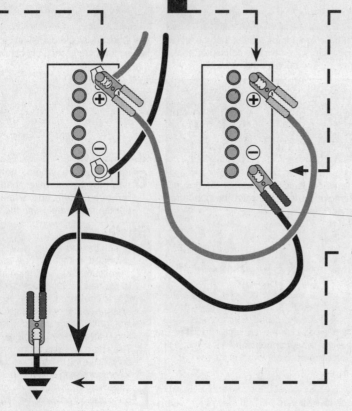

4 Connect the other end of the black jump lead to a bolt or bracket on the engine block, well away from the battery, on the vehicle to be started.

5 Make sure that the jump leads will not come into contact with the fan, drive-belts or other moving parts of the engine.

6 Start the engine using the booster battery and run it at idle speed. Switch on the lights, rear window demister and heater blower motor, then disconnect the jump leads in the reverse order of connection. Turn off the lights etc.

Wheel changing

⚠️ **Warning:** *Do not change a wheel in a situation where you risk being hit by other traffic. On busy roads, try to stop in a lay-by or a gateway. Be wary of passing traffic while changing the wheel – it is easy to become distracted by the job in hand.*

Preparation

- ☐ When a puncture occurs, stop as soon as it is safe to do so.
- ☐ Park on firm level ground, if possible, and well out of the way of other traffic.
- ☐ Use hazard warning lights if necessary.

- ☐ If you have one, use a warning triangle to alert other drivers of your presence.
- ☐ Apply the handbrake and engage first or reverse gear (or P on models with automatic transmission).

- ☐ Chock the wheel diagonally opposite the one being removed – a couple of large stones will do for this.
- ☐ If the ground is soft, use a flat piece of wood to spread the load under the jack.

Note: *On the Grand Scénic, the spare wheel is an optional extra. A tyre repair and inflation kit is provided – refer to the vehicle handbook under 'Punctures' for details on how this is used.*

Changing the wheel

1 On the Scénic, the spare wheel and tools are under boot carpet. Fold back the carpet, then lift out the tool tray, which contains the jack, wheelbrace, towing eye, and hub cap removal tool.

2 Unscrew the spare wheel retainer anti-clockwise, and lift out the spare wheel.

3 Remove the wheel trim or centre cap from the punctured wheel, using the tool provided. Use the wheelbrace to loosen each wheel bolt by half a turn.

4 Locate the jack head into the jacking point nearest the wheel to be changed. The jacking points are small 'cups' on the base of the door sill, indicated by an arrowhead marking. Only use the jack on firm, level ground.

5 Turn the jack handle clockwise until the wheel is raised clear of the ground. Remove the bolts and lift the punctured wheel clear.

6 Fit the spare wheel, noting that the tyre may be narrower than the one just removed. Refit the wheel bolts, and tighten moderately with the wheelbrace.

7 Lower the car to the ground, then finally tighten the wheel bolts in a diagonal sequence. Refit the wheel trim or centre cap, where possible. Ideally, the wheel bolts should be slackened and retightened to the specified torque at the earliest opportunity. Remove the wheel chocks and stow the jack and tools in the correct locations in the car.

Finally . . .

- ☐ Check the tyre pressure on the wheel just fitted. If it is low, or if you don't have a pressure gauge with you, drive slowly to the nearest garage and inflate the tyre to the right pressure. **Note:** *The tyre pressure monitoring system will register a fault until the punctured wheel is repaired and refitted – see Chapter 10.*
- ☐ The spare wheel is for temporary use only. Drive with extra care, especially when cornering – limit yourself to a maximum of 70 mph, and to the shortest possible journeys, while it is fitted.
- ☐ Have the damaged tyre or wheel repaired as soon as possible.

Identifying leaks

Puddles on the garage floor or drive, or obvious wetness under the bonnet or underneath the car, suggest a leak that needs investigating. It can sometimes be difficult to decide where the leak is coming from, especially if the engine bay is very dirty already. Leaking oil or fluid can also be blown rearwards by the passage of air under the car, giving a false impression of where the problem lies.

Warning: Most automotive oils and fluids are poisonous. Wash them off skin, and change out of contaminated clothing, without delay.

 The smell of a fluid leaking from the car may provide a clue to what's leaking. Some fluids are distinctively coloured. It may help to clean the car carefully and to park it over some clean paper overnight as an aid to locating the source of the leak.
Remember that some leaks may only occur while the engine is running.

Sump oil

Engine oil may leak from the drain plug...

Oil from filter

...or from the base of the oil filter.

Gearbox oil

Gearbox oil can leak from the seals at the inboard ends of the driveshafts.

Antifreeze

Leaking antifreeze often leaves a crystalline deposit like this.

Brake fluid

A leak occurring at a wheel is almost certainly brake fluid.

Power steering fluid

Power steering fluid may leak from the pipe connectors on the steering rack.

Towing

When all else fails, you may find yourself having to get a tow home – or of course you may be helping somebody else. Long-distance recovery should only be done by a garage or breakdown service. For shorter distances, DIY towing using another car is easy enough, but observe the following points:

☐ A towing eye is located with the jack in the luggage compartment (see *Wheel changing*). To fit the towing eye, prise out the cover on the side of the bumper, and remove it. Screw the towing eye in as far as it will go. Tighten the towing eye with the wheelbrace.

☐ Use a proper tow-rope – they are not expensive. The vehicle being towed must display an ON TOW sign in its rear window.

☐ Insert the keycard into its slot and press the starter button (to turn on the ignition) when the vehicle is being towed, so that the steering lock is released, and that the direction indicator and brake lights will work.

☐ Before being towed, release the handbrake and select neutral on the transmission. On models with automatic transmission, the car **must** be towed with its front wheels raised clear of the ground, or transmission damage may occur. Otherwise, the safe towing speed is no more than 12 mph, for no further than 18 miles.

☐ Note that greater-than-usual pedal pressure will be required to operate the brakes, since

the vacuum servo unit is only operational with the engine running.

☐ If the ignition is not switched on, or the battery is flat, the electric power steering may not work, resulting in very heavy steering.

☐ The driver of the car being towed must keep the tow-rope taut at all times to avoid snatching.

☐ Make sure that both drivers know the route before setting off.

☐ Only drive at moderate speeds and keep the distance towed to a minimum. Drive smoothly and allow plenty of time for slowing down at junctions.

Introduction

There are some very simple checks which need only take a few minutes to carry out, but which could save you a lot of inconvenience and expense.

These *Weekly checks* require no great skill or special tools, and the small amount of time they take to perform could prove to be very well spent, for example:

☐ Keeping an eye on tyre condition and pressures, will not only help to stop them wearing out prematurely, but could also save your life.

☐ Many breakdowns are caused by electrical problems. Battery-related faults are particularly common, and a quick check on a regular basis will often prevent the majority of these.

☐ If your car develops a brake fluid leak, the first time you might know about it is when your brakes don't work properly. Checking the level regularly will give advance warning of this kind of problem.

☐ If the oil or coolant levels run low, the cost of repairing any engine damage will be far greater than fixing the leak, for example.

Underbonnet check points

Note: *All models have electric power steering. As this is not a hydraulically-operated system, no power steering fluid reservoir is present.*

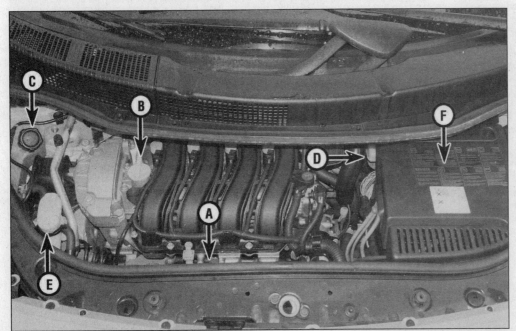

◀ **1.6 litre petrol engine (1.4 litre similar)**

A *Engine oil level dipstick*

B *Engine oil filler cap*

C *Coolant reservoir (expansion) tank*

D *Brake and clutch fluid reservoir*

E *Washer fluid reservoir*

F *Battery*

◀ **1.5 litre diesel engine (1.9 litre similar)**

A *Engine oil level dipstick*

B *Engine oil filler cap*

C *Coolant reservoir (expansion) tank*

D *Brake and clutch fluid reservoir*

E *Washer fluid reservoir*

F *Battery*

Engine oil level

Before you start

✔ Make sure that the car is on level ground.
✔ Check the oil level before the car is driven, or at least 5 minutes after the engine has been switched off.

HAYNES HINT *If the oil is checked immediately after driving the vehicle, some of the oil will remain in the upper engine components, resulting in an inaccurate reading on the dipstick.*

The correct oil

Modern engines place great demands on their oil. It is very important that the correct oil for your car is used (see *Lubricants and fluids*).

Car care

● If you have to add oil frequently, you should check whether you have any oil leaks. Place some clean paper under the car overnight, and check for stains in the morning. If there are no leaks, then the engine may be burning oil.
● Always maintain the level between the upper and lower dipstick marks (see photo 3). If the level is too low, severe engine damage may occur. Oil seal failure may result if the engine is overfilled by adding too much oil.

1 Pull out the dipstick. The dipstick is located at the front of the engine on all engines except the 1.9 litre diesel (see *Underbonnet check points* on page 0•11 for exact location). On 1.9 litre diesel engines, the dipstick is incorporated into the oil filler cap – unscrew and remove it.

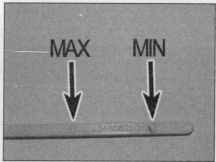

3 Note the oil level on the end of the dipstick, which should be within the 'hatched' area, between the upper and lower marks. Approximately 1.5 to 2.0 litres of oil will raise the level from the lower to the upper mark.

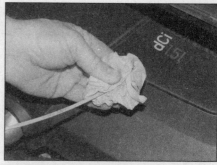

2 Using a clean rag or paper towel, wipe all the oil from the dipstick. Insert the clean dipstick into the tube (or screw the oil filler cap fully on) as far as it will go, then withdraw/unscrew it again.

4 Oil is added through the filler cap. Unscrew the filler cap, then top-up the level – a funnel is essential on many engines, due to the awkward access. Add the oil slowly, checking the level on the dipstick often. Don't overfill.

Coolant level

Warning: Do not attempt to remove the expansion tank pressure cap when the engine is hot, as there is a very great risk of scalding. Do not leave open containers of coolant about, as it is poisonous.

Car Care

● With a sealed-type cooling system, adding coolant should not be necessary on a regular basis. If frequent topping-up is required, it is likely there is a leak. Check the radiator, all hoses and joint faces for signs of staining or wetness, and rectify as necessary.

● It is important that antifreeze is used in the cooling system all year round, not just during the winter months. Don't top up with water alone, as the antifreeze will become diluted.

1 The coolant level varies with the temperature of the engine. The expansion tank (at the rear of the engine compartment, behind the right-hand headlight) has two sets of MAX and MIN level markings. When cold, the level should be between the two marks. When the engine is hot, the level may rise slightly above the MAX mark.

2 If topping-up is necessary, wait until the engine is cold, then remove the cap on the expansion tank.

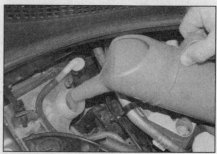

3 Add a mixture of water and antifreeze to the expansion tank, until the coolant is up to the MAX mark. Use antifreeze of the same type as that which is already in the system. Refit the cap securely.

Brake and clutch* fluid level

*The brake fluid reservoir also supplies fluid to the clutch master cylinder.

Safety first!

● If the reservoir requires repeated topping-up, this is an indication of a fluid leak somewhere in the system, which should be investigated immediately.

● The fluid level in the reservoir will drop slightly as the brake pads wear down, but the fluid level must never be allowed to drop below the MIN mark.

● If a leak is suspected, the car should not be driven until the braking system has been checked. Never take any risks where brakes are concerned.

 Warning: Brake fluid can harm your eyes and damage painted surfaces, so use extreme caution when handling and pouring it. Do not use fluid which has been standing open for some time, as it absorbs moisture from the air, which can cause a dangerous loss of braking effectiveness.

1 The MAX and MIN marks are indicated on the side of the reservoir, which is located at the back of the engine compartment, on the transmission side. The fluid level must be kept between these two marks.

2 If topping-up is necessary, unclip and lift off the engine top cover. For better access, also remove the battery cover, which is secured by a screw/clip at the front, and two bolts at the back.

3 Wipe the area around the filler cap with a clean rag, then unscrew the cap. When adding fluid, it's a good idea to inspect the reservoir. The fluid should be changed if it appears to be dark, or if dirt is visible.

4 Carefully add fluid, avoiding spilling it on surrounding paintwork. Use only the specified hydraulic fluid; mixing different types of fluid can cause damage to the system and/or a loss of braking effectiveness. After filling to the correct level, refit the cap securely. Wipe off any spilt fluid.

Screen washer fluid level

● Screenwash additives not only keep the windscreen clean during bad weather, they also prevent the washer system freezing in cold weather – which is when you are likely to need it most. Don't top-up using plain water, as the screenwash will become diluted, and will freeze in cold weather.

 Warning: On no account use engine coolant antifreeze in the screen washer system – this may damage the paintwork.

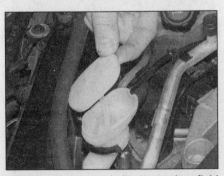

1 The windscreen/tailgate washer fluid reservoir filler neck is located at the front of the engine compartment, behind the right-hand headlight. Unclip and remove the cap.

2 When topping-up the reservoir, a screenwash additive should be added in the quantities recommended on the bottle.

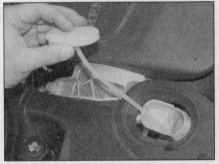

3 The bottle can safely be filled until the level is visible inside. Some models have a 'tube dipstick' attached to the cap – with these, place a finger over the hole in the cap, and withdraw the tube; if sufficient fluid is present, a level will be seen in the tube.

Tyre condition and pressure

It is very important that tyres are in good condition, and at the correct pressure – having a tyre failure at any speed is highly dangerous. Tyre wear is influenced by driving style – harsh braking and acceleration, or fast cornering, will all produce more rapid tyre wear. As a general rule, the front tyres wear out faster than the rears, and some people swap (or 'rotate') tyres from front to rear, to even up wear. However, if this is completely effective, you may incur the expense of replacing four tyres at once! **Note:** *The tyre pressure monitoring system on the Scénic will produce an error message if the tyres are rotated.*

Remove any nails or stones embedded in the tread before they penetrate the tyre to cause deflation. If removing a nail reveals a hole, refit the nail to mark the hole's position, then immediately change the wheel and have the tyre repaired.

Regularly check the tyres for damage in the form of cuts or bulges, especially in the sidewalls. Periodically remove the wheels, and clean any dirt or mud from the inside and outside surfaces. Examine the wheel rims for signs of corrosion or damage. Alloy wheels are easily damaged by 'kerbing' whilst parking; steel wheels may also become dented or buckled. A new wheel is very often the only way to overcome severe damage.

New tyres should be balanced when they are fitted, but it may become necessary to re-balance them as they wear, or if the balance weights fitted to the wheel rim should fall off. Unbalanced tyres will wear more quickly, as will the steering and suspension components. Wheel imbalance is normally signified by vibration particularly at a certain speed (typically around 50 mph). If this vibration is felt only through the steering, then it is likely that just the front wheels need balancing. If, however, the vibration is felt through the whole car, the rear wheels could be out of balance. Wheel balancing should be carried out by a tyre dealer or garage.

1 *Tread Depth - visual check*
The original tyres have tread wear safety bands (B), which will appear when the tread depth reaches approximately 1.6 mm. The band positions are indicated by a triangular mark on the tyre sidewall (A).

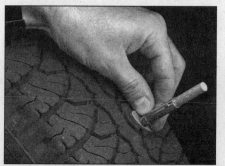

2 *Tread Depth - manual check*
Alternatively, tread wear can be monitored with a simple, inexpensive device known as a tread depth indicator gauge.

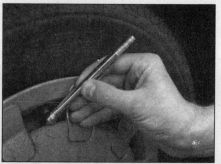

3 *Tyre Pressure Check*
Check the tyre pressures regularly with the tyres cold. Do not adjust the tyre pressures immediately after the vehicle has been used, or an inaccurate setting will result.

Tyre tread wear patterns

Shoulder Wear

Underinflation (wear on both sides)
Under-inflation will cause overheating of the tyre, because the tyre will flex too much, and the tread will not sit correctly on the road surface. This will cause a loss of grip and excessive wear, not to mention the danger of sudden tyre failure due to heat build-up.
Check and adjust pressures
Incorrect wheel camber (wear on one side)
Repair or renew suspension parts
Hard cornering
Reduce speed!

Centre Wear

Overinflation
Over-inflation will cause rapid wear of the centre part of the tyre tread, coupled with reduced grip, harsher ride, and the danger of shock damage occurring in the tyre casing.
Check and adjust pressures

If you sometimes have to inflate your car's tyres to the higher pressures specified for maximum load or sustained high speed, don't forget to reduce the pressures to normal afterwards.

Uneven Wear

Front tyres may wear unevenly as a result of wheel misalignment. Most tyre dealers and garages can check and adjust the wheel alignment (or "tracking") for a modest charge.
Incorrect camber or castor
Repair or renew suspension parts
Malfunctioning suspension
Repair or renew suspension parts
Unbalanced wheel
Balance tyres
Incorrect toe setting
Adjust front wheel alignment
Note: *The feathered edge of the tread which typifies toe wear is best checked by feel.*

Wiper blades

Check the condition of the wiper blades; if they are cracked or show any signs of deterioration, or if the glass swept area is smeared, renew them. For maximum clarity of vision, wiper blades should be renewed annually, as a matter of course.

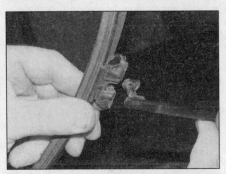

1 To remove a windscreen wiper blade, first slide the cover off the centre of the blade.

2 Pull the arm fully away from the screen until it locks. Unclip the blade from the arm.

3 Don't forget to check the tailgate wiper blade as well, which unclips directly from the arm.

Battery

Caution: Before carrying out any work on the vehicle battery, read the precautions given in 'Safety first!' at the start of this manual.

✔ Make sure that the battery tray is in good condition, and that the clamp is tight. Corrosion on the tray, retaining clamp and the battery itself can be removed with a solution of water and baking soda. Thoroughly rinse all cleaned areas with water. Any metal parts damaged by corrosion should be covered with a zinc-based primer, then painted.

✔ Periodically (approximately every three months), check the charge condition of the battery as described in Chapter 5A.

✔ If the battery is flat, and you need to jump start your vehicle, see *Roadside Repairs*.

1 The battery is located at the front of the engine compartment, behind the left-hand headlight. To access the battery, a cover has to be removed, secured by two bolts at the back, and one screw/clip at the front. The exterior of the battery should be inspected periodically for damage such as a cracked case or cover.

2 Check the tightness of the battery cable clamps to ensure good electrical connections. You should not be able to move them. Also check each cable for cracks and frayed conductors.

Battery corrosion can be kept to a minimum by applying a layer of petroleum jelly to the clamps and terminals after they are reconnected.

3 If corrosion (white, fluffy deposits) is evident, remove the cables from the battery terminals, clean them with a small wire brush, then refit them. Automotive stores sell a tool for cleaning the battery post . . .

4 . . . as well as the battery cable clamps.

Electrical systems

✔ Check all external lights and the horn. Refer to the appropriate Sections of Chapter 12 for details if any of the circuits are found to be inoperative.

✔ Visually check all accessible wiring connectors, harnesses and retaining clips for security, and for signs of chafing or damage.

If you need to check your brake lights and indicators unaided, back up to a wall or garage door and operate the lights. The reflected light should show if they are working properly.

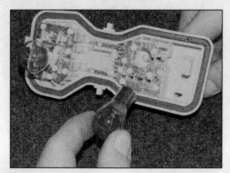

1 If a single indicator light, brake light or headlight has failed, it is likely that a bulb has blown and will need to be replaced. Refer to Chapter 12 for details. If both brake lights have failed, it is possible that the brake light switch operated by the brake pedal has failed. Refer to Chapter 9 for details.

2 If more than one indicator light or headlight has failed, it is likely that either a fuse has blown, or that there is a fault in the circuit (see Chapter 12). The main fuses are mounted behind a panel above the glovebox. Open the glovebox and pull down the fuse access panel at the back.

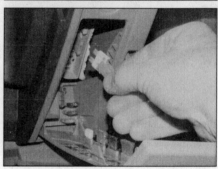

3 To replace a blown fuse, remove it using the plastic tweezer tool provided (where applicable). Fit a new fuse of the same rating, available from car accessory shops. It is important that you find the reason that the fuse blew (see Electrical fault finding in Chapter 12).

Lubricants and fluids

Petrol engine *	Engine oil, SAE 5W-30, 5W-40, 10W-30 or 10W-40, to specification ACEA A1, A3 or A5
Diesel engine *	Engine oil, SAE 5W-40, 10W-40 or 10W-50, to specification ACEA B3 or B4
Cooling system	Ethylene glycol-based antifreeze suitable for use in mixed-metal engines – Glacéol RX type D
Manual transmission	TransElf TRJ 75W-80 (Grand Scénic with 5-speed transmission – TransElf TRT 75W-80)
Automatic transmission	Elf Renaultmatic D3 Syn (Dexron III ATF)
Brake and clutch systems	Hydraulic fluid to DOT 4

*Oil viscosity 20W-50 should not be used. On diesel engines, oil viscosity 5W-30 or 10W-30 must not be used.

Tyre pressures

Note: *Pressures given here are a guide only, and apply to original-equipment tyres – the recommended pressures may vary if any other make or type of tyre is fitted. Check with the car handbook for latest recommendations, and for usage other than that quoted below.*

	Front	Rear
Scénic - Normal use*		
195/65 R15 and 205/55 R17 tyres	2.4 bar (35 psi)	2.2 bar (32 psi)
205/60 R16 and 205-650 R440 tyres	2.3 bar (33 psi)	2.1 bar (30 psi)
205/55 R16 tyres	2.2 bar (32 psi)	2.0 bar (29 psi)
Grand Scénic - Normal use*		
205/60 R16 tyres:		
1.6 petrol and 1.5 diesel models	2.2 bar (32 psi)	2.2 bar (32 psi)
1.9 diesel models	2.3 bar (33 psi)	2.2 bar (32 psi)
205/55 R17 tyres	2.4 bar (35 psi)	2.2 bar (32 psi)
Emergency spare tyre		
Typical pressure (front or rear)	2.5 bar (36 psi)	

*Normal use means no prolonged motorway driving, and in the case of the Grand Scénic, with less than 6 passengers. Consult the car's handbook for the increased pressures required for use under these conditions.

Chapter 1 Part A:
Routine maintenance and servicing – petrol models

Contents

Degrees of difficulty

| **Easy,** suitable for novice with little experience | | **Fairly easy,** suitable for beginner with some experience | | **Fairly difficult,** suitable for competent DIY mechanic | | **Difficult,** suitable for experienced DIY mechanic | | **Very difficult,** suitable for expert DIY or professional | 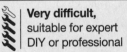 |

Lubricants and fluids

Refer to *Weekly checks* on page 0•17

Capacities

Engine oil (including oil filter)

1.4 and 1.6 litre engines . . . . 4.9 litres
Difference between MAX and MIN dipstick marks. . . . . 1.5 to 2.0 litres

Cooling system . . . . 6.0 to 6.5 litres

Manual transmission . . . . 2.8 litres

Automatic transmission . . . . 6.0 litres

Fuel tank . . . . 60 litres approx (13 gallons)

Auxiliary drivebelt

Belt tension:
   Models without air conditioning . . . . 233 ± 5 Hz (measured with Renault tool 1715)
   Models with air conditioning . . . . Automatic tensioner

Cooling system

Antifreeze mixture:	Antifreeze	Water
Protection to –23°C	35%	65%
Protection to –40°C	50%	50%

Fuel system

Specified idle speed (non-adjustable):
   1.4 litre engines . . . . 750 ± 50 rpm
   1.6 litre engines . . . . 700 ± 30 rpm
Idle mixture CO content (non-adjustable) . . . . 0.5% max (0.3% max at 2000 rpm)

Ignition system

Firing order 1-3-4-2
Location of No 1 cylinder . . . . Flywheel end
Ignition timing . . . . Controlled by ECU – see Chapter 5B

Spark plugs:

	Type	Electrode gap
All engines	Eyquem RFN 58 LZ	0.95 ± 0.05 mm
	Champion RC 87 YCL	0.95 ± 0.05 mm

Brakes

Brake pad friction material minimum thickness . . . . 1.5 mm
Handbrake adjustment dimension (nominal setting for new cables) . . . 17 mm

Torque wrench settings

	Nm	lbf ft
Roadwheel bolts.	130	96
Side support plate bolts	21	15
Spark plugs	25 to 30	18 to 22

The maintenance intervals in this manual are provided with the assumption that you, not the dealer, will be carrying out the work. These are the minimum maintenance intervals recommended by us for cars driven daily. If you wish to keep your car in peak condition at all times, you may wish to perform some of these procedures more often. We encourage frequent maintenance, because it enhances the efficiency, performance and resale value of your car.

If the car is driven in dusty areas, used to tow a trailer, or driven frequently at slow speeds (idling in traffic) or on short journeys, more frequent maintenance intervals are recommended.

When the car is new, it should be serviced by a factory-authorised dealer service department, in order to preserve the factory warranty.

Every 250 miles (400 km) or weekly
☐ Refer to Weekly checks

Every 9000 miles (15 000 km)
☐ Renew the engine oil and filter (Section 3)

Note: *Frequent oil and filter changes are good for the engine. We recommend changing the oil at the mileage specified here, or at least once a year.*

Every 18 000 miles (30 000 km) or 2 years, whichever comes first
In addition to all the items listed previously, carry out the following:
☐ Renew the pollen filter (Section 4)
☐ Check the braking system (Section 5)
☐ Check the operation of the clutch (Section 6)
☐ Check the condition of the auxiliary drivebelt (Section 7)
☐ Check the condition of the seat belts (Section 8)
☐ Check the operation of all electrical equipment (Section 9)
☐ Check the condition of the exhaust system and mountings (Section 10)
☐ Check the suspension and steering components (Section 11)
☐ Check the condition of the driveshaft gaiters (Section 12)
☐ Check the bodywork and underbody for damage and corrosion (Section 13)
☐ Check all underbonnet components and hoses for fluid leaks (Section 14)
☐ Carry out a road test (Section 15)

Every 36 000 miles (60 000 km) or 4 years, whichever comes first
In addition to all the items listed previously, carry out the following:
☐ Renew the spark plugs (Section 16)
☐ Renew the air filter element (Section 17)
☐ Check the manual transmission oil level (Section 18)
☐ Check the front wheel alignment (Section 19)
☐ Check the operation of the air conditioning system (Section 20)
☐ Renew the timing belt (Section 21)*
☐ Renew the brake fluid (Section 22)
☐ Renew the coolant (Section 23)

* Note: *Although the normal interval for timing belt renewal is 72 000 miles (120 000 km), it is strongly recommended that the interval is reduced to 36 000 miles (60 000 km) on cars which are subjected to intensive use, ie, mainly short journeys or a lot of stop-start driving. The actual belt renewal interval is therefore very much up to the individual owner, but bear in mind that severe engine damage may result if the belt breaks.*

Underbonnet view of a 1.6 litre engine model (1.4 litre similar)

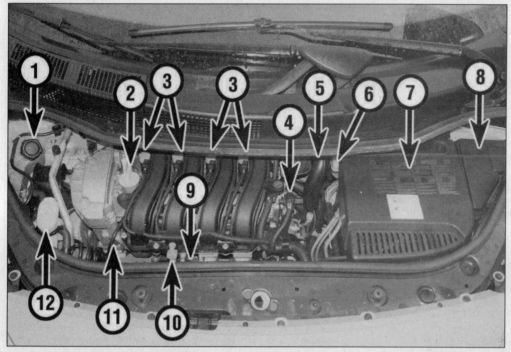

1. Coolant expansion tank
2. Engine oil filler cap
3. Ignition coil
4. Camshaft position sensor
5. Inlet air duct
6. Brake/clutch fluid reservoir
7. Battery cover
8. Engine compartment fusebox
9. Engine oil dipstick
10. Inlet air temperature sensor
11. Fuel supply hose
12. Washer fluid reservoir

Front underbody view

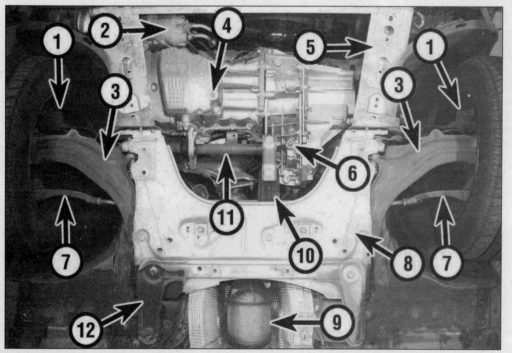

1. Front brake caliper
2. Air conditioning compressor
3. Front suspension lower arm
4. Engine oil drain plug
5. Radiator lower crossmember
6. Transmission oil drain plug
7. Track rod
8. Subframe
9. Catalytic converter
10. Engine rear mounting link
11. Right-hand driveshaft
12. Rear crossmember

Rear underbody view

1 Exhaust rear silencer
2 Spare wheel well
3 Rear shock absorber
4 Rear axle
5 Rear brake pipes/hoses
6 Handbrake cables
7 Exhaust mounting
8 Heat shield
9 Fuel tank
10 Charcoal canister

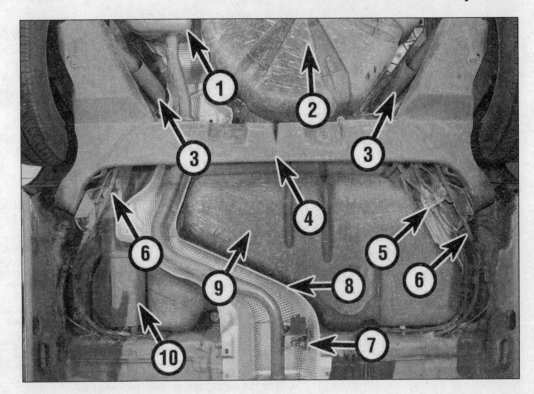

Maintenance procedures

1 Introduction

This Chapter is designed to help the home mechanic maintain his/her car for safety, economy, long life and peak performance.

The Chapter contains a master maintenance schedule, followed by Sections dealing specifically with each task in the schedule. Visual checks, adjustments, component renewal and other helpful items are included. Refer to the accompanying illustrations of the engine compartment and the underside of the car for the locations of the various components.

Servicing your car in accordance with the mileage/time maintenance schedule and the following Sections will provide a planned maintenance programme, which should result in a long and reliable service life. This is a comprehensive plan, so maintaining some items but not others at the specified service intervals, will not produce the same results.

As you service your car, you will discover that many of the procedures can – and should – be grouped together, because of the particular procedure being performed, or because of the proximity of two otherwise-unrelated components to one another. For example, if the car is raised for any reason, the exhaust can be inspected at the same time as the suspension and steering components.

The first step in this maintenance programme is to prepare yourself before the actual work begins. Read through all the Sections relevant to the work to be carried out, then make a list and gather all the parts and tools required. If a problem is encountered, seek advice from a parts specialist, or a dealer service department.

Resetting the service light

To reset the service warning light on the instrument panel, switch on the ignition, then scroll through the trip computer's displayed options until the 'mileage before next service' is displayed (accompanied by a spanner symbol). Now press and hold one of the reset buttons on the end of the wiper stalk for 10 seconds, until the display resets.

2 Regular maintenance

If, from the time the car is new, the routine maintenance schedule is followed closely, and frequent checks are made of fluid levels and high-wear items, as suggested throughout this manual, the engine will be kept in relatively good running condition, and the need for additional work will be minimised.

It is possible that there will be times when the engine is running poorly due to the lack of regular maintenance. This is even more likely if a used car, which has not received regular and frequent maintenance checks, is purchased. In such cases, additional work may need to be carried out, outside of the regular maintenance intervals.

If engine wear is suspected, a compression test (refer to Chapter 2A) will provide valuable information regarding the overall performance of the main internal components. Such a test can be used as a basis to decide on the extent of the work to be carried out. If, for example, a compression test indicates serious internal engine wear, conventional maintenance as described in this Chapter will not greatly improve the performance of the engine, and may prove a waste of time and money, unless extensive overhaul work is carried out first.

The following series of operations are those most often required to improve the performance of a generally poor-running engine:

Primary operations

a) *Clean, inspect and test the battery (refer to Weekly checks).*

b) *Check all the engine-related fluids (refer to Weekly checks).*

c) *Check the condition of the auxiliary drivebelt(s) (Section 7).*

d) *Check the condition of all hoses, and check for fluid leaks (Section 14).*

e) *Renew the spark plugs (Section 16).*

f) *Check the condition of the air filter, and renew if necessary (Section 17).*

If the above operations do not prove fully effective, carry out the following secondary operations:

Secondary operations

All items listed under *Primary operations*, plus the following:

a) *Check the charging system (Chapter 5A).*

b) *Check the ignition system (Chapter 5B).*

c) *Check the fuel system (refer to Chapter 4A).*

Every 9000 miles (15 000 km)

3 Engine oil and filter renewal

1 Frequent oil and filter changes are the most important preventative maintenance procedures which can be undertaken by the DIY owner. As engine oil ages, it becomes diluted and contaminated, which leads to premature engine wear.

2 Before starting this procedure, gather together all the necessary tools and materials. Also make sure that you have plenty of clean rags and newspapers handy, to mop up any spills. Ideally, the engine oil should be warm, as it will drain more easily, and more built-up sludge will be removed with it.

3 Take care not to touch the exhaust or any other hot parts of the engine when working under the car. To avoid any possibility of scalding, and to protect yourself from possible skin irritants and other harmful contaminants in used engine oils, it is advisable to wear gloves when carrying out this work.

4 With the handbrake applied, jack up the front of the car and support it on axle stands (see *Jacking and vehicle support*).

5 Remove the oil filler cap, then position a container beneath the sump. Where necessary, remove the fasteners and lower out the engine undertray. Clean the drain plug and the area around it, then slacken it half a turn – all models have a drain plug which requires an 8 mm square key to remove it **(see illustrations)**.

 HAYNES HINT *If possible, try to keep the plug pressed into the sump while unscrewing it by hand the last couple of turns. As the plug releases from the threads, move it away sharply so the stream of oil from the sump runs into the container, not up your sleeve.*

6 Allow some time for the old oil to drain, noting that it may be necessary to reposition the container as the oil flow slows to a trickle.

7 After all the oil has drained, wipe off the drain plug with a clean rag; fit a new sealing washer, where applicable. Clean the area around the drain plug opening, then refit and tighten the plug securely.

8 Move the container into position under the oil filter, which is located horizontally on the front face of the engine. Access is not easy, but it is possible without removing any body or engine components.

9 Using an oil filter removal tool where possible, slacken the filter initially. Loosely wrap some rags around the oil filter, then unscrew it and immediately position it with its open end uppermost to prevent further spillage of oil **(see illustration)**. Remove the oil filter from the engine compartment, and empty the oil into the container.

10 Use a clean rag to remove all oil, dirt and sludge from the filter sealing area on the engine. Check the old filter to make sure that the rubber sealing ring hasn't stuck to the engine. If it has, carefully remove it.

11 Apply a light coating of clean oil to the sealing ring on the new filter, then screw it into position on the engine **(see illustration)**.

3.5a **Removing the engine undertray**

3.5b **The engine oil drain plug is removed using a square-section key**

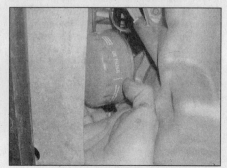

3.8 **Oil filter location on the front of the engine**

3.11 **Fitting the new oil filter**

Tighten the filter firmly by hand only – do not use any tools. Wipe clean the exterior of the oil filter.

12 Remove the old oil and all tools from under the car, refit the undertray where necessary, and lower the car to the ground.

13 Fill the engine with the specified quantity and grade of oil, as described in *Weekly checks*. Pour the oil in slowly, in small amounts, waiting each time for the oil to drain into the sump. When the oil level is up to the maximum mark on the dipstick, refit and tighten the oil filler cap **(see illustrations)**.

14 Start the engine and run it for a few minutes, checking that there are no leaks around the oil filter seal and the sump drain plug. Note that when the engine is first started, there will be a delay of a few seconds before the oil pressure warning light goes out while the new filter fills with oil. Do not race the engine while the warning light is on.

15 Switch off the engine and wait a few minutes for the oil to settle in the sump once more. With the new oil circulated and the filter now completely full, recheck the level on the dipstick and add more oil if necessary.

16 Dispose of the used engine oil safely with reference to *General repair procedures* in the Reference section of this manual.

3.13a Remove the oil filler cap . . .

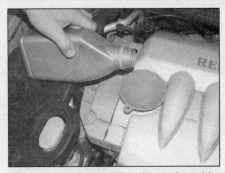

3.13b . . . and start filling the engine with oil

3.13c The engine oil dipstick is at the side of the inlet manifold (1.4 litre) . . .

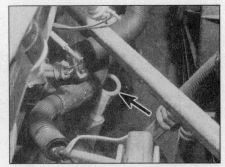

3.13d . . . or tucked down at the front of the engine (1.6 litre)

Every 18 000 miles (30 000 km) or 2 years

4 Pollen filter renewal

Note: *Only models with air conditioning are equipped with a pollen filter.*

1 Open the bonnet, then on 1.6 litre models, unclip and remove the engine top cover.

2 The filter access cover is located centrally below the windscreen cowl panel – turn the catches to the side to release and remove the cover **(see illustrations)**.

3 Squeeze the tabs on the filter to release it. The filter element should slide out of its location, but it may be necessary to break the filter frame to achieve this **(see illustration)**.

4 Before fitting the new filter, clean carefully inside the housing.

5 Fit the new filter into its slot, observing any direction-of-fitting markings – as for removal, it may be necessary to break part of the new filter frame to make it fit. Clip the access cover back into place to complete.

5 Braking system check

Handbrake check and adjustment

Note: *Handbrake adjustment is only possible on models with the conventional (non-automatic) handbrake. Refer to Chapter 9 in the event of any problems with the automatic handbrake.*

1 The handbrake should be capable of holding the parked car stationary, even on steep slopes, when applied with moderate force. The mechanism should be firm and positive in feel, with no trace of stiffness or sponginess from the cables, and should release immediately the handbrake lever is released. If the mechanism is faulty in any of these respects, it must be checked immediately as follows.

2 Handbrake adjustment is made inside the car, after removing the centre console as described in Chapter 11.

3 Check the exposed length of thread in front of the cable adjuster nut fitted behind the handbrake handle **(see illustration)**. The specified setting is for new cables, so those which have seen longer service may already be showing more thread than specified, to take up the slack.

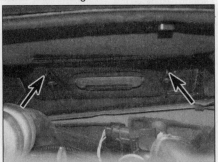

4.2a Turn the catches to the side . . .

4.2b . . . and remove the pollen filter access cover

4.3 Removing the pollen filter

5.3 Check the exposed length of thread on the handbrake adjuster

4 Jack up the rear of the car and support it on axle stands (see *Jacking and vehicle support*).
5 Operate the handbrake several times, and leave it applied as normal.
6 Check that the handbrake operating lever on each rear caliper is sitting off its stop by approximately 1 mm **(see illustration)**. If not, further adjustment may be required, or the cable on the side affected may have seized.
7 Check that the handbrake cables slide freely by pulling on their front ends, and check that the operating levers on the rear brake calipers move smoothly.
8 If the cables have stretched over time, the cables may need to be adjusted beyond the nominal setting. Bear in mind that the adjuster nut has a plastic insert, which loses its effectiveness over time – if the adjustment

For a quick check, the thickness of friction material remaining on each pad can be measured through the aperture on the caliper body.

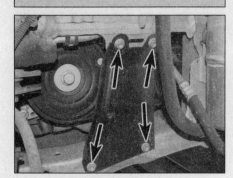

7.6a Remove the four bolts . . .

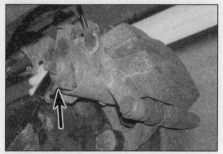

5.6 With the handbrake on, there should be a gap between the caliper lever and its stop

is being lost regularly, a new nut should be fitted.
9 Move both of the caliper operating levers as far rearwards as possible, then tighten the adjuster nut inside the car until all free play is removed from both cables. With the aid of an assistant, adjust the nut so that the operating lever on each rear brake caliper starts to move as the handbrake lever is moved between the first and second notch (click) of its ratchet mechanism **(see illustration)**.
10 After adjustment, release the handbrake fully, and check that the wheels are free to turn.
11 On completion, lower the car to the ground.

Brake pad and disc check

12 With the handbrake applied, jack up the front or rear of the car and support it securely on axle stands (see *Jacking and vehicle support*). Remove the roadwheels. Remember, the car has disc brakes all round, so all four calipers should be checked.
13 For a quick check, the thickness of friction material remaining on each brake pad can be measured through the aperture in the caliper body **(see Haynes Hint)**. If any pad's friction material is worn to the specified thickness or less, all four pads must be renewed as a set. Pad wear warning contacts may be fitted to the inboard pads, but this should not be used as an excuse for omitting a visual check.
14 For a comprehensive check, the brake pads should be removed and cleaned. This will allow the operation of the caliper to be checked, and the brake disc itself to be fully examined for condition on both sides. Refer to Chapter 9 for further information.

7.6b . . . and take out the side support plate

5.9 If necessary, use the nut to adjust the handbrake

6 Clutch check

Check that the clutch pedal moves smoothly and easily through its full travel, and that the clutch itself functions correctly, with no trace of slip or drag. If the clutch action is less than precise, this may indicate the need for bleeding the system – it could also indicate the presence of a fluid leak (see Chapter 6).

7 Auxiliary drivebelt checking, removal and refitting

Checking

1 The auxiliary drivebelt is located at the right-hand side of the engine, providing drive for the alternator and (where applicable) the air conditioning compressor.
2 The drivebelt configuration is surprisingly similar on all models, but there are three different types of belt tensioner. Where air conditioning is not fitted, an extra idler pulley is added.
3 Due to their function and material makeup, drivebelts are prone to failure after a period of time, and should therefore be inspected regularly. On models with air conditioning, an automatic tensioner precludes the need for checking the belt tension.
4 Loosen the right-hand front wheel bolts, then jack up the front of the car, and support it on axle stands (see *Jacking and vehicle support*). Remove the wheel.
5 Remove the screws and clips securing the wheel arch liner, and remove it, noting that it is in two pieces (refer to Chapter 11, Section 21 for more information).
6 Inside the wheel arch, remove the four bolts securing the side support plate to the support member and inner wing, and remove it **(see illustrations)**.
7 With the engine stopped, inspect the full length of the drivebelt for cracks and separation of the belt plies. Small cracks in the belt ribs are no cause for concern, unless they are deep into the belt itself. Also check for fraying, and glazing which gives the belt a shiny appearance.

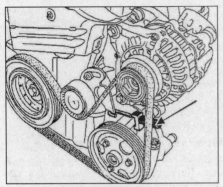

7.15 Using the Renault tool to pull the tensioner and adjust the belt

8 Turn the engine (using a spanner or socket on the crankshaft pulley bolt) so that the belt can be inspected thoroughly. Twist the belt between the pulleys so that both sides can be viewed. Check the pulleys for nicks, cracks, distortion and corrosion.

9 If the belt is satisfactory, refit the components removed to access it, then refit the wheel and lower the car to the ground. Tighten the wheel bolts to the specified torque.

Removal and refitting

10 If not already done, gain access to the belt as described in paragraphs 4 to 6.

Models without air conditioning

11 Before removing the belt, note its fitted position. On models without air conditioning, the pulleys have six grooves, the belt has five. In this case, the inner groove is left unused, so that the run of the belt is straight.

12 Loosen the two bolts securing the tensioner wheel bracket to the engine.

13 Turn the tensioner wheel bracket until the drivebelt can be removed from the pulleys.

14 Fit the drivebelt around the pulleys, making sure that it is correctly located in the grooves (refer to paragraph 11). Turn the tensioner wheel bracket to tension the belt, and tighten the bolts.

15 If the Renault special tools are not available, the belt tension will have to be set by feel – other than the 'frequency' specified, belt deflection is not quoted by Renault (**see illustration**). Test the belt deflection midway between the pulleys on the bottom run of the belt – as a guide only, aim for a deflection of around 5 mm either way. Setting the belt tension too high may cause wear in the belt, and in the alternator bearings.

16 Turn the engine through a few complete revolutions, using a spanner or socket on the crankshaft pulley bolt. With the belt settled on its pulleys, re-check the belt tension and adjust if necessary.

17 On completion, fully tighten the tensioner wheel bracket bolts.

18 If a new belt has been fitted, re-check the belt tension after (say) 500 miles, or earlier if there are signs that the belt is slipping. It is quite normal for a new belt to 'stretch' slightly in its first few miles of service (but don't over-tension a new belt to compensate).

7.19a Use a spanner on the hex fitting to turn the tensioner . . .

Models with air conditioning

19 Using a 16 mm spanner on the bolt or hex fitting close to the tensioner, turn the tensioner pulley clockwise to release the tension on the belt. Noting its routing, remove the drivebelt from the pulleys (**see illustrations**).

20 Fit the belt loosely around the main pulleys, making sure that it is correctly located in the grooves, then turn the tensioner the same way as previously until the belt can be fitted around the tensioner pulley also. Release the tensioner, and allow it to automatically tension the belt.

21 Turn the engine through a few complete revolutions, using a spanner or socket on the crankshaft pulley bolt. Check that the belt is running properly on its pulleys, and that the tensioner is working correctly (check that the belt is taut, midway along its bottom run).

All models

22 On completion, refit the components removed to access the belt, then refit the wheel and lower the car to the ground. Tighten the wheel bolts to the specified torque.

8 Seat belt check

1 Carefully examine the seat belt webbing for cuts, or any signs of serious fraying or deterioration. If the belt is of the retractable type, pull the belt all the way out of the inertia reel, and examine the full extent of the webbing.

2 Fasten and unfasten the belt, ensuring that

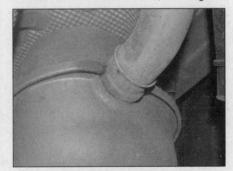

10.2 Check for exhaust leaks at pipe bends and joints

7.19b . . . and remove the belt from the pulleys

the locking mechanism holds securely, and releases properly when intended. If the belt is of the retractable type, check also that the retracting mechanism operates correctly when the belt is released.

3 Check the security of all seat belt mountings and attachments which are accessible without removing any trim or other components.

9 Electrical equipment check

1 Check the operation of all electrical equipment, ie, lights, direction indicators, horn, etc. Refer to the appropriate Sections of Chapter 12 for details if any of the circuits are found to be inoperative.

2 Note that stop-light switch adjustment is described in Chapter 9.

3 Visually check all accessible wiring connectors, harnesses and retaining clips for security, and for signs of chafing or damage. Rectify any faults found.

10 Exhaust system check

1 With the engine cold (at least an hour after the car has been driven), check the complete exhaust system from the engine to the end of the tailpipe. Ideally, the inspection should be carried out with the car on a hoist to permit unrestricted access, but if a hoist is not available, raise and support the car safely on axle stands (see *Jacking and vehicle support*).

2 Check the exhaust pipes and connections for evidence of leaks, severe corrosion and damage. Make sure that all brackets and mountings are in good condition and tight. Leakage at any of the joints or in other parts of the system will usually show up as a black sooty stain in the vicinity of the leak (**see illustration**).

3 Rattles and other noises can often be traced to the exhaust system, especially the brackets and mountings (**see illustration**). Try to move the pipes and silencers. If the components can come into contact with the body or suspension parts, secure the system

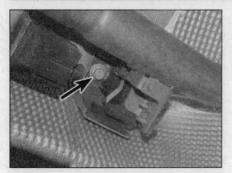

10.3 Check that the exhaust mounting-to-floor bolts are tight

with new mountings or if possible, separate the joints and twist the pipes as necessary to provide additional clearance.

4 Run the engine at idling speed. Have an assistant place a cloth or rag over the rear end of the exhaust pipe, and listen for any escape of exhaust gases that would indicate a leak.

5 On completion, lower the car to the ground.

11 Suspension and steering check

Front suspension and steering

1 Raise the front of the car, and securely support it on axle stands (see *Jacking and vehicle support*).

2 Visually inspect the balljoint dust covers and the steering rack-and-pinion gaiters for splits, chafing or deterioration **(see illustrations)**.

Any wear of these components will cause loss of lubricant, together with dirt and water entry, resulting in rapid deterioration of the balljoints or steering gear.

3 Grasp the roadwheel at the 12 o'clock and 6 o'clock positions, and try to rock it **(see illustration)**. Very slight free play may be felt, but if the movement is appreciable, further investigation is necessary to determine the source. Continue rocking the wheel while an assistant depresses the footbrake. If the movement is now eliminated or significantly reduced, it is likely that the hub bearings are at fault. If the free play is still evident with the footbrake depressed, then there is wear in the suspension joints or mountings.

4 Now grasp the wheel at the 9 o'clock and 3 o'clock positions, and try to rock it as before. Any movement felt now may again be caused by wear in the hub bearings or the steering track rod balljoints. If the outer balljoint is worn, the visual movement will be obvious. If the inner joint is suspect, it can be felt by placing a hand over the rack-and-pinion rubber gaiter and gripping the track rod. If the wheel is now rocked, movement will be felt at the inner joint if wear has taken place.

5 Using a large screwdriver or flat bar, check for wear in the suspension mounting bushes by levering between the relevant suspension component and its attachment point. Some movement is to be expected, as the mountings are made of rubber, but excessive wear should be obvious. Also check the condition of any visible rubber bushes, looking for splits, cracks or contamination of the rubber.

6 With the car standing on its wheels, have an assistant turn the steering wheel back-and-forth, about an eighth of a turn each way. There should be very little, if any, lost movement between the steering wheel and roadwheels. If this is not the case, closely observe the joints and mountings previously described. In addition, check the steering column universal joints for wear, and also check the rack-and-pinion steering gear itself.

Rear suspension

7 Chock the front wheels, then jack up the rear of the car and support securely on axle stands (see *Jacking and vehicle support*).

8 Working as described previously for the front suspension, check the rear hub bearings, the suspension bushes and the shock absorber mountings for wear **(see illustration)**. **Note:** *The handbrake must be released before checking the rear wheel bearings.*

Shock absorber check

9 Check for any signs of fluid leakage around the shock absorber body, or from the rubber gaiter around the piston rod **(see illustration)**. Should any fluid be noticed, the shock absorber is defective internally, and should be renewed. **Note:** *Shock absorbers should always be renewed in pairs on the same axle.*

10 The efficiency of the shock absorber may be checked by bouncing the car at each corner. Generally speaking, the body will return to its normal position and stop after being depressed. If it rises and returns on a rebound, the shock absorber is probably suspect.

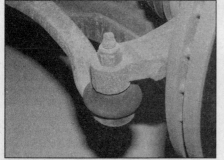

11.2a Check the balljoint rubber gaiters on the track rod ends . . .

11.2b . . . and on the anti-roll bar drop links

11.2c Check the steering rack gaiters for splitting

11.3 Check for wheel bearing wear by grasping the wheel and trying to rock it

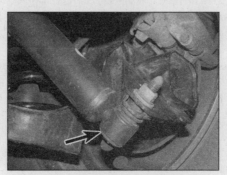

11.8 Check the rear shock absorber for fluid leaks and mounting damage

11.9 Check around the front strut piston rod gaiter for fluid leaks

Roadwheel bolt check

11 Remove the wheel trims or wheel centre caps, as applicable, then slacken the roadwheel bolts slightly.

12 Tighten the bolts to the specified torque, using a torque wrench.

12 Driveshaft gaiter check

1 With the car raised and securely supported on stands, turn the steering onto full lock, then slowly rotate the roadwheel. Inspect the condition of the outer constant velocity (CV) joint rubber gaiters while squeezing the gaiters to open out the folds. Check for signs of cracking, splits or deterioration of the rubber which may allow the grease to escape and lead to water and grit entry into the joint. Also check the security and condition of the retaining clips. Repeat these checks on the inner CV joints **(see illustrations)**. If any damage or deterioration is found, refer to Chapter 8.

2 At the same time, check the general condition of the CV joints themselves by first holding the driveshaft and attempting to rotate the wheel. Repeat this check by holding the inner joint and attempting to rotate the driveshaft. Any appreciable movement indicates wear in the joints, wear in the driveshaft splines, or a loose driveshaft retaining nut.

13 Bodywork and underbody condition check

1 Once the car has been washed and all tar spots and other surface blemishes have been cleaned off, carefully check all paintwork, looking closely for chips or scratches. Pay particular attention to vulnerable areas such as the front panels (bonnet and bumper), and around the wheel arches. Any damage to the paintwork must be rectified as soon as possible to comply with the terms of the manufacturer's anti-corrosion warranties; check with a Renault dealer for details.

2 If a chip or light scratch is found which is recent and still free from rust, it can be touched-up using the appropriate touch-up stick which can be obtained from Renault dealers. Any more serious damage, or rusted stone chips, can be repaired as described in Chapter 11, but if damage or corrosion is so severe that a panel must be renewed, seek professional advice as soon as possible.

3 Always check that the door and ventilation opening drain holes and pipes are completely clear, so that water can drain out.

4 The wax-based underbody protective coating should be inspected annually, preferably just prior to Winter, when the underbody should be washed down as thoroughly as possible without disturbing the protective coating (see Chapter 11, Section 2, regarding the use of

12.1a Check the outer CV joint gaiters for splits or signs of perishing

steam cleaners). Any damage to the coating should be repaired using a wax-based sealer. If any of the body panels are disturbed for repair or renewal, do not forget to replace the coating and to inject wax into door panels, sills and box sections, to maintain the level of protection provided by the manufacturer.

14 Hose and fluid leak check

1 Visually inspect the engine joint faces, gaskets and seals for any signs of water or oil leaks. Pay particular attention to the areas around the top of the engine, cylinder head, oil filter and sump joint faces **(see illustration)**. Bear in mind that, over a period of time, some very slight seepage from these areas is to be expected – what you are really looking for is any indication of a serious leak. Should a leak be found, renew the

14.1 Check along the sump joint for signs of oil leaks

14.3a Check the large-diameter radiator hoses for signs of damage

12.1b Similarly check the inner CV joint gaiters

offending gasket or oil seal by referring to the appropriate Chapters in this manual.

2 Also check the security and condition of all the engine-related pipes and hoses, and all hydraulic and braking system pipes and hoses **(see illustration)**. Ensure that all cable-ties or securing clips are in place, and in good condition. Clips which are broken or missing can lead to chafing of the hoses, pipes or wiring, which could cause more serious problems in the future.

3 Carefully check the radiator hoses and heater hoses along their entire length. Renew any hose which is cracked, swollen or deteriorated. Cracks will show up better if the hose is squeezed. Pay close attention to the hose clips that secure the hoses to the cooling system components. Hose clips can pinch and puncture hoses, resulting in cooling system leaks. If the crimped-type hose clips are used, it may be a good idea to use Jubilee clips **(see illustrations)**.

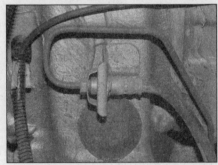

14.2 Check the brake pipes very carefully, especially at joints

14.3b Spring-type hose clips can pinch and puncture hoses

A leak in the cooling system will usually show up as white- or rust-coloured deposits on the area surrounding the joint.

4 Inspect all the cooling system components (hoses, joint faces, etc) for leaks **(see Haynes Hint)**. Where any problems are found on system components, renew the component or gasket with reference to Chapter 3.

5 With the car raised, inspect the fuel tank and filler neck for punctures, cracks and other damage. The connection between the filler neck and tank is especially critical **(see illustration)**. Sometimes a rubber filler neck or connecting hose will leak due to loose retaining clamps or deteriorated rubber.

6 Carefully check all rubber hoses and metal fuel lines leading away from the fuel tank. Check for loose connections, deteriorated hoses, crimped lines, and other damage. Pay particular attention to the vent pipes and hoses, which often loop up around the filler neck and can become blocked or crimped. Follow the lines to the front of the car, carefully inspecting them all the way. Renew damaged sections as necessary. Similarly, whilst the car is raised, take the opportunity to inspect all underbody brake fluid pipes and hoses.

7 From within the engine compartment, check the security of all fuel, vacuum and

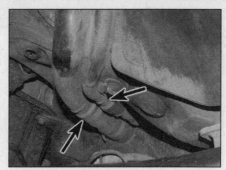

14.5 Check the fuel tank filler neck hoses for signs of leakage

brake hose attachments and pipe unions, and inspect all hoses for kinks, chafing and deterioration.

8 Where applicable, check the condition of the automatic transmission fluid cooler pipes and hoses.

15 Road test

Instruments and electrical equipment

1 Check the operation of all instruments and electrical equipment.

2 Make sure that all instruments read correctly, and switch on all electrical equipment in turn, to check that it functions properly.

Steering and suspension

3 Check for any abnormalities in the steering, suspension, handling or road 'feel'.

4 Drive the car, and check that there are no unusual vibrations or noises.

5 Check that the steering feels positive, with no excessive 'sloppiness', or roughness, and check for any suspension noises when cornering and driving over bumps.

Drivetrain

6 Check the performance of the engine, clutch, transmission and driveshafts.

7 Listen for any unusual noises from the engine, clutch and transmission.

8 Make sure that the engine runs smoothly when idling, and that there is no hesitation when accelerating.

9 Check that, where applicable, the clutch action is smooth and progressive, that the drive is taken up smoothly, and that the pedal travel is not excessive. Also listen for any noises when the clutch pedal is depressed.

10 Check that all gears can be engaged smoothly without noise, and that the gear lever action is not abnormally vague or 'notchy'.

11 Listen for a metallic clicking sound from the front of the car, as the car is driven slowly in a circle with the steering on full-lock. Carry out this check in both directions. If a clicking noise is heard, this indicates wear in a driveshaft joint (see Chapter 8).

Braking system

12 Make sure that the car does not pull to one side when braking, and that the wheels do not lock prematurely when braking hard.

13 Check that there is no vibration through the steering when braking.

14 Check that the handbrake operates correctly, without excessive movement of the lever, and that it holds the car stationary on a slope.

15 Test the operation of the brake servo unit as follows. Depress the footbrake four or five times to exhaust the vacuum, then start the engine. As the engine starts, there should be a noticeable 'give' in the brake pedal as vacuum builds up. Allow the engine to run for at least two minutes, and then switch it off. If the brake pedal is now depressed again, it should be possible to detect a hiss from the servo as the pedal is depressed. After about four or five applications, no further hissing should be heard, and the pedal should feel considerably harder.

Every 36 000 miles (60 000 km) or 4 years

16.2 Unclip and remove the engine upper cover

16 Spark plug renewal

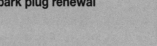

Warning: High voltages are produced by the electronic ignition system. Extreme care must be taken when working on the system with the ignition switched on. Persons with surgically-implanted cardiac pacemaker devices should keep well clear of the ignition circuits, components and test equipment.

1 The correct functioning of the spark plugs

is vital for the correct running and efficiency of the engine. It is essential that the plugs fitted are appropriate for the engine, the type being specified at the start of this Chapter. If the correct type of plug is used and the engine is in good condition, the spark plugs should not need attention between scheduled servicing intervals. Spark plug cleaning is rarely necessary, and should not be attempted unless specialised equipment is available, as damage can easily be caused to the firing ends.

2 To remove the plugs, first open the bonnet and on 1.6 litre engines, unclip the engine upper cover **(see illustration)**.

3 Remove the ignition HT coils from the top of the spark plugs as described in Chapter 5B.

4 It is advisable to remove any dirt from the spark plug recesses using a clean brush, a vacuum cleaner or compressed air before removing the plugs, to prevent the dirt dropping into the cylinders. However, since the plugs are deeply recessed in the engine, this may be difficult.

5 Unscrew the plugs using a spark plug spanner, box spanner or a deep socket and extension bar **(see illustrations)**. Keep the socket in alignment with the spark plug, otherwise if it is forcibly moved to either side, the ceramic top of the spark plug may be broken off. As each plug is removed, examine it as follows.

6 Examination of the spark plugs will give a good indication of the condition of the engine. If the insulator nose of the spark plug is clean and white, with no deposits, this is indicative of a weak mixture or too hot a plug (a hot plug transfers heat away from the electrode slowly, a cold plug transfers heat away quickly).

7 If the tip and insulator nose are covered with hard black-looking deposits, then this is indicative that the mixture is too rich. Should the plug be black and oily, then it is likely that the engine is fairly worn, as well as the mixture being too rich.

8 If the insulator nose is covered with light tan to greyish-brown deposits, then the mixture is correct and it is likely that the engine is in good condition.

9 If the spark plug has not completed its service interval, it may be refitted, however, check that the condition of the plug and the gap is correct before refitting. If, due to engine condition, the spark plug is not serviceable, it should be renewed.

10 The spark plug gap is of considerable importance as, if it is too large or too small, the size of the spark and its efficiency will be seriously impaired. For best results, the spark plug gap should be set in accordance with the Specifications at the start of this Chapter.

11 To set it, measure the gap with a feeler blade, and then bend open, or closed, the outer plug electrode until the correct gap is achieved **(see illustration)**. The centre electrode should never be bent, as this may crack the insulation and cause plug failure, if nothing worse.

12 Special spark plug electrode gap measuring and adjusting tools are available from most motor accessory shops **(see illustration)**.

13 Before fitting the spark plugs, check that the threaded connector sleeves are tight, and that the plug exterior surfaces and threads are clean. Apply a little anti-seize compound to the threads.

14 Insert each spark plug into the cylinder head and screw them in by hand, taking extra care to enter the plug threads correctly **(see Haynes Hint)**.

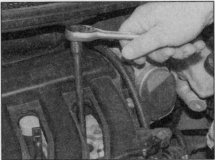

16.5a Unscrew the plugs using a long extension bar . . .

16.5b . . . and a suitable deep socket

16.11 Measuring the spark plug gap with a feeler blade

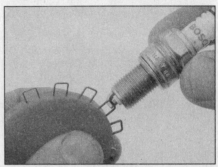

16.12 Measuring the spark plug gap with a wire gauge

15 Tighten the plugs to the specified torque using the spark plug socket and a torque wrench.

16 Before refitting the coils over the new plugs, Renault recommend that the rubber boots are first lightly lubricated inside, using fluorine grease (part number 82 00 168 855).

17 Refit the ignition HT coils with reference to Chapter 5B, then refit the engine cover to complete.

HAYNES HINT

It's often difficult to insert spark plugs into their holes without cross-threading them. To avoid this possibility, fit a short length of rubber or plastic hose over the end of the spark plug. The flexible hose acts as a universal joint, to help align the plug with the plug hole. Should the plug begin to cross thread, the hose will slip on the spark plug, preventing thread damage to the aluminium cylinder head.

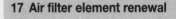

17 Air filter element renewal

Removal

1.4 litre engines

1 The air filter element is located at the left-hand rear of the engine. Remove the windscreen cowl panels as described in Chapter 11 for access.

2 Remove the single mounting bolt at the front, pull off the air inlet duct, then unclip and lift out the air inlet resonator box **(see illustrations)**.

3 Squeeze the quick-release fitting and pull off the brake servo vacuum supply hose from the inlet manifold **(see illustration)**.

4 Undo the two screws and unclip the air cleaner cover **(see illustrations)**.

17.2a Remove the front mounting bolt . . .

17.2b . . . then pull off the air duct and lift out the air resonator

17.3 Pull off the brake servo vacuum hose

17.4a Remove the securing screws . . .

17.4b . . . and pull out the air cleaner cover

5 Note how the element is fitted, then withdraw it from the air cleaner cover (see illustration).

1.6 litre engines

6 The air filter is located behind the battery. Remove the left-hand outer section of

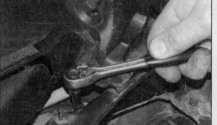

17.5 Withdraw the air filter element from the cover

the windscreen cowl panel for access, as described in Chapter 11.

7 Remove the two bolts from the air filter access panel, and lift it out (see illustrations).

8 If the air filter has never been disturbed

before, it may be necessary to cut the plastic side 'perforations' securing the access flap with a sharp knife, before hinging the flap upwards. We managed to remove the filter without doing this, as described later in this Section.

9 Remove the battery cover, which is secured by two bolts at the rear, and a screw/clip at the front (see illustration).

10 Unscrew and remove the two filter housing mounting screws – access to the one nearest the engine is hampered by the engine ECU, and may require the use of a stubby or cranked screwdriver (see illustrations).

11 Either hinge the access flap upwards, or carefully press it rearwards to provide clearance, then slide the filter housing out upwards to remove it (see illustration).

12 Withdraw the filter element from the housing (see illustration).

17.7a Remove the filter access panel bolt which can be seen . . .

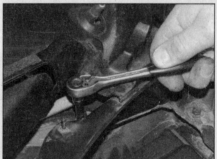

17.7b . . . and the one tucked inside . . .

17.9 Remove the battery cover

17.10a The filter housing screw one side is easy to access . . .

17.10b . . . but the other one may need a small or right-angled screwdriver

Note: between 17.7b and 17.9 there is caption **17.7c** . . . then lift out the panel

Refitting

13 Clean the inside of the air cleaner body and housing/cover, being careful not to get dirt into the inlet duct.
14 Fit the new element using a reversal of the removal procedure.

18 Manual transmission oil level check

1 Either position the car over an inspection pit, or jack up the front and rear of the car and support it on axle stands (see *Jacking and vehicle support*). The car must be level for the check to be accurate.
2 Remove the engine undertray or unclip the cover, as applicable, from the bottom of the transmission.
3 Locate the plastic filler/level plug, and clean the area around it before removal. The plug is located on the front-facing side of the transmission **(see illustration)**.
4 Unscrew and remove the plug – this could be very tight. Check the condition of the filler plug seal, and obtain a new one if necessary.
5 The oil level should be up to the lower edge of the filler/level plug aperture.
6 If necessary, top-up using the specified type of lubricant until the transmission oil level is correct. Fill the transmission until oil starts to flow out, and allow excess oil to drain out.

> *If using a typical transmission oil bottle, this will have to be positioned upside-down, which is itself quite difficult. To avoid the oil draining out of the bottle prematurely, fold over the plastic bottle's filler tube until the bottle is in the right position, then unfold it and insert into the filler hole.*

7 Once the transmission oil level is correct, refit the filler/level plug and tighten it securely – by hand only.
8 Refit the engine undertray cover or transmission bottom cover as applicable, then lower the car to the ground. Note that frequent need for topping-up indicates a leak,

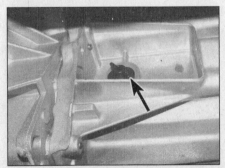

18.3 The transmission filler/level plug is on the front

17.11 Slide the filter housing upwards to remove, holding back the access flap

possibly through an oil seal. The cause should be investigated and rectified.

19 Front wheel alignment check

Refer to the information given in Chapter 10.

20 Air conditioning system check

The air conditioning system must be checked by a Renault dealer using dedicated test equipment.

21 Timing belt renewal

Refer to Chapter 2A.

22 Brake fluid renewal

> ⚠ *Warning: Brake hydraulic fluid can harm your eyes and damage painted surfaces, so use extreme caution when handling and pouring it. Do not use fluid that has been standing open for some time, as it absorbs moisture from the air. Excess moisture can cause a dangerous loss of braking effectiveness.*

1 The procedure is similar to that for the bleeding of the hydraulic system as described in Chapter 9, except that the brake fluid reservoir should be emptied by syphoning, using a clean poultry baster or similar before starting, and allowance should be made for the old fluid to be expelled when bleeding a section of the circuit.
2 Working as described in Chapter 9, open the first bleed screw in the sequence, and pump the brake pedal gently until nearly all the old fluid has been emptied from the master cylinder reservoir **(see illustration)**. Top-up to the MAX level with new fluid, and continue pumping until only the new fluid remains in the

17.12 Withdraw the air filter element from the housing

reservoir, and new fluid can be seen emerging from the bleed screw. Tighten the screw, and top the reservoir level up to the MAX level line.

> *Old hydraulic fluid is invariably much darker in colour than the new, making it easy to distinguish the two.*

3 Work through all the remaining bleed screws in the sequence until new fluid can be seen at all of them. Be careful to keep the master cylinder reservoir topped-up to above the MIN level at all times, or air may enter the system and greatly increase the length of the task.
4 When the operation is complete, check that all bleed screws are securely tightened, and that their dust caps are refitted. Wash off all traces of spilt fluid, and recheck the master cylinder reservoir fluid level.
5 Check the operation of the brakes before taking the car on the road.

23 Coolant renewal

Cooling system draining

> ⚠ *Warning: Wait until the engine is cold before starting this procedure. Do not allow antifreeze to come in contact with your skin, or with the car's painted surfaces. Rinse off spills immediately with plenty of water. Never*

22.2 Change the brake fluid using the same method as for brake bleeding

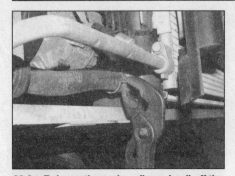

23.3a Release the spring clip and pull off the radiator lower hose (front bumper removed)

leave antifreeze lying around in an open container, or in a puddle in the driveway or on the garage floor. Children and pets are attracted by its sweet smell, but antifreeze can be fatal if ingested.

1 With the engine completely cold, remove the expansion tank filler cap. Turn the cap anti-clockwise, wait until any pressure remaining in the system is released, then unscrew it and lift it off.

2 Where applicable, remove the undertray, then position a container beneath the radiator bottom hose connection. For more complete draining, remove the smaller expansion tank hose at the side, right at the base of the radiator – however, access is difficult without removing the front bumper first, as described in Chapter 11.

3 Release the hose clip, pull off the hose and allow the coolant to drain into the container **(see illustrations)**.

4 To assist draining, open the cooling system bleed screw on the thermostat housing, and on the heater hose **(see illustrations)**.

5 If compressed air is available, Renault suggest inserting an air line into the expansion tank to drive out as much water as possible.

6 Flush the system if necessary as described in the following paragraphs, then refit the bottom hose. Use a new hose clip if necessary. Refill the system as described later in this Section.

Cooling system flushing

7 If coolant renewal has been neglected, or if the antifreeze mixture has become diluted, then in time, the cooling system may gradually

23.3b Direct the flow from the radiator into a suitable container

lose efficiency, as the coolant passages become restricted due to rust, scale deposits, and other sediment. The cooling system efficiency can be restored by flushing the system clean.

8 The simplest method for flushing the system is to loosely refit the radiator bottom hose, then refill the system with clean water. When the system is full, disconnect the radiator bottom hose and allow the water to drain a second time. Check the condition of the water drained – if it is clean, flushing is complete; if not, repeat the process.

Radiator flushing

9 Disconnect the top and bottom hoses and any other relevant hoses from the radiator, with reference to Chapter 3.

10 Insert a garden hose into the radiator top inlet. Direct a flow of clean water through the radiator, and continue flushing until clean water emerges from the radiator bottom outlet.

11 If after a reasonable period, the water still does not run clear, the radiator can be flushed with a good proprietary cleaning agent. It is important that the manufacturer's instructions are followed carefully. If the contamination is particularly bad, insert the hose in the radiator bottom outlet, and reverse-flush the radiator.

Engine flushing

12 To flush the engine, remove the thermostat as described in Chapter 3, and disconnect the bottom hose.

13 Insert a garden hose into the thermostat housing and direct a clean flow of water through the engine. Continue flushing until

clean water emerges from the radiator bottom hose.

14 On completion, refit the thermostat and reconnect the bottom hose. Where applicable, refit the engine undertray.

Antifreeze mixture

15 The antifreeze should always be renewed at the specified intervals. This is necessary not only to maintain the antifreeze properties, but also to prevent corrosion which would otherwise occur as the corrosion inhibitors become progressively less effective.

16 Always use an ethylene-glycol based antifreeze which is suitable for use in mixed-metal cooling systems. The quantity of antifreeze and levels of protection are given in the Specifications.

17 Before adding antifreeze, the cooling system should be completely drained, preferably flushed, and all hoses checked for condition and security.

18 After filling with antifreeze, a label should be attached to the expansion tank, stating the type and concentration of antifreeze used, and the date installed. Any subsequent topping-up should be made with the same type and concentration of antifreeze.

19 Do not use engine antifreeze in the windscreen/tailgate washer system, as it will cause damage to the vehicle's paintwork. A screenwash additive should be added to the washer system in the quantities stated on the bottle.

Cooling system filling

20 Before attempting to fill the cooling system, make sure that all hoses and clips are in good condition, and that the clips are tight. Note that an antifreeze mixture must be used all year round, to prevent corrosion of the engine components.

21 Remove the expansion tank filler cap **(see illustration)**.

22 If not already done, open the cooling system bleed screws.

23 Slowly fill the system until the coolant level reaches the MAX mark on the expansion tank. Close the bleed screws in turn when coolant free from air bubbles emerges from each one.

24 Start the engine, and run it at a fast idle speed (approx 2000 rpm). As soon as the

23.4a Open the bleed screw on the thermostat housing . . .

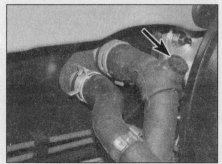

23.4b . . . and on the heater hose next to the bulkhead

23.21 Remove the coolant expansion tank filler cap

engine is running, top-up the level in the expansion tank if necessary, then refit and tighten the expansion tank filler cap – the cap should not normally be removed when the engine is running, nor when the system is hot.

25 Allow the engine to run at 2000 rpm until the cooling fan has cut in and out three times.

26 Stop the engine and allow the engine to cool for at least an hour, and preferably, overnight.

27 Recheck the coolant level with reference to *Weekly checks*. Top-up the level if necessary and refit the expansion tank filler cap.

Airlocks

28 If, after draining and refilling the system, symptoms of overheating are found which did not occur previously, then the fault is almost certainly due to trapped air at some point in the system, causing an airlock and restricting the flow of coolant; usually, the air is trapped because the system was refilled too quickly.

29 If an airlock is suspected, first try gently squeezing all visible coolant hoses. A coolant hose which is full of air feels quite different to one full of coolant, when squeezed. After refilling the system, most airlocks will clear once the system has cooled, and been topped up.

30 While the engine is running at operating temperature, switch on the heater and heater fan, and check for heat output. Provided there is sufficient coolant in the system, any lack of heat output could be due to an airlock in the system.

31 Airlocks can have more serious effects than simply reducing heater output – a severe airlock could reduce coolant flow around the engine. Check that the radiator top hose is hot when the engine is at operating temperature – a top hose which stays cold could be the result of an airlock (or a non-opening thermostat).

32 If the problem persists, stop the engine and allow it to cool down **completely**, before unscrewing the radiator and expansion tank caps, or loosening the hose clips and squeezing the hoses to bleed out the trapped air. In the worst case, the system will have to be at least partially drained (this time, the coolant can be saved for re-use) and flushed to clear the problem.

Chapter 1 Part B:
Routine maintenance and servicing – diesel models

Contents

Degrees of difficulty

Easy, suitable for novice with little experience	**Fairly easy,** suitable for beginner with some experience	**Fairly difficult,** suitable for competent DIY mechanic	**Difficult,** suitable for experienced DIY mechanic	**Very difficult,** suitable for expert DIY or professional

Lubricants and fluids

Refer to *Weekly checks* on page 0•17

Capacities

Engine oil (including oil filter)
1.5 litre engines . . . .   4.6 litres
1.9 litre engines . . . .   4.8 litres
Difference between MAX and MIN dipstick marks. . . . .   1.5 to 2.0 litres

Cooling system
1.5 litre engines . . . .   5.3 litres
1.9 litre engines . . . .   6.5 litres

Manual transmission
1.5 litre models (5-speed). . . . .   2.5 litres
1.9 litre models (6-speed). . . . .   2.1 litres

Automatic transmission. . . . .   6.0 litres

Fuel tank . . . .   60 litres approx. (13 gallons)

Cooling system

Antifreeze mixture: **Antifreeze**
   Protection to –23°C 35%
   Protection to –40°C 50%

Fuel system

Specified idle speed (non-adjustable):
   1.5 litre engines . . . .   805 ± 50 rpm
   1.9 litre engines . . . .   800 ± 50 rpm

Brakes

Brake pad friction material minimum thickness. . . . .   1.5 mm
Handbrake adjustment dimension (nominal setting for new cables) . . .   17 mm

Torque wrench settings

	Nm	lbf ft
Roadwheel bolts.	130	96
Side support plate bolts.	21	15

The maintenance intervals in this manual are provided with the assumption that you, not the dealer, will be carrying out the work. These are the minimum maintenance intervals recommended by us for vehicles driven daily. If you wish to keep your vehicle in peak condition at all times, you may wish to perform some of these procedures more often. We encourage frequent maintenance, because it enhances the efficiency, performance and resale value of your vehicle.

If the vehicle is driven in dusty areas, used to tow a trailer, or driven frequently at slow speeds (idling in traffic) or on short journeys, more frequent maintenance intervals are recommended.

When the vehicle is new, it should be serviced by a factory-authorised dealer service department, in order to preserve the factory warranty.

Every 250 miles (400 km) or weekly

☐ Refer to Weekly checks

Every 9000 miles (15 000 km)

☐ Renew the engine oil and filter (Section 3)

Note: *Frequent oil and filter changes are good for the engine. We recommend changing the oil at the mileage specified here, or at least once a year.*

Every 18 000 miles (30 000 km) or 2 years, whichever comes first

In addition to all the items listed previously, carry out the following:

☐ Renew the pollen filter (Section 4)
☐ Check the braking system (Section 5)
☐ Check the operation of the clutch (Section 6)
☐ Check the condition of the auxiliary drivebelt (Section 7)
☐ Drain any water from the fuel filter (Section 8)
☐ Check the condition of the seat belts (Section 9)
☐ Check the operation of all electrical equipment (Section 10)
☐ Check the condition of the exhaust system and mountings (Section 11)
☐ Check the suspension and steering components (Section 12)
☐ Check the condition of the driveshaft gaiters (Section 13)
☐ Check the bodywork and underbody for damage and corrosion (Section 14)
☐ Check all underbonnet components and hoses for fluid leaks (Section 15)
☐ Carry out a road test (Section 16)

Every 36 000 miles (60 000 km) or 4 years, whichever comes first

In addition to all the items listed previously, carry out the following:

☐ Renew the air filter element (Section 17)
☐ Renew the fuel filter element (Section 18)
☐ Check the manual transmission oil level (Section 19)
☐ Check the front wheel alignment (Section 20)
☐ Check the operation of the air conditioning system (Section 21)
☐ Renew the timing belt (Section 22)*
☐ Renew the brake fluid (Section 23)
☐ Renew the coolant (Section 24)

* Note: *Although the normal interval for timing belt renewal is 72 000 miles (120 000 km), it is strongly recommended that the interval is reduced to 36 000 miles (60 000 km) on vehicles which are subjected to intensive use, ie, mainly short journeys or a lot of stop-start driving. The actual belt renewal interval is therefore very much up to the individual owner, but bear in mind that severe engine damage may result if the belt breaks.*

Underbonnet view of a 1.5 litre engine model

1 Coolant expansion tank
2 Diesel priming bulb
3 Engine oil filler cap
4 Injectors
5 Intercooler air duct
6 Brake/clutch fluid reservoir
7 Engine management ECU
8 Air cleaner housing
9 Engine compartment fusebox
10 Battery negative terminal
11 Engine oil dipstick
12 Injection pump
13 Washer fluid reservoir

Underbonnet view of a 1.9 litre engine model

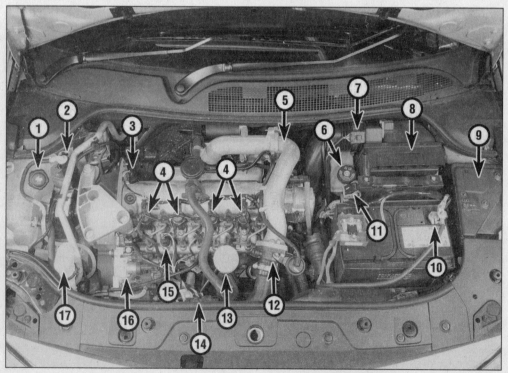

1 Coolant expansion tank
2 Hand priming bulb
3 Camshaft position sensor
4 Injectors
5 Intercooler air duct
6 Brake/clutch fluid reservoir
7 Airflow meter
8 Air cleaner housing
9 Engine compartment fusebox
10 Battery negative terminal
11 Engine management ECU
12 Engine cut-off device
13 Engine oil filler cap (and dipstick)
14 Turbo pressure sensor
15 Fuel rail pressure sensor
16 Injection pump
17 Washer fluid reservoir

Front underbody view (1.5 litre)

1 Front brake caliper
2 Air conditioning compressor
3 Engine oil drain plug
4 Radiator lower crossmember
5 Front suspension lower arm
6 Transmission oil drain plug
7 Track rod
8 Subframe
9 Engine rear mounting link
10 Right-hand driveshaft
11 Exhaust pipe
12 Rear crossmember

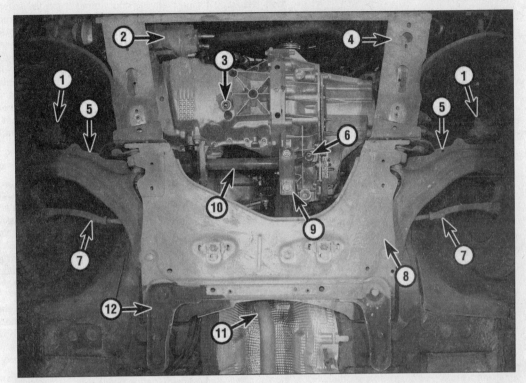

Rear underbody view

1 Rear shock absorber
2 Exhaust rear silencer
3 Automatic handbrake control
   unit
4 Handbrake cables
5 Rear brake pipes/hoses
6 Rear axle
7 Fuel tank
8 Heat shield

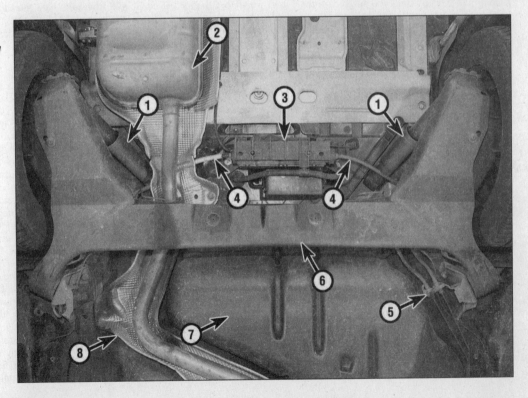

Maintenance procedures

1 Introduction

This Chapter is designed to help the home mechanic maintain his/her vehicle for safety, economy, long life and peak performance.

The Chapter contains a master maintenance schedule, followed by Sections dealing specifically with each task in the schedule. Visual checks, adjustments, component renewal and other helpful items are included. Refer to the accompanying illustrations of the engine compartment and the underside of the vehicle for the locations of the various components.

Servicing your vehicle in accordance with the mileage/time maintenance schedule and the following Sections will provide a planned maintenance programme, which should result in a long and reliable service life. This is a comprehensive plan, so maintaining some items but not others at the specified service intervals, will not produce the same results.

As you service your vehicle, you will discover that many of the procedures can – and should – be grouped together, because of the particular procedure being performed, or because of the proximity of two otherwise-unrelated components to one another. For example, if the vehicle is raised for any reason, the exhaust can be inspected at the same time as the suspension and steering components.

The first step in this maintenance programme is to prepare yourself before the actual work begins. Read through all the Sections relevant to the work to be carried out, then make a list and gather all the parts and tools required. If a problem is encountered, seek advice from a parts specialist, or a dealer service department.

Resetting the service light

To reset the service warning light on the instrument panel, switch on the ignition, then scroll through the trip computer's displayed options until the 'mileage before next service' is displayed (accompanied by a spanner symbol). Now press and hold one of the reset buttons on the end of the wiper stalk for 10 seconds, until the display resets.

2 Regular maintenance

If, from the time the vehicle is new, the routine maintenance schedule is followed closely, and frequent checks are made of fluid levels and high-wear items, as suggested throughout this manual, the engine will be kept in relatively good running condition, and the need for additional work will be minimised.

It is possible that there will be times when the engine is running poorly due to the lack of regular maintenance. This is even more likely if a used vehicle, which has not received regular and frequent maintenance checks, is purchased. In such cases, additional work may need to be carried out, outside of the regular maintenance intervals.

If engine wear is suspected, a compression test (refer to Chapter 2B or C) will provide valuable information regarding the overall performance of the main internal components.

Such a test can be used as a basis to decide on the extent of the work to be carried out. If, for example, a compression test indicates serious internal engine wear, conventional maintenance as described in this Chapter will not greatly improve the performance of the engine, and may prove a waste of time and money, unless extensive overhaul work is carried out first.

The following series of operations are those most often required to improve the performance of a generally poor-running engine:

Primary operations

a) Clean, inspect and test the battery (refer to Weekly checks).
b) Check all the engine-related fluids (refer to Weekly checks).
c) Check the condition of the auxiliary drivebelt (Section 7).
d) Check the condition of all hoses, and check for fluid leaks (Section 15).
e) Check the condition of the air filter, and renew if necessary (Section 17).
f) Check the fuel filter, and renew if necessary (Section 18).

If the above operations do not prove fully effective, carry out the following secondary operations:

Secondary operations

All items listed under *Primary operations*, plus the following:
a) Check the charging system (refer to Chapter 5A).
b) Check the preheating system (refer to Chapter 5C).
c) Check the fuel system (refer to Chapter 4B).

Every 9000 miles (15 000 km)

3 Engine oil and filter renewal

1 Frequent oil and filter changes are the most important preventative maintenance procedures which can be undertaken by the DIY owner. As engine oil ages, it becomes diluted and contaminated, which leads to premature engine wear.
2 Before starting this procedure, gather together all the necessary tools and materials. Also make sure that you have plenty of clean rags and newspapers handy, to mop up any spills. Ideally, the engine oil should be warm, as it will drain more easily, and more built-up sludge will be removed with it.
3 Take care not to touch the exhaust or any other hot parts of the engine when working under the car. To avoid any possibility of scalding, and to protect yourself from possible skin irritants and other harmful contaminants in used engine oils, it is advisable to wear gloves when carrying out this work.
4 With the handbrake applied, jack up the front of the car and support it on axle stands (see *Jacking and vehicle support*).
5 Remove the oil filler cap, then position a container beneath the sump. Where necessary, remove the fasteners and lower out the engine undertray. Clean the drain plug and the area around it, then slacken it half a turn – all models have a drain plug which requires an 8 mm square key to remove it **(see illustrations)**.

3.5a Remove the engine undertray

3.5b Engine oil drain plug (1.5 litre)

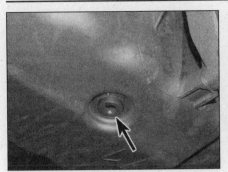

3.5c Engine oil drain plug (1.9 litre)

3.8a The 1.5 litre engine oil filter is angled upwards

3.8b Oil filter location on the front of the engine (1.9 litre – seen with bumper removed)

 HAYNES HiNT *If possible, try to keep the plug pressed into the sump while unscrewing it by hand the last couple of turns. As the plug releases from the threads, move it away sharply so the stream of oil from the sump runs into the container, not up your sleeve.*

6 Allow some time for the old oil to drain, noting that it may be necessary to reposition the container as the oil flow slows to a trickle.

7 After all the oil has drained, wipe off the drain plug with a clean rag; fit a new sealing washer, where applicable. Clean the area around the drain plug opening, then refit and tighten the plug securely.

8 Move the container into position under the oil filter, located on the front of the engine **(see illustrations)**. The oil filter is not easy to access – this is particularly true of 1.5 litre models. It may be advisable, once the engine oil has drained, to wait until the engine has cooled before attempting to reach the filter.

9 Using an oil filter removal tool, slacken the filter initially. Loosely wrap some rags around the oil filter, then unscrew it and immediately position it with its open end uppermost to prevent further spillage of oil. Remove the oil filter from the engine compartment and empty the oil into the container.

10 Use a clean rag to remove all oil, dirt and sludge from the filter sealing area on the

3.11 Oil the new filter sealing ring before fitting (1.5 litre)

engine. Check the old filter to make sure that the rubber sealing ring hasn't stuck to the engine. If it has, carefully remove it.

11 Apply a light coating of clean oil to the sealing ring on the new filter, then screw it into position on the engine **(see illustration)**. Tighten the filter firmly by hand only – do not use any tools. Wipe clean the exterior of the oil filter.

12 Remove the old oil and all tools from under the car, then, where necessary, refit the undertray and lower the car to the ground.

13 Fill the engine with the specified quantity and grade of oil, as described in *Weekly checks*. Pour the oil in slowly, in small amounts, waiting each time for the oil to drain into the sump. When the oil level is up to the maximum mark on the dipstick, refit and tighten the oil filler cap.

3.15 Once the engine has been run, check the oil level and add more if required

14 Start the engine and run it for a few minutes, checking that there are no leaks around the oil filter seal and the sump drain plug. Note that when the engine is first started, there will be a delay of a few seconds before the oil pressure warning light goes out while the new filter fills with oil. Do not race the engine while the warning light is on.

15 Switch off the engine and wait a few minutes for the oil to settle in the sump once more. With the new oil circulated and the filter now completely full, recheck the level on the dipstick and add more oil if necessary **(see illustration)**.

16 Dispose of the used engine oil safely with reference to *General repair procedures* in the Reference section of this manual.

Every 18 000 miles (30 000 km) or 2 years

4 Pollen filter renewal

Note: *Only models with air conditioning are equipped with a pollen filter.*

1 Open the bonnet, then unclip and remove the engine top cover.

2 The filter access cover is located centrally below the windscreen cowl panel – turn the catches to the side to release and remove the cover **(see illustrations)**.

3 Squeeze the tabs on the filter to release it. The filter element should slide out of its

4.2a Turn the catches to the side . . .

4.2b . . . and remove the pollen filter access cover

4.3 Removing the pollen filter

5.3 Check the exposed length of thread on the handbrake adjuster

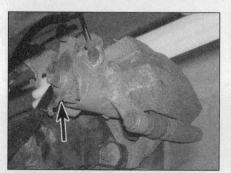

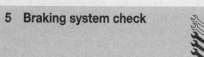

5.6 With the handbrake on, there should be a gap between the caliper lever and its stop

location, but it may be necessary to break the filter frame to achieve this **(see illustration)**.

4 Before fitting the new filter, clean carefully inside the housing.

5 Fit the new filter into its slot, observing any direction-of-fitting markings – as for removal, it may be necessary to break part of the new filter frame to make it fit. Clip the access cover back into place to complete.

5 Braking system check

Handbrake check and adjustment

Note: *Handbrake adjustment is only possible on models with the conventional (non-automatic) handbrake. Refer to Chapter 9 in the event of any problems with the automatic handbrake.*

1 The handbrake should be capable of holding the parked car stationary, even on steep slopes, when applied with moderate force. The mechanism should be firm and positive in feel, with no trace of stiffness or sponginess from the cables, and should release immediately the handbrake lever is released. If the mechanism is faulty in any of these respects, it must be checked immediately as follows.

2 Handbrake adjustment is made inside the car, after removing the centre console as described in Chapter 11.

3 Check the exposed length of thread in front of the cable adjuster nut fitted behind

5.9 If necessary, use the nut to adjust the handbrake

the handbrake handle **(see illustration)**. The specified setting is for new cables, so those which have seen longer service may already be showing more thread than specified, to take up the slack.

4 Jack up the rear of the car and support it on axle stands (see *Jacking and vehicle support*).

5 Operate the handbrake several times, and leave it applied as normal.

6 Check that the handbrake operating lever on each rear caliper is sitting off its stop by approximately 1 mm **(see illustration)**. If not, further adjustment may be required, or the cable on the side affected may have seized.

7 Check that the handbrake cables slide freely by pulling on their front ends, and check that the operating levers on the rear brake calipers move smoothly.

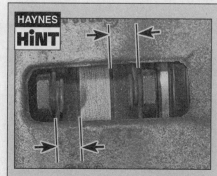

HAYNES HiNT

For a quick check, the thickness of friction material remaining on each pad can be measured through the aperture on the caliper body.

8 If the cables have stretched over time, the cables may need to be adjusted beyond the nominal setting. Bear in mind that the adjuster nut has a plastic insert, which loses its effectiveness over time – if the adjustment is being lost regularly, a new nut should be fitted.

9 Move both of the caliper operating levers as far rearwards as possible, then tighten the adjuster nut inside the car until all free play is removed from both cables. With the aid of an assistant, adjust the nut so that the operating lever on each rear brake caliper starts to move as the handbrake lever is moved between the first and second notch (click) of its ratchet mechanism **(see illustration)**.

10 After adjustment, release the handbrake fully, and check that the wheels are free to turn.

11 On completion, lower the car to the ground.

Brake pad and disc check

12 With the handbrake appled, jack up the front or rear of the car and support it securely on axle stands (see *Jacking and vehicle support*). Remove the roadwheels. Remember, the car has disc brakes all round, so all four calipers should be checked.

13 For a quick check, the thickness of friction material remaining on each brake pad can be measured through the aperture in the caliper body **(see Haynes Hint)**. If any pad's friction material is worn to the specified thickness or less, all four pads must be renewed as a set. Pad wear warning contacts may be fitted to the inboard pads, but this should not be used as an excuse for omitting a visual check.

14 For a comprehensive check, the brake pads should be removed and cleaned. This will allow the operation of the caliper to be checked, and the brake disc itself to be fully examined for condition on both sides. Refer to Chapter 9 for further information.

6 Clutch check

1 Check that the clutch pedal moves smoothly and easily through its full travel, and that the clutch itself functions correctly, with no trace of slip or drag. If the clutch action is less than precise, this may indicate the need for bleeding the system – it could also indicate the presence of a fluid leak (see Chapter 6).

7 Auxiliary drivebelt checking, removal and refitting

Checking

1 The auxiliary drivebelt is located at the right-hand side of the engine, providing drive for the alternator and (where applicable) the air conditioning compressor.

2 The drivebelt configuration is surprisingly similar on all models, but there are three different types of belt tensioner. Where air conditioning is not fitted, an extra idler pulley is added.

3 Due to their function and material makeup, drivebelts are prone to failure after a period of time, and should therefore be inspected regularly. On models with air conditioning, an automatic tensioner precludes the need for checking the belt tension.

4 Loosen the right-hand front wheel bolts, then jack up the front of the car, and support it on axle stands (see *Jacking and vehicle support*). Remove the wheel.

5 Remove the screws and clips securing the wheel arch liner, and remove it, noting that it is in two pieces (refer to Chapter 11, Section 21 for more information).

6 Inside the wheel arch, remove the four bolts securing the side support plate to the support member and inner wing, and remove it **(see illustrations)**.

7 With the engine stopped, inspect the full length of the drivebelt for cracks and separation of the belt plies. Small cracks in the belt ribs are no cause for concern, unless they are deep into the belt itself. Also check for fraying, and glazing which gives the belt a shiny appearance.

8 Turn the engine (using a spanner or socket on the crankshaft pulley bolt) so that the belt can be inspected thoroughly. Twist the belt between the pulleys so that both sides can be viewed. Check the pulleys for nicks, cracks, distortion and corrosion.

9 If the belt is satisfactory, refit the components removed to access it, then refit the wheel and lower the car to the ground. Tighten the wheel bolts to the specified torque.

Removal and refitting

10 If not already done, gain access to the belt as described in paragraphs 4 to 6.

Models without air conditioning

11 Before removing the belt, note its fitted position. On models without air conditioning, the pulleys have six grooves, the belt has five. In this case, the inner groove is left unused, so that the run of the belt is straight.

12 Loosen the two bolts securing the tensioner wheel bracket to the engine.

13 Turn the tensioner wheel bracket until the drivebelt can be removed from the pulleys.

14 Fit the drivebelt around the pulleys, making sure that it is correctly located in the grooves (refer to paragraph 11). Turn the tensioner wheel bracket to tension the belt, and tighten the bolts.

15 If the Renault special tools are not available, the belt tension will have to be set by feel – other than the 'frequency' specified, belt deflection is not quoted by Renault **(see illustration)**. Test the belt deflection midway between the pulleys on the bottom run of the belt – as a guide only, aim for a deflection of around 5 mm either way. Setting the belt

7.6a Remove the four bolts . . .

tension too high may cause wear in the belt, and in the alternator bearings.

16 Turn the engine through a few complete revolutions, using a spanner or socket on the crankshaft pulley bolt. With the belt settled on its pulleys, re-check the belt tension and adjust if necessary.

17 On completion, fully tighten the tensioner wheel bracket bolts.

18 If a new belt has been fitted, re-check the belt tension after (say) 500 miles, or earlier if there are signs that the belt is slipping. It is quite normal for a new belt to 'stretch' slightly in its first few miles of service (but don't over-tension a new belt to compensate).

Models with air conditioning

19 Using a 16 mm spanner on the bolt or hex fitting close to the tensioner, turn the tensioner pulley clockwise to release the tension on the belt. Noting its routing, remove the drivebelt from the pulleys **(see illustrations)**.

20 Fit the belt loosely around the main pulleys, making sure that it is correctly located in the grooves, then turn the tensioner the same way as previously until the belt can be fitted around the tensioner pulley also. Release the tensioner, and allow it to automatically tension the belt.

21 Turn the engine through a few complete revolutions, using a spanner or socket on the crankshaft pulley bolt. Check that the belt is running properly on its pulleys, and that the tensioner is working correctly (check that the belt is taut, midway along its bottom run).

All models

22 On completion, refit the components

7.19a Use a spanner on the hex fitting to turn the tensioner . . .

7.6b . . . and take out the side support plate

7.15 Using the Renault tool to pull the tensioner and adjust the belt

removed to access the belt, then refit the wheel and lower the car to the ground. Tighten the wheel bolts to the specified torque.

8 Fuel filter water draining

Note: *It is advisable to wear gloves when carrying out this procedure.*

1 The fuel filter is located under the right-hand wheel arch – remove the wheel arch liner as described in Chapter 11, Section 21 for access.

7.19b . . . and remove the belt from the pulleys

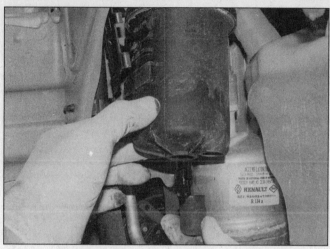

8.3 Pull off the rubber cover from the drain tap

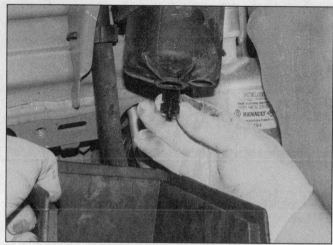

8.4 Place a container underneath, and open the drain tap

2 A water drain tap is provided at the base of the fuel filter housing, to which a suitable piece of tubing may be fitted.

3 Place a suitable container beneath the drain tap, and pull off the rubber cover **(see illustration)**.

4 Open the drain tap, and allow fuel and water to drain until water-free fuel emerges **(see illustration)**. Typically, only a very small amount should have to be drained – if a large amount of fuel is drained, the engine may have to be cranked for a long time before the engine will start. Close the drain tap securely.

5 Dispose of the drained fuel safely.

6 Start the engine. If difficulty is experienced, bleed the fuel system (Chapter 4B).

9 Seat belt check

1 Carefully examine the seat belt webbing for cuts, or any signs of serious fraying or deterioration. If the belt is of the retractable type, pull the belt all the way out of the inertia reel, and examine the full extent of the webbing.

2 Fasten and unfasten the belt, ensuring that the locking mechanism holds securely, and releases properly when intended. If the belt

is of the retractable type, check also that the retracting mechanism operates correctly when the belt is released.

3 Check the security of all seat belt mountings and attachments which are accessible without removing any trim or other components.

10 Electrical equipment check

1 Check the operation of all electrical equipment, ie, lights, direction indicators, horn, etc. Refer to the appropriate Sections of Chapter 12 for details if any of the circuits are found to be inoperative.

2 Note that stop-light switch adjustment is described in Chapter 9.

3 Visually check all accessible wiring connectors, harnesses and retaining clips for security, and for signs of chafing or damage. Rectify any faults found.

11 Exhaust system check

1 With the engine cold (at least an hour after the vehicle has been driven), check the

complete exhaust system from the engine to the end of the tailpipe. Ideally, the inspection should be carried out with the vehicle on a hoist to permit unrestricted access, but if a hoist is not available, raise and support the vehicle safely on axle stands (see *Jacking and vehicle support*).

2 Check the exhaust pipes and connections for evidence of leaks, severe corrosion and damage **(see illustrations)**. Make sure that all brackets and mountings are in good condition and tight. Leakage at any of the joints or in other parts of the system will usually show up as a black sooty stain in the vicinity of the leak.

3 Rattles and other noises can often be traced to the exhaust system, especially the brackets and mountings **(see illustration)**. Try to move the pipes and silencers. If the components can come into contact with the body or suspension parts, secure the system with new mountings or if possible, separate the joints and twist the pipes as necessary to provide additional clearance.

4 Run the engine at idling speed. Have an assistant place a cloth or rag over the rear end of the exhaust pipe, and listen for any escape of exhaust gases that would indicate a leak.

5 On completion, lower the car to the ground.

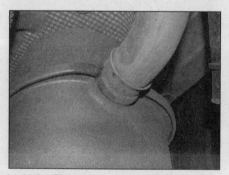

11.2a Check for exhaust leaks at pipe bends and joints . . .

11.2b . . . and at flexible sections

11.3 Check that the exhaust mounting-to-floor bolts are tight

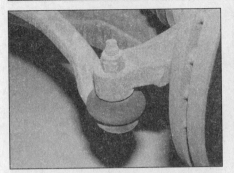

12.2a Check the balljoint rubber gaiters on the track rod ends . . .

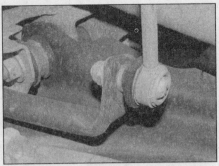

12.2b . . . and on the anti-roll bar drop links

12.2c Check the steering rack gaiters for splitting

12.3 Check for wheel bearing wear by grasping the wheel and trying to rock it

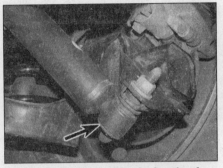

12.8 Check the rear shock absorber for fluid leaks and mounting damage

12.9 Check around the front strut piston rod gaiter for fluid leaks

12 Suspension and steering check

Front suspension and steering

1 Raise the front of the car, and securely support it on axle stands (see *Jacking and vehicle support*).

2 Visually inspect the balljoint dust covers and the steering rack-and-pinion gaiters for splits, chafing or deterioration **(see illustrations)**. Any wear of these components will cause loss of lubricant, together with dirt and water entry, resulting in rapid deterioration of the balljoints or steering gear.

3 Grasp the roadwheel at the 12 o'clock and 6 o'clock positions, and try to rock it **(see illustration)**. Very slight free play may be felt, but if the movement is appreciable, further investigation is necessary to determine the source. Continue rocking the wheel while an assistant depresses the footbrake. If the movement is now eliminated or significantly reduced, it is likely that the hub bearings are at fault. If the free play is still evident with the footbrake depressed, then there is wear in the suspension joints or mountings.

4 Now grasp the wheel at the 9 o'clock and 3 o'clock positions, and try to rock it as before. Any movement felt now may again be caused by wear in the hub bearings or the steering track rod balljoints. If the outer balljoint is worn, the visual movement will be obvious. If the inner joint is suspect, it can

be felt by placing a hand over the rack-and-pinion rubber gaiter and gripping the track rod. If the wheel is now rocked, movement will be felt at the inner joint if wear has taken place.

5 Using a large screwdriver or flat bar, check for wear in the suspension mounting bushes by levering between the relevant suspension component and its attachment point. Some movement is to be expected, as the mountings are made of rubber, but excessive wear should be obvious. Also check the condition of any visible rubber bushes, looking for splits, cracks or contamination of the rubber.

6 With the car standing on its wheels, have an assistant turn the steering wheel back-and-forth, about an eighth of a turn each way. There should be very little, if any, lost movement between the steering wheel and roadwheels. If this is not the case, closely observe the joints and mountings previously described. In addition, check the steering column universal joints for wear, and also check the rack-and-pinion steering gear itself.

Rear suspension

7 Chock the front wheels, then jack up the rear of the car and support securely on axle stands (see *Jacking and vehicle support*).

8 Working as described previously for the front suspension, check the rear hub bearings, the suspension bushes and the shock absorber mountings for wear **(see illustration)**. **Note:** *The handbrake must be released before checking the rear wheel bearings.*

Shock absorber check

9 Check for any signs of fluid leakage around the shock absorber body, or from the rubber gaiter around the piston rod **(see illustration)**. Should any fluid be noticed, the shock absorber is defective internally, and should be renewed. **Note:** *Shock absorbers should always be renewed in pairs on the same axle.*

10 The efficiency of the shock absorber may be checked by bouncing the car at each corner. Generally speaking, the body will return to its normal position and stop after being depressed. If it rises and returns on a rebound, the shock absorber is probably suspect.

Roadwheel bolt check

11 Remove the wheel trims or wheel centre caps, as applicable, then slacken the roadwheel bolts slightly.

12 Tighten the bolts to the specified torque, using a torque wrench.

13 Driveshaft gaiter check

1 With the car raised and securely supported on stands, turn the steering onto full lock, then slowly rotate the roadwheel. Inspect the condition of the outer constant velocity (CV) joint rubber gaiters while squeezing the gaiters to open out the folds. Check for signs of cracking, splits or deterioration of the rubber which may allow the grease to escape and lead to water and grit entry into the joint. Also check

13.1a Check the outer CV joint gaiters for splits or signs of perishing

the security and condition of the retaining clips. Repeat these checks on the inner CV joints **(see illustrations)**. If any damage or deterioration is found, refer to Chapter 8.

2 At the same time, check the general condition of the CV joints themselves by first holding the driveshaft and attempting to rotate the wheel. Repeat this check by holding the inner joint and attempting to rotate the driveshaft. Any appreciable movement indicates wear in the joints, wear in the driveshaft splines, or a loose driveshaft retaining nut.

14 Bodywork and underbody condition check

1 Once the car has been washed and all tar spots and other surface blemishes have been

15.1 Check along the sump joint for signs of oil leaks

15.3a Check the large-diameter radiator hoses for signs of damage

13.1b Similarly check the inner CV joint gaiters

cleaned off, carefully check all paintwork, looking closely for chips or scratches. Pay particular attention to vulnerable areas such as the front panels (bonnet and spoiler), and around the wheel arches. Any damage to the paintwork must be rectified as soon as possible to comply with the terms of the manufacturer's anti-corrosion warranties; check with a Renault dealer for details.

2 If a chip or light scratch is found which is recent and still free from rust, it can be touched-up using the appropriate touch-up stick which can be obtained from Renault dealers. Any more serious damage, or rusted stone chips, can be repaired as described in Chapter 11, but if damage or corrosion is so severe that a panel must be renewed, seek professional advice as soon as possible.

3 Always check that the door and ventilation opening drain holes and pipes are completely clear, so that water can drain out.

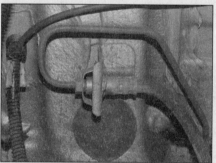

15.2 Check the brake pipes very carefully, especially at joints

15.3b Spring-type hose clips can pinch and puncture hoses

4 The wax-based underbody protective coating should be inspected annually, preferably just prior to Winter, when the underbody should be washed down as thoroughly as possible without disturbing the protective coating (see Chapter 11, Section 2, regarding the use of steam cleaners). Any damage to the coating should be repaired using a suitable wax-based sealer. If any of the body panels are disturbed for repair or renewal, do not forget to replace the coating and to inject wax into door panels, sills and box sections, to maintain the level of protection provided by the manufacturer.

15 Hose and fluid leak check

1 Visually inspect the engine joint faces, gaskets and seals for any signs of water or oil leaks. Pay particular attention to the areas around the top of the engine, cylinder head, oil filter and sump joint faces **(see illustration)**. Bear in mind that, over a period of time, some very slight seepage from these areas is to be expected – what you are really looking for is any indication of a serious leak. Should a leak be found, renew the offending gasket or oil seal by referring to the appropriate Chapters in this manual.

2 Also check the security and condition of all the engine-related pipes and hoses, and all hydraulic and braking system pipes and hoses **(see illustration)**. Ensure that all cable-ties or securing clips are in place, and in good condition. Clips which are broken or missing can lead to chafing of the hoses, pipes or wiring, which could cause more serious problems in the future.

3 Carefully check the radiator hoses and heater hoses along their entire length. Renew any hose which is cracked, swollen or deteriorated. Cracks will show up better if the hose is squeezed. Pay close attention to the hose clips that secure the hoses to the cooling system components. Hose clips can pinch and puncture hoses, resulting in cooling system leaks. If the crimped-type hose clips are used, it may be a good idea to use Jubilee clips **(see illustrations)**.

4 Inspect all the cooling system components (hoses, joint faces, etc) for leaks **(see Haynes Hint)**. Where any problems are found on system components, renew the component or gasket with reference to Chapter 3.

5 With the car raised, inspect the fuel tank and filler neck for punctures, cracks and other damage. The connection between the filler neck and tank is especially critical **(see illustration)**. Sometimes a rubber filler neck or connecting hose will leak due to loose retaining clamps or deteriorated rubber.

6 Carefully check all rubber hoses and metal fuel lines leading away from the fuel tank. Check for loose connections, deteriorated hoses, crimped lines, and other damage.

Pay particular attention to the vent pipes and hoses, which often loop up around the filler neck and can become blocked or crimped. Follow the lines to the front of the car, carefully inspecting them all the way. Renew damaged sections as necessary. Similarly, whilst the car is raised, take the opportunity to inspect all underbody brake fluid pipes and hoses.

7 From within the engine compartment, check the security of all fuel, vacuum and brake hose attachments and pipe unions, and inspect all hoses for kinks, chafing and deterioration.

8 Where applicable, check the condition of the automatic transmission fluid cooler pipes and hoses.

16 Road test

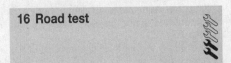

Instruments and electrical equipment

1 Check the operation of all instruments and electrical equipment.

2 Make sure that all instruments read correctly, and switch on all electrical equipment in turn, to check that it functions properly.

Steering and suspension

3 Check for any abnormalities in the steering, suspension, handling or road 'feel'.

4 Drive the car, and check that there are no unusual vibrations or noises.

5 Check that the steering feels positive, with no excessive 'sloppiness', or roughness, and check for any suspension noises when cornering and driving over bumps.

A leak in the cooling system will usually show up as white- or rust-coloured deposits on the area surrounding the joint.

Drivetrain

6 Check the performance of the engine, clutch, transmission and driveshafts.

7 Listen for any unusual noises from the engine, clutch and transmission.

8 Make sure that the engine runs smoothly when idling, and that there is no hesitation when accelerating.

9 Check that, where applicable, the clutch action is smooth and progressive, that the drive is taken up smoothly, and that the pedal travel is not excessive. Also listen for any noises when the clutch pedal is depressed.

10 Check that all gears can be engaged smoothly without noise, and that the gear lever action is not abnormally vague or 'notchy'.

11 Listen for a metallic clicking sound from the front of the car, as the car is driven slowly in a circle with the steering on full-lock. Carry out this check in both directions. If a

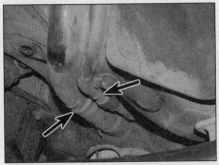

15.5 Check the fuel tank filler neck hoses for signs of leakage

clicking noise is heard, this indicates wear in a driveshaft joint (see Chapter 8).

Braking system

12 Make sure that the car does not pull to one side when braking, and that the wheels do not lock prematurely when braking hard.

13 Check that there is no vibration through the steering when braking.

14 Check that the handbrake operates correctly, without excessive movement of the lever, and that it holds the car stationary on a slope.

15 Test the operation of the brake servo unit as follows. Depress the footbrake four or five times to exhaust the vacuum, then start the engine. As the engine starts, there should be a noticeable 'give' in the brake pedal as vacuum builds up. Allow the engine to run for at least two minutes, and then switch it off. If the brake pedal is now depressed again, it should be possible to detect a hiss from the servo as the pedal is depressed. After about four or five applications, no further hissing should be heard, and the pedal should feel considerably harder.

Every 36 000 miles (60 000 km) or 4 years

17 Air filter element renewal

Removal

1 The air filter is located behind the battery.

Remove the left-hand outer section of the windscreen cowl panel for access, as described in Chapter 11.

2 Remove the two bolts from the air filter access panel, and lift it out **(see illustrations)**.

3 If the air filter has never been disturbed before, it may be necessary to cut the plastic

side 'perforations' securing the access flap with a sharp knife, before hinging the flap upwards. We managed to remove the filter without doing this, as described later in this Section.

4 Remove the battery cover, which is secured by two bolts at the rear, and a screw/clip at the front **(see illustration)**.

17.2a Remove the filter access panel bolt which can be seen . . .

17.2b . . . and the one tucked inside . . .

17.2c . . . then lift out the panel

17.4 Remove the battery cover

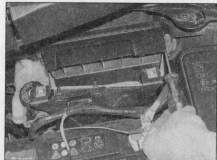

17.5a The filter housing screw one side is easy to access . . .

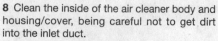
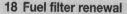

17.5b . . . but the other one may need a small or right-angled screwdriver

17.6 Slide the filter housing upwards to remove, holding back the access flap

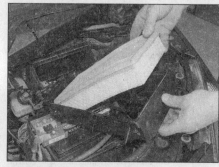

17.7 Withdraw the air filter element from the housing

Refitting

8 Clean the inside of the air cleaner body and housing/cover, being careful not to get dirt into the inlet duct.

9 Fit the new element using a reversal of the removal procedure.

18 Fuel filter renewal

Note: *It is advisable to wear gloves when carrying out this procedure.*

1 The fuel filter is located behind the right-hand headlight, and is accessed through the wheel arch.

2 Loosen the right-hand front wheel bolts, then jack up the front of the car, and support it on axle stands (see *Jacking and vehicle support*). Remove the wheel.

3 Remove the wheel arch liner as described in Chapter 11, Section 21 for access.

4 A water drain tap is provided at the base of the fuel filter housing, to which a suitable piece of tubing may be fitted. If wished, the fuel can be drained from the filter before removal, using a procedure similar to that for water draining, in Section 8.

5 Lift the filter upwards, and slide it out of the holder as far as possible **(see illustration)**.

6 Disconnect the wiring plug(s) from the filter unit, noting their fitted positions. Similarly, squeeze the quick-release fittings and disconnect the two fuel pipes, noting their fitted positions – anticipate some loss of fuel as this is done **(see illustrations)**. Remove the filter unit completely.

7 Unless a new filter is being fitted immediately, cap or plug the open fuel pipe connections, to prevent the entry of dirt into the system.

5 Unscrew and remove the two filter housing mounting screws – access to the one nearest the engine is hampered by the engine ECU, and may require the use of a stubby or cranked screwdriver **(see illustrations)**.

6 Either hinge the access flap upwards, or carefully press it rearwards to provide clearance, then slide the filter housing out upwards to remove it **(see illustration)**.

7 Withdraw the filter element from the housing **(see illustration)**.

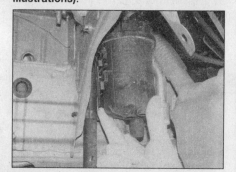

18.5 Lift and twist the filter to release it from its mounting bracket

18.6a Disconnect the fuel return pipe . . .

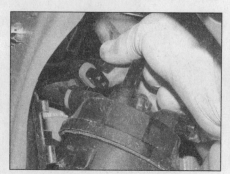

18.6b . . . the wiring plug . . .

18.6c . . . and the fuel supply pipe from the fuel filter

> **HAYNES HiNT**
> *When fitting a new filter, where possible, fill it with clean fuel before fitting. This will greatly reduce the length of time required for priming and bleeding the system on completion.*

18.9a Mark the position of the filter cover, relative to the bowl . . .

18.9b . . . then unscrew the bolt . . .

18.9c . . . remove the cover (over a suitable container) . . .

18.9d . . . take out the cover seal . . .

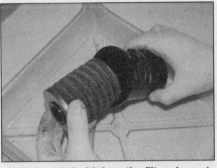

18.9e . . . and withdraw the filter element

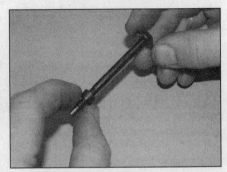

18.9f Fit a new seal to the securing bolt . . .

8 On 1.5 litre engines, the filter is renewed as a complete unit.

9 On 1.9 litre engines, mark the position of the filter assembly top cover, relative to the filter bowl. Unscrew the cover securing bolt, and remove the filter element. Check the condition of the cover seal and bolt seal, and fit new ones if necessary. Fit the new filter, then ensuring the marks on the bowl and cover are aligned, fit the cover securing bolt and tighten it securely **(see illustrations)**.

10 Fit the filter back into position under the wheel arch, making sure the fuel pipes and wiring plugs are reconnected correctly and securely.

11 On models with a drain plug on the base of the filter, open the drain plug and squeeze the hand-priming pump under the bonnet until the fuel flows through the filter, then securely tighten the drain plug.

12 On completion, refit the components removed to access the filter, then refit the wheel and lower the car to the ground. Tighten the wheel bolts to the specified torque. Reconnect the battery.

13 Squeeze the hand-priming pump a few times to prime the system, then start the engine as normal. If the engine is reluctant to start, refer to Chapter 4B for more information on priming and bleeding the fuel system.

14 With the engine running, check for any sign of fuel leakage under the wheel arch.

15 Dispose of the old filter correctly, remembering that it may still contain (or be soaked in) fuel.

18.9g . . . and to the cover . . .

19 Manual transmission oil level check

1 Either position the car over an inspection pit, or jack up the front and rear of the car and support it on axle stands (see *Jacking and vehicle support*). The car must be level for the check to be accurate.

2 Remove the engine undertray or unclip the cover, as applicable, from the bottom of the transmission.

3 Locate the filler/level plug, and clean the area around it before removal. On 5-speed transmissions, the plug is located on the front facing side of the transmission, while 6-speed units have the level plug on the left-hand end face, at the front **(see illustrations)**.

4 Unscrew and remove the plug – this will probably be very tight **(see illustration)**.

18.9h . . . when fitting the new filter

Check the condition of the filler plug seal, and obtain a new one if necessary.

5 The oil level should be up to the lower edge of the filler/level plug aperture.

6 If necessary, top-up using the specified

19.3a The transmission filler/level plug is on the front (5-speed) . . .

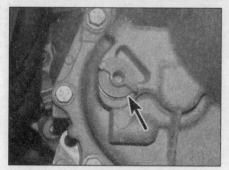

19.3b . . . or on the side (6-speed)

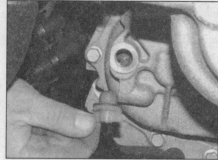

19.4 Unscrew the filler/level plug

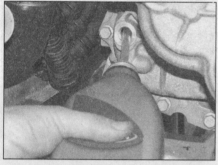

19.6 Top-up the oil level through the filler hole

type of lubricant until the transmission oil level is correct. Fill the transmission until oil starts to flow out and allow excess oil to drain out **(see illustration)**.

7 Once the transmission oil level is correct, refit the filler/level plug and tighten it securely.

8 Refit the engine undertray cover or transmission bottom cover as applicable, then lower the car to the ground. Note that frequent need for topping-up indicates a leak, possibly through an oil seal. The cause should be investigated and rectified.

20 Front wheel alignment check

Refer to the information given in Chapter 10.

23.2 Change the brake fluid using the same method as for brake bleeding

21 Air conditioning system check

The air conditioning system must be checked by a Renault dealer using dedicated test equipment.

22 Timing belt renewal

Refer to Chapter 2B or 2C.

23 Brake fluid renewal

⚠ **Warning: Brake hydraulic fluid can harm your eyes and damage painted surfaces, so use extreme caution when handling and pouring it. Do not use fluid that has been standing open for some time, as it absorbs moisture from the air. Excess moisture can cause a dangerous loss of braking effectiveness.**

1 The procedure is similar to that for the bleeding of the hydraulic system as described in Chapter 9, except that the brake fluid reservoir should be emptied by syphoning, using a clean poultry baster or similar before starting, and allowance should be made for the old fluid to be expelled when bleeding a section of the circuit.

24.3a Release the spring clip and pull off the radiator lower hose (front bumper removed)

2 Working as described in Chapter 9, open the first bleed screw in the sequence, and pump the brake pedal gently until nearly all the old fluid has been emptied from the master cylinder reservoir **(see illustration)**. Top-up to the MAX level with new fluid, and continue pumping until only the new fluid remains in the reservoir, and new fluid can be seen emerging from the bleed screw. Tighten the screw, and top the reservoir level up to the MAX level line.

HAYNES HiNT *Old hydraulic fluid is invariably much darker in colour than the new, making it easy to distinguish the two.*

3 Work through all the remaining bleed screws in the sequence until new fluid can be seen at all of them. Be careful to keep the master cylinder reservoir topped-up to above the MIN level at all times, or air may enter the system and greatly increase the length of the task.

4 When the operation is complete, check that all bleed screws are securely tightened, and that their dust caps are refitted. Wash off all traces of spilt fluid, and recheck the master cylinder reservoir fluid level.

5 Check the operation of the brakes before taking the car on the road.

24 Coolant renewal

Cooling system draining

⚠ *Warning: Wait until the engine is cold before starting this procedure. Do not allow antifreeze to come in contact with your skin, or with the painted surfaces of the vehicle. Rinse off spills immediately with plenty of water. Never leave antifreeze lying around in an open container, or in a puddle in the driveway or on the garage floor. Children and pets are attracted by its sweet smell, but antifreeze can be fatal if ingested.*

1 With the engine completely cold, remove the expansion tank filler cap. Turn the cap anti-clockwise, wait until any pressure remaining in the system is released, then unscrew it and lift it off.

2 Where applicable, remove the undertray, then position a container beneath the radiator bottom hose connection. For more complete draining, remove the smaller expansion tank hose at the side, right at the base of the radiator – however, access is difficult without removing the front bumper first, as described in Chapter 11.

3 Loosen the hose clip, pull off the hose and allow the coolant to drain into the container **(see illustrations)**.

4 To assist draining, open the cooling system bleed screw on the thermostat housing, and on the heater hose **(see illustrations)**. Models

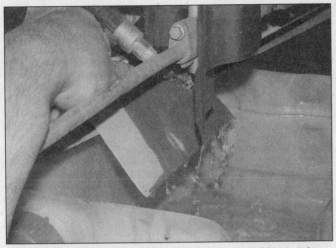

24.3b Direct the flow from the radiator into a suitable container

24.4a Open the bleed screw on the thermostat housing . . .

with the 1.9 litre engine may have an additional bleed screw at the rear of the engine, behind the EGR solenoid valve.

5 If compressed air is available, Renault suggest inserting an air line into the expansion tank to drive out as much water as possible.

6 Flush the system if necessary as described in the following paragraphs, then refit the bottom hose. Use a new hose clip if necessary. Refill the system as described later in this Section.

Cooling system flushing

7 If coolant renewal has been neglected, or if the antifreeze mixture has become diluted, then in time, the cooling system may gradually lose efficiency, as the coolant passages become restricted due to rust, scale deposits, and other sediment. The cooling system efficiency can be restored by flushing the system clean.

8 The simplest method for flushing the system is to loosely refit the radiator bottom hose, then refill the system with clean water. When the system is full, disconnect the radiator bottom hose and allow the water to drain a second time. Check the condition of the water drained – if it is clean, flushing is complete; if not, repeat the process.

Radiator flushing

9 Disconnect the top and bottom hoses and any other relevant hoses from the radiator, with reference to Chapter 3.

10 Insert a garden hose into the radiator top inlet. Direct a flow of clean water through the radiator, and continue flushing until clean water emerges from the radiator bottom outlet.

11 If after a reasonable period, the water still does not run clear, the radiator can be flushed with a good proprietary cleaning agent. It is important that the manufacturer's instructions are followed carefully. If the contamination is particularly bad, insert the hose in the radiator bottom outlet, and reverse-flush the radiator.

Engine flushing

12 To flush the engine, remove the thermostat as described in Chapter 3, and disconnect the bottom hose.

13 Insert a garden hose into the thermostat housing and direct a clean flow of water through the engine. Continue flushing until clean water emerges from the radiator bottom hose.

14 On completion, refit the thermostat and reconnect the bottom hose. Where applicable, refit the engine undertray.

Antifreeze mixture

15 The antifreeze should always be renewed at the specified intervals. This is necessary not only to maintain the antifreeze properties, but also to prevent corrosion which would otherwise occur as the corrosion inhibitors become progressively less effective.

16 Always use an ethylene-glycol based antifreeze which is suitable for use in mixed-metal cooling systems. The quantity of antifreeze and levels of protection are given in the Specifications.

17 Before adding antifreeze, the cooling system should be completely drained, preferably flushed, and all hoses checked for condition and security.

18 After filling with antifreeze, a label should be attached to the expansion tank, stating the type and concentration of antifreeze used, and the date installed. Any subsequent topping-up should be made with the same type and concentration of antifreeze.

19 Do not use engine antifreeze in the windscreen/tailgate washer system, as it will cause damage to the vehicle's paintwork. A screenwash additive should be added to the washer system in the quantities stated on the bottle.

Cooling system filling

20 Before attempting to fill the cooling system, make sure that all hoses and clips are in good condition, and that the clips are tight. Note that an antifreeze mixture must be used all year round, to prevent corrosion of the engine components.

21 Remove the expansion tank filler cap (see illustration).

22 If not already done, open the cooling system bleed screws.

23 Slowly fill the system until the coolant level reaches the MAX mark on the expansion tank. Close the bleed screws in turn when coolant free from air bubbles emerges from each one.

24 Start the engine, and run it at a fast idle speed (approx 2000 rpm). As soon as the

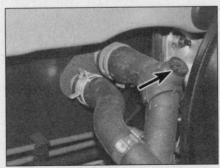

24.4b . . . and on the heater hose next to the bulkhead

24.21 Remove the coolant expansion tank filler cap

engine is running, top-up the level in the expansion tank if necessary, then refit and tighten the expansion tank filler cap – the cap should not normally be removed when the engine is running, nor when the system is hot.

25 Allow the engine to run at 2000 rpm until the cooling fan has cut in and out three times.

26 Stop the engine and allow the engine to cool for at least an hour, and preferably, overnight.

27 Recheck the coolant level with reference to *Weekly checks*. Top-up the level if necessary and refit the expansion tank filler cap.

Airlocks

28 If, after draining and refilling the system, symptoms of overheating are found which did not occur previously, then the fault is almost certainly due to trapped air at some point in the system, causing an airlock and restricting the flow of coolant; usually, the air is trapped because the system was refilled too quickly.

29 If an airlock is suspected, first try gently squeezing all visible coolant hoses. A coolant hose which is full of air feels quite different to one full of coolant, when squeezed. After refilling the system, most airlocks will clear once the system has cooled, and been topped up.

30 While the engine is running at operating temperature, switch on the heater and heater fan, and check for heat output. Provided there is sufficient coolant in the system, any lack of heat output could be due to an airlock in the system.

31 Airlocks can have more serious effects than simply reducing heater output – a severe airlock could reduce coolant flow around the engine. Check that the radiator top hose is hot when the engine is at operating temperature – a top hose which stays cold could be the result of an airlock (or a non-opening thermostat).

32 If the problem persists, stop the engine and allow it to cool down **completely**, before unscrewing the radiator and expansion tank caps, or loosening the hose clips and squeezing the hoses to bleed out the trapped air. In the worst case, the system will have to be at least partially drained (this time, the coolant can be saved for re-use) and flushed to clear the problem.

Chapter 2 Part A:
1.4 & 1.6 litre petrol engine in-car repair procedures

Contents

Degrees of difficulty

Easy, suitable for novice with little experience	**Fairly easy,** suitable for beginner with some experience	**Fairly difficult,** suitable for competent DIY mechanic	**Difficult,** suitable for experienced DIY mechanic	**Very difficult,** suitable for expert DIY or professional

Specifications

General

Type	Four-cylinder, in-line, 16-valve double overhead camshaft (DOHC), variable valve timing (VVT) on 1.6 litre
Designation:	
1.4 litre models	K4J 729 / 730
1.6 litre models	K4M 761 / 782
Bore	79.5 mm
Stroke:	
1.4 litre engine	70.0 mm
1.6 litre engine	80.5 mm
Capacity:	
1.4 litre engine	1390 cc
1.6 litre engine	1598 cc
Firing order	1-3-4-2 (No 1 cylinder at transmission end)
Direction of crankshaft rotation	Clockwise viewed from pulley end
Compression ratio:	
1.4 litre engine	10.0 : 1
1.6 litre engine	9.8 : 1

Camshaft

Endfloat	0.08 to 0.178 mm
Camshaft bearing journal diameters:	
No 1 to No 5 bearings	24.979 to 25.000 mm
No 6 bearing.	27.979 to 28.000 mm

Lubrication system

	Minimum	Maximum
System pressure:		
At idle	1.0 bar	
At 3000 rpm	3.0 bar	
Oil pump clearances:	**Minimum**	**Maximum**
Gear-to-body	0.110 mm	0.249 mm
Gear endfloat	0.020 mm	0.086 mm

Torque wrench settings

	Nm	lbf ft
Alternator support bracket:		
Bracket-to-engine bolts	40	30
Bracket-to-sump bolt	21	15
Camshaft phase-shifter (1.6 litre):		
Cover screws	15	11
Centre bolt	75	55
Camshaft sprocket nuts*		
Stage 1	30	22
Stage 2	Angle-tighten a further 84° ± 4°	
Connecting rod (big-end) cap – oiled	43	32
Coolant elbow mounting bolts	10	7
Crankshaft pulley bolt:		
Stage 1	40	30
Stage 2	Angle-tighten a further 115° ± 15°	
Cylinder block TDC blanking plug	20	15
Cylinder head bolts:		
Stage 1	20	15
Stage 2	Angle-tighten a further 240° ± 6°	
Cylinder head cover bolts:		
Stage 1 – bolts 22, 23, 20, 13	8	6
Stage 2 – bolts 1 to 12, 14 to 19, 21 to 24	15	11
Stage 3 – bolts 22, 23, 20, 13	Slacken fully	
Stage 4 – bolts 22, 23, 20, 13	15	11
Driveplate bolts*		
Stage 1	55	41
Stage 2	Angle-tighten a further 50° ± 5°	
Engine mountings:		
Left-hand mounting centre nut	62	46
Left-hand mounting outer nuts	105	78
Left-hand mounting stud-to-mounting	180	133
Left-hand mounting-to-body bolts	21	15
Left-hand mounting-to-transmission bolts	62	46
Lower mounting bolts	105	78
Right-hand mounting bracket-to-engine bolts	44	32
Right-hand mounting through-bolt	105	78
Right-hand mounting-to-wing bolts	62	46
Right-hand mounting-to-engine upper bolts	62	46
Exhaust manifold nuts	23	17
Exhaust mounting flange nuts	21	15
Flywheel bolts*	65	48
Main bearing cap:		
Stage 1	25	18
Stage 2	Angle-tighten a further 47° ± 5°	
Oil pump:		
Mounting bolts	25	18
Sprocket bolts	10	7
Oil separator to cylinder head upper section	13	10
Radiator lower crossmember:		
Front bolt	105	78
Rear nut (to subframe)	21	15
Side support plate bolts	21	15
Roadwheel bolts	130	96
Sump:		
Stage 1	8	6
Stage 2	14	10
Timing belt idler pulley	45	33
Timing belt tensioner pulley:		
Pre-tighten (initial setting)	7	5
Final setting	27	20
Timing cover (upper)	41	30
VVT solenoid bolt	10	7

*Use new nuts/bolts when refitting

1 General information

How to use this Chapter

This Part of Chapter 2 is devoted to in-car repair procedures for the 1.4 and 1.6 litre petrol engines. Similar information covering the other engine types can be found in Parts B and C. All procedures concerning engine removal and refitting, and engine block/cylinder head overhaul can be found in Part D of this Chapter.

Refer to *Vehicle identification numbers* in the Reference Section at the end of this manual for details of engine code locations.

Most of the operations included in this Part are based on the assumption that the engine is still installed in the car. Therefore, if this information is being used during a complete engine overhaul, with the engine already removed, many of the steps included here will not apply.

Engine description

The engine is of four-cylinder, in-line, double overhead camshaft (DOHC) type, mounted transversely in the front of the car.

The camshafts are mounted in the cylinder head on six plain bearings with matching caps, and are driven from the crankshaft by a toothed rubber timing belt, which also drives the water pump. On the 1.4 litre engines, the camshaft sprockets are both conventional; on the 1.6 litre engine, the inlet camshaft sprocket incorporates a phase-shifter which provides variable valve timing by advancing the inlet valve timing during certain operating conditions. The phase-shifter is activated by the engine management ECU, via an electrically-controlled solenoid valve located on the top right-hand side of the cylinder head. The camshafts operate the valves by hydraulic tappets and roller cam followers located below the camshafts in the cylinder head.

The cylinder block is of cast iron, with conventional dry liners bored directly into the cylinder block. The crankshaft is supported within the cylinder block on five shell-type main bearings. Thrustwashers are fitted at the upper centre main bearing to control crankshaft endfloat.

The connecting rods are attached to the crankshaft by horizontally-split shell-type big-end bearings and to the pistons by gudgeon pins which are an interference-fit in the connecting rods. The aluminium alloy pistons are fitted with three piston rings, comprising two compression rings and a scraper-type oil control ring.

A fully-enclosed crankcase ventilation system is employed; crankcase fumes are drawn from an oil separator on the cylinder head, and passed via a hose to the inlet manifold.

Lubrication is by pressure feed from a gear-type oil pump, which is chain-driven direct from the crankshaft.

Operations with engine in place

The following operations can be carried out without having to remove the engine from the car:

a) *Removal and refitting of the cylinder head.*
b) *Removal and refitting of the timing belt and sprockets.*
c) *Renewal of the camshaft oil seal.*
d) *Removal and refitting of the camshaft.*
e) *Removal and refitting of the sump.*
f) *Removal and refitting of the connecting rods and pistons*.*
g) *Removal and refitting of the oil pump.*
h) *Renewal of the crankshaft timing belt end oil seal.*
i) *Renewal of the engine mountings.*

* Note: *Although the operation marked with an asterisk can be carried out with the engine in the car after removal of the sump, it is better for the engine to be removed, in the interests of cleanliness and improved access. For this reason, these procedures are described in Part D of this Chapter.*

2 Compression test – description and interpretation

Note: *A compression gauge will be required for this test.*

1 A compression check will tell you what mechanical condition the top end (pistons, rings, valves, head gasket) of the engine is in. Specifically, it can tell you if the compression is down due to leakage caused by worn piston rings, defective valves and seats or a blown head gasket. **Note:** *The engine must be at normal operating temperature and the battery must be fully-charged, for this check.*

2 Begin by cleaning the area around the spark plugs before you remove them (compressed air should be used, if available, otherwise a small brush or even a bicycle tyre pump will work). The idea is to prevent dirt from getting into the cylinders as the compression check is being done.

3 Remove all the spark plugs from the engine (see Chapter 1A).

4 Disable the engine management system by removing the engine protection fuse from the engine compartment fusebox.

5 Fit the compression gauge into the No 1 spark plug hole – the type of tester which screws into the plug thread is to be preferred.

6 Have an assistant hold the accelerator pedal fully depressed, while at the same time cranking the engine over several times on the starter motor. Observe the compression gauge – the compression should build-up quickly in a healthy engine. Low compression on the first stroke, followed by gradually-increasing

pressure on successive strokes, indicates worn piston rings. A low compression reading on the first stroke, which does not build-up during successive strokes, indicates leaking valves or a blown head gasket (a cracked head could also be the cause). Deposits on the undersides of the valve heads can also cause low compression. Record the highest gauge reading obtained, then repeat the procedure for the remaining cylinders.

7 Add some engine oil (about three squirts from a plunger-type oil can) to each cylinder, through the spark plug hole and repeat the test.

8 If the compression increases after the oil is added, the piston rings are worn. If the compression does not increase significantly, the leakage is occurring at the valves or head gasket. Leakage past the valves may be caused by burned valve seats and/or faces, or warped, cracked or bent valves.

9 If two adjacent cylinders have equally low compression, there is a strong possibility that the head gasket between them is blown. The appearance of coolant in the combustion chambers or the crankcase would verify this condition.

10 Actual compression pressures for the engines covered by this manual are not specified by the manufacturer. However, bearing in mind the information given in the preceding paragraphs, the results obtained should give a good indication of engine condition and what course of action, if any, to take.

3 Top Dead Centre (TDC) for No 1 piston – locating

Note: *A TDC pin from a Renault dealer (Mot. 1489) or automotive tool shop is required for this operation.*

1 Top Dead Centre (TDC) is the highest point in the cylinder that each piston reaches as the crankshaft turns. Each piston reaches TDC at the end of the compression stroke, and again at the end of the exhaust stroke. However, for the purpose of timing the engine, TDC refers to the position of No 1 piston at the end of its compression stroke. No 1 piston is at the flywheel (transmission) end of the engine.

2 With the handbrake applied, jack up the front right-hand side of the car and support it on axle stands. Remove the right-hand roadwheel.

3 Remove the plastic liners from within the right-hand wheel arch to give access to the crankshaft pulley bolt (see Chapter 11, Section 21).

4 Remove the spark plugs as described in Chapter 1A.

5 The engine must now be turned in order to check for pressure in No 1 cylinder (nearest the flywheel) as the piston rises on the compression stroke. As the spark plug holes are deeply recessed, it is not possible

3.7 Using a screwdriver, prise the camshaft sealing plugs from the left-hand end of the cylinder head

3.8a Unscrew the TDC plug . . .

3.8b . . . obtain the TDC pin . . .

3.8c . . . and screw it into the cylinder block

3.9a The special Renault tool used to lock the camshafts in their TDC position

3.9b Home-made tool for locking the camshafts

to place a finger over them, however, the inverted handle of a screwdriver may be used instead, or alternatively simply listen for air being forced out of the No 1 spark plug hole. Turn the engine in a clockwise direction, using a socket or spanner on the crankshaft pulley bolt, until air is forced from No 1 cylinder; this indicates that No 1 piston is rising on its compression stroke.

6 Remove the air cleaner resonator box (1.4 litre) or the air inlet duct (1.6 litre) from the left-hand side of the engine, with reference to Chapter 4A. To further improve access to the left-hand side of the engine, the battery can be removed as described in Chapter 5A.

7 Using a screwdriver, pierce the centres of the two plastic plugs at the left-hand end of the cylinder head, and pull out the plugs **(see illustration)**. With No 1 piston approaching TDC, the grooves in the ends of the camshafts should be positioned approximately at 30° angle from the horizontal, with the offset below the centreline, downward ends at the rear of the engine.

8 Unscrew the TDC plug from the left-hand front of the cylinder block, then fully screw in the TDC pin **(see illustrations)**.

9 Carefully turn the crankshaft clockwise until the crankshaft web contacts the TDC pin. At this point, the No 1 piston is at TDC on its compression stroke, and the grooves in the ends of the camshafts will now be positioned horizontally. Renault technicians use a special tool to lock the camshafts in their TDC position. The tool is attached to the left-hand end of the cylinder head to hold the camshafts with their grooves horizontal, and a

similar tool may be fabricated from metal plate if necessary **(see illustrations)**.

10 Note that the crankshaft sprocket is not keyed to the crankshaft, therefore if the crankshaft pulley/sprocket is removed it is important to have an accurate method of determining the TDC position of No 1 piston.

---

4 Timing belt – removal, inspection and refitting

Note: *A Renault TDC pin (Mot. 1489) or approved alternative is required for this operation, and may be obtained from most car accessory shops. Also, a Renault camshaft locking bar (Mot. 1496) or alternative will be required (see text).*

Note: *Renault state that the timing belt must be renewed whenever it is removed, and*

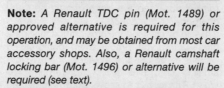

4.6 Support the right-hand end of the engine with a trolley jack

also that the tensioner and idler pulley must be renewed whenever the timing belt is renewed.

Caution: If the timing belt breaks in service, extensive engine damage may result. Renew the belt at the intervals specified in Chapter 1A, or earlier if its condition is at all doubtful.

Removal

1 Disconnect the battery negative lead, and move the lead away from the battery (see *Disconnecting the battery*).

2 With the handbrake applied, jack up the front right-hand side of the car and support on axle stands (see *Jacking and vehicle support*). Remove the right-hand roadwheel. Where fitted, remove the engine compartment undertray.

3 Remove the screws and clips securing the right-hand wheel arch liner, referring if necessary to Chapter 11, Section 21. For improved access to the right-hand side of the engine, we found it beneficial to remove the front bumper (see Chapter 11). The engine is very close to the right-hand inner body panel.

4 Remove the auxiliary drivebelt as described in Chapter 1A.

5 Set the engine at TDC for No 1 piston as described in Section 3.

6 Carefully position a trolley jack and a large block of wood under the sump to support the right-hand side of the engine. Raise the jack to just take the weight of the engine **(see illustration)**. If available, an engine support bar can be fitted, to take the weight of the engine from above.

7 Remove the windscreen cowl panels as described in Chapter 11, Section 8.

8 Remove the engine right-hand mounting from the engine and body with reference to Section 12. At this stage, we also removed the alternator for improved access – refer to Chapter 5A. It may also be beneficial to unbolt and remove the coolant expansion bottle – move it to one side without disconnecting the hoses.

9 Remove the wiring loom from the right-hand end of the engine by disconnecting it from the inlet manifold and unbolting the support bracket at the right-hand front of the cylinder head. Also unclip and disconnect the vacuum pipe from the inlet manifold. Release the loom from the upper timing cover and position it to one side (**see illustrations**).

10 Unclip the fuel pipe(s) from the lower timing cover, then remove the air cleaner as described in Chapter 4A.

11 Using a screwdriver, pierce the centres of the two plastic plugs at the left-hand end of the camshafts, and pull the plugs from the cylinder head. With No 1 piston approaching TDC, the grooves in the ends of the camshafts should be as shown (**see illustrations**).

12 Unscrew the TDC plug from the left-hand front of the cylinder block, then fully screw in the TDC pin (**see illustration**).

4.9a Unclip the vacuum pipes and wiring loom, and position to one side

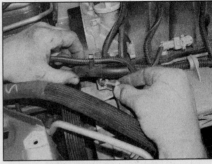

4.9b Unbolting the wiring support bracket from the right-hand front of the engine

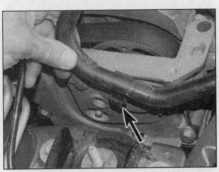

4.9c Note how the wiring loom conduit locates in the upper timing cover

4.11a Use a screwdriver to prise out the plastic plugs from the left-hand end of the cylinder head

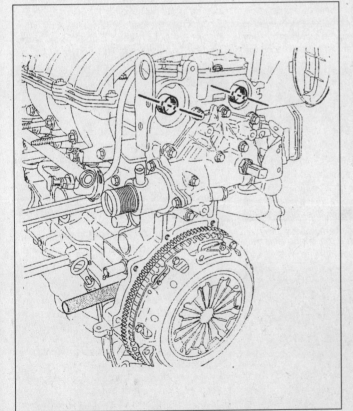

4.11b Turn the crankshaft until the slots in the camshafts are initially positioned at approximately a 30° angle from the horizontal, with the offsets below the centreline

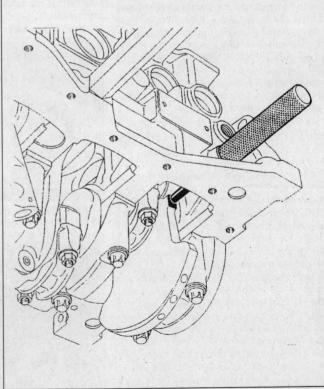

4.12 TDC pin on the left-hand front of the cylinder block

4.13a With the crankshaft at TDC the grooves in the end of the camshafts will be positioned horizontally

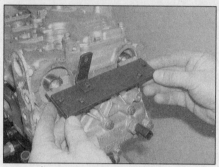

4.13b Engage the camshaft holding tool with the camshaft slots . . .

4.13c . . . and secure the tool using a suitable bolt screwed into the cylinder head

TOOL TIP

To make a camshaft holding tool, obtain a length of steel strip and cut it to length so that it will fit across the rear of the cylinder head. Obtain a second length of steel strip of suitable thickness to fit snugly in the slots in the camshafts. Cut the second strip into two lengths and drill accordingly so that they can be bolted to the first strip in the correct position to engage with the camshaft slots. Secure a suitably drilled small piece of steel angle to the first strip so that the tool can be bolted to the threaded hole in the cylinder head upper section.

13 Carefully turn the crankshaft clockwise until the crankshaft web is in contact with the TDC pin. At this point, the No 1 piston is at TDC on its compression stroke, and the grooves in the ends of the camshafts will now be positioned horizontally. Renault technicians use a special tool to lock the camshafts in their TDC position, however, a length of metal bar may be fabricated **(see illustrations and Tool Tip)**.

14 On 1.6 litre engines, further confirmation of the TDC position can be gained from the camshaft sprockets. At TDC, the Renault 'diamond' emblem on the exhaust camshaft sprocket and the etched mark on the inlet sprocket (with the VVT unit) will both be facing vertically upwards **(see illustration)**.

15 Before loosening the crankshaft pulley bolt, note that the crankshaft sprocket is **not** keyed to the crankshaft, therefore if the crankshaft pulley is removed, it is important to have an accurate

method of determining the TDC position of No 1 piston. Although the sprocket is not keyed to the crankshaft, there is still a groove in the crankshaft nose which is at the 12 o'clock position when piston No 1 is at TDC.

16 To prevent the crankshaft from rotating while the pulley bolt is unscrewed, first remove the metal bar from the camshafts then, on manual transmission models have an assistant engage top gear and firmly depress the brake pedal. Alternatively, and on automatic transmission models, the crankshaft may be held stationary by unbolting the crankshaft speed/position sensor from the top of the transmission and wedging a screwdriver in the starter ring gear teeth through the sensor's opening in the bellhousing.

17 Unscrew the crankshaft pulley bolt, then remove the pulley **(see illustrations)**. Note: *The bolt is very tight*. The bolt may be re-

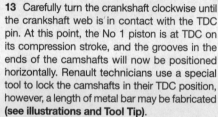

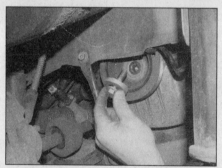

4.17a Unscrew the crankshaft pulley bolt . . .

4.17b . . . and remove the pulley

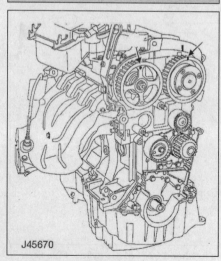

4.14 Camshaft sprocket marks at TDC (1.6 litre engines)

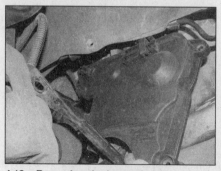

4.18a Removing the lower timing cover . . .

4.18b . . . and upper timing cover

used if its length from under the head to its end does not exceed 49.1 mm. If the length is greater than this, renew the bolt.

18 Unbolt the lower timing cover, followed by the upper timing cover **(see illustrations)**.

19 Loosen the timing belt tensioner, then turn the tensioner hub anti-clockwise to release the tension.

20 The belt should be marked with arrows to indicate its running direction – if it is to be re-used (which is not recommended), mark it to ensure correct refitting. Release the belt from the camshaft sprockets, water pump pulley, crankshaft sprocket, tensioner pulley and idler pulley and remove it from the engine.

21 Clean the sprockets, tensioner and idler and wipe them dry. Also clean the cylinder head and block behind the timing belt running area.

Inspection

22 Examine the timing belt carefully for any signs of cracking, fraying or general wear, particularly at the roots of the teeth. Renew the belt if there is any sign of deterioration of this nature, or if there is any oil or grease contamination. Renew any leaking oil seals. The belt **must** be renewed if it has completed the maximum mileage given in Chapter 1A.

23 When fitting a new belt, Renault recommend that a new tensioner and idler pulley are also fitted – these are often sold as a kit with a new belt, when purchased from a Renault dealer.

24 Thoroughly clean the nose of the crankshaft and the bore of the crankshaft sprocket, and also the contact surfaces of the sprocket and pulley. This is necessary to prevent the possibility of the sprocket, which is not keyed to the crankshaft, slipping in use and causing engine damage.

Refitting

25 Check that the lug on the rear of the tensioner is correctly located in the groove.

26 Check that the camshafts and No 1 piston are still at TDC. Fit the timing belt on the crankshaft sprocket, then locate it around the water pump and idler, over the camshafts and around the tensioner. Make sure that the belt is taut between the camshaft sprockets, and the correct way round if refitting the original.

27 Check that the idler retaining bolt is tightened to the specified torque.

28 On the 1.4 litre engine, two types of tensioner have been fitted; Version 1 is identified by having a fixed and adjustable pointer, whereas Version 2 has a fixed notched plate and adjustable pointer. On 1.6 litre engines, only the Version 2 tensioner is fitted. The adjustment procedure varies for each version.

Version 1 tensioner

29 With the belt fully engaged with the sprockets, slacken the tensioner and tension the belt. To do this, use a 6.0 mm Allen key to turn the index finger on the tensioner 7.0 to 8.0 mm to the right of the static index, then retighten the tensioner to the specified torque

(see illustration). Check that the camshafts and crankshaft are still at TDC.

30 Refit the crankshaft pulley and tighten the bolt to the specified torque. This can be done with the timing pin still tight in the cylinder block, and the crankshaft web resting against it. If the original bolt is being re-used, lightly lubricate the threads with engine oil. If a new bolt is being used it should be fitted dry.

31 Remove the locking tool from the camshafts and the TDC pin from the cylinder block. Turn the crankshaft clockwise two complete turns, then reset the piston to TDC as described earlier.

32 Remove the locking tool and TDC pin, then unscrew the tensioner fastener by one turn only. Using the Allen key, align the index finger with the static index pointer by turning it anti-clockwise. Tighten the tensioner fastener to the specified torque.

33 Turn the crankshaft two complete turns, and recheck the TDC position and tensioner index setting.

Version 2 tensioner

34 Using a 6.0 mm Allen key, turn the index pointer until it is opposite the shallow notch at the front of the fixed notched plate **(see illustration)**, then pre-tighten the nut to the specified initial torque. Check that the camshafts and crankshaft are still at TDC.

35 Refit the crankshaft pulley and tighten the bolt to the specified torque. This can be done with the timing pin still tight in the cylinder block, and the crankshaft web resting against it. If the original bolt is being re-used, lightly lubricate the threads with engine oil. If a new bolt is being used it should be fitted dry.

36 Remove the locking tool from the camshafts and the TDC pin from the cylinder block. Turn the crankshaft clockwise two complete turns, then recheck the TDC position and tensioner index setting. If necessary, loosen the nut and use the Allen key to reposition the index pointer in line with the shallow notch. Finally, fully tighten the tensioner to the specified final torque.

All engines

37 Refit the upper timing cover and lower timing cover, and tighten the bolts securely.

38 Refit the TDC plug to the cylinder block, and tighten it securely.

39 Fit two new plastic plugs in the cylinder head on the left-hand end of the camshafts. Renault technicians use special tools to drive the plugs into position, although suitable sockets or blocks of wood may be used instead **(see illustration)**.

40 Refit the air cleaner with reference to Chapter 4A.

41 Clip the fuel pipes to the lower timing cover.

42 Reconnect the vacuum pipe to the inlet manifold, and attach the wiring loom to the upper timing cover. Refit the support bracket and tighten the bolts, reconnect the wiring and attach it to the support.

43 Refit the engine right-hand mounting to

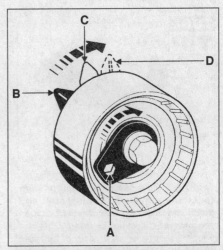

4.29 Version 1 timing belt tensioner pulley details

A *Slot for Allen key in tensioner arm*
B *Position of moving index pointer in the at-rest position*
C *Fixed index pointer*
D *Moving index pointer positioned 7.0 to 8.0 mm to the right of the fixed index pointer*

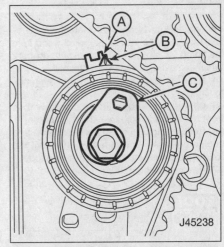

4.34 Version 2 timing belt tensioner pulley details

A *Shallow notch*   C *Eccentric*
B *Adjustable index*   *adjustment*

4.39 Fitting new plastic plugs to the cylinder head using a large socket

Tool Tip 1 *To make a camshaft holding tool, obtain a length of steel strip and cut it to length so that it will fit across the rear of the cylinder head. Obtain a second length of steel strip of suitable thickness to fit snugly in the slots in the camshafts. Cut the second strip into two lengths and drill accordingly so that they can be bolted to the first strip in the correct position to engage with the camshaft slots. Secure a suitably drilled small piece of steel angle to the first strip so that the tool can be bolted to the threaded hole in the cylinder head upper section.*

the engine and body with reference to Section 12. Lower the jack and block of wood from the sump (or remove the engine support bar). Where removed, refit the alternator at this stage.

44 Refit the auxiliary drivebelt with reference to Chapter 1A.

45 Where removed, refit the crossmember, front bumper and coolant expansion bottle.

46 Refit the right-hand wheel arch liners, and engine compartment undertray, then refit the roadwheel and lower the car to the ground.

47 Reconnect the battery negative lead.

Tool Tip 2 *To make a camshaft sprocket turning tool, obtain two lengths of steel strip 6 mm thick by 30 mm wide or similar, one 600 mm long, the other 200 mm long (all dimensions approximate). Bolt the two strips together to form a forked end, leaving the bolt slack so that the shorter strip can pivot freely. At the end of each 'prong' of the fork, drill a suitable hole and fit a nut and bolt to engage with the holes in the sprocket.*

5 Timing belt sprockets and tensioner – removal, inspection and refitting

Caution: The timing belt sprockets are not keyed to the camshafts, neither is the crankshaft sprocket keyed to the crankshaft. Before starting work, make sure that you have the necessary tooling to accurately set the camshafts and crankshaft to TDC.

Removal

1 Remove the timing belt as described in Section 4.

2 Slide the crankshaft sprocket from the nose of the crankshaft, noting which way round it is fitted.

3 Use a suitable tool to hold each camshaft sprocket stationary while the fasteners are loosened, then unscrew and remove the fasteners and withdraw the sprockets from the camshafts. **Note:** *On 1.4 litre engines, both sprockets are retained by nuts. On 1.6 litre engines, the inlet camshaft sprocket incorporates a phase-shifter, and it is necessary to unscrew a cover for access to the retaining bolt; the exhaust sprocket has a nut. In both cases, the sprocket nuts must be renewed on refitting.*

4 To remove the tensioner, unscrew the centre fastener and withdraw the unit from the stud on the water pump. Note the groove in the water pump cover for the tensioner lug.

5 To remove the idler, unscrew the centre bolt and withdraw it from the cylinder head.

Inspection

6 Inspect the teeth of the sprockets for signs of nicks and damage. Also examine the water pump pulley. The teeth are not prone to wear and should normally last the life of the engine.

7 Spin the tensioner pulley by hand and check it for any roughness or tightness. Do not attempt to clean it with solvent, as this may enter the bearing. If wear is evident, renew the tensioner. **Note:** *Renault state that the tensioner and idler pulley must be renewed whenever the timing belt is renewed.*

Refitting

8 Locate the idler on the cylinder head, then insert the bolt and tighten to the specified torque.

9 Locate the tensioner on the stud on the water pump cover, making sure that the lug engages the groove. Fit the fastener loosely at this stage.

10 Set the engine at TDC for No 1 piston as described in Section 3. Slip the crankshaft sprocket off the end of the crankshaft and check that the keyway in the crankshaft is uppermost. Note that although there is a keyway in both the crankshaft and crankshaft sprocket, a Woodruff key is not used.

11 Using a suitable solvent, thoroughly clean the end of the crankshaft, crankshaft sprocket

bore, and the crankshaft and sprocket mating faces. Similarly clean the camshaft ends, camshaft sprocket bores and mating faces. It is essential that all traces of oil and grease are removed from these areas to allow the sprockets to be securely clamped when the pulley and retaining bolt/nuts are refitted. If the sprockets slip in service, serious engine damage will result.

12 Check that the camshafts are still correctly positioned with their slots parallel to the join between the upper and lower cylinder head sections, and the offsets below the centreline. If necessary, temporarily refit the old camshaft sprocket fastener and turn the camshafts slightly using a spanner to correctly align the slots.

13 The camshafts must now be retained in this position either by using Renault special tool Mot. 1496, or by fabricating a home-made alternative **(see Tool Tip 1)**. Engage the Renault special tool or the home-made alternative with the slots in the camshafts and secure the tool to the cylinder head using a suitable bolt. With the crankshaft against the TDC pin and the camshafts secured with the holding tool, refit the crankshaft sprocket to the end of the crankshaft.

14 Locate the camshaft sprockets on the camshafts so that the Renault logo engraved spokes, or phase-shifter marking, are at the 12 o'clock position. Fit the sprocket fasteners loosely at this stage. A clearance of between 0.5 and 1.0 mm should exist between the fasteners and the sprockets. Where applicable on 1.6 litre engines, mark the rocker cover in line with the mark on the inlet camshaft phase-shifter, and check that the phase-shifter is neither advanced or retarded.

15 Slide the crankshaft sprocket onto the nose of the crankshaft, making sure it is the correct way round.

16 Locate the new timing belt over the crankshaft and camshaft sprockets, and around the tensioner pulley, making sure that the sprocket marks remain vertical.

17 Refit the crankshaft pulley and the retaining bolt and washer. If the original bolt is being re-used, lightly lubricate the threads with engine oil. If a new bolt is being used it should be fitted dry. Tighten the bolt so that there is approximately 2.0 to 3.0 mm clearance between the bolt and the pulley. The crankshaft and camshaft sprockets must all be free to turn for the timing belt to be tensioned correctly.

18 Using a 6.0 mm Allen key engaged with the hole in the tensioner pulley arm, turn the pointer to the setting positions described in Section 4 (according to tensioner version) and tighten the retaining fastener.

19 Turn the exhaust camshaft sprocket clockwise through three complete revolutions to initially settle and pre-tension the timing belt; use the mark on the sprocket and rocker cover to count the number of turns. Note that three revolutions of the camshaft sprockets will turn the crankshaft sprocket through six complete turns. The exhaust camshaft sprocket can be turned using a suitable forked tool engaged with the holes in the sprocket **(see Tool Tip 2)**. During this operation, ensure that the camshaft and crankshaft sprocket retaining nuts/bolts remain slack to allow the sprockets to turn freely.

20 On models fitted with the Version 1 tensioner (see Section 4), unscrew the tensioner fastener by one turn only, then use an Allen key to align the index finger with the static index pointer by turning it anti-clockwise. Tighten the tensioner to the specified torque.

21 On models fitted with the Version 2 tensioner (see Section 4), check that the tensioner pointer is still aligned with the shallow notch on the fixed plate, and if necessary, loosen the fastener and use the Allen key to reposition the pointer. Finally, fully tighten the fastener to the specified final torque on completion.

22 Tighten the crankshaft pulley bolt, either with the timing pin tight in the cylinder block, and the crankshaft web resting against it, or while an assistant holds the crankshaft stationary with a screwdriver engaged with the flywheel ring gear.

23 Check that the crankshaft is still set to TDC, then check that the camshaft locking tool is in position. The camshaft sprockets must now be held stationary while the fasteners are tightened to the specified torques. Renault technicians use a metal plate bolted to the cylinder head which clamps the two sprockets stationary, however, the tool used to hold the pulleys on removal can be used, provided care is taken not to move the camshafts or crankshaft during the tightening procedure.

24 Remove the timing rod and locking tool, then turn the crankshaft clockwise through two complete revolutions and recheck the timing for a final time. Remove the timing tools.

25 Where applicable, refit and tighten the cover on the phase-shifter sprocket.

26 Fit two new camshaft sealing caps to the left-hand end of the cylinder head, carefully tapping them into place with a large socket or similar tool.

27 Refit the upper timing cover and lower timing cover, and tighten the bolts securely.

28 Refit the TDC plug to the cylinder block, and tighten it securely.

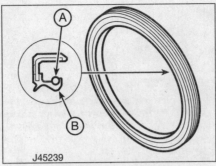

6.0a Camshaft oil seal version 1

A *Internal spring*
B *V-shaped sealing lip*

29 Refit the air cleaner with reference to Chapter 4A.

30 Clip the fuel pipes to the lower timing cover.

31 Reconnect the vacuum pipe to the inlet manifold and attach the wiring loom to the upper timing cover. Refit the support bracket and tighten the bolts, reconnect the wiring and attach it to the support.

32 Refit the engine right-hand mounting to the engine and body with reference to Section 12. Lower the jack and block of wood from the sump, or remove the engine support bar, as applicable.

33 Refit the auxiliary drivebelt with reference to Chapter 1A.

34 Refit the right-hand wheel arch liners, and engine compartment undertray, then refit the roadwheel and lower the car to the ground.

35 Reconnect the battery negative lead.

---

6   Camshaft oil seals – renewal

Note: *There are two versions of camshaft oil seal fitted (see illustrations); version 1 has an internal spring and V-shaped sealing lip, version 2 has a flat sealing lip without an internal spring. Version 2 is extremely fragile, and must only be handled by the protector/guide supplied with it. The oil seals are not interchangeable and the fitting procedure for each is different, as described in the following paragraphs.*

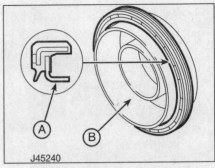

6.0b Camshaft oil seal version 2

A *Flat sealing lip*
B *Fitting protector*

1 Remove the camshaft sprocket as described in Section 5.

2 Note the fitted depth of the old oil seal. Using a small screwdriver, prise out the oil seal from the cylinder head taking care not to damage the sealing surface on the camshaft. Alternatively, the oil seal can be removed by drilling two small holes diagonally opposite each other and inserting self-tapping screws in them. A pair of grips can then be used to pull out the oil seals, by pulling on each side in turn.

3 Inspect the seal rubbing surface on the camshaft. If it is grooved or rough in the area where the old seal was fitted, the new seal should be fitted slightly less deeply, so that it rubs on an unworn part of the surface.

Version 1 oil seal

4 Wipe clean the oil seal seating, then smear a little oil on the outer perimeter and sealing lip of the new oil seal **(see illustration)**.

5 Locate the seal squarely in the cylinder head, then drive it into position using a metal tube or socket which has an external diameter slightly less than that of the bore in the cylinder head **(see illustration)**. Alternatively, the oil seal can be pressed into position using a metal tube, washer and nut.

Version 2 oil seal

6 Renault technicians use a special tool (Mot. 1632) to fit the oil seal. The tool consists of a threaded rod, metal tube and nut, and a machined shoulder to locate the protector/guide on **(see illustration)**. The rod is

6.4 Smear a little grease on the oil seal . . .

6.5 . . . before driving it into the cylinder head with a suitable socket

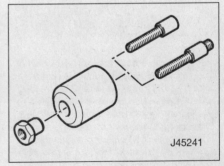

6.6 Renault tool for fitting the camshaft oil seal

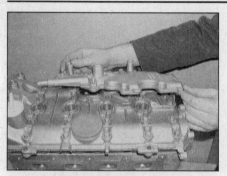

7.12 Undo the eight bolts and remove the oil separator housing

7.13 Removing the cylinder head cover/ bearing cap from the cylinder head

screwed into the end of the camshaft, and the protector/guide located on the shoulder. The metal tube is then fitted against the oil seal, and the nut tightened to press the seal into the cylinder head/bearing cap. If the Renault tool cannot be obtained, a similar tool can be made out of a threaded rod, metal tube, washer and nut.

7 Wipe clean the oil seal seating, then press the oil seal squarely into position. Note that the Renault tool is designed to locate the seal at the original depth, however, if the camshaft sealing surface is excessively worn, position it less deeply so that it locates on the unworn surface.

8 After fitting the oil seal, remove the protector/guide and tool.

All types

9 Wipe away any excess oil, then refit the camshaft sprocket as described in Section 5.

7	Camshafts –
	removal, inspection
	and refitting

Removal

1 Disconnect the battery negative lead, and move the lead away from the battery (see *Disconnecting the battery*).

2 On 1.6 litre engines, unclip the engine top cover.

3 Remove the timing belt as described in Section 4, and the camshaft sprockets as described in Section 5.

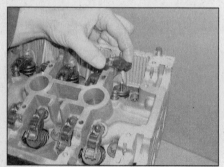

7.15 Lift out the cam followers and place them in a marked box or containers

4 Remove the throttle body, then disconnect the fuel supply and return hoses from the fuel rail, with reference to Chapter 4A.

5 Remove the fuel rail shield, then disconnect the wiring from the injectors and coils, and position it to one side.

6 On 1.6 litre engines, disconnect the wiring plug from the variable valve timing solenoid, located next to No 4 ignition coil.

7 Unscrew the three flange nuts and separate the exhaust pipe from the manifold.

8 Disconnect the wiring from the oxygen sensor – on the rear left-hand side of the engine (left as seen from the driver's seat).

9 Unbolt and remove the exhaust manifold support strut and the engine lifting eye.

10 Remove the inlet manifold as described in Chapter 4A.

11 Remove the ignition coils as described in Chapter 5B.

12 Unbolt and remove the oil separator unit **(see illustration)**

13 Progressively unscrew the cylinder head cover/bearing cap retaining bolts, then release the cover by using a copper mallet to tap the lugs at each rear corner and using a screwdriver to lever up the lugs on the front of the cover. Once the cover is free, lift it squarely from the cylinder head **(see illustration)**. The camshafts will rise up slightly under the pressure of the valve springs – be careful they don't tilt and jam. Remove the cover/bearing cap.

14 Identify each camshaft for location and TDC position, then carefully lift them from the cylinder head. The inlet camshaft should have

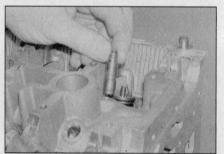

7.16 Lift out the tappets and place them upright in a marked box or containers filled with oil

the marking AM on it, and the exhaust should have the marking EM. If these are not visible, identify the camshafts with dabs of paint. Remove the oil seals from the camshafts, noting their fitted positions.

15 Obtain a box with sixteen compartments and mark the valve positions clearly on it. Remove each cam follower and place it in its compartment for safe-keeping **(see illustration)**.

16 Obtain a metal box with sixteen compartments identified with the valve positions, and fill it with fresh engine oil. Remove the hydraulic tappets from the cylinder head and place them in their correct compartments, making sure that they are completely immersed in the oil **(see illustration)**.

Inspection

17 Inspect the cam lobes and the camshaft bearing journals for scoring or other visible evidence of wear.

18 If the camshafts appear satisfactory, measure the bearing journal diameters and compare the figures obtained with those given in the Specifications. If the diameters are not as specified, consult a Renault dealer or engine overhaul specialist. Wear of the camshaft bearings will almost certainly be accompanied by similar wear of the bearings in the cylinder head, which will entail renewal of the cylinder head upper and lower sections together with the camshafts.

19 Inspect the cam followers and hydraulic tappets for scuffing, cracking or other damage and renew any components as necessary. Also check the condition of the tappet bores in the cylinder head. As with the camshafts, any wear in this area will necessitate cylinder head renewal.

Refitting

20 Clean the sealant from the mating surfaces of the cylinder head cover/bearing cap and cylinder head.

21 To prevent any possibility of the valves contacting the pistons when the camshafts are refitted, remove the TDC pin or dowel rod used to lock the crankshaft, and turn the crankshaft clockwise a quarter-turn.

22 Lubricate the tappet bores in the cylinder head with clean engine oil.

23 If the hydraulic tappets have not been kept immersed in oil, the oil will drain from them and they will need to be re-primed before refitting. To check whether they require re-priming, depress the top of the tappet with a thumb – if the piston goes down, the tappet requires re-priming. Renault recommend that the tappets are immersed in diesel fuel and operated until they are primed.

24 Remove the hydraulic tappets from their compartments, and insert them in their correct positions in the head.

25 One at a time, remove the cam followers from their compartments, and locate them on the hydraulic tappets and valve stems.

7.26a Refit the camshafts in the cylinder head . . .

7.26b Position the camshafts in their TDC position so that the grooves are horizontal and the offset is below the centreline

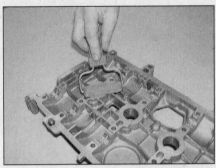

7.27 Apply an even coating of Loctite 518 gasket solution to the mating face of the cylinder head cover/bearing cap

26 Lubricate the bearings and journals of the inlet and exhaust camshafts with fresh engine oil, then carefully locate them on the cylinder head in their correct positions and at TDC as previously noted. The grooves at the left-hand end of the camshafts must be horizontal **(see illustrations)**.

27 Check that the cylinder head cover/ bearing cap mating surfaces are clean and dry, then apply Loctite 518 (or a suitable alternative) to the cover surface using a roller **(see illustration)**. Make several applications until the colour is **reddish**.

28 Locate the cylinder head cover/bearing cap on the cylinder head, insert the bolts, and progressively tighten them to the specified torque in the sequence and stages given in the Specifications **(see illustration)**. Make sure that the camshafts are located correctly on the cam followers and in the cover.

29 Check that the oil separator mating surfaces are clean and dry, then apply Loctite 518 (or a suitable alternative) to the separator surface using a roller **(see illustration)**. Make several applications until the colour is **reddish**.

30 Locate the oil separator on the cylinder head cover, insert the bolts, and tighten them to the specified torque in sequence **(see illustration)**.

31 Refit the ignition coils with reference to Chapter 5B.

32 Refit the engine lifting eye to the cylinder head and tighten the bolts securely.

33 Refit the support bracket to the right-hand side of the exhaust manifold, and tighten the bolts securely.

34 Reconnect the wiring to the oxygen sensor on the rear left-hand side of the engine.

35 Refit the throttle body, exhaust pipe and inlet manifold with reference to Chapter 4A.

36 Reconnect the wiring to the ignition coil and fuel injectors, and attach the wiring loom to the front of the engine.

37 Reconnect the fuel supply and return hoses to each end of the fuel rail, and tighten the clips.

38 Refit the fuel rail shield.

39 Refit the camshaft sprockets as described in Section 5.

40 Refit the timing belt with reference to Section 4 of this Chapter.

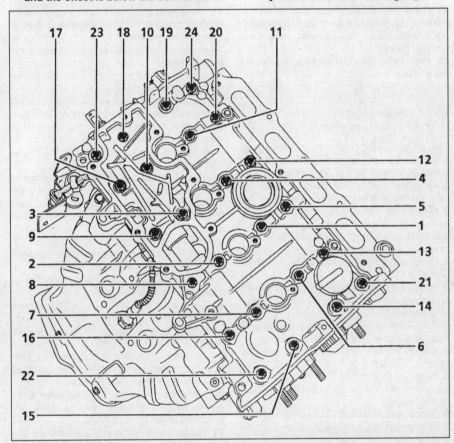

7.28 Cylinder head cover/bearing cap bolt identification

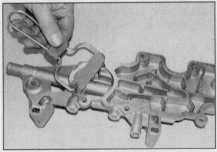

7.29 Apply an even coating of Loctite 518 gasket solution to the mating face of the oil separator housing

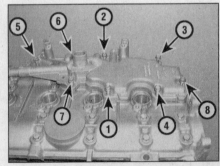

7.30 Oil separator housing bolt tightening sequence

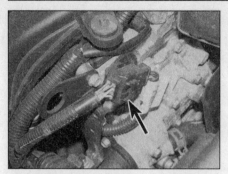

8.11 Disconnect the camshaft position sensor

41 Reconnect the battery negative lead, then where applicable, refit the engine top cover.
42 Top-up the engine oil, with reference to 'Weekly checks'.
43 Refit the engine undertray and lower the car to the ground.

8 Cylinder head –
removal, inspection and refitting

Note: *In addition to any other parts required, have a new timing belt, cylinder head and cylinder head cover gaskets and (possibly) a set of new cylinder head bolts ready for reassembly. Renault state that the tensioner and idler pulley must be renewed whenever the timing belt is renewed.*

1 Remove the battery as described in Chapter 5A.
2 Remove the engine undertray, then drain the cooling system and engine oil with reference to Chapter 1A.
3 On 1.4 litre engines, remove the air cleaner resonator box as described in Chapter 4A.
4 On 1.6 litre engines, unclip the engine top cover.
5 Remove the timing belt and camshaft sprockets with reference to Sections 4 and 5 of this Chapter.
6 Unbolt and remove the fuel rail shield.
7 Disconnect the fuel supply hose from the fuel rail.

8.34 Locate a new cylinder head gasket on the cylinder block . . .

8 Unbolt the engine wiring loom brackets at the transmission end of the head.
9 Remove the ignition coils as described in Chapter 5B.
10 On 1.6 litre engines, disconnect the wiring plug, then unscrew and remove the variable valve timing solenoid valve from the head (see Chapter 4A, Section 13).
11 Disconnect the camshaft position sensor wiring connector **(see illustration)**.
12 Remove the air temperature sensor, inlet manifold and throttle body with reference to Chapter 4A.
13 Disconnect the exhaust pipe from the manifold, and disconnect the oxygen sensor wiring.
14 Unscrew the bolts and remove the support bracket from the right-hand side of the exhaust manifold.
15 Unbolt the engine lifting eye from the cylinder head.
16 Unbolt the oil separator from the top of the cylinder head cover.
17 Progressively unscrew the cylinder head cover retaining bolts, then release the cover by using a copper mallet to tap the lugs at each rear corner and using a screwdriver to lever up the lugs on the front of the cover. Remove the cover.
18 Identify each camshaft for location and TDC position, then carefully lift them from the cylinder head. The inlet camshaft should have the marking AM on it and the exhaust should have the marking EM. If these are not visible, identify the camshafts with dabs of paint.
19 Obtain a box with sixteen compartments and mark the valve positions clearly on it. Remove each cam follower and place it in its compartment for safe-keeping.
20 Obtain a metal box with sixteen compartments identified with the valve positions, and fill it with fresh engine oil. Carefully remove the hydraulic tappets from the cylinder head and place them in their correct compartments, making sure that they are completely immersed in the oil.
21 Disconnect the wiring from the temperature sensor on the thermostat housing at the left-hand end of the cylinder head.
22 Release the clips and disconnect the radiator top hose, heater hoses and expansion tank hose from the thermostat housing.
23 Progressively unscrew and remove the cylinder head bolts in the **reverse** order of the tightening sequence shown later in this Section.
24 Make a final check round the head to ensure that nothing is still attached, nor anything in the way which would hinder it being lifted off.
25 Lift the head from the cylinder block, followed by the gasket. Though a new gasket should obviously be used when refitting, retain the old one to compare with the new.

Inspection

26 The mating faces of the cylinder head and block must be perfectly clean before refitting

the head. Use a scraper to remove all traces of gasket and carbon and also clean the tops of the pistons. Take particular care with the aluminium cylinder head, as the soft metal is easily damaged.
27 Also, make sure that debris is not allowed to enter the oil and water channels – this is particularly important for the oil circuit, as carbon could block the oil supply to the camshaft and cam followers or crankshaft bearings. Using adhesive tape and paper, seal the water, oil and bolt holes in the cylinder block. Clean the piston crowns in the same way.

> **HAYNES HiNT** *To prevent carbon entering the gap between the pistons and bores, smear a little grease in the gap. After cleaning the piston, rotate the crankshaft so that the piston moves down the bore, then wipe out the grease and carbon with a cloth rag.*

28 Check the block and head for nicks, deep scratches and other damage. If slight, they may be removed carefully with a file. It may be possible to repair more serious damage by machining, but this is a specialist job.
29 If warpage of the cylinder head is suspected, use a straight-edge to check it for distortion, as this can be associated with the head gasket blowing. No regrinding of the cylinder head is allowed. Refer to Part D of this Chapter for further information.
30 Clean out all the bolt holes in the block using a pipe cleaner, or a rag and screwdriver. Make sure that all oil is removed, otherwise there is a possibility of the block being cracked by hydraulic pressure when the bolts are tightened.
31 Examine the bolt threads and the threads in the cylinder block for damage. If necessary, use the correct-size tap to chase out the threads in the block and use a die to clean the threads on the bolts.
32 In view of the severe stresses to which they are subjected, owners may wish to renew the head bolts as a matter of course whenever they are disturbed. If any of the bolts shows the slightest sign of wear or of damage, all the bolts should be renewed as a set. The bolts may be re-used if their length between the bolt head underside and thread end does not exceed 117.7 mm – if any one bolt is longer than this dimension, renew all the bolts as a set.

Refitting

33 It is recommended that No 1 piston is positioned half-way down its cylinder before refitting the cylinder head, as a safeguard against the valves touching the tops of the pistons. Turn the crankshaft clockwise until No 1 piston falls to the mid-cylinder position.
34 Position a new gasket on the block, making sure it is the correct way up **(see illustration)**. Check that none of the holes in the block are being obscured by the gasket.

35 If the lower inlet manifold was removed, it can be refitted at this stage, with reference to Chapter 4A, making sure that the timing end is flush with the end of the cylinder head before tightening the bolts.

36 Carefully lower the cylinder head onto the block, making sure that the gasket is not displaced **(see illustration)**.

37 If new bolts are being fitted, **do not** lubricate their threads. If the old bolts are being refitted, lightly lubricate their threads with fresh engine oil. Insert the bolts and initially screw them in finger-tight.

38 Tighten the cylinder head bolts to the specified torques in sequence and in the stages given in the Specifications **(see illustrations)**. When angle-tightening the bolts, put paint marks on the bolt heads and cylinder head as a guide for the correct angle, or obtain a special angle-tightening tool.

39 Further refitting is a reversal of removal, noting the following points:

a) *Tighten all nuts/bolts securely, or to the specified torque.*

b) *Refit the camshafts, tappets and cylinder head cover as described in Section 7.*

c) *Refit the camshaft sprockets and timing belt as described in Sections 5 and 4.*

d) *Refit the throttle body, inlet manifold and exhaust pipe as described in Chapter 4A.*

e) *On completion, refill the engine with fresh oil, then fill and bleed the cooling system, with reference to Chapter 1A.*

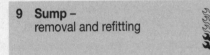

9	Sump –
	removal and refitting

Note: *An engine lifting hoist is required during this procedure.*

Removal

1 Disconnect the battery negative lead (refer to *Disconnecting the battery* in the Reference Section).

2 Jack up the front of the car and support on axle stands. Remove the engine compartment undertray.

3 Drain the engine oil referring to Chapter 1A, then refit and tighten the drain plug. Though not essential, it makes sense to fit a new oil filter on completion, before the sump is refilled with fresh oil.

4 Remove both front roadwheels, then remove both wheel arch liners (see Chapter 11, Section 21 if necessary).

5 Inside the wheel arch each side, remove the four bolts securing the support plate to the subframe and inner wing, and remove it.

6 Using cable-ties or string, tie the radiator up to the front crossmember – this is necessary, as the radiator lower crossmember must be removed.

7 Unbolt and remove the side supports each side, fitted between the subframe and radiator lower crossmember. Ensure that the radiator is adequately supported, as described in the

8.36 . . . and carefully lower the cylinder head into position

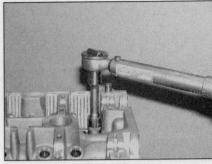

8.38a Tighten the cylinder head bolts to the Stage 1 torque using a torque wrench

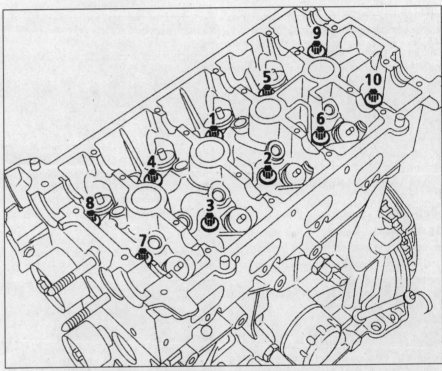

8.38b Cylinder head bolt tightening sequence

previous paragraph. Remove the front bolt and rear nut, then lower the crossmember to the floor.

8 Referring to the driveshaft removal procedure in Chapter 8, unscrew the two bolts securing the driveshaft collar to the support bearing on the back of the engine. The driveshaft itself does not have to be removed, however.

9 Remove the lowest bolt from the alternator mounting bracket fitted to the front of the engine. The bracket itself does not have to be removed, but the lowest bolt is screwed into the sump.

10 Unbolt and remove the engine lower mounting from the engine and subframe (refer to Section 12) – this will allow the engine to move slightly on its remaining right- and left-hand mountings, but providing they are not disturbed, this is not dangerous.

11 Loosen and remove the nineteen bolts used to secure the sump. In addition to

the bolts, the sump is secured by several spots of sealant – tap the sump with a hide or plastic mallet to break the seal, or prise it very carefully, so as not to damage the sealing surfaces. Lower the sump out from under the car, and recover the gasket – a new one should be used when refitting.

8.38c Using an angle gauge to tighten the cylinder head bolts through the Stage 2 angle

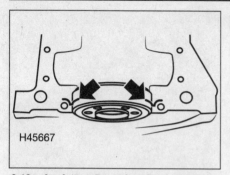

9.13a Apply two 5 mm beads of sealant to the areas shown (flywheel end)

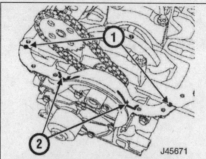

9.13b Apply a 7 mm diameter spot of sealant at (1) and a 5 mm bead at (2) – timing end

9.14 Locate a new gasket on the sump

9.15 Use a straight-edge to maintain the alignment between the left-hand end of the sump and cylinder block

Refitting

12 Thoroughly clean the mating surfaces of the sump and cylinder block. If required, the anti-emulsion plate inside the sump can also be unclipped and cleaned – when refitting, ensure that the five tabs on the plate sit properly in the cut-outs inside the sump.

13 Apply a total of four beads and two spots of suitable silicone sealant (Renault part number 7711219706, or equivalent) to the areas shown in the accompanying illustrations. Do not apply too much, otherwise the excess may end up inside the sump, where it could get sucked into the engine.

14 Locate the new gasket in position on the sump, and lift the sump into position on the cylinder block (**see illustration**). Insert the bolts and tighten them progressively in two stages to the specified torque – start with the centre bolts, and work in a diagonal sequence.

15 If the engine is removed from the car, use a straight-edge to maintain the alignment between the left-hand end of the sump and cylinder block (**see illustration**).

16 Further refitting is a reversal of removal, noting the following points:

a) *When refitting the radiator lower crossmember, fit the fasteners and side plates loosely, then insert a 10 mm spacer between it and the subframe, at the rear (refer to Chapter 7A, Section 8). We used a 10 mm diameter bolt – this should be withdrawn once the nuts have been tightened each side. The crossmember forms part of the deformable front structure of the car, and the gap left by using the spacer is essential.*

b) *Tighten all nuts/bolts to the specified torque.*

c) *Refer to Chapter 8 when refitting the right-hand driveshaft collar to the support bearing.*

d) *Allow sufficient time for the sealant used to cure, then fill the engine with fresh oil (see Chapter 1A). On completion, start the engine, and check for signs of leakage.*

10 Oil pump and sprockets
– removal, inspection and refitting

Removal

1 To remove the oil pump alone, first remove the sump as described in Section 9.

2 Unscrew the oil pump mounting bolts and the additional bolt(s) securing the anti-emulsion plate to the crankcase (**see illustration**).

3 Withdraw the oil pump slightly and remove the anti-emulsion plate. Tilt the pump to disengage its sprocket from the drive chain, and lift away the pump (**see illustrations**). If the locating dowels are displaced, refit them in their locations.

4 To remove the pump complete with its drive chain and sprockets, first remove the sump as described in Section 9, then remove the crankshaft timing belt end oil seal housing as described in Section 11.

5 Remove the oil pump as described in paragraphs 1 and 2 above.

6 Slide the drive sprocket together with the chain from the crankshaft (**see illustration**). Note that the drive sprocket is not keyed to the crankshaft, but relies on the pulley bolt being tightened correctly to clamp the sprocket.

10.2 Unscrew the anti-emulsion plate bolt(s)

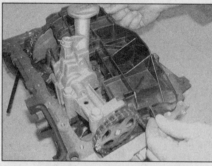

10.3a Remove the anti-emulsion plate . . .

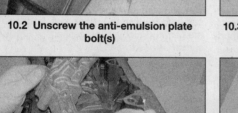

10.3b . . . then tilt the pump to disengage its sprocket from the drive chain

10.6 Slide the drive sprocket together with the chain from the crankshaft

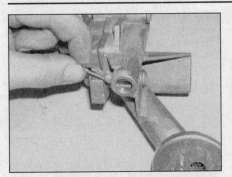

10.7a Extract the oil pressure relief valve retaining clip . . .

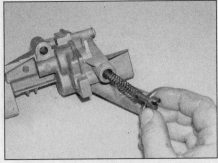

10.7b . . . remove the oil pressure relief valve spring retainer and spring . . .

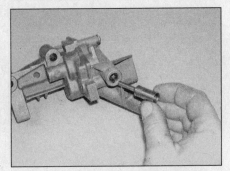

10.7c . . . followed by the plunger

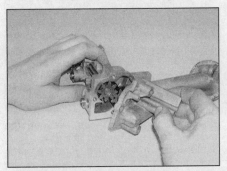

10.8 Unscrew the retaining bolts, and lift off the oil pump cover

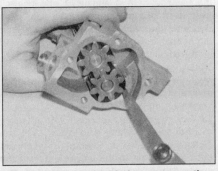

10.10a Using feeler blades, measure the clearance between the pump body and the gears . . .

10.10b . . . and measure the gear endfloat

Inspection

7 Extract the retaining clip, and remove the oil pressure relief valve spring retainer, spring and plunger **(see illustrations)**.

8 Unscrew the retaining bolts, and lift off the pump cover **(see illustration)**.

9 Carefully examine the gears, pump body and relief valve plunger for any signs of scoring or wear. Renew the pump complete if excessive wear is evident.

10 If the components appear serviceable, measure the clearance between the pump body and the gears using feeler blades. Also measure the gear endfloat, and check the flatness of the end cover **(see illustrations)**. If the clearances exceed the specified tolerances, the pump must be renewed.

11 If the pump is satisfactory, reassemble the components in the reverse order of removal. Fill the pump with oil, then refit the cover and tighten the bolts securely **(see illustration)**.

Refitting

12 Wipe clean the oil pump and cylinder block mating surfaces.

13 Locate the drive sprocket onto the end of the crankshaft, ensuring that it is fitted with the projecting boss facing away from the crankshaft **(see illustration)**. Engage the pump with the dowels, fit the two retaining bolts and tighten them to the specified torque.

14 Refit the anti-emulsion plate and secure with the retaining bolt(s).

15 Refit the oil seal housing as described in Section 11.

16 Refit the sump as described in Section 9.

11 Crankshaft oil seals
   – renewal

Timing belt end oil seal

1 Remove the timing belt and the crankshaft sprocket with reference to Sections 4 and 5. An alternative, though longer, method is to remove the sump and oil seal housing, and fit the new oil seal on the bench.

2 Note the fitted position of the old seal, then prise it out of the oil seal housing using a screwdriver or suitable hooked instrument. An alternative method of removing the oil seal is to drill carefully two small holes opposite each other in the oil seal and insert self-tapping screws, then pull on the screws with grips. Take care not

to damage the surface of the spacer or the seal housing.

3 With the oil seal removed, where applicable slide the spacer from the crankshaft, noting which way round it is fitted.

4 Examine the spacer for excessive oil seal wear and polish off any burrs or raised edges which may have caused the seal to fail in the first place. If necessary, the spacer can be refitted so that the new oil seal contacts an unworn area. Clean the oil seal seating in the housing.

5 Smear the lips and outer perimeter of the new seal with fresh engine oil, and locate it over the crankshaft with its closed side facing outwards. Using hand pressure, press the oil seal squarely into the housing a little way, then use a socket or metal tube to drive the oil seal to the previously noted position – take great care not to damage the seal lips during fitting

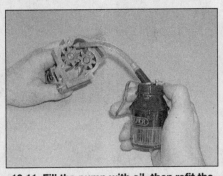

10.11 Fill the pump with oil, then refit the cover

10.13 The oil pump drive sprocket must be fitted the right way round

11.5 Using a socket to drive the new crankshaft oil seal into the housing

(see illustration). Do not drive it in too far or it will have to be removed and possibly renewed.

6 Slide the spacer onto the crankshaft and carefully press it into the oil seal, while twisting it to prevent damage.

7 Wipe away any excess oil, then refit the crankshaft sprocket and fit the new timing belt with reference to Sections 5 and 4.

Flywheel/driveplate end oil seal

8 Renewal of the crankshaft left-hand oil seal first requires the engine and transmission assembly to be removed as described in Chapter 2D. After the engine and transmission have been separated on the bench, the flywheel/driveplate must be removed (see Section 13 of this Chapter).

9 Prise out the old oil seal using a small screwdriver, taking care not to damage the surface on the crankshaft. Alternatively, the oil seal can be removed by drilling two small holes diagonally opposite each other and inserting self-tapping screws in them. A pair of grips can then be used to pull out the oil seal, by pulling on each side in turn.

10 Inspect the seal rubbing surface on the crankshaft. If it is grooved or rough in the area where the old seal was fitted, the new seal should be fitted slightly less deeply, so that it rubs on an unworn part of the surface.

11 Wipe clean the oil seal seating, then dip

11.11 Fitting a new crankshaft flywheel end oil seal

the new seal in fresh engine oil, and locate it over the crankshaft with its closed side facing outwards (see illustration). Make sure that the oil seal lip is not damaged as it is located on the crankshaft.

12 Using a metal tube, drive the oil seal squarely into the bore until flush. A block of wood cut to pass over the end of the crankshaft may be used instead.

13 Refit the flywheel/driveplate with reference to Section 13. Where applicable, refit the clutch as described in Chapter 6. Reconnect the transmission to the engine and refit the engine/transmission as described in the relevant Chapters of this manual.

12 Engine mountings – inspection and renewal

Inspection

1 With the handbrake applied, jack up the front of the car and support it on axle stands (see Jacking and vehicle support). Where fitted, remove the engine compartment undershield.

2 As far as possible, inspect the rubber sections of all the mountings for signs of cracking and deterioration. Careful use of a

lever will help to determine the condition of the rubber. If there is excessive movement in the mounting, or if the rubber has deteriorated, the mounting should be renewed.

3 Lower the car to the ground.

Renewal

Right-hand mounting

4 Support the right-hand end of the engine with a trolley jack and block of wood beneath the sump.

5 If available, an engine support bar may be used to support the engine from above.

6 Where applicable, remove the two rear bolts from the engine section of the mounting, and lift off the plate underneath (see illustration).

7 The wing and engine sections of the mounting are held together by a horizontal through-bolt, from the wing side – this must be loosened as far as possible, though it cannot be removed. Access to this bolt is hampered by the coolant expansion tank, and by the air conditioning pipes (where applicable).

8 Remove the three bolts securing the mounting to the engine, and lift it away.

9 Mark its position relative to the wing, then remove the four bolts securing the mounting to the inner wing, and lift it off (see illustrations).

10 If required, the mounting bracket on the engine can also be unbolted and removed.

11 Fit the mounting using a reversal of the removal procedure, but tighten the nuts/bolts to the specified torque wrench settings.

Left-hand mounting

12 Remove the air cleaner resonator or air inlet ducts from the left-hand side of the engine as applicable, for access to the engine/transmission left-hand mounting. Remove the battery and battery tray as described in Chapter 5A.

13 Support the left-hand end of the transmission with a trolley jack and block of wood beneath the transmission. If available,

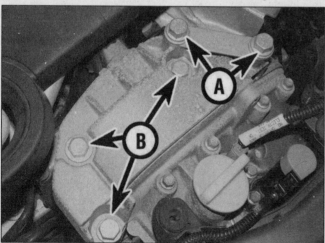

12.6 Engine section of the right-hand mounting – remove bolts (A) first, then three mounting-to-engine bolts (B)

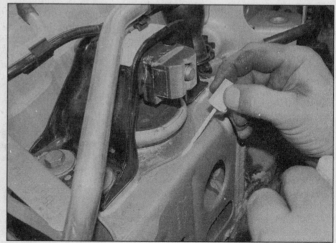

12.9a Mark its position on the inner wing . . .

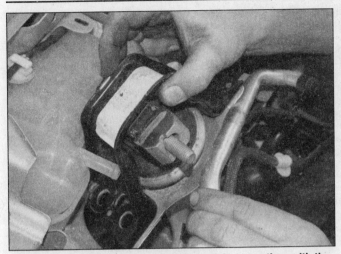

12.9b ... then lift out the wing section of the mounting, with the through-bolt

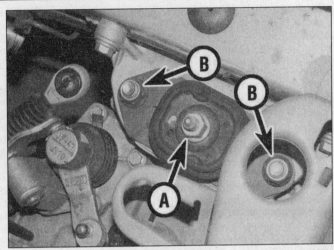

12.14 Left-hand (transmission) mounting centre (A) and outer (B) nuts

an engine support bar may be used to support the engine from above.

14 Unscrew the centre nut and the two outer nuts either side of it **(see illustration)**.

15 Remove the three bolts from the top of the transmission, and lower the transmission slightly **(see illustration)**.

16 Remove the four bolts securing the mounting to the inner wing, and lift it away.

17 Fit the mounting using a reversal of the removal procedure, but tighten the bolts to specified torque wrench settings.

Lower mounting

18 Jack up the front of the car, and support it securely on axle stands (see *Jacking and vehicle support*).

19 Remove the two bolts securing the lower mounting-to-engine plate – one of these bolts is also used to secure the front of the lower mounting link. This will separate the lower mounting from the engine, but leaves the mounting link in the way. If required, the mounting link rear bolt (to the subframe) can

also be unscrewed, and the mounting link removed completely **(see illustration)**.

20 Though removing the lower mounting will increase the amount of engine movement, the engine will remain safely supported on its right- and left-hand mountings.

21 Fit the mounting using a reversal of the removal procedure, but tighten the bolts to the specified torque wrench settings.

---

13 Flywheel/driveplate
– removal, inspection and refitting

Removal

1 Remove the transmission as described in Chapter 7A or 7B.

2 On manual transmission models, remove the clutch as described in Chapter 6.

3 Mark the flywheel/driveplate in relation to the crankshaft to aid refitting. Note that the

flywheel/driveplate can only be refitted in one position, as the bolts are unequally spaced.

4 The flywheel/driveplate must now be held stationary while the bolts are loosened. To do this, locate a long bolt in one of the transmission-to-engine mounting bolt holes to bear against, and either insert a wide-bladed screwdriver in the starter ring gear, or use a piece of bent metal bar engaged with the ring gear.

5 Unscrew the mounting bolts, and withdraw the flywheel/driveplate; be careful – it is heavy.

Inspection

6 Examine the flywheel/driveplate for wear or chipping of the ring gear teeth. If the ring gear is worn or damaged, it may be possible to renew it separately, but this job is best left to a Renault dealer or engineering works. The temperature to which the new ring gear must be heated for installation is critical and, if not done accurately, the hardness of the teeth will be destroyed.

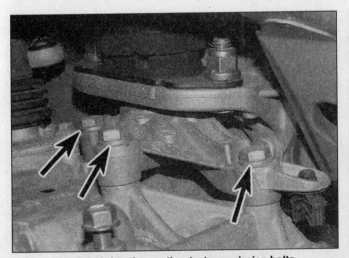

12.15 Left-hand mounting-to-transmission bolts

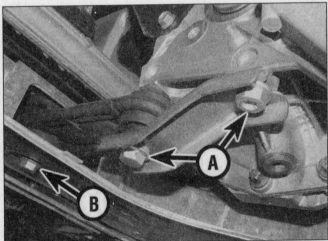

12.19 Engine lower mounting plate bolts (A) and mounting link rear bolt (B)

7 Check the flywheel/driveplate carefully for signs of distortion, and for hairline cracks around the bolt holes, or radiating outwards from the centre. If damage of this sort is found, it must be renewed.

8 Examine the flywheel for scoring of the clutch face. If the clutch face is scored, the flywheel may be machined until flat, but renewal is preferable.

Refitting

9 Clean the flywheel/driveplate and crankshaft mating surfaces, then locate the flywheel/driveplate on the crankshaft, making sure that any previously-made marks are aligned.

10 Apply a few drops of locking fluid to the mounting bolt threads, fit the bolts and tighten them in a diagonal sequence to the specified torque wrench setting.

11 Refit the clutch, if applicable (Chapter 6) and the transmission as described in Chapter 7A or 7B.

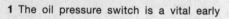

14 Oil pressure switch – removal and refitting

1 The oil pressure switch is a vital early warning of low oil pressure. The switch operates the oil warning light on the instrument panel – the light should come on with the ignition, and go out almost immediately when the engine starts.

2 If the light does not come on, there could be a fault on the instrument panel, the switch wiring, or the switch itself. If the light does not go out, low oil level, worn oil pump (or sump pick-up blocked), blocked oil filter, or worn main bearings could be to blame – or again, the switch may be faulty.

3 If the light comes on while driving, the best advice is to turn the engine off immediately, and not to drive the car until the problem has been investigated – ignoring the light could mean expensive engine damage.

Removal

4 The oil pressure switch is located on the front face of the engine, next to the oil filter.

5 Jack up the front of the car, and support it on axle stands (see *Jacking and vehicle support*) – to improve access, remove the oil filter, referring to Chapter 1A if necessary.

6 Disconnect the wiring plug from the switch.

7 Unscrew the switch from the block, and remove it together with its sealing washer. There should only be a very slight loss of oil when this is done.

Inspection

8 Examine the switch for signs of cracking or splits. If the top part of the switch is loose, this is an early indication of impending failure.

9 Check that the wiring terminals at the switch are not loose, then trace the wire from the switch connector until it enters the main loom – any wiring defects will give rise to apparent oil pressure problems.

Refitting

10 Refitting is the reverse of the removal procedure, noting the following points:
  a) *Clean the switch threads before fitting. Tighten the switch securely.*
  b) *Reconnect the switch connector, making sure it clicks home properly. Ensure that the wiring is routed away from any hot or moving parts.*
  c) *Lower the car to the ground, then check the engine oil level and top-up if necessary (see Weekly checks).*
  d) *Check for signs of oil leaks once the engine has been restarted and warmed-up to normal operating temperature.*

Chapter 2 Part B:
1.5 litre diesel engine in-car repair procedures

Contents

Degrees of difficulty

Easy, suitable for novice with little experience	Fairly easy, suitable for beginner with some experience	Fairly difficult, suitable for competent DIY mechanic	Difficult, suitable for experienced DIY mechanic	Very difficult, suitable for expert DIY or professional

Specifications

General

Type . . . .   Four-cylinder, in-line, 8-valve single overhead camshaft, direct common-rail injection

Designation:
    dCi 80 (80 bhp). K9K 722
    dCi 100 (100 bhp) K9K 728
Capacity . . . .   1461 cc
Bore . . . .   76.0 mm
Stroke. . . . .   80.5 mm
Firing order. . . . .   1-3-4-2 (No 1 cylinder at flywheel end)
Direction of crankshaft rotation . . . .   Clockwise viewed from timing belt end
Compression ratio 18.25:1

Compression pressures

Engine warm – approximately 80°C:
    Minimum pressure . . . .   20 bars
    Maximum difference between cylinders. . . . .   4 bars

Camshaft

Drive. . . . .   Toothed belt
Number of bearings   6
Camshaft endfloat . . . .   0.08 to 0.178 mm

Valve clearances

Inlet . . . .   0.20 + 0.05 – 0.075 mm
Exhaust. . . . .   0.40 + 0.05 – 0.075 mm

Lubrication system

System pressure (at 80°C):
    At idle speed. . . . .   1.2 bars minimum
    At 3000 rpm . . . .   3.5 bars minimum
Oil pump type. . . . .   Gear-type, chain-driven off the crankshaft right-hand end

Oil pump clearances:	Minimum	Maximum
Gear-to-body	0.110 mm	0.249 mm
Gear endfloat	0.020 mm	0.086 mm

Oil level sensor resistance . . . .   6.0 to 20 ohms

Torque wrench settings

	Nm	lbf ft
Air conditioning compressor	25	18
Alternator mounting bolts	21	15
Alternator support bracket:		
Bracket-to-engine bolts	40	30
Bracket-to-sump bolt	21	15
Auxiliary drivebelt tensioner mounting bolt:		
Models with air conditioning	40	30
Models without air conditioning	30	22
Big-end bearing caps:		
Stage 1	20	15
Stage 2	Angle-tighten a further 45° ± 6°	
Brake vacuum pump	21	15
Camshaft bearing caps	10	7
Camshaft sprocket:		
Stage 1	30	22
Stage 2	Angle-tighten a further 84°	
Crankshaft main bearing caps:		
Stage 1	27	20
Stage 2	Angle-tighten a further 47°	
Crankshaft pulley bolt (M12):		
Stage 1	60	44
Stage 2	Angle-tighten a further 100° ± 10°	
Crankshaft pulley bolt (M14):		
Stage 1	120	89
Stage 2	Angle-tighten a further 95° ± 15°	
Cylinder block TDC blanking plug	20	15
Cylinder head bolts*:		
Stage 1	25	18
Stage 2	Angle-tighten a further 255° ± 10°	
Cylinder head coolant outlet	10	7
Cylinder head cover	10	7
Driveplate bolts*:		
Stage 1	55	41
Stage 2	Angle-tighten a further 50° ± 5°	
Engine mountings:		
Left-hand mounting centre nut	62	46
Left-hand mounting outer nuts	105	78
Left-hand mounting stud-to-mounting	180	133
Left-hand mounting-to-body bolts	21	15
Left-hand mounting-to-transmission bolts	62	46
Lower mounting bolts	105	78
Right-hand mounting bracket-to-engine bolts	44	32
Right-hand mounting through-bolt	105	78
Right-hand mounting-to-wing bolts	62	46
Right-hand mounting-to-engine upper bolts	62	46
Engine right-hand cover:		
Stage 1 – bolts 1 and 6	8	6
Stage 2 – bolts 2 to 5 followed by 1 and 6	12	9
Exhaust gas recirculation valve	21	15
Exhaust manifold	26	19
Flywheel bolts*	65	48
Glow plugs	15	11
Heat exchanger connector	45	33
High-pressure fuel pump	21	15
High-pressure fuel pump sprocket:		
Stage 1	15	11
Stage 2	Angle-tighten a further 60° ± 10°	
High-pressure pipe	38	28
High-pressure rail	28	21
Injector flanges	28	21
Knock sensor	20	15
Oil filter housing	45	33
Oil level sensor	22	16
Oil pressure sensor	22	16
Oil pump mounting bolts	25	18

Torque wrench settings (continued)

	Nm	lbf ft
Radiator lower crossmember:		
Front bolt	105	78
Rear nut (to subframe)	21	15
Side support plate bolts	21	15
Roadwheel bolts.	130	96
Starter motor mounting bolts	44	32
Sump (refer to text):		
Stage 1 – bolts 1 to 8	8	6
Stage 2 – bolts 1 to 8	14	10
Stage 3 – bolts 9 to 20 followed by 1 and 2	8	6
Stage 4 – bolts 9 to 20 followed by 1 and 2	14	10
Timing belt tensioner	25	18
Turbocharger oil delivery pipe	23	17
Turbocharger oil return pipe	12	9
Turbocharger-to-exhaust manifold	26	19
Water pump bolts	11	8
Water pump inlet pipe	20	15

*Use new bolts

---

1 General information

How to use this Chapter

This Part of Chapter 2 is devoted to in-car repair procedures for the 1.5 litre diesel engine. Similar information covering the other engines can be found in Parts A and C. All procedures concerning engine removal and refitting, and engine block/cylinder head overhaul can be found in Part D of this Chapter.

Refer to *Vehicle identification numbers* in the Reference Section at the end of this manual for details of engine code locations.

Most of the operations included in this Part are based on the assumption that the engine is still installed in the car. Therefore, if this information is being used during a complete engine overhaul, with the engine already removed, many of the steps included here will not apply.

Engine description

The engine is of four-cylinder, in-line, single overhead camshaft type, mounted transversely at the front of the car.

The cylinder block is of cast iron, with conventional dry liners bored directly into the cylinder block. The crankshaft is supported in five shell-type main bearings. Thrustwashers are fitted to No 3 main bearing to control crankshaft endfloat.

The connecting rods are attached to the crankshaft by 'cracked' horizontally split shell-type big-end bearings and to the pistons by gudgeon pins. The gudgeon pins are fully-floating and are retained by circlips. The aluminium alloy pistons are fitted with three piston rings, comprising two compression rings and a scraper-type oil control ring.

The single overhead camshaft is mounted directly in the cylinder head, and is driven by the crankshaft via a toothed timing belt. The back of the timing belt also drives the water pump.

The camshaft operates the valves via inverted bucket-type tappets, which operate in bores machined directly in the cylinder head. The valve clearances are adjusted by changing the tappet buckets which are available in 25 different thicknesses. The inlet and exhaust valves are mounted vertically in the cylinder head and are each closed by a single valve spring.

The high-pressure fuel injection pump is driven by the timing belt and is described in further detail in Chapter 4B.

A semi-closed crankcase ventilation system is employed, and crankcase fumes are drawn from the cylinder block and passed via a hose to the inlet tract (see Chapter 4C for further details).

Engine lubrication is by pressure feed from a gear-type oil pump located beneath the crankshaft. Engine oil is fed through an externally-mounted oil filter to the main oil gallery feeding the crankshaft and camshaft. Oil spray jets are fitted to the cylinder block to supply oil to the underside of the pistons. An oil cooler is mounted between the oil filter and the cylinder block.

Operations with engine in place

The following operations can be carried out without having to remove the engine from the car:

a) Removal and refitting of the cylinder head.
b) Removal and refitting of the timing belt and sprockets.
c) Renewal of the camshaft oil seals.
d) Removal and refitting of the camshaft.
e) Removal and refitting of the sump.
f) Removal and refitting of the connecting rods and pistons*.
g) Removal and refitting of the oil pump.
h) Renewal of the crankshaft oil seals.
i) Renewal of the engine mountings.
j) Removal and refitting of the flywheel.

* Although the operation marked with an asterisk can be carried out with the engine in the car after removal of the sump, it is better for the engine to be removed in the interests of cleanliness and improved access. For this reason, the procedure is described in Chapter 2D.

2 Compression and leakdown tests – description and interpretation

Compression test

Note: *A compression tester specifically designed for diesel engines must be used for this test.*

1 When engine performance is down, or if misfiring occurs which cannot be attributed to a fault in the fuel system, a compression test can provide diagnostic clues as to the engine's condition. If the test is performed regularly it can give warning of trouble before any other symptoms become apparent.

2 A compression tester is connected to an adaptor which screws into the glow plug hole. It is unlikely to be worthwhile buying such a tester for occasional use, but it may be possible to borrow or hire one – if not, have the test performed by a garage.

3 Unless specific instructions to the contrary are supplied with the tester, observe the following points:

a) The battery must be in a good state of charge, the air filter must be clean and the engine should be at normal operating temperature.
b) All the glow plugs must be removed before starting the test and the wiring disconnected from the injectors.

4 There is no need to hold the accelerator pedal down during the test because the diesel engine air inlet is not throttled.

5 The actual compression pressures measured are not so important as the balance between cylinders. Values are given in the Specifications.

6 The cause of poor compression is less easy to establish on a diesel engine than on a petrol one. The effect of introducing oil into

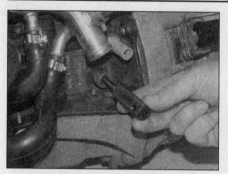

3.13 Fitting the crankshaft TDC pin

3.14 Fitting the camshaft TDC pin

the cylinders ('wet' testing) is not conclusive, because there is a risk that the oil will sit in the swirl chamber or in the recess on the piston crown instead of passing to the rings. However, the following can be used as a rough guide to diagnosis.

7 All cylinders should produce very similar pressures; any difference greater than that specified indicates the existence of a fault.

8 Note that the compression should build-up quickly in a healthy engine; low compression on the first stroke, followed by gradually increasing pressure on successive strokes, indicates worn piston rings. A low compression reading on the first stroke, which does not build-up during successive strokes, indicates leaking valves or a blown head gasket (a cracked head could also be the cause).

9 A low reading from two adjacent cylinders is almost certainly due to the head gasket having blown between them.

Leakdown test

10 A leakdown test measures the rate at which compressed air fed into the cylinder is lost. It is an alternative to a compression test and in many ways it is better, since the escaping air provides easy identification of where pressure loss is occurring (piston rings, valves or head gasket).

11 The equipment needed for leakdown testing is unlikely to be available to the home mechanic. If poor compression is suspected, have the test performed by a suitably-equipped garage.

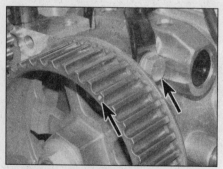

3.15 The high-pressure pump sprocket mark aligns with the bolt head on the cylinder head

3 Engine assembly/ valve timing holes – general information and usage

Note: Special Renault timing tools are required for this work, or tools obtained from an automotive accessory shop.

Caution: Do not attempt to rotate the engine whilst the crankshaft and camshaft timing pins are in position. If the engine is to be left in this state for a long period of time, it is a good idea to place suitable warning notices inside the car, and in the engine compartment. This will reduce the possibility of the engine being accidentally cranked on the starter motor, which would cause considerable damage.

1 Top Dead Centre (TDC) is the highest point in the cylinder that each piston reaches as the crankshaft turns. Each piston reaches TDC at the end of the compression stroke and again at the end of the exhaust stroke; however, for the purpose of timing the engine, TDC refers to the position of No 1 piston at the end of its compression stroke. No 1 piston is at the flywheel end of the engine.

2 When No 1 piston is at TDC, the timing hole in the camshaft sprocket will be aligned with the hole in the cylinder head so that the timing pin can be inserted. Additionally, if the crankshaft timing pin is fully screwed into the cylinder block, it will just contact the timing flat on the crankshaft web.

3 Setting the TDC timing is necessary to ensure that the valve timing is maintained during operations that require removal and refitting of the timing belt. Note that the engine does not have a conventional diesel injection pump, however, it is still necessary to align a mark on the pump sprocket with a bolt head on the cylinder head.

4 To set the engine at TDC, the right-hand engine mounting must be removed for access to the camshaft sprocket. First jack up the right-hand front of the car and support on axle stands. Remove the front right wheel, engine undertray and wheel arch liner.

5 Remove the auxiliary drivebelt with reference to Chapter 1B.

6 Support the right-hand end of the engine

with a support bar across the engine compartment, with a hoist, or alternatively with a jack and block of wood beneath the sump. Unbolt the right-hand engine mounting from the engine and body, and unclip the upper timing cover.

7 Unbolt the high-pressure pump position sensor from the lower timing cover.

8 Release the fuel pipes from the support clips, then remove the lower timing cover by releasing the clips and pulling out the plastic bolt. If necessary, slightly raise the engine to facilitate removal of the timing cover.

9 Unbolt and remove the engine mounting support bracket.

10 Unscrew and remove the plug from the TDC hole on the left-hand front of the cylinder block.

11 The crankshaft must now be turned using a spanner on the crankshaft pulley bolt. To turn the engine more easily, remove the glow plugs (Chapter 5C) or the fuel injectors (Chapter 4B). Before removing the injectors, consider that Renault stipulate the high-pressure fuel lines must be renewed after removing them – new high-pressure fuel lines are expensive.

12 Turn the crankshaft clockwise until the timing hole in the camshaft sprocket is approaching the hole in the cylinder head.

13 Insert and tighten the special TDC pin into the cylinder block timing hole (see illustration). *Note: If the pin is not available, an alternative method of determining the TDC position is to use a dial gauge on the top of piston No 1 after removing the fuel injector or glow plug.*

14 Slowly turn the crankshaft clockwise until its web contacts the timing pin. Now insert the remaining timing pin through the hole in the camshaft sprocket and into the cylinder head (see illustration). The engine is now positioned with No 1 piston at TDC on its compression stroke.

15 Check that the mark on the high-pressure injection pump sprocket is aligned with the bolt head on the cylinder head (see illustration).

16 On completion, remove the timing pins and refit all removed components.

4 Valve clearances – checking and adjustment

Note: This operation is not part of the maintenance schedule, and would normally only be required after a very high mileage, since an incorrect clearance would be most likely due to wear. It should be undertaken if noise from the valve gear becomes evident, or if loss of performance gives cause to suspect that the clearances may be incorrect. Adjustment involves removing the camshaft and changing the tappet buckets, which are available in 25 different thicknesses.

Checking

1 Unclip the engine top cover, and detach

4.1a Unclip the engine top cover

4.1b Remove the intercooler air duct support bolt

4.2 Disconnecting the crankcase ventilation hose from the cylinder head cover

the intercooler air duct which runs across the cylinder head cover – this may be bolted to the cover, with a hose clip securing it at the back of the engine (see illustrations).

2 Disconnect the crankcase ventilation hose from the cylinder head cover (see illustration).

3 Release the fuel return pipes from the clips on the cylinder head cover.

4 Unscrew the bolts and remove the cover from the top of the cylinder head (see illustration).

5 During the following procedure, the crankshaft must be turned using a spanner on the crankshaft pulley bolt. Loosen the right-hand wheel bolts, then jack up the front of the car, and support it on axle stands (see *Jacking and vehicle support*). Remove the wheel and wheel arch liner.

6 If desired, to turn the crankshaft more easily, remove the glow plugs (Chapter 5C) or the fuel injectors (Chapter 4B). Before removing the injectors, consider that Renault stipulate the high-pressure fuel lines must be renewed after removing them – new high-pressure fuel lines are expensive.

7 Draw the valve positions on a piece of paper, numbering them 1 to 8 from the flywheel end of the engine. Identify them as inlet or exhaust (ie, 1E, 2I, 3E, 4I, 5E, 6I, 7E, 8I).

VALVES ROCKING ON CYLINDER	CHECK CLEARANCE ON CYLINDER
1	4
3	2
4	1
2	3
	J45252

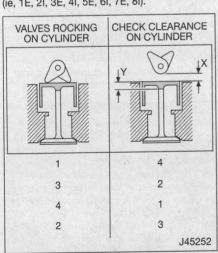

4.10 Valve clearance measurement

X Clearance   *Y Tappet thickness*

4.4 Cylinder head cover retaining bolts

8 Turn the crankshaft until the valves of No 1 cylinder (flywheel end) are 'rocking'. The exhaust valve will be closing and the inlet valve will be opening. The piston of No 4 cylinder will be at the top of its compression stroke, with both valves fully closed. The clearances for both valves of No 4 cylinder may be checked at the same time.

9 Insert a feeler blade of the correct thickness (see Specifications) between the cam lobe and the top of the tappet bucket, and check that it is a firm sliding fit (see illustration). If it is not, use the feeler blades to ascertain the exact clearance, and record this for use when calculating the thickness of the new tappet bucket required. Note that the inlet and exhaust valve clearances are different.

10 With No 4 cylinder valve clearances checked, turn the engine through half a turn so that No 3 valves are 'rocking', then check the valve clearances of No 2 cylinder in the same way.

4.11 Using a dial gauge to measure the thickness of the removed tappet

4.9 Using a feeler blade to check the valve clearances

Similarly check the remaining valve clearances in the sequence shown (see illustration).

Adjustment

Note: *A micrometer or dial gauge and probe will be required for this operation.*

11 Where a valve clearance differs from the specified value, the tappet bucket for that valve must be changed with a thinner or thicker one accordingly. On new tappets, the thickness is stamped on the bottom face of the tappet, however, the original tappets do have any thickness stamped on them. It is therefore prudent to use a micrometer or dial gauge to measure the true thickness of any tappet removed, as it may have been reduced by wear (see illustration).

12 To access the tappet buckets, first remove the camshaft as described in Section 8. Remove and refit each bucket separately, to avoid confusion (see illustration).

4.12 Removing a tappet bucket

13 The size of tappet required is calculated as follows. If the measured clearance is less than specified, subtract the measured clearance from the specified clearance, and deduct the result from the thickness of the existing tappet. For example:

Sample calculation – clearance too small
Clearance measured (A) = 0.10 mm
Desired clearance (B) = 0.20 mm
Difference (B – A) = 0.10 mm
Tappet bucket thickness fitted = 3.70 mm
Tappet bucket thickness required =
3.70 – 0.10 = 3.60 mm

14 If the measured clearance is greater than specified, subtract the specified clearance from the measured clearance, and add the result to the thickness of the existing tappet. For example:

Sample calculation – clearance too big
Clearance measured (A) = 0.50 mm
Desired clearance (B) = 0.40 mm
Difference (A – B) = 0.10 mm
Tappet bucket thickness fitted = 3.45 mm
Tappet bucket thickness required =
3.45 + 0.10 = 3.55 mm

15 Working on each separately, lift out the bucket to be renewed, then oil the new one and carefully locate it in the cylinder head **(see illustration)**.
16 Refit the camshaft with reference to Section 8.
17 Where removed, refit the glow plugs (Chapter 5C) or the fuel injectors (Chapter 4B).
18 Remove the spanner from the crankshaft pulley bolt.
19 Clean the contact surfaces on the cover and

4.15 Lubricate the tappet bucket before refitting it

cylinder head, then apply four beads of sealant, 2.0 mm wide, to the camshaft end bearing caps (Nos 1 and 6) **(see illustration 8.24)**.
20 Refit the cylinder head cover and tighten the bolts to the specified torque in the order given **(see illustration 8.25)**.
21 Secure the fuel return pipes in the clips on the cylinder head cover.
22 Reconnect the crankcase ventilation hose.
23 Refit the intercooler air duct, then refit the engine top cover.

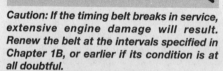

5 Timing belt – removal, inspection and refitting

Caution: If the timing belt breaks in service, extensive engine damage will result. Renew the belt at the intervals specified in Chapter 1B, or earlier if its condition is at all doubtful.

Removal

1 Disconnect the battery negative lead (refer to *Disconnecting the battery* in Reference).
2 Loosen the right-hand front wheel bolts, then jack up the right-hand front of the car and support on axle stands. Remove the front right wheel, engine/radiator undertray and wheel arch liner. Unclip and remove the engine top cover. Remove the windscreen cowl panels as described in Chapter 11, Section 8.
3 Remove the auxiliary drivebelt with reference to Chapter 1B, then unbolt and remove the drivebelt tensioner. For improved access, unscrew and remove the alternator upper mounting bolt and loosen the lower bolt, then swivel the alternator away from the cylinder head.
4 Support the right-hand end of the engine with a support bar across the engine compartment with a hoist, or alternatively with a jack and block of wood beneath the sump. If a hoist is being used, remove the bonnet with reference to Chapter 11.
5 Remove the engine right-hand mounting from the engine and body with reference to Section 14, then release and unclip the plastic upper timing cover **(see illustrations)**. There is no need to unscrew the centre mounting nut.
6 Unbolt the high-pressure pump position sensor from the lower timing cover, and disconnect the wiring **(see illustrations)**.
7 Release the fuel pipes from the support clips, then remove the lower timing covers by releasing the clips and unscrewing the plastic bolt **(see illustrations)**. Note that the bolt is refitted by simply pressing it into position. If

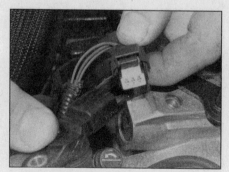

5.5a Release the clips . . .

5.5b . . . and remove the plastic upper timing cover

5.6a Removing the high-pressure pump position sensor . . .

5.6b . . . and disconnecting the wiring

5.7a Release the fuel pipes from the support clips . . .

5.7b . . . then remove the lower timing covers

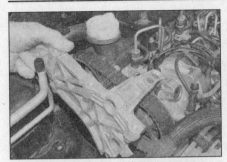

5.8 Removing the right-hand engine mounting support bracket (note the bracket extension is fitted *beneath* the timing belt)

5.9 TDC hole blanking plug

5.13 Using a bolt as a TDC pin through the camshaft sprocket

necessary, slightly raise the engine to facilitate removal of the timing cover.

8 Unbolt and remove the engine mounting support bracket **(see illustration)**.

9 Unscrew and remove the blanking plug from the TDC hole on the left-hand front of the cylinder block **(see illustration)**.

10 The crankshaft must now be turned to the TDC position using a spanner on the crankshaft pulley bolt. To enable the engine to be turned more easily, remove the glow plugs (Chapter 5C) or the fuel injectors (Chapter 4B). Before removing the injectors, consider that Renault stipulate the high-pressure fuel lines must be renewed after removing them. New high-pressure fuel lines are expensive.

11 Turn the crankshaft clockwise until the timing hole in the camshaft sprocket is approaching the hole in the cylinder head.

12 Insert and tighten the special TDC pin into the cylinder block timing hole.

13 Slowly turn the crankshaft clockwise until its web contacts the timing pin. Now insert the remaining timing pin (or a suitable bolt) through the hole in the camshaft sprocket and into the cylinder head **(see illustration)**. The engine is now positioned with No 1 piston at TDC on its compression stroke.

14 Check that the mark on the high-pressure injection pump sprocket is aligned with the bolt head on the cylinder head.

15 Temporarily remove the timing pins while the crankshaft pulley bolt is being loosened.

16 Before loosening the crankshaft pulley bolt, note that the crankshaft sprocket is **not** keyed to the crankshaft as is the normal arrangement, therefore if the crankshaft pulley is removed it is important to have an accurate method of determining the TDC position of No 1 piston. Although the sprocket is not keyed to the crankshaft, there is still a groove in the crankshaft nose which is at the 12 o'clock position when piston No 1 is at TDC.

17 Unscrew the crankshaft pulley bolt while holding the crankshaft stationary. Have an assistant engage 4th gear and depress firmly the brake pedal. Alternatively, remove the starter motor or where applicable remove the cover plate from the transmission bellhousing, and have an assistant insert a screwdriver or similar tool in the starter ring gear teeth. With the bolt removed, ease the pulley from the crankshaft **(see illustrations)**.

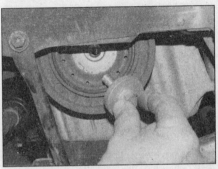

5.17a Unscrew and remove the crankshaft pulley bolt . . .

5.17b . . . and remove the pulley

18 Reposition the crankshaft at TDC and insert both timing pins again.

19 Loosen the tensioner locknut, then turn the tensioner clockwise to release the tension. If necessary, use a 6.0 mm Allen key in the eccentric hub plate to move the tensioner **(see illustration)**.

20 If the original belt is to be re-used (contrary to Renault's recommendation), check if the belt is marked with arrows to indicate its running direction, and if necessary mark it. Similarly, make accurate alignment marks on the belt, corresponding to the timing marks on the camshaft, high-pressure fuel injection pump and crankshaft sprockets. Check that there are 18 inclusive teeth between the timing marks on the camshaft and injection pump sprockets, then release the timing belt from the camshaft sprocket, high-pressure injection pump, water pump pulley, crankshaft sprocket and tensioner **(see illustration)**.

21 **Do not** turn the camshaft or the crankshaft whilst the timing belt is removed, as there is a risk of piston-to-valve contact. If it is necessary to turn the camshaft for any reason, before doing so, turn the crankshaft anti-clockwise (viewed from the timing belt end of the engine) by a quarter turn to position all four pistons half-way down their bores. Leave the TDC pin tightened into the cylinder block.

22 Clean the sprockets, water pump pulley and tensioner and wipe them dry, although do not apply excessive amounts of solvent to the water pump and tensioner pulleys otherwise the bearing lubricant may be contaminated. Also clean the rear timing belt cover, and the cylinder head and block.

Inspection

23 Examine the timing belt carefully for any signs of cracking, fraying or general wear, particularly at the roots of the teeth. Renew

5.19 Loosen the tensioner locknut . . .

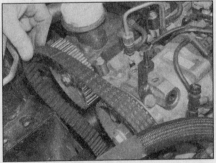

5.20 . . . then release the timing belt

5.29 Align the timing marks on the belt with those on the camshaft and fuel injection pump sprockets

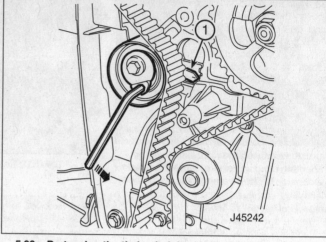

5.30a Pretension the timing belt by positioning the tensioner pointer (1) as shown

the belt if there is any sign of deterioration of this nature, or if there is any oil or grease contamination. The belt must, of course, be renewed if it has completed the maximum mileage given in Chapter 1B.

24 When fitting a new belt, Renault recommend that a new tensioner is also fitted – this is often sold as a kit with a new belt, when purchased from a Renault dealer.

25 Since the timing belt also drives the water pump, it makes sense to examine the pump carefully when a new belt is being fitted, since fitting a new pump will mean removing the belt again. If the pump shows any sign of leakage from the vent hole, or if the pulley sounds rough when spun, a new pump should be fitted as a precaution.

26 Thoroughly clean the nose of the crankshaft and the bore of the crankshaft sprocket, and also the contact surfaces of the sprocket and pulley. This is necessary to prevent the possibility of the sprocket, which is not keyed to the crankshaft, slipping in use and causing engine damage.

Refitting

27 Check that the crankshaft, camshaft and high-pressure fuel injection pump sprockets are still positioned at TDC, and that the groove in the crankshaft nose is pointing upwards. If the pistons have been positioned half-way down their bores, turn the crankshaft clockwise until the web contacts the TDC tool.

28 Check that the tensioner peg is correctly located in the groove in the cylinder head.

29 Align the timing marks on the belt with those on the camshaft and fuel injection pump sprockets **(see illustration)**, ensuring that the running direction arrows on the belt are pointing clockwise (viewed from the timing belt end of the engine). Note that the belt should be marked with lines across its width to act as timing marks. Fit the timing belt over the crankshaft sprocket first, followed by the water pump pulley, fuel injection pump sprocket, camshaft sprocket, and tensioner. There are 18 inclusive teeth between the timing marks on the camshaft and injection pump sprockets.

30 With the timing marks still aligned, use the 6.0 mm Allen key to pretension the belt by turning the tensioner anti-clockwise until the index pointer is positioned below the timing window **(see illustrations)**. Hold the tensioner stationary and tighten the locknut to the specified torque. This torque is critical, since if the nut were to come loose, considerable engine damage would result.

31 Refit the crankshaft pulley, then insert the bolt and tighten to the specified torque and angle. This can be done with the timing pin still tight in the cylinder block, and the crankshaft web resting against it. After tightening the bolt, remove the timing pins from the cylinder block and camshaft sprocket.

32 Turn the crankshaft two complete turns in the normal direction of rotation, but just before the camshaft sprockets are aligned, refit and tighten the crankshaft timing pin. Slowly turn the crankshaft clockwise until its web is contacting the timing pin, then check that it is possible to insert the remaining timing pin through the hole in the camshaft sprocket and into the cylinder head. If so, remove the timing pins.

5.30b Pretensioning the timing belt

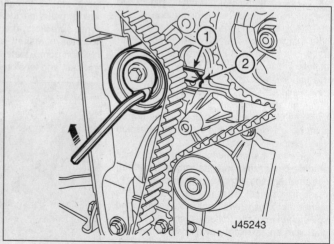

5.33 Position the pointer (1) to its final setting in the middle of the timing window (2)

33 Hold the tensioner with the Allen key, then loosen the locknut a maximum of one turn, and turn the tensioner clockwise until the index pointer is positioned in the middle of the timing window **(see illustration)**. Tighten the locknut to the specified torque.

34 Apply sealant to the threads, then refit the blanking plug to the cylinder block and tighten it to the specified torque.

35 Refit the engine mounting support bracket and tighten the bolts to the specified torque.

36 Refit the lower timing cover and locate the fuel pipes in their clips.

37 Refit the high-pressure pump position sensor on the lower timing cover and tighten the bolts.

38 Clip the upper timing cover onto the lower cover, then refit the right-hand engine mounting to the engine and body and tighten the bolts to the specified torque.

39 Refit the auxiliary drivebelt with reference to Chapter 1B.

40 Refit the engine undertray and wheel arch liner, the windscreen cowl panels and top cover.

41 Refit the front right wheel and lower the car to the ground. Tighten the wheel bolts to the specified torque.

42 Reconnect the battery negative lead (refer to *Disconnecting the battery* in the Reference Section).

43 If removed, refit the bonnet with reference to Chapter 11.

6	Timing belt sprockets, idler pulley and tensioner – removal and refitting

Crankshaft sprocket

Removal

1 Remove the timing belt as described in Section 5.

2 Slide the sprocket from the crankshaft, noting which way around it is fitted **(see illustration)**.

Refitting

3 Thoroughly clean the nose of the crankshaft and the bore of the crankshaft sprocket, and also the contact surfaces of the sprocket and pulley. This is necessary to prevent the possibility of the sprocket, which is not keyed to the crankshaft, slipping in use and causing engine damage.

4 Slide the sprocket onto the crankshaft the correct way around.

5 Refit the timing belt as described in Section 5.

Fuel injection pump sprocket

Note: *A suitable puller will be required for this operation.*

Removal

6 Note it is **strictly forbidden** to remove the high-pressure pump sprocket where it is marked with the number 070 575 **(see illustration)**. All other sprockets may be

6.2 Removing the crankshaft sprocket

removed as follows, however, note that if it is being removed for pump renewal, a special Renault tool is available to enable the pump to be removed without removing the timing belt; refer to Chapter 4B for details of the procedure which entails using a sprocket support tool.

7 Remove the timing belt as described in Section 5.

8 Hold the sprocket stationary using a suitable gear-holding tool. Alternatively, an old timing belt can be wrapped around the sprocket and held firmly with a pair of grips. Unscrew and remove the central securing nut.

9 Use a puller to release the sprocket from the taper on the pump shaft. Recover the Woodruff key from the groove in the pump shaft.

Refitting

10 Refitting is a reversal of removal, bearing in mind the following points:

a) Ensure that the Woodruff key is correctly engaged with the pump shaft and sprocket.

b) Tighten the sprocket securing nut to the specified torque.

c) Refit and tension the timing belt as described in Section 5. Make sure that the mark on the sprocket is aligned with the bolt on the cylinder head.

Camshaft sprocket

Removal

11 Remove the timing belt as described in Section 5.

6.13 Removing the sprocket from the end of the camshaft – note the integral spline

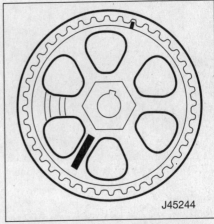

6.6 Do not remove the high-pressure injection pump sprocket marked 070 575

12 Hold the sprocket stationary using a suitable gear-holding tool. Alternatively, an old timing belt can be wrapped around the sprocket and held firmly with a pair of grips. Unscrew and remove the central securing nut.

13 Release the sprocket from the camshaft, noting the integral spline on the sprocket and the corresponding cut-out in the end of the camshaft **(see illustration)**.

14 Recover the Woodruff key from the end of the camshaft.

Refitting

15 Refit the camshaft sprocket, making sure that the integral spline locates in the camshaft cut-out. Insert the bolt and tighten it to the specified torque and angle, holding the sprocket stationary as during removal **(see illustration)**.

16 Refit and tension the timing belt as described in Section 5.

Tensioner

Removal

17 Remove the timing belt as described in Section 5.

18 Unscrew the securing nut and remove the washer and pivot bolt, then withdraw the tensioner assembly from the engine **(see illustration)**.

6.15 Angle-tightening the camshaft sprocket retaining bolt

6.18 Removing the timing belt tensioner

Refitting

19 Refitting is a reversal of removal. Refit and tension the timing belt as described in Section 5.

---

7 Camshaft oil seals – renewal

Timing belt end oil seal

Note: *There are two versions of camshaft oil seal fitted (see Chapter 2A, Section 6); version 1 has an internal spring and V-shaped sealing lip, version 2 has a flat sealing lip without an internal spring. Version 2 is extremely fragile, and must only be handled by the protector. The oil seals are not interchangeable and the fitting procedure for each is different, as described in the following paragraphs.*

1 Remove the camshaft sprocket as described in Section 6.

2 Note the fitted depth of the old oil seal. Using a small screwdriver, prise out the oil seal from the cylinder head taking care not to damage the sealing surface on the camshaft. Alternatively, the oil seal can be removed by drilling two small holes diagonally opposite each other and inserting self-tapping screws in them. A pair of grips can then be used to pull out the oil seals, by pulling on each side in turn.

3 Inspect the seal rubbing surface on the camshaft. If it is grooved or rough in the area where the old seal was fitted, the new seal should be fitted slightly less deeply, so that it rubs on an unworn part of the surface.

Version 1 oil seal

4 Wipe clean the oil seal seating, then dip the new seal in fresh engine oil, and locate it over the camshaft with its closed side facing outwards. Make sure that the oil seal lip is not damaged as it is located on the camshaft, and if necessary, temporarily wrap some tape around the end of the camshaft to protect it **(see illustration)**.

5 Locate the seal squarely in the cylinder head, then drive it into position using a metal tube or socket which has an external diameter slightly less than that of the bore in the cylinder head **(see illustration)**. Alternatively, the oil seal can be pressed into position using a metal tube, washer and nut.

Version 2 oil seal

6 Renault technicians use a tool (Mot. 1632) to

fit the oil seal. The tool consists of a threaded rod, metal tube and nut, and a machined shoulder to locate the protector/guide on. The rod is screwed into the end of the camshaft, and the protector/guide located on the shoulder. The metal tube is then fitted against the oil seal and the nut tightened to press the seal into the cylinder head/bearing cap **(see illustrations)**. If the Renault tool cannot be obtained, a similar tool can be made out of a threaded rod, metal tube, washer and nut.

7 Wipe clean the oil seal seating, then press the oil seal squarely into position. Note that the Renault tool is designed to locate the seal at the original depth, however, if the camshaft sealing surface is excessively worn, position it less deeply so that it locates on the unworn surface.

8 After fitting the oil seal, remove the protector/guide and tool.

All types

9 Wipe away any excess oil, then refit the camshaft sprocket as described in Section 6.

Flywheel end sealing

10 No oil seal is fitted to the flywheel end of the camshaft. The sealing is provided by a gasket between the cylinder head and the brake vacuum pump housing, and on certain models by an O-ring fitted between the vacuum pump and the housing. The gasket and the O-ring, where applicable, can be renewed after unbolting the vacuum pump from the cylinder head (see Chapter 9).

---

8 Camshaft and tappets – removal, inspection and refitting

Note: *A new camshaft oil seal will be required, and suitable sealant will be required for the camshaft bearing caps and cylinder head cover.*

Removal

1 Removal of the camshaft will normally only be required for access to the tappet buckets (eg, for valve clearance adjustment) or during cylinder head overhaul. For cylinder head overhaul, remove the head as described in Section 9.

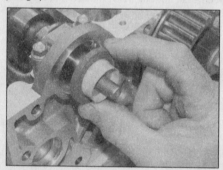

7.4 Locate the new oil seal on the end of the camshaft . . .

7.5 . . . then drive it into position using a socket

7.6a Screw the rod into the end of the camshaft . . .

7.6b . . . locate the new oil seal and protector onto the camshaft . . .

7.6c . . . then tighten the tool to press the seal into position

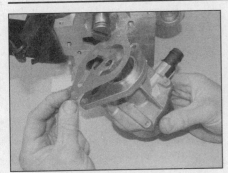

8.6a Removing the brake vacuum pump and gasket

8.6b Offset drive in the pump which engages the slot in the end of the camshaft

8.9 The camshaft bearing caps are numbered from the flywheel end of the engine

2 Remove the camshaft sprocket as described in Section 6.

3 Disconnect the crankcase ventilation hose and the fuel return pipes from the cylinder head cover.

4 Detach the intercooler air duct which runs across the cylinder head cover – this may be bolted to the cover, with hose clips either end.

5 Unscrew the bolts and remove the cover from the top of the cylinder head.

6 Remove the brake vacuum pump with reference to Chapter 9. Note the position of the offset drive inside the pump which engages the slot in the end of the camshaft **(see illustrations)**.

7 Using a dial gauge, measure the camshaft endfloat, and compare with the value given in the Specifications. This will give an indication of the amount of wear present on the thrust surfaces.

8 If the original camshaft is to be refitted, it is advisable to measure the valve clearances at this stage as described in Section 4, so that any different thickness tappets required can be obtained before the camshaft is refitted.

9 Check the camshaft bearing caps for identification marks, and if none are present, make identifying marks so that they can be refitted in their original positions and the same way round. Number the caps from the flywheel end of the engine **(see illustration)**.

10 Progressively slacken the bearing cap bolts until the valve spring pressure is relieved. Remove the bolts and the bearing caps themselves.

11 Lift out the camshaft together with the oil seal **(see illustration)**.

12 Remove the tappets, keeping each identified for position **(see illustration)**. Place them in a compartment box, or on a sheet of card marked into eight sections, so that they may be refitted to their original locations. If any of the valve clearances measured in paragraph 9 is incorrect, use a micrometer to measure the thickness of the old tappet from its upper surface to the inner surface which contacts the valve stem. Refer to Section 4 and obtain new tappets of the correct thickness.

Inspection

13 Examine the camshaft bearing surfaces

and cam lobes for wear ridges, pitting or scoring. Renew the camshaft if evident.

14 Renew the oil seal at the end of the camshaft as a matter of course. Lubricate the lips of the new seal before fitting, and store the camshaft so that its weight is not resting on the seal. Alternatively, the seal may be fitted after refitting the camshaft.

15 Examine the camshaft bearing surfaces in the cylinder head and bearing caps. Deep scoring or other damage means that the cylinder head must be renewed.

16 Inspect the tappet buckets for scoring, pitting and wear ridges. Renew as necessary.

Refitting

17 Oil the tappets (inside and out) and fit them to the bores from which they were removed; where applicable, fit the new tappets to their correct bores.

8.11 Removing the camshaft from the cylinder head

8.19a Apply 1.0 mm wide beads of sealant to the camshaft end bearing cap-to-cylinder head contact areas as shown

18 Oil the camshaft bearings. Place the camshaft without the oil seal onto the cylinder head.

19 Wipe clean the upper sealing edge of the cylinder head, then apply four beads of sealant, 1.0 mm wide, to the camshaft end bearing cap (Nos 1 and 6) contact areas as shown **(see illustrations)**.

20 Refit the camshaft bearing caps to their original locations, then insert the bearing cap bolts and progressively tighten them to the specified torque **(see illustration)**.

21 If a new camshaft has been fitted, measure the endfloat using a dial gauge, and check that it is within the specified limits.

22 Fit the new oil seal with reference to Section 7.

23 Refit the brake vacuum pump with reference to Chapter 9.

24 Wipe clean the contact surfaces on the

8.12 Removing the tappets

8.19b Apply the beads of sealant . . .

8.20 . . . then refit the camshaft bearing caps

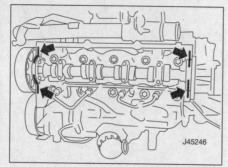

8.24 Apply 2.0 mm wide beads of sealant to the camshaft end bearing caps as shown

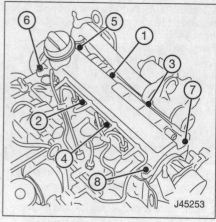

8.25 Cylinder head cover tightening sequence

cover and cylinder head, then apply four beads of sealant, 2.0 mm wide, to the camshaft end bearing caps (Nos 1 and 6) as shown **(see illustration)**.

25 Refit the cylinder head cover and tighten the bolts to the specified torque in the order given **(see illustration)**.

26 Refit the intercooler air duct, ensuring that the hose clips are securely tightened.

27 Secure the fuel return pipes in the clips on the cylinder head cover.

28 Reconnect the crankcase ventilation hose.

29 Refit the camshaft sprocket as described in Section 6.

9 Cylinder head – removal, inspection and refitting

Note: *A new cylinder head gasket must be*

fitted, and all cylinder head bolts must be renewed. Sealant for the cylinder head cover will also be required.

Removal

1 Before starting work, allow the engine to cool for as long as possible, to ensure the fuel pressure in the high-pressure lines, and the fuel temperature, are at a minimum (refer to Chapter 4B).

2 Remove the battery as described in Chapter 5A.

3 Remove the engine undertray, then drain the cooling system and engine oil with reference to Chapter 1A.

4 Remove the windscreen cowl panels as described in Chapter 11, Section 8.

5 Remove the timing belt (Section 5) and, if necessary, the camshaft sprocket (Section 6).

6 Disconnect the wiring from the following sensors **(see illustrations)**:

a) *Air intake temperature/pressure sensor.*

b) *EGR valve control.*

c) *Coolant temperature sensor.*

7 Detach the intercooler air duct which runs across the cylinder head cover – this may be bolted to the cover, with hose clips either end.

8 At the rear of the high-pressure injection pump, disconnect the wiring from the fuel temperature sensor and low pressure flow adjuster.

9 Disconnect the wiring from the four fuel injectors and glow plugs. If necessary, remove the glow plugs from the cylinder head. Before removing the injectors, consider that Renault stipulate the high-pressure fuel lines must be renewed after removing them. If the removal of the cylinder head is just to renew the gasket, leave the injectors in position together with the fuel lines and high-pressure pump. New high-pressure fuel lines are expensive.

10 Release the clip securing the fuel return pipe and wiring.

11 Remove the coolant hoses and temperature sensor from the left-hand end of the cylinder head **(see illustration)**.

12 Disconnect the exhaust downpipe and detach the catalytic converter from the turbocharger as described in Chapter 4B.

13 Unscrew the union nuts and remove the turbocharger oil return pipe from the cylinder block and turbocharger.

9.6a Disconnect the air temperature/boost pressure sensor . . .

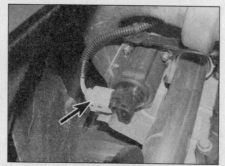

9.6b . . . EGR control solenoid . . .

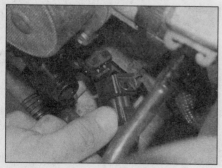

9.6c . . . and the coolant temperature sensor

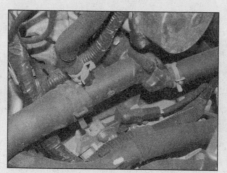

9.11 Coolant hoses on the left-hand end of the cylinder head

9.14 Removing the timing belt tensioner roller

14 Unbolt and remove the timing belt tensioner roller from the cylinder head (**see illustration**).

15 Unbolt and remove the auxiliary drivebelt tensioner from the cylinder block.

16 Unbolt and remove the inner timing cover from the cylinder block and head – loosen the alternator mountings and tilt the alternator forwards to make this easier (**see illustration**).

17 Disconnect the crankcase ventilation hose from the cylinder head cover (**see illustration**).

18 Release the injector fuel return pipes from the clips on the cylinder head cover (**see illustration**).

19 Unscrew the bolts and remove the cover from the top of the cylinder head (**see illustration**).

20 Refer to Chapter 4B and observe the precautions necessary when disconnecting the high-pressure fuel injection pipes. In particular, all disconnected pipes and components in the following paragraphs must be plugged to prevent entry of dust and dirt into the fuel system, and all removed high-pressure pipes must be renewed after removing (refer to paragraph 9).

21 Loosen the union nuts and disconnect the four high-pressure pipes between the fuel rail and injectors.

22 Loosen the union nut and disconnect the fuel supply pipe from the fuel rail.

23 Disconnect the wiring from the fuel pressure sensor on the fuel rail (**see illustration**).

24 Disconnect the quick-release vacuum pipe from the brake vacuum pump on the left-hand end of the cylinder head (**see illustration**).

25 Unbolt the engine oil level dipstick tube from the cylinder head and remove it from the sump (**see illustration**).

26 The cylinder head assembly, complete with high-pressure pump and ancillaries, is very heavy. If they are to be left attached, it is advisable to use a hoist and suitable lifting tackle connected to the lifting eyes to lift the cylinder head. Alternatively, have an assistant available to help lift it off.

27 Before removing the cylinder head, turn the crankshaft anti-clockwise (viewed from the timing belt end of the engine) by a quarter-turn to position all four pistons half-way down their bores. The TDC pin can remain in the cylinder block if necessary, however, remember that it is in position and do not turn the crankshaft further anti-clockwise.

28 Progressively slacken the cylinder head bolts in the **reverse** sequence to that shown (**see illustration 9.42**). With all the bolts loose, remove them (**see illustration**).

29 Make a final check round the head to ensure that nothing is still attached, nor anything in the way which would hinder it being lifted off.

30 Lift the cylinder head upwards off the cylinder block. If it is stuck, tap it with a hammer and block of wood to release it. **Do**

9.16 Removing the inner timing cover

9.18 Removing the injector fuel return pipes

not try to turn the cylinder head (it is located by two dowels), nor attempt to prise it free using a screwdriver inserted between the block and head faces.

31 If desired, the manifolds and high pressure pump can be removed from the cylinder head

9.23 Disconnecting the wiring from the fuel pressure sensor on the fuel rail

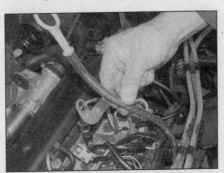

9.25 Removing the engine oil level dipstick tube

9.17 Disconnecting the crankcase ventilation hose from the cylinder head cover

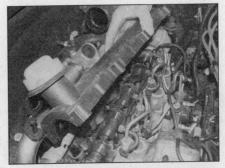

9.19 Removing the cylinder head cover

with reference to the relevant Sections of Chapter 4B.

Inspection

32 The mating faces of the cylinder head and block must be perfectly clean before refitting

9.24 Squeeze the tabs and pull off the pipe fitting from the brake vacuum pump

9.28 Removing the cylinder head bolts

9.39 Locate the new gasket on the cylinder block

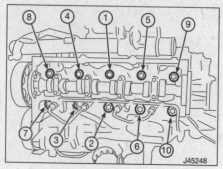

9.42 Cylinder head bolt tightening sequence

the head. Use a scraper to remove all traces of gasket and carbon, and also clean the tops of the pistons. Take particular care with the aluminium cylinder head, as the soft metal is easily damaged.

33 Also, make sure that debris is not allowed to enter the oil and water channels – this is particularly important for the oil circuit, as carbon could block the oil supply to the camshaft or crankshaft bearings. Using adhesive tape and paper, seal the water, oil and bolt holes in the cylinder block. Clean the piston crowns in the same way.

> **HAYNES HiNT** *To prevent carbon entering the gap between the pistons and bores, smear a little grease in the gap. After cleaning the piston, rotate the crankshaft so that the piston moves down the bore, then wipe out the grease and carbon with a cloth rag.*

34 Check the block and head for nicks, deep scratches and other damage. If slight, they may be removed carefully with a file. Machining of the cylinder head or cylinder block is not recommended by the manufacturers.

35 If warpage of the cylinder head is suspected, use a straight-edge to check it for distortion. Refer to Chapter 2D if necessary; if the warpage is more than the maximum, the cylinder head must be renewed, as regrinding is not allowed.

36 Clean out the cylinder head bolt holes in the block using a pipe cleaner, or a rag and screwdriver. Make sure that all oil is removed,

10.7 Removing the side support plates

otherwise there is a possibility of the block being cracked by hydraulic pressure when the bolts are tightened.

37 Examine the bolt threads in the cylinder block for damage, and if necessary, use the correct-size tap to chase out the threads. The cylinder head bolts must be renewed each time they are removed, and must not be oiled before being fitted.

Refitting

38 Where removed, refit the tappets, camshaft and camshaft sprocket with reference to Section 8 and 6. Turn the camshaft so that the sprocket is at its TDC position.

39 Ensure that the cylinder head locating dowels are fitted to the cylinder block, then fit the new gasket the right way round on the cylinder block **(see illustration)**.

40 It is recommended that No 1 piston is positioned half-way down its cylinder before refitting the cylinder head, as a safeguard against the valves touching the tops of the pistons. If not already done, turn the crankshaft clockwise until No 1 piston falls to the mid-cylinder position.

41 Carefully lower the cylinder head onto the dowels and gasket, then insert the new bolts and hand-tighten. **Do not** oil the threads or heads of the new bolts.

42 Tighten the bolts in sequence, and in the stages given in the Specifications **(see illustration)**. When angle-tightening the bolts, put paint marks on the bolt heads and cylinder head as a guide for the correct angle, or obtain a special angle-tightening tool.

43 Turn the crankshaft clockwise by a quarter-turn until the internal web contacts the TDC timing pin.

44 Refit the turbocharger, manifolds and injection pump to the cylinder head with reference to the relevant Sections of Chapter 4B.

45 Further refitting is a reversal of removal, noting the following points:

a) *Refit the cylinder head cover with reference to Section 8.*

b) *Tighten all nuts/bolts securely, or to the specified torque.*

c) *Refit the timing belt as described in Section 5.*

d) *On completion, refill the engine with fresh oil, then fill and bleed the cooling system, with reference to Chapter 1B.*

10 Sump – removal and refitting

Removal

1 Disconnect the battery negative lead (refer to *Disconnecting the battery* in the Reference Section).

2 Jack up the front of the car and support on axle stands. Remove the engine compartment undertray.

3 Drain the engine oil referring to Chapter 1B, then refit and tighten the drain plug. Though not essential, it makes sense to fit a new oil filter, before the sump is refilled with fresh oil.

4 Remove both front roadwheels, then remove both wheel arch liners.

5 Inside the wheel arch each side, remove the four bolts securing the support plate to the subframe and inner wing, and remove it.

6 Using cable-ties or string, tie the radiator up to the front crossmember – this is necessary, as the radiator lower crossmember must be removed.

7 Unbolt and remove the side supports each side, fitted between the subframe and radiator lower crossmember **(see illustration)**. Ensure that the radiator is adequately supported, as described in the previous paragraph. Remove the front bolt and rear nut, then lower the crossmember to the floor.

8 Referring to the driveshaft removal procedure in Chapter 8, unscrew the two bolts securing the driveshaft collar to the support bearing on the back of the engine. The driveshaft itself does not have to be removed, however.

9 Remove the lowest bolt from the alternator mounting bracket fitted to the front of the engine. The bracket itself does not have to be removed, but the lowest bolt is screwed into the sump.

10 Unbolt the catalytic converter support arm from the sump.

11 Unbolt and remove the engine lower mounting from the engine and subframe (see Section 14) – this will allow the engine to move slightly on its remaining right- and left-hand mountings, but providing they are not disturbed, this is not dangerous.

12 Loosen and remove the nineteen bolts used to secure the sump. In addition to the bolts, the sump is secured by several spots of sealant – tap the sump with a hide or plastic mallet to break the seal, or prise it very carefully, so as not to damage the sealing surfaces. Lower the sump out from under the car, and recover the gasket – a new one should be used when refitting.

Refitting

13 Thoroughly clean the mating surfaces of the sump and cylinder block. If required, the anti-emulsion plate inside the sump can also be unclipped and cleaned – when refitting, ensure that the five tabs on the plate sit properly in the cut-outs inside the sump.

14 Apply a total of four beads and two spots of suitable silicone sealant (Renault part number 7711219706, or equivalent) to the areas shown in Chapter 2A, Section 9. Do not apply too much, otherwise the excess may end up inside the sump, where it could get sucked into the engine.

15 Locate the new gasket in position, and lift the sump into position on the cylinder block. Insert the bolts and tighten them progressively in two stages to the specified torque – start with the centre bolts, and work in a diagonal sequence. If the engine is removed from the car, use a straight-edge to maintain the alignment between the left-hand end of the sump and cylinder block.

16 Further refitting is a reversal of removal, noting the following points:

a) *When refitting the radiator lower crossmember, fit the fasteners and side plates loosely, then insert a 10 mm spacer between it and the subframe, at the rear (refer to Chapter 7A, Section 8). We used a 10 mm diameter bolt – this should be withdrawn once the nuts have been tightened each side. The crossmember forms part of the deformable front structure of the car, and the gap left by using the spacer is essential.*

b) *Tighten all nuts/bolts to the specified torque.*

c) *Refer to Chapter 8 when refitting the right-hand driveshaft collar to the support bearing.*

d) *Allow sufficient time for the sealant used to cure, then fill the engine with fresh oil (see Chapter 1B). On completion, start the engine, and check for signs of leakage.*

11 Oil pump and sprockets – removal, inspection and refitting

Removal

1 Remove the sump as described in Section 10.

2 Unscrew the two mounting bolts and withdraw the oil pump, tilting it to disengage its sprocket from the drive chain. If the two locating dowels are displaced, refit them in their locations.

3 To remove the drive chain, first remove the crankshaft sprocket as described in Section 6, then unbolt the engine right-hand cover from the cylinder block. Prise out the oil seal with a screwdriver, and discard it as a new one must be fitted on reassembly. If necessary, the new oil seal may be fitted with the right-hand cover on the bench **(see illustration)**.

4 Slide the oil pump drive sprocket and drive chain from the nose of the crankshaft **(see illustrations)**. Note that the drive sprocket is not keyed to the crankshaft, but relies on the pulley bolt being tightened correctly to clamp the sprocket. It is most important that the pulley bolt is correctly tightened otherwise there is the possibility of the oil pump not functioning properly.

5 Unhook the drive chain from the drive sprocket.

Inspection

6 Unscrew the retaining bolts and lift the pump cover over the driveshaft. Withdraw the idler gear and the drivegear/shaft. Mark the gears before removal, so that they can be refitted in their original position.

7 Extract the retaining clip and remove the oil pressure relief valve spring retainer, spring, spring seat and plunger.

8 Clean the components and carefully examine the gears, pump body and relief valve plunger for any signs of scoring or wear. Renew the complete pump assembly if excessive wear is evident (no spare parts are available).

9 If the components appear serviceable, measure the clearance between the pump body and the gears using feeler gauges. Also measure the gear endfloat and check the flatness of the end cover. If the clearances exceed the specified tolerances, the pump must be renewed. There should be no discernible wear or distortion of the cover.

10 If the pump is satisfactory, reassemble the components in the reverse order of removal. Fill the pump with oil, then refit the cover and tighten the bolts securely.

Refitting

11 Wipe clean the oil pump and cylinder block mating surfaces and check that the two locating dowels are fitted in the cylinder block.

12 Engage the drive chain with the drive sprocket, then slide the sprocket onto the nose of the crankshaft.

13 Apply a 1.5 to 2.0 mm wide bead of silicone sealant (preferably Renault Threebond) to the right-hand cover sealing face, making sure that the bead runs below the bolt holes. Refit

11.3 Fitting a new oil seal to the right-hand cover

11.4a Oil pump and mounting bolts

11.4b Removing the oil pump and drive chain

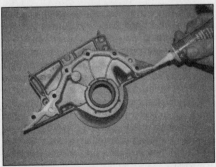

11.13a Apply sealant to the mating faces . . .

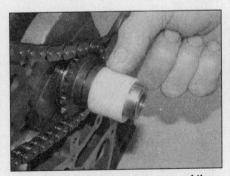

11.13b . . . wrap some tape around the nose of the crankshaft . . .

11.13c . . . and fit the right-hand cover

Oil seals can be removed by drilling a small hole and inserting a self-tapping screw. A pair of grips can then be used to pull out the oil seal by pulling on the screw. If difficulty is experienced, insert two screws diagonally opposite each other.

the engine right-hand cover, insert the bolts and tighten them to the specified torque in the stages given. If a new oil seal has already been fitted, wrap tape around the nose of the crankshaft to protect the oil seal, and remove it on completion **(see illustrations)**. First pre-tighten the bolts furthest from the crankshaft (Nos 1 and 6), then fully tighten the intermediate bolts (2 to 5), and finally fully bolts 1 and 6.

14 Tilt the oil pump and engage the sprocket with the drive chain, then position it on the dowels and insert the two mounting bolts. Tighten the bolts to the specified torque.

15 Refit the sump with reference to Section 10.

12 Crankshaft oil seals – renewal

Timing end cover oil seal

Note: *The new oil seal is extremely fragile and must only be handled by the protector. Do not touch the surface of the oil seal.*

1 Remove the crankshaft sprocket, as described in Section 6.

2 Note the fitted position of the old seal, then prise it out of the right-hand cover/housing using a screwdriver or suitable hooked instrument, taking care not to damage the surface of the crankshaft. Alternatively, the oil seal can be removed by drilling two small holes diagonally opposite each other and inserting self-tapping screws in them. A pair of

grips can then be used to pull out the oil seal, by pulling on each side in turn **(see Haynes Hint)**.

3 Inspect the seal rubbing surface on the crankshaft. If it is grooved or rough in the area where the old seal was fitted, the new seal should be fitted slightly less deeply, so that it rubs on an unworn part of the crankshaft surface.

4 Renault technicians use a tool (Mot. 1586) to fit the oil seal. The tool consists of a threaded rod, metal tube and nut, and a machined shoulder to locate the protector/guide on. The rod is screwed into the end of the crankshaft, and the protector/guide located on the shoulder. The metal tube is then fitted against the oil seal and the nut tightened to press the seal into the right-hand cover. If the Renault tool cannot be obtained, a similar tool can be made out of a threaded rod, metal tube, washer and nut.

5 Wipe clean the oil seal seating, then press the oil seal squarely into position. Note that the Renault tool is designed to locate the seal at the original depth, however, if the crankshaft sealing surface is excessively worn, position it less deeply so that it locates on the unworn surface.

6 After fitting the oil seal, remove the protector/guide and tool.

7 Refit the crankshaft sprocket as described in Section 6.

Flywheel end oil seal

8 Remove the flywheel as described in Section 13.

9 Renew the oil seal as described in paragraphs 2 to 6 inclusive **(see illustration)**.

10 Refit the flywheel with reference to Section 13.

13 Flywheel/driveplate – removal, inspection and refitting

Note: *New bolts must be used on refitting.*

Removal

1 Remove the transmission as described in Chapter 7A or 7B.

2 On manual transmission models, remove the clutch as described in Chapter 6.

3 Mark the flywheel/driveplate in relation to the crankshaft to aid refitting. Note that the flywheel/driveplate can only be refitted in one position, as the bolts are unequally spaced.

4 The flywheel/driveplate must now be held stationary while the securing bolts are loosened. To do this, locate a long bolt in one of the engine-to-gearbox mounting bolt holes and insert a wide-bladed screwdriver or length of bent metal bar in the starter ring gear or use a suitable locking tool **(see illustration)**.

5 Unscrew the mounting bolts, and withdraw the flywheel/driveplate; be careful – it is heavy. Discard the old bolts as new ones must be used on refitting.

Inspection

6 Examine the flywheel/driveplate for wear or chipping of the ring gear teeth. If the ring gear is worn or damaged, it may be possible to renew it separately, but this job is best left to a Renault dealer or engineering works. The temperature to which the new ring gear must be heated for installation is critical and, if not done accurately, the hardness of the teeth will be destroyed.

7 Check the flywheel/driveplate carefully for signs of distortion, and for hairline cracks around the bolt holes, or radiating outwards from the centre. If damage of this sort is found, it must be renewed.

8 Examine the flywheel for scoring of the clutch face. If the clutch face is scored, the flywheel may be machined until flat, but renewal is preferable.

12.9 Fitting a new oil seal to the flywheel end of the crankshaft

13.4 Hold the flywheel stationary using a screwdriver in the starter ring gear

Refitting

9 Clean the flywheel/driveplate and crankshaft mating surfaces, then locate the flywheel/driveplate on the crankshaft, making sure that any previously-made marks are aligned.

10 Locate the flywheel on the crankshaft and insert the new securing bolts, then tighten them in a diagonal sequence to the specified torque. Hold the flywheel stationary as during removal **(see illustration)**. **Do not** oil the new bolt threads, as they are supplied with locking compound.

11 Refit the clutch, if applicable (Chapter 6) and the transmission as described in Chapter 7A or 7B.

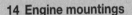

14 Engine mountings
– inspection and renewal

Inspection

1 With the handbrake applied, jack up the front of the car and support it on axle stands (see *Jacking and vehicle support*). Where fitted, remove the engine compartment undershield.

2 As far as possible, inspect the rubber

13.10 Fit new flywheel bolts

sections of all the mountings for signs of cracking and deterioration. Careful use of a lever will help to determine the condition of the rubber. If there is excessive movement in the mounting, or if the rubber has deteriorated, the mounting should be renewed.

3 Lower the car to the ground.

Renewal

Right-hand mounting

4 Support the right-hand end of the engine with a trolley jack and block of wood beneath the sump.

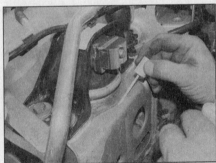

14.8a Mark its position on the inner wing . . .

5 If available, an engine support bar may be used to support the engine from above.

6 The wing and engine sections of the mounting are held together by a horizontal through-bolt, from the wing side – this must be loosened as far as possible, though it cannot be removed. Access to this bolt is hampered by the coolant expansion tank, and by the air conditioning pipes (where applicable).

7 Remove the small bolt at the rear of the mounting, then the three bolts securing the mounting to the engine, and lift it away **(see illustration)**.

8 Mark its position relative to the wing, then remove the four bolts securing the mounting to the inner wing, and lift it off **(see illustrations)**.

9 If required, the mounting bracket on the engine can also be unbolted and removed as described in Section 5, paragraph 8.

10 Fit the mounting using a reversal of the removal procedure, but tighten the nuts/bolts to the specified torque wrench settings.

Left-hand mounting

11 Remove the air inlet ducts from the left-hand side of the engine, for access to the engine/transmission left-hand mounting. Remove the battery and battery tray as described in Chapter 5A.

12 Support the left-hand end of the transmission with a trolley jack and block of wood beneath the transmission. If available, an engine support bar may be used to support the engine from above.

13 Unscrew the centre nut and the two outer nuts either side of it **(see illustration)**.

14 Remove the three bolts from the top of the transmission, and lower the transmission slightly **(see illustration)**.

15 Remove the four bolts securing the mounting to the inner wing, and lift it away.

16 Fit the mounting using a reversal of the removal procedure, but tighten the bolts to the specified torque wrench settings.

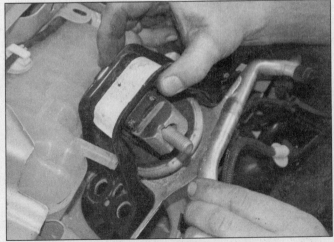

14.8b . . . then lift out the wing section of the mounting, with the through-bolt

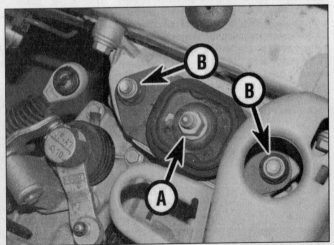

14.13 Left-hand (transmission) mounting centre (A) and outer (B) nuts

14.7 Engine section of the right-hand mounting – remove bolt (A) first, then three mounting-to-engine bolts (B)

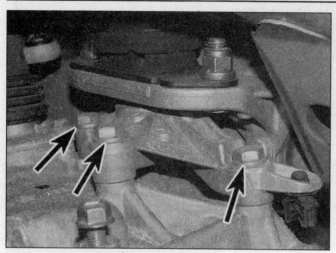

14.14 Left-hand mounting-to-transmission bolts

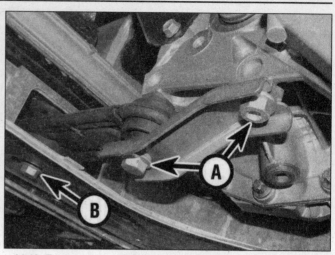

14.18 Engine lower mounting plate bolts (A) and mounting link rear bolt (B)

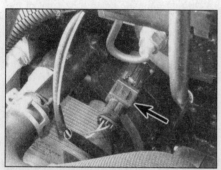

15.6 Disconnect the oil pressure warning light switch

Lower mounting

17 Jack up the front of the car, and support it securely on axle stands (see *Jacking and vehicle support*).

18 Remove the two bolts securing the lower mounting-to-engine plate – one of these bolts is also used to secure the front of the lower mounting link. This will separate the lower mounting from the engine, but leaves the mounting link in the way. If required, the mounting link rear bolt (to the subframe) can also be unscrewed, and the mounting link removed completely **(see illustration)**.

19 Though removing the lower mounting will increase the amount of engine movement, the engine will remain safely supported on its right- and left-hand mountings.

20 Fit the mounting using a reversal of the removal procedure, but tighten the bolts to the specified torque wrench settings.

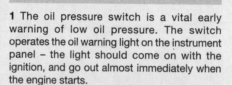

15 Oil pressure switch – removal and refitting

1 The oil pressure switch is a vital early warning of low oil pressure. The switch operates the oil warning light on the instrument panel – the light should come on with the ignition, and go out almost immediately when the engine starts.

2 If the light does not come on, there could be a fault on the instrument panel, the switch wiring, or the switch itself. If the light does not go out, low oil level, worn oil pump (or sump pick-up blocked), blocked oil filter, or worn main bearings could be to blame – or again, the switch may be faulty.

3 If the light comes on while driving, the best advice is to turn the engine off immediately, and not to drive the car until the problem has been investigated – ignoring the light could mean expensive engine damage.

Removal

4 The oil pressure switch is located on the front face of the engine, next to the oil filter.

5 Jack up the front of the car, and support it on axle stands (see *Jacking and vehicle support*) – to improve access, remove the oil filter, referring to Chapter 1B if necessary.

6 Disconnect the wiring plug from the switch **(see illustration)**.

7 Unscrew the switch from the block, and remove it together with its sealing washer. There should only be a very slight loss of oil when this is done.

Inspection

8 Examine the switch for signs of cracking or splits. If the top part of the switch is loose, this is an early indication of impending failure.

9 Check that the wiring terminals at the switch are not loose, then trace the wire from the switch connector until it enters the main loom – any wiring defects will give rise to apparent oil pressure problems.

Refitting

10 Refitting is the reverse of the removal procedure, noting the following points:

a) Clean the switch threads before fitting. Tighten the switch securely.

b) Reconnect the switch connector, making sure it clicks home properly. Ensure that the wiring is routed away from any hot or moving parts.

c) Lower the car to the ground, then check the engine oil level and top-up if necessary (see Weekly checks).

d) Check for signs of oil leaks once the engine has been restarted and warmed-up to normal operating temperature.

Chapter 2 Part C:
1.9 litre diesel in-car engine repair procedures

Contents

Degrees of difficulty

Easy, suitable for novice with little experience 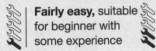	Fairly easy, suitable for beginner with some experience 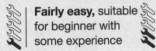	Fairly difficult, suitable for competent DIY mechanic 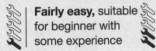	Difficult, suitable for experienced DIY mechanic 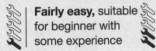	Very difficult, suitable for expert DIY or professional

Specifications

General

Type	Four-cylinder, in-line, 8-valve single overhead camshaft, direct common-rail injection
Designation	F9Q 812
Bore	80.0 mm
Stroke	93.0 mm
Capacity	1870 cc
Compression ratio	19.0:1
Firing order	1-3-4-2 (No 1 cylinder at flywheel end)
Direction of crankshaft rotation	Clockwise viewed from timing belt end

Compression pressures (engine warm)

Normal pressure	22 bars
Minimum pressure	20 bars
Maximum difference between cylinders	4 bars

Camshaft

Endfloat	0.05 to 0.13 mm

Valve clearances (engine cold)

Inlet	0.20 mm
Exhaust	0.40 mm

Timing belt tension

Setting	90 ± 15 Hz
Checking	80 ± 15 Hz

Lubrication system

Minimum oil pressure at 80°C:

	Minimum	Maximum
At 1000 rpm	1.2 bars	
At 3500 rpm	3.5 bars	
Oil pump clearances:		
Gear to body	0.100 mm	0.240 mm
Gear endfloat	0.020 mm	0.085 mm

Torque wrench settings

	Nm	lbf ft
Air conditioning compressor	25	18
Alternator support bracket-to-engine bolts	44	32
Auxiliary drivebelt tensioner mounting bolt:		
Models with air conditioning	40	30
Models without air conditioning	30	22
Camshaft bearing caps:		
8 mm diameter fasteners	20	15
6 mm diameter fasteners	10	7
Camshaft sprocket bolt	60	44
Connecting rod (big-end) cap bolts:		
Stage 1	20	15
Stage 2	Angle-tighten through 40° ± 6°	
Crankshaft pulley bolt:		
Stage 1	40	30
Stage 2	Angle-tighten a further 110° ± 10°	
Cylinder head bolts*:		
Non-metallic gasket:		
Stage 1 – all bolts	30	22
Stage 2 – all bolts	Angle-tighten through 100° ± 4°	
Stage 3	Wait for at least 3 minutes for the gasket to settle	
Stage 4 – bolts 1 and 2	Slacken fully	
Stage 5 – bolts 1 and 2	25	18
Stage 6 – bolts 1 and 2	Angle-tighten through 213° ± 7°	
Stage 7 – bolts 3 and 4	Slacken fully	
Stage 8 – bolts 3 and 4	25	18
Stage 9 – bolts 3 and 4	Angle-tighten through 213° ± 7°	
Stage 10 – bolts 5 and 6	Slacken fully	
Stage 11 – bolts 5 and 6	25	18
Stage 12 – bolts 5 and 6	Angle-tighten through 213° ± 7°	
Stage 13 – bolts 7 and 8	Slacken fully	
Stage 14 – bolts 7 and 8	25	18
Stage 15 – bolts 7 and 8	Angle-tighten through 213° ± 7°	
Stage 16 – bolts 9 and 10	Slacken fully	
Stage 17 – bolts 9 and 10	25	18
Stage 18 – bolts 9 and 10	Angle-tighten through 213° ± 7°	
Metallic gasket:		
Stage 1 – all bolts	30	22
Stage 2 – all bolts	Angle-tighten through 230° ± 6°	
Cylinder head cover nuts/bolts	12	9
Engine mountings:		
Left-hand mounting centre nut	62	46
Left-hand mounting stud-to-mounting	180	133
Left-hand mounting to body bolts	21	15
Left-hand mounting to transmission bolts	62	46
Left-hand mounting upper-to-lower section bolts	105	78
Lower mounting through-bolt	180	133
Lower mounting to engine bolts	62	46
Lower mounting to subframe through-bolt	105	78
Right-hand mounting rear link bolts	105	78
Right-hand mounting through-bolt	105	78
Right-hand mounting to body bolts	62	46
Right-hand mounting upper section to engine bolts	62	46
Flywheel bolts*	90	66
High-pressure fuel pump sprocket nut	70	52
Main bearing caps	60 to 65	44 to 48
Oil pump mounting bolts	25	18
Radiator lower crossmember:		
Front bolt	105	78
Rear nut (to subframe)	21	15
Side support plate bolts	21	15
Roadwheel bolts	130	96
Sump bolts:		
Stage 1	5	4
Stage 2	14	11
Timing belt tensioner nut	45	33

*Use new bolts

1 General information

How to use this Chapter

This Part of Chapter 2 is devoted to in-car repair procedures for the 1.9 litre diesel engine. Similar information covering the other engines can be found in Parts A and B. All procedures concerning engine removal and refitting, and engine block/cylinder head overhaul can be found in Part D of this Chapter.

Refer to *Vehicle identification numbers* in the Reference Section of this manual for details of engine code locations.

Most of the operations in Chapter 2C assume that the engine is still installed in the car. Therefore, if this information is being used during a complete engine overhaul, with the engine already removed, many of the steps included here will not apply.

Engine description

The engine is of four-cylinder, in-line, single overhead camshaft type, mounted transversely at the front of the car.

The crankshaft is supported in five shell-type main bearings. Thrustwashers are fitted to No 2 main bearing to control crankshaft endfloat.

The connecting rods are attached to the crankshaft by horizontally-split shell-type big-end bearings and to the pistons by gudgeon pins. The gudgeon pins are fully floating and are retained by circlips. The aluminium alloy pistons are of the slipper type and are fitted with three piston rings; two compression rings and a scraper-type oil control ring.

The single overhead camshaft is mounted in five plain bearings machined directly in the aluminium alloy cylinder head, and is driven by the crankshaft via a toothed timing belt. The back of the timing belt is also used to drive the water pump.

The camshaft operates the valves via inverted bucket-type followers, which operate in bores machined directly in the cylinder head. Valve clearance adjustment is by shims located externally between the followers and the cam lobes, or by different thickness followers. The inlet and exhaust valves are mounted vertically in the cylinder head and are each closed by a single valve spring.

The high-pressure fuel injection pump is driven by the timing belt and is described in further detail in Chapter 4B.

A semi-closed crankcase ventilation system is employed, and crankcase fumes are drawn from the cylinder block and passed via a hose to the inlet tract (see Chapter 4C for further details).

Engine lubrication is by pressure feed from a gear-type oil pump located beneath the crankshaft. Engine oil is fed through an externally-mounted oil filter to the main oil gallery feeding the crankshaft and camshaft.

Oil spray jets are fitted to the cylinder block to supply oil to the underside of the pistons. An oil cooler is mounted between the oil filter and the cylinder block.

Repair operations possible with the engine in the car

The following operations can be carried out without having to remove the engine from the car:

a) Removal and refitting of the cylinder head.
b) Removal and refitting of the timing belt and sprockets.
c) Renewal of the camshaft oil seals.
d) Removal and refitting of the camshaft.
e) Removal and refitting of the sump.
f) Removal and refitting of the connecting rods and pistons*.
g) Removal and refitting of the oil pump.
h) Renewal of the crankshaft oil seals.
i) Renewal of the engine mountings.

* **Note:** *Although the operation marked with an asterisk can be carried out with the engine in the car after removal of the sump, it is better for the engine to be removed in the interests of cleanliness and improved access. For this reason, the procedure is described in Chapter 2D.*

2 Compression and leakdown tests – description and interpretation

Compression test

Note: *A compression tester specifically designed for diesel engines must be used for this test.*

1 When engine performance is down, or if misfiring occurs which cannot be attributed to a fault in the fuel system, a compression test can provide diagnostic clues as to the engine's condition. If the test is performed regularly it can give warning of trouble before any other symptoms become apparent.

2 A compression tester specifically intended for diesel engines must be used, because of the higher pressures involved. The tester is connected to an adapter which screws into the glow plug hole. It is unlikely to be worthwhile buying such a tester for occasional use, but it may be possible to borrow or hire one – if not, have the test performed by a garage.

3 Unless specific instructions to the contrary are supplied with the tester, observe the following points:

a) *The battery must be in a good state of charge, the air filter must be clean and the engine should be at normal operating temperature.*
b) *The glow plugs should be removed before starting the test, as described in Chapter 5C.*
c) *Where applicable, it is advisable to disconnect the stop solenoid on the pump to reduce the amount of fuel discharged as the engine is cranked.*

4 There is no need to hold the accelerator pedal down during the test, because the diesel engine air inlet is not throttled.

5 The actual compression pressures measured are not as important as the balance between cylinders. Values are given in the Specifications.

6 The cause of poor compression is less easy to establish on a diesel engine than on a petrol one. The effect of introducing oil into the cylinders ('wet' testing) is not conclusive, because there is a risk that the oil will sit in the swirl chamber or in the recess on the piston crown instead of passing to the rings. However, the following can be used as a rough guide to diagnosis.

7 All cylinders should produce very similar pressures; any difference greater than that specified indicates the existence of a fault. Note that the compression should build-up quickly in a healthy engine; low compression on the first stroke, followed by gradually increasing pressure on successive strokes, indicates worn piston rings. A low compression reading on the first stroke, which does not build-up during successive strokes, indicates leaking valves or a blown head gasket (a cracked head could also be the cause).

8 A low reading from two adjacent cylinders is almost certainly due to the head gasket having blown between them.

Leakdown test

9 A leakdown test measures the rate at which compressed air fed into the cylinder is lost. It is an alternative to a compression test and in many ways it is better, since the escaping air provides easy identification of where pressure loss is occurring (piston rings, valves or head gasket).

10 The equipment needed for leakdown testing is unlikely to be available to the home mechanic. If poor compression is suspected, have the test performed by a suitably-equipped garage.

3 Top Dead Centre (TDC) for No 1 piston – locating

1 Top Dead Centre (TDC) is the highest point in the cylinder that each piston reaches as the crankshaft turns. Each piston reaches TDC at the end of the compression stroke and again at the end of the exhaust stroke; however, for the purpose of timing the engine, TDC refers to the position of No 1 piston at the end of its compression stroke. No 1 piston is at the flywheel end of the engine.

2 When No 1 piston is at TDC, the timing mark on the camshaft sprocket should be aligned with the pointer on the timing belt outer cover (the sprocket mark can be viewed through the cut-out in the cover, below the pointer). Additionally, the timing mark on the flywheel should be aligned with the TDC mark on the gearbox bellhousing.

3.4 To improve access, remove the side support plate

3.7 Flywheel timing mark aligned with TDC (0°) mark on bellhousing

3.8 Camshaft sprocket timing mark aligned with pointer on timing belt outer cover

3 To align the timing marks, the crankshaft must be turned. This should be done by using a spanner on the crankshaft pulley bolt. Improved access to the pulley bolt can be obtained by jacking up the front right-hand corner of the car and removing the roadwheel and the wheelarch liner (see Chapter 11, Section 21). If desired, to enable the engine to be turned more easily, remove the glow plugs (Chapter 5C).

4 To further improve access to the crankshaft pulley bolt, working inside the wheel arch, remove the four bolts securing the side support plate to the radiator lower crossmember and inner wing, and remove it **(see illustration)**.

5 Unclip and lift off the engine top cover.

6 Remove the battery and its tray as described in Chapter 5A.

7 Remove the access cover, and look through the timing aperture in the top of the gearbox bellhousing. Turn the crankshaft until the timing mark on the flywheel is aligned with the TDC (0°) mark on the bellhousing **(see illustration)**.

8 Check that the timing mark on the camshaft sprocket is aligned with the pointer on the timing belt outer cover **(see illustration)**. The engine is now positioned with No 1 piston at TDC on its compression stroke.

9 It is possible to check the crankshaft position as follows.

10 For absolute accuracy, the crankshaft position can be checked by inserting a timing pin – Renault tool Mot. 1054 **(see Tool tip)**. To do this, unscrew the blanking plug from the front transmission end of the cylinder block, next to the base of the oil level sensor **(see illustration)**.

11 Turn the engine slightly anti-clockwise (against the normal direction of rotation), so that the camshaft sprocket is half a tooth out of alignment with the cover pointer.

12 Insert the timing pin fully into the hole in the front of the engine, then carefully turn the engine clockwise, keeping light pressure on the end of the timing pin. At the TDC position, the pin should enter a slot in the crankshaft web, and the engine should be locked in position (rock the engine very slightly backwards or forwards to achieve engagement). In this position, the camshaft sprocket marks should also come into alignment **(see illustrations)**.

13 Once in place, it should be impossible to turn the crankshaft – if the crankshaft will still move to-and-fro slightly, then the timing pin has entered a balance hole in the crankshaft instead of the timing slot. **Note:** *Do not attempt to rotate the engine whilst the timing pin is in place. If the engine is to be left in this state for a long period of time, it is a good idea to place warning notices inside the car and in the engine compartment. This will reduce the possibility of the engine being accidentally cranked on the starter motor, which will cause severe damage if done with the timing pin in place.*

Caution: The timing pin is intended SOLELY for the purpose of checking the position of the crankshaft during various engine overhaul procedures. DO NOT use it as a locking tool to prevent crankshaft rotation while the pulley or flywheel bolts are unscrewed or tightened.

14 On completion, remove the timing pin and refit all removed components.

3.10 Remove the blanking plug from the cylinder block . . .

3.12a . . . and insert a suitable drill . . .

3.12b . . . or a purpose-made timing pin to check the crankshaft position

3.12c When the crankshaft is at TDC, the pin will go fully home

TOOL TIP *If the special Renault tool mentioned in this Section is not available, an 8 mm diameter rod or drill bit can be used instead. On some engines, however, an 8 mm diameter rod may be too slack a fit in the cylinder block plug aperture for the crankshaft position to be determined accurately – it will therefore be necessary in such cases to have a stepped pin made up, with an 8 mm diameter at its tip to engage in the crankshaft slot and a larger diameter as necessary to fit precisely in the cylinder block aperture.*

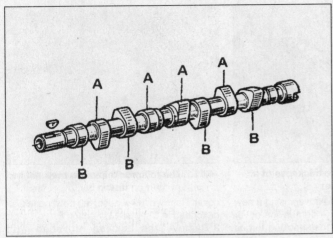

4.6 Valve location details

A Inlet   B Exhaust

4.8 Measuring a valve clearance

4 Valve clearances – checking and adjustment

Note: *This operation is not part of the maintenance schedule, and would normally only be required after a very high mileage, since an incorrect clearance would be most likely due to wear. It should be undertaken if noise from the valvegear becomes evident, or if loss of performance gives cause to suspect that the clearances may be incorrect. A new cylinder head cover gasket may be required on refitting.*
Note: *It is permissible to move adjustment shims to different followers to correct valve clearances, but swapping followers is not advisable, as the old followers will have worn into their bores.*

Checking

1 Unclip and lift off the engine top cover.
2 Where necessary for improved access, unclip any hoses which are routed across the top of the cylinder head cover and move them to one side out of the way. If fuel lines are disconnected, cover open unions to prevent dirt ingress. At the transmission end, removing the metal intercooler air duct may improve access (refer to Chapter 4B for details).
3 Unscrew the cylinder head cover retaining bolts and withdraw the cover from the engine. Recover the gasket.
4 During the following procedure, the crankshaft must be turned, using a spanner on the crankshaft pulley bolt. Improved access to the pulley bolt can be obtained by jacking up the front right-hand corner of the car and removing the roadwheel and the wheelarch liner (secured by plastic clips).
5 If desired, to enable the crankshaft to be turned more easily, remove the glow plugs as described in Chapter 5C.
6 Draw the valve positions on a piece of paper, numbering them 1 to 8 from the flywheel end of the engine. Identify them as

inlet or exhaust (ie, 1E, 2I, 3E, 4I, 5I, 6E, 7I, 8E) **(see illustration)**.
7 Turn the crankshaft until the valves of No 1 cylinder (flywheel end) are rocking – the exhaust valve will be closing and the inlet valve will be opening. The piston of No 4 cylinder will be at the top of its compression stroke, with both valves fully closed – the clearances for both valves of No 4 cylinder may now be checked.
8 Insert a feeler gauge of the correct thickness (see Specifications) between the cam lobe and the top of the follower or shim (early models) and check that it is a firm sliding fit **(see illustration)**. If it is not, use the feeler gauges to ascertain the exact clearance and record this for use when calculating the new follower/shim thickness required. Note that the inlet and exhaust valve clearances are different (see Specifications).
9 With No 4 cylinder valve clearances checked, turn the engine through half a turn

so that No 3 valves are rocking, then check the valve clearances of No 2 cylinder in the same way. Similarly check the remaining valve clearances in the sequence shown **(see illustration)**.

Adjustment

Note: *A micrometer will be required for this operation. Note that on most later models, a shim is not fitted, and the followers are available in different thicknesses for adjustment.*
10 Remove the camshaft as described in Section 8. Where shimless followers are fitted, the followers will also have to be removed. Separate shims, where fitted, have a round projection on their lower face which locates in a recess in the follower, which makes it very difficult to remove the shims with the camshaft installed. Special Renault tools are available to overcome this, but their use requires the removal of the manifolds and turbocharger, making removing the camshaft an easier option.
11 Where a valve clearance differs from the specified value, then the follower (or shim if applicable) for that valve must be substituted with a thinner or thicker one accordingly. The follower/shim thickness can be measured using a micrometer, and the thickness of new one required can be calculated as described below **(see illustrations)**.

VALVES ROCKING ON CYLINDER	CHECK CLEARANCE ON CYLINDER
1	4
3	2
4	1
2	3

4.9 Valve clearance checking sequence

4.11a Thickness is etched on the underside of each shim

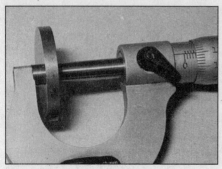

4.11b Checking a shim's thickness with a micrometer

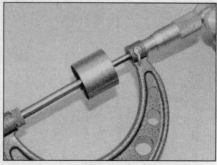

4.11c Measuring the thickness of a follower

4.11d The follower thickness may still be visible

12 The thickness of follower/shim required is calculated as follows. If the measured clearance is less than specified, subtract the measured clearance from the specified clearance and deduct the result from the thickness of the existing follower/shim. For example:

Sample calculation – clearance too small
Clearance measured (A) = 0.15 mm
Desired clearance (B) = 0.20 mm
Difference (B – A) = 0.05 mm
Follower/shim thickness fitted = 3.70 mm
Follower/shim required =
* 3.70 – 0.05 = 3.65 mm*

13 If the measured clearance is greater than specified, subtract the specified clearance from the measured clearance and add the result to the thickness of the existing follower/shim. For example:

Sample calculation – clearance too big
Clearance measured (A) = 0.50 mm
Desired clearance (B) = 0.40 mm
Difference (A – B) = 0.10 mm
Follower/shim thickness fitted = 3.45 mm
Follower/shim required =
* 3.45 + 0.10 = 3.55 mm*

14 Before refitting a shim, wipe the top of the follower and ensure that all the oil is removed from the shim locating recess in the follower's upper face. Fit the shim to the follower with the projection on the shim engaged with the follower's recess.

15 When all shims or followers have been selected, refit the camshaft (and followers, where applicable) as described in Section 8.

16 Remove the spanner from the crankshaft pulley bolt.

17 Refit the cylinder head cover, using a new gasket where necessary – tighten the cover retaining bolts evenly to the specified torque wrench setting.

18 Where applicable, refit the glow plugs (Chapter 5C).

19 Refit/reconnect any hoses which were moved for access. If fuel lines were disconnected, reconnect them, then prime and bleed the fuel system as described in Chapter 4B.

20 Refit the engine top cover.

5 Timing belt –
removal, inspection and refitting

Caution: If the timing belt breaks or slips in service, extensive engine damage may result. Renew the belt at the intervals specified in Chapter 1B, or earlier if its condition is at all doubtful.
Note: *A suitable tool will be required to check the timing belt tension on completion of refitting – see text. A suitable puller may be required to remove the crankshaft pulley.*

Removal

1 Disconnect the battery negative lead, and move the lead away from the battery (see *Disconnecting the battery*).

2 Loosen the right-hand front wheel bolts, then jack up the right-hand front of the car and support on axle stands. Remove the front right wheel, engine/radiator undertray and wheel arch liner. Remove the engine top

cover. Remove the windscreen cowl panels as described in Chapter 11, Section 8.

3 Remove the auxiliary drivebelt with reference to Chapter 1B, then unbolt and remove the drivebelt tensioner.

4 Support the right-hand end of the engine with a support bar across the engine compartment with a hoist, or alternatively with a jack and block of wood beneath the sump. If a hoist is being used, remove the bonnet with reference to Chapter 11.

5 Remove the engine right-hand mounting from the engine and body with reference to Section 13.

6 Unscrew the crankshaft pulley bolt while holding the crankshaft stationary. To hold the crankshaft, have an assistant firmly depress the footbrake pedal with 4th gear engaged while the bolt is loosened (note that at least two of the front wheel retaining bolts should be fitted on each side). Alternatively, remove the flywheel access cover from the top of the transmission bellhousing, and have an assistant insert a screwdriver or similar tool in the starter ring gear teeth.

7 Remove the bolt and the pulley from the crankshaft end **(see illustrations)**. Use a suitable puller if the pulley is tight.

8 Unscrew the four bolts and withdraw the timing belt outer cover, noting the location of any brackets secured by the bolts. The one-piece cover must be tilted to remove it **(see illustration)**.

9 Temporarily refit the crankshaft pulley bolt. Turn the crankshaft to position No 1 piston at TDC on the compression stroke and insert a

5.7a Remove the crankshaft pulley bolt . . .

5.7b . . . and the pulley

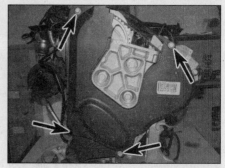

5.8 Remove the four bolts (arrowed) and take out the timing belt cover

timing pin to check the crankshaft position as described in Section 3 **(see illustrations)**.

10 If the original belt is to be re-used (contrary to Renault's recommendation), check that the belt is marked with arrows to indicate its running direction, and if necessary mark it. Similarly, note that the belt should be marked with bands across its width to act as timing marks corresponding to the timing marks on the camshaft and crankshaft sprockets. If the original timing bands have deteriorated, make accurate alignment marks on the belt.

11 Loosen the centre nut, then push back the tensioner to relieve the tension on the timing belt **(see illustration)**. Retighten the nut.

12 Release the belt first from the camshaft sprocket, then from the high-pressure pump, water pump, and crankshaft, and remove it from the engine.

13 Do not turn the camshaft or the crankshaft whilst the timing belt is removed, as there is a risk of piston-to-valve contact. If it is necessary to turn the camshaft for any reason, before doing so, remove the timing pin and turn the crankshaft anti-clockwise (viewed from the timing belt end of the engine) by a quarter-turn to position all four pistons halfway down their bores.

Inspection

Note: *Renault state that the timing belt must be renewed as a matter of course whenever it is removed.*

14 Clean the sprockets, idler pulley and tensioner, and wipe them dry – **do not** apply excessive amounts of solvent to the idler pulley and tensioner, otherwise the bearing lubricant may be removed. Also clean the timing belt inner cover and the related surfaces of the cylinder head and block.

15 Examine the timing belt carefully for any signs of cracking, fraying or general wear, particularly at the roots of the teeth. Renew the belt if there is any sign of deterioration of this nature, or if there is any oil or grease contamination. Renew any leaking oil seals. The belt **must**, of course, be renewed if it has completed the mileage given in the maintenance schedule in Chapter 1B.

16 Since the timing belt also drives the water pump, it makes sense to examine the pump carefully when a new belt is being fitted,

5.9a At TDC, the camshaft sprocket punch mark aligns with the mark on the belt backplate

since fitting a new pump will mean removing the belt again. If the pump shows any sign of leakage from the vent hole, or if the pulley sounds rough when spun, a new pump should be fitted as a precaution.

17 When fitting a new belt, Renault recommend that a new tensioner and crankshaft pulley are also fitted – these are often sold as a kit with a new belt, when purchased from a Renault dealer.

Refitting

18 Ensure that the crankshaft is at the TDC position for No 1 cylinder, with the timing pin in place to ensure complete accuracy, as described previously (Section 3). If the pistons have been positioned halfway down their bores, temporarily refit the timing belt outer cover and crankshaft pulley bolt.

19 Align the timing bands on the belt with

5.11 Loosen the tensioner centre nut, and push it back to relieve the belt tension

J45672

5.9b Crankshaft groove (2) should be between ribs (1), and timing mark (3) should be one tooth offset at TDC

the marks on the crankshaft and camshaft sprockets, ensuring that the running direction arrows on the belt are pointing clockwise (viewed from the timing belt end of the engine). Fit the timing belt over the crankshaft sprocket first, followed by the water pump pulley, high pressure pump sprocket, camshaft sprocket and tensioner **(see illustrations)**.

20 To enable the tensioner to be adjusted, screw a 6 mm bolt into the threaded hole provided in the timing belt inner cover **(see illustration)**.

21 Check that all the timing marks are still aligned and remove all slack from the timing

5.19a The running direction arrows on the belt must point clockwise

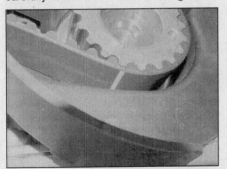

5.19b Align the timing bands on the belt with the crankshaft . . .

5.19c . . . and camshaft timing marks

5.20 M6 bolt fitted to timing belt inner cover to adjust timing belt tension

With experience, timing belt tension may be judged to be approximately correct when the belt can be twisted 45 to 90° with moderate pressure between the finger and thumb, checking midway between the sprockets on the belt's longest run.

belt by tightening the bolt just fitted to the timing belt inner cover. **Note:** *As a further check, count the number of timing belt tooth gaps between the camshaft sprocket's timing mark and the high pressure pump sprocket's timing mark – if the valve timing is correct, there will be 28 gaps.*

22 The belt tension must now be checked – this can be set or checked accurately **only** by using Renault special tools to pretension the belt and measure its vibration frequency. If this equipment is not available, set the belt's tension as carefully as possible **(see Haynes Hint)**, then take the car to a Renault dealer as soon as possible for the tension to be checked by qualified personnel using the special equipment.

23 If the adjustment is incorrect, the tensioner will have to be repositioned by loosening the tensioner nut and by screwing in or out the bolt fitted to the timing belt inner cover.

24 With the correct tension applied, retighten the tensioner nut to the specified torque. This torque is critical, since if the nut were to come loose, considerable engine damage would result. Unscrew the bolt fitted to the timing belt inner cover, and where necessary, refit the original.

25 Remove the crankshaft timing pin, then refit the crankshaft pulley and securing bolt. Prevent the crankshaft turning using the method described previously, and tighten the bolt to the specified torque (and angle) **(see illustration)**.

26 Check that the crankshaft is still positioned with No 1 piston at TDC (by temporarily refitting the crankshaft timing pin), then remove the timing pin and turn the crankshaft two complete turns in the normal direction of rotation, returning it to the TDC position again. Re-insert the timing pin in the cylinder block.

27 Temporarily refit the timing belt outer cover, and check that the sprocket timing mark still aligns with the pointer on the cover, as noted before removal (see Section 3).

28 Recheck the belt tension as described

5.25 Angle-tightening the crankshaft pulley bolt

previously. If the tension is incorrect, the setting and checking procedure must be repeated until the correct tension is achieved.

29 With the belt tensioned correctly, remove the adjuster bolt temporarily fitted to the timing belt inner cover, and replace it with the original bolt, where applicable. Remove the timing pin from the cylinder block, if not already done. Refit the blanking plug to the cylinder block and tighten it securely.

30 Refit the timing belt upper outer covers, ensuring that any brackets secured by the bolts are in position as noted before removal.

31 Refit the engine right-hand mounting as described in Section 13.

32 Refit the auxiliary drivebelt as described in Chapter 1B.

33 Refit the wheelarch liner and the roadwheel, and lower the car to the ground. Tighten the wheel bolts.

34 Refit the engine top cover, windscreen cowl panels and engine compartment undershield.

35 Reconnect the battery negative lead.

6 Timing belt sprockets and tensioner – removal and refitting

Crankshaft sprocket

Note: *A suitable puller may be required for this operation.*

Removal

1 Remove the timing belt as described in Section 5.

6.2 Removing the crankshaft sprocket

2 It should be possible simply to pull the sprocket off the crankshaft **(see illustration)**. However, in some cases, a puller may be required to draw off the sprocket.

3 Recover the Woodruff key if it is loose. Examine the oil seal for signs of oil leakage and, if necessary renew as described in Section 12.

Refitting

4 Refitting is a reversal of removal. Refit the Woodruff key to the crankshaft keyway and slide on the sprocket, making sure it is correctly engaged with the key; its flange should be against the cylinder block/timing belt inner cover.

5 Fit the new timing belt as described in Section 5.

Idler pulley

6 The timing belt idler pulley is the water pump drive pulley. If necessary, remove the water pump as described in Chapter 3.

High-pressure pump sprocket

Note: *A suitable puller may be required for this operation.*

Removal

7 Remove the timing belt (see Chapter 5).

8 Hold the sprocket stationary using a suitable gear-holding tool. Alternatively, the old timing belt can be wrapped around the sprocket and held firmly with a pair of grips.

9 Unscrew and remove the sprocket nut. Alternatively, depending on the type of puller to be used, leave it engaged with a few threads so that the puller will bear on the nut to prevent damage to the end of the shaft.

10 Using the puller, release the sprocket from the taper on the pump shaft. Note there is no location key.

Refitting

11 Refitting is a reversal of removal, but tighten the retaining nut to the specified torque, then refit the timing belt with reference to Section 5.

Camshaft sprocket

Note: *A suitable puller will be required for this operation.*

Removal

12 Remove the timing belt as described in Section 5. If it is necessary to turn the camshaft for any reason, before doing so, remove the timing pin and turn the crankshaft anti-clockwise (viewed from the timing belt end of the engine) by a quarter-turn to position all four pistons halfway down their bores.

13 Unscrew the bolts securing the engine right-hand mounting main bracket to the engine, and withdraw the bracket.

14 Unscrew the camshaft sprocket bolt. The sprocket can be held using a suitable socket and extension bar engaged with one of the timing belt inner cover securing bolts **(see illustrations)**. Alternatively, use the old timing

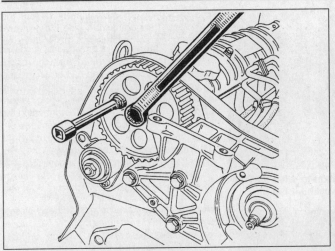

6.14a Using a socket and extension bar to hold the camshaft sprocket

6.14b Using a home-made tool to hold the camshaft sprocket stationary

belt wrapped around the pulley, held with a pair of grips. Recover the washer.

15 Remove the bolt, washer and sprocket from the camshaft **(see illustration)**. A suitable puller may be required, in which case ensure that the legs of the puller act on the holes in the sprocket, **not** on the sprocket teeth.

16 Recover the Woodruff key from the end of the camshaft if it is loose – note that on later engines, the key is an integral part of the sprocket.

Refitting

17 Refit the Woodruff key (where separate) to the camshaft keyway. Refit the sprocket with its projecting hub towards the cylinder head, ensuring that the key engages correctly with the keyway.

18 Ensure that the washer is in place, then refit the sprocket bolt and tighten it to the specified torque, holding the sprocket as during removal.

19 Refit the engine right-hand mounting main bracket to the engine and tighten the securing bolts. Where applicable, refit the upper two bolts to the holes in the bracket before the bracket is refitted.

20 Fit the new timing belt as described in Section 5.

Tensioner

Removal

21 Remove the timing belt as described in Section 5.

22 Remove the securing nut and its washer, then withdraw the tensioner assembly **(see illustration)**.

Refitting

23 Refitting is a reversal of removal, but check that the roller turns freely without binding or excessive play. Ensure that the peg on the cylinder block engages with the hole in the tensioner bracket.

24 Fit the new timing belt as described in Section 5.

6.15 Removing the sprocket from the camshaft

7 Camshaft oil seals – renewal

Timing belt end oil seal

1 Remove the camshaft sprocket as described in Section 6. For improved access, also remove the timing belt inner cover.

2 Remove the Woodruff key (where separate) from the end of the camshaft, if not already done.

3 Make a note of the fitted depth of the old seal then, using a small screwdriver, prise

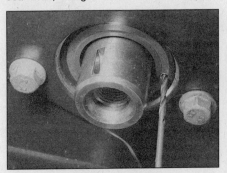

7.3a Drill a small hole . . .

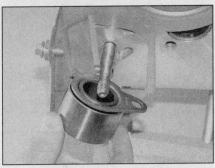

6.22 Removing the tensioner

it out of the cylinder head, taking care not to damage the surface of the camshaft. Alternatively, the oil seal can be removed by drilling a small hole and inserting a self-tapping screw. A pair of grips can then be used to pull out the oil seal, by pulling on the screw **(see illustrations)**. If difficulty is experienced, insert two screws diagonally opposite each other.

4 Wipe clean the oil seal seating in the cylinder head, then dip the new seal in fresh engine oil and locate it over the camshaft with its closed side facing outwards. Make sure that the oil seal lip is not damaged as it is located on the camshaft – to prevent this,

7.3b . . . and use a screw and pliers to pull out the seal

7.4 Wrap some adhesive tape over the end of the camshaft to prevent damage to the oil seal

7.5 Use a suitable socket to drive the new oil seal into the cylinder head

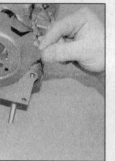

7.6a Refitting the inner timing cover . . .

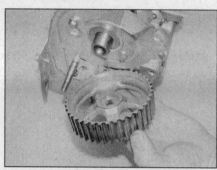

7.6b . . . and camshaft sprocket

wrap some adhesive tape over the end of the camshaft **(see illustration)**.

5 Using a tube of suitable diameter, drive the oil seal squarely into the housing to the previously noted depth **(see illustration)**. A block of wood cut to pass over the end of the camshaft may be used instead.

6 Refit the inner timing cover and camshaft sprocket as described in Section 6 **(see illustrations)**.

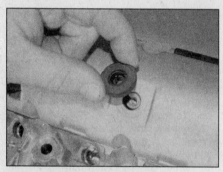

8.9a Unscrew the nuts . . .

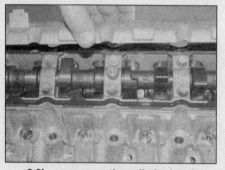

8.9b . . . remove the cylinder head cover . . .

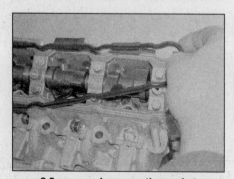

8.9c . . . and recover the gasket

8.10 Measuring camshaft endfloat

Flywheel end oil seal

7 No oil seal is fitted to the flywheel end of the camshaft. The sealing is provided by a gasket between the cylinder head and the brake vacuum pump housing and on certain models by an O-ring fitted between the pump and the housing. The gasket and the O-ring, where applicable, can be renewed after unbolting the pump from the cylinder head (see Chapter 9).

8 Camshaft and followers
– removal, inspection and refitting

Note: *A new camshaft timing belt end oil seal should be fitted and a new cylinder head cover gasket may be required on refitting. Suitable sealant will be required for the camshaft bearing caps and thread-locking compound for the bearing cap bolts.*

Removal

1 Remove the camshaft sprocket as described in Section 6.

2 Remove the timing belt tensioner as described in Section 6.

3 Unscrew the two bolts securing the timing belt upper inner cover to the cylinder head.

4 Unscrew the lower bolt(s) securing the timing belt upper inner cover to the cylinder block.

5 Remove the timing belt idler pulley securing bolt which also passes through the timing belt inner cover.

6 Manipulate the timing belt inner cover from the camshaft end and, where possible, withdraw the cover from the engine.

7 Remove the brake vacuum pump as described in Chapter 9.

8 Where necessary for improved access, unclip any hoses which are routed across the top of the cylinder head cover and move them to one side out of the way. If fuel lines are disconnected, cover open unions to prevent dirt ingress. At the transmission end, removing the metal intercooler air duct may improve access (refer to Chapter 4B for details).

9 Unscrew the cylinder head cover bolts and withdraw the cover. Recover the gasket **(see illustrations)**.

10 Using a dial gauge, measure the camshaft endfloat and compare with the value given in the Specifications **(see illustration)**. This will give an indication of the amount of wear present on the thrust surfaces. **Note:** *If preferred, the camshaft endfloat can be checked with the followers removed; this will make the checking procedure easier as the cam lobes will not be in contact with the followers.*

11 If the original camshaft is to be refitted, it is advisable to measure the valve clearances at this stage, as described in Section 4, so that the followers/shims required can be obtained before the camshaft is refitted.

12 Progressively slacken the bearing cap bolts until the valve spring pressure is relieved.

8.12a Unscrew the bolts . . .

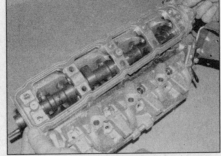

8.12b . . . and lift the camshaft bearing cap retainer from the cylinder head

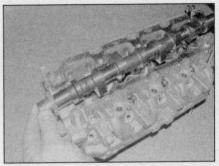

8.13 Lifting out the camshaft with oil seal

Remove the bolts (noting their locations to ensure correct refitting) and the bearing cap ladder itself **(see illustrations)**.

13 Lift out the camshaft with the oil seal **(see illustration)**.

14 Remove the followers, keeping each with its shim, where applicable **(see illustration)**. Place them in a compartmented box, or on a sheet of card marked into eight sections, so that they may be refitted to their original locations.

15 Write down the follower/shim thicknesses – they will be needed later if any of the valve clearances are incorrect. The thickness is etched on the follower/shim, but it is prudent to use a micrometer to measure the true thickness of any component removed, as it may have been reduced by wear.

Inspection

16 Examine the camshaft bearing surfaces and cam lobes for wear ridges, pitting or scoring. Renew the camshaft if evident.

17 Renew as a matter of course the oil seal at the timing belt end of the camshaft. Lubricate the lips of the new seal before fitting and store the camshaft so that its weight is not resting on the seal.

18 Examine the camshaft bearing surfaces in the cylinder head and bearing cap ladder. Deep scoring or other damage means that the cylinder head must be renewed.

19 Inspect the followers (and shims where applicable) for scoring, pitting and wear ridges. Renew as necessary.

Refitting

20 Ensure that the pistons are positioned halfway down their bores, as described for sprocket removal in Section 6.

21 Oil the followers and fit them to the bores from which they were removed **(see illustration)**. Where applicable, fit the correct shim, numbered side downwards, to each follower. **Note:** *If valve clearance adjustment is achieved by fitting different thickness followers (see Section 4) this will have to be done before refitting the camshaft.*

22 Oil the camshaft bearings. Place the camshaft onto the cylinder head. If necessary, the oil seal can be fitted at this stage, but make sure that it is positioned so that it is flush with the cylinder head face **(see illustrations)**.

8.14 Lifting out a cam follower

23 Use a short-haired roller to apply an even coating of Loctite 518 liquid gasket solution (or a suitable alternative) to the mating face of the camshaft bearing ladder until it is **reddish** in colour **(see illustration)**.

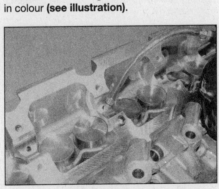

8.22a Oiling the camshaft bearing surfaces

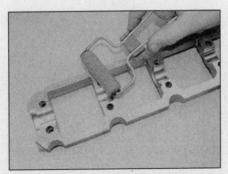

8.23 Applying Loctite 518 liquid gasket to the camshaft bearing ladder

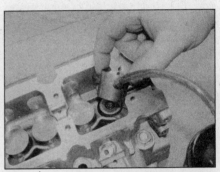

8.21 Oil the followers before refitting them in their correct bores

24 Refit the camshaft bearing cap ladder, ensuring that the right-hand oil seal is correctly located in the bearing cap **(see illustration)**.

25 Apply a few drops of thread-locking compound to the threads of the bearing cap

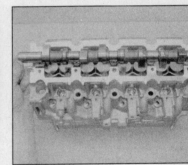

8.22b Refitting the camshaft

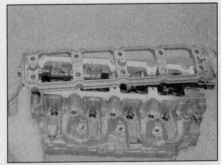

8.24 Refit the camshaft bearing ladder

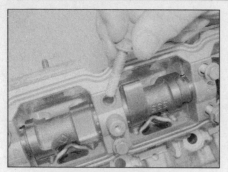

8.25a Insert the bolts . . .

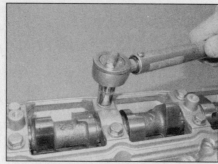

8.25b . . . and tighten them progressively to the specified torque

bolts. Fit the bolts and tighten them progressively to the specified torque **(see illustrations)**.

26 If a new camshaft has been fitted, measure the endfloat using a dial gauge and check that it is within the specified limits.

27 Refit the brake vacuum pump with reference to Chapter 9.

28 Refit the timing belt upper inner cover, then refit and tighten the bolts securing it to the cylinder block and to the head.

29 Refit and tighten the bolt securing the timing belt idler pulley assembly.

30 Refit the timing belt tensioner, ensuring that the peg on the cylinder block engages with the hole in the tensioner bracket.

31 Refit the camshaft sprocket as described in Section 6.

32 Check the valve clearances as described in Section 4 and take any corrective action necessary.

33 Refit the cylinder head cover, using a new

gasket where necessary – tighten the cover retaining bolts evenly to the specified torque wrench setting.

34 Refit/reconnect any hoses which were moved for access. If fuel lines were disconnected, reconnect them, then prime and bleed the fuel system as described in Chapter 4B.

35 Reconnect the battery negative lead.

---

9 Cylinder head – removal, inspection and refitting

Removal

1 Remove the battery and battery tray as described in Chapter 5A.

2 Remove the engine undertray, then drain the cooling system and engine oil with reference to Chapter 1A.

3 Remove the timing belt (Section 5) and, if necessary, the camshaft sprocket (Section 6).

4 Disconnect the hose from the vacuum pump on the left-hand end of the cylinder head **(see illustration)**.

5 Disconnect the air cleaner outlet duct and the intercooler air ducts with reference to Chapter 4B, and remove the air duct from the inlet manifold.

6 Disconnect the crankcase ventilation hose from the oil separator, and remove the separator itself.

7 Disconnect the wiring from the injectors and heater plugs, and from the EGR valve **(see illustrations)**.

8 Disconnect the wiring from the high pressure pump and the fuel temperature/pressure sensors on the fuel rail **(see illustrations)**. Unbolt the wiring support from the left-hand end of the cylinder head, and disconnect the plug.

9 Disconnect the wiring from the camshaft position sensor on the right-hand rear of the cylinder head. To provide access to the right-hand rear cylinder head bolt, remove the sensor completely **(see illustration)**.

10 Remove the remote vacuum reservoir from the back of the engine, disconnecting the wiring plug and vacuum hoses as necessary. The reservoir is held on by two bolts, as is the valve **(see illustrations)**.

11 Disconnect the fuel pipes from the filter and high pressure pump. Plug the apertures and ends of the pipes **(see illustrations)**.

12 Loosen the clips and disconnect the

9.4 Disconnect the hose from the brake vacuum pump

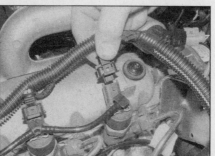

9.7a Disconnect the wiring plugs from the injectors . . .

9.7b . . . and from the EGR valve

9.8a Disconnect the pressure regulator from the pump . . .

9.8b . . . and the fuel pressure . . .

9.8c . . . and temperature sensors from the fuel rail

9.9 Disconnect the camshaft position sensor wiring plug

9.10a The remote vacuum reservoir is mounted at the back of the engine (bolts arrowed)

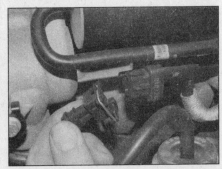

9.10b Disconnect the control valve wiring plug . . .

9.10c . . . then remove the two bolts and take off the valve

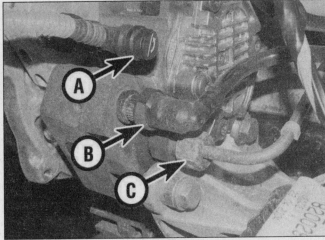

9.11a Supply pipe from fuel filter (A), return pipe from rail (B) and supply union to rail (C)

coolant hoses from the thermostat housing **(see illustration)**.

13 Disconnect the coolant temperature sensor wiring connector **(see illustration)**.

14 Remove the two rear mounting bolts from the high-pressure fuel pump **(see illustration)**.

15 Unscrew the nuts and disconnect the exhaust from the flange on the catalytic converter **(see illustration)**. Recover the gasket.

16 Unscrew and remove the catalytic converter mountings **(see illustration)**.

17 Unscrew the stay bolt from the bottom of the catalytic converter.

9.11b Use a small screwdriver to release the fittings . . .

9.11c . . . and cap the open unions

9.12 Disconnect the coolant hoses from the thermostat housing

9.13 Disconnect the coolant temperature sensor

9.14 Remove the two injection pump rear mounting bolts

9.15 Unscrew the nuts and disconnect the exhaust from the catalytic converter

9.16 Unbolt the stay from the catalytic converter

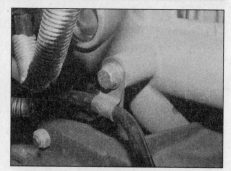

9.18a Turbo oil supply mounting bolt on the inlet manifold

9.18b Turbo oil supply union on top of the turbo

9.18c Turbo oil supply union on the block

9.20 Removing the catalytic converter

18 Unscrew the bolt from the turbocharger oil pipe support on the inlet manifold, the union nut on top of the turbocharger, and the union on the block **(see illustrations)**. Remove the pipe from the back of the engine.
19 Remove the oil return pipe from the turbocharger and cylinder block.
20 Unscrew the nuts and remove the catalytic converter from the turbocharger **(see illustration)**. Recover the gasket. If necessary, move the engine towards the radiator to provide additional working room.
21 Unscrew and remove the upper bolt securing the lower timing cover to the cylinder block **(see illustration)**, then loosen the remaining cover mounting bolts so that they are just on their last threads.
22 Working in the **reverse** of the tightening sequence shown later in this Section, progressively slacken the cylinder head bolts by half a turn at a time until all bolts can be

unscrewed by hand and removed. Discard the bolts, as the manufacturer states they must be renewed after removal.
23 Make a final check round the head to ensure that nothing is still attached, nor anything in the way which would hinder it being lifted off.
24 The cylinder head assembly, complete with ancillaries is heavy, and it is advisable to attach a hoist and suitable lifting tackle to the lifting brackets on the cylinder head to lift it from the engine. Alternatively, have an assistant available to help lift it off.
25 Lift the cylinder head (complete with manifolds, high pressure pump and timing belt upper inner cover) upwards and off the cylinder block. Take care not to damage the cylinder head or block mating surfaces as the assembly is lifted clear.
26 If the head is stuck, tap it upwards using a hammer and block of wood. **Do not** try to turn

the cylinder head (it is located by two dowels), nor attempt to prise it free using a screwdriver inserted between the block and head faces. If the locating dowels are a loose fit, remove them and store them with the head for safe-keeping. Make sure that the upper section of the inner timing cover clears the lower cover and bolt as the head is lifted.
27 Recover the gasket. Although it should obviously not be re-used, it should be kept for comparison with the new one. It is recommended that a Renault dealer is consulted before buying a new gasket, as its thickness is of considerable importance **(see illustration)**.
28 If desired, the manifolds, turbocharger and high-pressure pump can be removed from the cylinder head with reference to the relevant Sections of Chapter 4B.

Inspection

29 The mating faces of the cylinder head and block must be perfectly clean before refitting the head. Use a scraper to remove all traces of gasket and carbon and also clean the tops of the pistons. Take particular care with the aluminium cylinder head, as the soft metal is damaged easily.
30 Also, make sure that debris is not allowed to enter the oil and water channels – this is particularly important for the oil circuit, as carbon could block the oil supply to the camshaft or crankshaft bearings. Using adhesive tape and paper, seal the water, oil and bolt holes in the cylinder block. Clean the piston crowns in the same way.

9.21 Upper bolt securing the lower timing cover to the cylinder block

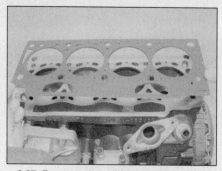

9.27 Recover the cylinder head gasket

HAYNES HiNT *To prevent carbon entering the gap between the pistons and bores, smear a little grease in the gap. After cleaning the piston, rotate the crankshaft so that the piston moves down the bore, then wipe out the grease and carbon with a cloth rag.*

31 Check the block and head for nicks, deep scratches and other damage. If slight, they may be removed carefully with a file. More serious damage may be repaired by machining, but this is a specialist job.

32 If warpage of the cylinder head is suspected, use a straight-edge to check it for distortion. Refer to Chapter 2D if necessary.

33 Clean out the cylinder head bolt holes in the block using a pipe cleaner, or a rag and screwdriver. Make sure that all oil is removed, otherwise there is a possibility of the block being cracked by hydraulic pressure when the bolts are tightened.

34 Examine the cylinder head bolt threads in the cylinder block for damage – if necessary, use the correct-size tap to chase out the threads in the block. The cylinder head bolts must be discarded and renewed, regardless of their apparent condition.

Refitting

35 Where applicable, refit the manifolds, turbocharger and high pressure pump to the cylinder head, with reference to the relevant Sections of Chapter 4B.

36 Remove the timing pin from the cylinder block and turn the crankshaft clockwise (viewed from the timing belt end) until Nos 1 and 4 pistons pass bottom dead centre (BDC) and begin to rise, then position them halfway up their bores (this is to prevent the possibility of piston-to-valve contact). Nos 2 and 3 pistons will also be at their midway positions, but descending their bores. Do not turn the crankshaft again until the timing belt is to be refitted.

37 Ensure that the cylinder head locating dowels are fitted to the cylinder block **(see illustration)**, then fit the correct gasket the right way round on the cylinder block, with the identification hole(s) at the front corner of the engine at the flywheel end.

38 Lower the cylinder head onto the block. Ensure that the timing belt upper inner cover engages correctly with the lower inner cover on the cylinder block. Where applicable, disconnect the lifting tackle and hoist.

39 The new cylinder head bolts must be fitted without oiling them. Insert the bolts, with their washers, and tighten them finger-tight **(see illustration)**.

40 Tighten the cylinder head bolts to the specified torques in the sequence shown, and in the stages given in the Specifications at the beginning of this Chapter. When angle-tightening the bolts, put paint marks on the bolt heads and cylinder head as a guide for

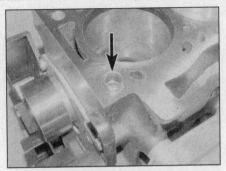

9.37 Cylinder head locating dowel on the block

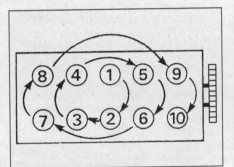

9.40a Cylinder head bolt tightening sequence

the correct angle, or obtain a special angle-tightening tool **(see illustrations)**.

41 Reset the engine to TDC on No 1 cylinder, using the information in Section 3.

42 Further refitting is a reversal of removal, noting the following points:
a) Refit the camshaft and followers with reference to Section 8.
b) Reconnect the exhaust to the turbocharger using a new gasket, as described in Chapter 4B.
c) Tighten all nuts/bolts securely, or to the specified torque.
d) Refit the timing belt as described in Section 5.
e) On completion, refill the engine with fresh oil, then fill and bleed the cooling system, with reference to Chapter 1B.

10 Sump –
removal and refitting

Removal

1 Disconnect the battery negative lead (refer to *Disconnecting the battery* in the Reference Section).

2 Jack up the front of the car and support on axle stands. Remove the engine compartment undertray.

3 Drain the engine oil referring to Chapter 1B, then refit and tighten the drain plug. Though not essential, it makes sense to fit a new oil filter on completion, before the sump is refilled with fresh oil.

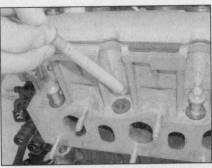

9.39 Inserting the cylinder head bolts

9.40b Angle-tightening the cylinder head bolts

4 Remove both front roadwheels, then remove both wheel arch liners (see Chapter 11, Section 21 if necessary).

5 Using cable-ties or string, tie the radiator up to the front crossmember – this is necessary, as the radiator lower crossmember must be removed.

6 Unbolt and remove the side supports each side, fitted between the inner wing and radiator lower crossmember. Ensure that the radiator is adequately supported, as described in the previous paragraph. Remove the front bolt and rear nut, then lower the crossmember to the floor.

7 Unbolt and remove the engine lower mounting from the engine and subframe (refer to Section 13) – this will allow the engine to move slightly on its remaining right- and left-hand mountings, but providing they are not disturbed, this is not dangerous.

8 Loosen and remove the nineteen bolts used to secure the sump. In addition to the bolts, the sump is secured by several spots of sealant – tap the sump with a hide or plastic mallet to break the seal, or prise it very carefully, so as not to damage the sealing surfaces.

9 Lower the sump out from under the car, and recover the gasket – a new one should be used when refitting.

Refitting

10 Thoroughly clean the mating surfaces of the sump and cylinder block.

11 Apply a total of four beads of suitable silicone sealant (Rhodorseal 5661, or equivalent) to the areas shown. Do not apply too much, otherwise the excess may end up

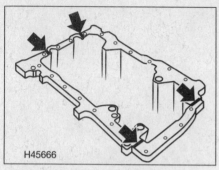

10.11 Apply beads of sealant in the areas shown before refitting the sump

10.12 Use a straight-edge to align the sump and block

2 Unscrew the two mounting bolts and withdraw the oil pump, tilting it to disengage its sprocket from the drive chain **(see illustrations)**. If the two locating dowels are displaced, refit them in their locations.

3 To remove the oil pump complete with its drive chain and sprockets, first remove the sump (Section 10), then unbolt the crankshaft timing belt end oil seal housing, as described in Section 12 **(see illustration)**. Where fitted, note the presence of the chain guide block and of its two locating dowels.

4 Where applicable, unscrew the bolts securing the sprocket to the oil pump hub. Use a screwdriver through one of the holes in the sprocket to hold it stationary.

5 Slide the drive sprocket from the crankshaft together with the chain **(see illustration)**. Note that the drive sprocket is not keyed to the crankshaft, but relies on the pulley bolt being tightened correctly to clamp the sprocket. It is most important that the pulley bolt is correctly tightened otherwise there is the possibility of the oil pump not functioning.

6 Unscrew the two mounting bolts and withdraw the oil pump, tilting it to disengage its sprocket from the drive chain. If the two locating dowels are displaced, refit them in their locations.

inside the sump, where it could get sucked into the engine **(see illustration)**.

12 Locate the new gasket in position, and lift the sump into position on the cylinder block. Insert the bolts and tighten them progressively in two stages to the specified torque – start with the centre bolts, and work in a diagonal sequence. If the engine is removed from the car, use a straight-edge to maintain the alignment between the left-hand end of the sump and cylinder block **(see illustration)**.

13 Further refitting is a reversal of removal, noting the following points:

a) When refitting the radiator lower crossmember, fit the fasteners and side plates loosely, then insert a 10 mm spacer between it and the subframe, at the rear (refer to Chapter 7A, Section 8). We used a 10 mm diameter bolt – this should be withdrawn once the nuts have been tightened each side. The crossmember

forms part of the deformable front structure of the car, and the gap left by using the spacer is essential.

b) Tighten all nuts/bolts to the specified torque.

c) Allow sufficient time for the sealant used to cure, then fill the engine with fresh oil (see Chapter 1B). On completion, start the engine, and check for signs of leakage.

11 Oil pump – removal, inspection and refitting

Removal

1 To remove the oil pump alone, first remove the sump, referring to Section 10. Where applicable, also unbolt and unclip the anti-emulsion panel **(see illustrations)**.

Inspection

7 Unscrew the retaining bolts and lift off the pump cover. Withdraw the idler gear and the drivegear/shaft. Mark the idler gear before removal, so that it can be refitted in its original position.

11.1a Unscrew the bolts . . .

11.1b . . . then unclip and remove the anti-emulsion panel

11.2a Oil pump mounting bolts

11.2b Disengaging the oil pump sprocket from the drive chain

11.3 Removing the timing belt end oil seal housing

11.5 Removing the oil pump drive sprocket and chain

11.8a Extract the retaining clip . . .

11.8b . . . and remove the oil pressure relief valve components

11.10a Measuring the oil pump gear-to-body clearance

11.10b Measuring the oil pump gear endfloat

11.10c Checking the flatness of the oil pump cover

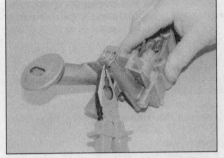

11.11 Bend the end of the retaining clip to ensure it remains in position

8 Extract the retaining clip and remove the oil pressure relief valve spring retainer, spring, spring seat and plunger (see illustrations).
9 Clean the components and carefully examine the gears, pump body and relief valve plunger for any signs of scoring or wear. Renew the complete pump assembly if excessive wear is evident (no spare parts are available).
10 If the components appear serviceable, measure the clearance between the pump body and the gears using feeler gauges. Also measure the gear endfloat and check the flatness of the end cover (see illustrations). If the clearances exceed the specified tolerances, the pump must be renewed. There should be no discernible wear or distortion of the end cover.
11 If the pump is satisfactory, reassemble the components in the reverse order of removal, but bend the end of the retaining clip to ensure it remains in position (see illustration). Fill the pump with oil, then refit the cover and tighten the bolts securely. Prime the oil pump by filling it with clean engine oil whilst rotating the driveshaft.

Refitting

12 Wipe clean the oil pump and cylinder block mating surfaces.
13 Check that the two locating dowels are fitted in the cylinder block, then position the oil pump on them and insert the two mounting bolts. Tighten the bolts securely.
14 Engage the sprockets on the chain (if removed), then refit both sprockets and the chain as an assembly. Slide the drive sprocket

fully onto the crankshaft and locate the driven sprocket on the oil pump hub.
15 Align the holes, then insert the sprocket bolts and tighten them securely while holding the sprocket stationary with a screwdriver.
16 Refit the oil seal housing as described in Section 12 – do not forget the chain guide block and its two locating dowels – and the sump (refer to Section 10).

12 Crankshaft oil seals – renewal

Timing belt end oil seal

1 Remove the crankshaft sprocket, as described in Section 6.
2 Note the fitted position of the old seal, then prise it out of the oil seal housing using a

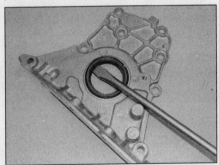

12.2 Removing the timing belt end oil seal (timing cover removed)

screwdriver or suitable hooked instrument. An alternative method of removing the oil seal is to drill carefully two small holes opposite each other in the oil seal and insert self-tapping screws, then pull on the screws with grips (see illustration). Take care not to damage the surface of the crankshaft or spacer, or the seal housing. **Note:** *On some models it may be necessary to remove the timing belt lower inner cover to allow the seal to be withdrawn. If this is the case, remove the idler pulley (see Section 6) then unbolt the cover.*
3 Clean the seal housing, and polish off any burrs or raised edges which may have caused the seal to fail in the first place. Inspect the seal rubbing surface on the crankshaft. If it is grooved or rough in the area where the old seal was fitted, the new seal should be fitted slightly less deeply, so that it rubs on an unworn part of the crankshaft surface.
4 Wipe clean the oil seal seating, then dip the new seal in fresh engine oil and locate it over the crankshaft with its closed side facing outwards. Make sure that the oil seal lip is not damaged as it is located on the crankshaft.
5 Using a tube of suitable diameter, drive the oil seal squarely into the housing to the previously noted position (see illustration) – take great care not to damage the seal lips during fitting. Note that if the surface of the shaft was noted to be badly scored, press the new seal slightly further into its housing so that its lip is running on an unmarked area of the shaft.
6 Where necessary, refit the timing belt lower inner cover/seal housing (see illustration)

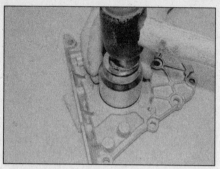

12.5 Using a socket to drive in the new oil seal

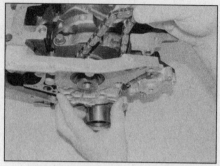

12.6 Refitting the oil seal housing

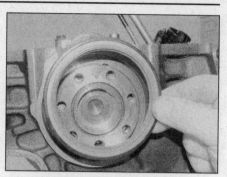

12.16 Removing the flywheel end crankshaft oil seal

and install the idler pulley as described in Section 6. Refit the crankshaft sprocket as described in Section 6 and fit the new timing belt as described in Section 5.

Timing belt end oil seal housing

7 Remove the timing belt as described in Section 5, and the crankshaft and auxiliary shaft/idler sprockets and the idler pulley with reference to Section 6. Remove the Woodruff key from the crankshaft keyway, then unbolt the timing belt lower inner cover from the cylinder block.

8 Unscrew the bolts (approximately four in number, depending on engine version) securing the sump to the oil seal housing.

9 Unscrew the retaining bolts and carefully withdraw the oil seal housing, noting the locating dowels around its two lower bolt holes. If it is stuck in place, a leverage point is provided on its upper edge (near the timing belt idler pulley) to allow a screwdriver or similar to be used gently to prise the housing away from the cylinder block without risking damage to the delicate mating surfaces of either. If the sump gasket is damaged, the sump will have to be removed to renew it.

10 The oil seal should be renewed whenever the housing is removed. Note the fitted position of the old seal, then prise it out with a screwdriver and wipe clean the seating. Smear the outer perimeter of the new seal with fresh engine oil and locate it squarely on the housing with its closed side facing outwards. Place the housing on a block of wood, then use a socket or metal tube to drive in the oil seal.

11 On refitting, clean all traces of sealant

from the housing, sump and block mating faces. Check that the chain guide block (where applicable) is correctly fitted and that the housing's locating dowels are in place.

12 Apply a 0.6 to 1.0 mm diameter bead of sealant (Renault recommend CAF 4/60 THIXO or Rhodorseal 5661) to the housing's gasket surfaces, around the inner edges of the bolt holes and apply a smear of sealant to the threads of the two bolts (nearest the oil seal) which project inside the cylinder block. Do **NOT** allow sealant to foul the oil gallery at the upper end of the housing. Refit the housing to the cylinder block and sump, tightening the bolts securely and evenly.

13 Refit the Woodruff key to the crankshaft keyway, then refit the timing belt lower inner cover to the cylinder block, tightening securely its retaining bolts.

14 Refit the crankshaft and idler pulley, and fit the new timing belt with reference to Sections 6 and 5.

Flywheel end oil seal

15 Renewal of the crankshaft left-hand oil seal requires the transmission to be removed so that the clutch and the flywheel can be withdrawn – refer to Chapter 7A and to Chapter 6. Remove the flywheel as described in Section 16.

16 Prise out the old oil seal using a small screwdriver, taking care not to damage the surface on the crankshaft **(see illustration)**. Alternatively, the oil seal can be removed by drilling two small holes diagonally opposite each other and inserting self-tapping screws in them. A pair of grips can then be used to

pull out the oil seal, by pulling on each side in turn.

17 Inspect the seal rubbing surface on the crankshaft. If it is grooved or rough in the area where the old seal was fitted, the new seal should be fitted slightly less deeply, so that it rubs on an unworn part of the surface.

18 Wipe clean the oil seal seating, then dip the new seal in fresh engine oil, and locate it over the crankshaft with its closed side facing outwards. Make sure that the oil seal lip is not damaged as it is located on the crankshaft.

19 Using a metal tube, drive the oil seal squarely into the bore until flush. A block of wood cut to pass over the end of the crankshaft may be used instead.

20 Refit the flywheel with reference to Section 16. Refit the clutch as described in Chapter 6, then refit the transmission as described in Chapter 7A.

13 Engine mountings – inspection and renewal

Inspection

1 With the handbrake applied, jack up the front of the car and support it on axle stands (see *Jacking and vehicle support*). Where fitted, remove the engine compartment undershield.

2 As far as possible, inspect the rubber sections of all the mountings for signs of cracking and deterioration. Careful use of a lever will help to determine the condition of the rubber. If there is excessive movement in the mounting, or if the rubber has deteriorated, the mounting should be renewed.

3 Lower the car to the ground.

Renewal

Right-hand mounting

4 Support the right-hand end of the engine with a trolley jack and block of wood beneath the sump. If available, an engine support bar may be used to support the engine from above.

5 Remove the clips and take off the engine compartment plastic trim panels from the right-hand side of the engine.

6 Remove the two bolts from the mounting link at the rear of the mounting, and lift off the link **(see illustrations)**.

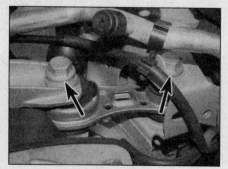

13.6a Unscrew the bolts from the mounting rear link . . .

13.6b . . . then lift the link out

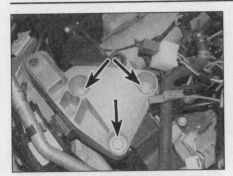

13.8a Unscrew the three bolts securing the mounting to the engine . . .

13.8b . . . and lift it away

13.9a Mark its position on the inner wing . . .

7 The wing and engine sections of the mounting are held together by a horizontal through-bolt, from the wing side – this must be loosened as far as possible, though it cannot be removed. Access to this bolt is hampered by the coolant expansion tank, and by the air conditioning pipes (where applicable).

8 Remove the three bolts securing the mounting to the engine, and lift it away **(see illustrations)**.

9 Mark its position relative to the wing, then remove the four bolts securing the mounting to the inner wing, and lift it off **(see illustrations)**.

10 If required, the mounting bracket on the engine can also be unbolted and removed **(see illustration)**.

11 Fit the mounting using a reversal of the removal procedure, but tighten the nuts/bolts to the specified torque wrench settings.

Left-hand mounting

12 Remove the air cleaner resonator or air inlet ducts from the left-hand side of the engine as applicable, for access to the engine/transmission left-hand mounting. Remove the battery and battery tray as described in Chapter 5A.

13 Support the left-hand end of transmission with a trolley jack and block of wood beneath the transmission. If available, an engine support bar may be used to support the engine from above.

14 Unscrew the centre nut and the two outer nuts either side of it **(see illustration)**.

15 Remove the three bolts from the top of the transmission, and lower the transmission slightly **(see illustration)**.

16 Remove the four bolts securing the mounting to the inner wing, and lift it away.

17 Fit the mounting using a reversal of the

removal procedure, but tighten the bolts to the specified torque wrench settings.

Lower mounting

18 Jack up the front of the car, and support it securely on axle stands (see *Jacking and vehicle support*).

19 Remove the two bolts securing the lower mounting link, and withdraw it from the subframe **(see illustration)**.

20 If required, the mounting link bracket (to the engine) can also be unbolted and removed **(see illustration)**.

21 Though removing the lower mounting will increase the amount of engine movement, the engine will remain safely supported on its right- and left-hand mountings.

22 Fit the mounting using a reversal of the removal procedure, but tighten the bolts to the specified torque wrench settings.

13.9b . . . then lift out the wing section of the mounting, with the through-bolt

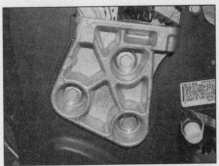

13.10 Unbolt and remove the mounting bracket on the engine if necessary

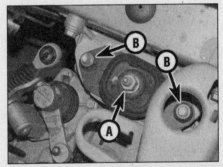

13.14 Left-hand (transmission) mounting centre (A) and outer (B) nuts

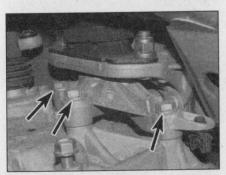

13.15 Left-hand mounting-to-transmission bolts

13.19 Engine lower mounting link bolts

13.20 Lower mounting link bracket on the back of the engine

14.4a Remove the oil filter mounting stud . . .

14.4b . . . then withdraw the oil cooler and recover the sealing ring

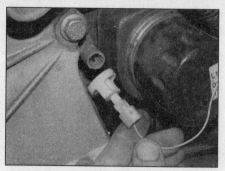

15.6 Disconnect the oil pressure switch wiring plug

14 Engine oil cooler – removal and refitting

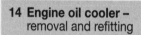

Removal

1 Drain the cooling system as described in Chapter 1B.
2 Remove the oil filter (refer to Chapter 1B).
3 Loosen the clips and disconnect the coolant hoses from the oil cooler.
4 Unscrew the oil filter mounting stud, which also secures the oil cooler and withdraw the oil cooler from the engine. Recover the sealing ring **(see illustrations)**.

Refitting

5 Refitting is a reversal of removal, but use a new sealing ring.

15 Oil pressure switch – removal and refitting

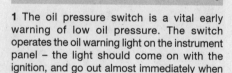

1 The oil pressure switch is a vital early warning of low oil pressure. The switch operates the oil warning light on the instrument panel – the light should come on with the ignition, and go out almost immediately when the engine starts.
2 If the light does not come on, there could be a fault on the instrument panel, the switch wiring, or the switch itself. If the light does not go out, low oil level, worn oil pump (or sump pick-up blocked), blocked oil filter, or worn

main bearings could be to blame – or again, the switch may be faulty.
3 If the light comes on while driving, the best advice is to turn the engine off immediately, and not to drive the car until the problem has been investigated – ignoring the light could mean expensive engine damage.

Removal

4 The oil pressure switch is located on the front face of the engine, next to the oil filter.
5 Jack up the front of the car, and support it on axle stands (see *Jacking and vehicle support*) – to improve access, remove the oil filter, referring to Chapter 1B if necessary.
6 Disconnect the wiring plug from the switch **(see illustration)**.
7 Unscrew the switch from the block, and remove it together with its sealing washer. There should only be a very slight loss of oil when this is done.

Inspection

8 Examine the switch for signs of cracking or splits. If the top part of the switch is loose, this is an early indication of impending failure.
9 Check that the wiring terminals at the switch are not loose, then trace the wire from the switch connector until it enters the main loom – any wiring defects will give rise to apparent oil pressure problems.

Refitting

10 Refitting is the reverse of the removal procedure, noting the following points:
a) Clean the switch threads before fitting. Tighten the switch securely.

b) Reconnect the switch connector, making sure it clicks home properly. Ensure that the wiring is routed away from any hot or moving parts.
c) Lower the car to the ground, then check the engine oil level and top-up if necessary (see Weekly checks).
d) Check for signs of oil leaks once the engine has been restarted and warmed-up to normal operating temperature.

16 Oil level sensor – removal and refitting

Removal

1 The sensor is fitted at the front of the engine, next to the oil filter. Access may be easiest from below.
2 Disconnect the wiring plug, then unscrew and withdraw the sensor from the engine block **(see illustrations)**.

Refitting

3 Refitting is a reversal of removal. Tighten the sensor securely, to prevent leaks.

17 Flywheel – removal, inspection and refitting

Note: *New flywheel bolts must be used on refitting.*

Removal

1 Remove the transmission as described in Chapter 7A.
2 Remove the clutch as described in Chapter 6.
3 Mark the flywheel in relation to the crankshaft to aid refitting. Note that the flywheel can only be refitted in one position, as the bolts are unequally spaced **(see illustration)**.
4 The flywheel must now be held stationary while the securing bolts are loosened. To do this, locate a long bolt in one of the engine-to-gearbox mounting bolt holes and insert a wide-bladed screwdriver or length of bent metal bar in the starter ring gear or use a suitable locking tool.

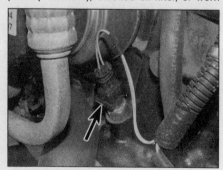

16.2a Disconnect the oil level sensor wiring plug . . .

16.2b . . . then unscrew and withdraw the sensor from the block

17.3 The flywheel bolts are unequally spaced

5 Unscrew the mounting bolts, and withdraw the flywheel; be careful – it is heavy. Discard the old bolts as new ones must be used on refitting.

Inspection

6 Examine the flywheel for wear or chipping of the ring gear teeth. If the ring gear is worn or damaged, it may be possible to renew it separately, but this job is best left to a Renault dealer or engineering works. The temperature to which the new ring gear must be heated for installation is critical and, if not done accurately, the hardness of the teeth will be destroyed.

7 Check the flywheel carefully for signs of distortion, and for hairline cracks around the bolt holes, or radiating outwards from the centre. If damage of this sort is found, it must be renewed.

8 Examine the flywheel for scoring of the clutch face. If the clutch face is scored, the flywheel may be machined until flat, but renewal is preferable.

Refitting

9 Clean the flywheel and crankshaft mating surfaces, then locate the flywheel/driveplate on the crankshaft, making sure that any previously-made marks are aligned.

10 Locate the flywheel on the crankshaft and insert the new securing bolts, then tighten them in a diagonal sequence to the specified torque. Hold the flywheel stationary as during removal. **Do not** oil the new bolt threads, as they are supplied with locking compound.

11 Refit the clutch (Chapter 6), and the transmission as described in Chapter 7A.

Chapter 2 Part D:
Engine removal and overhaul procedures

Contents

Degrees of difficulty

Easy, suitable for novice with little experience 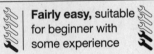	**Fairly easy,** suitable for beginner with some experience	**Fairly difficult,** suitable for competent DIY mechanic	**Difficult,** suitable for experienced DIY mechanic	**Very difficult,** suitable for expert DIY or professional

Specifications

General
Engine codes:

1.4 litre DOHC petrol engine	K4J
1.6 litre DOHC petrol engine	K4M
1.5 litre SOHC diesel engine	K9K
1.9 litre SOHC diesel engine	F9Q

Valves
Valve spring free length:

K4J engine	41.3 mm
K4M engine	51.83 mm
K9K engine	43.31 mm
F9Q engine	45.80 mm

Cylinder head
Height:

K4J and K4M engines	137.0 mm
K9K engine	127.0 mm
F9Q engine	162.0 mm
Maximum acceptable gasket face distortion	0.05 mm
Refinishing limit	No refinishing permitted
Valve protrusion/depth in relation to head surface	0.00 ± 0.07 mm

Cylinder block
Bore diameter:

K4J and K4M engines:

Class A	79.500 to 79.510 mm
Class B	79.510 to 79.520 mm
Class C	79.520 to 79.530 mm
K9K engine - nominal	76.000 mm
F9Q engine - nominal	80.000 mm

Pistons and piston rings

Piston diameter:
K4J engine (measured 45.7 mm from crown):
Class A	79.475 ± 0.005 mm
Class B	79.485 ± 0.005 mm
Class C	79.495 ± 0.005 mm

K4M engine (measured 42.0 mm from crown):
Class A	79.475 ± 0.005 mm
Class B	79.485 ± 0.005 mm
Class C	79.495 ± 0.005 mm
K9K engine (measured 56.0 mm from crown)	75.94 ± 0.007 mm
F9Q engine.	79.94 ± 0.007 mm

Piston ring end gaps (installed):
K4J and K4M engine:
Top compression	0.15 to 0.35 mm
Second compression	0.40 to 0.60 mm
Oil control (2 rails and expander)	0.20 to 0.90 mm

K9K and F9Q engines:
Top compression	0.2 to 0.35 mm
Second compression	0.7 to 0.9 mm
Oil control (2 rails and expander)	0.25 to 0.5 mm
Ring gap spacing (all engines)	120°
Piston protrusion (K9K engine).	0.192 ± 0.093 mm

Crankshaft

Main bearing journal diameter:
K4J, K4M and K9K engines:
Standard.	47.990 to 47.997 mm
1st undersize	47.997 to 48.003 mm
2nd undersize	48.003 to 48.010 mm

F9Q engine:
Standard.	54.790 ± 0.01 mm

Crankpin (big-end) journal diameter:
K4J, K4M and K9K engines:
Standard.	43.97 ± 0.01 mm

F9Q engine:
Standard.	48.00 ± 0.02 mm

Crankshaft endfloat:
K4J, K4M and K9K engines:
New.	0.045 to 0.252 mm
Maximum	0.852 mm

F9Q engine:
New.	0.070 to 0.230 mm

Torque wrench settings

Refer to Parts A, B, and C of this Chapter.

1 General information

How to use this Chapter

This Part of Chapter 2 is devoted to engine/transmission removal and refitting, to those repair procedures requiring the removal of the engine/transmission from the car, and to the overhaul of engine components. It includes only the Specifications relevant to those procedures. Refer to Parts A, B or C for additional Specifications, and for all torque wrench settings.

General information

The information ranges from advice concerning preparation for an overhaul and the purchase of new parts, to detailed step-by-step procedures covering removal and installation of internal engine components and the inspection of parts.

The following Sections have been written based on the assumption that the engine has been removed from the car. For information concerning in-car engine repair, as well as removal and installation of the external components necessary for the overhaul, see Parts A, B or C of this Chapter.

When overhauling the engine, it is essential to establish first exactly what replacement parts are available. At the time of writing, very few under- or oversized components are available for engine reconditioning (the exception being for the diesel engine). In many cases, it would appear that the easiest and most economically-sensible course of action is to replace a worn or damaged engine with an exchange unit.

2 Engine overhaul –
general information

It is not always easy to determine when, or if, an engine should be completely overhauled, as a number of factors must be considered.

High mileage is not necessarily an indication that an overhaul is needed, while low mileage does not preclude the need for an overhaul. Frequency of servicing is probably the most important consideration. An engine which has had regular and frequent oil and filter changes, as well as other required maintenance, will most likely give many thousands of miles of reliable service. Conversely, a neglected engine may require an overhaul very early in its life.

Excessive oil consumption is an indication that piston rings, valve stem oil seals and/

or valves and valve guides are in need of attention. Make sure that oil leaks are not responsible before deciding that the rings and/or guides are bad. Perform a cylinder compression check to determine the extent of the work required.

Check the oil pressure with a gauge fitted in place of the oil pressure warning light switch, and compare it with the value given in the Specifications. If it is extremely low, the main and big-end bearings and/or the oil pump are probably worn out.

Loss of power, rough running, knocking or metallic engine noises, excessive valve gear noise and high fuel consumption may also point to the need for an overhaul, especially if they are all present at the same time. If a complete tune-up does not remedy the situation, major mechanical work is the only solution.

An engine overhaul involves restoring all internal parts to the specification of a new engine. **Note:** *Always check first what replacement parts are available before planning any overhaul operation – refer to Section 1. Manufacturer main dealers, or a good engine reconditioning specialist/ automotive parts supplier, may be able to suggest alternatives which will enable you to overcome the lack of parts.*

During an overhaul, it is usual to renew the piston rings, and to rebore and/or hone the cylinder bores; where the rebore is done by an automotive machine shop, new oversize pistons and rings will also be installed – all these operations, of course, assume the availability of suitable parts. The main and big-end bearings are generally renewed and, if necessary, the crankshaft may be reground to restore the journals.

Generally, the valves are serviced as well during an overhaul, since they're usually in less-than-perfect condition at this point. While the engine is being overhauled, other components, such as the starter and alternator, can be renewed as well, or rebuilt, if the necessary parts can be found. The end result should be an as-new engine that will give many trouble-free miles.

Critical cooling system components such as the hoses, drivebelt, thermostat and coolant pump MUST be renewed when an engine is overhauled. The radiator should be checked carefully, to ensure that it isn't clogged or leaking (see Chapter 3). Also, as a general rule, the oil pump should be renewed when an engine is rebuilt.

Before beginning the engine overhaul, read through the entire procedure to familiarise yourself with the scope and requirements of the job. Overhauling an engine isn't difficult, but it is time-consuming. Plan on the car being off the road for a minimum of two weeks, especially if parts must be taken to an automotive machine shop for repair or reconditioning. Check on availability of parts, and make sure that any necessary special tools and equipment are obtained in advance. Most work can be done with typical

hand tools, although a number of precision measuring tools are required for inspecting parts to determine if they must be renewed. Often, an automotive machine shop will handle the inspection of parts, and will offer advice concerning reconditioning and renewal.

Always wait until the engine has been completely dismantled, and all components, especially the cylinder block/crankcase, have been inspected, before deciding what service and repair operations must be performed by an automotive machine shop. Since the block's condition will be the major factor to consider when determining whether to overhaul the original engine or buy a rebuilt one, never purchase parts or have machine work done on other components until the cylinder block/crankcase has been thoroughly inspected.

As a general rule, time is the primary cost of an overhaul, so it doesn't pay to install worn or sub-standard parts.

As a final note, to ensure maximum life and minimum trouble from a rebuilt engine, everything must be assembled with care, in a spotlessly-clean environment.

3 Engine removal – methods and precautions

If you have decided that an engine must be removed for overhaul or major repair work, several preliminary steps should be taken.

Locating a suitable place to work is extremely important. Adequate work space, with storage space for the car, will be needed. If a garage is not available, at the very least a flat, level, clean work surface is required.

Cleaning the engine compartment and engine before beginning the removal procedure will help keep tools clean and organised.

The engine can be removed complete with the transmission by unbolting the front-end components (bumper, radiator, etc) and lifting it out forwards. An engine hoist will be necessary; make sure the equipment is rated in excess of the combined weight of the engine and transmission. Safety is of primary importance, considering the potential hazards involved in removing the engine/transmission from the car.

If this is the first time you have removed an engine, a helper should ideally be available. Advice and aid from someone more experienced would also be useful. There are many instances when one person cannot simultaneously perform all of the operations required when removing the engine/transmission from the car.

Plan the operation ahead of time. Arrange for, or obtain, all of the tools and equipment you'll need prior to beginning the job. Some of the equipment necessary to perform engine/transmission removal and installation safely and with relative ease, and which may have to be hired or borrowed, includes (in addition to the

engine hoist) a heavy-duty trolley jack, a strong pair of axle stands, some wooden blocks, and an engine dolly (a low, wheeled platform capable of taking the weight of the engine/transmission, so that it can be moved easily when on the ground). A complete set of spanners and sockets (as described in the Reference section of this manual) will obviously be needed, together with plenty of rags and cleaning solvent for mopping-up spilled oil, coolant and fuel. If the hoist is to be hired, make sure that you arrange for it in advance, and perform all of the operations possible without it beforehand. This will save you money and time.

Plan for the car to be out of use for quite a while. A machine shop will be required to perform some of the work which the do-it-yourselfer can't accomplish without special equipment. These establishments often have a busy schedule, so it would be a good idea to consult them before removing the engine, to accurately estimate the amount of time required to rebuild or repair components that may need work.

Always be extremely careful when removing and installing the engine/transmission. Serious injury can result from careless actions. By planning ahead and taking your time, the job (although a major task) can be accomplished successfully.

4 Engine (petrol models) – removal and refitting

Note: *Read through the entire Section, as well as reading the advice in the preceding Section, before beginning this procedure. In this procedure, the engine and transmission are removed as a unit and lifted out of the engine bay. If preferred, the transmission can be removed from the engine first (as described in Chapter 7A or 7B) – this leaves the engine free to be lifted out on its own.*

Removal

1 Remove the battery and battery tray as described in Chapter 5A.

2 Though not essential, access to the engine will be improved (particularly for attaching the engine hoist) by removing the bonnet and the windscreen cowl panels as described in Chapter 11.

3 Jack up the front of the car, and support it on axle stands (see *Jacking and vehicle support*).

4 Remove the engine undertray, then drain the cooling system with reference to Chapter 1A. If the engine is to be dismantled, drain the engine oil also.

5 As part of the removal procedure, the driveshafts must be disconnected from the transmission, which will result in significant loss of oil/fluid. To avoid this, on manual transmission models, drain the transmission first, as described in Chapter 7A. Since the automatic transmission fluid level can

4.8 Unbolt and remove the side support plates

4.12a Remove the front bolt ...

4.12b ... and the rear nut each side ...

4.12c ... and lower out the radiator crossmember

only be determined by a Renault dealer using diagnostic equipment, it is strongly recommended that fluid loss is kept to a minimum – only drain the unit (as described in Chapter 7B) if all the fluid can be caught in a suitable container, for later refilling.

6 On models fitted with air conditioning, ideally the refrigerant circuit should be evacuated by a refrigeration specialist. The condenser is best removed to make room for the engine/transmission to come out, but with care, it could be tied to one side.

7 Remove both front roadwheels, then remove both wheel arch liners (see Chapter 11, Section 21).

8 Inside the wheel arch each side, remove the four bolts securing the radiator crossmember support plates to the subframe and inner wing, and remove them (see illustration).

9 Remove the front bumper as described in Chapter 11.

10 Unclip and remove the plastic side guards from the radiator, noting how they are clipped in place for refitting (refer to illustration 5.10).

11 Remove the radiator as described in Chapter 3. On models with air conditioning, either place the condenser to one side as described, or have the system evacuated and remove the condenser completely (this removes the possibility of it being damaged during engine removal). Cap the refrigerant unions to prevent dirt entry.

12 Remove the front bolt and rear nut at either side of the radiator crossmember, and lower out the crossmember (see illustrations).

13 Using the information in Chapter 12, Section 3, gain access to the engine compartment fusebox and remove the engine multiplex unit – this effectively disconnects the main engine wiring harness. Also disconnect the earth leads from the chassis.

14 Remove the air cleaner (and if not already done, the engine ECU) as described in Chapter 4A. On 1.4 litre models, it may be sufficient to remove just the air resonator, but removing the complete air cleaner will improve access.

15 Disconnect the fuel supply pipe from the fuel rail, and cap both open connections, to prevent fuel loss and dirt entry (see illustration).

16 Disconnect the brake servo vacuum hose from the inlet manifold (see illustration).

17 Disconnect the coolant hoses from the thermostat housing, and from the front of the engine.

18 On models with air conditioning, disconnect the compressor wiring plug, then unscrew the mounting bolts and withdraw the unit from the engine. Tie the compressor to one side without disconnecting the hoses (unless the system has been evacuated first – see paragraph 6) (refer to illustrations 5.18a, b, and c).

19 Referring to Chapter 7A or 7B as applicable, disconnect the gearchange control cables from the transmission. On automatic transmission models, disconnect the fluid cooler hoses and plug them, to prevent fluid loss and dirt entry.

20 On manual transmission models, disconnect the clutch hydraulic pipes at the transmission and on the bulkhead, referring to Chapter 6 if necessary. Plug the pipes to reduce fluid loss, and to prevent dirt entry.

21 Remove the driveshafts as described in Chapter 8.

22 Trace the wiring from the exhaust oxygen sensors to their connector plugs, and disconnect them.

23 Disconnect the exhaust downpipe from the manifold as described in Chapter 4A. Detach the front mountings and lower the exhaust.

24 Unbolt and remove the engine rear mounting as described in Chapter 2A.

25 Make a final check round the engine and transmission, to make sure nothing (apart from the left- and right-hand mountings) remains attached or in the way which will prevent it from being lifted out.

26 Securely attach the engine/transmission unit to a suitable engine crane or hoist, and raise it so that the weight is just taken off the two remaining engine mountings. It is helpful at this stage to have an assistant available, either to work the crane or to guide the engine out.

27 Referring to Chapter 2A, unbolt the left- and right-hand mountings from the body.

28 With the help of an assistant, lift the engine, and guide it out through the front of the car. When clear of the car, lower it to the ground. Be prepared to steady the engine when it touches down, to stop it toppling over.

Separation

29 To separate the transmission from the engine, first remove the starter motor with reference to Chapter 5A.

4.15 Disconnect the fuel supply pipe from the fuel rail (1.6 litre)

4.16 Disconnect the brake servo vacuum hose from the inlet manifold (1.4 litre)

Manual transmission models

30 Progressively unscrew and remove the transmission-to-engine bolts, noting where each one goes, and the location of any brackets attached, for guidance when refitting.

31 With the help of an assistant, withdraw the transmission directly from the engine, making sure that its weight is not allowed to bear on the clutch friction disc. Note that there are two locating dowels used.

Automatic transmission models

32 The torque converter is attached to the driveplate by three nuts which are accessed through the starter motor aperture. Turn the engine as required to position the nuts in the aperture, then unscrew and remove them. **Note:** *The nuts must be renewed every time they are removed.* Where applicable, unbolt the access plate from the bottom of the transmission.

33 Slacken and remove the remaining nut/bolts securing the transmission to the engine. Note the correct fitted positions of each nut/bolt, and the necessary brackets, as they are removed to use as a reference on refitting.

34 Carefully prise the transmission off the engine, to free its locating dowels. As the transmission is removed, make sure the torque converter is kept pushed fully onto the transmission shaft.

35 Once the transmission is free, secure the torque converter in position by bolting a length of metal bar to one of the housing holes, or by tying one of the studs to the TDC sensor aperture on the top of the housing.

Refitting

36 Refitting is a reversal of removal, noting the following additional points:

a) *Make sure that all mating faces are clean, and use new gaskets where necessary.*

b) *Tighten all nuts and bolts to the specified torque setting, where given.*

c) *If the transmission was removed, refit it to the engine as described in Chapter 7A or 7B, as applicable.*

d) *Delay fully tightening the engine left- and right-hand mountings until the engine has settled into place.*

e) *Fit new circlips to the grooves in the inner end of each driveshaft CV joint, and ensure that they fully engage as they are fitted into the transmission.*

f) *Check and if necessary adjust the transmission cables as described in Chapter 7A or 7B.*

g) *When refitting the radiator lower crossmember, fit the fasteners and side plates loosely, then insert a 10 mm spacer between it and the subframe, at the rear. We used a 10 mm diameter bolt – this should be withdrawn once the nuts have been tightened each side (see Chapter 7A, Section 8). The crossmember forms part of the deformable front structure of the car, and the gap left by using the spacer is essential.*

h) *Refill or top-up the transmission oil or fluid, with reference to Chapter 1A. On automatic transmission models, if the fluid drained is put back into the transmission, this should be sufficient to drive the car a short distance to a Renault dealer, where the fluid level can be properly checked.*

i) *On manual transmission models, top-up and bleed the clutch hydraulic system as described in Chapter 6.*

j) *Refill the cooling system as described in Chapter 1A.*

k) *On models with air conditioning, where the system was evacuated, new O-rings should be used when reconnecting the refrigerant unions. On completion, have the system recharged by a specialist or a Renault dealer.*

---

5 Engine (diesel models) – removal and refitting

Note: *Read through the entire Section, as well as reading the advice in the preceding Section, before beginning this procedure. In this procedure, the engine and transmission are removed as a unit and lifted out of the engine bay. If preferred, the transmission can be removed from the engine first (as described in Chapter 7A or 7B) – this leaves the engine free to be lifted out on its own.*

Removal

1 Remove the battery and battery tray as described in Chapter 5A.

2 Though not essential, access to the engine will be improved (particularly for attaching the engine hoist) by removing the bonnet and the windscreen cowl panels as described in Chapter 11.

3 Jack up the front of the car, and support it on axle stands (see *Jacking and vehicle support*).

4 Remove the engine undertray, then drain the cooling system with reference to Chapter 1B. If the engine is to be dismantled, drain the engine oil also.

5 As part of the removal procedure, the driveshafts must be disconnected from the transmission, which will result in significant loss of oil/fluid. To avoid this, on manual transmission models, drain the transmission first, as described in Chapter 7A. Since the automatic transmission fluid level can only be determined by a Renault dealer using diagnostic equipment, it is strongly recommended that fluid loss is kept to a minimum – only drain the unit (as described in Chapter 7B) if all the fluid can be caught in a suitable container, for later refilling.

6 On models fitted with air conditioning, ideally the refrigerant circuit should be evacuated by a refrigeration specialist. The condenser is best removed to make room for the engine/transmission to come out, but with care, it could be tied to one side.

5.10 Removing one of the radiator side guards (diesel model)

7 Remove both front roadwheels, then remove both wheel arch liners (see Chapter 11, Section 21).

8 Inside the wheel arch each side, remove the four bolts securing the radiator crossmember support plates to the subframe and inner wing, and remove them **(refer to illustration 4.8)**.

9 Remove the front bumper as described in Chapter 11.

10 Unclip and remove the plastic side guards from the radiator, noting how they are clipped in place for refitting **(see illustration)**.

11 Remove the radiator as described in Chapter 3. On models with air conditioning, either place the condenser to one side as described, or have the system evacuated and remove the condenser completely (this removes the possibility of it being damaged during engine removal). Cap the refrigerant unions to prevent dirt entry.

12 Remove the front bolt and rear nut at either side of the radiator crossmember, and lower out the crossmember **(refer to illustrations 4.12a, b and c)**.

13 Using the information in Chapter 12, Section 3, gain access to the engine compartment fusebox and remove the engine multiplex unit – this effectively disconnects the main engine wiring harness. Also disconnect the earth leads from the chassis **(see illustration)**.

14 Referring to Chapter 4B, disconnect the fuel supply and return lines, and the wiring connector, from the high-pressure fuel pump. Anticipate some fuel spillage, and cap or plug the open connections, to reduce fuel loss and prevent dirt entry.

5.13 Disconnect the earth leads from the chassis

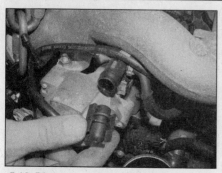

5.16 Disconnect the brake servo vacuum hose

5.18a Disconnect the wiring plug . . .

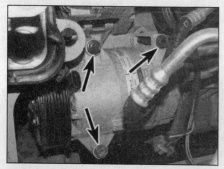

5.18b . . . then unscrew the mounting bolts . . .

5.18c . . . and withdraw the air conditioning compressor

15 Remove the air cleaner (and if not already done, the engine ECU) as described in Chapter 4B. It may be sufficient to remove just the air inlet duct, but removing the complete air cleaner will improve access.

16 Disconnect the brake servo vacuum hose from the vacuum pump **(see illustration)**.

17 Disconnect the coolant hoses from the thermostat housing, and from the front of the engine.

18 On models with air conditioning, disconnect the compressor wiring plug, then unscrew the mounting bolts and withdraw the unit from the engine. Tie the compressor to one side without disconnecting the hoses (unless the system has been evacuated first – see paragraph 6) **(see illustrations)**.

19 Referring to Chapter 7A or 7B as applicable, disconnect the gearchange control cables from the transmission. On automatic transmission models, disconnect the fluid cooler hoses and plug them, to prevent fluid loss and dirt entry.

20 On manual transmission models, disconnect the clutch hydraulic pipes at the transmission and on the bulkhead, referring to Chapter 6 if necessary. Plug the pipes to reduce fluid loss, and to prevent dirt entry.

21 Remove the driveshafts as described in Chapter 8.

22 Disconnect the exhaust downpipe from the manifold as described in Chapter 4B. Detach the front mountings and lower the exhaust.

23 Unbolt and remove the engine rear mounting as described in Chapter 2B or 2C.

24 Make a final check round the engine and

transmission, to make sure nothing (apart from the left- and right-hand mountings) remains attached or in the way which will prevent it from being lifted out.

25 Securely attach the engine/transmission unit to a suitable engine crane or hoist, and raise it so that the weight is just taken off the two remaining engine mountings. It is helpful at this stage to have an assistant available, either to work the crane or to guide the engine out.

26 Referring to Chapter 2B or 2C, unbolt the left- and right-hand mountings from the body.

27 With the help of an assistant, lift the engine, and guide it out through the front of the car **(see illustration)**. When clear of the car, lower it to the ground. Be prepared to steady the engine when it touches down, to stop it toppling over.

Separation

28 To separate the transmission from the

5.27 Removing the engine from the front

engine, first remove the starter motor with reference to Chapter 5A.

Manual transmission models

29 Progressively unscrew and remove the transmission-to-engine bolts, noting where each one goes, and the location of any brackets attached, for guidance when refitting.

30 With the help of an assistant, withdraw the transmission directly from the engine, making sure that its weight is not allowed to bear on the clutch friction disc. Note that there are two locating dowels used.

Automatic transmission models

31 The torque converter is attached to the driveplate by three nuts which are accessed through the starter motor aperture. Turn the engine as required to position the nuts in the aperture, then unscrew and remove them. **Note:** *The nuts must be renewed every time they are removed.* Where applicable, unbolt the access plate from the bottom of the transmission.

32 Slacken and remove the remaining nut/bolts securing the transmission to the engine. Note the correct fitted positions of each nut/bolt, and the necessary brackets, as they are removed to use as a reference on refitting.

33 Carefully prise the transmission off the engine, to free its locating dowels. As the transmission is removed, make sure the torque converter is kept pushed fully onto the transmission shaft.

34 Once the transmission is free, secure the torque converter in position by bolting a length of metal bar to one of the housing holes, or by tying one of the studs to the TDC sensor aperture on the top of the housing.

Refitting

35 Refitting is a reversal of removal, noting the following additional points:

a) *Make sure that all mating faces are clean, and use new gaskets where necessary.*

b) *Tighten all nuts and bolts to the specified torque setting, where given.*

c) *If the transmission was removed, refit it to the engine.*

d) *Delay fully tightening the engine left- and right-hand mountings until the engine has settled into place.*

e) *Fit new circlips to the grooves in the inner end of each driveshaft CV joint, and ensure that they fully engage as they are fitted into the transmission.*

f) *Check and if necessary adjust the transmission cables as described in Chapter 7A or 7B.*

g) *When refitting the radiator lower crossmember, fit the fasteners and side plates loosely, then insert a 10 mm spacer between it and the subframe, at the rear. We used a 10 mm diameter bolt – this should be withdrawn once the nuts have been tightened each side (see Chapter 7A, Section 8). The crossmember forms part of the deformable front structure of the*

6.3a Unclip and remove the coolant hoses from the engine/transmission

6.3b Remove the oil level sensor

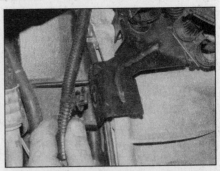

6.3c Unclip the wiring harness from the engine/transmission

car, and the gap left by using the spacer is essential.

h) *Refill or top-up the transmission oil or fluid, with reference to Chapter 1B. On automatic transmission models, if the fluid drained is put back into the transmission, this should be sufficient to drive the car a short distance to a Renault dealer, where the fluid level can be properly checked.*

i) *On manual transmission models, top-up and bleed the clutch hydraulic system as described in Chapter 6.*

j) *Refill the cooling system as described in Chapter 1B.*

k) *On models with air conditioning, where the system was evacuated, new O-rings should be used when reconnecting the refrigerant unions. On completion, have the system recharged by a specialist or a Renault dealer.*

6 Engine overhaul – dismantling sequence

1 It is much easier to dismantle and work on the engine if it is mounted on a portable engine stand. These stands can often be hired from a tool hire shop. Before the engine is mounted on a stand, the flywheel/driveplate should be removed (Part A, B or C of this Chapter) so that the stand bolts can be tightened into the end of the cylinder block/crankcase.

2 If a stand is not available, it is possible to dismantle the engine with it mounted on blocks, on a sturdy workbench or on the floor. Be extra careful not to tip or drop the engine when working without a stand.

3 If you are going to obtain a reconditioned engine, all external components must be removed first, to be transferred to the new engine (just as they will if you are doing a complete engine overhaul yourself). **Note:** *When removing the external components from the engine, pay close attention to details that may be helpful or important during refitting. Note the fitted position of gaskets, seals, spacers, pins, washers, bolts and other small items. These external components include the following:*

a) *Alternator, air conditioning compressor and mounting bracket (Chapter 5A).*

b) *Coolant hoses (see illustration).*

c) *Spark plugs or glow plugs (Chapter 1A or 5C).*

d) *Fuel system components (Chapter 4A or 4B).*

e) *Brake vacuum pump – diesel models (Chapter 9).*

f) *Thermostat and housing (Chapter 3).*

g) *Dipstick and tube, where applicable.*

h) *All electrical switches and sensors, and the related wiring harness (see illustrations).*

i) *Intake and exhaust manifolds (Chapter 4A or 4B).*

j) *Oil filter (Chapter 1A or 1B) and oil cooler, where applicable.*

k) *Engine/transmission mounting brackets (Chapter 2A, 2B or 2C).*

l) *Flywheel/driveplate (Chapter 2A, 2B or 2C).*

4 If you are obtaining a 'short' engine (which consists of the engine cylinder block/crankcase, crankshaft, pistons and connecting rods all assembled), then the cylinder head, sump, oil pump and timing belt will have to be removed also.

5 If you are planning a complete overhaul, the engine can be dismantled and the internal components removed in the following order:

a) *Alternator and mounting bracket (Chapter 5A).*

b) *Intake and exhaust manifolds (Chapter 4A or 4B).*

c) *Timing belt and pulleys (Chapter 2A, 2B or 2C).*

d) *Water pump (Chapter 3).*

e) *Cylinder head (Chapter 2A, 2B or 2C).*

7.4a Remove the split collets . . .

f) *Flywheel/driveplate (Chapter 2A, 2B or 2C).*

g) *Sump (Chapter 2A, 2B or 2C).*

h) *Oil pump (Chapter 2A, 2B or 2C).*

i) *Piston/connecting rod assemblies (Section 10).*

j) *Crankshaft (Section 11).*

6 Before beginning the dismantling and overhaul procedures, make sure that you have all of the correct tools necessary. Refer to the Reference section at the end of this manual for further information.

7 Cylinder head – dismantling

Note: *New and reconditioned cylinder heads are available from the manufacturers and from engine overhaul specialists. Due to the fact that some specialist tools are required for the dismantling and inspection procedures, and new components may not be readily available (refer to Section 1), it may be more practical and economical for the home mechanic to purchase a reconditioned head rather than to dismantle, inspect and recondition the original head.*

1 Referring to Chapter 2A, 2B or 2C, remove the camshaft(s), tappets, followers and shims, as applicable.

2 On diesel engines, remove the brake vacuum pump (see Chapter 9), thermostat housing, the fuel injectors, injection pump (if removed with the cylinder head) and glow plugs (Chapter 4B or 5C).

3 On all engines if necessary, remove the inlet and exhaust manifolds, the engine lifting eyes and top cover mountings, and the coolant outlet elbow.

4 Using a valve spring compressor, compress each valve spring in turn until the split collets can be removed. Release the compressor and lift off the cap and spring. If, when the valve spring compressor is screwed down, the valve spring cap refuses to free and expose the split collets, gently tap the top of the tool, directly over the cap, with a light hammer. This will free the cap **(see illustrations)**.

5 Remove the valves from the combustion chambers. It is essential that the valves and associated components are kept in their correct order, unless they are so badly worn

7.4b . . . then lift off the cap . . .

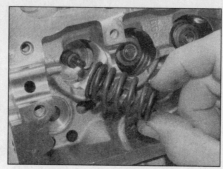

7.4c . . . and valve spring

7.4d . . . followed by the spring seat

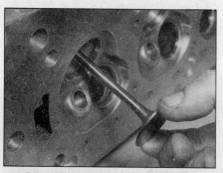

7.5a Withdrawing a valve from the combustion chamber

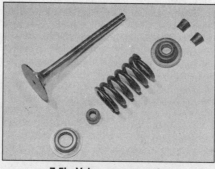

7.5b Valve components

7.5c Store the valve components in a labelled polythene bag

that they are to be renewed. If they are going to be kept and used again, place them in labelled polythene bags, or in a compartmented box **(see illustrations).**

6 On all petrol engines, the valve stem seals

7.7a Renault tool for measuring the fitted height of the old valve stem oil seals

7.7b Removing the oil seal from the top of the valve guide

are integral with the valve spring lower seats, and may be difficult to remove.

7 On the K9K diesel engine, before removing the valve stem oil seals, measure their fitted height above the cylinder head and record it. Renault technicians use a special tool which is adjusted according to the fitted height of the old seals; the tool is then used to tap the new seals to an identical height. Use a pair of pliers to pull the oil seals from the valve guides **(see illustrations).**

8 Cylinder head and valves – cleaning and inspection

1 Thorough cleaning of the cylinder head and valve components, followed by a detailed inspection, will enable you to decide how much valve service work must be carried out

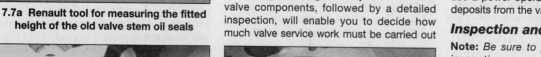

8.6 Checking the cylinder head surface for distortion with feeler blades

during the engine overhaul. **Note:** *If the engine has been severely overheated, and/or if the head gasket had failed, it is best to assume that the cylinder head is warped, and to check carefully for signs of this.*

Cleaning

2 Scrape away all traces of old gasket material and sealing compound from the cylinder head. Take care not to damage the cylinder head surfaces.

3 Scrape away the carbon from the combustion chambers and ports, then wash the cylinder head thoroughly with paraffin or a suitable solvent.

4 Scrape off any heavy carbon deposits that may have formed on the valves, then use a power-operated wire brush to remove deposits from the valve heads and stems.

Inspection and renovation

Note: *Be sure to perform all the following inspection procedures before concluding that the services of a machine shop or engine overhaul specialist are required. Make a list of all items that require attention.*

Cylinder head

5 Inspect the head very carefully for cracks, evidence of coolant leakage and other damage. If cracks are found, consult an automotive engineering specialist or manufacturer dealership, before purchasing a new head.

6 If warpage of the cylinder head gasket surface is suspected, use a straight-edge to check it for distortion **(see illustration).**

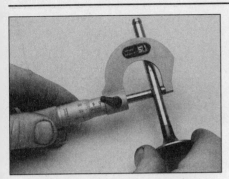

8.13 Measuring a valve stem using a micrometer

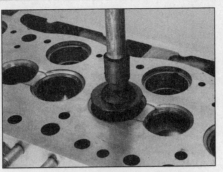

8.16 Grinding a valve to its seat – lift the valve to redistribute the paste

8.19 Checking a valve spring free length

If feeler blades are used, the degree of distortion can be assessed more accurately, and compared with the value specified. Check for distortion along the length and across the width of the head, and along both diagonals. If the head is warped, it may be possible to have it machined flat ('skimmed') at an engineering works – check with an engine specialist.

7 Examine the valve seats in each of the combustion chambers. If they are severely pitted, cracked or burned, then they will need to be renewed or recut by an engine overhaul specialist. If they are only slightly pitted, this can be removed by grinding-in the valve heads and seats with fine valve-grinding compound, as described below. Note that on diesel engines the valve seats can only be recut to a limited depth, to avoid decreasing the compression ratio. Using a dial test indicator, check that valve depth below the cylinder head gasket surface is within the limits given in the Specifications.

8 If the valve guides are worn, indicated by a side-to-side motion of the valve, new guides must be fitted.

9 The renewal of valve guides is best carried out by an engine overhaul specialist, since if it is not done skilfully, there is a risk of damaging the cylinder head.

10 If the valve seats are to be recut, consult an automotive engineering specialist or manufacturer dealership.

11 Check the tappet bores in the cylinder head for wear. If excessive wear is evident, the cylinder head must be renewed.

Valves

12 Examine the head of each valve for pitting, burning, cracks and general wear, and check the valve stem for scoring and wear ridges. Rotate the valve, and check for any obvious indication that it is bent. Look for pits and excessive wear on the tip of each valve stem. Renew any valve that shows any such signs of wear or damage.

13 If the valve appears satisfactory at this stage, measure the valve stem diameter at several points, using a micrometer **(see illustration)**. Any significant difference in the readings obtained indicates wear of the valve stem. Should any of these conditions be apparent, the valve(s) must be renewed.

14 If the valves are in satisfactory condition, they should be ground (lapped) into their respective seats, to ensure a smooth gas-tight seal. If the seat is only lightly pitted, or if it has been recut, fine grinding compound only should be used to produce the required finish. Coarse valve-grinding compound should not be used unless a seat is badly burned or deeply pitted; if this is the case, the cylinder head and valves should be inspected by an expert, to decide whether seat recutting, or even the renewal of the valve or seat insert, is required.

15 Valve grinding is carried out as follows. Place the cylinder head upside-down on a bench, with a block of wood at each end to give clearance for the valve stems.

16 Smear a trace of valve-grinding compound on the seat face, and press a suction grinding tool onto the valve head. With a semi-rotary action, grind the valve head to its seat, lifting the valve occasionally to redistribute the grinding compound **(see illustration)**. A light spring placed under the valve head will greatly ease this operation. If coarse grinding compound is being used, work only until a dull, matt even surface is produced on both the valve seat and the valve, then wipe off the used compound, and repeat the process with fine compound.

17 When a smooth unbroken ring of light grey matt finish is produced on both the valve and seat, the grinding operation is complete. Do not grind in the valves any further than absolutely necessary, or the seat will be prematurely sunk into the cylinder head.

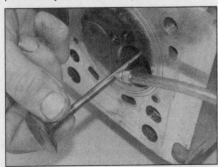

9.2 Lubricate the valve stems before inserting the valves

18 When all the valves have been ground-in, carefully wash off all traces of grinding compound, using paraffin or a suitable solvent, before reassembly of the cylinder head.

Valve components

19 Examine the valve springs for signs of damage and discoloration and also measure their free length using vernier calipers or a steel rule **(see illustration)** or by comparing the existing spring with a new component.

20 Stand each spring on a flat surface and check it for squareness. If any of the springs are damaged, distorted or have lost their tension, obtain a complete new set of springs.

Valve stem oil seals

21 The valve stem oil seals should be renewed as a matter of course.

9 Cylinder head – reassembly

1 Regardless of whether or not the head was sent away for repair work, make sure that it is clean before beginning reassembly. Be sure to remove any metal particles and abrasive grit that may still be present from operations such as valve grinding or head resurfacing. Use compressed air, if available, to blow out all the oil holes and passages.

2 Lubricate the valve stems, then insert the valves into their original locations. If new valves are being fitted, insert them into the locations to which they have been ground **(see illustration)**.

3 On petrol engines, ease the valve stem oil seals/seats over the valve stems, then press them onto the valve guides, using a large socket on the seat area. On the K9K diesel engine, press the new valve stem oil seals onto the guides to their previously-noted position, using the special guide to locate the seals over the valve stems **(see illustrations)**. **Do not** lubricate the oil seals before fitting them. Remove the guide after fitting the seal.

4 Working on each valve separately, locate the spring and cap over the valve stem. On the K9K diesel engine, the springs are tapered and the smaller-diameter taper must be positioned at the top.

9.3a Fit the special guide onto the valve stem . . .

9.3b . . . then fit the oil seal . . .

9.3c . . . and press it on to its previously-noted position on the guide

9.5 Use a little grease to hold the collets in place

9.8 Locating a new seal on the thermostat housing (diesel engine)

5 Compress the valve spring and locate the split collets in the recess in the valve stem. Release the compressor, then repeat the procedure on the remaining valves. Use a little grease to hold the collets in place (see illustration).

6 With all the valves installed, place the cylinder head on the bench supported by blocks of wood and, using a hammer and interposed block of wood, tap the end of each valve stem to settle the components.

7 Refit as necessary the manifolds, lifting eyes and coolant outlet elbow.

8 On diesel engines, refit the brake vacuum pump (see Chapter 9), thermostat housing with a new seal (see illustration), the fuel injectors, injection pump and glow plugs (Chapter 4B or 5C).

9 Referring to Chapter 2A, 2B or 2C, refit the tappets, followers and shims, and camshaft(s), as applicable.

10 Piston/connecting rod assemblies – removal

Note: *Although this task is theoretically possible with the engine in the car, in practice, owners are advised to remove the engine first. The following paragraphs assume the engine is removed from the car.*

1 With the cylinder head, sump and oil pump removed (see Chapter 2A, 2B or 2C), proceed as follows.

2 Rotate the crankshaft so that No 1 big-end cap (nearest the flywheel/driveplate position) is at the lowest point of its travel. If the big-end cap and rod are not already numbered, mark them with a centre-punch (see illustration). Mark both cap and rod to identify the cylinder they operate in.

3 Unscrew the big-end bearing cap nuts (K4J and K4M engines) or bolts (all other engines). Withdraw the cap, complete with shell bearing, from the connecting rod (see illustration).

4 If only the bearing shells are being attended to, push the connecting rod up and off the crankpin and remove the upper bearing shell (see illustration). Keep the bearing shells and cap together in their correct sequence if they are to be refitted.

5 Each piston has an arrow stamped on its crown, pointing towards the flywheel end of the engine.

6 Push the connecting rod up and remove the piston and rod from the top of the bore. Note that if there is a pronounced wear ridge at the top of the bore, there is a risk of damaging the piston rings as they foul the ridge. However, it is reasonable to assume that a rebore and new pistons will be required in any case if the ridge is so pronounced.

7 Repeat the procedure for the remaining piston/connecting rod assemblies. Ensure that the caps and rods are marked before removal, as described previously, and keep all components in order.

8 On diesel engines only, the gudgeon pins are a floating fit in the pistons, and can be removed after releasing the circlips. On petrol engines, do not attempt to separate the pistons from the connecting rods; have an engine overhaul specialist carry out the work.

10.2 Big-end caps marked with a centre-punch

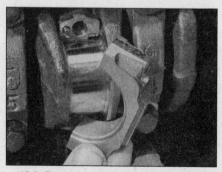

10.3 Removing a big-end bearing cap

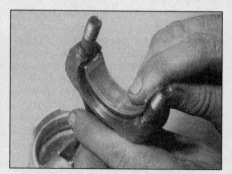

10.4 Removing a big-end bearing upper shell

11.3 Checking the crankshaft endfloat with a dial gauge

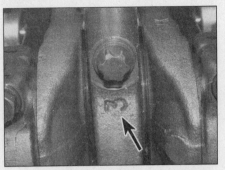

11.5 The main bearing caps are numbered for position

11.6 Removing a main bearing cap bolt

11 Crankshaft – removal

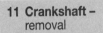

1 Remove the timing belt, crankshaft sprocket, oil pump (and drive sprocket), and flywheel/driveplate with reference to Chapters 2A, 2B or 2C. The pistons/connecting rods must be free of the crankshaft journals, however it is not essential to remove them completely from the cylinder block.

2 Unbolt the crankshaft left-hand oil seal housing from the cylinder block.

3 Before the crankshaft is removed, check the endfloat using a dial gauge in contact with the end of the crankshaft (see illustration). Push the crankshaft fully one way and then zero the gauge. Push the crankshaft fully the other way and check the endfloat. The result can be compared with the specified amount and will give an indication as to whether new thrustwashers are required.

4 If a dial gauge is not available, feeler gauges can be used. First push the crankshaft fully towards the flywheel/driveplate end of the engine, then slip the feeler gauge between the web of No 2 (or No 1) crankpin and the thrustwasher.

5 Identification numbers should already be cast onto the base of each main bearing cap, together with arrows pointing towards the flywheel/driveplate end of the engine. If not, number them 1 to 5 from the flywheel/driveplate end of the engine using a centre-punch, as was done for the connecting rods and caps (see illustration). Also mark the crankcase, so that the caps will be refitted the correct way round.

6 Unscrew the main bearing cap retaining bolts and withdraw the caps, complete with bearing shells (see illustration). Tap the caps with a wooden or copper mallet if they are stuck.

7 Carefully lift the crankshaft from the crankcase (see illustration).

8 Remove the thrustwashers where they are separate (diesel engines), then remove the bearing shell upper halves from the crankcase (see illustration). Place each shell with its respective bearing cap, noting that the grooved shells are fitted on the crankcase and the plain shells in the caps.

12 Cylinder block/crankcase – cleaning and inspection

Cleaning

1 For complete cleaning, remove all external components and brackets, and all electrical switches/sensors. The piston-cooling oil jets are pressed into the cylinder block, and must be drilled in order to fit a removal tool; this work is best left to a specialist. If necessary, the core plugs can be removed. Drill a small hole in them, then insert a self-tapping screw and pull out the plugs using a pair of grips or a slide-hammer.

2 Scrape all traces of gasket or sealant from the cylinder block, taking care not to damage the head and sump mating faces.

3 If the block is extremely dirty, it should be steam-cleaned.

4 After the block has been steam-cleaned, clean all oil holes and oil galleries one more time. Flush all internal passages with warm water until the water runs clear, dry the block thoroughly and wipe all machined surfaces with a light rust-preventative oil. If you have access to compressed air, use it to speed up the drying process and to blow out all the oil holes and galleries.

5 If the block is not very dirty, you can do an adequate cleaning job with hot soapy water and a stiff brush. Take plenty of time and do a thorough job. Regardless of the cleaning method used, be sure to clean all oil holes and galleries very thoroughly, dry the block

completely and coat all machined surfaces with light oil.

6 The threaded holes in the block must be clean to ensure accurate torque wrench readings during reassembly. Run the proper-size tap into each of the holes to remove rust, corrosion, thread sealant or sludge and to restore damaged threads. If possible, use compressed air to clear the holes of debris produced by this operation. Now is a good time to clean the threads on the head bolts and the main bearing cap bolts as well.

7 Refit the main bearing caps and tighten the bolts finger-tight.

8 After coating the mating surfaces of the new core plugs with suitable sealant, refit them in the cylinder block. Make sure that they are driven in straight and seated properly, or leakage could result. Special tools are available for this purpose, but a large socket, with an outside diameter that will just slip into the core plug, will work just as well.

9 If the engine is not going to be reassembled right away, cover it with a large plastic bag to keep it clean and prevent it rusting.

Inspection

10 Visually check the castings for cracks and corrosion. Look for stripped threads in the threaded holes. If there has been any history of internal coolant leakage, it may be worthwhile having an engine overhaul specialist check the cylinder block/crankcase for cracks with special equipment. If defects are found, have them repaired, if possible, or renew the assembly.

11 Check each cylinder bore for scuffing and scoring.

11.7 Lifting the crankshaft from the crankcase

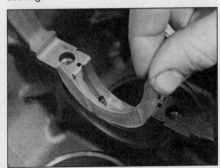

11.8 Removing the crankshaft thrustwashers (diesel engine)

13.2 Removing a piston ring with the aid of a feeler blade

13.12a Use the piston to push the rings into the cylinder bores . . .

13.12b . . . then measure the ring end gaps

12 If in any doubt as the condition of the cylinder block, have the block/bores inspected and measured by an engine reconditioning specialist. They will be able to advise on whether the block is serviceable, whether a rebore is necessary, and supply the appropriate replacement pistons and rings.

13 If the bores are in fairly good condition and not excessively worn, then it may only be necessary to renew the piston rings.

14 If this is the case, the bores should be honed, to allow the new rings to bed-in correctly and provide the best possible seal. Consult an engine reconditioning specialist

15 The cylinder block/crankcase should now be completely clean and dry, with all components checked for wear or damage, and repaired or overhauled as necessary. Refit as many ancillary components as possible, for safe-keeping. If reassembly is not to start immediately, cover the block with a large plastic bag to keep it clean, and protect the machined surfaces as described above to prevent rusting.

13 Piston/connecting rod assemblies – inspection

1 Before the inspection process can begin,

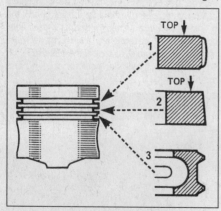

13.13 Piston ring profiles

1   *Top compression ring*
2   *Lower compression ring*
3   *Oil control ring*
Position the TOP markings as shown

the piston/connecting rod assemblies must be cleaned and the original piston rings removed from the pistons.

2 Carefully expand the old rings over the top of the pistons. The use of two or three old feeler blades will be helpful in preventing the rings dropping into empty grooves **(see illustration)**. Note that the oil control ring is in two sections.

3 Scrape away all traces of carbon from the top of the piston. A wire brush or a piece of fine emery cloth can be used once the majority of the deposits have been scraped away.

4 Remove the carbon from the ring grooves using a special groove-cleaning tool. If a tool is not available, use an old ring. Break the ring in half to do this. Be very careful to remove only the carbon deposits; do not remove any metal, or scratch the sides of the ring grooves. Protect your fingers – piston rings are sharp.

5 Once the deposits have been removed, clean the piston/connecting rod assembly with paraffin or a suitable solvent and dry thoroughly. Make sure the oil return holes in the ring grooves are clear.

6 If the pistons and cylinder bores are not damaged or worn excessively and if the cylinder block does not need to be rebored, the original pistons can be re-used. Normal piston wear appears as even vertical wear on the piston thrust surfaces and slight looseness of the top ring in its groove. New piston rings should always be used when the engine is reassembled.

7 Carefully inspect each piston for cracks around the skirt, at the gudgeon pin bosses and at the piston ring lands (between the piston ring grooves).

8 Look for scoring and scuffing on the sides of the skirt, holes in the piston crown and burned areas at the edge of the crown. If the skirt is scored or scuffed, the engine may have been suffering from overheating and/or abnormal combustion, which caused excessively-high operating temperatures. The cooling and lubricating systems should be checked thoroughly.

9 Scorch marks on the sides of the pistons show that blow-by has occurred and the rings are not sealing correctly. A hole in the piston crown is an indication that abnormal combustion (pre-ignition, knocking or

detonation) has been occurring. If any of the above problems exist, the causes must be corrected, or the damage will occur again.

10 Corrosion of the piston, in the form of small pits, indicates that coolant is leaking into the combustion chamber and/or the crankcase. Again, the cause must be corrected, or the problem may persist in the rebuilt engine.

11 Check the fit of the gudgeon pin by twisting the piston and connecting rod in opposite directions. Any noticeable play indicates excessive wear, which must be corrected. The piston/connecting rod assemblies should be taken to a dealer or engine reconditioning specialist to have the pistons, gudgeon pins and rods checked, and new components fitted as required.

12 Before refitting the rings to the pistons, check their end gaps by inserting each of them in their cylinder bores. Use the piston to make sure that they are square **(see illustrations)**. Renault rings are supplied pre-gapped; no attempt should be made to adjust the gaps by filing.

13 Refit the piston rings as follows. Where the original rings are being refitted, use the marks or notes made on removal, to ensure that each ring is refitted to its original groove and the same way up. New rings generally have their top surfaces identified by markings (often an indication of size, such as STD, or the word TOP) – the rings must be fitted with such markings uppermost **(see illustration)**. **Note:** *Always follow the instructions printed on the ring package or box.*

14 The oil control ring (lowest one on the piston) is usually installed first, and is composed of three separate elements. Slip the spacer/expander into the groove. Next, install the lower side rail. Place one end of the side rail into the groove between the spacer/expander and the ring land, hold it firmly in place, and slide a finger around the piston while pushing the rail into the groove. Next, install the upper side rail in the same manner **(see illustrations)**. After the three oil ring components have been installed, check that both the upper and lower side rails can be turned smoothly in the ring groove.

15 The second compression (middle) ring is installed next, followed by the top compression ring – ensure their marks are uppermost. Do not expand either ring any

13.14a Fit the oil control ring expander . . .

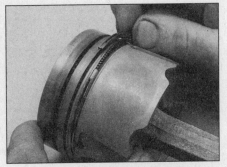

13.14b . . . followed by the ring

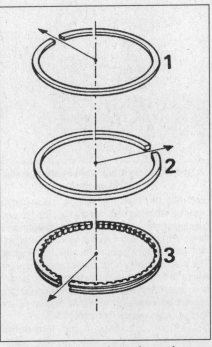

13.16 Position the piston ring end gaps 120° apart

1 *Top compression ring*
2 *Lower compression ring*
3 *Oil control ring*

more than necessary to slide it over the top of the piston.

16 With all the rings in position, space the ring gaps (including the elements of the oil control ring) uniformly around the piston at 120° intervals **(see illustration)**. Repeat the procedure for the remaining pistons and rings.

14 Crankshaft – inspection

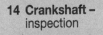

1 Clean the crankshaft and dry it with compressed air if available. Be sure to clean the oil holes with a pipe cleaner or similar probe.

 Warning: Wear eye protection when using compressed air.

2 Check the main and big-end bearing journals for uneven wear, scoring, pitting and cracking.

3 If the crankshaft has been reground, check for burrs around the crankshaft oil holes (the holes are usually chamfered, so burrs should not be a problem unless regrinding has been carried out carelessly). Remove any burrs with a fine file or scraper and thoroughly clean the oil holes as described previously.

4 Using a micrometer, measure the diameter of the main bearing and connecting rod journals and compare the results with the Specifications at the beginning of this Chapter **(see illustration)**. If in any doubt, take the crankshaft to an engine reconditioning specialist and have it measured.

14.4 Measuring a main bearing journal diameter using a micrometer

5 By measuring the diameter at a number of points around each journal's circumference, you will be able to determine whether or not the journal is out-of-round. Take the measurement at each end of the journal, near the webs, to determine if the journal is tapered.

6 If the crankshaft journals are damaged, tapered, out-of-round, or worn beyond the limits specified in this Chapter, the crankshaft must be taken to an engine overhaul specialist, who will regrind it, and who can supply the necessary undersize bearing shells, where available. **Note:** *Renault state that regrinding the crankshaft on the K9K diesel engine is not allowed.*

7 Check the oil seal journals at each end of the crankshaft for wear and damage. If either seal has worn an excessive groove in its journal, consult an engine overhaul specialist, who will be able to advise whether a repair is possible, or whether a new crankshaft is necessary.

15 Main and big-end bearings – inspection

1 Even though the main and big-end bearing shells should be renewed during the engine overhaul (where possible), the old shells should be retained for close examination, as they may reveal valuable information about the condition of the engine.

2 Bearing failure occurs because of lack of lubrication, the presence of dirt or other foreign particles, overloading the engine, and corrosion **(see illustration)**. Regardless of the cause of bearing failure, it must be corrected before the engine is reassembled, to prevent it from happening again.

3 When examining the bearing shells, remove them from the cylinder block/crankcase and main bearing caps and from the connecting rods and the big-end bearing caps, then lay them out on a clean surface in the same general position as their location in the engine. This will enable you to match any bearing problems with the corresponding crankshaft journal. Do not touch any shell's bearing surface with your fingers while checking it, or the delicate surface may be scratched.

4 Dirt or other foreign matter gets into the

engine in a variety of ways. It may be left in the engine during assembly, or it may pass through filters or the crankcase ventilation system. It may get into the oil, and from there into the bearings. Metal chips from machining operations and normal engine wear are often present. Abrasives are sometimes left in engine components after reconditioning, especially when parts are not thoroughly cleaned using the proper cleaning

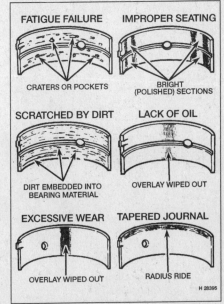

15.2 Typical bearing shell failures

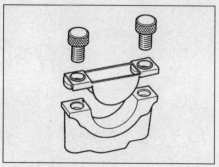

17.5a Tool for fitting main bearing shells (petrol engines)

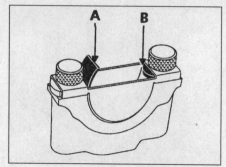

17.5b Press the bearing shell at (A) until it contacts (B)

methods. Whatever the source, these foreign objects often end up embedded in the soft bearing material, and are easily recognised. Large particles will not embed in the material, and will score or gouge the shell and journal. The best prevention for this cause of bearing failure is to clean all parts thoroughly, and to keep everything spotlessly-clean during engine assembly. Frequent and regular engine oil and filter changes are also recommended.

5 Lack of lubrication (or lubrication breakdown) has a number of inter-related causes. Excessive heat (which thins the oil), overloading (which squeezes the oil from the bearing face) and oil leakage (from excessive bearing clearances, worn oil pump or high engine speeds) all contribute to lubrication breakdown. Blocked oil passages, which usually are the result of misaligned oil holes in a bearing shell, will also starve a bearing of oil, and destroy it. When lack of lubrication is the cause of bearing failure, the bearing material is wiped or extruded from the shell's steel

backing. Temperatures may increase to the point where the steel backing turns blue from overheating.

6 Driving habits can have a definite effect on bearing life. Full-throttle, low-speed operation (labouring the engine) puts very high loads on bearings, which tends to squeeze out the oil film. These loads cause the shells to flex, which produces fine cracks in the bearing face (fatigue failure). Eventually, the bearing material will loosen in pieces, and tear away from the steel backing. Short-distance driving leads to corrosion of bearings, because insufficient engine heat is produced to drive off condensed water and corrosive gases. These products collect in the engine oil, forming acid and sludge. As the oil is carried to the engine bearings, the acid attacks and corrodes the bearing material.

7 Incorrect shell refitting during engine assembly will lead to bearing failure as well. Tight-fitting shells leave insufficient bearing running clearance, and will result in oil

starvation. Dirt or foreign particles trapped behind a bearing shell result in high spots on the bearing, which lead to failure. Do not touch any shell's bearing surface with your fingers during reassembly; there is a risk of scratching the delicate surface, or of depositing particles of dirt on it.

16 Engine overhaul – reassembly sequence

1 Before starting, ensure all new parts have been obtained and all necessary tools are available. Read through the entire procedure to familiarise yourself with the work involved and to ensure all items necessary for engine reassembly are at hand.

2 In addition to all normal tools and materials, obtain any necessary sealant and thread-locking fluid.

3 To save time and avoid problems, assembly can be carried out in the following order:
  a) *Crankshaft.*
  b) *Pistons/connecting rod assemblies.*
  c) *Oil pump.*
  d) *Sump.*
  e) *Flywheel/driveplate.*
  f) *Cylinder head.*
  g) *Timing belt and sprockets.*
  h) *Engine external components.*

4 At this stage, all engine components should be absolutely clean and dry, with all faults repaired. All components should be neatly arranged on a completely clean work surface or in individual containers.

17 Crankshaft – refitting

1 Crankshaft refitting is the first major step in engine reassembly. It is assumed at this point that the cylinder block/crankcase and crankshaft have been cleaned, inspected and repaired or reconditioned as necessary. Position the engine upside-down.

2 If temporarily refitted, remove the main bearing cap bolts, and lift out the caps. Lay the caps out in the proper order, to ensure correct installation.

3 If they are still in place, remove the old bearing shells from the block and the main bearing caps. Wipe the bearing recesses with a clean, lint-free cloth. They must be kept spotlessly clean.

4 Clean the backs of the new main bearing shells. Fit the shells with an oil groove in each main bearing location in the block. On petrol engines, the thrustwashers are integral with the No 3 (centre) upper main bearing shell, and on diesel engines the thrustwasher halves are fitted either side of No 2 or No 3 upper main bearing location. Fit the other shell from each bearing set in the corresponding main bearing cap.

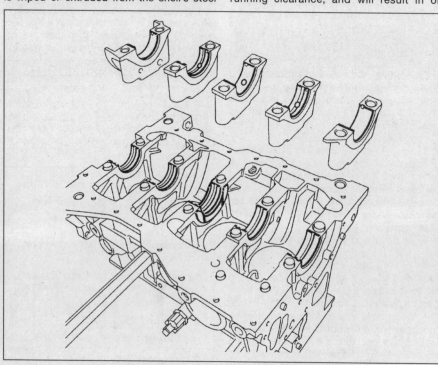

17.5c Bearing shell positions (petrol engines)

17.6a Smear a little grease on the crankshaft thrustwashers . . .

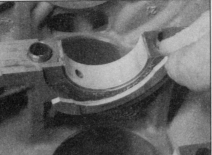

17.6b . . . and stick them to the centre main bearing

17.7 Lubricate the main bearing shells before fitting the crankshaft

5 Make sure the tag where fitted on each bearing shell fits into the notch in the block or cap/lower crankcase. On engines where tags are not incorporated in the shells, it is recommended that the Renault tool Mot. 1493 or 1493-01 is obtained, though if care is taken, the shells can be lined up accurately enough without it (see illustrations). Note that the oil holes in the block must line up with the oil holes in the bearing shell.

6 On diesel engines, fit the thrustwasher halves to No 2 (1.9 litre) or No 3 (1.5 litre) main bearing position and retain with grease (see illustrations). Do not hammer the shells into place, and do not nick or gouge the bearing faces.

7 Clean the bearing surfaces of the shells in the block, then apply a thin, uniform layer of clean molybdenum disulphide-based grease, engine assembly lubricant, or clean engine oil to each surface (see illustration). Coat the thrustwasher surfaces as well.

8 Lubricate the crankshaft oil seal journals with molybdenum disulphide-based grease, engine assembly lubricant, or clean engine oil.

9 Make sure the crankshaft journals are clean, then lay the crankshaft back in place in the block (see illustration).

10 Refit and tighten the main bearing caps as follows (see illustrations):

a) Clean the bearing surfaces of the shells in the caps, then lubricate them. Refit the caps in their respective positions, with the arrows pointing towards the flywheel/driveplate end of the engine.

b) Working on one cap at a time, from the centre main bearing outwards (and ensuring that each cap is tightened down squarely and evenly onto the block), tighten the main bearing cap bolts to the specified torque wrench setting.

11 Rotate the crankshaft a number of times by hand, to check for any obvious binding.

12 Check the crankshaft endfloat (see Section 10). It should be correct if the crankshaft thrustwashers are not worn or damaged, or have been renewed.

13 Refit the crankshaft left-hand oil seal housing and install a new seal (Chapters 2A, 2B or 2C).

17.9 Lay the crankshaft in position in the crankcase

17.10a Fitting No 5 main bearing cap (petrol engine)

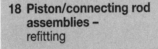

17.10b Tighten the main bearing cap bolts to the specified torque . . .

17.10c . . . and angle

14 Refit the flywheel/driveplate, oil pump (and drive sprocket), crankshaft sprocket and timing belt (Chapters 2A, 2B or 2C).

18 Piston/connecting rod assemblies – refitting

1 Clean the backs of the big-end bearing shells and the recesses in the connecting rods and big-end caps. If new shells are being fitted, ensure that all traces of the protective grease are cleaned off using paraffin. Wipe the shells and connecting rods dry with a lint-free cloth.

2 Press the big-end bearing shells into the connecting rods and caps in their correct positions. Note that locating tags are not incorporated in the shells and, to ensure correct fitting, it is recommended that the

Renault tool Mot. 1492 is obtained (see illustration). However, if care is taken and the shells are accurately fitted, the tool is not necessary.

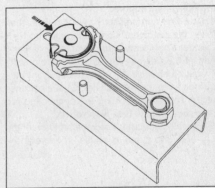

18.2 Using tool Mot. 1492 to fit the big-end shells

18.3a Lubricating the piston rings . . .

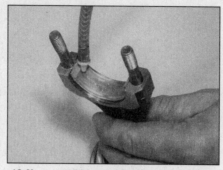

18.3b . . . and big-end bearing shell in the connecting rod

18.4 Using the wooden handle of a hammer to drive the piston into the bore

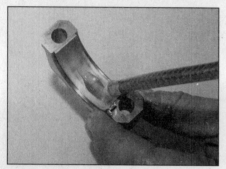

18.5a Lubricate the big-end cap bearing shell . . .

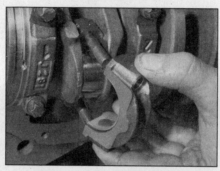

18.5b . . . then refit the cap . . .

18.5c . . . screw on the nuts . . .

18.5d . . . and tighten them to the specified torque and angle

3 Lubricate No 1 piston and piston rings and check that the ring gaps are still spaced at 120° intervals to each other. Also, lubricate the big-end bearing shell in the connecting rod **(see illustrations)**.

4 Fit a ring compressor to No 1 piston, then insert the piston and connecting rod into No 1 cylinder. The V arrow must point to the flywheel end of the engine. With No 1 crankpin at its lowest point, drive the piston carefully into the cylinder with the wooden handle of a hammer, at the same time guiding the connecting rod onto the crankpin **(see illustration)**.

5 Liberally lubricate the crankpin journal and big-end cap bearing shells, then refit the

correct cap and insert the nuts/bolts. Tighten them to the specified torque and angle **(see illustrations)**. Turn the crankshaft to make sure that it is free before moving on to the next assembly.

6 Repeat the above procedures on the remaining piston/connecting rod assemblies.

7 On completion, refit the oil pump, sump and cylinder head as described in Chapter 2A, 2B or 2C.

19 Engine –
initial start-up after overhaul

1 With the engine refitted in the car, double-check the engine oil and coolant levels. Make a final check that everything has been reconnected, and that there are no tools or rags left in the engine compartment.

2 On petrol models, carry out the following:
  a) *With the spark plugs removed and the fuel pump disabled by removing the fuel pump fuse from the engine compartment fusebox, crank the engine on the starter motor until the oil pressure light goes out.*
  b) *Refit the spark plugs and the fuse.*
  c) *Start the engine, noting that this may take a little longer than usual, due to the fuel system being empty.*

3 On diesel models, carry out the following:
  a) *Prime the fuel system as described in Chapter 4B.*
  b) *Start the engine as normal. Additional cranking may be necessary to bleed the fuel system before the engine starts.*

4 Once started, keep the engine running at fast tickover. Check that the oil pressure light goes out, then check that there are no leaks of oil, fuel and coolant. Do not be alarmed if there are some odd smells and smoke from parts getting hot and burning off oil deposits.

5 While the engine is idling, check for fuel, water and oil leaks.

6 Keep the engine idling until hot water is felt circulating through the top hose, indicating that the engine is at normal operating temperature, then switch it off.

7 After a few minutes, recheck the oil and water levels and top-up as necessary (see *Weekly checks*).

8 There is no requirement to retighten the cylinder head bolts.

9 If new pistons, rings or crankshaft bearings have been fitted, the engine must be run-in for the first 500 miles (800 km). Do not operate the engine at full-throttle, nor allow it to labour in any gear during this period. It is recommended that the oil and filter be changed at the end of this period.

Chapter 3
Cooling, heating and air conditioning systems

Contents

Degrees of difficulty

Easy, suitable for novice with little experience	**Fairly easy,** suitable for beginner with some experience	**Fairly difficult,** suitable for competent DIY mechanic	**Difficult,** suitable for experienced DIY mechanic	**Very difficult,** suitable for expert DIY or professional

Specifications

General

Cooling system type.	Pressurised sealed system, with timing belt-driven water pump, front-mounted radiator and electric cooling fan
Cooling system pressure	1.4 bar
Air conditioning refrigerant type	R134a

Thermostat

Starts to open	89°C
Fully open.	99°C
Travel (closed to fully open)	7.5 mm
Type	Wax

Coolant temperature sensor

Resistance:	
At 25°C.	2252 ± 112 ohms
At 80°C.	280 ± 8 ohms

Torque wrench settings

	Nm	lbf ft
Air conditioning compressor mounting bolts	25	18
Air conditioning condenser unions.	10	7
Water pump bolts*:		
1.4 and 1.6 litre petrol engines:		
Stage 1	8	6
Stage 2:		
M6 bolts	10	7
M8 bolts	22	16
1.5 litre diesel engine	11	8
1.9 litre diesel engine	10	7

*With thread-locking fluid applied – see text

1 General information

The cooling system is of the pressurised type. The main components are a timing belt-driven pump, an aluminium cross-flow radiator, an expansion bottle, an electric cooling fan, a thermostat, and the associated hoses. Diesel models also feature a coolant-fed oil cooler, mounted at the base of the oil filter

The system functions as follows. When the engine is cold, coolant is pumped around the cylinder block and head passages. After cooling the cylinder bores, combustion surfaces and valve seats, the coolant passes through the heater and inlet manifold, and is returned to the water pump.

When the coolant reaches a predetermined temperature, the thermostat opens, and the hot coolant passes through the top hose to the radiator. As the coolant circulates through the radiator, it is cooled by the inrush

2.3a Most of the coolant hose clips are of the spring type . . .

of air when the car is in motion. The airflow is supplemented by the action of the electric cooling fan when necessary. Upon reaching the bottom of the radiator, the coolant returns to the pump via the radiator bottom hose, and the cycle is repeated.

As the coolant warms up, it expands; the increased volume is accommodated in an expansion bottle. The bottle is 'hot', which means the coolant circulates through the bottle all the time the engine is running.

The electric cooling fan is mounted behind the radiator and is controlled by the engine ECU, see Section 7 for details.

For details of the air conditioning system (when fitted) refer to Section 14.

Precautions

⚠️ **Warning: Do not attempt to remove the expansion bottle filler cap, or to disturb any part of the cooling system, while the engine is hot, as there is a high risk of scalding. If the expansion bottle filler cap must be removed before the engine and radiator have fully cooled (even though this is not recommended), the pressure in the cooling system must first be relieved. Cover the cap with a thick layer of cloth to avoid scalding, and slowly unscrew the filler cap until a hissing sound is heard. When the hissing has stopped, indicating that the pressure has reduced, slowly unscrew the filler cap until it can be removed; if more hissing sounds are heard, wait until they have stopped before unscrewing the cap completely. At all times, keep well away from the filler cap opening, and protect your hands.**

2.5 Note that the radiator hose fittings are made of plastic

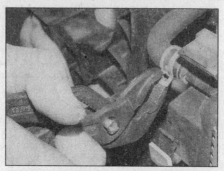

2.3b . . . released by squeezing the tangs together with pliers

⚠️ **Warning: Do not allow antifreeze to come into contact with your skin, or with the painted surfaces of the car. Rinse off spills immediately, with plenty of water. Never leave antifreeze lying around in an open container, or in a puddle in the driveway or on the garage floor. Children and pets are attracted by its sweet smell, but antifreeze can be fatal if ingested.**

⚠️ **Warning: If the engine is hot, the electric cooling fan may start rotating even if the engine is not running. Be careful to keep your hands, hair, and any loose clothing well clear when working in the engine compartment.**

⚠️ **Warning: Refer to Section 14 for precautions to be observed when working on models equipped with air conditioning.**

2 Cooling system hoses – renewal

Note: *Refer to the warnings given in Section 1 of this Chapter before proceeding. Hoses should only be disconnected once the engine has cooled sufficiently to avoid scalding.*

1 The number, routing and pattern of hoses will vary according to model, but the same basic procedure applies. Before commencing work, make sure that the new hoses are to hand, along with new hose clips if needed. It is good practice to renew the hose clips at the same time as the hoses.

2 Drain the cooling system, as described in Chapter 1A or 1B, saving the coolant if it is fit for re-use. Squirt a little penetrating oil onto the hose clips if they are rusty.

3 Release the hose clips from the hose concerned. Almost all the standard clips fitted at the factory are the spring type, released by squeezing its tangs together with pliers, at the same time working the clip away from the hose stub **(see illustrations)**. These clips can be awkward to use, can pinch old hoses, and may become less effective with age, so may have been replaced with Jubilee clips (released by turning the screw).

4 Unclip any wires, cables or other hoses which may be attached to the hose being removed. Make notes for reference when reassembling if necessary.

5 Note that the coolant unions are fragile (most are made of plastic); do not use excessive force when attempting to remove the hoses **(see illustration)**. If a hose proves to be difficult to remove, try to release it by rotating the hose ends before attempting to free it – if this fails, try gently prising up the end of the hose with a small screwdriver to 'break' the seal.

> **HAYNES HINT** *If the hose is stiff, use a little soapy water as a lubricant, or soften the hose by soaking it with hot water. If all else fails, cut the coolant hose with a sharp knife, then slit it so that it can be peeled off in two pieces. Although this may prove expensive if the hose is otherwise undamaged, it is preferable to buying a new radiator.*

6 Before fitting the new hose, smear the stubs with washing-up liquid or a suitable rubber lubricant to aid fitting. **Do not** use oil or grease, which may attack the rubber.

7 Fit the hose clips over the ends of the hose, then fit the hose over its stubs. Work the hose into position. When satisfied, locate and tighten the hose clips.

8 Refill the cooling system as described in Chapter 1A or 1B. Run the engine, and check that there are no leaks.

9 Recheck the tightness of the hose clips on any new hoses after a few hundred miles.

3 Radiator – removal, inspection, cleaning and refitting

Note: *If the radiator is to be removed for a period of more than 48 hours, precautions must be taken against internal corrosion. Either rinse the radiator with clean water and dry it thoroughly by blowing air through it, or fill it with coolant and plug the hose stubs.*

> **HAYNES HINT** *If the reason for removing the radiator is concern over coolant loss, note that minor leaks may be repaired by using a radiator sealant with the radiator in situ.*

Removal

1 Jack up the front of the car, and support it on axle stands (see *Jacking and vehicle support*).

2 Remove the front bumper as described in Chapter 11.

3 Remove the nut and bolt at either end of the bumper crossmember, and remove the crossmember from the front of the car **(see illustrations)**.

4 Unclip and withdraw the radiator plastic side guards at either side, noting how they are clipped in place for refitting **(see illustration)**.

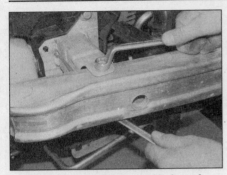

3.3a Unscrew the nut and bolt each end . . .

3.3b . . . then take off the bumper crossmember

3.4 Unclip and withdraw the radiator plastic side guards

5 To avoid the possibility of damage, it's advisable to unbolt and remove the bonnet release handle and the horn from the front crossmember (see illustrations). These could otherwise be left in place, with just the horn wiring plug needing to be disconnected as the crossmember itself is removed.

6 The front crossmember ('bonnet slam panel') must now be removed. First, disconnect the bonnet release cable at the in-line connector – unclip the cover, then prise up the top half of the connector, to detach the ballstud fitting. Unclip the air inlet duct and the washer filler neck from the back of the panel. Disconnect the horn wiring (if not already done) and unclip the wiring harness along the panel. Remove the bolt at either end of the panel, two further screws either side of the centre, and the panel can be removed (see illustrations).

7 Remove the engine undertray, then drain the

3.5a Unbolt and remove the bonnet release handle . . .

3.5b . . . then disconnect the wiring plug and unbolt the horn

cooling system with reference to Chapter 1A or 1B.

8 Disconnect the radiator hoses and cooling fan wiring plug (see illustrations).

9 On diesel models, remove the intercooler as described in Chapter 4B.

10 On models with air conditioning, lift the condenser from the radiator clips, so that

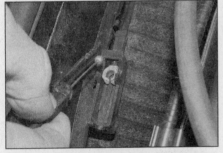

3.6a Unclip the cover from the bonnet release cable connector, and separate the ballstud fitting

3.6b Unclip the air inlet duct . . .

3.6c . . . and washer filler neck from the back of the panel

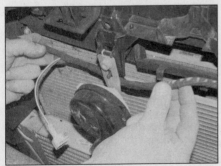

3.6d Disconnect the horn, and unclip the harness

3.6e Remove the bolt at each end, and two screws each side of the centre . . .

3.6f . . . then lift out the crossmember, unclipping the wiring as required

3.8a Release the spring clips, and disconnect the small . . .

3.8b . . . and large-diameter radiator hoses

3.8c Disconnect the cooling fan wiring plug

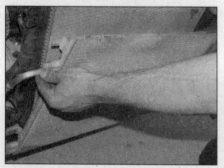

3.10a Lift the condenser out of its mounting clips . . .

3.10b . . . and place it to one side – use card to protect it while removed

3.11 Lift out the radiator

the condenser can be left behind without disconnecting the refrigerant unions. Lower the condenser down carefully to the ground, ensuring that the refrigerant pipes are not under strain – unfortunately, it cannot be moved very far out of the way, so protect it with card if it will be left out for long, or rest it back in place when the radiator is removed **(see illustrations)**.

11 Lift the radiator out, taking care not to damage the fins in the process, and remove it from the car **(see illustration)**. Recover the radiator rubber mountings.

Inspection and cleaning

12 If the radiator has been removed due to suspected blockage, reverse-flush it as described in Chapter 1A or 1B. Clean dirt and debris from the radiator fins, using an airline (in which case, wear eye protection) or a soft

brush. Be careful, as the fins are sharp, and easily damaged.

13 If necessary, a radiator specialist can perform a 'flow test' on the radiator, to establish whether an internal blockage exists.

14 A leaking radiator must be referred to a specialist for permanent repair. Do not attempt to weld or solder a leaking radiator, as damage to the plastic components may result.

15 If the radiator is to be sent for repair or renewed, remove all hoses and the cooling fan switch (where fitted).

16 Inspect the condition of the mounting rubbers, and renew them if necessary.

Refitting

17 Refitting is a reversal of removal, bearing in mind the following points:

  a) Take care not to damage the radiator fins

(nor the condenser, where applicable) during refitting.

  b) On diesel models, refit the intercooler as described in Chapter 4B.

  c) Refit the front bumper with reference to Chapter 11.

  d) On completion, refill the cooling system as described in Chapter 1A or 1B.

4 Expansion bottle – removal, inspection and refitting

Removal

1 With the engine cold, drain some coolant from the system (see Chapter 1A or 1B) until the expansion bottle is empty.

2 Undo the retaining nut at the bulkhead which secures the expansion bottle **(see illustration)**.

3 Remove the engine right-hand mounting as described in the relevant Part of Chapter 2.

4 To improve access, remove the front crossmember as described in Section 3, paragraph 6.

5 Disconnect the coolant hoses from the bottle.

6 As applicable, hold the air conditioning pipework and diesel fuel priming hose aside, and manoeuvre the bottle out from its location **(see illustration)**.

Inspection

7 Clean the bottle and inspect it for cracks and other damage. Renew it if necessary.

4.2 Unscrew and remove the bottle retaining nut

4.6 Hold the pipework aside, and remove the bottle

Also inspect the cap; if there is evidence that coolant has been vented through the cap, renew it.

Refitting

8 Refitting is a reversal of removal, noting the following points:
a) *Refit and tighten the engine mounting as described in the relevant Part of Chapter 2.*
b) *Refill and bleed the cooling system as described in Chapter 1A or 1B.*

5 Thermostat –
removal, testing and refitting

1 As the thermostat ages, it will become slower to react to changes in water temperature ('lazy'). Ultimately, the unit may stick in the open or closed position, and this causes problems. A thermostat which is stuck open will result in a very slow warm-up; a thermostat which is stuck shut will lead to rapid overheating.

2 Before assuming the thermostat is to blame for a cooling system problem, check the coolant level. If the system is draining due to a leak, or has not been properly filled, there may be an airlock in the system (refer to the coolant renewal procedure in Chapter 1A or 1B).

3 If the engine seems to be taking a long time to warm up (based on heater output), the thermostat could be stuck open. Don't necessarily believe the temperature gauge reading – some gauges never seem to register very high in normal driving.

4 A lengthy warm-up period might suggest that the thermostat is missing - it may have been removed or inadvertently omitted by a previous owner or mechanic. Don't drive the car without a thermostat - the engine management system's ECU will then stay in warm-up mode for longer than necessary, causing emissions and fuel economy to suffer.

5 If the engine runs hot, use your hand to check the temperature of the radiator top hose. If the hose isn't hot, but the engine clearly is, the thermostat is probably stuck

5.16a Thermostat housing location – petrol engine models

5.16b On diesel models, disconnect the large hose at the front, and the smaller one at the rear

closed, preventing the coolant inside the engine from escaping to the radiator - renew the thermostat. Again, this problem may also be due to an airlock (refer to the coolant renewal procedure in Chapter 1A or 1B).

6 If the radiator top hose is hot, it means that the coolant is flowing (at least as far as the radiator) and the thermostat is open. Consult the *Fault diagnosis* section at the end of this manual to assist in tracing possible cooling system faults, but a lack of heater output would now definitely suggest an airlock or a blockage.

7 To gain a rough idea of whether the thermostat is working properly when the engine is warming up, without dismantling the system, proceed as follows.

8 With the engine completely cold, start the engine and let it idle, while checking the temperature of the radiator top hose. Periodically check the temperature indicated on the coolant temperature gauge - if overheating is indicated, switch the engine off immediately.

9 The top hose should feel cold for some time as the engine warms up, and should then get warm quite quickly as the thermostat opens.

10 The above is not a precise or definitive test of thermostat operation, but if the system does not perform as described, remove and test the thermostat as described below.

11 The thermostat is located in the cylinder head outlet elbow housing on the left-hand side of the engine.

Removal

Note: *A new thermostat sealing ring may be required on refitting. Check with your local Renault dealer for the availability of parts.*

12 Partially drain the cooling system, as described in Chapter 1A or 1B, so that the coolant level is below the thermostat location.

13 Unclip the engine top cover, and remove it.

14 Remove the air cleaner resonator box (1.4 litre models) or air inlet hoses as necessary (all other models) to improve access, referring to Chapter 4A or 4B.

15 Though not essential, access to the thermostat housing will be improved by removing the battery as described in Chapter 5A.

16 Disconnect the hoses from the thermostat cover, noting their locations **(see illustrations).**

17 Unbolt the housing and remove it, recovering the sealing ring, where applicable. If the thermostat can be renewed separately, it should lift out of the housing – note how it is fitted (any vent hole should be at the top) **(see illustrations).** On some models, the thermostat cannot be removed from its housing, and the housing itself is renewed.

Refitting

18 Refitting is a reversal of removal, bearing in mind the following points:
a) *Where applicable, fit a new sealing ring.*
b) *On completion, refill the cooling system as described in Chapter 1A or 1B.*

5.17a Thermostat housing bolts – petrol models

5.17b On diesel models, remove the three mounting bolts. . .

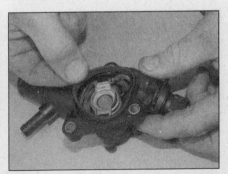
5.17c . . . take off the housing and remove the sealing ring

6.3 Lift the fan assembly to remove it from the radiator

6 Radiator cooling fan – removal and refitting

Removal

1 Disconnect the battery negative lead.
2 The front crossmember ('bonnet slam panel') must now be removed. First, disconnect the bonnet release cable at the in-line connector – unclip the cover, then prise up the top half of the connector, to detach the ballstud fitting. Either unclip the wiring harness along the panel, or disconnect the two plugs in the engine compartment fusebox relevant to this section of harness, and the screenwasher pump connector. Remove the bolt at either end of the panel, two further bolts either side of the centre, and the panel can be removed – unclip more wiring underneath as the panel is lifted out.
3 Disconnect the wiring plug from the fan, and unclip the wiring from the shroud. Lift the fan assembly to release it from the retaining clips either side, and lift it out **(see illustration)**.

Refitting

4 Refit by reversing the removal operations.

7 Radiator cooling fan switch – general information

The operation of the radiator fan is controlled

by the fuel injection ECU. On models with air conditioning, the fan has a slow- and high-speed setting, controlled when the air conditioning is switched on. **Note:** *If there is a fault on the slow-speed circuit, the fan will run at the high-speed setting.*

 a) *Slow speed – if the coolant temperature is greater than 99°C, the fan will operate at its slow speed. When the coolant temperature is lower than 96°C, the fan stops operating.*
 b) *High speed – if the coolant temperature is greater than 102°C, the fan will operate at its high speed. When the coolant temperature is lower than 99°C, the fan stops operating.*
 c) *The coolant temperature warning light will illuminate if the temperature is greater than 114°C. When the coolant temperature drops below 111°C, the light will go out.*

8 Coolant temperature sensor – testing, removal and refitting

1 The temperature sensor is located in the thermostat housing at the left-hand of the cylinder head **(see illustrations)**.

Testing

2 The temperature gauge is fed with a stabilised voltage from the instrument panel feed (via the ignition switch and a fuse). The gauge earth is controlled by the sender. The sender contains a thermistor – an electronic component whose electrical resistance decreases as its temperature rises. When the coolant is cold, the sender resistance is high, current flow through the gauge is reduced, and the gauge needle points towards the cold end of the scale. As the coolant temperature rises and the sender resistance falls, current flow increases, and the gauge needle moves towards the upper end of the scale. If the sender is faulty, it must be renewed.
3 The temperature warning light is fed with a voltage from the instrument panel. The light's earth is controlled by the sender. The sender is effectively a switch, which operates at a

predetermined temperature to earth the light and complete the circuit.
4 If the gauge develops a fault, first check the other instruments; if they do not work at all, check the instrument panel electrical feed. If the readings are erratic, there may be a fault in the voltage stabiliser, which will necessitate renewal of the stabiliser (the stabiliser is integral with the instrument panel printed circuit board – see Chapter 12). If the fault lies in the temperature gauge alone, check it as follows.
5 If the gauge needle remains at the 'cold' end of the scale when the engine is hot, disconnect the sender wiring plug, and earth the relevant wire to the cylinder head. If the needle then deflects when the ignition is switched on, the sender unit is proved faulty, and should be renewed. If the needle still does not move, remove the instrument panel (Chapter 12) and check the continuity of the wire between the sender unit and the gauge, and the feed to the gauge unit. If continuity is shown, and the fault still exists, then the gauge is faulty, and the gauge unit should be renewed.
6 If the gauge needle remains at the 'hot' end of the scale when the engine is cold, disconnect the sender wire. If the needle then returns to the 'cold' end of the scale when the ignition is switched on, the sender unit is proved faulty, and should be renewed. If the needle still does not move, check the remainder of the circuit as described previously.
7 The same basic principles apply to testing the warning light. The light should illuminate when the relevant sender wire is earthed.

Removal and refitting

8 Drain the cooling system as described in Chapter 1A or 1B. Alternatively, remove the expansion bottle cap to depressurise the system, and have the new temperature sensor or a suitable bung to hand.
9 Disconnect the multi-plug, then either release the securing clip and withdraw the temperature sensor from the coolant housing, or unscrew it **(see illustrations)**.
10 Refit the temperature sensor into the coolant housing using a reversal of the removal procedure. Make sure it is either securely held

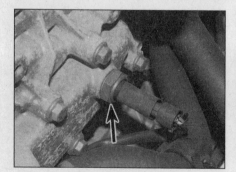

8.1a Temperature sensor location – petrol models

8.1b Temperature sensor location – 1.5 litre diesel models

8.9a Disconnect the wiring plug . . .

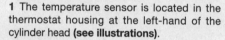

8.9b . . . then pull out the securing clip and withdraw the sensor

8.9c Recover the sensor sealing ring

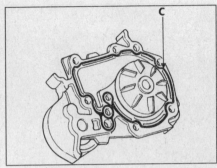

9.8 Apply a bead of sealant (C) to the coolant mating surface – petrol engines

by the clip, or screwed in tightly enough to prevent leaks.

11 Top-up or refill the cooling system, with reference to *Weekly checks*, Chapter 1A or 1B.

9 Water pump – removal and refitting

1 If the water pump is leaking, or is noisy in operation, it must be renewed. If in doubt as to whether a pump is leaking, examine the weep hole at the base of the pump – if water staining (typically white) can be seen around this hole, a new pump is needed. Note that a pump in this condition may only leak when the engine is running.
2 The water pump is driven by the engine's timing belt, which has to be removed when renewing the pump. In light of this, if a new timing belt is being fitted after a high mileage, for peace of mind, some owners will also fit a new pump.

Petrol engines

Note: *A tube of Loctite 518 sealant will be required on refitting.*

Removal

3 Drain the cooling system as described in Chapter 1A.
4 Remove the timing belt as described in Chapter 2A.
5 Slacken and remove the eight coolant pump retaining bolts, noting the locations of the different-size bolts.
6 Withdraw the pump from the block, tapping it with a soft-faced mallet if it is stuck.

Refitting

7 Commence refitting by thoroughly cleaning the mating surfaces of the pump and cylinder block, ensuring that all traces of sealant are removed.
8 Apply a 0.6 to 1.0mm wide band of Loctite 518 sealant to the pump mating face **(see illustration)**.
9 Locate the pump in position. Apply a little thread-locking fluid to water pump bolts 1 and 4 in the tightening sequence, and refit them to their correct locations.

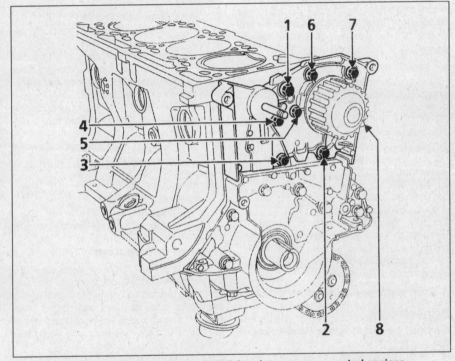

9.10 Coolant pump retaining bolt tightening sequence – petrol engines

10 Working in the sequence shown **(see illustration)**, tighten all the bolts to the specified torque setting. **Note:** *The tightening torque of the M6 bolts and M8 bolts are different (see Specifications at the start of this Chapter).*
11 Refit the timing belt as described in Chapter 2A – it is recommended that a new belt is fitted.
12 On completion, refill the cooling system as described in Chapter 1A.

1.5 litre diesel engine

Removal

13 Drain the cooling system as described in Chapter 1B.
14 Remove the timing belt as described in Chapter 2B.
15 Unbolt the auxiliary drivebelt tensioner and remove it.
16 Disconnect the alternator wiring, then

remove the alternator upper mounting bolt. Loosen the lower mounting bolt, and pivot the alternator forwards.
17 Undo the retaining bolts and remove the timing belt backplate from the cylinder block **(see illustration)**.

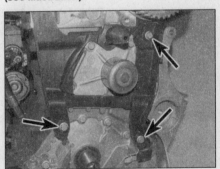

9.17 Unscrew the timing belt backplate securing bolts (arrowed)

9.18 Undo the pump retaining bolts (arrowed)

18 Unscrew the five retaining bolts, then manoeuvre the water pump out of position (see illustration). Recover the pump gasket and discard it; a new one must be used on refitting.

Refitting

19 Ensure that pump and cylinder block/housing mating faces are clean and dry, and that the locating dowels are correctly positioned.

20 Offer up the new gasket (dry) and fit the pump assembly. Apply a little thread-locking fluid to the pump retaining bolts, then refit and tighten them to their specified torque (see illustration).

21 Refit the timing belt backplate cover to the cylinder block, and securely tighten the retaining bolts.

22 Refit the timing belt as described in Chapter 2B – it is recommended that a new belt is fitted.

23 On completion, refill the cooling system as described in Chapter 1B.

1.9 litre diesel engine

Removal

24 Drain the cooling system as described in Chapter 1B.

25 Remove the timing belt as described in Chapter 2C.

26 Slacken and remove the five coolant pump retaining bolts, noting the locations of the different-size bolts (see illustration).

27 Withdraw the pump from the block, tapping it with a soft-faced mallet if it is stuck. Recover the gasket – a new one should be used when refitting.

11.4a Remove the two screws at the base of the surround panel . . .

9.20 Fitting a new gasket to the water pump

Refitting

28 Commence refitting by thoroughly cleaning the mating surfaces of the pump and cylinder block.

29 Locate the pump in position with a new gasket. Apply a little thread-locking fluid to the pump retaining bolts, then refit and tighten them to their specified torque.

30 Refit the timing belt as described in Chapter 2C – it is recommended that a new belt is fitted.

31 On completion, refill the cooling system as described in Chapter 1B.

10 Heating system – general information and checks

General information

1 The heater and fresh air ventilation unit works on the principle of mixing hot and cold air in the proportions selected by means of the central outer (temperature) control knob. Coolant flows through the heater radiator all the time that the engine is running, regardless of the temperature selected.

2 Air distribution is selected by the right-hand control knob. Additional control is possible by opening, closing or redirecting individual vents in the facia panel.

3 An air recirculation control (the left-hand knob) enables the outside air supply to be closed off, while the air inside the car is recirculated. This can be useful to prevent unpleasant odours entering from outside

11.4b . . . then unclip and lift off the panel

9.26 Coolant pump retaining bolts – 1.9 litre diesel engine

the car – for instance, when driving in heavy traffic – but should only be used briefly, as the recirculated air inside the car will soon become stale and may cause light misting.

4 A four-speed blower fan is controlled by the central inner knob.

5 For details of the air conditioning system fitted to some models, refer to Section 14.

Checks

6 Periodically check that all the controls operate as intended. Problems related to the temperature and air distribution controls may be due to cables being broken or disconnected (see Section 13).

7 If the blower does not operate at all, check the fuse and the blower multi-plug before condemning the motor. If one or two speeds do not work, the fault is almost certainly in the heater blower resistor (see Section 11).

8 Check the condition and security of the coolant hoses which feed the heater radiator. The radiator-to-hose joints are at the bulkhead under the bonnet. If water leaks inside the car seem to be coming from the heater, establish whether the leak is of coolant (indicating a leaking heater radiator) or of rainwater (indicating a defective scuttle seal). Cooling system antifreeze has a distinctive sweet smell.

11 Heater/ventilation system components – removal and refitting

Heater control panel

Removal

1 Disconnect the battery negative lead, and move the lead away from the battery (see *Disconnecting the battery*).

2 Remove the radio/CD player as described in Chapter 12.

3 Remove the gear lever housing as described in Chapter 11, Section 23.

4 Remove the two screws at the base of the surround panel, then unclip the surround panel from the facia (it is secured by two clips either side). Reach in behind and disconnect the wiring connectors from the card reader and starter button (see illustrations).

5 Remove the screw either side of the heater

11.4c Reach in behind, and disconnect the wiring plugs from the starter button . . .

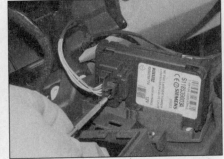

11.4d . . . and from the keycard reader

11.5 Remove the screw from either end of the heater control panel

control panel, then prise the panel out to gain access to the back **(see illustration)**.

6 Disconnect the wiring plug(s) from the back of the panel **(see illustrations)**. **Note:** *Models with automatic air conditioning (climate control) have more than one wiring plug, and no control cables, on the back of the panel.*

7 Where applicable, disconnect the three heater control cables from the back of the panel, as follows. Slide the retaining catch sideways to release the balljoint on the end of each cable, then unclip the cable outer and balljoint from the sockets on the back of the panel **(see illustrations)**. The cables are colour-coded as follows – note their locations for refitting:

 Recirculation control cable – black
 Distribution control cable – white
 Temperature control cable – grey

8 If required, the heater panel illumination bulbs can now be renewed if required. Use a pair of needle-nosed pliers to twist and remove the bulbholder, then pull out the wedge-base bulb **(see illustrations)**.

Refitting

9 Refitting is a reversal of removal. Ensure that the control cables are correctly and securely refitted – the cables do not require adjustment.

Temperature cable

Removal

10 Start by removing the heater control panel as described previously in this Section, and disconnect the cable from the back of

11.6a Disconnect the single wiring plug – manual air conditioning . . .

the panel. If just the cable is to be removed, the panel need not be removed completely, though removing it does improve working room.

11 Remove the glovebox as described in Chapter 11, Section 23. Unclip and remove

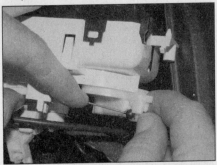

11.7a Release the balljoint on the end of the cable . . .

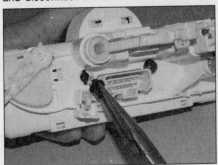

11.8a Twist and remove the bulbholder from the back of the heater panel . . .

11.8b . . . then pull out the wedge-base bulb

11.6b . . . or the three wiring plugs – automatic air conditioning

the air duct now visible, using the information later in this Section.

12 Trace the (grey) cable from the heater control panel to the operating lever on the side of the heater assembly, noting its routing **(see illustration)**.

11.7b . . . then unclip the cable outer

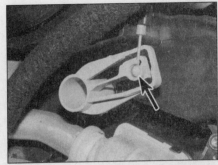

11.12 Trace the temperature cable to the lever above the heater matrix

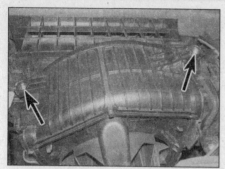

11.24a Remove the two screws from the top of the housing . . .

11.24b . . . and disconnect the wiring plug

11.25 Lift the fan assembly out of the heater housing

13 Using a small screwdriver, release the clip securing the cable outer, then twist and remove it. Press the tab to release the cable's balljoint end fitting, and separate the cable from the lever.

Removal

14 Refitting is a reversal of removal. Ensure the cable ends are securely reconnected, and check the cable operation before refitting the control panel.

Air distribution cable

15 Proceed as described previously in this Section for the temperature control cable. The air distribution control cable is white.

Recirculation cable

Removal

16 Proceed as described in paragraphs 10 and 11.
17 Remove the brake pedal cross-shaft as described in Chapter 9.
18 Trace the two rigid pipes forwards from the heater matrix to the point where they pass through the bulkhead. Remove the two bolts which secure the pipe support collar. Pull the collar out sideways at the bottom, then pull it down and remove it
19 Trace the (black) cable from the heater control panel to the operating lever on the side of the heater assembly, noting its routing.
20 Using a small screwdriver, release the clip securing the cable outer.
21 Press the tab to release the cable's balljoint end fitting, and separate the cable from the lever.

Removal

22 Refitting is a reversal of removal. Ensure the cable ends are securely reconnected, and check the cable operation before refitting the control panel.

Blower motor

Removal

23 Remove the facia panel as described in Chapter 11.
24 Remove the two screws from the top of the fan housing, then disconnect the fan wiring plug **(see illustrations)**.
25 Release the securing clip at the base of the housing, then lift the fan assembly out of the heater housing **(see illustration)**.

Refitting

26 Refit by reversing the removal operations.

Blower motor resistor

Note: *The resistor is located in the on top of the heater assembly, on the driver's side. It is switched into the circuit at low and intermediate speeds. If it fails, it is likely the fan will only run at full speed. On models with automatic air conditioning, note that this function is provided by the power module – see Section 14.*

Removal

27 Remove the facia panel as described in Chapter 11.
28 Remove the resistor mounting bolt, then unclip and withdraw it from its location.
29 There is no wiring connector for the resistor, so its two wires have to be cut in

order to remove it – leave as much wire behind on the heater assembly as possible.

Refitting

30 Refitting is a reversal of removal. Solder the new resistor wires to the old ones, observing the wire colour-coding, and insulate the two joints with tape or heat-shrink tubing.

Blower motor relays

Removal

31 Remove the interior multiplex module as described in Chapter 12.
32 The blower motor relays are located on the same bracket as the interior multiplex module. To remove the relay assembly, disconnect the wiring plug, then depress the central retaining catch and remove it from the bracket.

Refitting

33 Refitting is a reversal of removal.

Heater blower motor switch

Removal

34 Remove the heater control panel as described previously in this Section.
35 The switch is part of the panel, and cannot be renewed separately.

Refitting

36 Refitting is a reversal of removal.

Heater matrix

Removal

37 Disconnect the battery negative lead, and move the lead away from the battery (see *Disconnecting the battery*).
38 Working in the engine compartment, trace the two heater hoses to the bulkhead connections, which must be disconnected – do not confuse these coolant hoses with the additional rigid refrigerant pipes on models with air conditioning, which should not be disturbed **(see illustrations)**. The cooling system does not necessarily have to be drained for this operation – either clamp the hoses beforehand, or turn their hose ends upwards afterwards to minimise coolant loss.
39 Remove the glovebox as described in Chapter 11, Section 23.
40 Unclip and remove the air duct now visible, using the information later in this Section.

11.38a Release the spring clips and disconnect the heater hoses

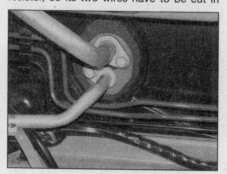

11.38b Do not disconnect the air conditioning rigid pipes

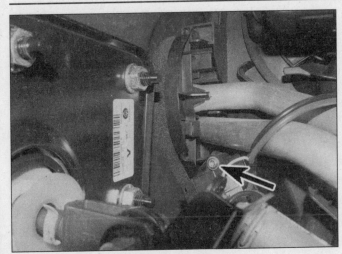

11.43a Remove the screw . . .

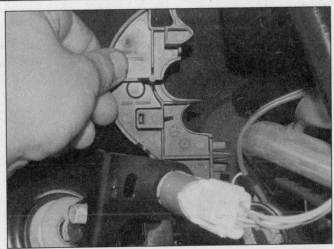

11.43b . . . and take off the pipe support collar at the bulkhead

41 Set the temperature control to the fully-cold position – this moves the heater assembly's control lever upwards, making room for the matrix to be withdrawn.

42 Remove the gear lever housing as described in Chapter 11, Section 23.

43 Trace the two rigid pipes forwards from the heater matrix to the point where they pass through the bulkhead. Remove the screw which secures the pipe support collar. Pull the collar cut sideways at the bottom, then pull it down and remove it – this may prove difficult, as it hits the studs for the brake pedal cross-shaft, but with a little effort, it can be achieved **(see illustrations)**.

44 Place a waterproof sheet inside the car, below the heater matrix, to protect it from coolant spillage. Have ready a shallow container to catch the coolant which will be lost when the heater pipes are disconnected (this applies even if the cooling system was drained, as coolant will remain in the matrix).

45 Loosen the pipe clips immediately in front of the matrix, and pull the pipes from the matrix stubs **(see illustrations)**.

46 Remove the two matrix mounting screws.

47 Move the rigid pipes forwards to clear the matrix, then withdraw the matrix sideways into the passenger footwell, keeping it level to avoid any further coolant spillage **(see illustration)**.

Refitting

48 Refitting is a reversal of removal, noting the following points:

a) *Check the condition of the heater matrix pipe sealing rings, and fit new ones if necessary.*

b) *On completion, fill and bleed the cooling system as described in Chapter 1A or 1B.*

Auxiliary heater

49 Refer to Section 14.

Heater assembly

> ⚠ *Warning: The air conditioning system must be discharged before starting this procedure. Discharging the air conditioning system must be carried out by a specialist, or by a Renault dealer.*

Removal

50 Have the air conditioning system professionally discharged, on models so equipped.

51 Working in the engine compartment, trace the two heater hoses to the bulkhead connections, which must be disconnected – do not confuse these coolant hoses with the additional rigid refrigerant pipes on models with air conditioning. The cooling system does not necessarily have to be drained for this operation – either clamp the hoses beforehand, or turn their hose ends upwards afterwards to minimise coolant loss.

52 On models with air conditioning, there will be four pipes visible (after unclipping the bulkhead soundproofing); the heater hoses are the pair nearest the passenger side, with the refrigerant pipes nearer the centre of the car. **Do not** disturb the refrigerant pipes unless the system has been discharged first (see Section 12) – for maximum personal safety, have these pipes disconnected by the engineer who discharges the system for you, and ensure the system is kept switched off afterwards.

53 Remove the facia panel as described in Chapter 11, including removal of the facia crossmember.

54 Working as described in paragraphs 43 to 45, disconnect the heater matrix pipes.

55 Work around the heater assembly, and remove the mounting nuts/bolts. When all these have been removed, have an assistant

11.45a Loosen the pipe clips – also note the matrix mounting screws (arrowed) . . .

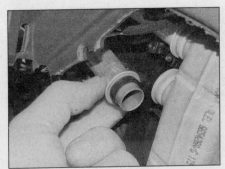

11.45b . . . and disconnect the pipes from the matrix

11.47 Withdraw the matrix sideways into the footwell

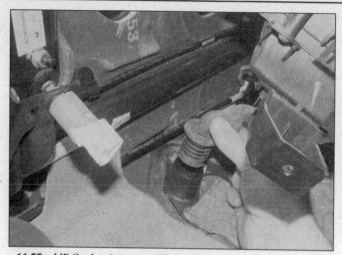

11.55a Lift the heater assembly to release the evaporator drain tube . . .

11.55b . . . and withdraw it from the bulkhead

on hand to withdraw it slowly into the car. On models with air conditioning, lift the assembly at the front to release the evaporator drain tube from its location in the floor **(see illustrations)**.

Refitting

56 Refitting is a reversal of removal, noting the following points:

a) *Check the condition of the heater matrix pipe sealing rings, and fit new ones if necessary.*

b) *On completion, fill and bleed the cooling system as described in Chapter 1A or 1B.*

c) *On models with air conditioning, have the refrigerant pipes reconnected (using new O-ring seals) and the system recharged by a specialist or a Renault dealer.*

Centre vents

57 The centre vents are attached to the heater control panel surround, which is removed as described in paragraphs 1 to 4. Once this is removed, it may be possible to unclip the vents from the surround panel.

Facia end vents

Note: *To remove the central vents, refer to the procedure earlier in this Section.*

Removal

58 Taking care not to mark the surface of the facia, prise out the vent.

11.65a Removing the passenger side duct . . .

59 Withdraw the vent from its location, and remove it.

Refitting

60 Refitting is a reversal of removal.

Air ducts

Removal

61 To remove the ducts supplying the facia side vents, the facia panel must first be removed as described in Chapter 11. The ducts can then be unclipped and removed.

62 To remove the facia-mounted air ducts which supply the footwells, first remove the footwell trim panel on the side concerned, as described in Chapter 11, Section 23.

63 To remove the driver's side duct, remove the driver's lower facia panel as described in Chapter 11, Section 23.

64 If the passenger side duct is being removed, the glovebox must be removed as described in Chapter 11, Section 23.

65 In both cases, the ducts are only clipped in position. Release them at each end, then noting the routing of any facia wiring or cables, unclip and withdraw the ducts – this may require that the duct is partially folded to manoeuvre it out, but try to keep this to a minimum **(see illustrations)**.

66 If required, the floor ducts supplying the rear footwells can also be removed. This

11.65b . . . and the one from the driver's side

involves removing the relevant front seat, and to release the carpet, the footwell and sill trim panels and centre console will also have to come out (see Chapter 11). Once access to the ducts has been gained, the ducts are then simply unclipped and removed.

Refitting

67 Refitting is a reversal of removal.

12 Air conditioning system – general information and precautions

General information

An air conditioning system is available on some models. It enables the temperature of incoming air to be lowered; it also dehumidifies the air, which makes for rapid demisting and increased comfort. Two types of air conditioning are fitted – manual and automatic (climate control).

The cooling side of the system works in the same way as a domestic refrigerator. Refrigerant gas is drawn into a belt-driven compressor, and passes into a condenser in front of the radiator, where it loses heat and becomes liquid. The liquid passes through an expansion valve to an evaporator, where it changes from liquid under high pressure to gas under low pressure. This change is accompanied by a drop in temperature, which cools the evaporator. The refrigerant returns to the compressor and the cycle begins again.

Air blown through the evaporator passes to the air distribution unit, where it is mixed with hot air blown through the heater matrix, to achieve the desired temperature in the passenger compartment. On models with climate control, an auxiliary electric heater is fitted, to provide 'instant' heat from cold, and to assist in maintaining the temperature which has been selected. Otherwise, the heating side of the system works in the same way as on models without air conditioning.

Precautions

⚠️ *Warning: The refrigerant is potentially dangerous, and should only be handled by qualified persons. If it is splashed onto the skin, it can cause frostbite. It is not itself poisonous, but in the presence of a naked flame (including a cigarette) it forms a poisonous gas.*

Uncontrolled discharging of the refrigerant is dangerous, and damaging to the environment. It follows that any work on the air conditioning system which involves opening the refrigerant circuit **must** only be carried out by a Renault dealer or an air conditioning specialist.

Do not operate the air conditioning system if it is known to be short of refrigerant; the compressor may be damaged.

13 Air conditioning system – checking and maintenance

Routine maintenance is limited to checking the tension and condition of the compressor (auxiliary) drivebelt, as described in Chapter 1A or 1B.

Periodic recharging of the system will be required, since there is inevitably a slow loss of refrigerant. It is suggested that the system be inspected by a specialist every year, or at once if a loss of performance is noticed **(see Tool Tip).**

14 Air conditioning system – component removal and refitting

⚠️ *Warning: Do not attempt to open the refrigerant circuit. Refer to the precautions at the end of Section 12.*

1 The only operations described here are those which can be carried out without discharging the refrigerant. All other operations must be referred to a specialist.

Compressor

2 If necessary, the compressor can be unbolted (three bolts) and moved aside, without disconnecting its flexible hoses, after removing the drivebelt (see Chapter 1A or 1B) and disconnecting the wiring plug **(see illustrations)**.

Compressor drivebelt

3 Refer to the auxiliary drivebelt procedures in Chapter 1A or 1B.

Condenser

4 To access the condenser, first remove the front bumper as described in Chapter 11.
5 Unbolt and remove the bumper crossmember, which is secured by a nut and bolt at each end **(see illustrations)**.
6 On diesel models, remove the intercooler as described in Chapter 4B.

Many car accessory shops sell one-shot air conditioning recharge aerosols. These generally contain refrigerant, compressor oil, leak sealer and system conditioner. Some also have a dye to help pinpoint leaks.

⚠️ *Warning: These products must only be used as directed by the manufacturer, and do not remove the need for regular maintenance.*

7 To remove the condenser completely requires that the system is discharged before unscrewing the unions, but with care, the condenser can be lifted from its clips on the radiator and moved aside without disturbing the unions. Protect the condenser while removed by wrapping it in card (or perhaps a piece of old carpet) **(see illustrations)**.

14.2a Disconnect the wiring plug . . .

14.2b . . . then remove the mounting bolts . . .

14.2c . . . and remove the compressor

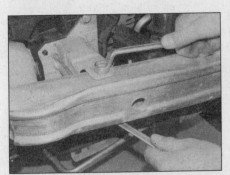

14.5a Unscrew the nut and bolt each end . . .

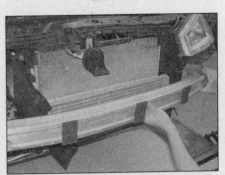

14.5b . . . then take off the bumper crossmember

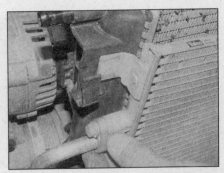

14.7a Lift the condenser out of its clips on the radiator . . .

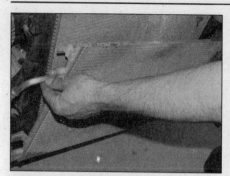

14.7b ... and carefully lower it without straining the pipes

14.7c Protect the condenser by wrapping it up while removed

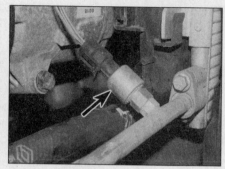

14.9 Pressure sensor location

Pressure sensor

Note: *The pressure sensor is located beside the condenser on the high-pressure pipe between the pressure relief valve and the dehydration canister. This can be removed without draining the system, as it is mounted on a 'Schrader' valve. Based on the pressure sensor information, the engine ECU controls the two-speed radiator cooling fan.*

8 Remove the front bumper for access to the sensor, as described in Chapter 11.

9 Disconnect the wiring connector from the sensor **(see illustration)**.

10 Slacken and remove the pressure sensor from the high-pressure pipe.

11 Refitting is a reversal of removal. Check the condition of the sensor seal, and fit a new one if necessary.

Power module

12 Fitted to models with automatic air conditioning, the power module provides the multiple fan speeds.

13 Remove the facia panel as described in Chapter 11.

14 The power module is located on top of the heater assembly, on the right-hand side.

15 Disconnect the two wiring plugs from the module. Remove the mounting screw, release the upper clip, and withdraw the module from the heater assembly.

16 Refitting is a reversal of removal.

Heating/ventilation control motors

Note: *On models with automatic air conditioning (climate control), electric motors*

replace the cables used on lesser models. Control cables are still used on models with manual air conditioning.

Recirculation motor

17 Remove the facia panel as described in Chapter 11.

18 The motor is located to the left of the fan housing – disconnect the wiring plug, then remove the two mounting bolts and withdraw the motor.

19 Refitting is a reversal of removal. If nothing has been disturbed while the motor was removed, it should fit straight back on – however, if necessary, turn the heater flap spindle until the mark corresponds to that on the motor.

Temperature and distribution motors

20 Remove the driver's lower facia trim panel as described in Chapter 11, Section 23.

21 The temperature motor is located just to the left of the clutch pedal upper switch.

22 To access the distribution motor, which is further forward, unclip the driver's air duct. It may also be necessary to remove the steering column as described in Chapter 10.

23 In both cases, disconnect the wiring plug, then remove the two mounting bolts and withdraw the motor

24 Refitting is a reversal of removal. If nothing has been disturbed while the motor was removed, it should fit straight back on – however, if necessary, turn the heater flap spindle until the mark corresponds to that on the motor.

Auxiliary heater

25 Only fitted to models with automatic air conditioning (climate control), this is an electric heater element fitted to the base of the main heater assembly. It provides 'instant' heat from cold when required, and will also be employed to supplement the heat from the main heater matrix as necessary, to maintain the selected cabin temperature.

26 The auxiliary heater is located just below the heater matrix. To gain access, remove the glovebox and the gear lever housing as described in Chapter 11, Section 23.

27 Slide the wiring plug locking catch upwards to release it, and pull off the plug **(see illustration)**.

28 Remove the two screws from the heater end plate **(see illustration)**.

29 Withdraw the heater unit by sliding it sideways into the footwell **(see illustration)**.

Evaporator

30 Remove the heater assembly as described in Section 11.

31 Turn the assembly upside-down, and remove the four screws from the evaporator cover **(see illustration)**.

32 Release the side catches using a screwdriver, then lift off the cover **(see illustrations)**.

33 Hold the foam gasket clear to allow the refrigerant pipes to clear it, and slide the evaporator up out of the heater housing **(see illustration)**.

34 Refitting is a reversal of removal.

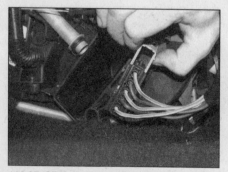

14.27 Slide the wiring plug locking catch upwards to release

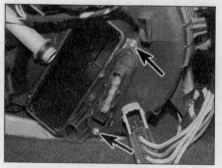

14.28 Remove the auxiliary heater mounting screws

14.29 Withdraw the heater unit into the footwell

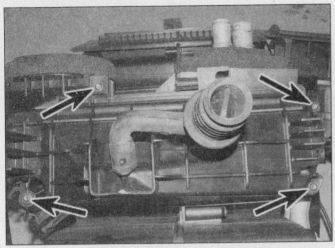

14.31 Remove the four screws . . .

14.32a . . . then release the side catches . . .

Cabin temperature sensor

35 On models with automatic air conditioning (climate control), two sensors monitor the passenger compartment temperature and humidity, and whether the car is parked in strong sunlight, in order to maintain the selected temperature as closely as possible.
36 The temperature sensor is located in front of the interior mirror. Using a small screwdriver, carefully prise off the mirror surround front section. Slide the mirror surround rear cover rearwards to remove **(see illustrations)**.
37 Disconnect the sensor wiring plug, then unscrew the two sensor mounting bolts and remove the sensor **(see illustrations)**.
38 Refitting is a reversal of removal.

Cabin sun sensor

39 Using a small screwdriver, and taking care to protect the finish, prise up and remove the sensor from the centre of the facia panel, right behind the windscreen **(see illustration)**.
40 Disconnect the wiring plug from the sensor, and remove it.
41 Refitting is a reversal of removal.

Exterior temperature sensor

42 The exterior temperature sensor is located in the right-hand exterior mirror.

14.32b . . . and lift off the evaporator cover

14.33 Hold the foam gasket aside when lifting out the evaporator

14.36a Prise off the interior mirror surround front section . . .

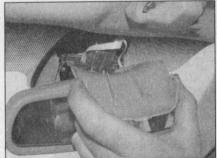

14.36b . . . and remove it

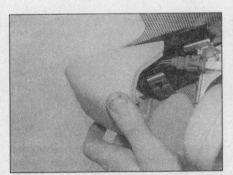

14.36c Slide the mirror surround rear section off towards the windscreen

14.37a Disconnect the sensor wiring plug . . .

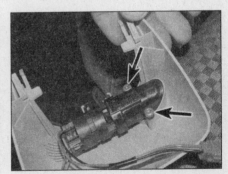

14.37b . . . then remove the screws and take out the sensor

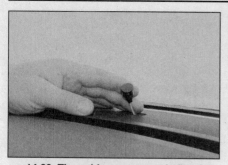

14.39 The cabin sun sensor is fitted centrally on the facia, behind the windscreen

14.44 Unclip the exterior temperature sensor from the door mirror

43 Remove the mirror glass and the mirror front shell as described in Chapter 11.

44 Unclip the sensor from its mounting on the mirror body **(see illustration)**.

45 No wiring plug is provided, so the two sensor wires have to be cut to remove the sensor. When doing this, leave as much wire as possible on the car, to make fitting the new sensor easier.

46 Refitting is a reversal of removal. Solder the new sensor wires to the old ones, observing the wire colour-coding, and insulate the two joints with tape or heat-shrink tubing.

Chapter 4 Part A:
Petrol engine fuel & exhaust systems

Contents

Degrees of difficulty

| **Easy,** suitable for novice with little experience | 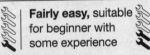 | **Fairly easy,** suitable for beginner with some experience | | **Fairly difficult,** suitable for competent DIY mechanic | | **Difficult,** suitable for experienced DIY mechanic | | **Very difficult,** suitable for expert DIY or professional | |

Specifications

System type
All models . . . . Sagem 3000 sequential multi-point injection

Fuel system data
Air temperature sensor resistance:
At -10°C	9539 ± 915 ohms
At 25°C	2051 ± 123 ohms

Coolant temperature sensor resistance:
At 25°C	2252 ± 112 ohms
At 80°C	280 ± 8 ohms
Crankshaft sensor	200 to 270 ohms at 23°C
Fuel pressure regulator control pressure	3.5 ± 0.06 bars
Fuel pump flow output (minimum)	80 to 120 litres/hour
Idle mixture CO content (non-adjustable)	0.5% maximum at 2500 rpm
Injector resistance	14.5 ± 0.7 ohms at 20°C

Specified idle speed (non-adjustable):
1.4 litre engines	750 ± 50 rpm
1.6 litre engines	700 ± 30 rpm

Throttle potentiometer:
Voltage	5.0 volts
Resistance	1000 ± 250 ohms

Recommended fuel
Minimum octane rating . . . . 95 or 98 RON unleaded (if unavailable, 91 RON may be used). Leaded fuel or LRP must **not** be used

Torque wrench settings

	Nm	lbf ft
Engine right-hand mounting bracket bolts	44	32
Exhaust joining sleeve clamp nut	25	18
Exhaust manifold:		
Heat shield bolts	10	7
Manifold-to-downpipe nuts	20	15
Mounting nuts	23	17
Fuel rail mounting bolts	9	7
Fuel tank	21	15
Inlet manifold bolts:		
Plastic upper section	9	7
Metal lower section	21	16
Knock sensor	20	15
Oxygen sensor	45	33
Throttle body mounting bolts	13	10

1 General information and precautions

The fuel system consists of a fuel tank which is mounted under the rear of the car with an electric fuel pump and fuel filter immersed in it, and a fuel feed line leading to the fuel rail on the engine. A further line from the fuel tank leads to the charcoal canister located beneath the right-hand front wing. Unlike earlier models, there is no return line to the fuel tank. The fuel pump supplies fuel to the fuel rail, which acts as a reservoir for the four fuel injectors which inject fuel into the inlet tracts. The fuel pressure regulator is located in the base of the fuel pump.

The amount of fuel supplied by the injectors is precisely controlled by the Electronic Control Unit (ECU), located behind the battery. The unit uses the signals from the crankshaft position sensor and the camshaft position sensor, to trigger each injector separately in cylinder firing order (sequential injection), with benefits in terms of better fuel economy and leaner exhaust emissions.

The ECU is the heart of the entire engine management system, controlling the fuel injection, ignition and emissions control systems. The module receives information from various sensors which is then computed and compared with pre-set values stored in its memory, to determine the required period of injection.

Information on crankshaft position and engine speed is generated by a crankshaft position sensor. The inductive head of the sensor runs just above the engine flywheel and scans a series of protrusions on the flywheel periphery. As the crankshaft rotates, the sensor transmits a pulse to the system's ignition module every time a protrusion passes it. There is one missing protrusion in the flywheel periphery at a point corresponding to 90° BTDC. The ignition module recognises the absence of a pulse from the crankshaft position sensor at this point to establish a reference mark for crankshaft position. Similarly, the time interval between absent pulses is used to determine engine speed. This information is then fed to the ECU for further processing.

The camshaft position sensor is located on the cylinder head so that it registers with a lobe on the camshaft. The sensor functions in the same way as the crankshaft position sensor, producing a series of pulses; this gives the ECU a reference point, to enable it to determine the firing order, and operate the injectors in the appropriate sequence.

Engine temperature information is supplied by the coolant temperature sensor. The sensor is an NTC (Negative Temperature Coefficient) thermistor – that is, a semi-conductor whose electrical resistance decreases as its temperature increases. The sensor provides the ECU with a constantly-varying (analogue) voltage signal, corresponding to the temperature of the engine coolant. This is used to refine the calculations made by the module, when determining the correct amount of fuel required to achieve the ideal air/fuel mixture ratio.

Inlet air temperature information is provided by another NTC sensor fitted to the inlet manifold. The MAP (manifold absolute pressure) sensor is located on the inlet manifold or throttle housing, and provides the ECU with information on engine load.

The engine features a throttle which is electronically-controlled – an accelerator cable is not fitted. Instead, a throttle position sensor fitted to the accelerator pedal provides the ECU with the throttle opening signal, and this is relayed to a motor-driven throttle valve. This system also enables the ECU to control the engine idle speed, varying the throttle opening as required by changes in engine temperature and load.

Road speed information is provided by the anti-lock braking system (ABS) wheel sensors.

An oxygen sensor in the exhaust system provides the module with constant feedback – 'closed-loop' control – which enables it to adjust the mixture to provide the best possible operating conditions for the catalytic converter. A further sensor is fitted, downstream of the converter, to monitor the converter's operation, and this provides an even finer degree of emission control.

The air inlet side of the system consists of an air cleaner housing, the MAP sensor, an inlet hose and duct, a throttle housing, and a two-piece inlet manifold.

Both the idle speed and mixture are under the control of the ECU, and cannot be adjusted.

Precautions

⚠️ **Warning: Many of the procedures in this Chapter require the removal of fuel lines and connections, which may result in some fuel spillage. Before carrying out any operation on the fuel system, refer to the precautions given in Safety first! at the beginning of this manual, and follow them implicitly. Petrol is a highly-dangerous and volatile liquid, and the precautions necessary when handling it cannot be overstressed.**

Note 1: Residual pressure will remain in the fuel lines long after the car was last used. When disconnecting any fuel line, first depressurise the fuel system as described in Section 3. Even after this is done, fuel will still be present – always have clean rag handy to catch any spillage.

Note 2: Before disconnecting any of the fuel injection system sensor wiring plugs, ensure at least that the ignition is switched off (ideally, disconnect the battery). If a sensor is disconnected while 'live', it could result in a fault code being logged in the system memory, and may even cause damage to the component concerned.

2 Unleaded petrol – general information and usage

All petrol models are designed to run on fuel with an octane rating of 95 or 98 RON, however, if unavailable, 91 octane fuel may be used. All models have a catalytic converter, and so must be run on unleaded fuel **only**. Under no circumstances should leaded fuel or LRP be used, as this will damage the converter.

4.1a Remove the single front mounting bolt . . .

4.1b . . . then pull off the air inlet duct and remove the resonator box

4.2 Squeeze the quick-release fitting and disconnect the servo hose

3 Fuel system – depressurisation

Note: *Refer to the warning note in Section 1 before proceeding.*

⚠️ **Warning: The following procedures will merely relieve the pressure in the fuel system – remember that fuel will still be present in the system components, and take precautions accordingly before disconnecting any of them.**

1 The fuel system referred to in this Chapter is defined as the fuel tank and tank-mounted fuel pump/fuel gauge sender unit, the fuel rail, the fuel injectors, and the metal pipes and flexible hoses of the fuel lines between these components. All these contain fuel, which will be under pressure while the engine is running and/or while the ignition is switched on.

2 The pressure will remain for some time after the ignition has been switched off, and must be relieved before any of these components is disturbed for servicing work.

3 Whichever depressurisation method is used, bear in mind the following points:

a) *Plug the disconnected pipe ends, to minimise fuel loss and prevent the entry of dirt into the fuel system.*

a) *Note that, once the fuel system has been depressurised and drained (even partially), it will take significantly longer to restart the engine – perhaps several seconds of cranking – before the system is refilled and pressure restored.*

Method 1

4 The simplest depressurisation method is to disconnect the fuel pump electrical supply by removing the fuel pump fuse (refer to the wiring diagrams or the label on the relevant fusebox for exact location) and starting the engine; allow the engine to idle until it stops through lack of fuel. Turn the engine over once or twice on the starter to ensure that all pressure is released, then switch off the ignition; do not forget to refit the fuse when work is complete.

Method 2

5 Place a suitable container beneath the

connection or union to be disconnected, and have a large rag ready to soak up any escaping fuel not being caught by the container. Slowly loosen the connection or union nut to avoid a sudden release of pressure, and position the rag around the connection, to catch any fuel spray which may be expelled.

4 Air cleaner and inlet ducts – removal and refitting

Removal

1.4 litre engine

1 Remove the front mounting bolt, then pull off the air inlet duct and lift out the resonator box, noting how it is clipped to the main air cleaner body at the back **(see illustrations)**.

2 Disconnect the brake servo vacuum hose

4.3a Remove the two air cleaner cover screws . . .

4.3c . . . and take out the filter element

from the inlet manifold, and move the hose to one side **(see illustration)**.

3 Unscrew the two air cleaner cover screws at the top, then remove the cover and take out the filter element **(see illustrations)**.

4 To improve access to the air cleaner, remove the windscreen cowl panels as described in Chapter 11.

5 Disconnect the oxygen sensor wiring plug at the rear of the engine, and unbolt the air cleaner retaining bracket just in front of it **(see illustration)**.

6 Unscrew and remove the two air cleaner mounting bolts, one either side of the throttle body **(see illustrations)**, then carefully lift the air cleaner off the throttle body and away from the rear of the engine.

1.6 litre engine

7 Remove the battery and battery tray as described in Chapter 5A. Detach the support

4.3b . . . then remove the cover . . .

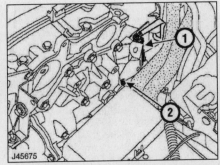

4.4 Disconnect the oxygen sensor wiring plug (1) and unbolt the bracket (2)

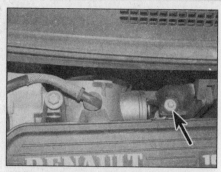

4.6a Unscrew the air cleaner mounting bolt to the left . . .

4.6b . . . and to the right of the throttle body

4.9a Slacken the hose clips . . .

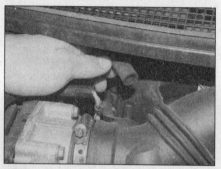

4.9b . . . then pull off the breather hose . . .

4.9c . . . and remove the air cleaner inlet duct

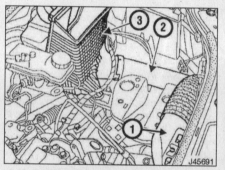

4.14 Inlet air duct (1), duct from resonator box (2) and air cleaner (3)

bracket for the ECU, and remove it together with the ECU.

8 Remove the larger left-hand section of the windscreen cowl panel for access, as

described in Chapter 11. Remove the air filter access panel – See Chapter 1A, Section 17. If the air filter has never been disturbed before, it may be necessary to cut the plastic side 'perforations' securing the access flap with a sharp knife, before hinging the flap upwards.

9 Slacken the hose clips at either end of the air duct between the air cleaner and throttle body, then pull off the breather hose and lift the duct out **(see illustrations)**.

10 Loosen the left-hand front wheel bolts, then jack up the front of the car, and support it on axle stands (see *Jacking and vehicle support*). Remove the front wheel.

11 Working in the wheel arch, remove the screws and clips securing the plastic liner, and pull it down to remove it – note that the arch liner is in two sections.

12 Remove the resonator box and tube from the front of the wheel arch.

13 Back in the engine compartment, unclip the inlet air ducting from the front panel and from the base of the air cleaner.

14 Finally, lift the air cleaner out, noting how it fits into its mounting points **(see illustration)**.

Refitting

15 Refitting is a reversal of removal. On 1.4 litre engines, apply a little grease to the throttle body seal before fitting the air cleaner.

5.2 Accelerator pedal mounting bolts

5 Accelerator pedal – removal and refitting

Removal

1 Remove the driver's side facia lower trim panel from under the steering column, as described in Chapter 11, Section 23.

2 Remove the two pedal mounting bolts, and carefully withdraw the pedal assembly **(see illustration)**.

3 Disconnect the wiring plug from the accelerator pedal sensor, and remove the assembly completely **(see illustration)**.

4 If required, the pedal sensor can be removed by first prise off the pedal link rod's ball fitting (where applicable), then unscrewing the three nuts **(see illustration)**.

5 Examine the pedal and pivot for signs of wear and renew as necessary.

Refitting

6 Refitting is a reversal of removal.

5.3 Disconnect the wiring plug from the pedal sensor

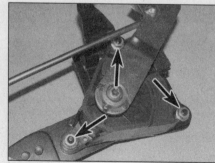

5.4 Pedal sensor mounting nuts

6 Fuel pump/fuel pressure – checking

Note: *Refer to the warning note in Section 1 before proceeding.*

Fuel pump

1 Switch on the ignition, and listen for the fuel pump (the sound of an electric motor running, audible from beneath the rear seats). Assuming there is sufficient fuel in the tank, the pump should start and run for approximately one or two seconds, then stop, each time the ignition is switched on. **Note:** *If the pump runs continuously all the time the ignition is switched on, the electronic control system is running in the backup (or 'limp-home') mode. This almost certainly indicates a fault has been logged in the ECU fault memory, and the car should therefore be taken to a Renault dealer for a full test of the complete system, using the correct diagnostic equipment; do not waste time or risk damaging the components by trying to test the system without such facilities.*
2 If the pump does not run at all, check the fuse and wiring (see Chapter 12).

Fuel pressure

3 A fuel pressure gauge will be required for this check, and should be connected in the fuel line at the front of the inlet manifold, where the fuel supply pipe joins the fuel rail. Always follow the gauge maker's instructions.

4 Start the engine and allow it to idle. Note the gauge reading as soon as the pressure stabilises, and compare it with the regulated fuel pressure figure listed in the Specifications.
  a) *If the pressure is high, check for a restricted fuel return line. If the line is clear, this indicates a fuel pressure regulator fault.*
  b) *If the pressure is low, this may indicate a blocked or kinked fuel line, blocked fuel filter, failing fuel pump, or again, a pressure regulator fault.*
5 The fuel pump, filter and pressure regulator are contained in a single unit, immersed in the fuel tank. It appears that a fault in any one of the three will require a complete new unit, but check for spares availability.
6 Carefully disconnect the fuel pressure gauge, depressurising the system first as described in Section 2. Be sure to cover the fitting with a rag before slackening it. Mop up any spilt petrol.
7 Run the engine, and check that there are no fuel leaks.

7 Fuel pump/sender unit – removal and refitting

Note: *Refer to the warning note in Section 1 before proceeding.*
  Proceed as described in Chapter 4B, Section 4 for the diesel models, noting that there is no fuel return pipe on petrol models.

8 Fuel gauge sender unit and pressure regulator – testing, removal and refitting

Testing

1 The fuel gauge sender unit is supplied as part of the fuel pump assembly, however it is possible to test its operation and remove it.
2 To test the sender unit, first remove the pump as described in Section 7.
3 Disconnect the wiring plug from the cover and connect an ohmmeter to the two terminals **(see illustration)**.
4 With the pump assembly upright on the bench, measure the resistance of the sender unit with the float at different heights **(see illustration)**. The exact resistances are not important, but it should be clear if the sender unit is not operating correctly.

Removal

5 To remove the sender unit, first release the wiring from the clips, then unclip the unit from the main body **(see illustrations)**.
6 To remove the fuel pressure regulator, unclip the base cover, then pull out the retaining spring clip and remove the regulator **(see illustrations)**.
7 Use a screwdriver to prise off the gauze filter. Clean any sediment from the filter and cover.

Refitting

8 Refitting is a reversal of removal, but test the unit before refitting the pump assembly to the tank.

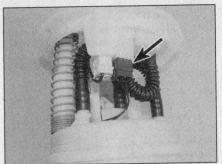

8.3 Disconnect the wiring from the cover

8.4 Testing the sender unit with an ohmmeter

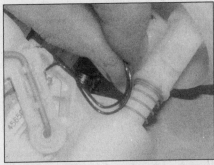

8.5a Remove the wiring from the clips . . .

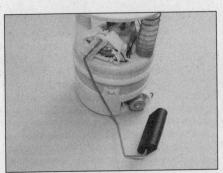

8.5b . . . then unclip the unit from the main body

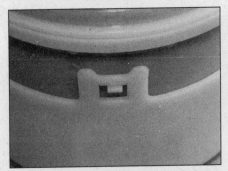

8.6a Release the clips and remove the base cover . . .

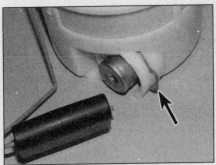

8.6b . . . then pull out the spring clip to remove the pressure regulator

9.5a Remove the three screws . . .

9.5b . . . and take out the access plate

9.7 Prise up the plastic cover

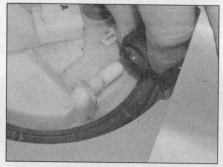

9.9 Disconnect the fuel supply hose

9 Fuel tank – removal and refitting

Note: *Refer to the warning note in Section 1 before proceeding.*

Removal

1 Before removing the fuel tank, as much fuel as possible must be drained from it. Since a drain plug is not provided, it is preferable to carry out the removal operation when the tank is nearly empty.

2 Disconnect the battery negative lead (refer to *Disconnecting the battery* in the Reference Section).

3 Remove the rear seats as described in Chapter 11 (centre row on Grand Scénic) for access to the fuel pump cover.

4 Carefully prise the retaining plugs out to release the carpet, then unclip the rear seat mountings and move the carpet clear. Detach and remove the soundproofing under the carpet.

5 Remove the three screws and take out the floor access plate **(see illustrations)**.

6 Where applicable, remove the radio tuner/amplifier from its floor location as described in Chapter 12.

7 Unclip the wiring, then prise up the plastic cover to expose the sender unit **(see illustration)**.

8 Disconnect the wiring connector from the fuel pump, and tape the connector to the car body, to prevent it disappearing behind the tank.

9 Disconnect the quick-release fitting on the fuel supply hose by squeezing together the locking button, then pull off the hose **(see illustration)**.

10 Loosen the rear wheel bolts. Chock the front wheels, then jack up the rear of the car and support on axle stands (see *Jacking and vehicle support*). Remove the rear wheels.

11 Remove the rear exhaust silencer, then

unhook and lower the exhaust as much as possible, referring to Section 15. For maximum working room, the complete exhaust system (from the manifold back) should be removed.

12 Remove the bolts and clips securing the tank heat shield, then remove the shield, manoeuvring it out from the rear axle.

13 Unclip the charcoal canister from the front left of the fuel tank – it should pull off to the side **(see illustration)**. Disconnect the breather hose and the two quick-release hoses at the front, noting their locations for correct refitting.

14 On models with the optional xenon headlights, disconnect the wiring from the height adjustment sensor, then unclip the linkage from the rear axle.

15 Unclip the brake and fuel pipes from the side and front of the tank. As far as possible, move or tie them clear of the tank, so that they cannot get caught up when the tank is lowered.

16 Loosen the hose clips, then disconnect the filler hose, and the smaller vent hose, from the tank – anticipate fuel spillage when this is done. If necessary, obtain some new Jubilee hose clips for refitting **(see illustration)**.

17 Place a trolley jack with an interposed block of wood beneath the tank, then raise the jack until it is supporting the weight of the tank.

18 Loosen and remove the three tank mounting bolts **(see illustration)**, taking care to steady the tank on the jack as necessary (especially if the tank has not been fully drained, as the fuel inside may cause the tank to tilt). When the bolts are free, have an assistant help to lower the tank out. The tank will have to be tilted around the rear axle and exhaust pipe (if the system was not removed). Check all the way down that no pipes or cables have become caught up. Remove the tank from under the car.

Inspection

19 If the tank is contaminated with sediment or water, remove the fuel pump/sender unit (Section 7), and swill the tank out with clean fuel. The tank is injection-moulded from a synthetic material – if seriously damaged, it should be renewed. However, in certain cases, it may be possible to have small leaks or minor damage repaired. Seek the advice of a specialist before attempting to repair the fuel tank.

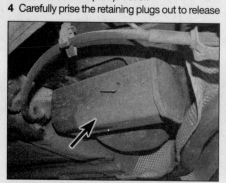

9.13 The charcoal canister is a large plastic box on the left of the tank

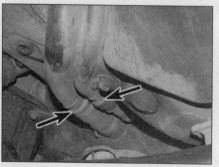

9.16 Loosen the hose clips and disconnect the tank filler and vent hoses

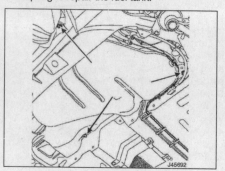

9.18 Fuel tank mounting bolts

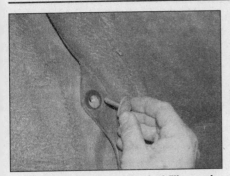

10.3 Removing one of the fuel filler neck bolts inside the wheel arch

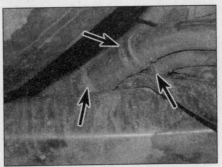

10.4 Loosen the filler and vent pipe hose clips

10.5 Filler neck securing screws inside filler cap

20 Whilst the fuel tank is removed from the car, it should be placed in a safe area where sparks or open flames cannot ignite the fumes coming out of the tank. Be especially careful inside garages where a natural-gas type appliance is located, because the pilot light could cause an explosion.

Refitting

21 Refitting is the reverse of the removal procedure, noting the following points:
a) *When lifting the tank back into position, take care to ensure that the hoses are not trapped between the tank and car body.*
b) *Ensure that all pipes and hoses are correctly routed, and make sure they are securely clipped in position.*
c) *If evidence of contamination was found, do not return any previously-drained fuel to the tank unless it is carefully filtered first.*
d) *On completion, refill the tank with a small amount of fuel, and check for signs of leakage prior to taking the car out on the road.*
e) *On models with xenon headlights, have the system reset by a Renault dealer on completion.*

10 Fuel tank filler neck – removal and refitting

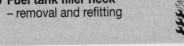

Note: *Refer to the warning note in Section 1 before proceeding.*

Removal

1 Run the fuel level as low as possible prior to removing the tank, to reduce the amount of fuel spillage when the neck is removed.
2 Loosen the right-hand rear wheel bolts, then raise and support the rear of the car, and support it on axle stands (see *Jacking and vehicle support*). Remove the right-hand rear wheel.
3 Remove the two bolts securing the filler neck and vent pipe support bracket to the wheel arch **(see illustration)**.
4 At the lower end of the filler neck, release the clips securing the flexible filler and vent hoses which lead to the tank, and disconnect the hoses **(see illustration)**. Have a container ready, to catch any spilt fuel. If necessary, obtain some new Jubilee hose clips for refitting.

5 Open the fuel filler cap, and remove the two screws inside which secure the top of the filler neck **(see illustration)**.
6 Returning to the wheel arch, pull the filler neck downwards and remove it. Also disconnect the vent hose **(see illustration)**.

Refitting

7 Refitting is a reversal of removal.

11 Throttle body – removal and refitting

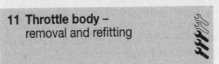

Note: *Refer to the warning note in Section 1 before proceeding.*

Removal

1 Depressurise the fuel system with reference to Section 3.
2 Disconnect the battery negative lead (refer to *Disconnecting the battery* in the Reference Section) and proceed as described under the relevant heading.
3 Remove the engine top cover, and the windscreen cowl panels as described in Chapter 11.

1.4 litre engine

4 Remove the air cleaner as described in Section 4.
5 Disconnect the throttle body wiring plug **(see illustration)**.
6 Disconnect the vapour hose from the canister-purge solenoid to the side of the throttle body **(see illustration)**.

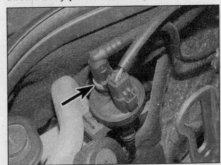

11.6 Disconnect the canister-purge solenoid vapour hose

10.6 Disconnect the fuel filler vent hose

7 Unscrew the three mounting bolts, and remove the throttle body **(see illustration)**. Recover the rubber seal – a new one should be used whenever it is disturbed.
8 Clean the mating faces of the throttle body and inlet manifold.

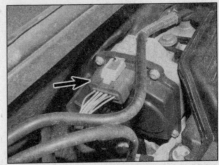

11.5 Disconnect the throttle body wiring plug

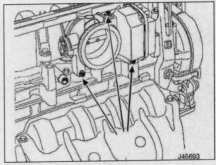

11.7 Throttle body mounting bolts – 1.4 litre

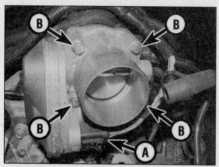

11.12 Throttle body wiring plug (A) and mounting bolts (B – one hidden)

1.6 litre engine

9 Slacken the hose clips at either end of the air duct between the air cleaner and throttle body, then pull off the breather hose and lift the duct out **(refer to illustrations 4.9a, b and c)**.
10 Disconnect the throttle body wiring plug.
11 Disconnect the vapour hose from the back of the throttle body which leads to the canister-purge solenoid.
12 Unscrew the four mounting bolts, and remove the throttle body **(see illustration)**. Recover the rubber seal – a new one should be used whenever it is disturbed.
13 Clean the mating faces of the throttle body and inlet manifold.

Refitting

14 Refitting is a reversal of removal, noting the following points:
a) Use a new throttle body seal, lightly greased on 1.4 litre engines.
b) Tighten the throttle body mounting bolts to the specified torque.
c) If a new throttle body has been fitted, it will need to be initialised and set up using Renault diagnostic equipment before it will function correctly.

12 Fuel injection system
– checking

Note: Refer to the warning note in Section 1 before proceeding.
1 If a fault appears in the fuel injection system, first ensure that all the system wiring connectors

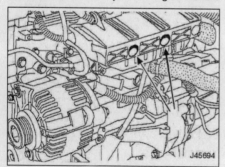

13.2 Fuel rail shield mounting nuts – 1.4 litre

12.2 Remove the centre console front cover panel to access the diagnostic connector

are securely connected and free of corrosion – also refer to paragraphs 6 to 9 below. Then ensure that the fault is not due to poor maintenance; ie, check that the air filter element is clean, the spark plugs are in good condition and correctly gapped, the cylinder compression pressures are correct, the ignition system wiring is in good condition and securely connected, and the engine breather hoses are clear and undamaged, referring to Chapters 1A, 2A and 5B.
2 If these checks fail to reveal the cause of the problem, the car should be taken to a suitably-equipped Renault dealer for testing. A diagnostic connector is fitted behind a cover at the front of the centre console, into which dedicated electronic test equipment can be plugged **(see illustration)**. The test equipment is capable of 'interrogating' the engine management system ECU electronically and accessing its internal fault log (reading fault codes).
3 Fault codes can only be extracted from the ECU using a dedicated fault code reader. A Renault dealer will obviously have such a reader, but they are also available from other suppliers. It is unlikely to be cost-effective for the private owner to purchase a fault code reader, but a well-equipped local garage or auto-electrical specialist will have one.
4 Using this equipment, faults can be pinpointed quickly and simply, even if their occurrence is intermittent. Testing all the system components individually in an attempt to locate the fault by elimination is a time-consuming operation that is unlikely to be fruitful (particularly if the fault occurs dynamically), and carries a high risk of damage to the ECU's internal components.

13.3 Disconnect the fuel supply hose by squeezing the quick-release fitting

5 Experienced home mechanics equipped with an accurate tachometer and a carefully-calibrated exhaust gas analyser may be able to check the exhaust gas CO content and the engine idle speed; if these are found to be out of specification, then the car must be taken to a suitably-equipped Renault dealer for assessment. Neither the air/fuel mixture (exhaust gas CO content) nor the engine idle speed are manually adjustable; incorrect test results indicate the need for maintenance (possibly, injector cleaning) or a fault within the fuel injection system.
6 Certain faults, such as failure of one of the engine management system sensors, will cause the system will revert to a backup (or 'limp-home') mode. This is intended to be a 'get-you-home' facility only – the engine management warning light will come on when this mode is in operation.
7 In this mode, the signal from the defective sensor is substituted with a fixed value (it would normally vary), which may lead to loss of power, poor idling, and generally-poor running, especially when the engine is cold.
8 However, the engine may in fact run quite well in this situation, and the only clue (other than the warning light) would be that the exhaust CO emissions (for example) will be higher than they should be.
9 Bear in mind that, even if the defective sensor is correctly identified and renewed, the engine will not return to normal running until the fault code is erased, taking the system out of backup mode. This also applies even if the cause of the fault was a loose connection or damaged piece of wire – until the fault code is erased, the system will continue in backup mode.

13 Fuel injection system components
– removal and refitting

Note: Refer to the warning note in Section 1 before proceeding.

Fuel rail and injectors

Note: If a faulty injector is suspected, before condemning the injector, it is worth trying the effect of one of the proprietary injector-cleaning treatments.

1 Depressurise the fuel system as described in Section 3, then disconnect the battery negative lead (see Disconnecting the battery).

1.4 litre engine

2 Unscrew the two nuts securing the fuel rail shield, and take off the shield **(see illustration)**.
3 Disconnect the fuel supply pipe from the fuel rail – plug or tape over the exposed connections **(see illustration)**.
4 Disconnect the wiring plugs from the four injectors and the knock sensor on the front of the engine, and move the wiring loom to one side.

1.6 litre engine

5 Remove the upper section of the inlet manifold as described in Section 14.

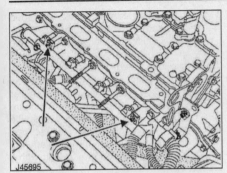

13.7a Fuel rail mounting bolts – 1.4 litre

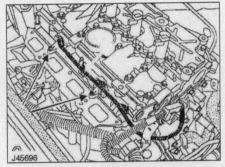

13.7b Fuel rail mounting bolts – 1.6 litre

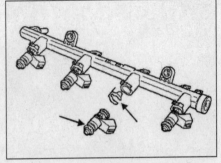

13.8 Remove the clips and pull out the injectors

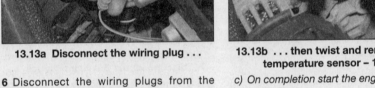

13.13a Disconnect the wiring plug . . .

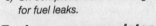

13.13b . . . then twist and remove the air temperature sensor – 1.6 litre

13.13c Air temperature sensor – 1.4 litre

6 Disconnect the wiring plugs from the injectors, and move the wiring loom to one side.

All engines

7 Unscrew and remove the two mounting bolts, and carefully ease the fuel rail together with the injectors from the inlet manifold **(see illustrations)**.

8 Note the fitted positions of the injectors, then remove the clips and ease the injectors from the fuel rail **(see illustration)**.

9 Remove the sealing rings from the grooves at each end of the injectors and obtain new ones.

10 Refitting is a reversal of the removal procedure, noting the following points:

a) *Renew all sealing rings, using a smear of engine oil to aid installation.*

b) *Refit the fuel rail assembly to the manifold, making sure the sealing rings remain correctly positioned, and tighten the retaining bolts to the specified torque.*

c) *On completion start the engine and check for fuel leaks.*

Fuel pressure regulator

11 The pressure regulator is located on the fuel pump inside the fuel tank, and may be removed after removing the pump (see Section 7).

Inlet air temperature sensor

Removal

12 The air temperature sensor is located on the upper section of the inlet manifold.

13 To remove the sensor, first disconnect the wiring plug, then twist and remove the sensor **(see illustrations)**.

Refitting

14 Refitting is a reversal of removal. Check the condition of the sensor's O-ring seal, and if necessary fit a new one.

Coolant temperature sensor

15 The sensor is located on the thermostat housing at the left-hand end of the cylinder head, above the transmission bellhousing. Refer to Chapter 3 for removal and refitting details.

Knock sensor

16 The knock sensor is located on the front of the cylinder block. Refer to Chapter 5B for the removal and refitting procedures.

Manifold absolute pressure (MAP) sensor

Removal

17 The MAP sensor is mounted on the rear of the upper section of the inlet manifold.

18 Disconnect the wiring and (where applicable) the vacuum hose from the sensor **(see illustration)**.

19 Unscrew the mounting bolts and remove the sensor.

Refitting

20 Refitting is a reversal of removal.

Fuel system and fuel pump relays

21 The switching functions for the fuel injection system are contained within the engine multiplex module (also known as the protection and switching unit) – see Chapter 12, Section 3 for more details.

Crankshaft speed/position sensor

Removal

22 The sensor is mounted on the top of the transmission bellhousing at the left-hand end of the cylinder block **(see illustration)**.

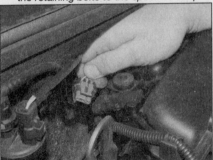

13.18 Disconnect the wiring plug from the MAP sensor – 1.6 litre

13.22 Crankshaft speed/position sensor location

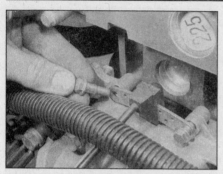

13.26 Unscrew and remove the crankshaft speed/position sensor

13.28 On 1.6 litre models, unclip the engine top cover

13.29a Disconnect the valve timing solenoid wiring plug . . .

13.29b . . . then remove the single bolt and withdraw the solenoid

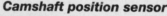

13.32 Camshaft position sensor wiring plug

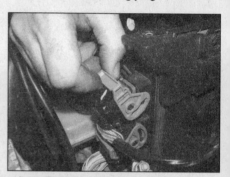

13.40 Slide the locking catches back and disconnect the ECU wiring plugs

23 Remove the air cleaner resonator box (1.4 litre) or air hoses as necessary (1.6 litre) to improve access, referring to Section 4.

24 Remove the battery and battery tray as described in Chapter 5A.

25 Trace the wiring back from the sensor to the wiring connector, and disconnect it from the main harness.

26 Unscrew the retaining bolts and remove the sensor (see illustration).

Refitting

27 Refitting is a reversal of removal. Ensure that the sensor retaining bolts are securely tightened – note that only the special shouldered bolts originally fitted must be used to secure the sensor; these bolts locate the sensor precisely to give the correct air gap between the sensor tip and the flywheel/driveplate.

Variable valve timing solenoid

28 Only fitted to 1.6 litre engines, the solenoid

13.41 Remove the ECU with its mounting bracket

is mounted on top of the engine, near the timing belt end. Unclip and remove the engine top cover for access (see illustration).

29 Disconnect the wiring plug, then unscrew the single mounting bolt and withdraw the solenoid from the top of the engine (see illustrations).

30 Refitting is a reversal of removal. Ensure that the mounting bolt and the wiring plug are secure.

Camshaft position sensor

31 The sensor is mounted at the transmission end of the inlet camshaft. On 1.6 litre engines, unclip and remove the engine top cover for access.

32 Disconnect the sensor wiring plug, then unscrew the mounting bolt and withdraw the sensor from the cylinder head (see illustration).

33 Refitting is a reversal of removal. Ensure

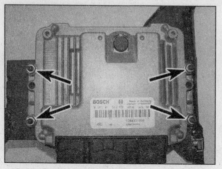

13.42 Separate the ECU by removing the four mounting bracket bolts

that the mounting bolt and the wiring plug are secure.

Electronic control unit (ECU)

Note: *The ECU is electronically-coded to match the engine immobiliser and certain other engine components. If the ECU is being removed in order to fit a new unit, it is highly recommended that the work be carried out by a Renault dealer.*

Caution: The ECU wiring plugs should only be disconnected after the disconnecting battery. If the ECU is unplugged 'live', it could be damaged.

Removal – 1.4 litre engine

34 Remove the windscreen cowl panels as described in Chapter 11. Remove the clips and take off the battery cover.

35 Disconnect the battery negative lead, and move the lead away from the battery (see *Disconnecting the battery*).

36 Slide back the locking catches, and disconnect the wiring plugs from the ECU.

37 Remove the four mounting bolts and lift out the ECU.

Removal – 1.6 litre engine

38 Remove the windscreen cowl panels as described in Chapter 11. Unclip and remove the engine top cover.

39 Remove the battery and battery tray as described in Chapter 5A.

40 Slide back the locking catches, and disconnect the wiring plugs from the ECU (see illustration).

41 Detach the ECU and its mounting bracket, and remove it complete (see illustration).

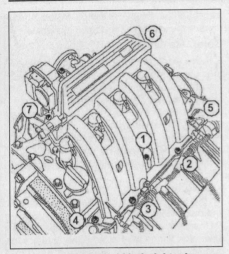

14.6 Inlet manifold bolt tightening sequence – 1.4 litre

42 If required, the ECU can be separated from the bracket, after removing the four mounting bolts **(see illustration)**.

Refitting

43 Refitting is a reversal of removal. Ensure that the ECU wiring plugs are securely reconnected.

14 Manifolds – removal and refitting

Inlet manifold

1 To improve access to the manifolds and related components from above, remove the windscreen cowl panels as described in Chapter 11.

2 Disconnect the battery negative lead, and move the lead away from the battery (see *Disconnecting the battery*).

Upper section – 1.4 litre

3 Remove the throttle body as described in Section 11.

4 Disconnect the wiring plugs from the ignition coils, MAP sensor and air temperature sensor – note their positions for refitting. Move the wiring harness to one side.

5 Remove the seven manifold mounting bolts – five along the front joint, two at the rear. Lift the manifold upper section away. Recover the rubber seals – new ones must be used when refitting.

6 Refitting is a reversal of removal. Use new seals on the manifold and throttle body, and tighten the manifold bolts in the sequence shown to the specified torque **(see illustration)**.

Upper section – 1.6 litre

7 Remove the air cleaner duct from the throttle body as described in Section 4.

8 Disconnect the throttle body wiring plug, and the vapour hose from the back of the throttle body which leads to the canister-

purge solenoid. Unclip the vapour hose from the manifold.

9 Disconnect the brake servo vacuum hose from the manifold.

10 Disconnect the wiring plugs from the ignition coils, MAP sensor and air temperature sensor – note their positions for refitting. Unclip the wiring harness from the manifold, and move it to one side.

11 Depressurise the fuel system as described in Section 2, then disconnect the fuel supply pipe from the fuel rail at the front of the manifold – plug or tape over the exposed connections.

12 Remove the eight manifold mounting bolts – five along the front joint, three at the rear. Lift the manifold upper section away. Recover the rubber seals – new ones must be used when refitting. If required, the throttle valve can be unbolted and removed as described in Section 11.

13 Refitting is a reversal of removal. Use new seals on the manifold and throttle body (where applicable), and tighten the manifold bolts in the sequence shown to the specified torque **(see illustration)**.

Lower section

14 Depressurise the fuel system as described in Section 2.

15 Remove the upper section as described previously in this Section.

16 Remove the fuel rail and injectors as described in Section 13.

17 On 1.4 litre engines, at the transmission end of the cylinder head, remove the nut securing the wiring harness. Unbolt the dipstick tube.

18 The manifold lower section is secured by a total of eleven bolts – ten manifold bolts, and one engine right-hand mounting bracket bolt at the timing end. Remove the bolts, then withdraw the lower section. Recover the gasket – a new one must be used when refitting.

19 Refitting is a reversal of removal, noting the following points:

a) Use a new gasket.

b) Offer the manifold into position, and fit the engine mounting bracket bolt finger-tight.

c) Fit and tighten the manifold bolts in a diagonal sequence to the specified torque, then fully tighten the engine mounting bracket bolt.

d) Refit the fuel rail and injectors, using new O-ring seals, as described in Section 13.

e) Refit the manifold upper section as described previously.

Exhaust manifold

20 On 1.4 litre engines, remove the air cleaner as described in Section 4.

21 Remove the inlet manifold upper section as described previously.

22 Jack up the front of the car, and support it on axle stands (see *Jacking and vehicle support*).

23 Trace the wiring forwards from the rear oxygen sensor, and disconnect it at the plug.

14.13 Inlet manifold bolt tightening sequence – 1.6 litre

24 Unbolt the exhaust manifold support bracket from the front of the engine. Unscrew and remove the manifold-to-downpipe flange joint nuts. If the nuts are in poor condition, obtain some new ones for reassembly.

25 To create enough movement in the system to separate the flange joint, unbolt the exhaust mountings as necessary (mark their fitted positions) until the exhaust rear section can be lowered. Do not pull down on the system, nor allow the pipes to hang unsupported under the car, as an old system in particular could suffer unnecessary damage.

26 Trace the wiring back from the upper oxygen sensor, and disconnect it. The manifold can be removed with the sensor in place (providing care is taken not to damage the sensor), or the sensor can be unscrewed and removed.

27 Remove the five bolts securing the heatshield over the manifold, and take off the heatshield **(see illustration)**. It's likely that these bolts may be in very poor condition, having suffered corrosion damage - make sure the spanner or socket used to remove them is a good fit, and spray the bolts with penetrating

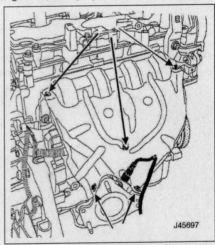

J45697

14.27 Exhaust manifold heat shield retaining bolts

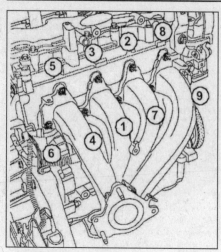

14.30 Exhaust manifold nut tightening sequence

lubricant before trying to remove them. If the bolts are found to be in poor condition, it is advisable to obtain new bolts for reassembly.

28 Unscrew a total of nine nuts and withdraw the exhaust manifold from the cylinder head. Recover the manifold gaskets – fit new ones at the head and downpipe joints when refitting the manifold. If the nuts are badly corroded or otherwise damaged, obtain a new set for reassembly.

29 If any studs were removed with the nuts, these can be refitted to the head using two nuts tightened against each other. Again, however, if the studs are badly corroded, it's best to fit new ones when reassembling.

30 Refitting is a reversal of removal, noting the following points:

a) Ensure that the cylinder head and manifold mating surfaces are clean.
b) Use new gaskets and tighten the mounting nuts in the sequence shown to the specified torque (see illustration).

15 Exhaust system – general information, removal and refitting

General information

1 On new cars, the exhaust system is in one piece, attached to the manifold by a bolted flange joint. This single section includes the catalytic converter (behind the front suspension subframe), a centre silencer, and a rear silencer. The system fits over the rear suspension, so the only way to remove it (other than to remove the suspension) is to cut it off.

2 The rear section can be renewed in three separate sections (each including the catalyst or a silencer) by cutting it off at the points indicated between two punched marks on the pipe (see illustration). Renault state that the entire exhaust is of stainless steel, which should at least mean corrosion damage is less of a problem.

3 The system is suspended throughout its entire length by rubber mountings, bolted to the car floor.

Removal

4 To remove a part of the system, first jack up the front or rear of the car, and support it on axle stands (see *Jacking and vehicle support*). Alternatively, position the car over an

inspection pit, or on car ramps. Where fitted, remove the engine compartment undertray.

Complete system

5 If the exhaust merely has to be removed to allow other work to be carried out, it can be unbolted and lowered as follows. As stated previously, the one-piece rear system cannot be removed without first unbolting the rear suspension, or cutting the exhaust as described in the rear silencer removal procedure. For renewal of an individual section, refer to the relevant sub-heading below.

6 Trace the wiring forwards from the rear oxygen sensor (behind the catalytic converter), and disconnect it at the plug.

7 Unscrew and remove the manifold-to-downpipe flange joint nuts. If the nuts are in poor condition, obtain some new ones for reassembly.

8 Mark their positions for accurate alignment when refitting, then unbolt the rubber mounting blocks from the car floor in the centre, and behind the rear silencer.

9 Lower the system at the front to clear the manifold, and draw it to the rear as far as possible. If the system is to be left unbolted during other servicing work, support it as necessary so that the pipes are not under strain. Protect the rear oxygen sensor and catalytic converter from damage – both may be damaged if carelessly handled.

Catalytic converter

10 Trace the wiring forwards from the rear oxygen sensor (behind the catalytic converter), and disconnect it at the plug.

11 Locate the cutting point behind the catalytic converter, indicated by two punch marks on the pipe. The pipe must be cut exactly between these marks, which are 80 mm apart – measure and mark the central point, and cut through (see illustration). If a new section is being fitted, if possible offer the new one up alongside to ensure the cut is made at the best place.

12 Unscrew and remove the manifold-to-downpipe flange joint nuts (see illustration). If the nuts are in poor condition, obtain some new ones for reassembly.

13 As the catalytic converter section is being withdrawn, treat it with care – rough handling will damage the ceramic element inside. Also take care with that the rear oxygen sensor does not suffer damage.

14 Clean off any burrs on the cut pipe(s) which might interfere with the joining sleeve and prevent a gas-tight joint being achieved.

15 Refitting is a reversal of removal, noting the following points:

a) Obtain a new manifold-to-downpipe gasket and a pipe joining sleeve for reassembly (see illustration). Old joining sleeves should not be re-used.
b) If a new converter section is being fitted, the pipe may require trimming to mate up with the old rear section – offer it roughly into position first to check.

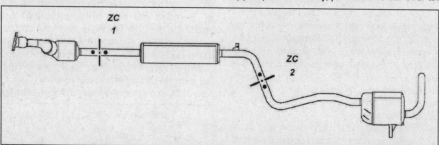

15.2 Cut the original exhaust at the cut zones (ZC1 and ZC2) indicated by the punched marks

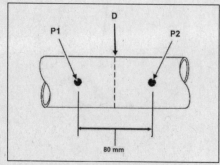

15.11 Mark a central point (D) between the punch marks (P1 and P2)

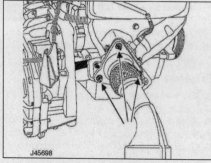

15.12 Manifold-to-downpipe flange nuts

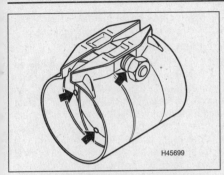

15.15 Pipe joining sleeve – insert pipe ends up to inner marks

c) *Reconnect the manifold-to-downpipe joint, using a new gasket. Tighten the nuts to the specified torque.*

d) *Apply exhaust jointing compound evenly around the inside of the joining sleeve, and fit it to one 'half' of the pipe. Ensure that both pipes to be joined enter the sleeve by an equal amount (position the sleeve centrally over the joint).Tighten the clamp nut to the specified torque, indicated by a 'click' from the nut – do not over-tighten, as this may deform the pipe and cause a leak.*

Centre silencer

16 Locate the cutting points in front of and behind the centre silencer, indicated by two punch marks on the pipe. The pipe must be cut exactly between these marks, which are 80 mm apart – measure and mark each central point, and cut through. If a new section is being fitted, if possible offer the new one up alongside to ensure the cut is made at the best place.

17 Mark it for position, then unbolt the centre silencer mounting block from the underside of the car **(see illustration)**. Remove the centre silencer. If a new silencer is being fitted, transfer the mounting to the new component.

18 Clean off any burrs on the cut pipe(s)

which might interfere with the joining sleeve and prevent a gas-tight joint being achieved.

 To make refitting easier, it may help to unbolt the rear silencer's rear mounting (mark it for position first). Once the centre silencer's front joining sleeve is in place, the old rear section can then be slid into position in the rear sleeve.

19 Refitting is a reversal of removal, noting the following points:

a) *Obtain two new pipe joining sleeves for reassembly – old ones should not be re-used.*

b) *If a new silencer section is being fitted, the pipes may require trimming to mate up with the old sections – offer it roughly into position first to check.*

c) *Apply exhaust jointing compound evenly around the inside of the joining sleeves, and fit them to the old pipes. Ensure that both pipes to be joined enter the sleeve by an equal amount (position the sleeve centrally over the joint).Tighten the clamp nut to the specified torque, indicated by a 'click' from the nut – do not over-tighten, as this may deform the pipe and cause a leak.*

d) *Align the exhaust mountings with the marks made before removal, and tighten their bolts securely.*

Rear silencer

20 Locate the cutting point in front the rear silencer, indicated by two punch marks on the pipe. The pipe must be cut exactly between these marks, which are 80 mm apart – measure and mark each central point, and cut through. If a new section is being fitted, if possible offer the new one up alongside to ensure the cut is made at the best place.

21 Mark it for position, then unbolt the rear silencer mounting block from the underside

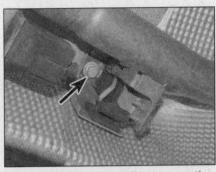

15.17 Unbolt the centre silencer mounting block under the car

of the car. Remove the rear silencer, twisting and feeding the pipe over the rear suspension (remove the rear wheel to improve access). If a new silencer is being fitted, transfer the mounting to the new component.

22 Clean off any burrs on the cut pipe(s) which might interfere with the joining sleeve and prevent a gas-tight joint being achieved.

23 Refitting is a reversal of removal, noting the following points:

a) *Obtain a new pipe joining sleeve for reassembly – old ones should not be re-used.*

b) *If a new silencer section is being fitted, the new pipe may require trimming to mate up with the old pipe – offer it roughly into position first to check.*

c) *Apply exhaust jointing compound evenly around the inside of the joining sleeve, and fit it to the old pipe. Ensure that both pipes to be joined enter the sleeve by an equal amount (position the sleeve centrally over the joint).Tighten the clamp nut to the specified torque, indicated by a 'click' from the nut – do not over-tighten, as this may deform the pipe and cause a leak.*

d) *Align the exhaust mounting with the marks made before removal, and tighten its bolts securely.*

Chapter 4 Part B:
Diesel engine fuel & exhaust systems

Contents

Degrees of difficulty

Easy, suitable for novice with little experience	**Fairly easy,** suitable for beginner with some experience	**Fairly difficult,** suitable for competent DIY mechanic	**Difficult,** suitable for experienced DIY mechanic	**Very difficult,** suitable for expert DIY or professional

Specifications

General

Type:
   1.5 litre engine . . . . Lucas-Delphi
   1.9 litre engine . . . . Bosch CP3
System type . . . . Rear-mounted fuel tank, high-pressure pump with common-rail, direct injection, turbocharger
Firing order. . . . . 1-3-4-2 (number 1 at flywheel end)

Fuel system data

Idle speed:
   1.5 litre engine . . . . 805 ± 50 rpm
   1.9 litre engine . . . . 800 ± 50 rpm
Maximum no-load speed:
   1.5 litre engine . . . . 5000 ± 100 rpm
   1.9 litre engine . . . . 4850 ± 150 rpm
Maximum under-load speed:
   1.5 litre engine . . . . 4800 ± 100 rpm
   1.9 litre engine . . . . 4500 ± 100 rpm
High-pressure pump:
   Type:
      1.5 litre engine . . . . Delphi
      1.9 litre engine . . . . Bosch
   Direction of rotation . . . . Clockwise viewed from sprocket end
Injectors:
   Type . . . . Delphi or Bosch solenoid injector
   Maximum pressure. . . . . 1600 bar (Delphi) 1300 bar (Bosch)
Sensor resistances:
   1.5 litre engine:
      Engine speed sensor . . . . 760 ohms
      Fuel flow actuator (on pump) . . . . 5.3 ± 0.5 ohms
      Fuel temperature sensor (on pump) . . . . 2200 ohms
      Turbocharger air temperature/pressure sensor . . . . 2511 ± 109 ohms @ 20°C
   1.9 litre engine:
      Engine speed sensor . . . . 800 ± 80 ohms
      Fuel temperature sensor (on pump) . . . . 2050 ohms
Glow plug resistance . . . . 0.6 ohms
Turbocharger . . . . Garrett

Torque wrench settings

	Nm	lbf ft
Catalytic converter:		
Converter to turbocharger	26	19
Rear mounting plate bolts	21	15
Support strut to engine:		
1.5 litre engine	44	32
1.9 litre engine	50	37
Support strut to converter:		
1.5 litre engine	25	18
1.9 litre engine	30	22
EGR air pipe bolts	21	15
EGR valve:		
1.5 litre engine	21	15
1.9 litre engine	10	7
EGR valve heat shield	12	9
Engine lifting eye	21	15
Exhaust joining sleeve clamp nut	25	18
Exhaust manifold (1.5 litre engine)	26	19
Fuel injectors to cylinder head:		
1.5 litre engine	28	21
1.9 litre engine	25	18
Fuel pressure regulator (1.9 litre)	6	4
Fuel rail pressure sensor (1.9 litre)	35	26
Fuel tank	21	15
Fuel temperature sensor (1.5 litre)	15	11
Glow plugs	15	11
High-pressure fuel rail:		
1.5 litre engine	28	21
1.9 litre engine	22	16
High-pressure pipe union nuts:		
1.5 litre engine	38	28
1.9 litre engine	25	18
High-pressure pump front support (1.9 litre engine):		
To cylinder block	44	32
To cylinder head:		
Stage 1	20	15
Stage 2	Angle-tighten a further 80°	
Support-to-pump bolts	30	22
High-pressure pump rear mounting bolts:		
1.5 litre engine	21	16
1.9 litre engine	30	22
High-pressure pump sprocket nut:		
1.5 litre engine:		
Stage 1	15	11
Stage 2	Angle-tighten a further 60° ± 10°	
1.9 litre engine	70	52
Inlet and exhaust manifolds (1.9 litre engine)	28	21
Knock sensor (1.5 litre)	20	15
Turbocharger oil supply pipe unions	23	17
Turbocharger oil return pipe union	12	9
Turbocharger to exhaust manifold	26	19

1 General information and precautions

General information

The fuel system consists of a rear-mounted fuel tank, a fuel filter with integral water separator, a high-pressure pump with common-rail injection system, electronic injectors and associated components.

The main components of the system are as follows:

a) Electronic control unit (ECU)
b) High-pressure pump
c) Fuel filter
d) Injector rail
e) Four electronic solenoid injectors
f) Airflow meter
g) Fuel temperature sensor
h) Coolant temperature sensor
i) Cylinder reference sensor
j) Engine speed sensor
k) Turbocharging pressure sensor
l) EGR valve

The common-rail injection system operates as follows. Fuel is drawn from the fuel tank to the high-pressure pump by a low-pressure transfer pump integrated in the high-pressure pump. Before reaching the high-pressure pump, the fuel passes through a fuel filter, where foreign matter and water are removed. As the fuel passes through the filter, it is heated by an electric heater. On reaching the high-pressure pump, the fuel is pressurised according to demand, and accumulates in the injection common-rail. The pressure in the rail is accurately maintained using a pressure sensor in the rail and a pressure regulator under the control of the engine management ECU. This arrangement keeps heat generation to a minimum, and improves engine output. The rail pressure is also maintained by the injectors themselves; short electrical pulses which are not long enough to open the injector, allow fuel into the return (leak-off) circuit, and also the normal pulses which open the injectors cause a reduction in pressure. The ECU determines the exact timing and duration of the injection period according to engine operating conditions.

The four fuel injectors inject a homogeneous spray of fuel into the combustion chambers located in the cylinder head. The injectors operate sequentially according to the firing order of the cylinders, and each injector needle is lubricated by fuel, which accumulates in the spring chamber. Each injector has its own unique flow characteristics which are used by the system ECU to calculate the exact quantity of fuel to inject.

In terms of the sensors used by the ECU to control a modern common-rail diesel system, these engines are very similar to their petrol equivalents. The ECU determines engine speed and position from a TDC sensor fitted to the transmission bellhousing, which detects a reference tooth on the flywheel ring gear, and signals the ECU. A similar sensor is fitted to monitor the camshaft, to give a reference for No 1 cylinder. Further sensors are used to monitor airflow into the engine, air temperature, and turbocharging pressure. On the fuel side, fuel pressure, temperature and flow rate are all monitored, according to model, via sensors on the high-pressure pump and/or the fuel rail. As with the petrol-engined models, an 'electronic' throttle is fitted, with an accelerator position sensor replacing the mechanical cable previously used. The knock sensor fitted to 1.5 litre models is mounted on the cylinder block to inform the ECU when the fuel injection timing needs to be retarded, in order to regain optimum engine efficiency.

Provided that the specified maintenance is carried out, the fuel injection equipment will give long and trouble-free service. The main potential cause of damage to the high-pressure pump and injectors is dirt or water in the fuel. It is highly recommended that a set of fuel line plugs is obtained – these are available from motor accessory shops and better motor factors.

Servicing of the high-pressure pump, injectors, and electronic equipment and sensors is very limited for the home mechanic, and any dismantling or adjustment other than that described in this Chapter must be entrusted to a Renault dealer or fuel injection specialist.

If a fault appears in the injection system, first ensure that all the system wiring connectors are securely connected and free of corrosion. Should the fault persist, the car should be taken to a Renault dealer or specialist who can test the system on a diagnostic tester. The tester will locate the fault quickly and simply, alleviating the need to test all the system components individually, which is a time-consuming operation that carries a risk of damaging the ECU. It is advisable to have any faulty components renewed by the dealer as in many instances the tester is required to reprogram the ECU in the event of component or sensor renewal.

2.4 Disconnect the airflow meter wiring plug

2.5b . . . then unclip the vacuum hoses . . .

Precautions

⚠️ *Warning: It is necessary to take certain precautions when working on the fuel system components, particularly the fuel injectors and high-pressure pump. Before carrying out any operations on the fuel system, refer to the precautions given in Safety first! at the beginning of this manual. Allow the engine to cool for 5 to 10 minutes to ensure the fuel pressure and temperature are at a minimum.*

⚠️ *Warning: Exercise extreme caution when working on the high-pressure fuel system. Do not attempt to test the fuel injectors or disconnect the high-pressure lines with the engine running. Never expose the hands or any part of the body to injector spray, as the high working pressure can cause the fuel to penetrate the skin, with possibly*

2.6 Unclip the duct from the base of the air cleaner

2.5a Loosen the hose clips at each end of the air duct . . .

2.5c . . . and lift it out

fatal results. You are strongly advised to have any work which involves testing the injectors under pressure carried out by a dealer or fuel injection specialist.

2 Air cleaner and inlet ducts
– removal and refitting

Removal

1 Remove the battery and battery tray as described in Chapter 5A.

2 Remove the engine ECU as described in Section 8.

3 Remove the larger left-hand section of the windscreen cowl panel for access, as described in Chapter 11. Remove the air filter access panel – See Chapter 1B, Section 17. If the air filter has never been disturbed before, it may be necessary to cut the plastic side 'perforations' securing the access flap with a sharp knife, before hinging the flap upwards.

4 Disconnect the airflow meter wiring plug **(see illustration)**.

5 Loosen the hose clips at each end of the air cleaner air duct, then unclip the two small hoses from the duct, and lift it out **(see illustrations)**.

6 Twist and unclip the plastic inlet air duct from the base of the air cleaner, and remove it **(see illustration)**.

7 The air cleaner is located on rubber pegs. Pull the air cleaner forwards to free the pegs, and remove it from the engine compartment **(see illustration)**.

2.7 Pull the air cleaner forwards off the mounting pegs

8 If required, the upper inlet air duct can also be unclipped and removed from the front panel **(see illustration)**.

Refitting

9 Refitting is a reversal of removal.

4.4a Remove the three screws . . .

4.6 Prise up the plastic cover to expose the sender unit

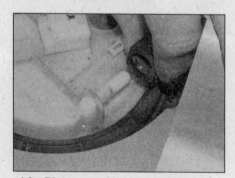

4.8a Disconnect the fuel supply hose . . .

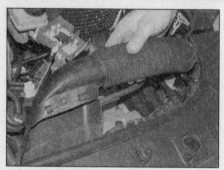

2.8 Removing the upper air duct

3 Accelerator pedal – removal and refitting

Refer to Chapter 4A, Section 5.

4.4b . . . and take out the access plate . . .

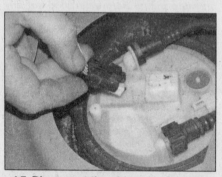

4.7 Disconnect the wiring plug from the top of the sender

4.8b . . . and the return hose

4 Fuel gauge sender unit – removal, testing and refitting

Note: *Refer to the precautions in Section 1 before proceeding.*

Removal

1 Disconnect the battery negative lead (refer to *Disconnecting the battery* in the Reference Section).

2 Remove the rear seats as described in Chapter 11 (centre row on Grand Scénic) for access to the fuel pump cover.

3 Carefully prise the retaining plugs out to release the carpet, then unclip the rear seat mountings and move the carpet clear. Detach and remove the soundproofing under the carpet.

4 Remove the three screws and take out the floor access plate **(see illustrations)**.

5 Where applicable, remove the radio tuner/ amplifier from its floor location as described in Chapter 12.

6 Unclip the wiring, then prise up the plastic cover to expose the sender unit **(see illustration)**.

7 Disconnect the wiring connector, and tape the connector to the car body, to prevent it disappearing behind the tank **(see illustration)**.

8 Note that the fuel supply and return hoses are equipped with a quick-release fitting to ease removal. To disconnect the supply hose (colour-coded green), squeeze the fitting at the sides; the return connection is released by depressing the red-coloured catch on top of the fitting **(see illustrations)**.

9 Check for alignment arrows on the cover, to indicate its correct fitted position – if none are visible, make your own **(see illustration)**.

10 Unscrew the locking ring and remove it from the tank. This can be accomplished by using a screwdriver on the raised ribs of the locking ring – carefully tap the screwdriver to turn the ring anti-clockwise until it can be unscrewed by hand. Alternatively a removal tool can be fabricated out of metal bar and two bolts **(see illustrations)**.

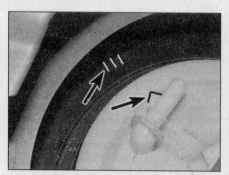

4.9 The triangular projection should align with the three line marks

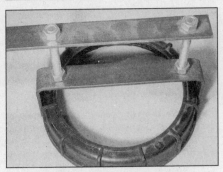

4.10a Home-made locking ring removal tool

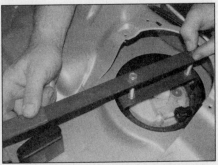

4.10b Using a home-made tool if necessary . . .

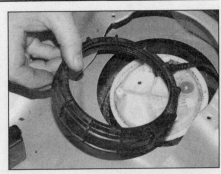

4.10c . . . unscrew the locking ring

11 Carefully lift the sender unit assembly out of the fuel tank, taking great care not to damage the fuel level gauge sender arm, or to spill fuel in the interior of the car (**see illustration**).
12 Remove the rubber sealing ring and check it for deterioration; if it is in good condition, it may be re-used, however if the pump is to remain out of the fuel tank for several hours, the locking ring should be refitted temporarily to prevent the sealing ring from distorting. If the sealing ring is unserviceable, obtain a new one (**see illustration**).
13 Note that the gauge sender unit is only available as a complete assembly – no components are available separately.

Refitting

14 Ensure that the pick-up filter is clean and free of debris. Fit the sealing ring to the top of the fuel tank.
15 Carefully manoeuvre the assembly into the fuel tank.
16 Align the arrow on the cover with the arrow on the fuel tank, then refit the locking ring. Securely tighten the locking ring, then recheck that the cover and tank marks are all correctly aligned.
17 Reconnect the hoses in their previously-noted positions.
18 Reconnect the wiring connector.
19 Reconnect the battery and start the engine. Check the fuel pump and hose(s) for signs of leakage.
20 Refit the plastic cover, access plate and the rear seat cushion.

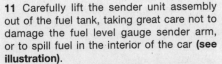

5 Fuel tank – removal and refitting

Note: *Refer to the warning note in Section 1 before proceeding.*

Proceed as described in Chapter 4A, Section 9 for the petrol models, noting that there is no pump on diesel models, and therefore no wiring plug to disconnect. Also, no charcoal canister is fitted to diesel models.

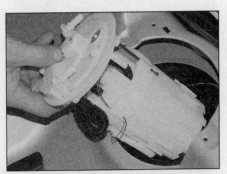

4.11 Lift out the sender unit assembly

6 Fuel system – priming and bleeding

Note: *Refer to the precautions in Section 1 before proceeding.*

⚠️ *Warning: Do not attempt to bleed the system by loosening any of the unions on the high-pressure circuit. Disconnecting any of the system sensors, or the fuel injectors, will result in a fault code being logged by the system ECU, which must then be cleared by a Renault dealer.*

1 After disconnecting part of the fuel supply system or running out of fuel, it is necessary to prime the system low-pressure circuit before restarting the engine.

6.2 Remove the clips and take off the left-hand plastic trim panel

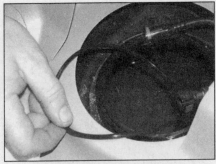

4.12 Recover the sealing ring

2 All models are fitted with a hand-operated priming bulb located behind the coolant expansion tank (**see illustration**).
3 Squeeze the priming bulb several times to purge the low-pressure circuit of air.
4 Attempt to start the engine normally, however, do not operate the starter motor for more than 5 seconds. If necessary, operate the starter motor in 4 to 5 second bursts followed by pauses of 8 to 10 seconds. As soon as the engine starts, let it run at fast idle speed until a regular idle speed is reached. If difficulty in purging the air from the system is experienced (engine may hunt), disconnect the blue high-pressure return pipe from the fuel filter and plug this hole, then place the end of the pipe in a container and continue to squeeze the priming bulb until the air is removed. Reconnect the return pipe and start the engine.

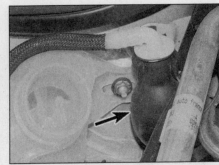

6.3 The hand priming bulb is located behind the coolant expansion tank

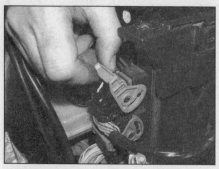

8.3 Slide back the locking levers, and disconnect the ECU wiring plugs

8.4 Unhook the boost pressure solenoid valve from the ECU bracket

8.5 Unhook and remove the ECU with its mounting bracket

8.6 ECU-to-mounting bracket bolts

7 Idle speed – general

1 The engine management ECU uses the following inputs to calculate the recommended idle speed according to the varying load on the engine by peripheral electrical or mechanical components.

   a) *Engine coolant temperature.*
   b) *Battery voltage.*
   c) *The gear selected.*
   d) *Electrical consumers (heater fan, climate control system, thermo-plungers, etc.).*

2 At normal engine temperature with no electrical consumers switched on and neutral selected, the engine idle speed will be in the range specified.

3 If the accelerator pedal sensor is faulty, the ECU will override the idle speed to 1100 rpm,

and the injection warning light will be illuminated on the instrument panel. If the brake pedal is depressed, the idle speed will revert to its normal level.

4 If there is an injector fault, the idle speed will be set to 1300 rpm and the warning light will be illuminated.

5 Should the idle speed be repeatedly incorrect, the car should be taken to a Renault dealer who will have the necessary diagnostic equipment to pin-point the faulty component responsible.

8 Engine management ECU – removal and refitting

Note: *The engine management ECU is electronically-coded for the car to which it is fitted, therefore new units are supplied without a code. If the ECU is being removed to enable*

a new unit to be fitted, the new unit must be programmed with the information from the old ECU by a Renault dealer. The information includes configuration for items such as the injectors, immobiliser, power-assisted steering pump and climate control system.

Removal

1 Remove the windscreen cowl panels as described in Chapter 11. Unclip and remove the engine top cover.

2 Remove the battery and battery tray as described in Chapter 5A.

3 Slide back the locking catches, and disconnect the wiring plugs from the ECU **(see illustration)**.

4 Where applicable, unhook the turbo boost pressure regulation solenoid valve from the ECU mounting bracket, and move it to one side without disconnecting the vacuum hoses **(see illustration)**.

5 Unhook the ECU and its mounting bracket, and remove it complete **(see illustration)**.

6 If required, the ECU can be separated from the bracket, after removing the four mounting bolts **(see illustration)**.

Refitting

7 Refitting is a reversal of removal. Ensure that the ECU wiring plugs are securely reconnected.

9 High-pressure pump – removal and refitting

Note: *Refer to the precautions in Section 1 before proceeding.*

Removal

1 Disconnect the battery negative lead (refer to *Disconnecting the battery* in the Reference Chapter).

2 Loosen the right-hand front wheel bolts, then jack up the front of the car and support on axle stands. Remove the right front wheel, engine undertray and wheel arch liner.

3 Remove the auxiliary drivebelt as described in Chapter 1B, and the timing belt with reference to Chapter 2B or 2C.

1.5 litre engine

4 Disconnect the intercooler duct which runs across the top of the engine, and either remove it or move it to one side.

5 Unbolt and remove the dipstick tube, pulling it out of the engine block, and tape over the resulting hole to prevent dirt entry.

6 Disconnect the wiring from the flow actuator and fuel temperature sensor on the rear of the high-pressure pump **(see illustration)**.

7 Disconnect the wiring from the injectors and glow plugs **(see illustrations)**.

8 Clean the area around the fuel supply and return pipes, then disconnect them from the high-pressure pump. The pipes are fitted with quick-release clips which must be depressed. Fit protector plugs to the open apertures and lines **(see illustrations)**.

9.6 Disconnect the wiring from the rear of the high-pressure pump

9.7a Disconnecting the wiring from the injectors . . .

9.7b . . . and glow plugs

9.8a Clean the area around the fuel supply and return pipes before disconnecting them

9.8b The fuel supply and return pipes on the high-pressure pump

9.8c Fuel supply pipe on the high-pressure pump

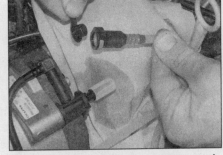

9.8d Fit plugs to the open apertures and fuel lines

9.15a Disconnect the wiring plug from the fuel filter . . .

9 Disconnect the wiring from the following components, then unclip the harness and lay it to one side:
  a) The fuel rail pressure sensor (at the far end of the fuel rail).
  b) The knock sensor (on the front of the engine).
  c) The oil level sensor (below the knock sensor).
  d) The cylinder reference sensor (on the timing belt cover).
10 Unscrew and remove the neck nut fitted to the fuel rail, near the fuel pressure sensor.
11 Loosen the fuel rail mounting nuts a few turns
12 Disconnect the high-pressure pipe connecting the pump to the fuel rail. To do this, unscrew the nut on the pump followed by the nut on the fuel rail, then move the nut along the tube while keeping the oval-shaped handle in contact with the taper. Tape over or plug the open connections. **Note:** *A new high-pressure fuel pipe should be obtained for refitting.*
13 Unscrew the three pump mounting bolts, and withdraw the high-pressure pump from the engine.

1.9 litre engine

14 Disconnect the crankcase breather hose which runs across the top of the engine, and move it to one side.
15 Disconnect the wiring plugs from the following fuel system components (**see illustrations**):
  a) The fuel filter (under the wing – see Chapter 1B).
  b) The glow plugs.

  c) The fuel pressure regulator (back of the pump).
  d) The fuel pressure sensor (at the pump end of the fuel rail).
16 Disconnect the fuel supply and return

9.15b . . . glow plugs . . .

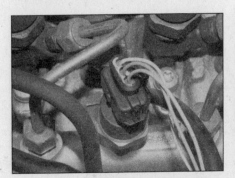

9.15d . . . and fuel pressure sensor

pipes from the injection pump (**see illustration**). Unclip the pipes as necessary, once disconnected. Cap or plug the open connections, to reduce fuel loss, and to prevent the entry of dirt.

9.15c . . . fuel pressure regulator . . .

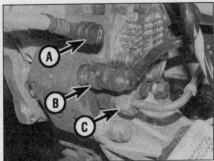

9.16 Supply pipe from fuel filter (A), fuel rail return hose (B) and pump-to-rail pipe (C)

9.17 One of the fuel rail mounting bolts

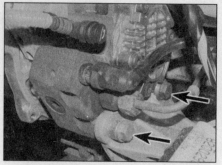

9.19a Injection pump rear mounting bolts

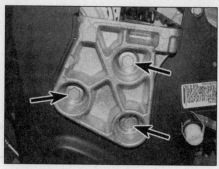

9.19b Injection pump front support bolts

17 Loosen the fuel rail mounting bolts by a few turns, so that the rail is still fitted, but loose **(see illustration)**.

18 Unscrew the unions and remove the pump-to-rail high-pressure fuel pipe. Again, cap or plug the open connections, to reduce fuel loss, and to prevent the entry of dirt. **Note:** *A new high-pressure fuel pipe should be obtained for refitting.*

19 Remove the two pump rear mounting bolts, then the three from the front support (which forms the mounting point for the engine right-hand mounting), and carefully lift the pump out with the front support attached **(see illustrations)**.

20 Separating the pump from the front support means removing the pump sprocket to access the support bolts. Removing the pump sprocket will require a suitable puller (the sprocket is located on a taper), and some means of holding the sprocket while the nut is loosened. Once the sprocket has been removed, three further bolts secure the front support. It may be preferable to entrust this part of the job to a Renault dealer or well-equipped workshop.

Refitting

21 Refitting is a reversal of removal, noting the following points:
  a) *Fit a new high-pressure pipe as follows. Some pipes may be supplied with a sachet of lubricant, which should be used on the union nut threads before fitting – if no lubricant is provided, none should be applied. Finger-tighten the nuts before tightening them to the specified torque.*

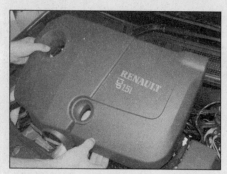

10.2 Unclip and remove the engine top cover

  Take care not to place the new high-pressure pipe under any stress when the unions are tightened.
  b) *Tighten all nuts and bolts to the specified torque.*
  c) *Fit a new timing belt as described in Chapter 2B or 2C.*
  d) *On completion, prime and bleed the fuel system as described in Section 6. Run the engine, and check for fuel leaks.*

10 Fuel system sensors and components – removal and refitting

Note: *Refer to the precautions in Section 1 before proceeding.*

1 Disconnect the battery negative lead (refer to *Disconnecting the battery* in the Reference Chapter).

1.5 litre engine

Flow actuator

2 Remove the engine top cover **(see illustration)**.

3 Disconnect the wiring from the flow actuator (inner) and fuel temperature sensor (outer) located on the rear of the high-pressure pump **(see illustration)**.

4 Wrap some cloth rag over the fuel return hose, then disconnect it by depressing the quick-release fitting **(refer to illustration 10.3)**.

5 Wrap some cloth rag over the union nuts, then unscrew them and remove the high-pressure pipe for No 4 injector. **Note:** *The*

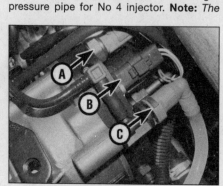

10.3 Fuel temperature sensor (A), fuel flow actuator (B) and fuel return hose (C)

manufacturers stipulate that the pipe is renewed whenever removed. Plug or tape over the fuel apertures.

6 Disconnect the wiring from the glow plugs and injectors for cylinders 3 and 4.

7 Unscrew the retaining bracket bolts and withdraw the flow actuator from the high-pressure pump. **Do not** pull on the wiring connector, but ease it out by hand only.

8 Only remove the new unit from its packaging just before fitting it, and do not lubricate it with used fuel or grease.

9 Carefully locate the actuator on the pump, making sure that the seal is not damaged. Insert the mounting bolts and tighten securely.

10 Reconnect all wiring, then fit the new high-pressure pipe and tighten the union nuts to the specified torque.

11 Refit the fuel return pipe and engine top cover.

Fuel temperature sensor

12 Remove the engine top cover.

13 Disconnect the wiring from the fuel temperature sensor located on the rear of the high-pressure pump. The sensor is nearest the outer edge of the pump **(refer to illustration 10.3)**.

14 Wrap some cloth rag over the sensor, then unscrew and remove it and recover the O-ring seal.

15 Lubricate the new O-ring seal with the lubricant supplied with the new sensor, then locate it on the sensor.

16 Fit the sensor and seal to the pump and tighten to the specified torque. Reconnect the wiring and refit the engine top cover.

Fuel pressure sensor

17 The sensor is mounted below the fuel rail, at the transmission end **(see illustration)**. The sensor is not available separately from the fuel rail, and no attempt should be made to remove it.

Crankshaft speed/position sensor

18 Remove the battery and battery tray as described in Chapter 5A, and the injection ECU as described in Section 8.

19 The sensor is located on top of the transmission bellhousing. Disconnect the wiring plug, then remove the sensor mounting bolt and withdraw it.

10.17 Fuel pressure sensor location

10.26a Disconnect the sensor wiring plug . . .

10.26b . . . then prise it from its location . . .

20 Check the sensor for signs of damage, and clean it before refitting. Refitting is a reversal of removal.

Accelerator pedal position sensor

21 Refer to Section 3.

Camshaft position sensor

22 Remove the engine top cover for access to the sensor, which is located on the timing belt top cover.
23 Disconnect the sensor wiring plug, then unscrew the mounting bolt and withdraw the sensor.
24 Refitting is a reversal of removal. Make sure the sensor is clean before refitting.

Turbocharging pressure sensor

25 The pressure sensor is located on the air duct leading into the inlet manifold, at the transmission end of the engine.
26 Disconnect the wiring plug from the sensor, then carefully prise it from its location. Recover the small O-ring seal, and check its condition – fit a new one if necessary **(see illustrations)**.
27 Refitting is a reversal of removal.

Turbocharger boost pressure solenoid

28 Remove the battery as described in Chapter 5A.
29 Unhook the solenoid from the ECU mounting bracket **(refer to illustration 10.73)**.

10.26c . . . and remove it – check the condition of the O-ring seal

30 Disconnect the solenoid wiring plug and the two vacuum hoses from the valve (noting their positions for refitting), and remove the valve **(refer to illustrations 10.74a and b)**.
31 Refitting is a reversal of removal.

Airflow and air temperature sensor

32 The airflow meter fitted to the main air cleaner body has an integral air temperature sensor.
33 Remove the air inlet duct between the air cleaner body and the turbocharger, using the information in Section 2 **(see illustration)**.
34 Disconnect the wiring plug, then remove the mounting screw at the top, and withdraw the airflow meter from the air cleaner **(see**

10.33 Remove the air inlet duct . . .

illustration). Check the condition of the sealing ring, and renew if necessary.
35 Refitting is a reversal of removal.

Knock sensor

36 Remove the engine top cover, and the engine compartment plastic trim panels as necessary to gain access to the sensor, which is fitted centrally on the front of the block, above the oil filter.
37 Disconnect the sensor wiring plug, then unscrew and remove the sensor from the block (a 24 mm spanner or deep socket will be needed) **(see illustration)**.
38 Refitting is a reversal of removal. It is vital for the correct operation of the sensor that it be tightened to the specified torque.

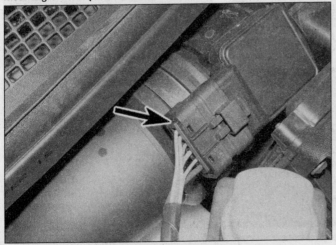

10.34 . . . then disconnect the airflow meter wiring plug

10.37 Disconnect the knock sensor wiring plug

Protection and switching unit

39 This unit is located in the engine compartment, next to the battery. The unit contains several engine-related fuses, and several internal (non-removable) relays, including the 'ignition' relay, fan control relay, and air conditioning compressor relay. The unit controls the air conditioning (where fitted), the radiator fan and the pre/post-heating system, and forms a central part of the car's multiplex wiring system. For the purposes of this manual, the unit is also known as the engine multiplex module – for more details, see Chapter 12, Section 3.

1.9 litre engine

Fuel pressure regulator

40 Remove the engine top cover.
41 Disconnect the battery negative lead, and move the lead away from the battery (see *Disconnecting the battery*).
42 Disconnect the wiring plug from the fuel pressure regulator located on the rear of the high-pressure pump **(see illustration)**.
43 Clean the area around the base of the regulator, then remove the three regulator mounting bolts **(see illustration)**.
44 Ease the regulator out of position – any resistance is due to the O-ring seals – without using any tools. Once the regulator is free, recover any O-ring seals which were left behind – new seals should be obtained for refitting.
45 Fit the new seals, lubricated with clean diesel fuel, to the regulator.

46 Wash the regulator mating face and mounting aperture on the pump with clean diesel fuel, then wipe clean – it is most important that no dirt is introduced into the pump during refitting.
47 Offer up the regulator, and push it gently into position, twisting it slightly to help enter the O-rings. Once it is fully home, refit the bolts and tighten by hand initially.
48 Tighten the three bolts evenly to the specified torque.
49 Reconnect the regulator wiring plug and the battery negative lead.
50 On completion, start the engine and check for signs of leakage before refitting the engine top cover.

Fuel rail pressure sensor

51 The fuel rail pressure sensor is screwed directly into the fuel rail, between the pipes feeding Nos 1 and 2 injectors.
52 Remove the engine top cover **(see illustration)**.
53 Disconnect the wiring plug from the pressure sensor, then unscrew and remove it from the rail **(see illustration)**. Recover the sealing washer – a new one must be used when refitting. If the sensor is to be removed for a long period, cap the open connection on the fuel rail, to prevent dirt entry.
54 Refitting is a reversal of removal. Use a new sealing washer, and tighten the sensor to the specified torque. On completion, and before refitting the engine top cover, run the engine and check for signs of fuel leakage.

Fuel temperature sensor

55 The temperature sensor is clipped to the front of the fuel rail, and is tapped into the low-pressure fuel return circuit.
56 Remove the engine top cover.
57 Squeeze and disconnect the connector on the top of the sensor **(see illustration)**.
58 The two remaining sensor pipes are heat-shrunk plastic, and may prove difficult to remove without causing damage. If suitable pieces of rubber joining sleeve can be found, the plastic could be cut off, providing the sensor stubs underneath are not damaged – the rubber sleeves can then be used when refitting, providing careful checks are made for signs of leaks. If the sensor is not being renewed, trace the pipes to the quick-release connector on the pump, and to the rubber sleeve on the leak-off pipes, and disconnect there.
59 Unclip the sensor from the fuel rail, and remove it.
60 Refitting is a reversal of removal. Check for signs of leakage from any of the pipes which were disturbed.

Crankshaft speed/position sensor

61 Remove the battery and battery tray as described in Chapter 5A, and the injection ECU as described in Section 8.
62 The sensor is located on the front of the transmission bellhousing. Disconnect the wiring plug, then remove the sensor mounting bolt and withdraw it **(see illustrations)**.
63 Check the sensor for signs of damage, and clean it before refitting. Refitting is a reversal of removal.

10.42 Disconnect the fuel pressure regulator wiring plug

10.43 Fuel pressure regulator mounting bolts (arrowed – one hidden)

10.52 Unclip and remove the engine top cover

10.53 Disconnect the fuel rail pressure sensor

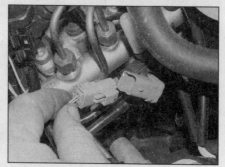

10.57 Disconnect the fuel temperature sensor

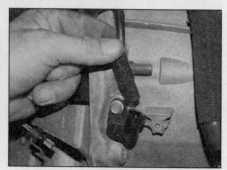

10.62a Disconnect the crankshaft sensor wiring plug . . .

Accelerator pedal position sensor

64 Refer to Section 3.

Camshaft position sensor

65 The camshaft position sensor is fitted to the cylinder head cover, at the timing belt end.
66 Remove the engine top cover.
67 Disconnect the wiring plug from the camshaft position sensor, then unscrew the mounting bolt underneath, and withdraw it from the engine (**see illustrations**). Check the condition of the sensor seal, and if necessary, fit a new one.
68 Refitting is a reversal of removal.

Turbocharging pressure sensor

69 The turbocharging pressure sensor is fitted to the intercooler upper air duct, which runs along behind the engine front panel.
70 Disconnect the wiring plug from one side of the sensor, then slide back the locking clip at the opposite end. Carefully pull the sensor out of the duct, noting that it has a small O-ring seal, and remove it (**see illustrations**). Check the condition of the sensor seal, and if necessary, fit a new one.
71 Refitting is a reversal of removal.

Turbocharger boost pressure solenoid

72 Remove the battery as described in Chapter 5A.
73 Unhook the solenoid from the ECU mounting bracket (**see illustration**).
74 Disconnect the solenoid wiring plug and the two vacuum hoses from the valve (noting their positions for refitting), and remove the valve (**see illustrations**).
75 Refitting is a reversal of removal.

10.62b ... then unscrew the mounting bolt and withdraw the sensor from the transmission

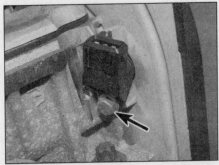

10.67b ... then unscrew the mounting bolt and remove it

Engine cut-off device

76 This device is a vacuum-operated flap in the air inlet duct, which is activated when the engine is switched off. When the flap closes, the engine is starved of air, and stops

10.67a Disconnect the camshaft position sensor ...

10.70a Disconnect the turbo pressure sensor wiring plug ...

immediately. The device is fed from a vacuum reservoir, via a solenoid valve, mounted on the back of the inlet manifold.
77 Loosen the hose clip and disconnect the duct from the front of the cut-off device (**see illustration**).

10.70b ... then slide back the locking clip ...

10.74a Disconnect the wiring plug ...

10.70c ... and prise out the sensor, noting its O-ring seal

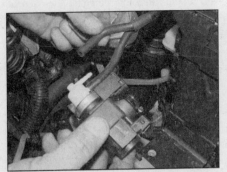

10.74b ... and the vacuum hoses, then remove the solenoid

10.73 Unhook the boost pressure solenoid from the ECU bracket

10.77 Loosen the hose clip and disconnect the duct from the cut-off device

10.79 Remove the engine cut-off device mounting bolts

10.80a Disconnect the vacuum control solenoid valve . . .

10.80b . . . then remove the Allen screws from the solenoid . . .

10.80c . . . and from the reservoir

10.85a Disconnect the airflow meter wiring plug . . .

85 Disconnect the wiring plug, then remove the two mounting screws, and withdraw the airflow meter from the air cleaner. Check the condition of the sealing ring, and renew if necessary **(see illustrations)**.

86 Refitting is a reversal of removal.

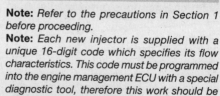

11 Fuel injectors –
testing, removal and refitting

Note: *Refer to the precautions in Section 1 before proceeding.*

Note: *Each new injector is supplied with a unique 16-digit code which specifies its flow characteristics. This code must be programmed into the engine management ECU with a special diagnostic tool, therefore this work should be entrusted to a Renault dealer.*

Testing

1 It is not possible to test the fuel injectors without specialist equipment, therefore, if they are thought to be faulty, consult a Renault dealer or diesel specialist.

Removal

Note: *Take care not to allow dirt into the injectors or fuel pipes during this procedure; clean around the area before commencing work. Note that all high-pressure pipes removed must be renewed as a matter of course. The injector flame shield washers must also be renewed.*

2 Disconnect the battery negative lead (refer to *Disconnecting the battery*).

3 Remove the engine top cover, then thoroughly clean the area around the injectors **(see illustration)**.

4 Unclip the wiring loom conduit from the high-pressure fuel rail as necessary **(see illustration)**.

5 On 1.5 litre engines, remove the engine oil level dipstick guide and tape over the hole.

6 Loosen the fuel rail mounting nuts/bolts a few turns, then disconnect the fuel return pipe from the high-pressure pump.

7 Disconnect the fuel injector wiring **(see illustration)**.

8 Using a screwdriver, release the clips from the two pairs of injector pipes **(see illustrations)**.

10.85b . . . remove the mounting screws . . .

10.85c . . . and withdraw the unit, with its sealing ring

78 Disconnect the vacuum hose from the vacuum diaphragm housing.

79 Remove the three bolts securing the device to the inlet duct, and withdraw it **(see illustration)**. Check the condition of the

device's O-ring seal, and if necessary, renew it.

80 To remove either the vacuum reservoir or the solenoid valve, first note the routing of the vacuum hoses. Disconnect the solenoid valve wiring plug. Unscrew the small Allen screws securing the solenoid and reservoir to the back of the inlet manifold, and remove – disconnect the hoses as necessary **(see illustrations)**.

81 Refitting is a reversal of removal.

Protection and switching unit

82 This is identical to the unit fitted to the 1.5 litre engine, described previously in this Section.

Airflow and air temperature sensor

83 The airflow meter fitted to the main air cleaner body has an integral air temperature sensor.

84 Remove the air cleaner as described in Section 2.

11.3 Thoroughly clean the area around the injectors

11.4 Releasing the wiring loom conduit from the fuel rail

11.7 Disconnecting the fuel injector wiring

11.8a Use a screwdriver . . .

11.8b . . . to prise off the injector pipe clips

11.9a Injector high-pressure pipe and unions – 1.9 litre engine

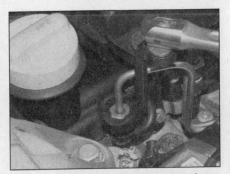

11.9b Unscrew the high-pressure pipe union nuts . . .

9 While holding the injectors with one spanner, unscrew the high-pressure pipe union nuts with a further spanner. Take care not to damage the leak-off stubs on the injectors, and wrap them in cloth rag before loosening them. Similarly, unscrew the union

nuts from the fuel rail, then remove the pipes. Move the nuts and olives along the pipes when releasing the pipes from the rail and injectors **(see illustrations)**.
10 Disconnect the fuel leak-off pipes from the injectors. Tape over or plug all fuel

apertures to prevent entry of dust and dirt **(see illustrations)**.
11 Using a Torx key, unscrew the bolt securing each injector clamp plate to the cylinder head. Lift off the clamp plates and remove the injectors then recover the flame

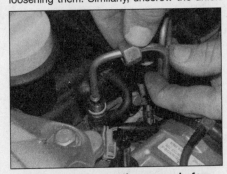

11.9c . . . and move them away before releasing the pipe from the injector

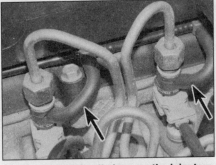

11.10a Fuel leak-off pipes on the injectors – 1.5 litre engine

11.10b On 1.9 litre engines, pull out the clips and lift off the leak-off pipes

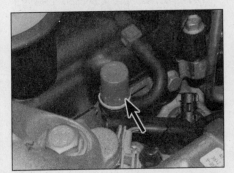

11.10c Fit protective caps to prevent entry of dust

11.11a Unscrew the securing bolt . . .

11.11b . . . and remove the clamp plate . . .

11.11c . . . then remove the injector from the cylinder head . . .

11.11d . . . and recover the flame shield washer

11.11e Fuel injector removed from the cylinder head

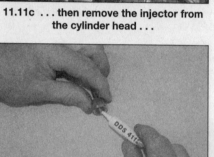

11.14a Lubricate the threads of the union nuts before tightening them

11.14b Fitting the plastic clips to the high-pressure fuel pipes – 1.5 litre

shield washers between the injectors and the cylinder head **(see illustrations)**. Take care not to drop the injectors or allow the needles at their tips to become damaged. The injectors are precision-made to fine limits and must not be handled roughly. In particular, do not mount them in a bench vice.

Refitting

12 Clean the cylinder head and injectors, taking care to prevent foreign matter entering the fuel apertures.
13 Fit new sealing shims between the injectors and the cylinder head. Insert the injectors then fit the clamp plates. Tighten the clamp plate bolts to the specified torque.
14 Refit the leak-off pipes, then fit the new high-pressure fuel pipes (together with the retaining clips, where applicable). Some pipes may be supplied with a sachet of lubricant, which should be used on the union nut threads before fitting – if no lubricant is provided, none should be applied. Finger-tighten the nuts before tightening them to the specified torque. On 1.5 litre engines, use pliers to fit the retaining clips onto the fuel pipes **(see illustrations)**.
15 Reconnect the fuel injector wiring.
16 Fit the new fuel return pipe to the high-pressure pump and fuel rail.
17 Refit the engine oil level dipstick guide (1.5 litre engines), the clip on the fuel rail, and the engine top cover.
18 Reconnect the battery negative lead (refer to *Disconnecting the battery* in the Reference Chapter).
19 Start the engine. If difficulty is experienced, bleed the fuel system as described in Section 6.

12 Injector rail (common rail) – removal and refitting

Note: *Refer to precautions in Section 1 before proceeding. After switching off the engine, allow several minutes for the fuel pressure to subside before disconnecting any of the high-pressure fuel pipes. Take care not to allow dirt into the fuel pipes during this procedure; clean around the area before commencing work. Note that all high-pressure pipes removed must be renewed as a matter of course.*

Removal

1 Disconnect the battery negative lead (refer to *Disconnecting the battery* in the Reference Chapter).
2 Remove the engine top cover.
3 Disconnect the following wiring, according to model:
 a) *Flow actuator and fuel temperature sensor on the rear of the high-pressure pump, and fuel pressure sensor on the fuel rail (1.5 litre engine).*
 b) *Fuel pressure regulator on the high-pressure pump, fuel pressure and temperature sensors on the fuel rail (1.9 litre engine).*
 c) *Fuel injectors.*
 d) *Heater (glow) plugs.*
4 Disconnect the fuel supply and return pipes from the high-pressure pump.
5 Unclip the wiring loom conduit from the high-pressure fuel rail as necessary.
6 On 1.5 litre engines, remove the engine oil

level dipstick guide and tape over the hole. Release the clips from the two pairs of high-pressure injector pipes.
7 While holding the injectors with one spanner, unscrew the high-pressure pipe union nuts with a further spanner. As a precaution against remaining pressure in the pipes, first wrap them loosely in cloth rag. Take care not to damage the leak-off stubs on the injectors. Similarly, unscrew the union nuts from the fuel rail, then remove the pipes. Move the nuts and olives along the pipes when releasing the pipes from the rail and injectors.
8 Tape over or plug all fuel apertures to prevent entry of dust and dirt into the fuel system.
9 Unbolt and remove the fuel rail.

Refitting

10 Refitting is a reversal of removal, noting the following points:
 a) *Tighten all nuts and bolts to the specified torque.*
 b) *Fit a new high-pressure pipe between the pump and rail. Some pipes may be supplied with a sachet of lubricant, which should be used on the union nut threads before fitting – if no lubricant is provided, none should be applied. Finger-tighten the nuts before tightening them to the specified torque. Take care not to place the new high-pressure pipe under any stress when the unions are tightened.*
 c) *When tightening the pipe union nuts onto the injectors, counter-hold the injectors with a further spanner.*
 d) *On completion, prime and bleed the fuel system as described in Section 6. Run the engine, and check for fuel leaks.*

13 Manifolds – removal and refitting

Removal

1 To improve access to the manifolds and related components from above, remove the windscreen cowl panels as described in Chapter 11.

1.5 litre engine

2 The inlet manifold is incorporated into the

cylinder head and therefore cannot be removed separately. To remove the exhaust manifold, ensure the handbrake is applied, then jack up the front of the car and support it on axle stands (see *Jacking and vehicle support*).

3 Disconnect the exhaust downpipe from the catalytic converter, and support it to one side with reference to Section 17.

4 Remove the turbocharger as described in Section 15. If the reason of removing the manifold is simply to renew the gasket, the turbocharger can remain attached to the manifold.

5 Loosen the two clamps, then remove the EGR metal tube between the inlet and exhaust manifolds. The manufacturers recommend that the metal tube and clamps are renewed as a matter of course. Unscrew the mounting bolts and remove the EGR unit from the inlet manifold.

6 Progressively unscrew the mounting nuts and remove the exhaust manifold from the studs on the cylinder head. Recover the metal gasket **(see illustrations)**.

1.9 litre engine

7 The manifolds are removed together – although the manifolds are separate, they are retained by the same nuts, since the stud holes are split between the manifold flanges.

8 Remove the engine top cover.

9 Loosen the hose clip at the front of the metal air duct situated across the top of the engine, and disconnect the intercooler duct from it. Disconnect the vacuum hose from the inlet air shut-off flap. Remove the single nut securing the metal duct to the top of the engine, and the two bolts from its flange to the inlet manifold, and remove the duct, unclipping the vacuum hoses **(see illustrations)**.

10 On models with the heat exchanger-type EGR valve, remove the valve assembly as described in Chapter 4C, Section 3.

11 Remove the two small Allen screws securing the vacuum reservoir to the rear of the inlet manifold. Move the reservoir clear, disconnecting as few of the hoses as possible. Remove two further screws, then disconnect the wiring plug and remove the vacuum control solenoid fitted below the reservoir **(see illustration)**.

12 Unbolt the vacuum hose support bracket from the rear of the inlet manifold, then unclip the rest of the hoses from the front and top, noting how they are fitted and routed. Also unclip the engine breather hose from the inlet manifold.

13 Disconnect the wiring plug from the EGR solenoid **(see illustration)**.

14 Unbolt the turbo oil supply pipe from the back of the inlet manifold. Anticipating some small loss of oil, unbolt the oil pipe unions at the engine and turbo, and remove the pipe completely. Cover the union connection on the turbo, to prevent the entry of dirt.

15 Remove the turbocharger as described in Section 15.

16 Release the clips at each end of the EGR

13.6a Removing the exhaust manifold together with the turbocharger

13.6b Removing the exhaust manifold gasket

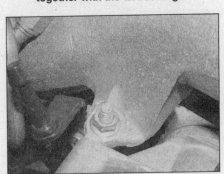

13.9a Remove the nut securing the intercooler duct to the top of the engine

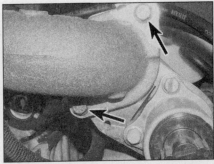

13.9b Remove the two bolts securing the intercooler duct to the inlet manifold

connecting pipe **(see illustration)**. Leave the pipe in place for now – remove it as required when the manifolds are free to move, and can be separated. Note that new clips may be required when refitting.

17 Unscrew the two bolts securing the engine lifting eye, and remove it from the exhaust manifold **(see illustration)**.

18 Progressively unscrew the nine nuts securing the inlet and exhaust manifolds, and withdraw them from the cylinder head. Recover the manifold gasket **(see illustrations)**.

13.11 Disconnect the wiring plug from the vacuum control solenoid

13.13 Disconnect the wiring plug from the EGR solenoid

13.16 Release the clips from the EGR valve connecting pipe

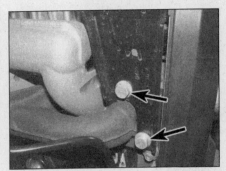

13.17 Unscrew the two engine lifting eye bolts

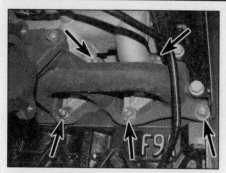

13.18a Remove the nine nuts securing the manifolds, and withdraw them

13.18b Recover the manifold gasket

Refitting

1.5 litre engine

19 Clean the surfaces of the cylinder head and exhaust manifold.

20 Locate a new gasket on the cylinder head studs.

21 Refit the exhaust manifold and finger-tighten the retaining nuts. Tighten the nuts to the specified torque, working in a clockwise direction from the centre of the manifold.

22 Refit the EGR unit to the inlet manifold and tighten the mounting nuts to the specified torque.

23 Fit the new metal tube between the inlet and exhaust manifolds and secure with new clamps. Renault technicians use a special tool to tighten the clamps, however, it should be possible to tighten them using pliers and a screwdriver if care it taken.

24 Refit the turbocharger with reference to Section 15.

1.9 litre engine

25 Refitting is a reversal of removal, bearing in mind the following points:

a) *Ensure that the cylinder head and manifold mating surfaces are clean, and use a new gasket. Note that the central lower four mounting nuts and washers may be started on their studs before refitting the exhaust manifold, as the manifold is slotted. Tighten all fixings to the specified torque.*

b) *Refit the turbocharger with reference to Section 15.*

c) *Ensure that the vacuum hoses are correctly routed and reconnected as noted before removal.*

14 Turbocharger – description

1 A turbocharger increases engine efficiency by raising the pressure in the inlet manifold above atmospheric pressure. Instead of the air simply being sucked into the cylinders, it is forced in. Additional fuel is supplied in proportion to the increased air intake.

2 Energy for the operation of the turbocharger

comes from the exhaust gas. The gas flows through a specially-shaped housing (the turbine housing) and in so doing, spins the turbine wheel. The turbine wheel is attached to a shaft, at the end of which is another vaned wheel known as the compressor wheel. The compressor wheel spins in its own housing and compresses the inducted air on the way to the inlet manifold.

3 Between the turbocharger and the inlet manifold on certain engine types, the compressed air passes through an intercooler. This is an air-to-air heat exchanger, mounted behind the front bumper, between the air conditioning condenser and the coolant radiator. The purpose of the intercooler is to remove, from the inducted air, some of the heat gained in being compressed. Because cooler air is denser, removal of this heat further increases engine efficiency.

4 Boost pressure (the pressure in the inlet manifold) is limited by a wastegate, which diverts the exhaust gas away from the turbine wheel in response to a pressure-sensitive actuator. Turbocharging pressure is controlled by a solenoid unit mounted on top of the air cleaner (1.5 litre) or on the ECU mounting bracket (1.9 litre), with a pressure sensor located on one of the air ducts – refer to Section 10.

5 The turbo shaft is pressure-lubricated by an oil feed pipe from the main oil gallery. The shaft 'floats' on a cushion of oil. A drain pipe returns the oil to the sump.

Precautions

6 The turbocharger operates at extremely high speeds and temperatures. Certain precautions must be observed to avoid premature failure of the turbo or injury to the operator.

7 Do not race the engine immediately after start-up, especially if it is cold. Give the oil a few seconds to circulate.

8 Always allow the engine to return to idle speed before switching it off – do not blip the throttle and switch off, as this will leave the turbo spinning without lubrication.

9 Allow the engine to idle for several minutes before switching off after a high-speed run.

10 Observe the recommended intervals for oil and filter changing, and use a reputable oil of the specified quality. Neglect of oil changing,

or use of inferior oil, can cause carbon formation on the turbo shaft and subsequent failure.

⚠️ *Warning: Do not operate the turbo with any parts exposed. Foreign objects falling onto the rotating vanes could cause excessive damage and (if ejected) personal injury.*

15 Turbocharger – removal and refitting

Note: New oil supply pipe O-rings and copper washers must be used on refitting.

Removal

1 Disconnect the battery negative lead (refer to *Disconnecting the battery* in the Reference Chapter).

2 Remove the engine top cover, then remove the air cleaner and inlet ducts as described in Section 2.

3 With the handbrake applied, jack up the front of the car, and support securely on axle stands (see *Jacking and vehicle support*). Remove the right-hand front roadwheel and the engine undertray.

1.5 litre engine

4 Loosen the hose clip and disconnect the air inlet duct from the resonator on top of the engine. Unbolt the resonator mounting bracket and EGR solenoid heat shield, and remove them.

5 Similarly, loosen the hose clip and disconnect the duct from the turbocharger. Unbolt the duct from the top of the engine, and remove it.

6 Disconnect the wiring plugs from the turbo pressure sensor and from the EGR solenoid.

7 Disconnect the vacuum hose from the wastegate.

8 Referring to Section 17 if necessary, unscrew the nuts and separate the exhaust downpipe from the catalytic converter.

9 Unbolt the catalytic converter mounting at the transmission end from the converter, and remove it from the transmission. Similarly, unbolt and remove the mounting strut from the other side of the converter.

10 Unscrew the four turbo-to-converter nuts, and withdraw the converter from under the car.

11 Unscrew the union and disconnect the oil supply pipe from the turbocharger, collect the copper sealing rings, then unscrew the union nut and disconnect the pipe from the cylinder head **(see illustrations)**. Cover the oil pipe connection on the turbo to prevent dirt entry.

12 Unscrew the bolts and detach the oil return pipe from the bottom of the turbocharger – if necessary, remove the pipe from the cylinder block **(see illustrations)**.

13 Unscrew the turbocharger upper and lower mounting nuts **(see illustrations)**, then remove the turbocharger.

15.11a Removing the oil supply pipe and copper sealing rings from the turbocharger

15.11b Removing the oil supply pipe from the cylinder head

15.12a Oil return pipe flange bolts on the bottom of the turbocharger

15.12b Removing the oil return pipe

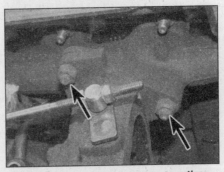

15.13a Turbocharger upper mounting nuts . . .

15.13b . . . and lower mounting nut

1.9 litre engine

14 Referring to Section 17 if necessary, unscrew the nuts and separate the exhaust downpipe from the catalytic converter.

15 Remove the four bolts securing the catalytic converter support plate at the transmission end, and remove the plate from under the car. Similarly, remove the support strut from the other end of the converter **(see illustrations)**.

16 Referring to Chapter 2C if necessary, unbolt and remove the engine lower mounting link.

17 Remove the three mounting nuts, and withdraw the catalytic converter from under the car **(see illustration)**. Recover the gasket – a new one will be needed for refitting.

18 Disconnect the engine breather hose from the turbocharger air inlet duct, by squeezing the quick-release fitting **(see illustration)**.

19 Disconnect the vacuum hose from the turbo wastegate **(see illustration)**.

20 Unscrew the turbo oil supply pipe union from the top of the unit, then remove the pipe mounting bolt from the inlet manifold, and finally the union from the engine block **(see illustrations)**. Remove the oil supply pipe, anticipating a small amount of oil spillage and recovering the sealing rings. Cover the oil pipe connection on the turbo to prevent dirt entry.

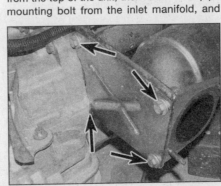

15.15a Undo the four bolts (one from behind) from the converter support plate . . .

15.15b . . . and remove the strut from the other side

15.17 Remove the catalytic converter from under the car

15.18 Engine breather hose on turbo air duct

15.19 Wastegate vacuum hose (arrowed)

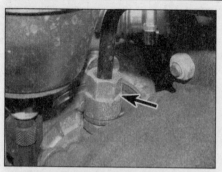

15.20a Unscrew the oil supply pipe union on top of the turbo . . .

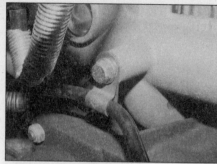

15.20b . . . the pipe mounting bolt from the manifold . . .

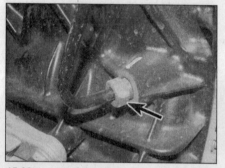

15.20c . . . and the pipe union on the block

15.22 Turbocharger air duct hose clips

21 Unscrew the two bolts from the oil return pipe flange on the base of the unit. If required, the pipe can be removed from the cylinder block.

22 Loosen the hose clips and disconnect the air ducts from the turbocharger (see illustration).

23 Unscrew the three turbocharger mounting nuts, then remove the unit from the exhaust manifold. Recover the gasket – a new one should be used when refitting.

Refitting

24 Refitting is a reversal of removal, noting the following points:

a) Renew any rusty or damaged nuts or bolts as necessary. Fit new gaskets, O-rings and seals.

b) On 1.5 litre engines, apply thread-locking fluid to the oil supply pipe union nut threads before refitting.

c) To ensure an immediate oil supply to the turbo before the engine is started, Renault specify that the engine first be prevented from firing by disconnecting the fuel flow actuator (1.5 litre engine) or the fuel pressure regulator (1.9 litre engine) on the high-pressure pump. Crank the engine for several seconds, then reconnect the components and start as normal. However, doing this may introduce a fault code in the engine ECU, which would then have to be cleared by a Renault dealer.

d) Run the engine at idle speed, and check the turbocharger oil unions for leakage.

e) After the engine has been run, check the engine oil level, and top-up if necessary.

16 Intercooler – removal and refitting

Removal

1 The intercooler is located in front of the radiator and air conditioning condenser (where applicable).

2 Remove the front bumper as described in Chapter 11.

3 Remove the single nut and bolt at either end, then withdraw the bumper crossmember from the front of the car (see illustrations).

4 Unclip and remove the plastic trim panel from either side of the radiator (see illustration).

5 Loosen the hose clips and disconnect the air ducts from the base and side of the intercooler (see illustrations).

6 Lift the intercooler at both sides, and lift it off the plastic mounting lugs on the radiator side

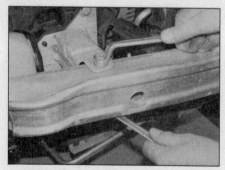

16.3a Unscrew the nut and bolt each end . . .

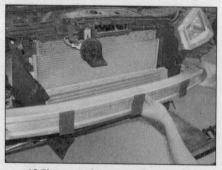

16.3b . . . and remove the bumper crossmember

16.4 Unclip the radiator plastic side guards

16.5a Disconnect the air ducts from the side . . .

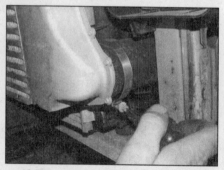

16.5b . . . and base of the intercooler

16.6 Removing the intercooler

16.7a Disconnect the duct on top of the engine . . .

16.7b . . . and where applicable, disconnect the pressure sensor wiring

tanks (see illustration). Remove it from the car, taking care not to damage the intercooler fins, nor the ones on the radiator or condenser (as applicable).

7 To remove the intercooler upper duct, loosen the hose clip and disconnect the duct from the top of the engine. On 1.9 litre engines, disconnect the wiring plug from the turbo pressure sensor (see illustrations). Withdraw the duct from the front of the car.

8 The metal section of the upper duct is bolted to the valve cover and secured by a hose clip at the EGR housing (1.5 litre engines), or by a nut at the back of the valve cover, and by two bolts to the EGR housing (1.9 litre engines) (see illustrations).

9 To remove the lower duct, remove the battery and battery tray as described in Chapter 5A, and the air cleaner as described in Section 2. Loosen the hose clip at the rear of the metal duct, then remove the single mounting nut and lift the duct from the top of the transmission (see illustrations).

Refitting

10 Before refitting the intercooler, check inside the duct connection stubs for significant amounts of oil. If present, this can be cleaned out with a suitable solvent, but it does indicate that the turbocharger oil seals have failed – the turbo should be removed for inspection as described in Section 15.

11 Refitting is a reversal of removal, but tighten all hose clips securely, to avoid air leaks. Refit the bumper as described in Chapter 11.

17 Exhaust system –
general information and component renewal

General information

1 On new cars, the exhaust system is in one piece, attached to the manifold by a bolted flange joint. This single section includes the catalytic converter (bolted to the back of the engine), a centre pipe, and a rear silencer. The system fits over the rear suspension, so the only way to remove it (other than to remove the suspension) is to cut it off.

16.8a The metal section is bolted to the valve cover – 1.5 litre . . .

2 The rear section can be renewed in two separate sections by cutting it off at the points indicated between two punched marks on the pipe (see illustration). Renault state that the entire exhaust is of stainless steel, which

16.8b . . . or secured using a nut . . .

should at least mean corrosion damage is less of a problem.

3 The system is suspended throughout its entire length by rubber mountings, bolted to the car floor.

16.9a Loosen the hose clip . . .

16.8c . . . and two bolts to the EGR housing – 1.9 litre

16.9b . . . then unscrew the mounting nut . . .

16.9c . . . and remove the lower duct from the transmission

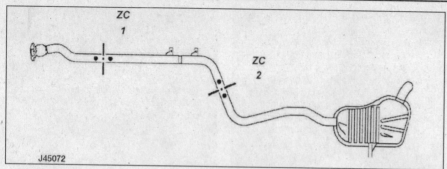

17.2 Cut the original exhaust at the cut zones (ZC1 and ZC2) indicated by the punched marks

Removal

4 To remove a part of the system, first jack up the front or rear of the car, and support it on axle stands (see *Jacking and vehicle support*). Alternatively, position the car over an inspection pit, or on car ramps. Where fitted, remove the engine compartment undertray.

Complete system

5 If the exhaust merely has to be removed to allow other work to be carried out, it can be unbolted and lowered as follows. As stated previously, the one-piece rear system cannot be removed without first unbolting the rear suspension, or cutting the exhaust as described in the rear silencer removal procedure. For renewal of an individual section, refer to the relevant sub-heading below.

6 Unscrew and remove the catalytic converter-to-downpipe flange joint nuts **(see**

illustration). If the nuts are in poor condition, obtain some new ones for reassembly.

7 Mark their positions for accurate alignment when refitting, then unbolt the rubber mounting blocks from the car floor in the centre, and behind the rear silencer.

8 Lift the system at the front to clear the converter studs, and draw it to the rear as far as possible. If the system is to be left unbolted during other servicing work, support it as necessary so that the pipes are not under strain.

Catalytic converter

9 Separate the downpipe from the converter as described in paragraphs 6 to 8.

10 Unbolt the catalytic converter mounting bracket (mounting plate on 1.9 litre engines) at the transmission end from the converter, and remove it from the transmission. Similarly, unbolt and remove the mounting strut from the other side of the converter **(refer to illustrations 15.15a and b)**.

17.6 Catalytic converter-to-downpipe nuts

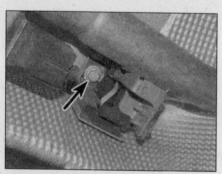

17.13 Unbolt the centre silencer mounting block under the car

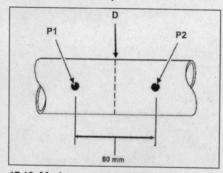

17.12 Mark a central point (D) between the punch marks (P1 and P2)

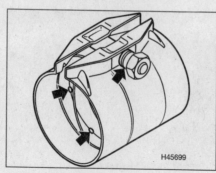

17.15 Pipe joining sleeve – insert pipe ends up to inner marks

11 Unscrew the turbo-to-converter nuts, and withdraw the converter from under the car **(refer to illustration 15.17)**. Recover the gasket – a new one will be needed for refitting.

Centre pipe

12 Locate the two cutting points along the centre pipe, indicated by two punch marks on the pipe. The pipe must be cut exactly between these marks, which are 80 mm apart – measure and mark each central point, and cut through **(see illustration)**. If a new section is being fitted, if possible offer the new one up alongside to ensure the cut is made at the best place.

13 Mark it for position, then unbolt the centre silencer mounting block from the underside of the car **(see illustration)**. Remove the centre pipe. If a new pipe is being fitted, transfer the mounting to the new component.

14 Clean off any burrs on the cut pipe(s) which might interfere with the joining sleeve and prevent a gas-tight joint being achieved.

> *To make refitting easier, it may help to unbolt the rear silencer's rear mounting (mark it for position first). Once the centre pipe's front joining sleeve is in place, the old rear section can then be slid into position in the rear sleeve.*

15 Refitting is a reversal of removal, noting the following points:

a) *Obtain two new pipe joining sleeves for reassembly – old ones should not be re-used* **(see illustration)**.

b) *If a new pipe section is being fitted, the pipes may require trimming to mate up with the old sections – offer it roughly into position first to check.*

c) *Apply exhaust jointing compound evenly around the inside of the joining sleeves, and fit them to the old pipes. Ensure that both pipes to be joined enter the sleeve by an equal amount (position the sleeve centrally over the joint). Tighten the clamp nut to the specified torque, indicated by a 'click' from the nut – do not over-tighten, as this may deform the pipe and cause a leak.*

d) *Align the exhaust mountings with the marks made before removal, and tighten their bolts securely.*

Rear silencer

16 Locate the cutting point in front the rear silencer, indicated by two punch marks on the pipe. The pipe must be cut exactly between these marks, which are 80 mm apart – measure and mark each central point, and cut through. If a new section is being fitted, if possible offer the new one up alongside to ensure the cut is made at the best place.

17 Mark it for position, then unbolt the rear silencer mounting block from the underside of the car. Remove the rear silencer, twisting and feeding the pipe over the rear suspension (remove the rear wheel to improve access). If a new silencer is being fitted, transfer the mounting to the new component.

18 Clean off any burrs on the cut pipe(s) which might interfere with the joining sleeve and prevent a gas-tight joint being achieved.

19 Refitting is a reversal of removal, noting the following points:

a) *Obtain a new pipe joining sleeve for reassembly – old ones should not be re-used.*

b) *If a new silencer section is being fitted, the new pipe may require trimming to mate up with the old pipe – offer it roughly into position first to check.*

c) *Apply exhaust jointing compound evenly around the inside of the joining sleeve, and fit it to the old pipe. Ensure that both pipes to be joined enter the sleeve by an equal amount (position the sleeve centrally over the joint).Tighten the clamp nut to the specified torque, indicated by a 'click' from the nut – do not over-tighten, as this may deform the pipe and cause a leak.*

d) *Align the exhaust mounting with the marks made before removal, and tighten its bolts securely.*

Notes

Chapter 4 Part C:
Emissions control systems

Contents

Degrees of difficulty

Easy, suitable for novice with little experience	**Fairly easy,** suitable for beginner with some experience	**Fairly difficult,** suitable for competent DIY mechanic	**Difficult,** suitable for experienced DIY mechanic	**Very difficult,** suitable for expert DIY or professional

Specifications

General

Oxygen sensor resistance (petrol engines) – typical:	
Upstream sensor	9.0 ohms
Downstream sensor	3.4 ohms

Torque wrench settings

	Nm	lbf ft
EGR pipe flange mounting bolts	20	15
EGR solenoid valve mounting bolts	9	7
EGR valve/heat exchanger assembly mounting bolts	10	7
Oxygen (lambda) sensor	45	33

1 General information and precautions

Petrol models

1 All petrol engines are designed to use unleaded petrol, and also have various other features built into the fuel system to help minimise harmful emissions.

2 All models are equipped with a crankcase emissions control system, a catalytic converter and an evaporative emissions control system.

3 The emissions control systems function as follows.

Crankcase emissions control

4 To reduce the emission of unburned hydrocarbons from the crankcase into the atmosphere, the engine is sealed and the blow-by gases and oil vapour are drawn from inside the crankcase, into the inlet manifold to be burned by the engine during normal combustion.

5 Under all conditions the gases are forced out of the crankcase by the (relatively) higher crankcase pressure.

6 The crankcase ventilation hoses and restrictors should be periodically cleaned to ensure correct operation of the system.

Exhaust emissions control

7 To minimise the amount of pollutants which escape into the atmosphere, all models are fitted with a catalytic converter in the exhaust system. The system is of the closed-loop type, in which two oxygen sensors in the exhaust system provide the fuel injection/ignition system ECU with constant feedback, enabling the ECU to adjust the mixture to provide the best possible conditions for the converter to operate. One oxygen sensor is located in the exhaust manifold, with the second downstream of the catalytic converter, to monitor the converter's efficiency.

8 The oxygen (lambda) sensor has a heating element built-in that is controlled by the ECU through the sensor relay to bring the sensor's tip to an efficient operating temperature quickly. The sensor's tip is sensitive to oxygen and sends the ECU a varying voltage depending on the amount of oxygen in the exhaust gases; if the inlet air/fuel mixture is too rich, the exhaust gases are low in oxygen, so the sensor sends a low voltage signal, the voltage rising as the mixture weakens and the amount of oxygen rises in the exhaust gases.

9 Peak conversion efficiency of all major pollutants occurs if the inlet air/fuel mixture is maintained at the chemically correct ratio for the complete combustion of petrol of 14.7 parts (by weight) of air to 1 part of fuel (the 'stoichiometric' ratio). The sensor output voltage alters in a large step at this point, the ECU using the signal change as a reference point and correcting the inlet air/fuel mixture accordingly by altering the fuel injector pulse width.

Evaporative emissions control

10 To minimise the escape into the atmosphere of unburned hydrocarbons, an evaporative emissions control system is also fitted to all models. The fuel tank filler cap is sealed, and a charcoal canister is mounted on the side of the fuel tank. The canister collects the petrol vapours generated in the tank when the car is parked and stores them until they can be cleared from the canister (under the control of the fuel injection/ignition system ECU) via the purge valve into the inlet manifold to be burned by the engine during normal combustion.

11 To ensure that the engine runs correctly when it is cold and/or idling, and to protect the catalytic converter from the effects of an over-rich mixture, the purge control valve is not opened by the ECU until the engine has warmed-up, and the engine is under load; the valve solenoid is then modulated on and off to allow the stored vapour to pass into the inlet manifold.

Diesel models

12 All diesel engine models are designed to meet strict emission requirements, and are also equipped with a crankcase emissions control system. In addition to this, all models are fitted with an unregulated catalytic converter to reduce harmful exhaust emissions. To further reduce emissions, an exhaust gas recirculation (EGR) system is also fitted.

13 The emissions control systems function as follows.

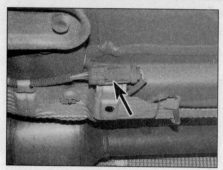

2.9a Disconnect the sensor wiring plug under the car . . .

Crankcase emissions control

14 To reduce the emission of unburned hydrocarbons from the crankcase into the atmosphere, the engine is sealed. Blow-by gases and oil vapour are drawn from inside the crankcase, through the cylinder head cover, then through a pressure-sensitive recirculation valve into the turbocharger. From the turbocharger, the gases enter the inlet manifold to be burned by the engine during normal combustion.

15 There are no restrictors in the system hoses, since the minimal depression in the inlet manifold remains constant during all engine operating conditions.

Exhaust emissions control

16 To minimise the amount of pollutants which escape into the atmosphere, an unregulated catalytic converter is fitted in the exhaust system. The catalytic converter consists of a canister containing a fine mesh impregnated with a catalyst material, over which the exhaust gases pass. The catalyst speeds up the oxidation of harmful carbon monoxide, unburnt hydrocarbons and soot, effectively reducing the quantity of harmful products reaching the atmosphere. The catalytic converter operates remotely in the exhaust system, and there is no oxygen sensor as fitted to the petrol engines.

Exhaust gas recirculation system

17 The system is designed to recirculate small quantities of exhaust gas into the inlet tract, and therefore into the combustion process, reducing the level of oxides of nitrogen present in the final exhaust gas which

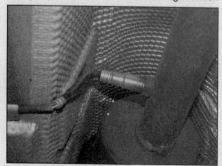

2.9b . . . then unscrew the sensor from the front pipe

is released into the atmosphere. The system is controlled by the engine management ECU, which uses several inputs to determine when to operate the system, including coolant and air temperature, engine and vehicle speed, injection flow rate, and atmospheric pressure.

18 Typically, the system will be in operation under most normal conditions, with the car moving and the engine above idle speed.

19 The volume of exhaust gas recirculated is controlled by an electrically-operated exhaust gas recirculation (EGR) solenoid valve on the exhaust manifold, activated by the engine management ECU.

Catalytic converter precautions

20 For long life and satisfactory operation of the catalytic converter, certain precautions must be observed. These are listed in Section 4 of this Chapter.

2 Petrol engine emissions control systems – testing and component renewal

Crankcase emissions control

Testing

1 There is no specific test procedure for the crankcase emissions control system. If problems are suspected, check that the hoses are clean internally, and that the restrictors are not blocked or missing.

Component renewal

2 This is self-evident. Mark the various hoses before disconnecting them if there is any possibility of confusion on reassembly.

Exhaust emissions control

Testing

3 An exhaust gas analyser (CO meter) will be needed. The ignition system must be in good condition, the air cleaner element must be clean, and the engine must be in good mechanical condition.

4 Bring the engine to normal operating temperature, then connect the exhaust gas analyser in accordance with the equipment maker's instructions.

5 Run the engine at 2500 rpm for about 30 seconds, then allow it to idle and check the CO level (Chapter 4A Specifications). If the CO level is within the specified limits, the system is operating correctly.

6 If the CO level is higher than specified, try the effect of disconnecting the oxygen sensor wiring. If the CO level rises when the sensor is disconnected, this suggests that the oxygen sensor is OK and that the catalytic converter is faulty. If disconnecting the sensor has no effect, this suggests a fault in the sensor.

7 Renew the oxygen sensor if it is proved faulty.

Oxygen sensor – renewal

8 To remove the upstream sensor, trace the

wiring from the sensor located on the exhaust manifold to the connector and disconnect it. Unscrew the sensor from the manifold using a deep socket.

9 To remove the downstream sensor, raise the front of the car and support it on axle stands (see *Jacking and vehicle support*). Trace the sensor wiring up from the sensor, which is located behind the catalytic converter at the rear of the front subframe, and disconnect it at the plug. Unscrew the sensor from the exhaust, and remove it **(see illustrations)**.

10 Clean the threads of the sensor (if it is to be refitted) and the threads in the exhaust pipe or manifold.

11 If the sensor wires are broken, the sensor must be renewed – no attempt should be made to repair them.

12 Apply high-temperature anti-seize compound to the sensor threads. Screw the sensor in by hand, then tighten it to the specified torque.

13 Reconnect the sensor wiring, and where applicable, lower the car to the ground.

Catalytic converter – renewal

14 The catalytic converter is renewed as part of the exhaust system. Refer to Part A of this Chapter.

Evaporative emissions control

Testing

15 The operating principle of the system is that the solenoid valve is open only when the engine is warm with the throttle at least at the part-throttle position.

16 Bring the engine to normal operating temperature, then switch it off. Connect a vacuum gauge (range 0 to 1000 mbars) into the hose from the canister to the solenoid valve. Connect a voltmeter to the solenoid valve terminals.

17 Start the engine and allow it to idle. There should be no vacuum shown on the gauge, and no voltage present at the solenoid.

18 If manifold vacuum is indicated although no voltage is present, the solenoid valve may be stuck open. Temporarily disconnect the hoses from the solenoid valve and blow through the outlets to dislodge any particles of carbon.

19 If voltage is present at idle, there is a fault in the wiring or the computer.

20 Depress the accelerator slightly. Voltage should appear momentarily at the solenoid terminals, and manifold vacuum be indicated on the gauge.

21 If vacuum is not indicated even though voltage is present, either there is a leak in the hoses, or the valve is not opening.

22 If no voltage appears, there is a fault in the wiring or the computer.

Canister renewal

23 Chock the front wheels, then jack up the rear of the car and support it on axle stands (see *Jacking and vehicle support*).

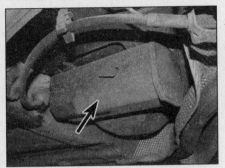

2.25 The charcoal canister is a box mounted on the side of the tank

24 Disconnect the battery negative lead (refer to *Disconnecting the battery* in the Reference Chapter).

25 The canister is mounted on the side of the fuel tank **(see illustration)**. To remove it, first pull it sideways off its mounting lug.

26 Note their locations, then squeeze the quick-release connections on the pipe fittings and disconnect them. If required, the breather pipe can also be disconnected. Remove the canister from under the car.

27 Dispose of the old canister safely, bearing in mind that it may contain liquid fuel and/or fuel vapour.

28 Fit the new canister using a reversal of the removal procedure. Make sure that the hoses are connected correctly.

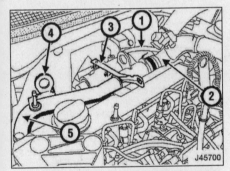

3.11 EGR valve removal details (1.5 litre)

1 Turbo boost control solenoid vacuum pipe	3 Bracket
	4 Engine lifting eye
	5 Metal air inlet duct
2 Air inlet duct	

3.13 Removing the metal air inlet duct

2.30 Charcoal canister purge control solenoid valve

Solenoid valve

29 The solenoid valve is located on the engine compartment bulkhead, on the right-hand side (right as seen from the driver's seat). To improve access, remove the windscreen cowl panels as described in Chapter 11.

30 Disconnect the wiring plug and the vacuum hose from the valve **(see illustration)**.

31 Unscrew the retaining nuts, and withdraw the valve complete with its bracket.

32 Refitting is a reversal of removal, ensuring that the vacuum hoses are securely reconnected.

3 Diesel engine emissions control systems – testing and component renewal

Crankcase emissions control

Testing

1 If the system is thought to be faulty, firstly, check that the hoses are unobstructed. On high-mileage cars, particularly when regularly used for short journeys, a jelly-like deposit may be evident inside the system hoses and oil separators. If excessive deposits are present, the relevant component(s) should be removed and cleaned.

2 Periodically inspect the system components for security and damage, and renew them as necessary.

Component renewal

3 This is self-evident. Mark the various hoses before disconnecting them if there is any possibility of confusion on reassembly.

3.15a Release the clamps . . .

Exhaust emissions control

Testing

4 The system can only be tested accurately using a suitable exhaust gas analyser (suitable for use with diesel engines).

Catalytic converter – renewal

5 The catalytic converter is renewed as part of the exhaust system. Refer to Part B of this Chapter.

Exhaust gas recirculation

Testing

6 Testing of the EGR system is best left to a Renault dealer who will have the dedicated equipment necessary to carry out the test.

EGR valve – 1.5 litre (type 1)

7 The EGR valve is mounted on the inlet manifold at the rear of the cylinder head, and is connected to the exhaust manifold by a convoluted metal tube, and to the inlet manifold by an air duct.

8 Remove the engine top cover, then remove the air cleaner unit as described in Chapter 4B. If necessary, to further improve access, remove the windscreen cowl panels as described in Chapter 11.

9 Disconnect the wiring from the EGR solenoid valve and downstream air temperature sensor.

10 Disconnect the hose from the turbo-charging pressure control valve on the air duct.

11 Loosen the clips and remove the air duct from between the EGR unit and turbocharger **(see illustration)**.

12 Unbolt and remove the right-hand rear engine lifting eye.

13 Unscrew the bolt and remove the metal air inlet duct **(see illustration)**.

14 Where fitted, remove the heat shield from over the EGR solenoid valve.

15 Loosen both clamps and remove the EGR convoluted metal tube from the EGR valve and exhaust manifold **(see illustrations)**.

16 Unscrew the mounting bolts and remove the EGR valve unit from its location on the inlet manifold. Note that the solenoid valve is not available separately **(see illustration)**.

17 Refitting is a reversal of removal, but renew the air inlet duct O-rings. Check the condition of the convoluted metal tube retaining clamps and if necessary, renew them – if the special

3.15b . . . and remove the EGR convoluted metal tube

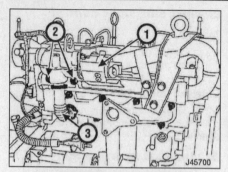

**3.16 EGR valve details (1.5 litre) –
seen from rear of engine**

1 *EGR solenoid heat shield*
2 *EGR valve mounting bolts*
3 *Convoluted metal tube*

tool is not available, use a pair of pincers to
tighten the clamps until the clip is engaged.

EGR valve – 1.5 litre (type 2)

18 Later 1.5 litre engines appear to be fitted
with a simpler EGR valve arrangement.
19 Unclip and remove the engine top cover
for access to the valve. If necessary, to further
improve access, remove the windscreen cowl
panels as described in Chapter 11.
20 Disconnect the wiring plug, then remove
the mounting nuts and withdraw the valve
from the manifold **(see illustration)**.
21 Refitting is a reversal of removal.

EGR solenoid – 1.9 litre engines

22 On some 1.9 litre engines (including the
car seen in our project workshop), the EGR
system simply comprises a solenoid mounted
on the inlet manifold, which has an integral
valve housing, joined to the exhaust manifold
by a convoluted metal tube. Other models
have a more elaborate system, with a coolant-
fed heat exchanger to cool the exhaust gases
before they enter the inlet manifold – this
system is covered later in this Section.
23 Remove the engine top cover. Access to
the solenoid may be improved by removing
the air cleaner (or at least, the air cleaner inlet
duct) as described in Chapter 4B, but this is
not essential. If necessary, to further improve
access, remove the windscreen cowl panels
as described in Chapter 11.
24 Disconnect the solenoid wiring plug **(see
illustration)**.

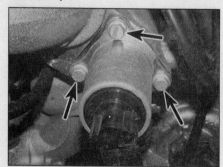

**3.25 Remove the three mounting bolts,
and withdraw the valve**

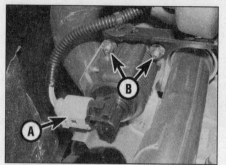

**3.20 EGR valve wiring plug (A) and
mounting nuts (B)**

25 Unscrew the three mounting bolts, and
withdraw the solenoid from the inlet manifold
(see illustration).
26 Refitting is a reversal of removal.

EGR unit (heat exchanger type) –
1.9 litre engines

27 Drain the cooling system as described in
Chapter 1B.
28 Remove the air cleaner and ducts as
described in Chapter 4B. If necessary, to further
improve access, remove the windscreen cowl
panels as described in Chapter 11.
29 Squeeze the quick-release fitting on the
crankcase breather pipe and disconnect it
from the turbocharger inlet duct. Lift the pipe,
disconnect its clip on top of the inlet manifold,
and move it clear of the back of the engine.
30 Unscrew the two small Allen screws
securing the vacuum reservoir, and remove the
reservoir from the back of the inlet manifold,
disconnecting as few of the hoses from it as
possible. Move the reservoir and hoses clear.
31 Disconnect the wiring plug from the EGR
solenoid. If required, the solenoid can now be
removed by unscrewing the three mounting
bolts.
32 Release the spring-type hose clips, then
disconnect the heat exchanger coolant hoses

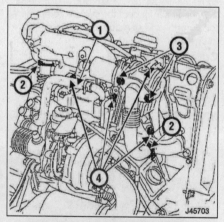

**3.32 EGR valve details (1.9 litre –
heat exchanger type)**

1 *Coolant supply hose*
2 *Tube clips*
3 *EGR valve pipe flange bolts*
4 *EGR valve/heat exchanger assembly bolts*

**3.24 Disconnect the EGR solenoid wiring
plug**

from the back of the thermostat housing, and
from the EGR heat exchanger, noting how
they are routed **(see illustration)**.
33 Prise off and release the metal clips
securing the two convoluted metal pipes
to the inlet and exhaust manifolds. If care is
taken, these clips may be re-used, but if they
have seen long service, new ones should be
obtained for refitting.
34 Remove the two bolts securing the pipe
flange to the EGR valve housing.
35 Unscrew the four mounting bolts securing
the valve and heat exchanger assembly to the
back of the engine, and withdraw it.
36 Refitting is a reversal of removal, noting
the following points:
  a) *Fit new exhaust manifold seals, and new
  EGR pipe clips as necessary.*
  b) *Refill and bleed the cooling system as
  described in Chapter 1B – note that a
  heat exchanger bleed screw is fitted,
  located behind the EGR solenoid.*

4 Catalytic converter –
general information
and precautions

General information

1 The catalytic converter reduces harmful
exhaust emissions by chemically converting
the more poisonous gases to ones which (in
theory at least) are less harmful. The chemical
reaction is known as an 'oxidising' reaction, or
one where oxygen is 'added'.
2 Inside the converter is a honeycomb
structure, made of ceramic material and
coated with the precious metals palladium,
platinum and rhodium (the 'catalyst' which
promotes the chemical reaction). The chemical
reaction generates heat, which itself promotes
the reaction - therefore, once the car has been
driven several miles, the body of the converter
will be very hot.
3 The ceramic structure contained within
the converter is understandably fragile, and
will not withstand rough treatment. Since
the converter runs at a high temperature,
driving through deep standing water (in flood
conditions, for example) is to be avoided,
since the thermal stresses imposed when
plunging the hot converter into cold water may

well cause the ceramic internals to fracture, resulting in a 'blocked' converter - a common cause of failure. A converter which has been damaged in this way can be checked by shaking it (do not strike it) - if a rattling noise is heard, this indicates probable failure.

Precautions

4 The catalytic converter is a reliable and simple device which needs no maintenance in itself, but there are some facts of which an owner should be aware if the converter is to function properly for its full service life.

Petrol models

a) *DO NOT use leaded petrol (or lead-replacement petrol, LRP) in a car equipped with a catalytic converter - the lead (or other additives) will coat the precious metals, reducing their converting efficiency and will eventually destroy the converter.*

b) *Always keep the ignition and fuel systems well-maintained in accordance with the manufacturer's schedule (see Chapter 1A).*

c) *If the engine develops a misfire, do not drive the car at all (or at least as little as possible) until the fault is cured.*

d) *DO NOT push or tow start the car – this will soak the catalytic converter in unburned fuel, causing it to overheat when the engine does start.*

e) *DO NOT switch off the ignition at high engine speeds - ie do not 'blip' the throttle immediately before switching off the engine.*

f) *DO NOT use fuel or engine oil additives – these may contain substances harmful to the catalytic converter.*

g) *DO NOT continue to use the car if the engine burns oil to the extent of leaving a visible trail of blue smoke.*

h) *Remember that the catalytic converter operates at very high temperatures. DO NOT, therefore, park the car on dry undergrowth, over long grass or piles of dead leaves after a long run.*

i) *As mentioned above, driving through deep water should be avoided if possible. The sudden cooling effect may fracture the ceramic honeycomb, damaging it beyond repair.*

j) *Remember that the catalytic converter is FRAGILE - do not strike it with tools during servicing work, and take care handling it when removing it from the car for any reason.*

k) *In some cases, a sulphurous smell (like that of rotten eggs) may be noticed from the exhaust. This is common to many catalytic converter-equipped cars, and has more to do with the sulphur content of the brand of fuel being used than the converter itself.*

l) *If a substantial loss of power is experienced, remember that this could be due to the converter being blocked. This can occur simply as a result of high mileage, but may be due to the ceramic element having fractured and collapsed internally (see paragraph 3). A new converter is the only cure in this instance.*

m) *The catalytic converter, used on a well-maintained and well-driven car, should last at least 100 000 miles – if the converter is no longer effective, it must be renewed.*

Diesel models

5 The catalytic converter fitted to diesel models is simpler than that fitted to petrol models, but it still needs to be treated with respect to avoid problems:

a) *DO NOT use fuel or engine oil additives - these may contain substances harmful to the catalytic converter.*

b) *DO NOT continue to use the car if the engine burns (engine) oil to the extent of leaving a visible trail of blue smoke.*

c) *Remember that the catalytic converter operates at very high temperatures. DO NOT, therefore, park the car in dry undergrowth, over long grass or piles of dead leaves after a long run.*

d) *As mentioned above, driving through deep water should be avoided if possible. The sudden cooling effect will fracture the ceramic honeycomb, damaging it beyond repair.*

e) *Remember that the catalytic converter is FRAGILE - do not strike it with tools during servicing work, and take care handling it when removing it from the car for any reason.*

f) *If a substantial loss of power is experienced, remember that this could be due to the converter being blocked. This can occur simply as a result of high mileage, but may be due to the ceramic element having fractured and collapsed internally (see paragraph 3). A new converter is the only cure in this instance.*

g) *The catalytic converter, used on a well-maintained and well-driven car, should last at least 100 000 miles - if the converter is no longer effective, it must be renewed.*

Notes

Chapter 5 Part A:
Starting and charging systems

Contents

Degrees of difficulty

Easy, suitable for novice with little experience	**Fairly easy,** suitable for beginner with some experience	**Fairly difficult,** suitable for competent DIY mechanic	**Difficult,** suitable for experienced DIY mechanic	**Very difficult,** suitable for expert DIY or professional

Specifications

Battery

Type	Lead-acid, 'maintenance-free'
Charge condition:	
Poor	11.5 volts
Normal	12.0 volts
Good.	12.5 volts

Alternator

Type	Valeo or Bosch
Output:	
Except 1.9 litre diesel engines	110 or 150 amps
1.9 litre diesel engines	125 or 155 amps
Regulated voltage	13.5 to 14.8 volts

Starter motor

Type	Valeo or Mitsubishi

Torque wrench settings

	Nm	lbf ft
Alternator mounting bolts.	25	18
Starter motor mounting bolts.	44	32

1 General information, precautions and battery disconnection

General information

The engine electrical system consists mainly of the charging and starting systems. Because of their engine-related functions, these components are covered separately from the body electrical devices such as the lights, instruments, etc (which are covered in Chapter 12). On petrol engine models, refer to Part B for information on the ignition system, and on diesel models, refer to Part C for information on the preheating system.

The electrical system is of the 12-volt negative-earth type.

The original-equipment battery is of the 'maintenance-free' (sealed for life) type, and is charged by the alternator, which is belt-driven from the crankshaft pulley.

The starter motor is of the pre-engaged type, incorporating an integral solenoid. On starting, the solenoid moves the drive pinion into engagement with the flywheel ring gear before the starter motor is energised. Once the engine has started, a one-way clutch prevents the motor armature being driven by the engine until the pinion disengages from the flywheel.

Precautions

It is necessary to take extra care when working on the electrical system to avoid damage to semi-conductor devices (diodes and transistors), and to avoid the risk of personal injury. In addition to the precautions given in Safety first! at the beginning of this manual, observe the following when working on the system:

Always remove rings, watches, etc before working on the electrical system. Even with the battery disconnected, capacitive discharge could occur if a component's live terminal is earthed through a metal object. This could cause a shock or nasty burn.

Do not reverse the battery connections. Components such as the alternator, electronic control units, or any other components having semi-conductor circuitry could be irreparably damaged.

If the engine is being started using jump leads and a slave battery, connect the batteries positive-to-positive and negative-to-negative (see Jump starting). This also applies when connecting a battery charger.

Never disconnect the battery terminals, the alternator, any electrical wiring or any test instruments when the engine is running.

Do not allow the engine to turn the alternator when the alternator is not connected.

Never 'test' for alternator output by 'flashing' the output lead to earth.

Never use an ohmmeter of the type

incorporating a hand-cranked generator for circuit or continuity testing.

Always ensure that the battery negative lead is disconnected when working on the electrical system.

Before using electric-arc welding equipment on the car, disconnect the battery, alternator and components such as the fuel injection/ignition electronic control unit to protect them from the risk of damage.

Battery disconnection

Refer to the precautions listed in *Disconnecting the battery*, in the Reference section of this manual.

2 Electrical fault finding – general information

Refer to Chapter 12.

3 Battery – testing and charging

Testing

Low-maintenance battery

1 If the car covers a small annual mileage, it is worthwhile checking the specific gravity of the electrolyte every three months to determine the state of charge of the battery. Use a hydrometer to make the check and compare the results with the following table. Note that the specific gravity readings assume an electrolyte temperature of 15°C (60°F); for every 10°C (18°F) below 15°C (60°F) subtract 0.007. For every 10°C (18°F) above 15°C (60°F) add 0.007.

	Ambient temperature	
	Above 25°C	Below 25°C
Fully-charged	1.210 to 1.230	1.270 to 1.290
70% charged	1.170 to 1.190	1.230 to 1.250
Discharged	1.050 to 1.070	1.110 to 1.130

2 If the battery condition is suspect, first check the specific gravity of electrolyte in each cell. A variation of 0.040 or more between any cells indicates loss of electrolyte or deterioration of the internal plates.

3 If the specific gravity variation is 0.040 or more, the battery should be renewed. If the cell variation is satisfactory but the battery is discharged, it should be charged as described later in this Section.

Maintenance-free battery

4 In cases where a 'sealed for life' maintenance-free battery is fitted, topping-up and testing of the electrolyte in each cell is not possible. The condition of the battery can therefore only be tested using a battery condition indicator or a voltmeter.

All battery types

5 If testing the battery using a voltmeter, connect the voltmeter across the battery and compare the result with those given in the Specifications under 'charge condition'. The test is only accurate if the battery has not been subjected to any kind of charge for the previous six hours. If this is not the case, switch on the headlights for 30 seconds, then wait four to five minutes before testing the battery after switching off the headlights. All other electrical circuits must be switched off, so check that the doors and tailgate/bootlid are fully shut when making the test.

6 If the voltage reading is less than 12.0 volts, then the battery is discharged.

7 If the battery is to be charged, remove it from the car (Section 4) and charge it as described later in this Section.

Charging

Low-maintenance battery

Note: *The following is intended as a guide only. Always refer to the manufacturer's recommendations (often printed on a label attached to the battery), and always disconnect both terminal leads before charging a battery.*

8 Charge the battery at a rate of 3.5 to 4 amps and continue to charge the battery at this rate until no further rise in specific gravity is noted over a four hour period.

9 Alternatively, a trickle charger charging at the rate of 1.5 amps can safely be used overnight.

10 Specially rapid 'boost' charges which are claimed to restore the power of the battery in 1 to 2 hours are not recommended, as they can cause serious damage to the battery plates through overheating.

11 While charging the battery, note that the temperature of the electrolyte should never exceed 37.8°C (100°F).

Maintenance-free battery

Note: *The following is intended as a guide only. Always refer to the manufacturer's recommendations (often printed on a label attached to the battery), and always disconnect both terminal leads before charging a battery.*

12 This battery type takes considerably longer to fully recharge than the standard type, the time taken being dependent on the extent of discharge, but it can take anything up to three days.

13 A constant voltage type charger is required, to be set, when connected, to 13.9 to 14.9 volts with a charger current below 25 amps. Using this method, the battery should be usable within three hours, giving a voltage reading of 12.5 volts, but this is for a partially-discharged battery and, as mentioned, full charging can take considerably longer.

14 If the battery is to be charged from a fully-discharged state (condition reading less than 12.2 volts), have it recharged by your Renault dealer or local automotive electrician, as the charge rate is higher and constant supervision during charging is necessary.

4 Battery – removal and refitting

Note: *Refer to the precautions given in Safety first! and in Section 1 of this Chapter.*

Removal

1 The battery is located at the front left-hand corner of the engine compartment, under a plastic cover.

2 Remove the two bolts at the back of the battery cover, and the screw/clip in front, then lift the cover away **(see illustrations)**.

3 Each battery terminal has a number of additional leads attached, some of which have to be removed to gain better access to the main terminal nuts, or to enable the main leads to be moved aside. Disconnect the negative lead first, then the positive. Move the leads well clear of the battery terminals **(see illustration)**.

4 Where applicable, pull out the battery vent pipe from the top of the battery, and move it

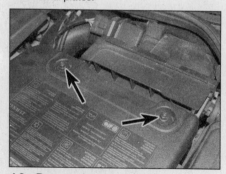

4.2a **Remove the two screw/clips from the rear of the battery cover . . .**

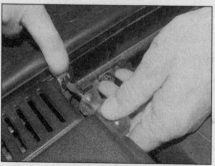

4.2b **. . . and a further one from the engine front panel . . .**

4.2c **. . . and lift off the cover for access to the battery**

4.3a Each battery terminal has several extra leads attached . . .

4.3b . . . which it is helpful to remove, to access the terminal clamp bolt

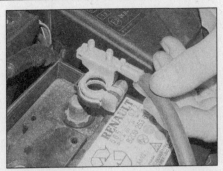

4.3c Disconnecting the negative terminal

4.3d Remove any additional leads from the positive terminal also . . .

4.3e . . . then loosen the clamp bolt . . .

4.3f . . . and remove the terminal/fusible link assembly

to one side **(see illustration)**. Make sure the vent pipe cannot be trapped when the battery is refitted.

5 Using a socket and long extension, unscrew the battery clamp plate nut, and remove the clamp **(see illustration)**.

6 Lift out the battery, using the handles provided on top where applicable **(see illustration)**. Particularly on diesel models, the battery is heavy.

7 If required, the battery tray can also be removed. First, unclip the wiring harness from

the tray, using a wide-bladed tool to avoid damaging the wire insulation. Where necessary, also unbolt the wiring support bracket nut at the front of the tray **(see illustrations)**.

8 Remove the three bolts securing the battery tray, and lift it out **(see illustrations)**.

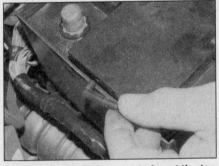

4.4 Pull out the battery vent pipe at the top

4.5 Removing the battery clamp plate

4.6 Lifting out the battery

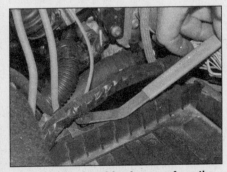

4.7a Unclip the wiring harness from the battery tray

4.7b Unscrew the wiring support bracket nut at the front

4.8a Remove the three bolts . . .

4.8b . . . and lift out the battery tray

9 If the tray is being removed to gain access to other components, it may also be useful to remove the engine ECU as described in Chapter 4A or 4B.

Refitting

10 Refitting is a reversal of removal. Smear petroleum jelly on the battery terminals after reconnecting the leads, to reduce corrosion. Always reconnect the positive lead first, and the negative lead last.

5 Charging system – testing

Note: *Refer to the warnings given in* **Safety first!** *and in Section 1 of this Chapter before starting work.*

1 If the no-charge warning light fails to illuminate when the ignition is switched on,

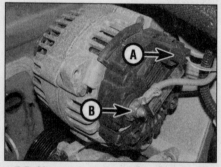

7.5 Alternator main wiring plug (A) and battery supply lead (B)

7.6b . . . and withdraw the auxiliary drivebelt tensioner

first check the alternator wiring connections for security. If satisfactory, check that the warning light bulb has not blown, and that the bulbholder is secure in its location in the instrument panel (see Chapter 12). If the light still fails to illuminate, check the continuity of the warning light feed wire from the alternator to the bulbholder. If all is satisfactory, the alternator is at fault, and should be renewed or taken to an auto-electrician for testing and repair.

2 If the ignition warning light illuminates when the engine is running, stop the engine and check that the drivebelt is correctly tensioned (see Chapter 1A or 1B) and that the alternator connections are secure. If all is so far satisfactory, have the alternator checked by an auto-electrician for testing and repair.

3 If the alternator output is suspect even though the warning light functions correctly, the regulated voltage may be checked as follows.

4 Connect a voltmeter across the battery terminals and start the engine.

5 Increase the engine speed until the voltmeter reading remains steady; the reading should be between 13.2 and 14.8 volts.

6 Switch on as many electrical accessories (eg, the headlights, heated rear window and heater blower) as possible, and check that the alternator maintains the regulated voltage between 13.2 and 14.8 volts.

7 If the regulated voltage is not as stated, the fault may be due to worn brushes, weak brush springs, a faulty voltage regulator, a faulty diode, a severed phase winding, or worn or

7.6a Remove the mounting bolt . . .

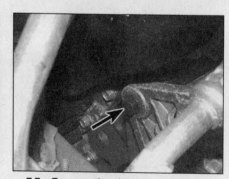

7.7a Remove the alternator upper . . .

damaged slip rings. The alternator should be renewed or taken to an auto-electrician for testing and repair.

6 Alternator – testing

If the alternator is thought to be suspect, it should be removed from the vehicle and taken to an auto-electrician for testing. Most auto-electricians will be able to supply and fit brushes at a reasonable cost. However, check on the cost of repairs before proceeding, as it may prove more economical to obtain a new or exchange alternator.

7 Alternator – removal and refitting

Removal

1 Disconnect the battery negative lead (refer to *Disconnecting the battery* in the Reference Chapter).

2 Remove the auxiliary drivebelt as described in Chapter 1A or 1B.

3 On all except 1.5 litre diesel models, remove the radiator as described in Chapter 3. While this itself involves a significant amount of work, we found that access to the alternator is so limited, this is preferable to any other method.

4 On 1.5 litre diesel models, remove the engine top cover. Loosen the hose clip and remove the air duct from the resonator on the top of the engine. Anticipating a small amount of diesel spillage, disconnect the fuel inlet and return hoses from the high-pressure pump. Cap the pipe connections on the pump at least, to prevent dirt entry into the system.

5 Disconnect the alternator wiring plug, then (after removing the access cap if necessary) unscrew the nut and remove the main battery supply lead from the terminal **(see illustration)**.

6 On all except 1.5 litre diesel models, working under the wheel arch, unbolt and remove the auxiliary drivebelt tensioner pulley – this is necessary, to gain access to the alternator lower mounting bolt **(see illustrations)**.

7 Remove the alternator lower and upper mounting bolts **(see illustrations)**. Note that the upper bolt cannot be fully withdrawn, as it hits the inner wing, but the upper mounting is slotted, to allow the partially-withdrawn bolt to pass out forwards with the alternator itself.

8 It is likely that (thanks to the spacers fitted to its mounting lugs) the alternator will prove difficult to remove from its mountings, and may even have to be prised forwards – take care when prising to avoid damaging it or any surrounding components. Remove the alternator from the engine **(see illustrations)**. On 1.5 litre diesel models, clearance is tight,

but it should just be possible to remove the unit upwards – where applicable, hold the air conditioning hose back against the engine to allow the alternator to pass.

Refitting

9 Refitting is a reversal of removal. Refer to the relevant part of Chapter 1A or 1B for details of fitting (and tensioning, where necessary) the auxiliary drivebelt. Note that the alternator mounting holes are fitted with adjustable spacers which are clamped to the mounting bracket when the bolts are tightened. This makes the task of refitting the alternator difficult, and it is suggested that the spacers are tapped out slightly to provide additional clearance **(see illustration)**.

8 Starting system – testing

Note: *Refer to the precautions given in* **Safety first!** *and in Section 1 of this Chapter before starting work.*

1 If the starter motor fails to operate, the following may be the possible causes:
  a) *The battery is faulty.*
  b) *The electrical connections between the starter button, solenoid, battery and starter motor are somewhere failing to pass the necessary current from the battery through the starter to earth.*
  c) *The solenoid is faulty.*
  d) *The starter motor is mechanically or electrically defective.*

2 To check the battery, switch on the headlights. If they dim after a few seconds, this indicates that the battery is discharged – recharge (see Section 3) or renew the battery. If the headlights glow brightly, press the starter button and observe the lights. If they dim, then this indicates that current is reaching the starter motor, therefore the fault must lie in the starter motor. If the lights continue to glow brightly (and no clicking sound can be heard from the starter motor solenoid), this indicates that there is a fault in the circuit or solenoid – see the following paragraphs. If the starter motor turns slowly when operated, but the battery is in good condition, then this indicates that either the starter motor is faulty, or there is considerable resistance somewhere in the circuit.

3 If a fault in the circuit is suspected, disconnect the battery leads (including the earth connection to the body), the starter/solenoid wiring and the engine/transmission earth strap. Thoroughly clean the connections, and reconnect the leads and wiring, then use a voltmeter or test light to check that full battery voltage is available at the battery positive lead connection to the solenoid, and that the earth is sound. Smear petroleum jelly around the battery terminals to prevent corrosion – corroded connections are amongst the most frequent causes of electrical system faults.

7.7b . . . and lower mounting bolts

7.8b . . . then withdraw the alternator from the engine (1.9 litre)

7.8a Pull back the upper mounting bolt as far as possible . . .

7.9 Using the mounting bolt to reposition the spacers before refitting the alternator

4 If the battery and all connections are in good condition, check the circuit by disconnecting the wire from the solenoid blade terminal. Connect a voltmeter or test light between the wire end and a good earth (such as the battery negative terminal), and check that the wire is live when the starter button is pressed. If it is, then the circuit is sound – if not the circuit wiring can be checked as described in Chapter 12.

5 The solenoid contacts can be checked by connecting a voltmeter or test light between the battery positive feed connection on the starter side of the solenoid and earth. When the starter button is pressed, there should be a reading or lighted bulb, as applicable. If there is no reading or lighted bulb, the solenoid is faulty and should be renewed.

6 If the circuit and solenoid are proved sound, the fault must lie in the starter motor. In this event, it may be possible to have the starter motor overhauled by a specialist, but check on the cost of spares before proceeding, as it may prove more economical to obtain a new or exchange motor.

9 Starter motor – removal and refitting

1 On most models, the starter motor is located on the back of the engine, and access is not easy. The exception is the 1.5 litre diesel engine, where the starter is fitted on the front.

Removal

2 Disconnect the battery negative lead (refer to *Disconnecting the battery*).

Petrol engines

3 Remove the air cleaner and ducts as described in Chapter 4A, and the windscreen cowl panels as described in Chapter 11.
4 Disconnect the wiring plug from the oil level sensor.
5 Noting their locations, disconnect the wires from the starter motor and solenoid.
6 Unscrew the three starter motor mounting bolts, and withdraw the starter motor from the transmission **(see illustration)**. Check that the centring dowel has not fallen out as the motor is removed, and refit to the transmission face if necessary.

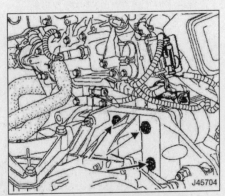

9.6 Starter motor mounting bolts – petrol engines

9.10a Remove the mounting bolts . . .

9.10b . . . and withdraw the starter motor (1.5 litre)

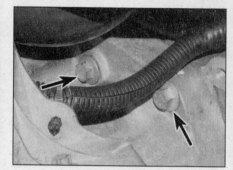

9.10c Remove the two bolts from the transmission side . . .

9.10d . . . and one from the engine side . . .

Diesel engines

7 On 1.9 litre engines, remove the catalytic converter as described in Chapter 4B.

9.10e . . . and withdraw the starter motor (1.9 litre)

8 Remove the windscreen cowl panels as described in Chapter 11, and the engine top cover.

9 Noting their locations, disconnect the wires from the starter motor and solenoid. To improve access to the starter motor mounting bolts, loosen the hose clips and disconnect the air ducts from the turbocharger.

10 Unscrew the three starter motor mounting bolts (two on 1.5 litre engines), and withdraw the starter motor from the transmission **(see illustrations)**. Check that the centring dowel has not fallen out as the motor is removed, and refit to the transmission face if necessary.

Refitting

11 Refitting is a reversal of removal – position the starter motor on the location dowel as it is offered into place. Finally, tighten the mounting bolts to the specified torque.

Chapter 5 Part B:
Ignition system – petrol engines

Contents

Degrees of difficulty

Easy, suitable for novice with little experience	Fairly easy, suitable for beginner with some experience	Fairly difficult, suitable for competent DIY mechanic	Difficult, suitable for experienced DIY mechanic	Very difficult, suitable for expert DIY or professional

Specifications

General

Ignition system type	Fully-electronic, computer-controlled, with four individual ignition coils, one on each spark plug
Firing order	1-3-4-2
Location of No 1 cylinder	Flywheel end

Ignition timing
Controlled by the ECU

Ignition HT coil resistances
Typical:

Primary resistance	0.54 ± 0.02 ohms
Secondary resistance	9.0 to 12.5 kohms

Torque wrench settings

	Nm	lbf ft
Ignition coil	15	11
Knock sensor	20	15
Spark plugs	25 to 30	18 to 22

1 General information and precautions

General information

The ignition system is integrated with the fuel injection system to form a combined engine management system under the control of one ECU (see Chapter 4A for further information). All engines are fitted with a distributorless ignition system.

The ignition system uses one coil for each cylinder, with each coil mounted on the relevant spark plug. The coils are fed in series, two at a time, and the system operates on the 'wasted spark' principle, where each plug sparks twice for every cycle of the engine, once on the compression stroke and once on the exhaust stroke.

The crankshaft speed/position sensor (see Chapter 4A, Section 13) is used to determine piston position as well as engine speed.

The power module for the ignition is integrated in the engine management ECU. The ECU uses the inputs from the sensors to calculate the required ignition advance setting and coil charging time – an integral amplifier circuit within the ECU switches the ignition coil primary (LT) circuit.

The knock sensor is mounted on the cylinder block to inform the ECU when the engine is 'pinking'. Its sensitivity to a particular frequency of vibration allows it to detect the impulses which are caused by the shock waves set up when the engine starts to 'pink' (pre-ignite). The knock sensor sends an electrical signal to the ECU which retards the ignition advance setting until the 'pinking' ceases – the ignition timing is then gradually returned to the 'normal' setting. This maintains the ignition timing as close to the knock threshold as possible – the most efficient setting for the engine under normal running conditions.

3.2a On 1.6 litre engines, unclip the engine top cover

Precautions

• The following precautions must be observed, to prevent damage to the ignition system components and to reduce risk of personal injury.
  a) *Ensure the ignition is switched off before disconnecting any of the ignition wiring.*
  b) *Ensure that the ignition is switched off before connecting or disconnecting any ignition test equipment, such as a timing light.*
  c) *Do not earth the coil primary or secondary circuits.*

⚠️ *Warning: Voltages produced by an electronic ignition system are considerably higher than those produced by conventional ignition systems. Extreme care must be taken when working on the system with the ignition switched on. Persons with surgically-implanted cardiac pacemaker devices should keep well clear of the ignition circuits, components and test equipment*

2 Ignition system – testing

1 The components of ignition systems are normally very reliable; most faults are far more likely to be due to loose or dirty connections, or to 'tracking' of HT voltage due to dirt, dampness or damaged insulation than to the failure of any of the system's components. Always check all wiring thoroughly before condemning an electrical component and

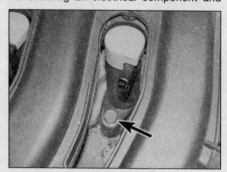

3.3a Unscrew the mounting bolt . . .

3.2b Disconnect the wiring plug from each coil

work methodically to eliminate all other possibilities before deciding that a particular component is faulty.

2 The old practice of checking for a spark by holding the live end of a spark plug HT lead (or in this case, the individual coils) a short distance away from the engine is not recommended; not only is there a high risk of a powerful electric shock, but the coil or ECU may be damaged. However, if necessary each plug can be checked individually by removing it, then reconnecting the coil and connecting the body of the spark plug to a suitable earthing point on the engine using a battery jumper lead. It is important to make a good earth connection if using this method. Never try to 'diagnose' misfires by pulling off one coil at a time.

Engine will not start

3 If the engine either will not turn over at all, or only turns very slowly, first check the battery and starter motor as described in Chapter 5A.
4 Use an ohmmeter to check the resistances of the coils, and compare with the information given in the Specifications.
5 If these checks fail to reveal the cause of the problem, the vehicle should be taken to a Renault dealer for testing. A wiring block connector is incorporated in the engine management circuit, into which a special electronic diagnostic tester can be plugged. The tester will locate the fault quickly and simply, alleviating the need to test all the system components individually, which is a time-consuming operation that carries a high

3.3b . . . and withdraw the coil from the engine

---

risk of damaging the ECU. If necessary, the system wiring and wiring connectors can be checked as described in Chapter 12, ensuring that the ECU wiring connector is first disconnected with the ignition switched off.

Engine misfires

6 An irregular misfire suggests either a loose connection or intermittent fault in the primary circuit, or an HT fault between the coils and spark plugs.
7 With the ignition switched off, check carefully through the system ensuring that all connections are clean and securely fastened.
8 Check that the HT coils and their associated wiring connections are clean and dry.
9 Regular misfiring of one spark plug may be due to a faulty spark plug, faulty injector, a faulty coil or loss of compression in the relevant cylinder. Regular misfiring of cylinders 1 and 4 only, or 2 and 3 only suggests a fault on the relevant coil. Regular misfiring of all the cylinders suggests a fuel supply fault, such as a clogged fuel filter or faulty fuel pump.

3 Ignition HT coils – removal, testing and refitting

Removal

1 Disconnect the battery negative lead (refer to *Disconnecting the battery* in Reference).
2 The ignition coils are accessible through the holes in the inlet manifold. On 1.6 litre engines, unclip and remove the engine top cover, then carefully disconnect the wiring from each coil. Take care not to damage the connectors **(see illustrations)**.
3 Unscrew the single mounting bolt and withdraw each coil from its spark plug **(see illustrations)**.
4 Check the condition of the O-rings where the coils enter the valve cover, and if necessary renew them.

Testing

5 Each coil can be tested as described in the previous Section, using an ohmmeter to check for the resistances given in the Specifications.
6 Further testing of the ignition system should be carried out by a Renault dealer using specialised equipment connected to the engine management diagnostic socket.

Refitting

7 Refitting is a reversal of removal, noting the following points:
  a) *Before refitting the coils over the plugs, Renault recommend that the rubber boots are first lightly lubricated inside, using fluorine grease (part number 82 00 168 855).*
  b) *Tighten the mounting bolts to the specified torque, and ensure that the wiring connectors are correctly and securely refitted.*

4 Knock sensor – removal and refitting

Removal

1 The knock sensor is located on the front, right-hand side of the cylinder block **(see illustration)**.

2 To remove the sensor, first disconnect the wiring, then unscrew it from the cylinder block.

Refitting

3 Refitting is a reversal of removal. Ensure that the sensor and its seating on the cylinder block or head are completely clean and tighten the sensor to the specified torque wrench setting. It is essential that these measures are scrupulously observed, as if the sensor is not correctly secured to a clean mating surface it may not be able to detect the impulses caused by pre-ignition. If this were to happen, the correction of ignition timing would not take place, with the consequent risk of severe engine damage.

5 Ignition timing – checking and adjustment

With the type of ignition fitted, the ignition timing is constantly being monitored and adjusted by the engine management ECU, and nominal checking values cannot be given. Therefore, it is not possible for the home mechanic to check the ignition timing. The only way in which the ignition timing can be checked is using special electronic test equipment, connected to the engine

4.1 Knock sensor location

management system diagnostic connector (refer to Chapter 4A). No adjustment of the ignition timing is possible. Should the ignition timing be incorrect, then a fault must be present in the engine management system.

Chapter 5 Part C:
Pre/post-heating system – diesel engines

Contents

Degrees of difficulty

Easy, suitable for novice with little experience	Fairly easy, suitable for beginner with some experience	Fairly difficult, suitable for competent DIY mechanic	Difficult, suitable for experienced DIY mechanic	Very difficult, suitable for expert DIY or professional

Specifications

Glow plugs

Type	Beru or Champion
Resistance	0.6 ohms

Torque wrench setting	Nm	lbf ft
Glow plugs	15	11

1 General information

The preheating/post-heating system consists of glow plugs screwed into the combustion chambers, a control unit mounted under the left-hand front wheel arch, and a coolant temperature sensor located on the thermostat housing (see Chapter 3). The control unit is itself activated by the engine management ECU (see Chapter 4B).

The glow plugs are supplied with current from the control unit in several phases, namely variable preheating, fixed pre-heating, starting heating, and variable post-heating.

The variable preheating phase occurs when the ignition is switched on, and during this phase the preheating warning light is illuminated on the instrument panel. The period of preheating depends on the temperature of the coolant and battery voltage. The maximum period of 15 seconds occurs if the coolant temperature is low and the battery voltage is less than 9.3 volts. The period varies from 15 seconds to zero seconds according to the temperature of the coolant, and when the temperature reaches 80°C, no preheating occurs. With normal battery voltage the maximum period is 10 seconds.

The fixed preheating phase occurs immediately after the variable phase finishes, after the warning light has extinguished, and lasts for up to 5 seconds. Normally, the driver will start the engine at some point during this phase.

During the period when the starter motor is in operation, the glow plugs are continuously supplied with current.

The variable post-heating phase occurs immediately after the engine has been started, and the period of post-heating depends on the temperature of the coolant. The maximum period of variable post-heating is 60 seconds, at which point the system is switched off. Variable post-heating will cease if the coolant temperature exceeds 80°C.

2 Pre/post-heating system – testing

1 If the system malfunctions, testing is best carried out by a Renault dealer using dedicated test equipment, however, some preliminary checks may be made as follows.

2 Connect a voltmeter or 12-volt test light between the glow plug supply cable and earth (engine or vehicle metal). Make sure that the live connection is kept clear of the engine and bodywork. Have an assistant switch on the ignition and check that voltage is applied to the glow plugs. Note the time for which the warning light is lit and the total time for which voltage is applied before the system cuts out, and compare to the times given in the description above.

3 If there is no supply at all, the relay, control unit or associated wiring is at fault.

4 To locate a defective glow plug, disconnect the main supply cable and the interconnecting wire from the top of the glow plugs. Using an ohmmeter, check for continuity between each glow plug terminal and earth. The resistance of a glow plug in good condition is very low (less than 1 ohm), so if the test light does not light or the continuity tester shows a high resistance, the glow plug is defective.

5 If an ammeter is available, the current draw of each glow plug can be checked. After an initial surge of around 15 to 20 amps, each plug should draw around 10 amps. Any plug which draws much more or less than 10 amps is probably defective.

6 As a final check, the glow plugs can be removed and inspected as described in Section 2.

7 If the pre/post-heating system is faulty, first check the wiring to each individual component. If this does not locate the fault, ideally each component should be substituted with known good units until the fault is located. If this is not possible, take the vehicle to a Renault dealer or diesel specialist who will have the diagnostic equipment necessary to pin-point the fault quickly.

3 Glow plugs – removal, inspection and refitting

Caution: If the preheating system has just been energised, or if the engine has been running, the glow plugs may be very hot.

Removal

1 Disconnect the battery negative (earth) lead and position it away from the terminal (refer to *Disconnecting the battery* in the Reference Section).

3.3 Disconnect the wiring connector from the glow plugs

3.4a Clean the surrounding area with a soft brush . . .

3.4b . . . then unscrew . . .

3.4c . . . and remove the glow plugs

4.2 Pre/post-heating control unit location – mounting nut arrowed

2 On 1.5 litre engines, detach the intercooler air duct which runs across the cylinder head cover – this may be bolted to the cover, with a hose clip securing it at the back of the engine. To gain access at the rear, it may be necessary to remove the windscreen cowl panels as described in Chapter 11.

3 Disconnect the wiring plugs from the glow plugs **(see illustration)**.

4 Clean the surrounding area, then unscrew and remove the glow plugs from the cylinder head. Note that access to No 4 glow plug is difficult, but once loosened, a suitable tight-fitting hose may be used to unscrew it **(see illustrations)**.

Inspection

5 Inspect the glow plugs for physical damage. Burnt or eroded glow plug tips can be caused by a bad injector spray pattern. Have the injectors checked if this sort of damage is found.

6 If the glow plugs are in good physical condition, check them electrically using a 12-volt test light or continuity tester with reference to the previous Section.

7 The glow plugs can be energised by applying 12 volts to them to verify that they heat up evenly and in the required time. Observe the following precautions:

a) *Support the glow plug by clamping it carefully in a vice or self-locking pliers. Remember it will become red-hot.*

b) *Make sure that the power supply or test lead incorporates a fuse or overload trip to protect against damage from a short-circuit.*

c) *After testing, allow the glow plug to cool for several minutes before attempting to handle it.*

8 A glow plug in good condition will start to glow red at the tip after drawing current for 5 seconds or so. Any plug which takes much longer to start glowing, or which starts glowing in the middle instead of at the tip, is defective.

Refitting

9 Refit by reversing the removal operations. Apply a smear of copper-based anti-seize compound to the plug threads and tighten the glow plugs to the specified torque. Do not overtighten, as this can damage the glow plug element.

---

4 Pre/post-heating system control unit – *removal and refitting*

Removal

1 Disconnect the battery negative lead, and move the lead away from the battery (see *Disconnecting the battery*).

2 The pre/post-heating control unit is located under the left-hand front wheel arch, at the front **(see illustration)**. Loosen the left-hand front wheel bolts, then jack up the front of the car, and support it on axle stands (see *Jacking and vehicle support*). Remove the front wheel.

3 Remove the front half section of the wheel arch liner, which is secured by a number of screws and clips (refer to Chapter 11, Section 21 for more details).

4 Slide up the plastic protective boot fitted at the top of the unit, over the wiring plug, then disconnect the plug from the unit.

5 Unscrew the unit mounting nut at the base, and remove it from its locating stud.

Refitting

6 Refitting is a reversal of removal.

Chapter 6
Clutch

Contents

Degrees of difficulty

Easy, suitable for novice with little experience	**Fairly easy,** suitable for beginner with some experience	**Fairly difficult,** suitable for competent DIY mechanic	**Difficult,** suitable for experienced DIY mechanic	**Very difficult,** suitable for expert DIY or professional

Specifications

General
Clutch type . . . . Single dry plate, diaphragm spring, hydraulically-operated release mechanism

Clutch disc
Diameter:
Petrol engines	200.0 mm
1.5 litre diesel engines	215.0 mm
1.9 litre diesel engines	239.0 mm
Friction material thickness (new)	7.0 mm (approximate)

Torque wrench settings

	Nm	lbf ft
Clutch pedal mounting bracket nuts	21	16
Clutch slave cylinder/release bearing	21	16
Clutch slave cylinder flange bolts (5-speed transmission)	9	7
Pressure plate-to-flywheel bolts:		
Petrol engines	20	15
1.5 litre diesel engines	15	11
1.9 litre diesel engines	12	9

1 General information

The clutch consists of a friction disc, a pressure plate assembly, a release bearing and hydraulic slave cylinder; all of these components are contained in the large cast-aluminium alloy bellhousing, sandwiched between the engine and the transmission.

The hydraulic master cylinder is located in the pedal bracket on the bulkhead, and the clutch fluid reservoir is shared with the brake fluid reservoir on the top of the brake master cylinder. Inside the reservoir each circuit has its own compartment, so that in the event of fluid loss in the clutch circuit, the brake circuit remains fully operational.

The clutch disc (friction disc) is fitted between the engine flywheel and the clutch pressure plate, and is allowed to slide on the transmission input shaft splines.

The pressure plate assembly is bolted to the engine flywheel. When the engine is running, drive is transmitted from the crankshaft, via the flywheel, to the friction disc (these components being clamped securely together by the pressure plate assembly) and from the friction disc to the transmission input shaft.

To interrupt the drive, the spring pressure must be relaxed by the hydraulically-operated release mechanism. Depressing the clutch pedal operates the master cylinder which in turn operates the slave cylinder and presses the release bearing against the pressure plate spring fingers. This causes the springs to deform and releases the clamping force on the pressure plate.

When the pedal is released, the diaphragm spring forces the pressure plate into contact with the friction linings on the friction disc. The disc is now firmly sandwiched between the pressure plate and the flywheel, thus transmitting engine power to the transmission.

Wear of the friction material on the friction disc is automatically compensated for by

the operation of the hydraulic system. As the friction material on the disc wears, the pressure plate moves towards the flywheel causing the clutch diaphragm spring inner fingers to move outwards. When the clutch pedal is released, excess fluid is expelled through the master cylinder into the fluid reservoir.

 Warning: Hydraulic fluid is poisonous; wash off immediately and thoroughly in the case of skin contact, and seek immediate medical advice if any fluid is swallowed or gets into the eyes. Certain types of hydraulic fluid are flammable, and may ignite when allowed into contact with hot components; when servicing any hydraulic system, it is safest to assume that the fluid is flammable, and to take precautions against the risk of fire as though it is petrol that is being handled. Hydraulic fluid is also an effective paint stripper, and will attack plastics; if any is spilt, it should be washed off immediately, using copious quantities of fresh water. Finally, it is hygroscopic (it absorbs moisture from the

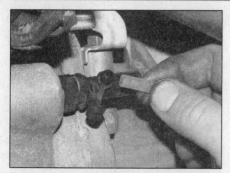

2.4 Connect a piece of tubing over the bleed nipple

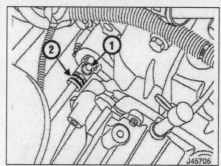

2.5a Bleed nipple (1) and hose clip (2) – 5-speed transmission

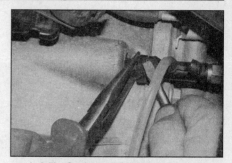

2.5b On 6-speed models, use a screwdriver to press the clip, before pulling the pipe outwards

2.8a Disconnect the wiring plug from the upper . . .

2.8b . . . and lower clutch pedal switches

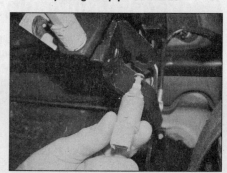

2.8c Twist and remove the switches from the pedal bracket

air) – old fluid may be contaminated and unfit for further use. When topping-up or renewing the fluid, always use the recommended type, and ensure that it comes from a freshly-opened sealed container.

2 Clutch master cylinder – removal and refitting

Note: *Refer to the warning in Section 1 before proceeding.*

Removal

1 Remove the battery and battery tray as described in Chapter 5A.
2 Remove the engine ECU, and the air cleaner and inlet ducts as described in Chapter 4A or 4B, as applicable.
3 Unscrew the brake fluid reservoir cap.
4 Connect a piece of tubing which is a tight

fit over the clutch bleed nipple located on the pipe at the front of the transmission **(see illustration)**. Place the other end of the tube into a container large enough to hold the contents of the brake fluid reservoir.
5 On 5-speed models, remove the clip on the fluid pipe; on 6-speed models, depress the spring clip using a flat-bladed screwdriver. Pull the clutch fluid pipe outwards by one 'click' **(see illustrations)**.
6 At this point, fluid will flow slowly into the container. Let the fluid flow until the reservoir is empty. Depress the clutch pedal a few times to empty the master cylinder and pipes.
7 Remove the driver's lower facia trim panel as described in Chapter 11, Section 23.
8 Disconnect the wiring plugs from the clutch pedal switches, noting their fitted positions. Twist the switches through a quarter-turn and remove them from the pedal mounting bracket **(see illustrations)**.

9 Place some absorbent cloth below the pipe connections on the master cylinder. Remove the clips from the master cylinder unions, and disconnect the pipes **(see illustration)**. Cap or tape over the open pipe connections, to prevent further loss of fluid.
10 Prise the master cylinder balljoint fitting from the pedal.
11 Unscrew the four pedal bracket mounting nuts, and withdraw the pedal from the bulkhead.
12 Release the master cylinder by turning it a quarter-turn clockwise, and remove it.
13 If the master cylinder is faulty it must be renewed – at the time of writing, repair kits are not available. Check, however, on parts availability from other sources before purchasing a new unit.

Refitting

14 Refitting is a reversal of removal, noting the following points:
  a) *Check the condition of the pipe seals, and renew if necessary.*
  b) *Ensure that all fluid hose connections are clean, and are securely made.*
  c) *Tighten the clutch pedal mounting bracket nuts to the specified torque.*
  d) *Before refitting the clutch pedal switches, pull out the switch plungers by a few clicks – either during refitting, or when the pedal is first used, the switches will then self-adjust correctly.*
  e) *Fill and bleed the clutch system on completion, as described in Section 5. Also check the operation of the brakes, and if necessary, bleed the system as described in Chapter 9.*

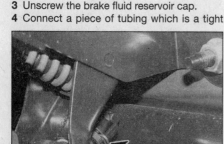

2.9a Pull out the clip and disconnect the upper . . .

2.9b . . . and lower pipes from the master cylinder

3.2a Unscrew the two mounting bolts . . .

3.2b . . . and withdraw the release bearing and slave cylinder

3.3 On 6-speed models, pull out the clip to separate the slave cylinder

3 Clutch slave cylinder – removal and refitting

Note: *Refer to the warning in Section 1 before proceeding.*

Removal

1 Remove the transmission as described in Chapter 7A.

2 Inside the bellhousing, unscrew and remove the two mounting bolts, then withdraw the slave cylinder and release bearing over the transmission input shaft **(see illustrations)**.

3 To separate the slave cylinder, either remove the two bolts and separate the pipe flanges (5-speed transmission), or pull out the joining clip (6-speed transmission) **(see illustration)**.

Refitting

4 Refitting is a reversal of removal, noting the following points:

a) *Renew the slave-cylinder-to-release bearing seal.*

b) *Tighten the flange bolts to the specified torque (5-speed transmissions).*

c) *Tighten the release bearing mounting bolts to the specified torque.*

d) *Refit the transmission as described in Chapter 7A.*

e) *On completion, bleed the clutch as described in Section 5.*

4 Clutch hydraulic hoses – removal and refitting

Note: *Refer to the warning in Section 1 before proceeding.*

Removal

1 Remove the battery and battery tray as described in Chapter 5A.

2 Remove the engine ECU as described in Chapter 4A or 4B, as applicable.

3 Remove the air cleaner and inlet ducts as described in Chapter 4A or 4B, as applicable.

4 Unscrew the brake fluid reservoir cap.

5 Empty the system of fluid as described in Section 2, paragraphs 4 to 6.

6 On 5-speed models, the slave cylinder pipe

can be pulled off. Plug or tape over the slave cylinder connection, to prevent further fluid loss.

7 On 6-speed models, prise the slave cylinder pipe clip out carefully (do not try to remove the clip completely), and pull the pipe off **(see illustration)**. Plug or tape over the slave cylinder connection, to prevent further fluid loss.

8 Trace the pipe back to the bulkhead connections, releasing it from the mounting clips.

9 Remove the driver's lower facia trim panel and the glovebox as described in Chapter 11, Section 23.

10 Disconnect the wiring plugs from the clutch pedal switches, noting their fitted positions. Twist the switches through a quarter-turn and remove them from the pedal mounting bracket **(refer to illustrations 2.8a, b, and c)**.

11 Place some absorbent cloth below the pipe connections on the master cylinder. Remove the clips from the master cylinder unions, and disconnect the pipes **(refer to illustrations 2.9a and b)**. Cap or tape over the open pipe connections, to prevent further loss of fluid.

12 Trace the pipes along inside the car, disconnecting them from the bulkhead clips.

13 Place some absorbent cloth below the pipe connections on the bulkhead, at the front of the passenger footwell. Remove the clips from the unions where the pipes pass through the bulkhead, and separate the pipes **(see illustration)**.

14 Twist the pipe mounting plate a quarter-turn clockwise to release it from the bulkhead.

4.7 Disconnect the fluid supply pipe from the slave cylinder

Refitting

15 Refitting is a reversal of removal, noting the following points:

a) *Before refitting the clutch pedal switches, pull out the switch plungers by a few clicks – either during refitting, or when the pedal is first used, the switches will then self-adjust correctly.*

b) *Fill and bleed the clutch system on completion, as described in Section 5. Also check the operation of the brakes, and if necessary, bleed the system as described in Chapter 9.*

5 Clutch hydraulic system – bleeding

Note: *Refer to the warning in Section 1 before proceeding.*

1 The correct operation of any hydraulic system is only possible after removing all air from the components and circuit; this is achieved by bleeding the system.

2 During the bleeding procedure, add only clean, unused hydraulic fluid of the recommended type; never re-use fluid that has already been bled from the system. Ensure that sufficient fluid is available before starting work.

3 If there is any possibility of incorrect fluid being already in the system, the hydraulic circuit must be flushed completely with uncontaminated, correct fluid.

4 If hydraulic fluid has been lost from the system, or air has entered because of a leak,

4.13 Master cylinder pipe connections at the bulkhead (passenger footwell)

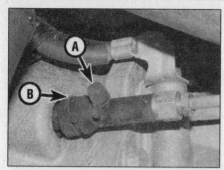

5.5 Clutch slave cylinder bleed nipple (A) and spring clip (B) – 6-speed transmission

ensure that the fault is cured before continuing further.

5 The bleed nipple (note that it is not a screw) is fitted to the slave cylinder at the front of the transmission bellhousing **(see illustration)**.

6 Remove the battery and battery tray as described in Chapter 5A.

7 Remove the engine ECU as described in Chapter 4A or 4B, as applicable.

8 Remove the air cleaner and inlet ducts as described in Chapter 4A or 4B, as applicable.

9 Unscrew the brake fluid reservoir cap, and top-up the fluid level to the MAX mark. Keep an eye on the fluid level as bleeding progresses, and keep it topped-up above the MIN mark throughout.

10 Referring to Section 2, paragraphs 4 and 5, connect a piece of tube to the bleed nipple, and open the circuit as described – bleeding and filling the system is done by gravity.

11 If the system is known to be empty (or if new parts have been fitted), have an assistant hold the clutch pedal depressed until the flow of bubbles seen in the pipe ceases. Depress and release the clutch pedal a few times, to purge the air from the master cylinder and pipes. Top-up the fluid level as necessary.

12 When no more bubbles are seen in the fluid, release the clutch pedal, then press the slave cylinder pipe firmly back into place.

13 Top-up the fluid level to the MAX mark, and refit the reservoir cap.

14 Check the operation of the clutch – any lack of response indicates the need for further bleeding.

15 If the clutch system was emptied, check the brakes for any sign of 'sponginess' in the pedal, which would mean the brakes also require bleeding, as described in Chapter 9.

16 Discard any hydraulic fluid that has been bled from the system; it will not be fit for re-use.

17 If the clutch is not operating correctly after repeated bleeding, the master cylinder or slave cylinder may be faulty.

6 Clutch pedal – removal and refitting

The clutch pedal is removed as an assembly with the clutch master cylinder – refer to Section 2. If required, the pedal could be removed, after unhooking the return spring, unscrewing the pivot shaft nut, and withdrawing the pivot shaft.

7 Clutch pedal switches – removal and refitting

1 Two clutch pedal switches are fitted to the Scénic. The one on top of the pedal bracket has a grey connector, and signals the start of pedal travel; the one on the pedal itself has a green connector, and signals the end of pedal travel **(see illustrations)**.

2 The signals from both switches may be used by the engine ECU, to permit smoother gearchanging, and to enable other related control functions, such as idle speed control when the pedal is depressed.

3 The end of pedal travel switch is used by the keyless card system, to signal that the clutch is fully depressed, to allow the engine to be started.

Removal

4 Remove the driver's lower facia trim panel as described in Chapter 11, Section 23.

5 Disconnect the wiring plugs from the relevant switch.

6 Twist the switch through a quarter-turn, and remove it from the pedal mounting bracket **(see illustration)**.

Refitting

7 Refitting is a reversal of removal, noting the following points:

a) Before refitting the switches, pull out the switch plungers by a few clicks – either during refitting, or when the pedal is first used, the switches will then self-adjust correctly **(see illustration)**.

b) Confirm the correct switch operation as follows. With the handbrake applied, make sure there is nothing in front of the car, as it could move forwards. Select a high gear, and try to start the engine without depressing the clutch – nothing should happen. With the clutch depressed, the engine should start.

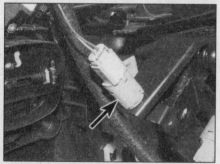

7.1a Start of pedal travel switch

7.1b End of pedal travel switch

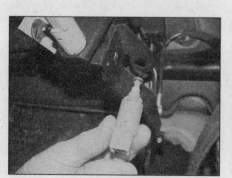

7.6 Twist and remove the switches from the pedal bracket

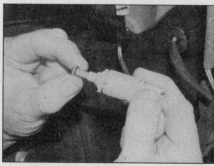

7.7 Pull out the switch plungers before refitting

8 Clutch assembly – removal, inspection and refitting

⚠️ **Warning: Dust created by clutch wear and deposited on the clutch components may contain asbestos, which is a health hazard. DO NOT blow it out with compressed air, or inhale any of it. DO NOT use petrol or petroleum-based solvents to clean off the dust. Brake system cleaner or methylated spirit should be used to flush the dust into a suitable receptacle. After the clutch components are wiped clean with rags, dispose of the contaminated rags and cleaner in a sealed, marked container.**

Note: Although some friction materials may no longer contain asbestos, it is safest to assume that they do, and to take precautions accordingly.

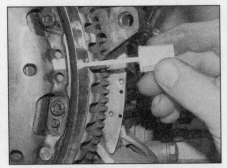

8.2 Mark the relationship of the pressure plate to the flywheel

8.3 Using a screwdriver in the ring gear teeth while unscrewing the clutch cover bolts

8.5a Withdraw the pressure plate assembly . . .

8.5b . . . and the friction disc, noting which way round it is fitted

8.7 Inspect the friction disc linings (A), springs (B – where applicable) and splines (C)

Removal

1 Unless the complete engine/transmission has to be removed from the car (see Chapter 2D), the clutch can be reached by removing the transmission as described in Chapter 7A.

2 Before disturbing the clutch, use chalk or a marker pen to mark the relationship of the pressure plate assembly to the flywheel.

3 Hold the flywheel stationary using a suitable tool engaged with the starter ring gear teeth – a piece of metal can be tightened to one of the bolt holes, or alternatively an assistant can use a wide-bladed screwdriver engaged with the teeth **(see illustration)**.

4 Working in a diagonal sequence, slacken the pressure plate bolts by half a turn at a time, until spring pressure is released and the bolts can be unscrewed by hand. Discard the bolts – new ones should be used when refitting.

5 Prise the pressure plate assembly off its locating dowels, and collect the friction disc, noting which way round the disc is fitted **(see illustrations)**.

Inspection

Note: *Due to the amount of work necessary to remove and refit clutch components, it is usually considered good practice to renew the clutch friction disc, pressure plate assembly and release bearing (slave cylinder)* as a matched set, even if only one of these is actually worn enough to require renewal. It is also worth considering the renewal of the clutch components on a preventive basis if the engine and/or transmission have been removed for some other reason.

6 When cleaning clutch components, read first the warning at the beginning of this Section; remove the dust using a clean, dry cloth, and working in a well-ventilated atmosphere.

7 Check the friction disc linings for signs of wear, damage or oil contamination. If the friction material is cracked, burnt, scored or damaged, or if it is contaminated with oil or grease (shown by shiny black patches), the friction disc must be renewed **(see illustration)**. Check the depth of the rivets below the friction material surface. If any are at or near the surface of the friction material, then the friction disc must be renewed.

8 If the friction material is still serviceable, check that the centre boss splines are unworn, that the torsion springs are in good condition and securely fastened (5-speed models only), and that all the rivets are tight. If any wear or damage is found, the friction disc must be renewed.

9 If the friction material is fouled with oil, this must be due to an oil leak from the crankshaft oil seal, from the sump-to-cylinder block joint, or from the transmission input shaft. Renew the seal or repair the joint, as appropriate, as described in the appropriate part of Chapter 2 or 7, before installing the new friction disc.

10 Check the pressure plate assembly for obvious signs of wear or damage; shake it to check for loose rivets or worn or damaged fulcrum rings, and check that the drive straps securing the pressure plate to the cover do not show signs of overheating (such as a deep yellow or blue discoloration). If the diaphragm spring is worn or damaged, or if its pressure is in any way suspect, the pressure plate assembly should be renewed **(see illustration)**.

8.10 Check the diaphragm spring fingers for wear, especially at the tips

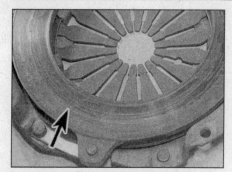

8.11 Check the machined face of the pressure plate

11 Examine the machined bearing surfaces of the pressure plate and of the flywheel; they should be clean, completely flat, and free from scratches or scoring **(see illustration)**. If either is discoloured from excessive heat, or shows signs of cracks, it should be renewed – although minor damage of this nature can sometimes be polished away using emery paper.

12 Check that the release bearing contact surface rotates smoothly and easily, with no sign of noise or roughness. Also check that the surface itself is smooth and unworn, with no signs of cracks, pitting or scoring. If there is any doubt about its condition, the bearing must be renewed.

Refitting

6-speed transmissions

13 The clutch pressure plate on models with the 6-speed transmission is unusual, in that there is a pre-adjustment mechanism to compensate for wear in the friction disc. This mechanism must be reset before refitting the pressure plate. A new plate may be supplied pre-set, in which case this procedure can be ignored.

14 A large-diameter bolt (M14 at least) long enough to pass through the pressure plate, a matching nut, and several large-diameter washers, will be needed for this procedure. Mount the bolt head in the jaws of a sturdy bench vice, with one large washer fitted **(see illustration)**.

15 Offer the plate over the bolt, friction disc surface facing down, and locate it centrally

8.14 Mount a large bolt and washer into a vice, then fit the pressure plate over it

over the bolt and washer – the washer should bear on the centre hub.

16 Fit several further large washers over the bolt, so that they bear on the ends of the spring fingers, then add the nut and tighten by hand to locate the washers **(see illustration)**.

17 The purpose of the procedure is to turn the plate's internal adjuster disc so that the three small green coil springs visible on the plate's outer surface are fully compressed. Tighten the nut just fitted until the adjuster disc is free to turn. Using a pair of thin-nosed or circlip pliers in one of the three windows on the top surface, open the jaws of the pliers to turn the adjuster disc anti-clockwise, so that the springs are fully compressed **(see illustrations)**.

18 Hold the pliers in this position, then unscrew the centre nut. Once the nut is released, the adjuster disc will be gripped in position, and the pliers can be removed. Take the pressure plate from the vice, and it is ready to fit.

All transmissions

19 On reassembly, ensure that the disc contact surfaces of the flywheel and pressure plate are completely clean, smooth, and free from oil or grease. Use solvent to remove any protective grease from new components.

20 Fit the friction disc so that its spring hub assembly faces away from the flywheel (5-speed transmissions); on 6-speed transmissions, the friction plate has a protruding small-diameter centre bush which locates into the crankshaft spigot bearing.

8.16 Fit large washers and a nut to the bolt, and hand-tighten

There may also be a marking showing which way round the plate is to be refitted. Depending on the type of centralising tool being used, the friction disc may be held in position at this stage.

21 Refit the pressure plate assembly, aligning the marks made on dismantling (if the original pressure plate is re-used), and locating the pressure plate on its locating dowels. Fit the pressure plate bolts, but tighten them only finger-tight, so that the friction disc can still be moved.

22 The friction disc must now be centralised, so that when the transmission is refitted, its input shaft will pass through the splines at the centre of the friction disc.

23 Centralisation can be achieved by passing a screwdriver or other long bar through the friction disc and into the hole in the crankshaft; the friction disc can then be moved around until it is centred on the crankshaft hole.

24 Alternatively, a clutch-aligning-tool can be used to eliminate the guesswork; these can be obtained from most accessory shops. The normal type consists of a spigot bar with several different adapters, but a home-made aligning tool can be fabricated from a length of metal rod or wooden dowel which fits closely inside the crankshaft hole, and has insulating tape wound around it to match the diameter of the friction disc splined hole **(see illustration)**.

25 A more recent type of aligning tool works by clamping the friction disc to the pressure plate before locating the two items on the flywheel **(see illustrations)**.

26 When the friction disc is centralised,

8.17a Tighten the nut until the spring adjuster is free to turn . . .

8.17b . . . then open up the jaws of suitable pliers to compress the springs

8.24 Using a clutch alignment tool to centralise the friction disc

tighten the pressure plate bolts evenly and in a diagonal sequence to the specified torque setting **(see illustration)**.

27 Renault recommend not greasing the splines the transmission input shaft, to avoid potential damage to the clutch release bearing.

28 Refit the transmission as described in Chapter 7A.

9 Clutch release bearing – removal, inspection and refitting

Removal

1 For access to the clutch release bearing, the transmission must be removed as described in Chapter 7A.

2 Remove the slave cylinder as described in Section 3.

Inspection

3 Note that it is often considered worthwhile to renew the release bearing as a matter of course regardless of its condition, considering the amount of work necessary to access it. Check that the contact surface rotates smoothly and easily, with no sign of noise or roughness, and that the surface itself is smooth and unworn, with no signs of cracks, pitting or scoring. If there is any doubt about its condition, the bearing (and slave cylinder) must be renewed.

8.25a Centralise the pressure plate on the disc . . .

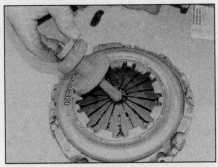

8.25b . . . fit the tool and tighten to clamp the disc to the pressure plate . . .

8.25c . . . then locate the assembly on the flywheel

8.26 Hold the flywheel stationary while tightening the clutch cover bolts

Refitting

4 Refit the slave cylinder as described in Section 3.

5 Refit the transmission with reference to Chapter 7A.

Chapter 7 Part A:
Manual transmission

Contents

Degrees of difficulty

Easy, suitable for novice with little experience	**Fairly easy,** suitable for beginner with some experience	**Fairly difficult,** suitable for competent DIY mechanic	**Difficult,** suitable for experienced DIY mechanic	**Very difficult,** suitable for expert DIY or professional

Specifications

General
Type . . . . Five or six forward speeds (all synchromesh) and reverse, cable-operated gearchange mechanism. Final drive differential integral with main transmission

Designation
1.4 and 1.6 litre petrol engines	JH3, 5-speed
1.5 litre diesel engines	JR5, 5-speed
1.9 litre diesel engines	ND0, 6-speed

Lubrication
Type	See *Lubricants and fluids* on page 0•17
Capacity:	
JH3 transmission	2.8 litres
JR5 transmission	2.5 litres
ND0 transmission	2.1 litres

Torque wrench settings
	Nm	lbf ft
Radiator lower crossmember:		
Front bolt	105	78
Rear nut (to subframe)	21	15
Side support plate bolts	21	15
Roadwheel bolts	130	96
Starter motor mounting bolts	44	32
Transmission bellhousing to engine	44	32
Transmission mounting:		
Centre nut	62	46
Mounting stud-to-mounting	180	133
Mounting-to-body bolts	21	15
Mounting-to-transmission bolts	62	46
Outer nuts	105	78
Transmission oil drain plug	25	18

1 General information

The transmission is equipped with five or six forward gears, one reverse gear and a final drive differential, incorporated in one casing bolted to the left-hand end of the engine. The transmission type code is stamped into the transmission casing, either on top or on the underside.

Drive is transmitted from the crankshaft via the clutch to the input shaft which rotates in sealed ball-bearings, and has a splined extension to accept the clutch friction disc. From the input shaft, drive is transmitted to the output shaft, which rotates in a roller bearing at its right-hand end, and a sealed ball-bearing at its left-hand end. From the output shaft, drive is transmitted to the

2.2 Remove the engine compartment undertray

2.3a On 5-speed models, the filler plug is on the front . . .

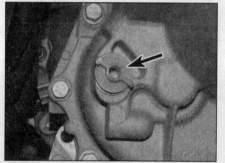

2.3b . . . while 6-speed models have the plug on the side

differential crown wheel, which rotates with the differential case and planetary gears, thus driving the side gears and driveshafts. The rotation of the planetary gears on their shaft allows the inner roadwheel to rotate

2.3c The 5-speed unit drain plug is underneath, with a square fitting . . .

at a slower speed than the outer roadwheel when the car is cornering.

The input and output shafts are arranged side-by-side, parallel to the crankshaft and driveshafts, so that their gear pinion teeth are in constant mesh. In the neutral position, the output shaft gear pinions rotate freely, so that drive cannot be transmitted to the crown wheel. Synchromesh is provided on all forward speeds. Gear selection is via a facia-mounted lever and twin cable mechanism.

The transmission selector cable causes the appropriate selector fork to move its respective synchro-sleeve along the shaft, in order to lock the gear pinion to the synchro-hub. Since the synchro-hubs are splined to the output shaft, this locks the pinion to the shaft, so that drive can be transmitted. To ensure that gearchanging can be made quickly and quietly, a synchromesh system is fitted to all forward gears, consisting of

baulk rings and spring-loaded fingers, as well as the gear pinions and synchro-hubs. The synchromesh cones are formed on the mating faces of the baulk rings and gear pinions.

2 Transmission oil – draining and refilling

1 This operation is much quicker and more efficient if the car is first taken on a journey of sufficient length to warm the engine/transmission up to operating temperature.
2 Park the car on level ground, switch off the engine and ensure the handbrake is applied. For improved access, jack up the car and support it securely on axle stands (see *Jacking and vehicle support*), or alternatively position the car over an inspection pit or on car ramps. Note that, to ensure accuracy, the car must be level when checking the oil level. Remove the engine compartment undertray **(see illustration)**.
3 Remove all traces of dirt from around the drain and filler/level plugs. On 5-speed transmissions, the filler/level plug is located on the front-facing side of the transmission, while 6-speed units have the plug on the left-hand end face, at the front. The drain plug on 5-speed transmissions is underneath, while the 6-speed transmission drain plug is on the left-hand face, at the rear (10 mm hex fitting) **(see illustrations)**.
4 Unscrew and remove the filler/level plug – this will probably be very tight **(see illustration)**.
5 Position a suitable container under the transmission, then unscrew the drain plug and allow the oil to drain completely into the container **(see illustration)**. If the oil is hot, take precautions against scalding. Clean both the filler/level and the drain plugs, being especially careful to wipe any metallic particles off the magnetic inserts, where applicable. The sealing washers should be renewed whenever they are disturbed.
6 When the oil has finished draining, clean the drain plug threads and those of the transmission casing, and refit the drain plug, tightening it securely.
7 Refilling the transmission is an extremely awkward operation. Above all, allow plenty of time for the oil level to settle properly before checking it. Note that the car must be level when checking the oil level.

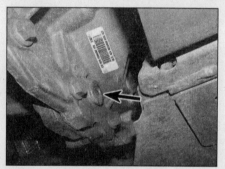

2.3d . . . while the 6-speed version is at the rear, with a hex fitting

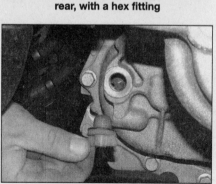

2.4 Unscrew the filler/level plug

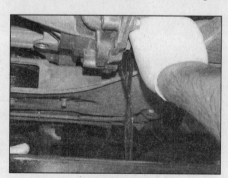

2.5 Unscrew the drain plug, and allow the oil to drain

> **HAYNES HiNT** *If using a typical transmission oil bottle, this will have to be positioned upside-down, which is itself quite difficult. To avoid the oil draining out of the bottle prematurely, fold over the plastic bottle's filler tube until the bottle is in the right position, then unfold it and insert into the filler hole.*

8 Refill the transmission with the exact amount of the specified type of oil, then check the oil level as described in Chapter 1A or 1B. When the level is correct, refit the filler/level plug and tighten securely **(see illustration)**.

9 Refit the engine undertray, then lower the car to the ground.

3 Gearchange mechanism – adjustment

Note: *Adjustment is only possible on the 6-speed transmission.*

1 Inside the car, unclip the base of the gear lever gaiter, and pull it upwards.
2 Select 4th gear.
3 Remove the battery and battery tray as described in Chapter 5A.
4 Remove the engine ECU as described in Chapter 4B.
5 Release the locking catch on the selector cable (marked with an 'N' on the cable sleeve) by sliding the sleeve forwards and pressing the catch sideways.
6 Have an assistant hold the gear lever in the 4th gear position.
7 Under the bonnet, set the cable to the required length, then re-fasten the locking catch on the selector cable by pushing it sideways and secure by sliding the catch backwards.
8 Check that all gears can be selected satisfactorily, then refit the removed components. Road-test the car to confirm the adjustment.

4 Gearchange mechanism – removal and refitting

Removal

1 Referring to Chapter 11, remove the gear lever housing (Section 23) and windscreen cowl panels (Section 8).
2 Ensure that the gear lever is in Neutral.
3 Remove the battery and battery tray as described in Chapter 5A.
4 Remove the engine ECU as described in Chapter 4A or 4B, as applicable.
5 To release the cables from their operating levers on top of the transmission, squeeze together the orange catches and lift the cable ends off **(see illustrations)**. On the 6-speed transmission, take care not to disturb the locking clip just behind the cable end fitting on the (blue) selector cable.
6 Work back along the cables to the clips which secure them into the cast lugs on the transmission. Slide the locking catches rearwards to release the cables, and lift them out **(see illustration)**.
7 Back inside the car, unscrew the three mounting nuts on the rear of the gearchange

mechanism, and the nut/bolt securing the support bar on the right-hand side. Lower the assembly away from the facia **(see illustrations)**.

8 To remove the gearchange mechanism completely, the heater assembly must be removed as described in Chapter 3.
9 Unscrew the three mounting nuts from the

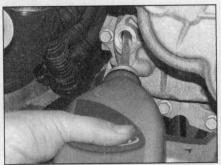
2.8 Filling the transmission with oil

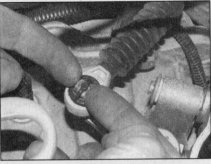
4.5a Squeeze the orange clips together . . .

4.5b . . . and lift off the cable end fittings

4.6 Release the cables from the transmission lugs

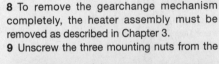

4.7a Remove the two nuts inside at the top . . .

4.7b . . . one more nut at the back . . .

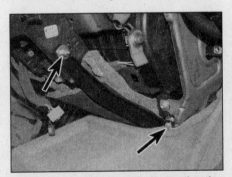
4.7c . . . and the nut and bolt securing the support bar . . .

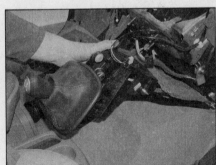
4.7d . . . then lower the assembly to the floor

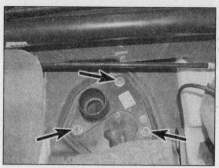

4.9 Remove the nuts from the gear cables seal on the bulkhead

5.7a Tap the new seal into position using a socket or metal tube . . .

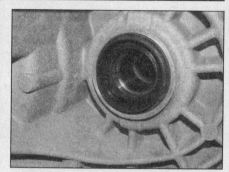

5.7b . . . until it is at the required fitted depth

cable bulkhead seal, and detach it and the cables **(see illustration)**.

10 Jack up the front of the car, and support it on axle stands (see *Jacking and vehicle support*).

11 Referring to Chapter 4A or 4B as necessary, disconnect the exhaust pipe at the front joint, then unbolt the floor mountings and move the exhaust aside. Remove the fasteners securing the front heat shield, and lower it for access to the cable run.

12 Feed the gear cables from the engine compartment back into the car through the bulkhead, and remove the gearchange mechanism.

Refitting

13 Refitting is a reversal of removal. If necessary, check the cable adjustment as described in Section 3.

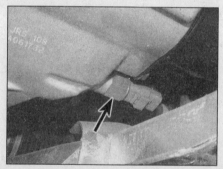

6.1a The reversing light switch is on the end of the 5-speed transmission . . .

6.1b . . . while 6-speed units have the switch on top

5 Oil seals – renewal

Driveshaft seals

1 With the handbrake applied, jack up the front of the car and support it on axle stands (see *Jacking and vehicle support*). Remove the right-hand wheel.

2 Drain the transmission oil as described in Section 2.

3 Referring to Chapter 8, disconnect the driveshaft from the transmission.

4 Wipe clean the old oil seal, and measure its fitted depth below the casing edge. This is necessary to determine the correct fitted position of the new oil seal.

5 Free the old oil seal, either by levering it out, or using a small drift to tap the outer edge of the seal inwards so that the opposite edge of the seal tilts out of the casing.

6 Wipe clean the oil seal seating in the casing.

7 Apply a smear of grease to the sealing lip of the new oil seal and, making sure its sealing lip is facing inwards, carefully slide it into position. Press the seal squarely into the transmission until it is positioned at the same depth as the original was prior to removal. If necessary, the seal can be tapped into position using a piece of metal tube or a socket which bears only on the hard outer edge of the seal **(see illustrations)**.

8 Reconnect the driveshaft to the transmission as described in Chapter 8.

9 Refill the transmission with oil as described in Section 2.

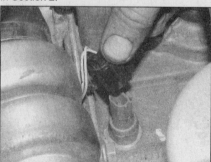

6.5 Disconnect the switch wiring plug, then unscrew and remove it

10 Refit the roadwheel and lower the car to the ground. Tighten the wheel bolts to the specified torque.

Input shaft seal

11 It is not possible to renew the input shaft oil seal without first dismantling the transmission. The guide tube assembly is a press-fit in the housing, and is removed inwards. Oil seal renewal should therefore be entrusted to a Renault dealer or transmission overhaul specialist.

6 Reversing light switch – testing, removal and refitting

Testing

1 The reversing light circuit is controlled by a plunger-type switch. On 5-speed units, the switch is screwed into the left-hand side of the transmission casing, next to the driveshaft inner joint, while 6-speed units have the switch on the top of the casing **(see illustrations)**. If a fault develops in the circuit, first ensure that the circuit fuse has not blown.

2 To test the switch, disconnect the wiring connector, and use a multimeter (set to the resistance function) or a battery-and-bulb test circuit to check that there is continuity between the switch terminals only when reverse gear is selected. If this is not the case, and there are no obvious breaks or other damage to the wires, the switch is faulty, and must be renewed.

Removal

5-speed models

3 With the handbrake applied, then jack up the front of the car and support it on axle stands (see *Jacking and vehicle support*). Where fitted, remove the engine compartment undertray.

6-speed models

4 Remove the battery and battery tray as described in Chapter 5A.

All models

5 Disconnect the wiring, then unscrew the switch from the transmission **(see illustration)**. Recover the sealing washer.

Refitting

6 Fit a new sealing washer to the switch, then screw it back into the transmission casing and tighten it securely. Reconnect the wiring, and test the operation of the circuit. If any oil was lost when the switch was removed, check the oil level as described in Chapter 1A or 1B.

7 Neutral switch – testing, removal and refitting

Testing

1 The neutral switch is an integral part of the keyless card system fitted to the Scénic. In order to start the engine, the clutch pedal must be depressed, or the transmission must be in neutral – the neutral switch, fitted to the rear of the gearchange mechanism on top of the transmission, informs the engine ECU when this is the case.

2 To test the switch, disconnect the wiring connector, and use a multimeter (set to the resistance function) or a battery-and-bulb test circuit to check that there is continuity between the switch terminals only when neutral is selected. If this is not the case, and there are no obvious breaks or other damage to the wires, the switch is faulty, and must be renewed.

Removal

3 It may be possible to access the switch from below, but the front subframe hinders this. To get to the switch from above, the air cleaner at least must be removed, as described in Chapter 4A or 4B.

4 Disconnect the wiring, then unscrew the switch from the gearchange mechanism **(see illustration)**.

Refitting

5 Refitting is a reversal of removal.

8 Manual transmission – removal and refitting

Note: *This Section describes the removal of the transmission leaving the engine in position in the car. Alternatively, the engine and transmission can be removed together, as described in Chapter 2D, then separated on the bench.*

Removal

1 With the handbrake applied, jack up the front of the car and support it on axle stands (see *Jacking and vehicle support*). Remove the engine compartment undertray and both front roadwheels.

2 Remove the engine top cover, and the windscreen cowl panels as described in Chapter 11.

3 Remove the battery and battery tray as described in Chapter 5A.

4 Remove the engine ECU, and the air cleaner, as described in Chapter 4A or 4B.

5 Drain the transmission oil as described in Section 2.

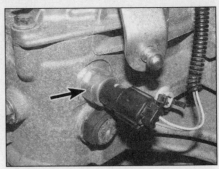

7.4 Neutral switch location at the back of the transmission

6 Remove the driveshafts as described in Chapter 8.

7 Remove the radiator as described in Chapter 3.

8 Unbolt the radiator lower crossmember side supports, then remove the front bolt and rear nut at either side of the crossmember, and lower it to the ground **(see illustrations)**.

9 Where applicable, release the clip securing the coolant pipes to the front of the transmission, and move the pipes to one side **(see illustration)**.

10 Release the clips securing the wiring harness to the transmission, and move the wiring to one side **(see illustration)**.

11 Using the information in Chapter 6, Section 2, first drain the clutch system via the bleed nipple, then disconnect the hydraulic fluid pipe from the slave cylinder.

12 Disconnect the gearchange cables from the top of the transmission, as described in Section 4.

8.8a Unbolt and remove the side support plates . . .

8.8b . . . then remove the front bolt . . .

8.8c . . . and rear nut . . .

8.8d . . . and lower out the radiator crossmember

8.9 Release the clip securing the coolant pipes to the front of the transmission

8.10 Unclip the wiring harness from the transmission

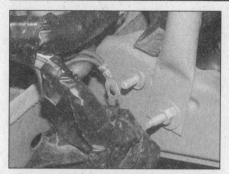

8.15 Unbolt the earth lead from the chassis leg

8.16a On diesel models, loosen the hose clip . . .

8.16b . . . then remove the mounting nut . . .

8.16c . . . and disconnect the intercooler air duct

8.19 6-speed models have an engine-to-transmission stud at the front

8.21 With care, the transmission can be supported from below

13 Disconnect the reversing light and neutral switch wiring connectors using the information in Sections 6 and 7.

14 Disconnect the crankshaft speed/position sensor wiring connector as described in Chapter 4A or 4B.

15 Unscrew the nut securing the wiring harness earth lead to the chassis leg on the transmission side (see illustration).

16 On diesel models, loosen the hose clip and disconnect the intercooler air duct, then remove the nut securing the duct mounting bracket to the top of the transmission (see illustrations).

17 Remove the starter motor as described in Chapter 5A.

18 On models with the 6-speed transmission, remove the front suspension subframe as described in Chapter 10. The 6-speed unit is physically bigger than the 5-speed, and there

is insufficient room for it to be lowered out with the subframe in place.

19 Loosen the transmission-to-engine nuts, bolts and studs – do not remove all of them at this stage (see illustration).

20 Referring to the relevant Part of Chapter 2, unbolt and remove the engine lower mounting.

21 The weight of the transmission must now be supported, as the engine left-hand mounting must be unscrewed and removed. Although this can be accomplished from below, with the aid of an assistant, it is recommended that an engine support bar or engine crane is used, to support the weight from above (see illustration). Note that, especially with the 6-speed unit, it will be necessary to lower the engine/transmission at the transmission end during the removal procedure.

22 With the transmission weight supported,

loosen and remove the three bolts securing the engine left-hand mounting to the top of the transmission – access to the rear bolt in particular is not easy (see illustration).

23 Lower the transmission until the housing is clear of the chassis on the left-hand side.

24 Unscrew and remove the transmission-to-engine nuts, bolts and studs, noting that some of them are used to retain other mounting brackets (see illustration).

25 Withdraw the transmission off the engine, taking care that its weight is not allowed to hang on the input shaft (see illustration). The 6-speed transmission in particular is a heavy unit, and it is recommended that an assistant is on hand to help. Lower the unit to the ground, and remove from under the car.

Refitting

26 Refitting is a reversal of removal, noting the following additional points:

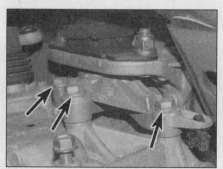

8.22 Unscrew the three left-hand mounting-to-transmission bolts

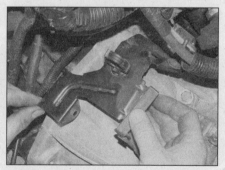

8.24 Note that some of the engine-to-transmission bolts also secure brackets

8.25 Withdraw the transmission off the engine

a) Make sure that the location dowels are correctly positioned in the transmission.

b) Renault recommend not greasing the splines the transmission input shaft, to avoid potential damage to the clutch release bearing.

c) When refitting the radiator lower crossmember, fit the fasteners and side plates loosely, then insert a 10 mm spacer between it and the subframe, at the rear. We used a 10 mm diameter bolt – this should be withdrawn once the nuts have been tightened each side (see illustrations). The crossmember forms part of the deformable front structure of the car, and the gap left by using the spacer is essential.

d) Check the transmission oil level with reference to Chapter 1A or 1B.

e) Tighten all nuts and bolts to the specified torque.

f) On 6-speed transmissions, adjust the gearchange mechanism if necessary, as described in Section 3.

9 Manual transmission overhaul – general information

Overhauling a manual transmission is a difficult and involved job for the DIY home mechanic. In addition to dismantling and

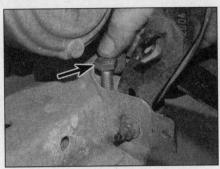

8.26a Insert a suitable 10 mm spacer (such as this M10 bolt) . . .

8.26b . . . and tighten the crossmember-to-subframe mountings with it in place

reassembling many small parts, clearances must be precisely measured and, if necessary, changed by selecting shims and spacers. Transmission internal components are also often difficult to obtain, and in many instances, extremely expensive. Because of this, if the transmission develops a fault or becomes noisy, the best course of action is to have the unit overhauled by a specialist repairer, or to obtain an exchange reconditioned unit.

Nevertheless, it is not impossible for the more experienced mechanic to overhaul a transmission, provided the special tools are available and the job is done in a deliberate step-by-step manner so that nothing is overlooked.

The tools necessary for an overhaul include internal and external circlip pliers, bearing pullers, a slide-hammer, a set of pin punches, a dial test indicator, and possibly a hydraulic press. In addition, a large, sturdy workbench and a vice will be required.

During dismantling of the transmission, make careful notes of how each component is fitted, to make reassembly easier and more accurate.

Before dismantling the transmission, it will help if you have some idea what area is malfunctioning. Certain problems can be closely related to specific areas in the transmission, which can make component examination and renewal easier. Refer to the *Fault finding* Section at the end of this manual for more information.

Chapter 7 Part B:
Automatic transmission

Contents

Degrees of difficulty

Easy, suitable for novice with little experience	**Fairly easy,** suitable for beginner with some experience	**Fairly difficult,** suitable for competent DIY mechanic	**Difficult,** suitable for experienced DIY mechanic	**Very difficult,** suitable for expert DIY or professional

Specifications

General
Type . . . .   Electronically-controlled with four forward speeds and reverse. Final drive differential integral with transmission
Transmission type code DP0
Application . . . .   1.6 litre petrol engine models

Ratios
1st. . . . .   2.73 : 1
2nd . . . .   1.50 : 1
3rd . . . .   1.00 : 1
4th . . . .   0.71 : 1
Reverse . . . .   3.17 : 1

Lubrication
Type . . . .   See *Lubricants and fluids* on page 0•17
Capacity (from dry). . . . .   6.0 litres
Drain and refill initial quantity (see text) . . . .   3.5 litres

Torque wrench settings

	Nm	lbf ft
Drain plug.	25	18
Fluid cooler bolt	50	37
Multi-function switch mounting bolts.	10	7
Radiator lower crossmember:		
Front bolt	105	78
Rear nut (to subframe)	21	15
Side support plate bolts.	21	15
Roadwheel bolts.	130	96
Starter motor mounting bolts	44	32
Torque converter-to-driveplate nuts*	37	27
Transmission bellhousing to engine	44	32
Transmission mounting:		
Centre nut.	62	46
Mounting stud-to-mounting	180	133
Mounting-to-body bolts	21	15
Mounting-to-transmission bolts	62	46
Outer nuts.	105	78
Transmission selector lever nut	10	7

*Use new nuts when refitting

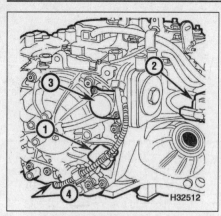

1.2 Sensor locations on the automatic transmission

1 Input speed sensor
2 Output speed sensor
3 Fluid cooler flow control solenoid
4 Line pressure sensor

1 General information

Automatic transmission models are fitted with a fully-automatic four-speed, electronically-controlled transmission.

The transmission consists of a torque converter, an epicyclic geartrain, hydraulically-operated clutches and brakes, and an electronic control unit incorporated into the engine management ECU. Sensors fitted to the transmission include an input speed sensor, output speed sensor, fluid cooler flow control solenoid valve and a line pressure sensor **(see illustration)**.

The torque converter provides a fluid coupling between the engine and transmission, and acts as an automatic clutch, also providing a degree of torque multiplication when accelerating. The torque converter incorporates a lock-up function whereby the engine and transmission can be

2.4a Combined drain plug and level checking plug unit (A)

directly coupled by means of a small clutch unit inside the torque converter. The lock-up function is controlled by the ECU according to operating conditions.

The epicyclic geartrain provides the forward gears or reverse gear, depending on which of its component parts are held stationary or allowed to turn. The components of the geartrain are held or released by brakes and clutches which are activated by a hydraulic control unit. A fluid pump within the transmission provides the necessary hydraulic pressure to operate the brakes and clutches.

Impulses from switches and sensors connected to the transmission throttle and selector linkages are directed to the ECU, which determines the ratio to be selected from the information received. The computer activates solenoid valves, which in turn open or close ducts within the hydraulic control unit. This causes the clutches and brakes to hold or release the various components of the geartrain, and provide the correct ratio for the particular engine speed or load. The information from the computer module can be overridden by use of the selector lever, and a particular gear can be held if required, regardless of engine speed. The selector lever also incorporates a shift-lock feature, which prevents the selector lever being moved from the P position unless the brake pedal is depressed.

The automatic transmission fluid is cooled by passing it through a cooler located on the top of the transmission. Coolant from the cooling system passes through the cooler.

Due to the complexity of the automatic transmission, any repair or overhaul work must be left to a Renault dealer with the necessary special equipment for fault diagnosis and repair. The contents of the following Sections are therefore confined to supplying general information, and any service information and instructions that can be used by the owner.

2 Automatic transmission fluid – draining and refilling

Note: The transmission is a 'sealed-for-life' unit, and fluid renewal is not required. The following procedure should only be necessary if repair work requiring the fluid to be drained is to be carried out. The transmission fluid filling and level checking procedure is particularly complicated, and the home mechanic cannot accurately ensure the correct fluid level after draining. If the fluid drained is carefully stored, however, the transmission may be refilled using the old fluid, or, if the amount of fluid drained is carefully measured, the same amount of fresh fluid could be used when refilling. This will allow the car to be driven a short distance to a Renault dealer to have the level checked properly.

Draining

1 Take the car on a short run, to warm the transmission up to normal operating temperature.
2 Park the car on level ground, then switch off the engine and ensure the handbrake is applied. Jack up the front of the car and support it securely on axle stands (see Jacking and vehicle support).
3 Remove the engine compartment undertray.
4 Position a suitable container under the transmission – if the fluid is to be re-used (see note above), the container must be spotlessly clean. Unscrew the transmission drain plug and allow the fluid to drain completely into the container, taking care to lose as little of the fluid as possible. Note that the drain plug and level checking plug are incorporated into one unit – the drain plug is the larger of the two hexagonal-headed plugs forming the draining/level checking unit **(see illustrations)**.

 Warning: If the fluid is hot, take precautions against scalding.

5 When the fluid has finished draining, clean the drain plug threads and those of the transmission casing. Fit a new sealing washer to the drain plug, and refit the plug to the transmission, tightening it securely.
6 If the fluid is to be re-used, it must be kept clean – transfer it into a clean container which can be sealed, if possible.

Refilling

7 Refer to Chapter 5A and remove the battery and its tray for access to the transmission filler plug. Unscrew the filler plug from the top of the transmission **(see illustration)**. Add either the fluid drained, or an equal amount of fresh fluid, to the transmission via the filler plug opening, using a clean funnel with a fine-mesh filter, then refit the plug.
8 An initial-fill quantity is given in the specifications at the start of this Chapter, but it is recommended this is only used if the quantity of old fluid drained is not known.

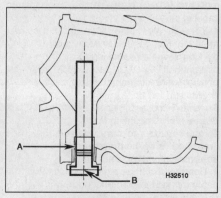

2.4b Cross-section of the combined drain/level plug unit

A Drain plug
B Level (overflow) plug

Renault mechanics run the transmission to a specific fluid temperature, then drain some of the fluid added, a process which is repeated until the correct level is established.

9 The car should be driven as little as possible until the fluid level can be checked accurately by a Renault dealer.

3 Selector cable – adjustment

1 Move the selector lever inside the car to the N position.

2 Disconnect the selector cable end fitting from the multi-function switch on top of the transmission. To improve access to the cable, remove the battery and its tray as described in Chapter 5A.

3 Check that the multi-function switch is in the N position, and if necessary set it accordingly.

4 Depress the tab on the side of the cable end fitting and suitably retain it in the released position **(see illustration)**.

5 Reconnect the selector cable to the multi-function switch then release the tab on the end fitting to lock the cable. Refit the battery and tray as described in Chapter 5A.

6 Check that the selector lever moves freely, and that the starter motor will only operate with P or N selected. Also check that the Park function operates correctly.

4 Selector lever assembly – removal and refitting

Removal

1 Remove the battery and its tray as described in Chapter 5A.

2 Inside the car, set the selector lever in the N position – keep it in this position throughout.

3 Under the bonnet, depress the tab on the cable end fitting and lift it off the selector lever on top of the transmission – take care not to move the transmission selector lever once the cable has been disconnected.

4 Release the cable outer from the cast retaining lug on the transmission housing by turning the two locking rings in opposite directions. Trace the cable back as far as possible, releasing any cable clips or ties as necessary.

5 Remove the gear/selector lever housing as described in Chapter 11.

6 Back inside the car, unscrew the three mounting nuts on the rear, and lower the assembly away from the facia.

7 Unscrew the three mounting bolts from the cable bulkhead seal, and detach it and the selector cable.

8 Jack up the front of the car, and support it on axle stands (see *Jacking and vehicle support*).

9 Referring to Chapter 4A as necessary,

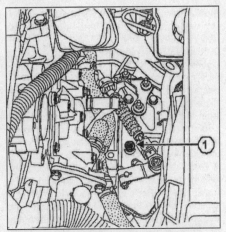

2.7 Transmission fluid filler plug (1)

disconnect the exhaust pipe at the front joint, then unbolt the floor mountings and move the exhaust aside. Remove the fasteners securing the front heat shield, and lower it for access to the cable run.

10 Feed the selector cable from the engine compartment back into the car through the bulkhead, and remove the assembly.

Refitting

11 Refitting is the reverse of removal. On completion, check the operation of the selector lever and, if necessary, adjust the cable as described in Section 3.

5 Selector cable – removal and refitting

Removal

1 Remove the selector lever assembly as described in Section 4.

2 Release the cable end from the base of the selector lever, and remove it.

Refitting

3 Reconnect the cable to the base of the lever, then place the lever in the N position – keep it there for the duration of refitting.

4 Refit the selector lever as described in Section 4. Adjust the cable as described in Section 3.

6 Fluid seals – renewal

Driveshaft seals

1 With the handbrake applied, jack up the front of the car and support it on axle stands (see *Jacking and vehicle support*). Remove the relevant roadwheel.

2 Drain the transmission fluid as described in Section 2.

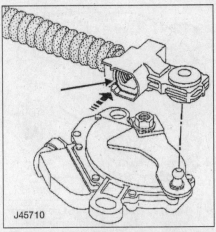

J45710

3.4 Depress the side tab on the cable end fitting to release the cable

3 Referring to Chapter 8, disconnect the complete driveshaft assembly from the transmission on the side being worked on.

4 Note the fitted depth of the old seal, then carefully lever the seal out of position using a flat-bladed screwdriver. Be careful not to drop the seal or its inner spring into the automatic transmission.

5 Wipe clean the oil seal seating in the casing and apply a smear of oil to the seal lip. Making sure the seal lip is facing inwards, carefully ease the new seal into position. Press the seal squarely into the transmission until it is positioned at the same depth as the original was prior to removal. If necessary the seal can be tapped into position using a piece of metal tube or a socket which bears only on the hard outer edge of the seal.

6 Refit the driveshaft assembly with reference to Chapter 8.

7 Refill the transmission with new fluid as described in Section 2.

8 Refit the roadwheel, lower the car to the ground and tighten the wheel bolts to the specified torque.

Torque converter seal

9 Remove the transmission from the engine as described in Section 9.

J45711

4.7 Selector lever assembly mounting bolts

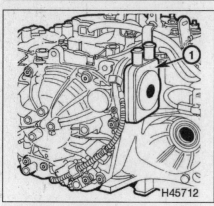

7.1 The fluid cooler is located on the rear left-hand side of the transmission

10 Remove the retaining strap and carefully slide the torque converter from the transmission shaft. Be prepared for fluid loss as the converter is removed.

11 Using a flat-bladed screwdriver carefully lever the seal out from the centre of the torque converter, taking great care not to mark the metal bush.

12 Press the new seal squarely into position, making sure its sealing lip is facing inwards.

13 Lubricate the lip of the seal with clean transmission fluid and carefully slide the converter onto the transmission shaft.

14 Make sure the torque converter is correctly engaged with the transmission shaft splines then refit the transmission as described in Section 9.

7 Fluid cooler – removal and refitting

Removal

1 The fluid cooler is located on the rear left-hand side of the transmission **(see**

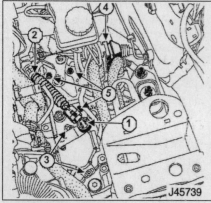

8.6 Multi-function switch removal details

1 *Selector cable end fitting*
2 *Selector cable outer locking rings*
3 *Multi-function switch mounting bolts*
4 *Transmission wiring modular connector*
5 *Modular connector support plate bolts*

illustration). To gain access to the cooler, remove the air cleaner and inlet duct as described in Chapter 4A.

2 To minimise coolant loss, clamp the coolant hoses on either side of the fluid cooler. Alternately, drain the cooling system as described in Chapter 1A.

3 Loosen the clips and disconnect the hoses from the fluid cooler – be prepared for some coolant spillage. Wash off any spilt coolant immediately with cold water, and dry the surrounding area before proceeding further.

4 Slacken and remove the mounting bolt(s), and remove the fluid cooler from the transmission. There will be some loss of fluid, so some clean rags should be placed around the cooler to absorb spillage. Make sure that dirt is prevented from entering the hydraulic system.

5 Remove the sealing ring from each mounting bolt and the sealing rings fitted between the cooler and transmission. Discard all sealing rings; new ones must be used on refitting.

Refitting

6 Lubricate the new seals with clean automatic transmission fluid, then fit the two new seals to the base of the fluid cooler, and a new seal to each mounting bolt.

7 Locate the fluid cooler on the top of the transmission housing, ensuring its lower seals remain in position. Refit the mounting bolt(s) and tighten to the specified torque.

8 Reconnect the coolant hoses to the fluid cooler, and securely tighten their retaining clips. Remove the hose clamps (where used).

9 Refit the air cleaner and inlet duct with reference to Chapter 4A.

10 On completion, top-up the cooling system and check the automatic transmission fluid level as described in Section 2.

8 Multi-function switch – removal, refitting and adjustment

1 The multi-function switch informs the electronic control unit of the selector lever position, prevents the starter motor operating when the transmission is in gear and also controls the reversing lights. The switch is located on the top of the transmission.

Removal

2 Remove the battery and its tray as described in Chapter 5A.

3 Remove the engine ECU and the air cleaner, as described in Chapter 4A.

4 Inside the car, set the selector lever in the N position – keep it in this position throughout.

5 Under the bonnet, depress the tab on the cable end fitting, and lift it off the selector lever on top of the transmission.

6 Release the cable outer from the cast retaining lug on the transmission housing by turning the two locking rings in opposite directions **(see illustration)**.

7 Mark the selector lever in relation to its splined shaft, then remove its retaining nut and take the lever off.

8 Undo the two multi-function switch mounting bolts.

9 Pull out the locking tab and disconnect the transmission wiring harness modular connector located at the rear of the unit.

10 Unscrew the three bolts securing the modular connector support plate, then remove two further nuts from the connector block itself.

11 Pull out the locking clip and disconnect the green wiring plug from the multi-function switch, then remove the switch assembly **(see illustration)**.

Refitting

12 Refit the switch assembly using a reversal of the removal procedure, but leave the two switch mounting bolts loose until the switch has been adjusted as follows.

13 Connect an ohmmeter across the two test terminals on the side of the multi-function switch. Turn the switch body until the internal switch contacts close, and 0 ohms is indicated on the ohmmeter. Hold the switch body in this position, and tighten the two retaining bolts.

14 Refit the selector lever to the transmission shaft, aligning the marks made prior to removal. Tighten the nut to the specified torque.

15 Further refitting is a reversal of removal. Adjust the selector cable as described in Section 3.

9 Automatic transmission – removal and refitting

Note: *If a new transmission and/or torque converter is being fitted, note that the ECU auto-adaptive values must be reset by a Renault dealer.*

Removal

1 With the handbrake applied, jack up the front of the car and support it on axle stands (see *Jacking and vehicle support*). Remove the engine compartment undertray and both front roadwheels.

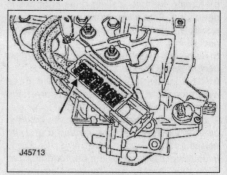

8.11 Disconnect the multi-function switch wiring plug

2 Remove the engine top cover, and the windscreen cowl panels as described in Chapter 11.

3 Remove the battery and battery tray as described in Chapter 5A.

4 Remove the engine ECU, and the air cleaner, as described in Chapter 4A.

5 Drain the transmission fluid as described in Section 2.

6 Remove the driveshafts as described in Chapter 8.

7 Remove the radiator as described in Chapter 3.

8 Unbolt the radiator lower crossmember side supports, then remove the front bolt and rear nut at either side of the crossmember, and lower it to the ground (see illustrations).

9 Where applicable, release the clip securing the coolant pipes to the front of the transmission, and move the pipes to one side.

10 Remove the multi-function switch assembly as described in Section 8.

11 Release the clips securing the wiring harness to the transmission, and move the wiring to one side.

12 Remove the crankshaft speed/position sensor as described in Chapter 4A.

13 Either drain the cooling system as described in Chapter 1A, or clamp the coolant hoses feeding the fluid cooler, before disconnecting the hoses.

14 Remove the left-hand front wheelarch liner, for access to the transmission ECU, which is mounted at the front of the wheelarch. Release and disconnect the transmission ECU wiring connector (see illustration), then trace the wiring harness back along its length, releasing it from the various clips and ties.

15 Unscrew the nut securing the wiring harness earth lead to the chassis leg on the transmission side.

16 Unscrew the exhaust manifold-to-downpipe nuts, and separate the flange joint.

17 Loosen the transmission-to-engine nuts/bolts – do not remove them at this stage.

18 Referring to the relevant Part of Chapter 2, unbolt and remove the engine lower mounting.

19 Remove the starter motor as described in Chapter 5A.

20 The torque converter is attached to the driveplate by three nuts which are accessed through the starter motor aperture. Turn the engine as required to position the nuts in the aperture, then unscrew and remove them. **Note:** *The nuts must be renewed every time they are removed.* Where applicable, unbolt the access plate from the bottom of the transmission.

21 The weight of the transmission must now be supported, as the engine left-hand mounting must be unscrewed and removed. Although this can be accomplished from below, with the aid of an assistant, it is recommended that an engine support bar or engine crane is used, to support the weight from above. Note that it will be necessary to lower the engine/transmission at the transmission end during the removal procedure.

9.8a Unbolt and remove the side support plates . . .

9.8c . . . and rear nut . . .

22 With the transmission weight supported, loosen and remove the three bolts securing the engine left-hand mounting to the top of the transmission – access to the rear bolt in particular is not easy.

23 Lower the transmission until the housing is clear of the chassis on the left-hand side.

24 Unscrew and remove the transmission-to-engine nuts, bolts and studs, noting that some of them are used to retain other mounting brackets.

25 Withdraw the transmission off the engine, taking care that the torque converter stays pushed fully into the transmission as it is removed – it is recommended that an assistant is on hand to help. Lower the unit to the ground, and remove from under the car.

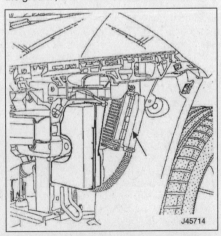

9.14 Disconnect the transmission ECU wiring connector

9.8b . . . then remove the front bolt . . .

9.8d . . . and lower out the radiator crossmember

26 Secure the torque converter in position by bolting a length of metal bar to one of the housing holes, or by tying one of the studs to the crankshaft sensor aperture on the top of the housing (see illustration).

Refitting

27 The transmission is refitted using a reversal of the removal procedure, bearing in mind the following points:

a) *Keep the torque converter pushed fully onto the transmission. Apply a smear of high-melting point grease (Renault recommend the use of Molykote BR2) to the converter centring ring.*

b) *Ensure the locating dowels are correctly*

9.26 Torque converter secured in the transmission with string tied through the TDC sensor aperture

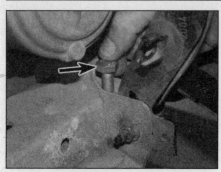

9.27a Insert a suitable 10 mm spacer (such as this M10 bolt) . . .

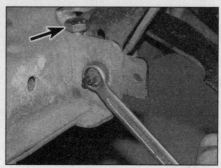

9.27b . . . and tighten the crossmember-to-subframe mountings with it in place

positioned prior to installation and clean the torque converter-to-driveplate stud threads.

c) Align the torque converter studs with the driveplate holes as the transmission is refitted. Apply thread-locking compound (Renault recommend the use of Loctite Frenbloc) to the new retaining nuts and tighten them to the specified torque.

d) When refitting the radiator lower crossmember, fit the fasteners and side plates loosely, then insert a 10 mm spacer between it and the subframe, at the rear on each side. We used a 10 mm diameter bolt – this should be withdrawn once the nuts have been tightened each side (see illustrations). The crossmember forms part of the deformable front structure of the car, and the gap left by using the spacer is essential.

e) Tighten all nuts and bolts to the specified torque (where given).
f) Refit the driveshafts as described in Chapter 8.
g) Adjust the selector cable as described in Section 3.
h) On completion, refill the transmission as described in Section 2.

10 Automatic transmission overhaul – general information

In the event of a fault occurring with the transmission, it is first necessary to determine whether it is of an electrical, mechanical or hydraulic nature, and to do this special test equipment is required. It is therefore essential to have the work carried out by a Renault dealer if a transmission fault is suspected.

Do not remove the transmission from the car for possible repair before professional fault diagnosis has been carried out, since most tests require the transmission to be in the car.

Chapter 8
Driveshafts

Contents

Degrees of difficulty

Easy, suitable for novice with little experience	**Fairly easy,** suitable for beginner with some experience	**Fairly difficult,** suitable for competent DIY mechanic	**Difficult,** suitable for experienced DIY mechanic	**Very difficult,** suitable for expert DIY or professional

Specifications

General

Driveshaft type . . . . Solid steel shafts, splined to inner and outer constant velocity joints, vibration damper fitted on some right-hand driveshafts

Torque wrench settings

	Nm	lbf ft
Anti-roll bar link rod nut	44	32
Driveshaft retaining nut*	280	207
Driveshaft support bearing bolts	44	32
Lower balljoint nut	62	46
Roadwheel bolts.	130	96
Track rod end balljoint nut	37	27

Use new nuts

1 General information

Drive is transmitted from the differential to the front wheels by means of two, unequal-length driveshafts.

Each driveshaft is fitted with an inner and outer constant velocity (CV) joint. The inner constant velocity joint is of the spider-and-yoke type and the outer joint is of the ball-and-cage type. Each outer joint is splined to engage with the wheel hub, and is threaded so that it can be fastened to the hub by a large nut. The inner joint is also splined to engage with the differential sunwheel.

On the right-hand driveshaft, the inner constant velocity (CV) joint is located approximately halfway along the shaft length, and the joint is supported by the rear of the cylinder block via a support bearing and bracket.

2 Driveshaft –
removal and refitting

Removal

1 Drain the transmission oil/fluid as described in Chapter 7A or 7B.
2 Remove the wheel trim/centre cap (as applicable), then slacken the driveshaft nut with the car resting on its wheels **(see illustration)**. Also slacken the wheel bolts.
3 Chock the rear wheels, then with the handbrake applied, jack up the front of the car and support it on axle stands (see *Jacking and vehicle support*). Remove the appropriate front roadwheel.
4 If the driveshaft nut was not slackened with the wheels on the ground (see paragraph 1), refit at least two roadwheel bolts to the front hub, tightening them securely, then have an assistant firmly depress the brake pedal to prevent the front hub from rotating, whilst you slacken and remove the driveshaft retaining nut. Alternatively, a tool can be fabricated from two lengths of steel strip (one long, one short) and a nut and bolt; the nut and bolt forming the pivot of a forked tool **(see Tool Tip)**.

2.2 Slacken the driveshaft nut with the car resting on its wheels

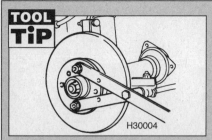

TOOL TiP

H30004

Using a fabricated tool to hold the front hub stationary whilst the driveshaft nut is slackened.

2.5a Loosen the track rod end balljoint nut . . .

2.5b . . . then use a balljoint separator tool . . .

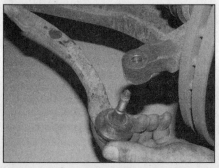

2.5c . . . to disconnect the track rod end balljoint

2.6a Unscrew the link rod upper nut, using an Allen key to hold the stud . . .

2.6b . . . and separate the link rod from the strut bracket

5 Slacken the nut securing the steering gear track rod end balljoint to the swivel hub, but leave the nut attached by just a few threads. Release the balljoint tapered shank using a universal balljoint separator, then unscrew the

nut completely, and separate the joint **(see illustrations)**.
6 Unscrew the upper nut from the anti-roll bar link rod, using an Allen key to prevent the stud turning. Pull the link rod

away from the strut mounting bracket **(see illustrations)**.
7 Disconnect the ABS wheel sensor wiring connector from the base of the swivel hub, using a small screwdriver to help release it. Unclip the ABS wiring from the subframe, then unclip the in-line wiring connector and disconnect that also **(see illustrations)**.
8 Unscrew and remove the lower balljoint retaining nut, and tap out the bolt **(see illustrations)**.
9 The lower balljoint must now be separated, by pulling the lower arm downwards. On our project car, this proved extremely difficult, due to corrosion between the balljoint and the hub. Apply plenty of penetrating spray to begin with. We used a long pole, fitted into a wooden block under the car, with a chain wrapped around the end of the lower arm, to provide sufficient leverage. Tapping in a tapered punch between the 'jaws' for the

2.7a Disconnect the spade connector from the ABS wheel sensor . . .

2.7b . . . then unclip the ABS wiring from the subframe . . .

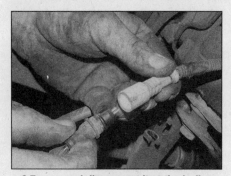

2.7c . . . and disconnect it at the in-line connector

2.8a Unscrew the lower arm balljoint nut . . .

2.8b . . . and tap out the bolt

2.9a Using a long pole, wood block and chain to lever down the lower arm . . .

2.9b . . . with a tapered punch to spread the location in the hub . . .

2.9c . . . the balljoint was separated from the lower arm

2.12 Pull the disc/hub out, and turn it to remove the driveshaft splined end

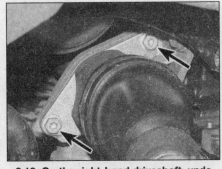

2.13 On the right-hand driveshaft, undo the two support plate bolts

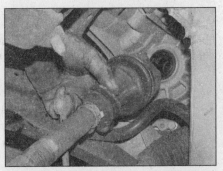

2.14a Removing the left-hand driveshaft

balljoint on the hub also proved useful (see illustrations).

10 The splined end of the driveshaft now has to be released from its location in the hub. It's likely that the splines will be very tight (corrosion may even be a factor, if the driveshaft has not been disturbed for some time), and considerable force may be needed. Tap the end of the shaft with a plastic or hide mallet only – if an ordinary hammer is used, place a small piece of wood over the end of the driveshaft – and leave the old nut loosely in place on the end to avoid damaging the splines.

11 Once the splines have been released, remove the driveshaft nut and discard it – the nut is only intended to be used once.

12 Pull the disc/hub outwards, and turn it to allow the driveshaft to be withdrawn through the hub. It's helpful to have an assistant on hand here, to pull the hub outwards, while you slide out the driveshaft (see illustration). **Note:** *Once the left-hand driveshaft has been removed from the hub, there is nothing to prevent it dropping out of the transmission – be prepared to catch it.*

13 If working on the right-hand driveshaft, unscrew the two bolts securing the driveshaft collar to the support bearing on the back of the engine (see illustration).

14 Pull the driveshaft out of the transmission, and remove it, ensuring that neither of the CV joints is bent excessively during the procedure. Also take care that the joint gaiters do not suffer unnecessary damage during removal. On the right-hand driveshaft, recover

the support bearing collar, noting how it fits, and the support bearing O-ring seal (see illustrations).

Refitting

15 Refitting is a reversal of removal, noting the following points:

a) *Whenever a driveshaft is removed, the driveshaft oil seals in the transmission should be inspected, and if necessary, new ones fitted as described in Chapter 7A or 7B. Similarly, check the condition of the O-ring fitted to the right-hand shaft's support bearing.*

b) *Clean and grease the driveshaft support bearing, and apply a little grease to the driveshaft oil seals and splines.*

c) *Tighten all nuts and bolts to the specified torque.*

d) *Once the driveshaft has been re-inserted in the hub, tighten the new*

2.14b Take off the support collar as the right-hand driveshaft is removed . . .

driveshaft nut as fully as possible by hand initially – delay tightening to the specified torque until the car is resting back on its wheels.

3 Driveshaft gaiters and CV joints – renewal

Few would argue that the Scénic is a unique and distinctive car. It does, however, have one feature not readily visible from the outside – driveshafts for which there are apparently no service parts available. This means that, at the time of writing, there are no gaiter ('boot') kits available, and it would appear also that the joints cannot be renewed separately – no procedures on joint or gaiter removal are given by Renault. The only option, therefore, in the event of the slightest problem with

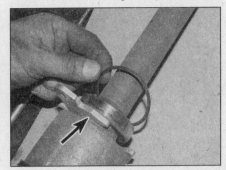

2.14c . . . noting how it fits, and recover the bearing's O-ring seal

either shaft, would appear to be a complete replacement driveshaft.

It is hoped that, in time, repair kits and exchange driveshafts will become available, possibly from sources independent of Renault. In the meantime, readers are advised to seek advice from the better motor factors. While not something we would normally endorse, repairing a damaged gaiter could be accomplished using one of the universal 'sticky-boot' kits, where a new gaiter is fitted around the damaged one. Also, don't overlook the possibility of sourcing a secondhand shaft from a breakers – try and obtain one from a Scénic with the same transmission.

4 Driveshaft overhaul – general information

If any of the checks described in Chapter 1A or 1B reveal wear in a driveshaft joint, first remove the roadwheel trim or centre cap (as appropriate) and check that the driveshaft retaining nut is still correctly tightened; if in doubt, use a torque wrench to check it. Refit the centre cap or trim, and repeat the check on the other driveshaft.

Road test the car, and listen for a metallic clicking from the front as the car is driven slowly in a circle on full-lock. If a clicking noise is heard, this indicates wear in the outer constant velocity joint.

If vibration, consistent with road speed, is felt through the car when accelerating, there is a possibility of wear in the inner constant velocity joints.

At the time of writing, wear in either joint can only be rectified by renewing the driveshaft. This is necessary since no driveshaft components are available separately.

Chapter 9
Braking system

Contents

Degrees of difficulty

Easy, suitable for novice with little experience	Fairly easy, suitable for beginner with some experience	Fairly difficult, suitable for competent DIY mechanic	Difficult, suitable for experienced DIY mechanic	Very difficult, suitable for expert DIY or professional

Specifications

General

System type	Servo-assisted hydraulic circuit, split diagonally with ABS anti-locking braking system
Front brakes	Disc, with single-piston sliding caliper
Rear brakes	Disc, with single-piston sliding caliper
Handbrake	Cable-operated, to rear wheels. Automatic handbrake on most models

Front brakes

Disc diameter:
Except 1.9 litre diesel models:		
Scénic	280 mm	
Grand Scénic	300 mm	
1.9 litre diesel models	300 mm	
Disc run-out (all models)	0.07 mm maximum	

Disc thickness:	New	Minimum
All models	24.0 mm	21.8 mm
Brake pad thickness (friction material and backing plate)	18.0 mm	6.0 mm

Rear brakes

Disc diameter:
Scénic	270 mm
Grand Scénic	274 mm
Disc run-out	0.07 mm maximum

Disc thickness:
New	8.0 mm
Minimum	6.5 mm

Brake pad thickness (friction material and backing plate):
New	16.0 mm
Minimum	6.0 mm

Vacuum servo

Pushrod setting dimension	133.2 mm

Torque wrench settings

	Nm	lbf ft
ABS system components:		
Hydraulic unit brake pipe union nuts	17	13
Hydraulic unit mounting bolts	65	48
Brake caliper mounting bracket bolts*	105	77
Brake disc retaining screw	15	11
Brake hose and pipe unions	17	13
Brake pedal mounting nuts	21	15
Front brake caliper guide pin bolts*	32	24
Master cylinder brake pipe union nuts	17	13
Master cylinder mounting nuts	50	37
Rear brake caliper guide pin bolts*	36	27
Rear hub nut**	220	162
Roadwheel bolts	130	96
Vacuum servo unit mounting bolts	21	15

*Use thread-locking fluid
**Use a new nut

1 General information

The braking system is of the servo-assisted, dual circuit hydraulic type. All models are fitted with front and rear disc brakes. An anti-lock braking system (ABS) is fitted to all models as standard. Refer to Sections 18 and 19 for further information on ABS operation and components.

The front and rear disc brakes are actuated by single-piston sliding type calipers, which ensure that equal pressure is applied to each disc pad.

The rear disc brake calipers incorporate mechanical handbrake mechanisms, providing an independent mechanical means of rear brake application. Most Scénic models have an unusual automatic handbrake, with a facia-mounted control and electronic control unit, intended to free up storage space between the front seats.

The vacuum servo unit uses inlet manifold depression (generated only when a petrol engine is running) to boost the effort applied by the driver at the brake pedal and transmits this increased effort to the master cylinder pistons. Because there is no throttling of the inlet manifold on a diesel engine, it is not a suitable source of vacuum for brake servo operation. Vacuum is therefore derived from a separate vacuum pump, driven via a pushrod operated by an eccentric on the camshaft.

Precautions

The car's braking system is one of its most important safety features. When working on the brakes, there are a number of points to be aware of, to ensure that your health (or even your life) is not being put at risk.

⚠ *Warning: Brake fluid is poisonous. Take care to keep it off bare skin, and in particular not to get splashes in your eyes. The fluid also attacks paintwork and plastics – wash off spillages immediately with cold water. Finally, brake fluid is highly inflammable, and should be handled with the same care as petrol.*

Make sure the ignition is off (take out the keycard) before disconnecting any braking system hydraulic union, and do not switch it on until after the hydraulic system has been bled. Failure to do this could lead to air entering the ABS hydraulic unit. If air enters the hydraulic unit pump, it will prove very difficult (in some cases impossible) to bleed the unit (see Section 6).

When servicing any part of the system, work carefully and methodically – do not take short-cuts; also observe scrupulous cleanliness when overhauling any part of the hydraulic system.

Always renew components in axle sets, where applicable – this means replacing brake pads on BOTH sides, even if only one set of pads is worn, or one wheel cylinder is leaking (for example). In the instance of uneven brake wear, the cause should be investigated and fixed (on front brakes, sticking caliper pistons is a likely problem).

Use only genuine Renault replacement parts, or at least those of known good quality.

Although genuine Renault brake pads are asbestos-free, the dust created by wear of non-genuine parts may contain asbestos, which is a health hazard. Never blow it out with compressed air, and don't inhale any of it.

DO NOT use petroleum-based solvents to clean brake parts; use brake cleaner or methylated spirit only.

DO NOT allow any brake fluid, oil or grease to contact the brake pads or disc.

2 Brake pedal – removal and refitting

Removal

1 Renault recommend removing the facia panel (Chapter 11) and the steering column (Chapter 10) to improve access to the brake pedal. While this is undoubtedly true, it appears perfectly possible to remove the brake pedal with these components in place.
2 Remove the accelerator pedal as described in Chapter 4A or 4B.
3 Carefully slide off the spring clip which secures the pedal-to-cross-shaft clevis pin (see illustration), then slide out the pin and disconnect the shaft.
4 Unscrew the five nuts securing the pedal mounting bracket to the bulkhead (see illustration), then remove the pedal, twisting it sideways to release it.
5 Check the condition of the clevis pin and its spring clip – these are vital components connecting the brake pedal to the cross-shaft, and if their condition is at all suspect, new parts should be fitted.

Refitting

6 Refitting is a reversal of removal, noting the following points:
  a) Tighten the pedal mounting bracket nuts to the specified torque.

2.3 Remove the square spring clip securing the clevis pin

2.4 Brake pedal mounting bracket nuts

3.3 Removing the ventilation system air duct below the glovebox

b) Ensure that the pedal-to-cross-shaft clevis pin's spring clip is securely refitted.

c) Check the operation of the brakes before taking the car out on the road.

3 Brake pedal cross-shaft – removal and refitting

Removal

1 Remove the brake pedal as described in Section 2. As with brake pedal removal, it should not be necessary to remove the facia panel (Chapter 11) for this operation, although it will make access easier.

2 Remove the glovebox as described in Chapter 11, Section 23.

3 To further improve access, unclip and remove the plastic air duct fitted below the glovebox location **(see illustration)**.

4 Working in the passenger footwell, disconnect the wiring plug from the brake light switch at the top of the servo operating lever. Turn the brake light switch 90° anti-clockwise and remove it.

5 Unscrew the two nuts securing the cross-shaft to the servo operating lever **(see illustration)**.

6 Prise up the tabs of the star washer used to secure the servo operating lever clevis pin **(see illustration)**. **Note:** *A new star washer should be used when refitting – this is a small but vital component in the braking system.*

7 The servo operating lever clevis pin has a spring clip fitted, attached to the servo pushrod. Disconnect the clip by twisting it downwards, then slide the clevis pin out.

8 Taking care not to damage the clutch master cylinder pipes, withdraw the cross-shaft into the driver's footwell, and remove it from the car.

9 If required, the servo operating lever's mounting plate can be removed from the bulkhead, after removing the mounting nuts.

10 Examine the shaft, and all related components, very carefully. If there are signs of damage to any component, new parts should be fitted – never take risks where brakes are concerned.

Refitting

11 Refitting is a reversal of removal, noting the following points:

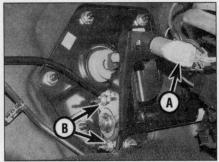

3.5 Disconnect the brake light switch (A) and remove the cross-shaft end nuts (B)

a) Use a new star washer on the servo operating lever clevis pin, and ensure that it is fitted tightly.

b) Tighten all fasteners securely, or to the specified torque.

c) Refit the glovebox as described in Chapter 11, and the brake pedal as described in Section 2.

d) Check the operation of the brakes before taking the car out on the road.

4 Vacuum servo unit – testing, removal and refitting

Testing

1 To test the operation of the servo unit, depress the footbrake several times to exhaust the vacuum, then start the engine whilst keeping the pedal firmly depressed.

2 As the engine starts, there should be a noticeable 'give' in the brake pedal as the vacuum builds up. Allow the engine to run for at least two minutes, then switch it off. If the brake pedal is now depressed it should feel normal, but further applications should result in the pedal feeling firmer, with the pedal stroke decreasing with each application.

3 If the servo does not operate as described, inspect the servo unit check valve as described in Section 4.

4 If the servo unit still fails to operate satisfactorily, the fault lies within the unit itself. Apart from external components, no spares are available, so a defective servo must be renewed.

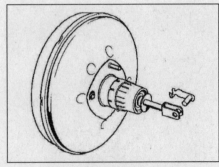

4.10 Remove the spring clip from the servo pushrod

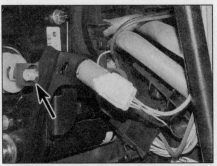

3.6 Prise up the tabs of the star washer

Removal

5 Remove the master cylinder as described in Section 8.

6 On manual transmission models, release the upper cable on top of the transmission. Squeeze together the orange catches and lift the cable end off. Work back along the cable to the clip securing it to the cast lug on the transmission. Slide the locking catch rearwards to release the cable, and lift it out.

7 Remove the glovebox as described in Chapter 11, Section 23.

8 To further improve access, unclip and remove the plastic air duct fitted below the glovebox location.

9 Prise up the tabs of the star washer used to secure the servo operating lever clevis pin. **Note:** *A new star washer should be used when refitting – this is a small but vital component in the braking system.*

10 The servo operating lever clevis pin has a spring clip fitted, attached to the servo pushrod. Disconnect the clip by twisting it downwards, then slide the clevis pin out **(see illustration)**.

11 Prise out the servo check valve from the front of the servo unit, and move the hose to one side.

12 On 1.9 litre diesel engine models, remove the EGR solenoid valve as described in Chapter 4C.

13 Unscrew and remove the two servo mounting bolts **(see illustration)**.

14 Carefully withdraw the servo unit through the bulkhead into the engine compartment, and remove it.

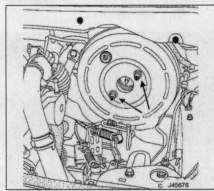

4.13 Remove the two servo mounting bolts

Refitting

15 Prior to refitting, check that the servo unit pushrod is adjusted to the correct specified dimension.

16 Refitting is a reversal of removal, noting the following points:

a) *Use a new star washer on the servo operating lever clevis pin, and ensure that it is fitted tightly.*

b) *Tighten all fasteners securely, or to the specified torque.*

c) *Refit the glovebox as described in Chapter 11, and the brake pedal as described in Section 2.*

d) *Check the operation of the brakes before taking the car out on the road.*

5 Vacuum servo unit check valve – removal, testing and refitting

Removal

1 Referring to Chapter 4A or 4B if necessary, remove the air cleaner duct for access to the servo unit vacuum hose **(see illustration)**.

2 Withdraw the valve from its rubber sealing grommet, using a pulling and twisting motion **(see illustration)**. Remove the grommet from the servo.

3 To remove the hose completely, squeeze the tabs at the other end of the hose, and disconnect it from the inlet manifold or vacuum pump **(see illustrations)**.

5.1 Remove the air cleaner duct to access the check valve

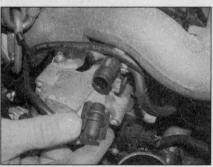

5.3a Disconnect the servo hose from the vacuum pump (diesel) . . .

Testing

4 Examine the check valve for signs of damage, and renew if necessary. The valve may be tested by blowing through it in both directions. Air should flow through the valve in one direction only – when blown through from the servo unit end of the valve. Renew the valve if this is not the case.

5 Examine the rubber sealing grommet and flexible vacuum hose for signs of damage or deterioration, and renew as necessary.

Refitting

6 Fit the sealing grommet into position in the servo unit.

7 Ease the check valve into position, taking care not to displace or damage the grommet. Reconnect the vacuum hose to the inlet manifold or vacuum pump.

8 On completion, start the engine and check that there are no air leaks. Check the operation of the brakes before taking the car onto the road.

6 Hydraulic system – bleeding

Note: *Refer to the precautions in Section 1 before proceeding.*

Caution: Make sure the ignition is off (take out the keycard) before bleeding the system.

General

1 The correct operation of any hydraulic

5.2 The check valve is located in the front of the servo

5.3b . . . or inlet manifold (petrol)

system is only possible after removing all air from the components and circuit; this is achieved by bleeding the system.

2 During the bleeding procedure, add only clean, unused hydraulic fluid of the recommended type; never re-use fluid that has already been bled from the system. Ensure that sufficient fluid is available before starting work.

3 If there is any possibility of incorrect fluid being already in the system, the system must be flushed completely with uncontaminated, correct fluid, and new seals should be fitted to the various components.

4 If air has entered the hydraulic system because of a leak, ensure that the fault is cured before proceeding further.

5 Park the car on level ground, switch off the engine, remove the keycard and select first or reverse gear (or P on automatic transmission models). Chock the wheels and release the handbrake.

6 Check that all pipes and hoses are secure, unions tight and bleed screws closed. Clean any dirt from around the bleed screws – if they have not been opened for some time, apply a maintenance spray such as WD-40, and allow time for it to soak in.

7 Unscrew the master cylinder reservoir cap and top the master cylinder reservoir up to the MAX level line; refit the cap loosely. Remember to maintain the fluid level at least above the MIN level line throughout the procedure, or there is a risk of further air entering the system.

8 There is a number of one-man, do-it-yourself brake bleeding kits currently available from motor accessory shops. It is recommended that one of these kits is used whenever possible, as they greatly simplify the bleeding operation, and also reduce the risk of expelled air and fluid being drawn back into the system. If such a kit is not available, the basic (two-man) method must be used, which is described in detail below.

9 If a kit is to be used, prepare the car as described previously, and follow the kit manufacturer's instructions. The procedure may vary slightly according to the type of kit being used; general procedures are as outlined below in the relevant sub-section.

10 Whichever method is used, the same sequence must be followed (paragraphs 11 and 12) to ensure the removal of all air from the system.

Bleeding sequence

11 If the system has been only partially disconnected, and the correct precautions were taken to minimise fluid loss, it should be necessary only to bleed that part of the system (ie, the primary or secondary circuit).

12 If the complete system is to be bled, then it should be done working in the following sequence:

a) *Right-hand rear brake.*

b) *Left-hand front brake.*

c) *Left-hand rear brake.*

d) *Right-hand front brake.*

Bleeding

Basic (two-man) method

13 Collect a clean glass jar, a length of plastic or rubber tubing which is a tight fit over the bleed screw, and a ring spanner to fit the screw. The help of an assistant will also be required.

14 Remove the dust cap from the first screw in the sequence. Fit the spanner and tube to the screw, place the other end of the tube in the jar, and pour in sufficient fluid to cover the end of the tube.

15 Ensure that the master cylinder reservoir fluid level is maintained at least above the MIN level line throughout the procedure.

16 Have the assistant fully depress the brake pedal several times to build-up pressure, then maintain it on the final stroke.

17 While pedal pressure is maintained, unscrew the bleed screw (approximately one turn) and allow the compressed fluid and air to flow into the jar. The assistant should maintain pedal pressure, following it down to the floor if necessary, and should not release it until instructed to do so. When the flow stops, tighten the bleed screw again. Have the assistant release the pedal slowly.

18 Repeat the steps given in paragraphs 16 and 17 until the fluid emerging from the bleed screw is free from air bubbles. Remember to recheck the fluid level in the master cylinder reservoir every five strokes or so. If the master cylinder has been drained and refilled, and air is being bled from the first screw in the sequence, allow approximately five seconds between strokes for the master cylinder passages to refill.

19 When no more air bubbles appear, tighten the bleed screw securely, remove the tube and spanner, and refit the dust cap. Do not overtighten the bleed screw.

20 Repeat the procedure on the remaining screws in the sequence until all air is removed from the system and the brake pedal feels firm.

Using a one-way valve kit

21 As their name implies, these kits consist of a length of tubing with a one-way valve fitted to prevent expelled air and fluid being drawn back into the system; some kits include a translucent container, which can be positioned so that the air bubbles can be more easily seen flowing from the end of the tube **(see illustration)**.

22 The kit is connected to the bleed screw, which is then opened. The user returns to the driver's seat and depresses the brake pedal with a smooth, steady stroke and slowly releases it; this is repeated until the expelled fluid is clear of air bubbles.

23 Note that these kits simplify work so much that it is easy to forget the master cylinder reservoir fluid level; ensure that this is maintained at least above the MIN level line at all times.

Using a pressure-bleeding kit

24 These kits are usually operated by the reservoir of pressurised air contained in the spare tyre, although it may be necessary to reduce the pressure in the tyre to lower than normal; refer to the instructions supplied with the kit.

25 By connecting a pressurised, fluid-filled container to the master cylinder reservoir, bleeding can be carried out simply by opening each screw in turn (in the specified sequence) and allowing the fluid to flow out until no more air bubbles can be seen in the expelled fluid.

26 This method has the advantage that the large reservoir of fluid provides an additional safeguard against air being drawn into the system during bleeding.

27 Pressure-bleeding is particularly effective when bleeding 'difficult' systems, or when bleeding the complete system at the time of routine fluid renewal.

All methods

28 When bleeding is complete and firm pedal feel is restored, wash off any spilt fluid, tighten the bleed screws securely and refit their dust caps.

29 Check the hydraulic fluid level, and top-up if necessary (see *Weekly checks*).

30 Discard any hydraulic fluid that has been bled from the system; it will not be fit for re-use.

31 Check the feel of the brake pedal. If it feels at all spongy, air must still be present in the system, and further bleeding is required. Failure to bleed satisfactorily after several repetitions of the bleeding procedure may be due to worn master cylinder seals.

7 Hydraulic pipes and hoses – renewal

Note: *Refer to the precautions in Section 1 before proceeding.*

1 If any pipe or hose is to be renewed, minimise fluid loss by removing the master cylinder reservoir cap and then tightening it down onto a piece of polythene (taking care not to damage the sender unit) to obtain an airtight seal. Alternatively, flexible hoses can be sealed, if required, using a proprietary brake hose clamp; metal brake pipe unions can be plugged (if care is taken not to allow dirt into the system) or capped immediately

6.21 Using a one-man brake bleeding kit

they are disconnected. Place a wad of rag under any union that is to be disconnected, to catch any spilt fluid.

2 If a flexible hose is to be disconnected, unscrew the brake pipe union nut before removing the spring clip which secures the hose to its mounting bracket **(see illustrations)**.

3 To unscrew the union nuts, it is preferable to obtain a brake pipe spanner of the correct size (split ring); these are available from motor accessory shops. Failing this, a close-fitting open-ended spanner will be required, though if the nuts are tight or corroded, their flats may be rounded off if the spanner slips. In such a case, a self-locking wrench is often the only way to unscrew a stubborn union, but it follows that the pipe and the damaged nuts must be renewed on reassembly. Always clean a union and surrounding area before disconnecting it. If disconnecting a component with more than one union, make a careful note of the connections before disturbing any of them.

4 If a brake pipe is to be renewed, it can be obtained, cut to length and with the union nuts and end flares in place, from Renault dealers. All that is then necessary is to bend it to shape, following the line of the original, before fitting it to the car. Alternatively, most motor accessory shops can make up brake pipes from kits, but this requires very careful measurement of the original to ensure that the new pipe is of the correct length. The safest answer is usually to take the original to the shop as a pattern.

5 On refitting, do not over tighten the union nuts. The specified torque wrench settings

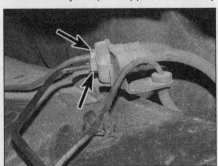

7.2a Unscrew the union nuts . . .

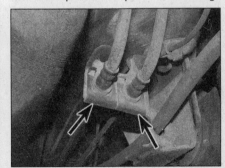

7.2b . . . and pull out the spring clips securing the hoses

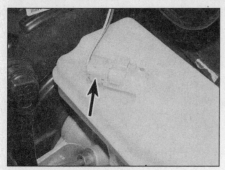

8.3 Disconnect the fluid level sender wiring connector

8.6 Master cylinder mounting nuts

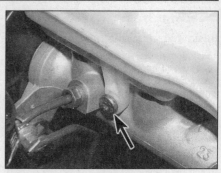

8.8 Reservoir-to-master cylinder mounting bolt

(where given) are not high, and it is not necessary to exercise brute force to obtain a sound joint.

6 Ensure that the pipes and hoses are correctly routed with no kinks, and that they are secured in the clips or brackets provided. In the case of flexible hoses, make sure that they cannot contact other components during movement of the steering and/or suspension assemblies.

7 After fitting, remove the polythene from the reservoir (or remove the plugs or clamps, as applicable), and bleed the hydraulic system as described in Section 6. Wash off any spilt fluid, and check carefully for fluid leaks.

8 Master cylinder – removal and refitting

Note: *Refer to the precautions in Section 1 before proceeding.*

Removal

1 Remove the battery as described in Chapter 5A.

2 Remove the engine ECU and the air cleaner (or just the resonator on 1.4 litre petrol engines) as described in Chapter 4A or 4B.

3 Remove the master cylinder reservoir cap, having disconnected the sender unit wiring connector, and syphon the hydraulic fluid from the reservoir **(see illustration)**. Note: *Do not syphon the fluid by mouth, as it is poisonous; use a syringe or an old antifreeze hydrometer.* Alternatively, open any convenient pair of

bleed screws in the system (one in each hydraulic circuit) and gently pump the brake pedal to expel the fluid through plastic tubes connected to the screws (see Section 6).

4 Release the clip and disconnect the clutch fluid supply hose.

5 Wipe clean the area around the brake pipe unions on the side of the master cylinder, and place absorbent rags beneath the pipe unions to catch any surplus fluid. Make a note of the correct fitted positions of the unions, then unscrew the union nuts and carefully withdraw the pipes. Plug or tape over the pipe ends and master cylinder orifices, to minimise the loss of brake fluid and to prevent the entry of dirt into the system. Wash off any spilt fluid immediately with cold water.

6 Unscrew and remove the two master cylinder-to-servo nuts **(see illustration)**.

7 Unclip the bulkhead soundproofing as necessary, then remove the master cylinder from the servo.

8 If necessary, the reservoir can be separated from the cylinder after removing the mounting bolt **(see illustration)**.

9 At the time of writing it was not possible to obtain internal components for the master cylinder, although it is worth checking with a Renault dealer and the larger motor factors. If parts are not available, it must be renewed as a complete unit. The O-ring seal fitted between the master cylinder and the vacuum servo must be renewed as a matter of course whenever the unit is removed, as a leak at this point will allow atmospheric pressure into the servo unit.

Refitting

10 Remove all traces of dirt from the master cylinder and servo unit mating surfaces. Fit a new O-ring seal to the groove on the master cylinder body.

11 Fit the master cylinder to the servo, ensuring that the servo pushrod enters the master cylinder bore centrally. Refit the master cylinder mounting nuts, and tighten them to the specified torque.

12 Wipe clean the brake pipe unions, then refit them to the master cylinder ports. Tighten the union nuts to the specified torque.

13 Further refitting is a reversal of removal, noting the following points:

a) On completion, fill the reservoir with fresh fluid and bleed the brakes as described in Section 6.

b) Bleed the clutch as described in Chapter 6.

c) Check the operation of the brakes before taking the car out on the road.

9 Front brake pads – renewal

Note: *Refer to the precautions in Section 1 before proceeding. Always renew the pads on both front brakes, never just on one side.*

1 With the handbrake applied, jack up the front of the car and support it on axle stands (see *Jacking and vehicle support*). Remove the front roadwheels.

2 Unscrew and remove the caliper lower guide pin bolt – this may require the use of a second spanner on the guide pin's outer hex fitting to prevent it from turning **(see illustration)**.

3 With the lower guide pin bolt removed, swing the caliper body upwards for access to the pads **(see illustration)**. If necessary, to prevent strain on the flexible brake hose, unclip the hose from the suspension strut.

4 The pads are clipped into place in the caliper mounting bracket – pull them out at the top to release them from their spring clips **(see illustrations)**.

5 First measure the thickness of each brake pad (friction material and backing plate). If any pad is worn at any point to the specified minimum thickness or less, all four pads

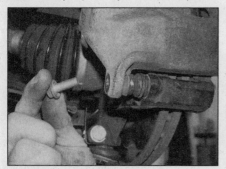

9.2 Remove the caliper lower guide pin bolt . . .

9.3 . . . then swing the caliper upwards for access to the pads

must be renewed. Also, the pads should be renewed if any are fouled with oil or grease; there is no satisfactory way of degreasing friction material once contaminated.

6 If any of the brake pads are worn unevenly or fouled with oil or grease, trace and rectify the cause before reassembly. New brake pads and spring kits are available from Renault dealers.

 If the pads are wearing unevenly, the calipers are probably seized, which will also wear the discs prematurely. Just removing the pads and pushing the piston fully back into its bore (see paragraph 9) may unseize the piston enough to restore correct operation. If not, remove and overhaul the calipers as described in Section 10.

7 If the brake pads are still serviceable, carefully clean them using a clean, fine wire brush or similar, paying particular attention to the sides and back of the metal backing. Carefully clean the pad locations in the caliper body/mounting bracket.

8 Prior to fitting the pads, check that the guide sleeves are free to slide easily in the caliper body, and check that the rubber guide sleeve gaiters are undamaged. Brush the dust and dirt from the caliper and piston, but *do not inhale it, as it may be a health hazard.* Inspect the dust seal around the piston for damage, and the piston for evidence of fluid leaks, corrosion or damage. If attention to any of these components is necessary, refer to Section 10. Also inspect the brake disc as described in Section 11.

9 The caliper piston must be pushed back into the caliper to make room for the new pads – this may require considerable effort. Either use a G-clamp, sliding-jaw (water pump) pliers, or suitable pieces of wood as levers **(see illustration)**.
Caution: Pushing back the piston causes a reverse-flow of brake fluid, which has been known to 'flip' the master cylinder rubber seals, resulting in a total loss of braking. To avoid this, clamp the caliper flexible hose and open the bleed screw – as the piston is pushed back, the fluid can be directed into a suitable container using a hose attached to the bleed screw. Close the screw just before the piston is pushed fully back, to ensure no air enters the system.

10 If the recommended method of opening a bleed screw before pushing back the piston is not used, the fluid level in the reservoir will rise, and possibly overflow. Make sure that there is sufficient space in the brake fluid reservoir to accept the displaced fluid, and if necessary, syphon some off first. Any brake fluid spilt on paintwork should be washed off with clean water, without delay – brake fluid is also a highly-effective paint-stripper.

11 Genuine Renault pads appear to have an anti-squeal coating applied to the pad

9.4 Unclip the pads from the caliper mounting bracket

9.11 Apply a little copper grease to the backs of the pads

backplates. If other pads are being fitted, or if there is any doubt, apply a little copper brake grease to the backs of the pads (none should be applied to the friction material) before fitting **(see illustration)**.

12 Install the pads in the caliper mounting bracket, ensuring that the friction material of each pad is against the brake disc **(see illustration)**.

13 Lower the caliper over the pads. If the caliper will not fit properly, the piston has not been pushed back far enough (see paragraph 9). If removed, clip the brake hose back onto the suspension strut.

14 Refit the lower guide pin bolt, and tighten to the specified torque, preventing the bolt from turning using another spanner on the pin's outer hex fitting.

15 Depress the brake pedal several times to bring the pads into firm contact with the brake disc.

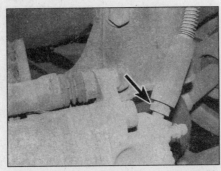

10.3 Loosen the brake hose union nut

9.9 Push back the caliper piston using a G-clamp and block of wood, with the bleed screw open

9.12 Clip the pads into the caliper mounting bracket

16 Repeat the above procedure on the other front brake caliper.

17 Refit the roadwheels, then lower the car to the ground and tighten the bolts to the specified torque.

18 Check the hydraulic fluid level as described in *Weekly checks*.

19 If new pads have been fitted, full braking efficiency will not be obtained until the linings have bedded-in. Be prepared for longer stopping distances, and avoid harsh braking as far as possible for the first hundred miles or so after fitting new pads.

10 Front brake caliper – removal, overhaul and refitting

Note: *Refer to the precautions in Section 1 before proceeding.*

Removal

1 With the handbrake applied, jack up the front of the car and support it on axle stands (see *Jacking and vehicle support*). Remove the appropriate roadwheel.

2 Minimise fluid loss, either by removing the master cylinder reservoir cap and then tightening it down onto a piece of polythene to obtain an airtight seal (taking care not to damage the sender unit), or by using a brake hose clamp, a G-clamp or a similar tool with protected jaws to clamp the flexible hose.

3 Clean the area around the hose union, then loosen the brake hose union nut **(see illustration)**.

10.4 Unscrew the guide pin bolts using a second spanner on the pin's hex fitting

4 Slacken and remove the upper and lower caliper guide pin bolts, using a slim open-ended spanner to prevent the guide pin itself from rotating **(see illustration)**.

5 With the guide pin bolts removed, lift the caliper away from the brake disc **(see illustration)**. Unclip the brake hose from the clip on the suspension strut, then unscrew the caliper from the end of the brake hose. Note that the brake pads need not be disturbed, and can be left in position in the caliper mounting bracket.

Overhaul

Note: *Ensure that an appropriate caliper overhaul kit is obtained before starting work.*

6 With the caliper on the bench, wipe away all traces of dust and dirt, but avoid inhaling the dust, as it is injurious to health.

7 Using a small flat-bladed screwdriver, carefully prise the dust seal retaining clip out of the caliper bore.

8 Withdraw the partially-ejected piston from the caliper body and remove the dust seal. The piston can be withdrawn by hand, or if necessary forced out by applying compressed air to the union bolt hole.

Caution: The piston may be ejected with some force. Only low pressure should be required, such as is generated by a foot pump.

9 Extract the piston hydraulic seal using a blunt instrument such as a knitting needle or a crochet hook, taking care not to damage the caliper bore.

10 Withdraw the guide sleeves or pins from the caliper body or mounting bracket (as applicable) and remove the rubber gaiters.

11 Thoroughly clean all components using only methylated spirit, isopropyl alcohol or clean hydraulic fluid as a cleaning medium. Never use mineral-based solvents, such as petrol or paraffin, which will attack the hydraulic system rubber components. Dry the components immediately, using compressed air or a clean, lint-free cloth. Use compressed air to blow clear the fluid passages.

12 Check all components and renew any that are worn or damaged. Check particularly the cylinder bore and piston; if they are scratched, worn or corroded in any way, they must be renewed (note that this means the renewal of the complete body assembly). Similarly check

10.5 Lift the caliper off the disc, then unscrew it from the brake hose

the condition of the guide sleeves or pins and their bores; they should be undamaged and (when cleaned) a reasonably tight sliding fit in the body or mounting bracket bores. If there is any doubt about the condition of a component, renew it.

13 If the assembly is fit for further use, obtain the appropriate repair kit.

14 Renew all rubber seals, dust covers and caps disturbed on dismantling as a matter of course; these should never be re-used.

15 Before commencing reassembly, ensure that all components are absolutely clean and dry.

16 Dip the piston and the new piston (fluid) seal in clean hydraulic fluid. Smear clean fluid on the cylinder bore surface.

17 Fit the new piston (fluid) seal, using only the fingers to manipulate it into the cylinder bore groove. Fit the new dust seal to the piston. Refit the piston to the cylinder bore using a twisting motion, ensuring that the piston enters squarely into the bore. Press the piston fully into the bore, then press the dust seal into the caliper body.

18 Install the dust seal retaining clip, ensuring that it is correctly seated in the caliper groove.

19 Apply the grease supplied in the repair kit, or a good quality high-temperature brake grease or anti-seize compound to the guide sleeves or pins. Fit the sleeves or pins to the caliper body or mounting bracket. Fit the new rubber gaiters, ensuring that they are correctly located in the grooves on both the sleeve or pin, and body or mounting bracket (as applicable).

11.3 Checking the disc thickness with a micrometer

Refitting

20 Screw the caliper body fully onto the flexible hose union nut. Check that the brake pads are still correctly fitted in the caliper mounting bracket.

21 Slide the caliper over the pads. Refit the guide pin bolts, and tighten them to the specified torque.

22 Clip the brake hose back into position on the suspension strut, making sure it is not twisted.

23 Tighten the brake hose union nut to the specified torque.

24 Remove the brake hose clamp or polythene, where fitted, and bleed the hydraulic system as described in Section 6. Providing the precautions described were taken to minimise brake fluid loss, it should only be necessary to bleed the relevant front brake.

25 Refit the roadwheel, then lower the car to the ground and tighten the roadwheel bolts to the specified torque.

11 Front brake disc – inspection, removal and refitting

Note: *Refer to the precautions in Section 1 before proceeding.*

Inspection

1 Chock the front wheels, firmly apply the handbrake, jack up the front of the car and support on axle stands (see *Jacking and vehicle support*). Remove the appropriate front roadwheel.

2 Slowly rotate the brake disc so that the full area of both sides can be checked; remove the brake pads, as described in Section 9, if better access is required to the inboard surface. Light scoring is normal in the area swept by the brake pads, but if heavy scoring is found, the disc must be renewed.

3 It is normal to find a lip of rust and brake dust around the disc's perimeter; this can be scraped off if required. If, however, a lip has formed due to wear of the brake pad swept area, the disc thickness must be measured using a micrometer **(see illustration)**. Take measurements at several places around the disc at the inside and outside of the pad swept area; if the disc has worn at any point to the specified minimum thickness or less, it must be renewed.

4 If the disc is thought to be warped, it can be checked for run-out, ideally by using a dial gauge mounted on any convenient fixed point, while the disc is slowly rotated **(see illustration)**. In the absence of a dial gauge, use feeler blades to measure (at several points all around the disc) the clearance between the disc and a fixed point such as the caliper mounting bracket.

5 If the measurements obtained are at the specified maximum or beyond, the disc is excessively warped, and must be renewed;

11.4 Checking for disc run-out with a dial gauge

11.9a Remove the two Torx screws securing the brake disc . . .

11.9b . . . then remove the disc from the hub

11.10a Apply copper grease to the hub before fitting the disc

11.10b Apply locking fluid to the caliper mounting bracket bolts . . .

11.10c . . . then fit and tighten them to the specified torque

however, it is worth checking first that the hub bearing is in good condition (Chapters 1A or 1B and 10). Also try the effect of removing the disc and turning it through 180° to reposition it on the hub; if run-out is still excessive, the disc must be renewed.

6 Check the disc for cracks (especially around the wheel bolt holes), and for any other wear or damage. Renew the disc if necessary.

Removal

7 Remove the brake caliper and pads as described in Sections 9 and 10.

8 Unscrew the two bolts securing the brake caliper mounting bracket to the swivel hub, and slide the bracket off the disc.

9 If the same disc is to be refitted, use chalk or paint to mark the relationship of the disc to the hub. Remove the two screws securing the brake disc to the hub, and remove the disc (see illustrations). If it is tight, lightly tap its rear face with a hide or plastic mallet.

Refitting

10 Refitting is the reverse of the removal procedure, noting the following points:

a) Ensure that the mating surfaces of the disc and hub are clean and flat. To reduce the risk of corrosion, apply copper grease to the hub before fitting the disc (ensure that the grease does not get on the disc friction surfaces) (see illustration).

b) If applicable, align the marks made on removal.

c) Securely tighten the disc retaining screws.

d) If a new disc has been fitted, use a suitable solvent to wipe any preservative

coating from the disc before refitting the caliper.

e) Apply locking fluid to the threads of the brake caliper mounting bolts, and tighten them to the specified torque (see illustrations).

f) Refit the roadwheel, then lower the car to the ground and tighten the roadwheel bolts to the specified torque. On completion, depress the brake pedal several times to bring the brake pads into contact with the disc.

12 Rear brake pads – inspection and renewal

Note: Refer to the precautions in Section 1 before proceeding. Always renew the pads on both rear brakes, never just on one side.

Inspection

1 Chock the front wheels, engage reverse gear (or P) and release the handbrake. Jack up the rear of the car and support it on axle stands (see Jacking and vehicle support). Remove the rear wheels.

2 The pad thicknesses can be viewed without removing them from the caliper. Unlike some, the rear pads do not feature wear grooves. Wear rates for rear pads are generally far lower than for front pads, but if the friction material remaining is low, remember that this may also adversely affect the operation of the handbrake.

3 If either pad is worn at any point to the

specified minimum thickness or less, all four pads must be renewed. Also, the pads should be renewed if any are fouled with oil or grease – there is no satisfactory way of degreasing friction material once contaminated. If any of the brake pads are worn unevenly, or fouled with oil or grease, trace and rectify the cause before reassembly. New brake pads and spring kits are available from Renault dealers.

Renewal

4 Unscrew the caliper guide pin bolts, using a second spanner on the pin outer hex fitting to prevent the pin turning (see illustration). Note: To just access the pads, only the lower pin need be unscrewed – the caliper could then be swung upwards. However, fitting new pads involves 'screwing' the caliper piston back into the caliper, which is more easily achieved with the caliper removed from its mounting bracket, which means removing both guide pin bolts.

12.4 Unscrew the caliper guide pin bolts, using two spanners

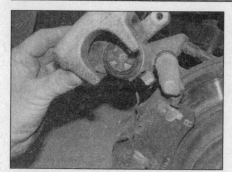

12.5 Lift the caliper off the mounting bracket

12.6 Unclip the brake pads from the mounting bracket

12.9a Turn and press the caliper piston firmly clockwise using suitable pliers

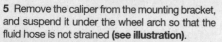
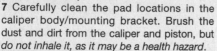
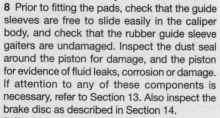

12.9b Special tools are available to retract the piston

12.11 Apply copper grease to the backs of the pads

12.14 Tighten the caliper guide pin bolts using two spanners as for removal

5 Remove the caliper from the mounting bracket, and suspend it under the wheel arch so that the fluid hose is not strained **(see illustration)**.

6 Unclip the inner and outer pads from the caliper mounting bracket, and remove them **(see illustration)**.

7 Carefully clean the pad locations in the caliper body/mounting bracket. Brush the dust and dirt from the caliper and piston, but *do not inhale it, as it may be a health hazard*.

8 Prior to fitting the pads, check that the guide sleeves are free to slide easily in the caliper body, and check that the rubber guide sleeve gaiters are undamaged. Inspect the dust seal around the piston for damage, and the piston for evidence of fluid leaks, corrosion or damage. If attention to any of these components is necessary, refer to Section 13. Also inspect the brake disc as described in Section 14.

9 If new brake pads are to be fitted, it will be necessary to retract the piston fully into the caliper bore by rotating it in a clockwise direction. This can be achieved using sturdy circlip pliers, noting that as well as being turned, the piston has to be pressed in very firmly. Special tools are available from companies such as Draper to achieve this with less effort **(see illustrations)**.

Caution: Pushing back the piston causes a reverse-flow of brake fluid, which has been known to 'flip' the master cylinder rubber seals, resulting in a total loss of braking. To avoid this, clamp the caliper flexible hose and open the bleed screw – as the piston is pushed back, the fluid can be directed into a suitable container using a hose attached to the bleed screw. Close the screw just

before the piston is pushed fully back, to ensure no air enters the system.

10 If the recommended method of opening a bleed screw before pushing back the piston is not used, the fluid level in the reservoir will rise, and possibly overflow. Make sure that there is sufficient space in the brake fluid reservoir to accept the displaced fluid, and if necessary, syphon some off first. Any brake fluid spilt on paintwork should be washed off with clean water, without delay – brake fluid is also a highly-effective paint-stripper.

11 Genuine Renault pads appear to have an anti-squeal coating applied to the pad backplates. If other pads are being fitted, or if there is any doubt, apply a little copper brake grease to the backs of the pads (none should be applied to the friction material) before fitting **(see illustration)**.

12 Install the pads in the caliper mounting bracket, ensuring that the friction material of each pad is against the brake disc.

13 Lower the caliper over the pads. If the caliper will not fit properly, the piston has not been pushed back far enough (see paragraph 9). If removed, clip the brake hose back onto the suspension strut.

14 Refit the lower guide pin bolt, and tighten to the specified torque, preventing the bolt from turning using another spanner on the pin's outer hex fitting **(see illustration)**.

15 Depress the brake pedal several times to bring the pads into firm contact with the brake disc.

16 Repeat the above procedure on the other front brake caliper.

17 Refit the roadwheels, then lower the car

to the ground and tighten the bolts to the specified torque.

18 Check the hydraulic fluid level as described in *Weekly checks*.

19 Check the handbrake cable adjustment as described in Chapter 1A or 1B.

20 If new pads have been fitted, full braking efficiency will not be obtained until the linings have bedded-in. Be prepared for longer stopping distances, and avoid harsh braking as far as possible for the first hundred miles or so after fitting new pads.

13 Rear brake caliper – removal, overhaul and refitting

Note: Before starting work, refer to the warnings at the beginning of Section 6 concerning the dangers of hydraulic fluid, and at the beginning of Section 17 concerning the dangers of asbestos dust.

Removal

1 Chock the front wheels, engage reverse gear (or P) and release the handbrake. Jack up the rear of the car and support it on axle stands (see *Jacking and vehicle support*). Remove the relevant rear wheel.

2 Free the handbrake inner cable from the caliper handbrake operating lever, then unclip the outer cable from its bracket on the caliper body **(see illustrations)**.

3 Minimise fluid loss, either by removing the master cylinder reservoir cap and then tightening it down onto a piece of polythene to obtain an airtight seal (taking care not to damage the sender unit), or by using a brake hose clamp, a G-clamp or a similar tool with protected jaws to clamp the flexible hose at the nearest convenient point to the brake caliper.

4 Wipe away all traces of dirt around the brake pipe union on top of the caliper, and unscrew the union nut. Carefully ease the pipe out of position, and plug or tape over its end to prevent dirt entry. Wipe off any spilt fluid immediately.

5 Unscrew the caliper guide pin bolts, using a second spanner on the pin outer hex fitting to prevent the pin turning. Lift the caliper off the pads, and remove it.

Overhaul

Note: *Ensure the correct caliper overhaul kit is obtained before starting work.*

6 With the caliper on the bench, wipe away all traces of dust and dirt, but avoid inhaling the dust, as it is injurious to health.

7 Using a small screwdriver, carefully prise out the dust seal from the caliper bore, taking care not to damage the piston.

8 Remove the piston from the caliper bore by rotating it in an anti-clockwise direction. This can be achieved by using a square-section bar, such as the shaft of a screwdriver, which locates snugly in the caliper piston slots. Once the piston turns freely but does not come out any further, the piston can be withdrawn by hand, or if necessary pushed out by applying compressed air to the union bolt hole.

Caution: The piston may be ejected with some force – only low pressure should be required, such as is generated by a foot pump.

9 Using a blunt instrument such as a knitting needle or a crochet hook, extract the piston hydraulic seal, taking care not to damage the caliper bore.

10 Withdraw the guide sleeves from the caliper body, and remove the guide sleeve gaiters.

11 Inspect the caliper components as described in Section 10 for the front calipers. Renew as necessary, noting that the inside of the caliper piston must not be dismantled. If necessary, the handbrake mechanism can be overhauled as described in the following paragraphs. If it is not wished to overhaul the handbrake mechanism, proceed to paragraph 16.

12 Release the handbrake dust cover retaining clip, and peel the cover away from the rear of the caliper. Make a note of the correct fitted positions of the relative components to use as a guide on reassembly. Remove the circlip from the base of the operating lever shaft, then compress the adjusting screw spring washers, and withdraw the operating lever and dust cover from the caliper body. With the lever withdrawn, remove the return spring, plunger cam, adjusting screw, spring washers and thrustwasher from the rear of the caliper body. Using a pin punch, carefully tap

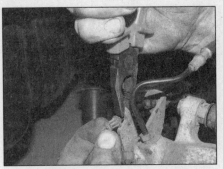

13.2a Release the handbrake cable end fitting from the lever . . .

the adjusting screw bush out of the caliper body and remove the O-ring.

13 Clean all the handbrake components in methylated spirit, and examine them for wear. If there is any sign of wear or damage, the complete handbrake mechanism assembly should be renewed.

14 Ensure that all components are clean and dry. Install the O-ring, then press the adjusting screw bush into position until its outer edge is flush with the rear of the caliper body; if necessary, tap the bush into position using a tubular drift. Fit the thrustwasher, then install the adjusting screw and spring washers, ensuring that the washers are correctly positioned. Locate the plunger cam in the end of the adjusting screw, and position the return spring in the caliper housing.

15 Fit the new dust cover to the operating lever, then compress the adjusting screw spring washers and insert the lever shaft through the caliper body, ensuring that it is correctly engaged with the return spring and plunger cam. Secure the operating lever in position with the circlip, then release the spring washers and check the operation of the handbrake mechanism. Apply a smear of high-melting point grease to the operating lever shaft and adjusting screw. Slide the dust cover over the caliper body, and secure it in position with a cable tie.

16 Soak the piston and the new piston (fluid) seal in clean hydraulic fluid. Smear clean fluid on the cylinder bore surface.

17 Fit the new piston (fluid) seal, using only the fingers to manipulate it into the cylinder bore groove, and refit the piston assembly. Turn the piston in a clockwise direction, using the method employed on dismantling, until it is fully retracted into the caliper bore.

18 Fit the dust seal to the caliper, ensuring that it is correctly located in the caliper and also the groove on the piston.

19 Apply the grease supplied in the repair kit, or a good-quality high-temperature brake grease or anti-seize compound to the guide sleeves. Fit the guide sleeves to the caliper body, and fit the new gaiters, ensuring that the gaiters are correctly located in the grooves on both the guide sleeve and caliper body.

Refitting

20 Position the caliper over the brake disc.

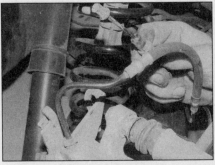

13.2b . . . then unclip the cable outer from its bracket

Refit the two caliper guide pin bolts and tighten to the specified torque.

21 Wipe clean the brake pipe union. Refit the pipe to the caliper, and tighten its union nut securely.

22 Remove the clamp from the brake hose, or the polythene from the master cylinder reservoir (as applicable).

23 Clip the handbrake outer cable into position, then reconnect the inner cable to the caliper operating lever.

24 Bleed the hydraulic system as described in Section 6. Note that, providing the precautions described were taken to minimise brake fluid loss, it should only be necessary to bleed the relevant rear brake.

25 Repeatedly apply the brake pedal to bring the pads into contact with the disc. Check and if necessary adjust the handbrake cable as described in Chapter 1A or 1B.

26 Refit the roadwheel, lower the car to the ground and tighten the wheel bolts to the specified torque. On completion, check the hydraulic fluid level as described in *Weekly checks*.

14 Rear brake disc –
inspection, removal
and refitting

Note: *Refer to the precautions in Section 1 before proceeding.*

Inspection

1 Chock the front wheels, engage reverse gear (or P) and release the handbrake. Jack up the rear of the car and support it on axle stands (see *Jacking and vehicle support*). Remove the appropriate rear roadwheel.

2 Inspect the disc as described in Section 11.

Removal

3 Remove the brake pads as described in Section 12.

4 Remove the two caliper mounting bracket bolts, and lift the bracket off **(see illustrations)**.

5 Using a hammer and a suitable punch (or a large flat-bladed screwdriver), carefully tap and prise the cap out of the centre of the brake disc **(see illustrations)**.

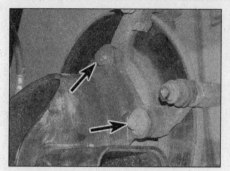

14.4a Unscrew the mounting bolts . . .

14.4b . . . and lift off the caliper mounting bracket

14.5a Using a hammer and punch . . .

14.5b . . . tap off and remove the centre cap

14.6 Unscrew and remove the rear hub nut

14.7 Withdraw the disc from the stub axle

6 Using a socket and long bar, slacken and remove the rear hub nut – this will be very tight, so ensure that the car is well-supported, and that only good-quality, close-fitting tools are used **(see illustration)**. Discard the hub nut; a new nut must be used on refitting.

7 It should now be possible to withdraw the brake disc and hub bearing assembly from the stub axle by hand **(see illustration)**. If the disc is tight, tap the periphery of the disc using a hide or plastic mallet.

Refitting

8 If new discs are being fitted, use a suitable solvent to wipe any preservative coating from its surface. Note that new discs (or at least genuine Renault ones) are supplied with new rear wheel bearings pre-fitted – the bearings can, however, be renewed separately as described in Chapter 10.

9 Before refitting the disc, carefully clean the ABS magnetic ring on the back, surrounding the hub bearing **(see illustration)**.

10 Fit the new rear hub nut and tighten it to the specified torque. Tap the cap back into position in the centre of the disc (if the cap is in poor condition, a new one should be fitted) **(see illustrations)**.

11 Apply a few drops of locking fluid to the threads of the caliper mounting bracket bolts **(see illustration)**. Offer up the bracket and refit the bolts, tightening them to the specified torque.

12 Refit the brake pads as described in Section 12.

13 Check the handbrake cable adjustment as described in Chapter 1A or 1B.

14 Refit the roadwheels and lower the car to the ground. Tighten the roadwheel bolts to the specified torque.

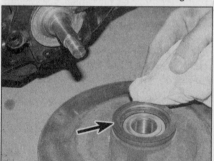

14.9 Clean the magnetic ring on the back of the disc/hub

14.10a Fit the new rear hub nut . . .

14.10b . . . then tap the centre cap into position

14.11 Apply thread-locking fluid to the caliper mounting bolts

15 Handbrake (manual) – component removal and refitting

Handbrake lever

1 Chock the front wheels, engage reverse gear (or P) and release the handbrake. Jack

15.3 Measure the length of exposed thread on the handbrake adjuster

15.4 Loosen the handbrake adjuster nut, then unhook the rear cables

15.5 Disconnect the handbrake warning light switch wiring plug

15.6 The handbrake lever is secured by four mounting nuts

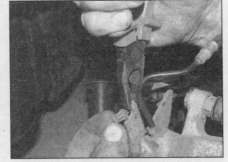

15.12a Release the handbrake cable end fitting from the lever . . .

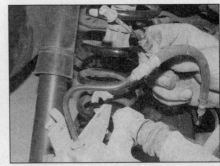

15.12b . . . then unclip the cable outer from its bracket

up the rear of the car and support it on axle stands (see *Jacking and vehicle support*).

2 Remove the centre console as described in Chapter 11. Though not essential, access to the handbrake is greatly improved by removing one of the front seats (also Chapter 11).

3 Before slackening the handbrake adjuster nut, measure the length of exposed thread on the adjuster rod, and make a note of it – this way, the adjustment can be reset to its original setting when refitting **(see illustration)**.

4 Loosen the adjuster nut until both handbrake cables can be unhooked from the equaliser bar, by moving them sideways **(see illustration)**.

5 Disconnect the wiring plug from the handbrake warning light switch **(see illustration)**.

6 Unscrew the four handbrake lever mounting nuts **(see illustration)**, and lift the lever assembly out of the car.

7 Refitting is a reversal of removal. Adjust the handbrake as described in Chapter 1A or 1B, setting the adjuster nut to the dimension noted on removal as a starting point.

Operating cables

8 The right- and left-hand cables are linked to the lever assembly by an equaliser plate. Each cable can be removed individually as follows.

9 Chock the front wheels, engage reverse gear (or P) and release the handbrake. Jack up the rear of the car and support it on axle stands (see *Jacking and vehicle support*).

10 To access the cables, remove the centre console and one front seat as described in Chapter 11.

11 Loosen the handbrake adjuster nut, and

disconnect the cables from the equaliser bar, as described in paragraphs 3 and 4.

12 Disengage the inner cable from the caliper handbrake lever, then unclip the outer cable from its mounting bracket **(see illustrations)**.

13 Working along the length of the cable, remove any retaining bolts and screws, and free the cable from the retaining clips and ties **(see illustrations)**. Remove the cable from under the car.

14 Refitting is a reversal of removal. Adjust the handbrake as described in Chapter 1A or 1B.

16 Handbrake (automatic) – component removal and refitting

Description

1 The automatic handbrake is fitted on many Scénics primarily to increase the storage

capacity between the front seats. Some models feature a capacious storage bin as the centre console.

2 However, the system does offer a number of other advantages. In normal use, the handbrake control unit applies the handbrake when the engine is turned off. When the car is about to move off, as signalled by the throttle position sensor and/or the clutch pedal switches, the handbrake is released. The system prevents the car from rolling backwards on a hill start, thanks to a gradient sensor built into the control unit, and the ABS sensors.

3 The handbrake can be operated manually using the facia control, and the status of the system is displayed on the instrument panel. The control unit contains an electric motor, which operates the handbrake cables from the rear of the car. In an emergency, the handbrake can be over-ridden using a separate catch under the boot floor.

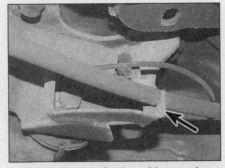

15.13a The handbrake cables may be supported in metal holders . . .

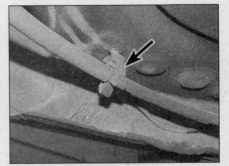

15.13b . . . or retained in plastic clips to the underside of the car

16.5a Remove the two screws under the control switch . . .

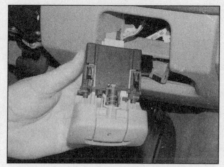

16.5b . . . then withdraw the switch . . .

16.5c . . . and disconnect its wiring plug

16.9 Pull the emergency handbrake release handle

16.10a Unhook the release handle from the cable . . .

16.10b . . . then feed the cable down and unclip the floor grommet

Facia control

4 Remove the headlight adjuster switch panel as described in Chapter 12.

5 Remove the two screws below the handbrake control, then free the control from the facia panel and disconnect the wiring plug (see illustrations).

6 Refitting is a reversal of removal.

Control unit

Scénic

7 Disconnect the battery negative lead, and move the lead away from the battery (see *Disconnecting the battery*).

8 Chock the front wheels, then jack up the rear of the car and support on axle stands (see *Jacking and vehicle support*).

9 Open the tailgate, and remove the cover panel from the handbrake emergency handle under the boot floor. Pull the handle – this will

release the handbrake, accompanied by a noise from the cables (see illustration).

10 Detach the cable from the emergency handle, then feed the cable down through the grommet in the floor under the car. The grommet has to be unclipped from the floor to release it (see illustrations).

11 Note how the handbrake operating cables are routed from the control unit to the brake calipers – the left-hand cable is routed under the exhaust heat shield, which will have to be removed first. Remove the circlips securing the cable outers to the calipers, then unhook the cable end fittings from the caliper operating levers, and unclip the cables from the floor clips (see illustrations).

12 Remove the two cable anchorage support bolts from the centre of the floor.

13 Remove the two control unit mounting bolts, then lower the unit and disconnect the wiring plug.

14 With the help of an assistant, slide the control unit and the anchorage support to the left of the car, until the anchorage cover can be unclipped. Remove the unit from under the car.

15 Refitting is a reversal of removal.

Grand Scénic

16 Proceed as described in paragraphs 7 to 11.

17 Unclip the floor trim panel in front of the rearmost rear seats, and undo the two control unit mounting bolts underneath (see illustrations).

18 Under the car, disconnect the wiring plug from the control unit. Remove the unit's single remaining mounting bolt, and withdraw the unit from under the car (see illustrations).

19 Refitting is a reversal of removal.

Operating cables

20 Removing the cables is as described in the control unit removal and refitting procedure,

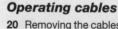

16.11a Slide out the circlip from the cable outer . . .

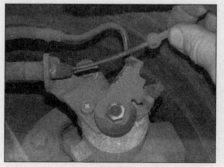

16.11b . . . then unhook the cable from the operating lever . . .

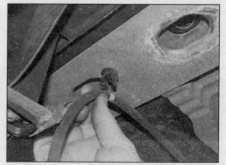

16.11c . . . and unclip the cable from the floor

16.17a Unclip the floor trim panel . . .

16.17b . . . then unscrew the two unit upper mounting bolts

16.18a Open the locking lever and disconnect the unit's wiring plug . . .

previously in this Section. The cables are not available separately, at least not from Renault at the time of writing.

Throttle position sensor

21 Refer to Chapter 4A or 4B.

Clutch pedal switches

22 Refer to Chapter 6.

17 Stop-light switch –
removal, refitting and adjustment

Removal

1 The stop-light switch is located on the passenger-side end of the brake pedal cross-shaft, and is accessed from the front passenger footwell.

2 Remove the glovebox as described in Chapter 11, Section 23.

3 To further improve access, unclip and remove the plastic air duct fitted below the glovebox location **(see illustration)**.

4 Disconnect the wiring plug from the brake light switch, then turn the switch 90° anti-clockwise and remove it **(see illustration)**.

Refitting and adjustment

5 Refitting is a reversal of removal. Before fitting the switch, the plunger should be reset as follows. Pull the plunger out firmly – it should extend on its ratchet mechanism by several clicks **(see illustrations)**. When the switch is refitted and the pedal pressed for the first few times, the plunger will be pushed back in automatically to the correct setting.

6 On completion, check the operation of the stop-lights.

18 Anti-lock braking system (ABS) –
general information

The purpose of the system is to prevent the wheel(s) locking during heavy braking. This is achieved by automatic release of the brake on the relevant wheel before it can lock up, followed by rapid reapplication of the brake.

The main components of the system are four wheel sensors (one per wheel), and a

16.18b . . . then remove the single remaining bolt . . .

16.18c . . . and lower the unit out from under the car

modulator block which contains the ABS computer, the hydraulic solenoid valves and accumulators, and an electrically-driven return pump.

The solenoids are controlled by the computer, which receives signals from the

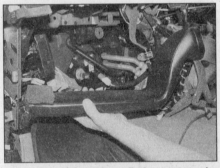

17.3 Removing the ventilation system air duct below the glovebox

17.4 Disconnect the brake light switch plug, then twist and remove it

wheel sensors. The sensors detect the speed of rotation of a reluctor ring, attached to the wheel hub. By comparing the speed signals from the four wheels, the computer can determine when a wheel is decelerating at an abnormal rate, and can therefore predict

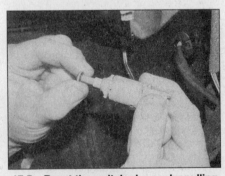

17.5a Reset the switch plunger by pulling it out by a few clicks

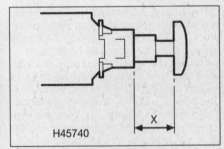

```
H45740
```

17.5b Check how far the switch plunger has been pulled out

x = 17 to 18 mm

19.5a Prise up the plastic clips . . .

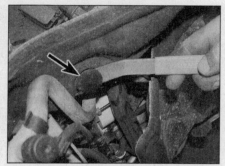

19.5b . . . along the length of the bulkhead . . .

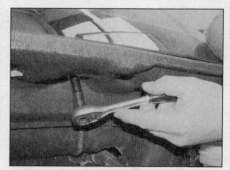

19.5c . . . then remove the central bolt . . .

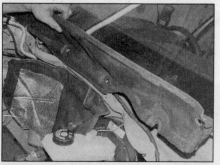

19.5d . . . and lift out the fabric trim panel

19.5e Remove the clips securing the lower soundproofing panel

when a wheel is about to lock. During normal operation, the system functions in the same way as a non-ABS braking system does.

If the computer senses that a wheel is about to lock, the ABS system enters the 'pressure-maintain' phase. The computer operates the relevant solenoid valve in the modulator block; this isolates the brake on the wheel in question from the master cylinder, effectively sealing-in the hydraulic pressure.

If the speed of rotation of the wheel continues to decrease at an abnormal rate, the ABS system then enters the 'pressure-decrease' phase. The return pump operates and pumps the hydraulic fluid back into the master cylinder, releasing pressure on the brake. When the speed of rotation of the wheel returns to an acceptable rate, the pump stops and the solenoid valve opens, allowing hydraulic pressure to return and reapply the brake. This cycle can be carried out at up to 10 times a second.

The action of the solenoid valves and return pump creates pulses in the hydraulic circuit. When the ABS system is functioning, these pulses can be felt through the brake pedal.

The Scénic is also equipped with an additional safety feature built into the ABS system, called EBD (Electronic Brake force Distribution), which automatically apportions braking effort between the front and rear wheels. The EBD function is built into the system's software, and the intention is to limit braking effort (fluid pressure) to the rear wheels, to prevent them locking up under heavy braking.

Another feature of the ABS is Brake Assist,

which monitors how rapidly the brake pedal is pressed, and determines whether an emergency stop is required – in this case, maximum braking effort is applied more quickly than the driver would normally be able to, unaided.

The Electronic Stability Programme (ESP) is available as an option. This system uses the ABS to prevent wheel spin or skidding during acceleration or cornering, by selectively and partially applying the brakes individually or in pairs, to either 'steer' the car, or slow the front wheels (traction control). A yaw sensor mounted under the driver's seat informs the system ECU of the lateral (sideways) forces acting on the car, indicating the direction and speed of cornering. An integral steering angle sensor in the steering system is used to indicate the amount of steering lock applied. A front-wheel-drive car will typically understeer (run wide) if excess power is used when cornering on a slippery road – if the yaw sensor detects this condition, one or more brakes will be applied to help turn the car, and engine power will be momentarily reduced. Similarly, the traction control function uses the front wheel sensors to detect abnormally-fast wheel rotation, relative to the vehicle speed – when wheel spin is occurring, the engine power will be reduced, and the front brakes applied slightly

The operation of the ABS system is entirely dependent on electrical signals. To prevent the system responding to any inaccurate signals, a built-in safety circuit monitors all signals received by the computer. If an inaccurate signal or low battery voltage is detected, the

ABS system is automatically shut down, and the warning light on the instrument panel is illuminated to inform the driver that the ABS system is not operational. Normal braking is unaffected, apart from the loss of the Electronic Brake force Distribution function (which may result in premature rear wheel lock-up under braking).

If a fault does develop in the ABS system, the car must be taken to a Renault dealer for fault diagnosis and repair. Check first, however, that the problem is not due to loose or damaged wiring connections, or badly-routed wiring picking up spurious signals from the ignition system.

19 Anti-lock braking system (ABS) components – removal and refitting

Note: *Refer to the precautions in Section 1 before proceeding. Note that the system fitted to the Scénic is more 'integrated' than those seen previously, which unfortunately means renewing several components is more difficult.*

Hydraulic unit

Removal

1 The hydraulic unit is located in the far right-hand rear corner of the engine compartment (right as seen from the driver's seat), tight against the bulkhead. Access to the unit is far from easy.

2 Disconnect the battery negative lead (refer to *Disconnecting the battery* in the Reference Section).

3 Remove the engine top cover, and the windscreen cowl panels as described in Chapter 11.

4 Unbolt the engine lifting eye from the back of the cylinder head.

5 Prise up the plastic clips and remove the central bolt, then lift out the shaped fabric trim panel fitted at the base of the windscreen. Similarly, remove the soundproofing panel fitted to the bulkhead below the trim panel just removed (see illustrations).

6 On petrol models, remove the inlet manifold as described in Chapter 4A to improve access to the hydraulic unit.

19.9 Unscrew the nut and disconnect the unit's earth lead

19.10 Turn the locking catch and disconnect the unit wiring plug

7 On models with air conditioning, it may be necessary to disconnect some of the air conditioning pipework to allow the hydraulic unit to be removed. Disconnecting these pipes should not be attempted until the system has been discharged by a Renault dealer or air conditioning specialist (refer to Chapter 3).

8 Again on models with air conditioning, unclip the rubber condensation drain hose fitted in front of the hydraulic unit.

9 Unscrew the nut and disconnect the hydraulic unit's earth lead from the inner wing **(see illustration)**.

10 Turn the locking catch on the unit's wiring connector plug, then disconnect the plug and move the harness to one side **(see illustration)**.

11 Before removing the hydraulic unions from the unit, it may be advisable to mark them for position, perhaps by attaching labels, or marked pieces of tape, to each pipe.

12 Loosen the hydraulic unions, then disconnect and unclip the pipes from the unit – avoid bending the pipes at all costs.

13 Unscrew the three bolts securing the unit's mounting bracket, then remove the unit/bracket assembly from its location. If required, the unit and bracket can be separated after removal.

Caution: Do not attempt to dismantle the hydraulic unit assembly. Overhaul of the unit is a complex job, and should be entrusted to a Renault dealer.

Refitting

14 Refitting is the reverse of the removal procedure, noting the following points:
  a) *Tighten the hydraulic unit mounting bolts to the specified torque.*
  b) *Refit the brake pipes to the correct unions, and tighten the union nuts to the specified torque.*
  c) *Reconnect the wiring plug securely.*
  d) *Before reconnecting the battery, bleed the complete braking system as described in Section 6. Ensure the system is bled in*

the correct order, to prevent air entering the return pump.

ABS computer

15 The computer is an integral part of the hydraulic unit assembly, and cannot be renewed separately. If renewal is necessary, the hydraulic unit must be renewed as a complete assembly, as described in this Section.

Wheel sensors

16 The wheel sensors are an unusual design, and cannot easily be renewed. In the event of a fault arising with a sensor, its wiring plug can be disconnected and sprayed with a maintenance spray such as WD-40 (the wiring to the sensor should also be checked for damage).

17 For further advice on the best way to proceed with fixing any wheel sensor problems, the car should be referred to a Renault dealer.

Front wheel sensor

18 Front wheel sensors can be removed only after pressing out the wheel bearing, as described in Chapter 10. The bearing itself contains the magnetic ring (reluctor).

Rear wheel sensor

19 The rear wheel sensor is a press fit

20.3 Disconnect the servo hose from the vacuum pump

over the stub axle. Remove the brake disc as described in Section 14 – this will allow inspection and cleaning of the sensor's magnetic ring (reluctor) fitted to the rear of the disc. Presumably, the sensor could be prised off and a new one pressed on if required, though no procedure for this is given by Renault.

20 Vacuum pump (diesel engines) – removal and refitting

Removal

1 Unclip and remove the engine cover.

2 If required, to give better access to the vacuum pump, remove the air filter ducts as described in Chapter 4B.

3 Squeeze together the tabs on the hose end fitting, and disconnect the vacuum hose from the pump **(see illustration)**.

4 Slacken and remove the two mounting bolts securing the pump to the end of the cylinder head **(see illustration)**, then remove the pump. Recover the pump gasket and discard it; a new one should be used on refitting.

Refitting

5 Ensure that the pump and cylinder head

20.4 Remove the two pump mounting bolts (arrowed) – one out of view

20.5 Use a new gasket when fitting the vacuum pump

mating surfaces are clean and dry, and fit the new gasket to the head **(see illustration)**.

6 Manoeuvre the pump into position, then refit the pump mounting bolts and tighten them securely.

21 Vacuum pump (diesel engines) – testing and overhaul

1 The operation of the braking system vacuum pump can be checked using a vacuum gauge.

2 Disconnect the vacuum pipe from the pump, and connect the gauge to the pump union using a length of hose.

3 Start the engine and allow it to idle, then measure the vacuum created by the pump. As a guide, after one minute, a minimum of approximately 500 mm Hg should be recorded. If the vacuum registered is significantly less than this, it is likely that the pump is faulty. However, seek the advice of a Renault dealer before condemning the pump.

4 Overhaul of the vacuum pump may not be possible; check for availability of spares.

Chapter 10
Suspension and steering

Contents

Degrees of difficulty

Easy, suitable for novice with little experience	**Fairly easy,** suitable for beginner with some experience	**Fairly difficult,** suitable for competent DIY mechanic	**Difficult,** suitable for experienced DIY mechanic	**Very difficult,** suitable for expert DIY or professional

Specifications

Front suspension

Type	Independent, MacPherson struts, with coil springs and integral shock absorbers. Anti-roll bar fitted to all models
Hub bearing endfloat	0 to 0.05 mm

Rear suspension

Type	Semi-independent twist-beam axle, telescopic dampers and separate coil springs
Hub bearing endfloat	0 to 0.05 mm

Steering

Type	Power-assisted steering, rack-and-pinion, assistance provided by electric motor integrated into steering column

Tyres

Tyre sizes and pressures	See end of Weekly checks on page 0•17

Wheel alignment and steering angles

Front wheel toe setting (vehicle unladen):

Angle setting	+0° 10' ± 10' toe-out
Measurement setting:	
15-inch wheels	+1.1 mm ± 1.1 mm toe-out
16-inch wheels	+1.2 mm ± 1.2 mm toe-out
17-inch wheels	+1.3 mm ± 1.3 mm toe-out

Castor angle at ride height* (W2 minus W1) stated:

84 mm	4° 54' ± 30'
74 mm	5° 12' ± 30'
50 mm	6° 00' ± 30'
47 mm	6° 12' ± 30'
Maximum difference between left- and right-hand sides	0° 30'

Front wheel camber angle at ride height* (R1 minus W1) stated:

124 mm	0° 00' ± 0° 30'
130 mm	-0° 00' ± 0° 30'
149 mm	-0° 10' ± 0° 30'
155 mm	-0° 13' ± 0° 30'
Maximum difference between left- and right-hand sides	0° 30'

Wheel alignment and steering angles (continued)

Steering axis/kingpin inclination at ride height* (R1 minus W1) stated:

124 mm.	10° 52' ± 0° 30'
130 mm.	11° 00' ± 0° 30'
149 mm.	11° 18' ± 0° 30'
155 mm.	11° 28' ± 0° 30'
Maximum difference between left- and right-hand sides.	0° 30'
Rear wheel toe setting (vehicle unladen)	-0° 35' ± 20' toe-in
Rear wheel camber setting (vehicle unladen)	-1° 30' ± 20'

*Refer to Section 13 for details of measuring ride height

Roadwheels

Type	Pressed-steel or aluminium alloy
Size.	6.5J x 15, 6.5J x 16 or 6.5J x 17
Maximum run-out at rim.	1.2 mm

Torque wrench settings

	Nm	lbf ft
Front suspension		
Anti-roll bar link rod balljoint nut	44	32
Anti-roll bar mounting clamp bolts.	21	15
Driveshaft (hub) nut*.	280	207
Lower arm balljoint clamp bolt.	60	44
Lower arm mounting bolts/nuts.	70	52
Radiator crossmember:		
Front mounting bolt	105	77
Rear mounting nuts	21	15
Side support plate bolts.	21	15
Rear crossmember bolts	62	46
Strut lower pinch-bolt.	105	77
Strut piston rod nut	62	46
Strut upper mounting bolt (to body).	21	15
Subframe bolts*	105	77
Rear suspension		
Hub nut*.	220	162
Rear axle-to-chassis securing bolts.	62	46
Rear trailing arm pivot bolt nut.	125	92
Shock absorber lower mounting bolt.	105	77
Shock absorber upper mounting bolt	62	46
Steering		
Steering column mounting nuts.	21	15
Steering column universal joint nut/bolt*	24	18
Steering gear mounting bolts*	105	77
Steering wheel bolt.	44	32
Track rod end balljoint-to-swivel hub retaining nut	37	27
Track rod end locknut.	53	39
Roadwheels		
Wheel bolts.	130	96

* Use a new nut/bolt

---

1 General information

The independent front suspension is of the MacPherson strut type, incorporating coil springs and integral telescopic shock absorbers. The MacPherson struts are located by transverse lower suspension arms, which utilise rubber inner mounting bushes and incorporate a balljoint at the outer ends. The front swivel hubs, which carry the wheel bearings, brake calipers and the hub/disc assemblies, are bolted to the MacPherson struts and connected to the lower arms via the balljoints. A front anti-roll bar is fitted to all models. The anti-roll bar is rubber-mounted onto the subframe, and connects both the lower suspension arms.

The rear suspension is a twist-beam axle, with coil springs and separate telescopic dampers. At the pivot points (in front of the 'trailing arms') the axle is attached to the vehicle underbody by rubber bushes, and the rear ends are located by the inclined shock absorbers, which are bolted to the underbody at their upper ends. The coil springs are mounted separately from the shock absorbers, and act directly between the axle and the underbody.

The steering column is connected by a universal joint to an intermediate shaft, which has a second universal joint at its lower end. The lower universal joint is attached to the steering gear pinion by means of an eccentric clamp bolt.

The steering gear is mounted onto the front subframe. It is connected by two track rods and balljoints to steering arms projecting rearwards from the swivel hubs. The track rod ends are threaded to enable wheel alignment (toe) adjustment.

An electrically-powered motor is used to provide the steering's power assistance, rather than the conventional engine-driven hydraulic

2.1 Loosen the driveshaft nut while the car is resting on its wheels, if possible

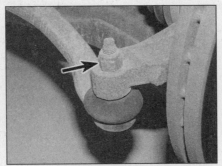

2.3a Unscrew the track rod end balljoint nut . . .

2.3b . . . then use a balljoint separator tool to free the balljoint . . .

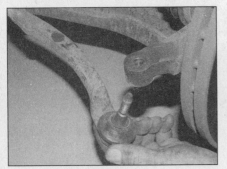

2.3c . . . and disconnect the track rod end from the hub

2.4a Unscrew the anti-roll bar drop link nut, using an Allen key to hold the stud . . .

2.4b . . . then separate the link rod from the strut

pump. The motor is attached to the steering column, and at the time of writing could only be purchased as a complete unit with the steering column shaft – check with your local dealer for availability of parts.

2 Front swivel hub assembly – removal and refitting

Removal

1 Remove the wheel trim or wheel centre cap, as applicable. Have an assistant firmly apply the footbrake, then slacken the driveshaft nut – the nut is extremely tight, so use good-quality, close-fitting tools **(see illustration)**.
2 Loosen the front wheel bolts, then jack up the front of the car and support it on axle stands (see *Jacking and vehicle support*). Remove the front wheel.
3 Loosen the track rod end balljoint nut, unscrewing it almost to the end of its threads (if the nut will not unscrew, hold the balljoint stud on top using a small spanner). Use a balljoint separator tool to free the balljoint, then unscrew the nut completely, and disconnect the track rod from the swivel hub **(see illustrations)**.
4 Unscrew the upper nut from the anti-roll bar drop link, using an Allen key if necessary to prevent the balljoint stud turning as this is done **(see illustrations)**.
5 Disconnect the wiring plug from the ABS sensor at the back of the hub. Unclip the sensor wiring from the subframe, and

disconnect it at the in-line connector **(see illustrations)**.
6 Unscrew the nut from the lower balljoint bolt, then tap out the bolt and remove it **(see illustrations)**.

7 The lower balljoint must now be separated, by pulling the lower arm downwards. On our project car, this proved extremely difficult, due to corrosion between the balljoint and the hub. Apply plenty of penetrating spray to

2.5a Disconnect the ABS sensor wiring plug . . .

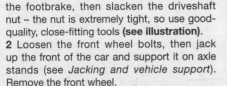
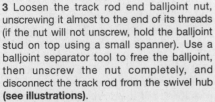
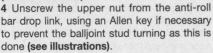

2.5c . . . and separate the in-line connector

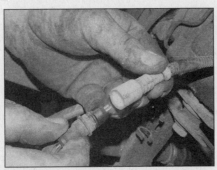

2.5b . . . then unclip the sensor wiring . . .

2.6a Unscrew the nut . . .

2.6b ... then tap out the lower balljoint bolt

2.7a Using a long pole, wood block and chain to lever down the lower arm ...

2.7b ... with a tapered punch to spread the location in the hub ...

2.7c ... the balljoint was separated from the lower arm

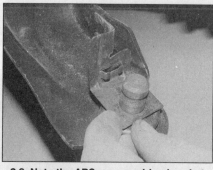

2.8 Note the ABS sensor wiring bracket fitted over the balljoint

2.10 Pull out the disc/hub, and remove the driveshaft to the inside

begin with. We used a long pole, fitted into a wooden block under the car, with a chain wrapped around the end of the lower arm, to provide sufficient leverage. Tapping in a tapered punch between the 'jaws' for the

balljoint on the hub also proved useful (see illustrations).

8 Recover the metal bracket from the balljoint, used to secure the ABS sensor wiring. Leave in position on the lower arm if possible, so

it does not get left out when refitting (see illustration).

9 The splined end of the driveshaft now has to be released from its location in the hub, and it's possible that the splines will be very tight (corrosion may even be a factor, if the driveshaft has not been disturbed for some time). Tap the end of the shaft with a plastic or hide mallet. If an ordinary hammer is used, place a small piece of wood over the end of the driveshaft – in addition to the loosened driveshaft nut, this will protect the threads from damage.

10 Pull the disc/hub outwards, and turn it to allow the driveshaft to be withdrawn through the hub. It's helpful to have an assistant on hand here, to pull the hub outwards, while you slide out the driveshaft (see illustration). Note: *Once the left-hand driveshaft has been removed from the hub, there is nothing to prevent it dropping out of the transmission – tie the shaft up at its outer end, to make this less likely.*

11 At the top of the swivel hub, apply penetrating spray (such as WD-40) to the joint between the hub and the base of the strut (see illustration).

12 Unscrew and remove the pinch-bolt from the base of the strut, noting which way round it is fitted, and that it may also be used to secure the brake hose mounting bracket (see illustration).

13 Using a hammer and block of wood if necessary, tap the hub downwards to separate it from the base of the strut. Pull the lower arm downwards as far as possible, and remove the hub from the car (see illustrations).

2.11 Apply penetrating spray to the hub/strut joint

2.12 Remove the pinch-bolt at the base of the strut

2.13a Separate the hub from the base of the strut ...

2.13b ... and remove it

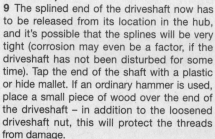
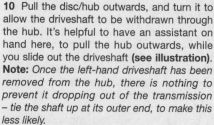
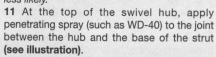

Refitting

14 Refitting is a reversal of removal, noting the following points:

a) *When offering the hub back up to the base of the strut, align the locating flange on the back of the strut with the slot in the top of the hub (see illustration).*

b) *Lubricate the driveshaft splines with a little grease before inserting into the hub.*

c) *Tighten all nuts/bolts to the specified torque, but delay tightening the driveshaft nut fully until the car it back on the ground.*

d) *Remember to refit the ABS sensor wiring bracket to the lower balljoint, before fitting the balljoint to the hub.*

e) *Ensure that the brake hose and ABS wiring are routed correctly, and clipped into their respective brackets securely.*

f) *On completion, if new components have been fitted, it is advisable to have the wheel alignment checked.*

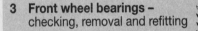

3 Front wheel bearings – checking, removal and refitting

Note: *The bearing is a sealed, pre-adjusted and pre-lubricated, double-row roller type, and is intended to last the car's entire service life without maintenance or attention. Do not attempt to remove the bearing unless absolutely necessary, as it will be damaged during the removal operation. Never over-tighten the driveshaft nut in an attempt to 'adjust' the bearing.*

2.14 Align the flange on the back of the strut with the slot in the hub

Note: *A press will be required to dismantle and rebuild the assembly; if such a tool is not available, a large bench vice, big nuts/bolts and spacers (such as large sockets) will serve as an adequate substitute. A punch or chisel will also be needed to remove the bearing inner race from the hub flange.*

Checking

1 Wear in the front hub bearings can be checked for as described in Chapter 1A or 1B. However, the most common first symptom of bearing wear is a rumbling noise, noted at a particular road speed, or when the offending wheel is loaded-up during cornering. In this case, besides rocking the wheel, spin it and listen carefully, to distinguish between the sound of the brake pads rubbing the disc, and the rumble of bearing wear. Compare the sound with the other front wheel to confirm.

2 Wheel bearings do not have to be renewed

in pairs. However, if the bearing on one side has worn, it may only be a short while before the other one needs renewal.

Removal

3 With the swivel hub removed as described in Section 2, proceed as follows.

4 The hub flange must first be removed from the bearing/swivel hub assembly. It is preferable to use a press to do this, but it is possible to drive out the hub using a metal tube of suitable diameter. Alternatively, a suitable puller can be used.

5 Securely support the hub carrier, on two metal bars for instance, with the inner face uppermost then, using a metal bar or tube of suitable diameter, press or drive out the hub flange – we used a bolt and large washer (the same diameter as the end of the hub's splined end) **(see illustrations)**. Alternatively, use the puller to separate the hub flange from the bearing. Note that the bearing inner race will remain on the hub.

6 The bearing inner race left on the hub flange must now be removed. To do this, grip the edge of the flange in a vice, and tap the race off with a chisel **(see illustrations)**. Tap the race at the top and both sides (even turn the flange over in the vice) to stop it jamming as it comes off.

7 To remove the bearing itself, the retaining circlip must first be removed, which requires the use of a sturdy pair of circlip pliers **(see illustrations)**. A new circlip should be used when refitting – one is supplied in the bearing kits supplied by Renault dealers.

3.5a Insert a large bolt and flanged nut of the right diameter . . .

3.5b . . . and using a large hammer . . .

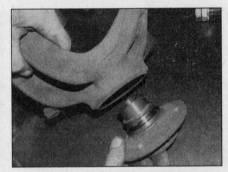

3.5c . . . drive out the hub flange

3.6a Using a hammer and suitable chisel . . .

3.6b . . . tap the inner race off the hub flange

3.7a Using circlip pliers in the holes provided . . .

3.7b ... compress the circlip ...

3.7c ... and remove it from the hub

3.8a Apply some spray lubricant ...

3.8b ... then use a nut, bolt, and some suitable spacers ...

3.8c ... 'wind' out the bearing from the hub

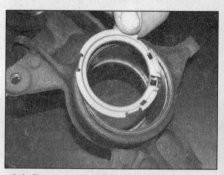

3.9 Recover the ABS wheel sensor from the hub

8 Now the bearing itself must be removed. After applying a generous amount of spray lubricant, we were able to pull the bearing out, using another old bearing, together with a large nut and bolt, and several washers/ spacers (**see illustrations**). Mount the swivel hub in a vice, then tighten the nut and bolt to apply pressure to the bearing – this, and a few hammer blows, should be enough to get the bearing moving, and extract it.

9 Once the bearing has been removed, recover the ABS wheel sensor, noting which way round it is fitted (**see illustration**).

10 Using emery paper, clean off any burrs or raised edges from the hub flange and hub, which might stop the components going back together (**see illustration**). Clean and lightly lubricate the bearing location in the hub.

11 Insert the ABS wheel sensor into the bearing location, with the sensor wiring connector facing the cut-out section at the base (**see illustration**). Renault-supplied bearing kits include a new sensor, but there appears to be no reason why the old one cannot be re-used, provided it is clean. As the new bearing is fitted, it is essential that the wiring connector remains in this hub 'window', otherwise it will not be possible to reconnect it.

12 The new bearing has a magnetic reluctor ring fitted to its inner face (for the ABS sensor), which means that it should not be roughly handled during fitting. This means that, unlike a normal bearing, heavy hammer blows cannot be used to drive it into the swivel hub. It also means that the new bearing should be kept clean, and the protective cover fitted over the magnetic ring should only be removed just prior to fitting (**see illustration**).

13 As for removal, mount the swivel hub in a sturdy bench vice. First, start the bearing into position by gently tapping it squarely into the hub, using a small hammer and protective wooden block.

14 Using the same nut/bolt and spacers as for removal, tighten the nut and bolt to press the bearing into place. As this is done, check

3.10 Clean any burrs from the hub flange

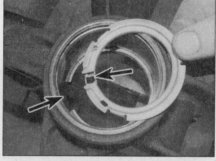

3.11 Align the sensor with the cut-out at the base of the bearing location

3.12 Remove the protective cover from the bearing's magnetic surface

3.14a Using a nut/bolt and spacers to press the new bearing into place

that the wiring connector for the ABS sensor is still central in the hub 'window' – until the bearing is fully fitted, the sensor can be turned using a small screwdriver as necessary **(see illustrations)**.

15 The bearing is fully seated when the circlip groove is visible. Fit the new circlip using suitable circlip pliers to retain the bearing **(see illustration)**.

16 The hub flange can be pressed into the new bearing using a very similar method to the one just used **(see illustrations)**.

17 On completion, refit the swivel hub as described in Section 2.

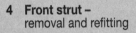

4 Front strut – removal and refitting

Removal

1 Loosen the relevant front wheel bolts, then jack up the front of the car and support it on axle stands *(see Jacking and vehicle support)*. Remove the appropriate roadwheel.

2 Unclip the brake hose and ABS wiring from the strut assembly **(see illustration)**.

3 Unscrew the upper nut from the anti-roll bar drop link, using an Allen key if necessary to prevent the balljoint stud turning as this is done **(see illustrations)**.

4 At the top of the swivel hub, apply penetrating spray (such as WD-40) to the joint between the hub and the base of the strut **(see illustration)**.

3.14b Check during fitting that the sensor wiring connector is central in the hub 'window'

3.16a Fit the hub flange into the new bearing . . .

5 Unscrew and remove the pinch-bolt from the base of the strut, noting which way round it is fitted, and that it may also be used to secure the brake hose mounting bracket **(see illustration)**.

3.15 Fit the new circlip into the hub to retain the bearing

3.16b . . . and press it into place using the nut/bolt and spacer method

6 Using a hammer and block of wood if necessary, tap the hub downwards to separate it from the base of the strut. Pull the lower arm downwards as far as possible, and pull the strut to the side **(see illustration)**.

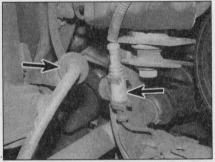

4.2 Unclip the brake hose and ABS wiring

4.3a Unscrew the anti-roll bar drop link nut, using an Allen key to hold the stud . . .

4.3b . . . then separate the link rod from the strut

4.4 Apply penetrating spray to the hub/strut joint

4.5 Remove the pinch-bolt at the base of the strut

4.6 Separate the hub from the base of the strut

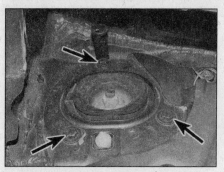

4.9a Unscrew the three strut upper mounting bolts . . .

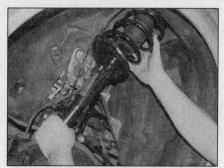

4.9b . . . and lower the strut out from under the wheel arch

4.10 Align the flange on the back of the strut with the slot in the hub

7 On the left-hand side especially, once the strut has been separated from the hub, there is a danger that the driveshaft may be pulled out of the transmission. To avoid this possibility, support the hub assembly underneath the lower arm, or tie it up.

8 Remove the windscreen cowl panels as described in Chapter 11. This is necessary to gain access to the strut upper mounting bolts in the engine compartment.

9 Unscrew and remove the three strut upper mounting bolts – do not loosen the centre nut at this stage. Lower the strut assembly out from under the wheel arch **(see illustrations)**.

Refitting

10 Refitting is a reversal of removal, noting the following points:
  a) Lightly lubricate the base of the strut where it enters the top of the swivel hub.
  b) When offering the base of the strut into

the hub, align the locating flange on the back of the strut with the slot in the top of the hub **(see illustration)**. This can be difficult to achieve, as the lower arm must also be pulled down, which itself introduces the risk of pulling the left-hand driveshaft out of the transmission. Have an assistant available to help, or remove the swivel hub as described in Section 2 to make refitting easier.
  c) Tighten all nuts/bolts to the specified torque.

5 Front strut – dismantling, inspection and reassembly

⚠️ **Warning: Before attempting to dismantle the front suspension strut, a special tool to hold**

the coil spring in compression must be obtained. Adjustable coil spring compressors are readily available, and are recommended for this operation. Any attempt to dismantle the strut without such a tool is likely to result in damage or personal injury.

Dismantling

1 With the strut removed from the car as described in Section 4, clean away all external dirt.

2 Fit the spring compressor, and compress the coil spring until all tension is relieved from the upper mounting plate. Ensure that the compressor tool is securely located on the spring according to the tool manufacturer's instructions. We found that the type of compressor which hooks onto the spring coils was insufficient, and had to use one with 'plates' or 'cups' for trapping the spring coils **(see illustration)**.

3 Slacken and remove the strut piston rod nut (18 mm on our car), using a 6 mm Allen key to prevent the rod from turning as this is done **(see illustrations)**.

4 Remove the upper mounting plate/bearing and the upper spring seat **(see illustration)**.

5 Carefully remove the coil spring, complete with the spring compressor, and store in a safe place for refitting **(see illustration)**. If the spring will not be refitted for some time, it may be safer to release the spring compressor from the spring while it is stored.

6 Slide the rubber bump stop/dust cover off the strut piston **(see illustration)**.

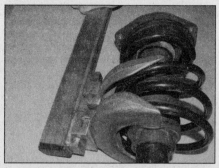

5.2 Fit a spring compressor, and tighten until the strut upper plate is released

5.3a Hold the piston rod using an Allen key, while the nut is loosened . . .

5.3b . . . and removed

5.4 Remove the upper plate/bearing and the spring seat . . .

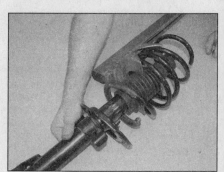

5.5 . . . followed by the spring and compressor

5.6 Finally, remove the bump stop/dust cover from the strut piston

5.12a Ensure that the spring ends are located against the stops at the strut base . . .

5.12b . . . and against the spring seat at the top

Inspection

7 With the strut assembly now completely dismantled, examine all the components for wear, damage or deformation, and check the upper bearing for smoothness of operation. Renew any of the components as necessary.

8 Examine the strut for signs of fluid leakage. Check the strut piston for signs of pitting along its entire length, and check the strut body for signs of damage. Test the operation of the strut, while holding it in an upright position, by moving the piston through a full stroke and then through short strokes of 50 to 100 mm. In both cases, the resistance felt should be smooth and continuous. If the resistance is jerky or uneven, or if there is any visible sign of wear or damage, renewal is necessary.

9 If any doubt exists about the condition of the coil spring, gradually release the spring compressor (if not already done), and check the spring for distortion and signs of cracking. Since no minimum free length is specified by Renault, the only way to check the tension of the spring is to compare it to a new component. Renew the spring if it is damaged or distorted, or if there is any doubt as to its condition.

10 Inspect all other components for signs of damage or deterioration, and renew any that are suspect.

Reassembly

Note: *Apply grease between the ends of the spring and its stops.*

11 Ensure that all components are clean and dry. Slide the bump stop/dust cover into position over the strut piston.

12 Refit the compressed coil spring, followed by the upper spring seat. Ensure that both ends of the spring are correctly located in the spring seats **(see illustrations)**.

13 Refit the strut upper mounting plate/ bearing. Fit a new piston rod nut, and tighten it while holding the rod using the Allen key as for removal. There is a specified torque for the piston rod nut, which should be observed where possible, but if the required special tools for tightening it are not available, ensure the nut is tightened very securely.

14 Slowly and carefully release the spring compressor, watching to make sure that both ends of the spring remain correctly located in the spring seats.

15 Refit the strut to the car as described in Section 4.

6 Front anti-roll bar – removal and refitting

Removal

1 Loosen the front wheel bolts, then jack up the front of the car and support it on axle stands *(see Jacking and vehicle support)*. Remove both front roadwheels.

2 The anti-roll bar drop link rods can be renewed by unscrewing the nuts at either end, using an Allen key if necessary to prevent the balljoint stud turning as this is done **(see illustrations)**.

3 To remove the anti-roll bar itself, remove the front subframe as described in Section 8.

4 Unscrew the anti-roll bar clamp bolts, and remove the anti-roll bar **(see illustration)**.

5 Carefully examine the anti-roll bar components for signs of wear, damage or deterioration, paying particular attention to the mounting bushes. Renew worn components as necessary.

Refitting

6 Refitting is a reversal of removal, noting the following points:
 a) *The anti-roll bar mountings have pegs which locate into holes in the subframe.*
 b) *Tighten the clamp bolts to the specified torque.*
 c) *Refit the subframe as described in Section 8.*
 d) *Tighten the drop link nuts to the specified torque while holding the balljoint studs with an Allen key.*

7 Front lower arm – removal, overhaul and refitting

Removal

1 As the radiator lower crossmember must be removed as part of this procedure, the radiator must first be supported by tying it up to the front panel, using string or cable-ties.

2 Loosen the relevant front wheel bolts, then jack up the front of the car and support it on axle stands *(see Jacking and vehicle support)*. Remove the appropriate front roadwheel.

6.2a Unscrew the anti-roll bar drop link nut, using an Allen key to hold the stud . . .

6.2b . . . then separate the link rod from the strut

6.4 Unscrew the anti-roll bar clamp bolts, and remove the bar from the subframe

7.4 Remove the radiator crossmember side support plates

7.5a Remove the front bolts . . .

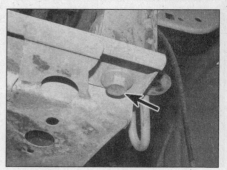

7.5b . . . and rear nuts . . .

7.5c . . . and remove the radiator crossmember

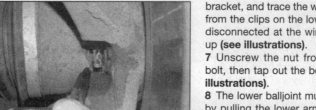

7.6a Disconnect the ABS sensor from the back of the wheel hub . . .

bracket, and trace the wiring back, releasing it from the clips on the lower arm until it can be disconnected at the wiring connector further up **(see illustrations)**.

7 Unscrew the nut from the lower balljoint bolt, then tap out the bolt and remove it **(see illustrations)**.

8 The lower balljoint must now be separated, by pulling the lower arm downwards. On our project car, this proved extremely difficult, due to corrosion between the balljoint and the hub. Apply plenty of penetrating spray to begin with. We used a long pole, fitted into a wooden block under the car, with a chain wrapped around the end of the lower arm, to provide sufficient leverage. Tapping in a tapered punch between the 'jaws' for the balljoint on the hub also proved useful **(see illustrations)**.

9 Recover the metal bracket from the balljoint, used to secure the ABS sensor wiring (see

3 Remove the wheel arch liners on both sides, and the engine undertray.

4 Remove the four bolts each side securing the radiator crossmember side support plates, and remove the plate from each side **(see illustration)**.

5 Remove the front bolts and rear nuts, then remove the radiator crossmember and lower it to the ground **(see illustrations)**.

6 Disconnect the ABS wheel sensor wiring plug from the back of the swivel hub. Unclip the sensor wiring from the lower balljoint

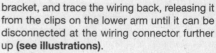

7.6b . . . then unclip the wiring from the lower balljoint bracket . . .

7.6c . . . and the clips along the lower arm . . .

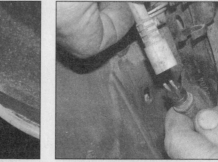

7.6d . . . then finally disconnect the large wiring plug under the wheel arch

7.7a Unscrew the nut . . .

7.7b . . . then tap out the lower balljoint bolt

7.8a Using a long pole, wood block and chain to lever down the lower arm . . .

7.8b . . . with a tapered punch to spread the location in the hub . . .

7.8c . . . the balljoint was separated from the lower arm

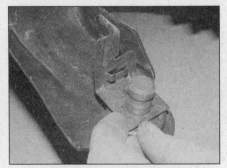

7.9 Recover the ABS sensor wiring bracket from the balljoint

7.10 Unscrew the anti-roll bar drop link lower nut, and separate the link

7.11a Unscrew the nut and take out the front pivot bolt . . .

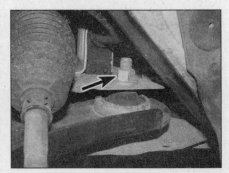

7.11b . . . then remove the nut and rear bolt, then take down the lower arm

illustration). Leave in position on the lower arm if possible, so it does not get left out when refitting.

10 Unscrew the lower nut from the anti-roll bar drop link, using an Allen key if necessary to prevent the balljoint stud turning as this is done (see illustration).

11 Unscrew the nut and remove the lower arm front pivot bolt. Remove the rear mounting nut and bolt, then take down the lower arm (see illustrations).

Overhaul

12 At the time of writing, no lower arm components were available separately. If the bushes or lower balljoint are worn, a complete new arm should be fitted. Check with a Renault dealer or reputable motor factors to see whether this is still the case, as repair kits may become available over time.

Refitting

13 Refitting is a reversal of removal, noting the following points:
  a) Tighten the suspension arm pivot and rear bolt nuts by hand only until the car is resting on its wheels.
  b) Tighten all nuts and bolts to the specified torque.
  c) When refitting the radiator lower crossmember, fit the fasteners and side plates loosely, then insert a 10 mm spacer between it and the subframe, at the rear on each side. We used a 10 mm diameter bolt

– this should be withdrawn once the nuts have been tightened each side. The crossmember forms part of the deformable front structure of the car, and the gap left by using the spacer is essential.
  d) Remember to refit the ABS sensor wiring bracket to the lower balljoint, before fitting the balljoint to the hub.
  e) Ensure that the ABS wiring is routed correctly, and clipped into its brackets securely.
  f) On completion, with the car resting on its wheels, tighten the suspension arm pivot and rear bolt nuts to the specified torque.
  g) If new components have been fitted, it is advisable to have the wheel alignment checked.

8 Front subframe – removal and refitting

Removal

1 Set the front wheels in the straight-ahead position.

2 Inside the car, pull back the floor covering at the base of the steering column, then unscrew the universal joint bolt and separate the column from the steering gear pinion (see illustrations).

3 Renault state that a new universal joint nut/bolt must be used when refitting. The nut is housed in a cage, which must be prised off (the cage does not have to be refitted, once removed) (see illustration).

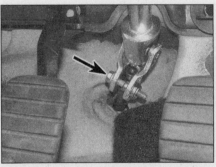

8.2a Pull back the carpet, then unscrew the bolt . . .

8.2b . . . and separate the column from the steering gear

8.3 To renew the nut, the metal cage must be prised off

8.5a Unscrew the track rod end balljoint nut . . .

8.5b . . . then use a balljoint separator tool to free the balljoint . . .

8.5c . . . and disconnect the track rod end from the hub

8.6 Disconnect the engine lower mounting – 1.9 litre diesel engine

6 Working at the rear of the subframe, disconnect the engine lower mounting tie-bar from the engine **(see illustration)**.

7 Support the weight of the subframe, using at least two sturdy jacks.

8 Remove the two small bolts each side from the rear crossmember fitted at the rear of the subframe **(see illustration)**.

9 Loosen a total of four bolts securing the subframe to the car. Note that two of the bolts are also used to secure the rear crossmember – remove these bolts first, and lower the crossmember out from under the car **(see illustrations)**.

10 The two front mounting bolts also secure plastic brackets used to attach wiring, etc. Unclip the wiring from these plates as necessary, then remove the bolts and lower the subframe carefully to the floor **(see illustration)**. Discard the subframe bolts – new ones should be used when refitting.

4 Disconnect the lower arms as described in Section 7, paragraphs 1 to 10.

5 Loosen the track rod end balljoint nut each side, unscrewing it almost to the end of its threads (if the nut will not unscrew, hold the

balljoint stud on top using a small spanner). Use a balljoint separator tool to free the balljoint, then unscrew the nut completely, and disconnect the track rods from the swivel hubs **(see illustrations)**.

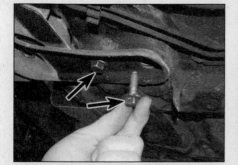

8.8 Remove the two small bolts from the rear crossmember

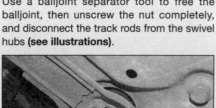

8.9a Remove the subframe rear mounting bolts . . .

8.9b . . . and lower out the rear crossmember

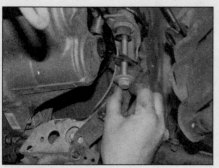

8.10 With the subframe supported, remove the front bolts and plastic brackets

8.11a Tightening the rear crossmember bolts

8.11b Tighten the new steering column universal joint nut/bolt to the specified torque

Refitting

11 Refitting is a reversal of removal, noting the following points:

a) *Use new subframe bolts.*

b) *Tighten all nuts/bolts to the specified torque* **(see illustration).**

c) *Refer to Section 7 when reconnecting the lower arms and the radiator lower crossmember.*

d) *Fit a new nut and bolt when reconnecting the steering column universal joint* **(see illustration).**

e) *On completion, it is advisable to have the wheel alignment checked.*

9 Rear wheel bearings – checking, removal and refitting

Note: *The bearing is a sealed, pre-adjusted and pre-lubricated, double-row tapered-roller type, and is intended to last the car's entire service life without maintenance or attention. Never overtighten the hub nut in an attempt to 'adjust' the bearings.*

Checking

1 Wear in the rear hub bearings can be checked for as described in Chapter 1A or 1B. However, the most common first symptom of bearing wear is a rumbling noise, noted at a particular road speed, or when the offending wheel is loaded-up during cornering. In this case, besides rocking the wheel, spin it and listen carefully, to distinguish between the sound of the brake pads rubbing the disc, and the rumble of bearing wear. Compare the sound with the other rear wheel to confirm.

2 Wheel bearings do not have to be renewed in pairs. However, if the bearing on one side has worn, it may only be a short while before the other one needs renewal.

Removal

3 Remove the rear brake disc as described in Chapter 9. **Note:** *New rear discs supplied by Renault dealers come with new wheel bearings pre-fitted, but wheel bearing kits are also available.*

4 To remove the bearing, the retaining circlip must first be removed, which requires the use of a sturdy pair of circlip pliers **(see illustrations).** A new circlip should be used when refitting – one is supplied in the bearing kits supplied by Renault dealers.

5 Care must be taken during bearing renewal, as there is a magnetic (reluctor) ring fitted to the rear of the disc/hub which must not be damaged. Mount the disc over the open jaws of a sturdy bench vice, with the magnetic ring facing upwards **(see illustration).**

6 After applying a generous amount of spray lubricant, we were able to pull the bearing out, using two blocks of wood, together with a large nut and bolt, and several washers/spacers **(see illustration).**

7 Tighten the nut and bolt to apply pressure

to the bearing – this, and a few hammer blows, should be enough to get the bearing moving, and extract it **(see illustration).**

Refitting

8 Using emery paper, clean off any burrs or

9.4a Insert a pair of circlip pliers into the holes . . .

9.4b . . . then compress the circlip and remove it from the disc/hub

9.5 Mount the disc over the open jaws of a vice . . .

9.6 . . . then fit a large bolt, nut, spacers and two blocks of wood . . .

raised edges from the hub, which might stop the components going back together – take care not to damage the magnetic ring. Clean and lightly lubricate the bearing location in the hub **(see illustrations).**

9 Offer the bearing into position, and using a

9.7 . . . to extract the bearing

9.8a Clean off any burrs from the bearing location

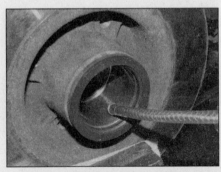

9.8b Lightly oil the bearing location

9.9a Offer the bearing into place . . .

9.9b ... then tap it gently to start it into the hub

9.10a Fit the same nut, bolt and spacers used for removal ...

9.10b ... then tighten the nut/bolt to press the bearing into place

suitable spacer, tap it gently around its edge to start it squarely into the disc/hub **(see illustrations)**.
10 Using the same nut/bolt and spacers as for removal, tighten the nut and bolt to press the bearing into place **(see illustrations)**.

9.11 Fit the new bearing retaining circlip

11 The bearing is fully seated when the circlip groove is visible. Fit the new circlip using suitable circlip pliers to retain the bearing **(see illustration)**.
12 Refit the brake disc or drum as described in Chapter 9.

10 Rear shock absorber
– removal, testing and refitting

Removal

1 Chock the front wheels and engage reverse gear (or P). Loosen the relevant rear wheel bolts, then jack up the rear of the car and support it on axle stands *(see Jacking and vehicle support)*. Remove the appropriate rear roadwheel.
2 Prise out the large plastic clip which secures the plastic cover fitted under the trailing arm and rear axle, then unscrew the small bolt underneath the trailing arm and lower the plastic cover for access to the shock absorber lower mounting **(see illustrations)**.
3 Using a jack and block of wood under the rear spring cup, lift the trailing arm slightly **(see illustration)**.
4 Unscrew the nut and disengage the shock absorber lower mounting bolt from the trailing arm **(see illustrations)**.
5 Inside the boot area, lift the floor carpet to gain access to the shock absorber upper mounting bolt **(see illustrations)**.
6 Unscrew the upper mounting bolt, then remove the shock absorber from under the car **(see illustration)**.

Testing

7 Mount the shock absorber in a vice, and test as described in Section 5 for the front suspension strut. Also check the

10.2a Prise out the large plastic clip ...

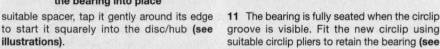

10.2b ... and remove it ...

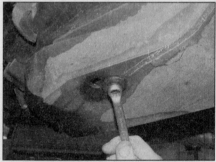

10.2c ... then unscrew the small bolt ...

10.2d ... and lower the plastic cover from the trailing arm

10.3 Raise the trailing arm slightly using a jack

10.4a Unscrew the lower mounting nut ...

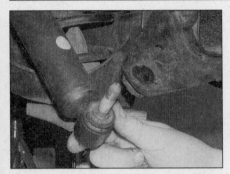

10.4b . . . and detach the shock absorber from the trailing arm

10.5a Lift up the boot floor carpet . . .

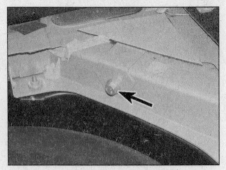

10.5b . . . for access to the shock absorber upper mounting bolt

10.6 Lower the shock absorber out from under the wheel arch

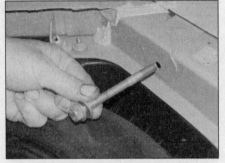

10.8 Insert the shock absorber mounting bolt, and tighten by hand initially

10.11 With the car back on the ground, tighten the shock absorber mountings

rubber mounting bushes for damage and deterioration. Renew the shock absorber complete if any damage or wear is evident; the mounting bushes are not available separately. Inspect the mounting bolts for signs of wear or damage, and renew as necessary. Shock absorbers should always be renewed in pairs.

Refitting

8 Offer the shock absorber into position in its upper mounting, then insert the bolt and tighten by hand only at this stage **(see illustration)**.
9 Similarly, locate the lower mounting bolt, and tighten its nut by hand. If a new unit is being fitted, it may be restrained in its fully-compressed state by a special cord or strap – once the unit is in place, this restraining device should be cut.
10 Remove the jack supporting the trailing arm. Refit the roadwheel, lower the car to the

ground and tighten the roadwheel bolts to the specified torque.
11 Rock the car to settle the shock absorber in position, then tighten both the upper and lower mountings to the specified torque **(see illustration)**.
12 Refit the plastic cover to the trailing arm, securing with the bolt and round clip.

11 Rear coil spring – removal and refitting

Removal

1 Disconnect the shock absorber lower mounting on the side concerned as described in Section 10, paragraphs 1 to 4.
2 Before removing the spring, mark it for position relative to the car – the spring should already have a paint code mark on it, which

can be used to ensure it is orientated properly when refitting.
3 Carefully lower the jack supporting the trailing arm, and remove the coil spring and its lower mounting rubber from the trailing arm. Lever the trailing arm down slightly if necessary to remove the spring **(see illustration)**.
4 Check the condition of the lower mounting rubber, and renew if necessary **(see illustration)**. If new springs are being fitted, note that these should always be fitted in pairs.
5 If required, the spring upper mounting/ bump stop can be unclipped from the body, and a new one fitted **(see illustration)**.

Refitting

6 Refitting is a reversal of removal, remembering the following points:
a) *Align the spring as noted before removal, so that it sits properly in the trailing arm.*

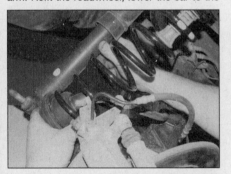

11.3 Lower the trailing arm, and remove the spring

11.4 Check the condition of the lower mounting rubber

11.5 If necessary, unclip the upper mounting/bump stop

12.3 Disconnect the rear wheel ABS sensors

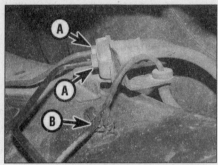

12.5 Disconnect the brake pipe/hose unions (A) – also unclip the ABS wiring (B)

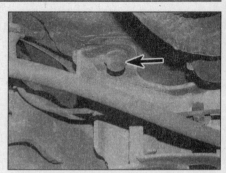

12.9 One of the rear axle mounting plate bolts

b) Refit the shock absorber lower mounting as described in Section 10, noting that the nut/bolt should not be tightened until the car is resting on its wheels.

12 Rear axle –
removal and refitting

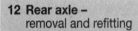

Note: *Renewal of the rear axle bushes requires the use of a press. Check on parts availability before removing the rear axle for bush renewal.*

Removal

1 Chock the front wheels and engage reverse gear (or P on automatic models). Loosen the rear wheel bolts, then jack up the rear of the car and support it on axle stands. Remove both rear roadwheels.

2 If a new rear axle is to be fitted, remove the brake discs as described in Chapter 9. Otherwise, to make refitting the axle easier, remove the rear brake pads and tie up the calipers as described in Chapter 9.

3 Disconnect the wiring plugs from the ABS rear wheel sensors (behind the discs, facing forwards) **(see illustration)**. Trace the wiring back, and unclip it from the axle.

4 Unhook the handbrake cable ends from the operating levers on the calipers, then unclip the cable outers from the calipers. Trace the cables back, and ensure they are disconnected from the clips relevant to the rear axle. On models with the automatic handbrake, remove the control unit as described in Chapter 9.

5 Use a brake hose clamp, a G-clamp or a similar tool with protected jaws to clamp the brake flexible hoses at the nearest convenient point. Disconnect the rear brake pipes at the flexible hose unions which are clipped to the axle crossmember **(see illustration)**. Plug or tape over the union ends to prevent dirt entry. Wash off any spilt fluid immediately.

6 Disconnect the rear shock absorber lower mountings as described in Section 10, paragraphs 2 to 4.

7 Remove the rear springs as described in Section 11, paragraphs 2 and 3.

8 On models with the optional xenon headlights, it may be necessary to disconnect

the wiring from, and to unbolt the ride height level sensor attached to the rear axle.

9 Clean the area under the car around the axle mounting plates, and mark their positions relative to the floor using paint. Loosen the three axle mounting plate bolts either side **(see illustration)**.

10 With the aid of an assistant, position two sturdy jacks under the ends of the axle, and just take its weight.

11 Remove the three mounting plate bolts each side progressively, then, with the assistant on hand to steady the axle on the jacks, lower the axle out from under the car.

12 If a new axle is being fitted, remove the brake pipes from the original and fit them to the new axle. Also transfer the brake assemblies using the information in Chapter 9.

Refitting

13 Refitting is a reversal of removal, noting the following points:

a) Align the axle mounting plates with the marks made prior to removal, then tighten the bolts to the specified torque.

b) Refit the springs and reconnect the shock absorbers as described in Sections 11 and 10.

c) Refit the brake components, then on completion bleed the braking system as described in Chapter 9.

d) On completion, it may be advisable to have the rear wheel alignment checked by a Renault dealer or competent specialist. On models with xenon headlights, the headlight system should also be set up by a Renault dealer on completion.

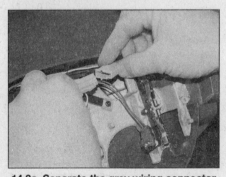

14.3a Separate the grey wiring connector at the top of the wheel . . .

13 Ride height –
general information and checking

General information

1 The ride height measurements are used to ensure accuracy when checking the front suspension and steering angles (see Section 19). This is because the angles will vary slightly according to the ride height of the car (see Specifications). The ride height measuring points are as follows:

R1   Dimension between the front wheel axle and the ground.
W1   Dimension between the front subframe rear mounting bolt and the ground.
R2   Dimension between the rear wheel axle and the ground.
W2   Dimension between the rear axle pivot bolt and the ground.

Checking

2 Position the unladen car on a level surface, with the tyres correctly inflated and the fuel tank full.

3 Measure and record the required dimensions as necessary.

4 Note that no adjustment of the ride height is possible.

5 If further checks are required, take your car to your local dealer who will have the specialised equipment to do this.

14 Steering wheel –
removal and refitting

Removal

1 Set the front wheels in the straight-ahead position.

2 Remove the driver's airbag (referring to the warnings) as described in Chapter 12. Note that, once the battery has been disconnected as required, the steering will be locked.

3 Disconnect the grey horn wiring connector at the top of the wheel, and the earth wire on the front **(see illustrations)**.

4 Unscrew and remove the steering wheel

14.3b . . . and the spade connector on the front

14.4 Unscrew and remove the steering wheel bolt

14.5 Note the alignment punch marks on the wheel and column

bolt, holding the wheel rim with one hand, and loosening the bolt with the other – do not rely on the steering lock to prevent the wheel turning, otherwise it may be damaged **(see illustration)**.

5 Before removing the wheel, note that there should be punched alignment markings on the wheel and the end of the column, to ensure that the wheel is correctly refitted. If not, make your own marks with a pin punch or paint **(see illustration)**.

6 Pull the wheel from its splines, then feeding the wiring through the wheel, remove it completely **(see illustration)**. Note: *Do not turn the airbag contact ring assembly or the steering column shaft whilst the steering wheel is removed.*

Refitting

7 Refitting is a reversal of removal, bearing in mind the following points:

a) *Make sure the steering wheel splines are aligned correctly, using the marks noted prior to removal.*

b) *Fit a new steering wheel bolt, and tighten to the specified torque (see illustration).*

c) *Check that all the wiring plugs are connected securely.*

d) *Refit the airbag as described in Chapter 12 (referring to the warnings).*

14.6 Pull the steering wheel from its splines, and feed through the wiring

15 Steering column – removal, overhaul and refitting

Removal

1 Disconnect the battery negative lead.

2 Remove the steering wheel as described in Section 14.

3 Remove the steering column switch assembly as described in Chapter 12

4 Remove the driver's side facia lower trim panel as described in Chapter 11, Section 23.

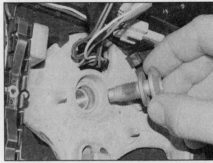

14.7 Fit a new steering wheel bolt, and tighten to the specified torque

5 Remove the driver's side air duct from below the column, referring if necessary to Chapter 3.

6 Remove the instrument panel trim pieces and the steering column lock as described in Chapter 12.

7 Pull back the floor covering at the base of the steering column, then unscrew the universal joint bolt and separate the column from the steering gear pinion. Renault state that a new universal joint nut/bolt must be used when refitting. The nut is housed in a cage, which must be prised off (the cage does not have to be refitted, once removed) **(see illustrations)**.

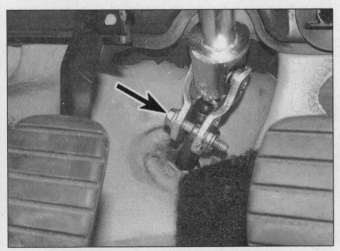

15.7a Pull back the carpet, then unscrew the bolt . . .

15.7b . . . and separate the column from the steering gear

15.7c To renew the nut, the metal cage must be prised off

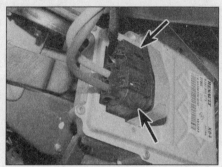

15.8a Disconnect the two wiring plugs from the motor . . .

8 Disconnect the remaining wiring plugs from the steering column motor. Unclip the wiring harness so that the column is free to be removed **(see illustrations)**.

9 The column is mounted to the facia cross-member by four nuts – the top nut is accessible through the instrument panel aperture, with three more underneath **(see illustrations)**.

10 Unscrew the nuts, then lower the column/motor assembly into the footwell and remove it from the car – note that the assembly is heavy, and it may be advisable to enlist the help of an assistant **(see illustration)**.

Overhaul

11 Check the steering shaft for signs of free play in the column bushes, and check the universal joints for signs of damage or roughness in the joint bearings. If damage or wear is found on the steering shaft universal joints or shaft bushes, the column must be renewed as an assembly.

Steering motor

12 The electric power steering motor is not available separately at the time of writing,

and must be renewed with the column as an assembly.

Steering lock

13 The (electric) steering column lock is attached using a bolt with a **left-hand thread**. The lock can in fact be removed with the column in place, as described in Chapter 12.

14 Refer to Chapter 12 for information on removing the keycard reader slot.

Refitting

15 Refitting is a reversal of removal, noting the following points:

a) *Tighten the column mounting nuts to the specified torque.*

b) *Check very carefully that the motor wiring plugs are securely connected – if the plugs were to work loose, this could result in a loss of power assistance.*

c) *Fit a new nut and bolt when reconnecting the steering column universal joint.*

d) *When the battery has been reconnected, the steering must be initialised by turning it to full lock in either direction a few times, holding in the full-lock position for a few seconds each time.*

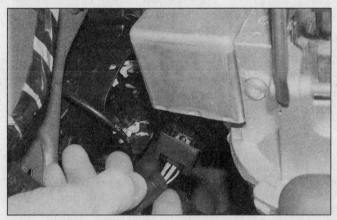

15.8b . . . and the steering column lock wiring plug

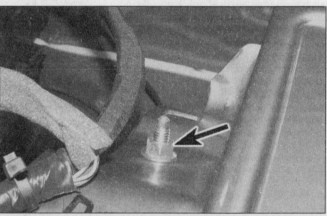

15.9a The top mounting nut can be reached via the instrument panel

15.9b One of the three steering column lower mounting nuts

15.10 Lowering out the column/motor assembly

16 Steering gear rubber gaiter – renewal

1 Disconnect the track rod end balljoint from the swivel hub, using the information in Section 18. The track rod end does not have to be removed completely, though it is advisable to tape over the track rod balljoint threads, to avoid damaging the new gaiter during fitting.

2 Mark the correct fitted position of the gaiter on the track rod. Release or cut the retaining clips, and slide the gaiter off the steering gear housing and track rod end.

3 Thoroughly clean the track rod and the steering gear housing, using fine abrasive paper to polish off any corrosion, burrs or sharp edges which might damage the sealing lips of the new gaiter on installation.

4 Recover the grease from inside the old gaiter. If it is uncontaminated with dirt or grit, apply it to the track rod inner balljoint. If the old grease is contaminated, or it is suspected that some has been lost, apply some new molybdenum disulphide grease.

5 Grease the inside of the new gaiter. Carefully slide the gaiter onto the track rod, and locate it on the steering gear housing. Align the outer edge of the gaiter with the mark made on the track rod prior to removal, then secure it in position with new retaining clips.

6 Reconnect the track rod balljoint as described in Section 18.

17 Steering gear assembly – removal, inspection and refitting

Removal

1 Remove the front subframe as described in Section 8.

2 Unscrew the two steering gear mounting bolts, and remove the steering gear assembly from the subframe **(see illustration)**. Discard the steering gear mounting bolts – new ones must be used when refitting.

Inspection

3 Renewal procedures for the gaiters and track rod end balljoints are given in Sections 16 and 18 respectively.

4 Examine the steering gear assembly for signs of wear or damage. Check that the rack moves freely over the full length of its travel, with no signs of roughness or excessive free play between the steering gear pinion and rack. Internal wear or damage can only be cured by renewing the steering gear assembly.

5 Overhaul of the steering rack and pinion assembly is not possible. The only components which can be renewed are the steering gear gaiters and track rod balljoints.

Refitting

6 Refitting is a reversal of removal, noting the following points:
  a) *Fit new steering gear mounting bolts, and tighten them to the specified torque.*
  b) *Refit the subframe as described in Section 8.*
  c) *When the battery has been reconnected, the steering must be initialised by turning it to full lock in either direction a few times, holding in the full-lock position for a few seconds each time.*
  d) *On completion, it is advisable to have the wheel alignment checked.*

18 Track rod end balljoint – removal and refitting

Removal

1 With the handbrake applied, jack up the front of the car and support it on axle stands (see *Jacking and vehicle support*). Remove the appropriate front roadwheel.

2 If the balljoint is to be re-used, use a straight-edge and a scriber, or similar, to mark its relationship to the track rod.

3 Loosen the track rod end balljoint nut, unscrewing it almost to the end of its threads (if the nut will not unscrew, hold the balljoint stud on top using a small spanner). Use a balljoint separator tool to free the balljoint, then unscrew the nut completely, and disconnect the track rod from the swivel hub **(see illustrations)**.

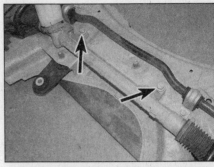

17.2 Unscrew and remove the steering gear mounting bolts

4 Holding the balljoint on the hex fitting provided, unscrew its locknut by half a turn only – do not move the locknut from this position as it will serve as a reference mark on refitting **(see illustration)**.

5 Counting the **exact** number of turns necessary to do so, unscrew the balljoint from the track rod end.

6 Count the number of exposed threads between the end of the balljoint and the locknut, and record this figure. If a new balljoint is to be fitted, unscrew the locknut from the old balljoint.

7 Carefully clean the balljoint and the threads. Renew the balljoint if its movement is sloppy or if it is too stiff, if it is excessively worn, or if it is damaged in any way. Carefully check the shank taper and threads. If the balljoint gaiter is damaged, the complete balljoint must be renewed; it is not possible to obtain the gaiter separately.

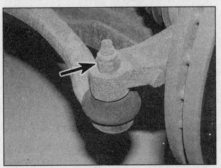

18.3a Unscrew the track rod end balljoint nut . . .

18.3b . . . then use a balljoint separator tool to free the balljoint . . .

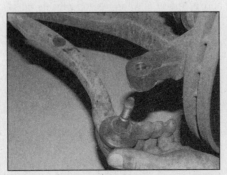

18.3c . . . and disconnect the track rod end from the hub

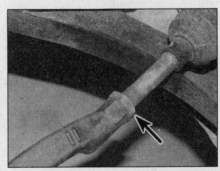

18.4 Hold the track rod end, and unscrew the locknut (arrowed)

Refitting

8 If applicable, screw the locknut onto the new balljoint, and position it so that the same number of exposed threads are visible as was noted prior to removal.

9 Screw the balljoint into the track rod by the number of turns noted on removal. This should bring the balljoint locknut to within a quarter of a turn of the end of the track rod, with the alignment marks that were made (if applicable) on removal lined up. Tighten the balljoint locknut to the specified torque.

10 Refit the balljoint shank to the swivel hub, and tighten the retaining nut to the specified torque. If difficulty is experienced due to the balljoint shank rotating, jam it by exerting pressure on the underside of the balljoint, using a tyre lever or a jack – alternatively, hold the balljoint stud on top using a small spanner.

11 Refit the roadwheel, lower the car to the ground and tighten the roadwheel bolts to the specified torque.

12 Have the front wheel toe setting checked on completion.

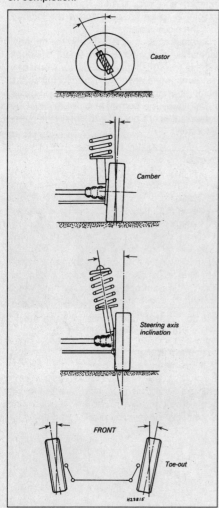

19.1 Wheel alignment and steering angles

19 Wheel alignment and steering angles – general information

General information

1 A car's steering and suspension geometry is defined in four basic settings **(see illustration)**. For this purpose, all angles are expressed in degrees (toe settings are also expressed as a measurement of length). The steering axis is defined as an imaginary line drawn through the axis of the suspension strut, extended where necessary to contact the ground.

2 Camber is the angle between each roadwheel and a vertical line drawn through its centre and tyre contact patch, when viewed from the front or rear of the car. Positive camber is when the roadwheels are tilted outwards from the vertical at the top; negative camber is when they are tilted inwards.

3 Camber is not adjustable. Values are given for reference only. Checking is possible using a camber checking gauge, but if the figure obtained is significantly different from that specified, the car must be taken for careful checking by a professional. Wrong camber settings can only be caused by wear or damage to the body or suspension components.

4 Castor is the angle between the steering axis and a vertical line drawn through each roadwheel's centre and tyre contact patch, when viewed from the side of the car. Positive castor is when the steering axis is tilted so that it contacts the ground ahead of the vertical; negative castor is when it contacts the ground behind the vertical.

5 Castor is not adjustable. As with camber, values are given for reference only; deviation can only be due to wear or damage.

6 Steering axis inclination/SAI – also known as **kingpin inclination/KPI** – is the angle between the steering axis and a vertical line drawn through each roadwheel's centre and tyre contact patch, when viewed from the front or rear of the car.

7 SAI/KPI is not adjustable, and is given for reference only.

8 Toe is the amount by which the roadwheels point outwards or inwards, viewed from above. Toe-in is when the roadwheels point inwards, towards each other at the front, while toe-out is when they splay outwards from each other at the front. The value for toe can be expressed as an angle (taking the centre-line of the car as zero), or as a measurement of length (taking measurements between the inside rims of the wheels at hub height).

9 The front wheel toe setting is adjusted by screwing the balljoints in or out of their track rods to alter the effective length of the track rod assemblies.

10 Rear wheel toe setting is not adjustable, and is given for reference only. While it can be checked, if the figure obtained is significantly different from that specified, the

car must be taken for careful checking by a professional, as the fault can only be caused by wear or damage to the body or suspension components.

Checking – general

11 Due to the special measuring equipment necessary to check the wheel alignment, and the skill required to use it properly, the checking and adjustment of these settings is best left to a Renault dealer or similar expert. Most tyre-fitting shops now possess sophisticated checking equipment.

12 For accurate checking, the car must be at the kerb weight specified in *Dimensions and weights* in the Reference Section.

13 Before starting work, check first that the tyre sizes and types are as specified, then check tyre pressures and tread wear. Also check roadwheel run-out, the condition of the hub bearings, the steering wheel free play and the condition of the front suspension components (Chapter 1A or 1B). Correct any faults.

14 Park the car on level ground, with the front roadwheels in the straight-ahead position. Rock both ends to settle the suspension. Release the handbrake and roll the car backwards 1 metre (3 feet), then forwards again, to relieve any stresses in the steering and suspension components.

Front wheel toe setting

Checking

15 Two methods are available to the home mechanic for checking the front wheel toe setting. One method is to use a gauge to measure the distance between the front and rear inside edges of the roadwheels. The other method is to use a scuff plate, in which each front wheel is rolled across a movable plate which records any deviation, or scuff, of the tyre from the straight-ahead position as it moves across the plate. Such gauges are available in relatively-inexpensive form from accessory outlets. It is up to the owner to decide whether the expense is justified, in view of the small amount of use such equipment would normally receive.

16 Prepare the car as described previously in paragraphs 12 to 14.

17 If the measurement procedure is being used, carefully measure the distance between the front edges of the roadwheel rims and the rear edges of the rims. Subtract the rear measurement from the front measurement, and check that the result is within the specified range. If not, adjust the toe setting as described in paragraph 19.

18 If scuff plates are to be used, roll the car backwards, check that the roadwheels are in the straight-ahead position, then roll it across the scuff plates so that each front roadwheel passes squarely over the centre of its respective plate. Note the angle recorded by the scuff plates. To ensure accuracy, repeat the check three times, and take the average of the three readings. If the road-wheels are running parallel, there will of course be no angle recorded; if a deviation value is shown on the scuff plates, compare the reading obtained for each wheel with that specified. If the value recorded is outside the specified tolerance, the toe setting is incorrect, and must be adjusted as follows.

Adjustment

19 With the handbrake applied, jack up the front of the car and support it securely on axle stands (see *Jacking and vehicle support*). Turn the steering wheel onto full-left lock, and record the number of exposed threads on the right-hand track rod end. Now turn the steering onto full-right lock, and record the number of threads on the left-hand side. If there are the same number of threads visible on both sides, then subsequent adjustment should be made equally on both sides. If there are more threads visible on one side than the other, it will be necessary to compensate for this during adjustment. **Note:** *It is important that, after adjustment, the same number of threads be visible on each track rod end.*

20 First clean the track rod threads; if they are corroded, apply penetrating fluid before starting adjustment. Release the rubber gaiter outboard clips, then peel back the gaiters and apply a smear of grease, so that both gaiters are free and will not be twisted or strained as their respective track rods are rotated.

21 Use a straight-edge and a scriber or similar to mark the relationship of each track rod to its balljoint. Holding each track rod in turn, unscrew its locknut fully.

22 Alter the length of the track rods, bearing in mind the note in paragraph 19, by screwing them into or out of the balljoints. Rotate the track rod using an open-ended spanner fitted to the flats provided **(see illustration)**. Shortening the track rods (screwing them onto their balljoints) will reduce toe-in and increase toe-out. Each complete turn of the track rod effectively adjusts the toe setting by 30' or 3 mm (depending on the method being used).

23 When the setting is correct, hold the track rods and securely tighten the balljoint locknuts or clamps. Check that the balljoints are seated correctly in their sockets, and count the exposed threads. If the number of threads exposed is not the same on both sides, then the adjustment has not been made equally, and problems will be encountered with tyre scrubbing in turns; also, the steering wheel spokes will no longer be horizontal when the wheels are in the straight-ahead position.

24 When the track rod lengths are the same,

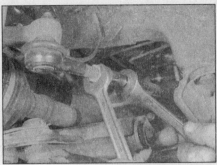

19.22 Hold the track rod end with one spanner, and adjust with another

lower the car to the ground and recheck the toe setting; readjust if necessary. Ensure that the rubber gaiters are seated correctly and are not twisted or strained; secure them in position with new retaining clips.

Rear wheel toe setting

25 The procedure for checking the rear toe setting is same as described for the front in paragraph 17. However, no adjustment is possible.

20 Tyre pressure monitoring system – general information

This system, offered as an option, continuously monitors the tyre pressures of the four tyres in use on the car, and warns of any tyre pressure issues as they develop.

A sensor unit is fitted to each wheel, and forms an integral assembly with the tyre valve **(see illustration)**. Besides the conventional valve, the unit contains sensors for pressure, temperature and acceleration, a radio transmitter and a non-removable battery. Each sensor is programmed to monitor one 'corner' of the car, meaning that the wheels cannot be interchanged without a fault being signalled – a coloured band around the valve indicates each sensor's intended working position, as shown below. The units can be transferred between wheels once the tyres have been removed.

Green	Front left
Yellow	Front right
Red	Rear left
Black	Rear right

Information on the pressure, temperature and acceleration of each tyre is sent to the multiplex unit inside the car, via the radio senders. The multiplex unit then processes this information, determines whether a fault

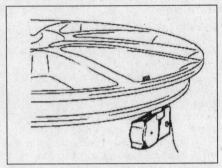

20.2 Tyre pressure sensor unit – seen with tyre removed

is present, and signals the driver using the information display in the centre of the instrument panel. The system warns the driver in the event of:

a) *Overinflation.*

b) *Moderate or extreme underinflation.*

c) *A puncture.*

d) *A tyre pressure which is inappropriate for the vehicle speed.*

e) *Slow punctures between left- and right-hand tyres.*

f) *Pressure left-right imbalance when starting.*

g) *Sensor failure.*

Precautions

The spare wheel is not equipped with a sensor, so while the spare is in use, a fault will be signalled continuously. A spare wheel sensor would not work with this system, since each sensor is coded for one position on the car – the spare wheel gets fitted wherever it is needed.

Similarly, even the four wheels with sensors cannot be interchanged (from front to rear, for instance, to compensate for uneven tyre wear) with this system, otherwise a fault will be signalled.

When new tyres are being fitted, make sure the fitter is made aware of the special sensor units, which have integrated valves, not the 'disposable' kind more commonly used. It is common practice for new valves to be fitted with new tyres, but this should not be attempted. Care is also required when removing old tyres (and when fitting new ones), as the sensors are located just inside the rim edge.

If new sensors have been fitted, they must be programmed to the multiplex module using Renault diagnostic equipment before they will work properly. Any problems with the system should also be referred to a Renault dealer.

Chapter 11
Bodywork and fittings

Contents

Degrees of difficulty

| **Easy,** suitable for novice with little experience | **Fairly easy,** suitable for beginner with some experience | **Fairly difficult,** suitable for competent DIY mechanic | **Difficult,** suitable for experienced DIY mechanic | **Very difficult,** suitable for expert DIY or professional |

Specifications

Torque wrench settings	Nm	lbf ft
Centre console (automatic handbrake type) baseplate nuts	21	15
Front seat mounting bolts	35	26
Grand Scénic third-row seat mounting bolts	21	15
Rear seat rail mounting bolts	21	15
Seat belt mountings:		
Grand Scénic third-row seat belt centre stalks bolt	44	32
Other mounting bolts	21	15

1 General information

The bodyshell and floorpan are manufactured from pressed-steel, and form an integral part of the car's structure (monocoque), without the need for a separate chassis. The Scénic is available only as a 5-door Hatchback, but the 7-seater Grand Scénic is a long-wheelbase variation on this theme.

Various areas of the structure are strengthened to provide for suspension, steering and engine mounting points, and load distribution.

All models are fitted with front wings manufactured from a polymer compound, which can withstand an impact of up to 10 mph (16 km/h) without sustaining permanent damage.

Corrosion protection is applied to all new cars. Various anti-corrosion preparations are used, including galvanising, zinc phosphatisation, and PVC underseal. An 'anti-gravel' undercoat is applied to the front section of the bonnet, to prevent corrosion and paint chipping caused by stones and other road debris hitting the front of the car. Protective wax is injected into the box sections and other hollow cavities.

Extensive use is made of plastic for peripheral components, such as the radiator grille, bumpers and wheel trims, and for much of the interior trim. Plastic wheel arch liners are fitted, to protect the metal body panels against corrosion due to a build-up of road dirt.

2 Maintenance – bodywork and underframe

The general condition of a car's bodywork is the one thing that significantly affects its value. Maintenance is easy, but needs to be regular. Neglect, particularly after minor damage, can lead quickly to further deterioration and costly repair bills. It is important also to keep watch on those parts of the car not immediately visible, for instance the underside, inside all the wheel arches, and the lower part of the engine compartment.

The basic maintenance routine for the bodywork is washing – preferably with a lot of water, from a hose. This will remove all the loose solids which may have stuck to the car. It is important to flush these off in such a way as to prevent grit from scratching the finish. The wheel arches and underframe need washing in the same way, to remove any accumulated mud which will retain moisture and tend to encourage rust. Strange as it sounds, the best time to clean the underframe and wheel arches is in wet weather, when the mud is thoroughly wet and soft. In very wet weather, the underframe is usually cleaned of large accumulations automatically, and this is a good time for inspection.

Periodically, except on cars with a wax-based underbody protective coating, it is a good idea to have the whole of the underframe of the car steam-cleaned, engine compartment included, so that a thorough inspection can be carried out to see what minor repairs and renovations are necessary. Steam-cleaning is available at many garages, and is necessary for the removal of the accumulation of oily grime, which sometimes is allowed to become thick in certain areas. If steam-cleaning facilities are not available, there are one or two excellent grease solvents available, which can be brush-applied; the dirt can then be simply hosed off. Note that these methods should not be used on cars with wax-based underbody protective coating, or the coating will be removed. Such cars should be inspected annually, preferably just prior to Winter, when the underbody should be washed down, and any damage to the wax coating repaired. Ideally, a completely fresh coat should be applied. It would also be worth considering the use of such wax-based protection for injection into door panels, sills, box sections, etc, as an additional safeguard against rust damage, where such protection is not provided by the car manufacturer.

After washing paintwork, wipe off with a chamois leather to give an unspotted clear finish. A coat of clear protective wax polish will give added protection against chemical pollutants in the air. If the paintwork sheen has dulled or oxidised, use a cleaner/polisher combination to restore the brilliance of the shine. This requires a little effort, but such dulling is usually caused because regular washing has been neglected. Care needs to be taken with metallic paintwork, as special non-abrasive cleaner/polisher is required to avoid damage to the finish. Always check that the door and ventilator opening drain holes and pipes are completely clear, so that water can be drained out. Brightwork should be treated in the same way as paintwork. Windscreens and windows can be kept clear of the smeary film which often appears, by the use of proprietary glass cleaner. Never use any form of wax or other body or chromium polish on glass.

3 Maintenance – upholstery and carpets

Mats and carpets should be brushed or vacuum-cleaned regularly, to keep them free of grit. If they are badly stained, remove them from the car for scrubbing or sponging, and make quite sure they are dry before refitting. Seats and interior trim panels can be kept clean by wiping with a damp cloth. If they do become stained (which can be more apparent on light-coloured upholstery), use a little liquid detergent and a soft nail brush to scour the grime out of the grain of the material. Do not forget to keep the headlining clean in the same way as the upholstery. When using liquid cleaners inside the car, do not over-wet the surfaces being cleaned. Excessive damp could get into the seams and padded interior, causing stains, offensive odours or even rot. If the inside of the car gets wet accidentally, it is worthwhile taking some trouble to dry it out properly, particularly where carpets are involved. *Do not leave oil or electric heaters inside the car for this purpose.*

4 Minor body damage – repair

Repair of minor scratches

If the scratch is very superficial, and does not penetrate to the metal of the bodywork, repair is very simple. Lightly rub the area of the scratch with a paintwork renovator, or a very fine cutting paste, to remove loose paint from the scratch, and to clear the surrounding bodywork of wax polish. Rinse the area with clean water.

In the case of metallic paint, the most commonly-found scratches are not in the paint, but in the lacquer top coat, and appear white. If care is taken, these can sometimes be rendered less obvious by very careful use of paintwork renovator (which would otherwise not be used on metallic paintwork); otherwise, repair of these scratches can be achieved by applying lacquer with a fine brush.

Apply touch-up paint to the scratch using a fine paint brush; continue to apply fine layers of paint until the surface of the paint in the scratch is level with the surrounding paintwork. Allow the new paint at least two weeks to harden, then blend it into the surrounding paintwork by rubbing the scratch area with a paintwork renovator or a very fine cutting paste. Finally, apply wax polish.

Where the scratch has penetrated right through to the metal of the bodywork, causing the metal to rust, a different repair technique is required. Remove any loose rust from the bottom of the scratch with a penknife, then apply rust-inhibiting paint, to prevent the formation of rust in the future. Using a rubber or nylon applicator, fill the scratch with bodystopper paste. If required, this paste can be mixed with cellulose thinners, to provide a very thin paste which is ideal for filling narrow scratches. Before the stopper-paste in the scratch hardens, wrap a piece of smooth cotton rag around the top of a finger. Dip the finger in cellulose thinners, and quickly sweep it across the surface of the stopper-paste in the scratch; this will ensure that the surface of the stopper-paste is slightly hollowed. The scratch can now be painted over as described earlier in this Section.

Repair of dents

When deep denting of the car's bodywork has taken place, the first task is to pull the dent out, until the affected bodywork almost attains its original shape. There is little point in trying to restore the original shape completely, as the metal in the damaged area will have stretched on impact, and cannot be reshaped fully to its original contour. It is better to bring the level of the dent up to a point which is about 3 mm below the level of the surrounding bodywork. In cases where the dent is very shallow anyway, it is not worth trying to pull it out at all. If the underside of the dent is

accessible, it can be hammered out gently from behind, using a mallet with a wooden or plastic head. Whilst doing this, hold a block of wood firmly against the outside of the panel, to absorb the impact from the hammer blows and thus prevent a large area of the bodywork from being 'belled-out'.

Should the dent be in a section of the bodywork which has a double skin, or some other factor making it inaccessible from behind, a different technique is called for. Drill several small holes through the metal inside the area – particularly in the deeper section. Then screw long self-tapping screws into the holes, just sufficiently for them to gain a good purchase in the metal. Now the dent can be pulled out by pulling on the protruding heads of the screws with a pair of pliers.

The next stage of the repair is the removal of the paint from the damaged area, and from an inch or so of the surrounding 'sound' bodywork. This is accomplished most easily by using a wire brush or abrasive pad on a power drill, although it can be done just as effectively by hand, using sheets of abrasive paper. To complete the preparation for filling, score the surface of the bare metal with a screwdriver or the tang of a file, or alternatively, drill small holes in the affected area. This will provide a really good 'key' for the filler paste.

To complete the repair, see the Section on filling and respraying.

Repair of rust holes or gashes

Remove all paint from the affected area, and from an inch or so of the surrounding 'sound' bodywork, using an abrasive pad or a wire brush on a power drill. If these are not available, a few sheets of abrasive paper will do the job most effectively. With the paint removed, you will be able to judge the severity of the corrosion, and therefore decide whether to renew the whole panel (if this is possible) or to repair the affected area. New body panels are not as expensive as most people think, and it is often quicker and more satisfactory to fit a new panel than to attempt to repair large areas of corrosion.

Remove all fittings from the affected area, except those which will act as a guide to the original shape of the damaged bodywork (e.g. headlight shells etc). Then, using tin snips or a hacksaw blade, remove all loose metal and any other metal badly affected by corrosion. Hammer the edges of the hole inwards, in order to create a slight depression for the filler paste.

Wire-brush the affected area to remove the powdery rust from the surface of the remaining metal. Paint the affected area with rust-inhibiting paint; if the back of the rusted area is accessible, treat this also.

Before filling can take place, it will be necessary to block the hole in some way. This can be achieved by the use of aluminium or plastic mesh, or aluminium tape.

Aluminium or plastic mesh, or glass-fibre matting is probably the best material to use for a large hole. Cut a piece to the approximate size and shape of the hole to be filled, then position it in the hole so that its edges are below the level of the surrounding bodywork. It can be retained in position by several blobs of filler paste around its periphery.

Aluminium tape should be used for small or very narrow holes. Pull a piece off the roll, trim it to the approximate size and shape required, then pull off the backing paper (if used) and stick the tape over the hole; it can be overlapped if the thickness of one piece is insufficient. Burnish down the edges of the tape with the handle of a screwdriver or similar, to ensure that the tape is securely attached to the metal underneath.

Filling and respraying

Before using this Section, see the Sections on dent, deep scratch, rust holes and gash repairs.

Many types of bodyfiller are available, but generally speaking, those proprietary kits which contain a tin of filler paste and a tube of resin hardener are best for this type of repair. A wide, flexible plastic or nylon applicator will be found invaluable for imparting a smooth and well-contoured finish to the surface of the filler.

Mix up a little filler on a clean piece of card or board – measure the hardener carefully (follow the maker's instructions on the pack), otherwise the filler will set too rapidly or too slowly. Using the applicator, apply the filler paste to the prepared area; draw the applicator across the surface of the filler to achieve the correct contour and to level the surface. As soon as a contour that approximates to the correct one is achieved, stop working the paste – if you carry on too long, the paste will become sticky and begin to 'pick-up' on the applicator. Continue to add thin layers of filler paste at 20-minute intervals, until the level of the filler is just proud of the surrounding bodywork.

Once the filler has hardened, the excess can be removed using a metal plane or file. From then on, progressively-finer grades of abrasive paper should be used, starting with a 40-grade production paper, and finishing with a 400-grade wet-and-dry paper. Always wrap the abrasive paper around a flat rubber, cork, or wooden block – otherwise the surface of the filler will not be completely flat. During the smoothing of the filler surface, the wet-and-dry paper should be periodically rinsed in water. This will ensure that a very smooth finish is imparted to the filler at the final stage.

At this stage, the 'dent' should be surrounded by a ring of bare metal, which in turn should be encircled by the finely 'feathered' edge of the good paintwork. Rinse the repair area with clean water, until all of the dust produced by the rubbing-down operation has gone.

Spray the whole area with a light coat of – this will show up any imperfections in the surface of the filler. Repair these imperfections

with fresh filler paste or bodystopper, and once more smooth the surface with abrasive paper. If bodystopper is used, it can be mixed with cellulose thinners, to form a really thin paste which is ideal for filling small holes. Repeat this spray-and-repair procedure until you are satisfied that the surface of the filler, and the feathered edge of the paintwork, are perfect. Clean the repair area with clean water, and allow to dry fully.

The repair area is now ready for final spraying. Paint spraying must be carried out in a warm, dry, windless and dust-free atmosphere. This condition can be created artificially if you have access to a large indoor working area, but if you are forced to work in the open, you will have to pick your day very carefully. If you are working indoors, dousing the floor in the work area with water will help to settle the dust which would otherwise be in the atmosphere. If the repair area is confined to one body panel, mask off the surrounding panels; this will help to minimise the effects of a slight mis-match in paint colours. Bodywork fittings (e.g. chrome strips, door handles etc) will also need to be masked off. Use genuine masking tape, and several thicknesses of newspaper, for the masking operations.

Before commencing to spray, agitate the aerosol can thoroughly, then spray a test area (an old tin, or similar) until the technique is mastered. Cover the repair area with a thick coat of primer; the thickness should be built up using several thin layers of paint, rather than one thick one. Using 400 grade wet-and-dry paper, rub down the surface of the primer until it is really smooth. While doing this, the work area should be thoroughly doused with water, and the wet-and-dry paper periodically rinsed in water. Allow to dry before spraying on more paint.

Spray on the top coat, again building up the thickness by using several thin layers of paint. Start spraying at the top of the repair area, and then, using a side-to-side motion, work downwards until the whole repair area and about 2 inches of the surrounding original paintwork is covered. Remove all masking material 10 to 15 minutes after spraying on the final coat of paint.

Allow the new paint at least two weeks to harden, then, using a paintwork renovator or a very fine cutting paste, blend the edges of the paint into the existing paintwork. Finally, apply wax polish.

Plastic components

With the use of more and more plastic body components by the car manufacturers (e.g. bumpers, spoilers, wings and in some cases major body panels), rectification of more serious damage to such items has become a matter of either entrusting repair work to a specialist in this field, or renewing complete components. Repair of such damage by the DIY owner is not really feasible, owing to the cost of the equipment and materials required

for effecting such repairs. The basic technique involves making a groove along the line of the crack in the plastic, using a rotary burr in a power drill. The damaged part is then welded back together, using a hot air gun to heat up and fuse a plastic filler rod into the groove. Any excess plastic is then removed, and the area rubbed down to a smooth finish. It is important that a filler rod of the correct plastic is used, as body components can be made of a variety of different types (e.g. polycarbonate, ABS, polypropylene).

Damage of a less serious nature (abrasions, minor cracks etc) can be repaired by the DIY owner using a two-part epoxy filler repair. Once mixed in equal, this is used in similar fashion to the bodywork filler used on metal panels. The filler is usually cured in twenty to thirty minutes, ready for sanding and painting.

If the owner is renewing a complete component himself, or if he has repaired it with epoxy filler, he will be left with the problem of finding a suitable paint for finishing which is compatible with the type of plastic used. At one time, the use of a universal paint was not possible, owing to the complex range of plastics encountered in body component applications. Standard paints, generally speaking, will not bond to plastic or rubber satisfactorily, but suitable paints to match any plastic or rubber finish, can be obtained from dealers. However, it is now possible to obtain a plastic body parts finishing kit which consists of a pre-primer treatment, a primer and coloured top coat. Full instructions are normally supplied with a kit, but basically, the method of use is to first apply the pre-primer to the component concerned, and allow it to dry for up to 30 minutes. Then the primer is applied, and left to dry for about an hour before finally applying the special-coloured top coat. The result is a correctly-coloured component, where the paint will flex with the plastic or rubber, a property that standard paint does not normally posses.

5 Major body damage – repair

Where serious damage has occurred, or large areas need renewal due to neglect, it means that complete new panels will need welding-in, and this is best left to professionals. If the damage is due to impact, it will also be necessary to check completely the alignment of the bodyshell, and this can only be carried out accurately by a Renault dealer using special jigs. If the body is left misaligned, it is primarily dangerous, as the car will not handle properly, and secondly, uneven stresses will be imposed on the steering, suspension and possibly transmission, causing abnormal wear, or complete failure, particularly to such items as the tyres.

6.3 Remove the three front bolts from the engine undertray

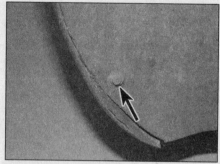

6.4a Remove the two bumper edge screws each side . . .

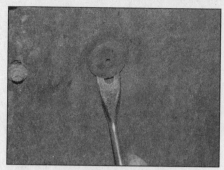

6.4b . . . then prise out the wheel arch liner securing clips . . .

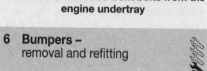

6 Bumpers – removal and refitting

Front bumper

1 On models fitted with front foglights, make sure the ignition is off (take out the keycard).
2 To improve access, jack up the front of the car and support it securely on axle stands (see *Jacking and vehicle support*).
3 Remove three central bolts from the underside of the bumper, where it joins the engine undertray **(see illustration)**.
4 Inside the wheel arch each side, remove the two screws securing the outer edge of the bumper. Prise out the large clips and remove (or just fold back) the front section of the wheel arch liner for access to the bumper-to-

wing bolt, which should also be unscrewed **(see illustrations)**.
5 Prise out the plastic clips and remove the various screws (noting their locations) from the top edge of the bumper, between the headlights **(see illustration)**.
6 Carefully unclip the bumper end from the wing each side.
7 On models with front foglights, reach inside the left-hand side of the bumper and disconnect the main supply wiring plug **(see illustration)**.
8 Pull the bumper ends outwards on each side, lift and unhook the inner 'skin' from between the headlights, then pull forwards to remove it **(see illustration)**. Check as this is done that no wiring is being placed under strain, and release as necessary. On models with headlight washers, the washer tubing must be disconnected before the bumper can

be fully removed – the washer jets themselves are each secured by a single nut.
9 Refitting is a reversal of removal.

Rear bumper

10 To improve access, chock the front wheels, then jack up the rear of the car and support it securely on axle stands (see *Jacking and vehicle support*).
11 Remove the rear light units as described in Chapter 12.
12 Prise out the two plastic clips each side securing the top of the bumper, at the base of each rear light aperture **(see illustrations)**.
13 On models with rear parking sensors, disconnect the wiring plug in the left-hand rear light aperture.
14 Remove two screws inside each wheel arch securing the outer edge of the bumper **(see illustration)**.

6.4c . . . and fold back the liner to access the bumper-to-wing bolt

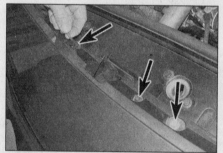

6.5 Prise up the clips and remove the screws from the bumper panel between the headlights

6.7 Disconnect the front foglight supply plug inside the left-hand end of the bumper

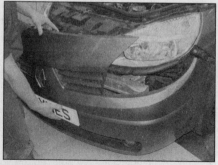

6.8 Unhook the bumper from between the headlights, and remove forwards

6.12a Inside the rear light apertures, there are two clips . . .

6.12b . . . which should be prised out and removed

15 On the underside of the bumper, remove one screw on the right-hand side, and four more bolts across the centre **(see illustrations)**.

16 Unclip the outer cover from the tailgate stop each side, then remove the mounting screw and take off the stops **(see illustrations)**.

17 Remove the two bumper upper bolts each side, below the tailgate sealing strip **(see illustration)**.

18 Pull the bumper ends outwards at each side to release the clips, then remove it **(see illustrations)**.

19 Refitting is a reversal of removal.

7 Radiator grille panel
– removal and refitting

The grille is part of the front bumper assembly, which is removed as described in Section 6. With the bumper removed, it appears that the grille panel can be unclipped and unscrewed as required. For availability of parts, you will need to check with your local Renault dealer.

8 Windscreen cowl panels
– removal and refitting

Removal

1 Open the bonnet (for the best access, we

6.14 Remove the two bumper end screws inside the wheel arch

6.15b . . . and four more screws across the centre

removed the bonnet as described later in this Chapter, but this is definitely not essential).

2 Unclip the foam panel at each end of the rubber weatherseal, then peel up the weatherseal and remove it **(see illustration)**.

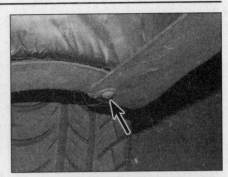

6.15a Remove the outer screw underneath . . .

6.16a Using a small screwdriver . . .

Outer cowl panel

3 To remove the left-hand outer cowl panel (left as seen from the driver's seat), the wiper arms do not have to be removed. The panel is secured by three plastic nuts at the front

6.16b . . . unclip and remove the tailgate bump stop cover . . .

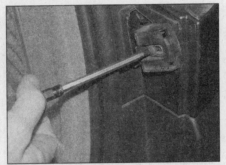

6.16c . . . then remove the mounting screw . . .

6.16d . . . and slide off the bump stop

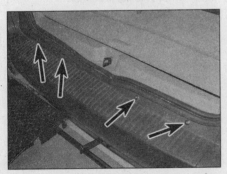

6.17 Remove a total of four screws under the tailgate sealing strip

6.18a Unclip the bumper ends . . .

6.18b . . . and withdraw the bumper from the car

8.2 Peel off the rubber weatherseal

8.3a Unscrew the plastic nuts . . .

8.3b . . . then lift off the outer cowl panel

8.6a Unscrew the remaining plastic nut . . .

8.6b . . . and the end screws

8.7 Unclip the end trim, noting how it is fitted

– remove the nuts, then lift off the panel and remove it **(see illustrations)**.

Lower cowl panel

4 Remove the outer cowl panel as described in the previous paragraph.

5 Remove the windscreen wiper arms as described in Chapter 12.
6 Remove the remaining plastic nut from the right-hand side of the panel, and the Torx screw from each end **(see illustrations)**.

7 Unclip the trim piece from each end of the panel, noting how it is clipped onto its mounting bracket **(see illustration)**.
8 The lower cowl panel is secured by a number of clips to the base of the windscreen – starting at one end, carefully pull the panel down and forwards to remove it **(see illustrations)**.

Metal scuttle panel

9 Remove the cowl panels as described previously in this Section.
10 Access to the panel is easier with the wiper motor and linkage removed as described in Chapter 12, but this is not essential.
11 Remove the two bolts in the centre securing the stay bracket between the scuttle panel and the base of the windscreen. Lift off the stay and remove it **(see illustration)**.
12 Remove the air filter access panel, which is secured by two bolts – one of which is easily seen, with the other tucked inside the panel recess **(see illustrations)**.

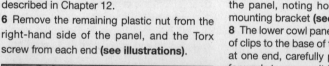

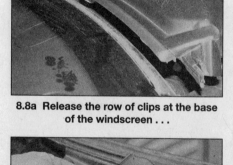

8.8a Release the row of clips at the base of the windscreen . . .

8.8b . . . and withdraw the lower cowl panel

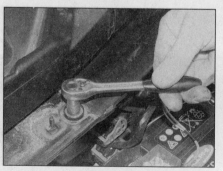

8.11 Unbolt and remove the central stay bracket

8.12a Remove the bolt which is easily seen . . .

8.12b . . . and the one hidden inside the recess . . .

13 Remove the two bolts each side securing the scuttle panel, then ease it from its location (see illustrations).

14 If required, the soundproofing panels fitted below the scuttle panel may also be removed – these are secured by large plastic clips (see illustration).

Refitting

15 Refitting is a reversal of removal.

9 Bonnet – removal and refitting

Removal

1 Have an assistant support the bonnet in the open position.

2 Where applicable, unclip the soundproofing panel from the inside of the bonnet to access the washer tubing.

3 Disconnect the windscreen washer hose at the T-piece, then trace it back to the right-hand hinge (right as seen from the driver's seat), unclipping it from the locations under the bonnet (see illustrations).

4 If the original bonnet is to be refitted, mark the position of the hinges on the bonnet to aid alignment on refitting (a line can be drawn around the hinge using a suitable pen).

5 Remove the bolts securing the bonnet to the hinges (two bolts at each side), then carefully withdraw the bonnet from the car (see illustration).

Refitting

6 Refitting is a reversal of removal, bearing in mind the following points:

   a) *Where applicable, align the hinges with the marks made on the bonnet before removal.*

   b) *Close the bonnet (carefully, in case it fouls the surrounding bodywork), and check the alignment with the surrounding body panels.*

   c) *If necessary, the alignment of the bonnet can be adjusted by altering the position of the bonnet on the hinges, using the elongated holes provided.*

10 Bonnet lock components – removal and refitting

Lock assembly

Removal

1 Open the bonnet.

2 At the rear of the bonnet crossmember ('slam panel'), trace the bonnet release cable to the rectangular joining section. Unclip the plastic cover, then prise off the ball fitting and separate the cable sections (see illustrations).

3 Note and mark the position of the lock

8.12c . . . then withdraw the air filter access panel

8.13b . . . and withdraw the metal scuttle panel

on the panel, to aid correct alignment when refitting.

4 Unscrew the two securing bolts (see illustration), then remove the lock assembly

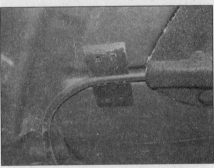

9.3a At the right-hand side, unclip the washer tubing from the bonnet recess . . .

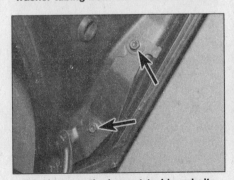

9.5 Unscrew the bonnet-to-hinge bolts

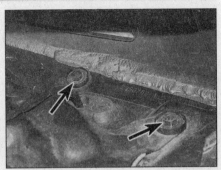

8.13a Remove the two bolts each side . . .

8.14 The soundproofing panels are secured with large plastic clips

from below the panel, unclipping the release cable as necessary.

Refitting

5 Refitting is a reversal of removal, but align

9.3b . . . and from the support clip by the hinge

10.2a Unclip the cover from the bonnet cable joiner . . .

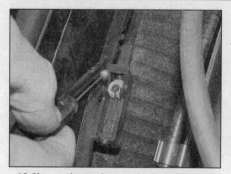

10.2b . . . then prise up the ball fitting to separate the cable

10.4 Bonnet lock securing bolts

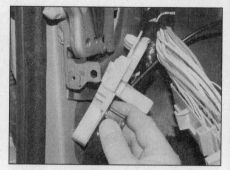

10.8a Unclip the bonnet release lever mounting bracket . . .

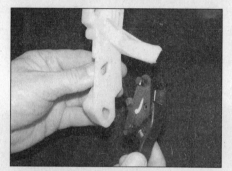

10.8b . . . then remove the lever itself

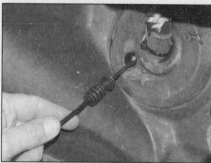
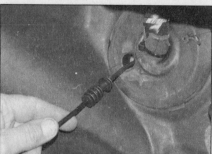
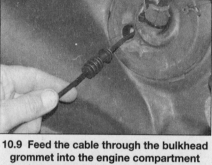

10.9 Feed the cable through the bulkhead grommet into the engine compartment

8 Unclip the lever mounting bracket from the facia crossmember, then unclip the bonnet release lever from the mounting bracket **(see illustrations)**.

9 Unhook the cable end and outer from the release lever, then feed the cable through the bulkhead grommet into the engine compartment **(see illustration)**.

10 Separate the cable sections as described in paragraph 2. Trace the cable back from the joining section, noting its routing and releasing it from all clips and ties. Remove the cable from the engine compartment.

Refitting

11 Refitting is a reversal of removal, but ensure that the bulkhead grommet is securely located in the bulkhead. Route the cable as noted during removal. Make sure that the cable sections are securely joined, and that the cable is working correctly before closing the bonnet.

Release catch

Removal

12 The release catch is secured to the bonnet crossmember by two Torx screws. Open the bonnet and remove the screws, then feed the release handle through the radiator grille and remove it **(see illustrations)**.

Refitting

13 Refitting is a reversal of removal.

10.12a Remove the bonnet release catch securing screws . . .

10.12b . . . and take off the release handle

the assembly with the marks made on the panel before removal.

6 Make sure that the cable sections are securely joined before closing the bonnet.

Lock release cable/lever

Removal

7 Remove the glovebox as described in Section 23.

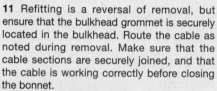

11 Doors –
removal and refitting

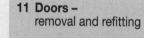

Removal

1 To remove a door, open it fully, and support it under its lower edge on blocks covered with pads of rag. Alternatively, have an assistant on hand to support the door.

2 Disconnect the battery negative lead.

3 Disconnect the door wiring connector by swinging the securing catch upwards, then pull the connector from its socket **(see illustrations)**.

4 Have an assistant support the door, then unscrew the upper and lower hinge nuts and withdraw it from the car **(see illustrations)**.

11.3a Swing the locking catch upwards . . .

11.3b . . . and pull out the door wiring connector

Refitting

5 Refitting is a reversal of removal. Tighten the hinge nuts to the specified torque, and check the operation of the door. If the same doors are refitted, no adjustment should be required.

Adjustment

6 Door closure may be most easily adjusted by altering the position of the lock striker on the body pillar **(see illustration)**.

7 The hinges are secured in position with a nut and bolt, and their position can be adjusted if required **(see illustration)**.

---

12 Door handle and lock components – removal and refitting

Door interior handle

1 Prise out the trim cover, and remove the single screw securing the door interior handle to the door **(see illustrations)**.

2 Prise out the handle and unclip the operating cable from the rear of it. Remove the handle from the door **(see illustrations)**.

3 Refitting is a reversal of removal.

Front door lock cylinder/trim

4 Open the door, and prise out the trim cap from the back edge **(see illustration)**.

5 Release the door lock cylinder retaining catch by inserting a hooked piece of wire into the hole, and pulling the catch outwards **(see illustrations)**.

11.4a Unscrew the door upper . . .

11.6 Door lock striker Torx bolts

6 Protect the paint on the outside of the door, then prise out the door lock cylinder and remove it **(see illustrations)**.

7 Refitting is a reversal of removal. Re-engage the door lock cylinder catch on completion by pushing it forwards.

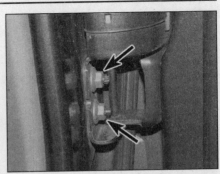

11.4b . . . and lower hinge nuts

11.7 Loosen the hinge nut and bolt to adjust their position

Door exterior handle

8 On models with 'hands-free' locking (identifiable by the pushbutton on the handle), remove the door trim panel as described in Section 13 until access is gained to the inside

12.1a Prise out the trim cover . . .

12.1b . . . and remove the screw behind it

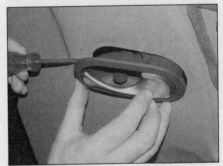

12.2a Prise out the handle . . .

12.2b . . . then unclip the operating cable from it

12.4 Prise out the trim cap at the rear of the door

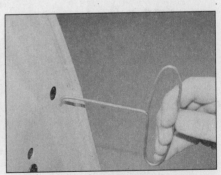

12.5a Insert a piece of hooked wire into the hole . . .

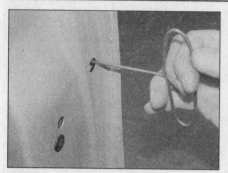

12.5b . . . and pull outwards to disengage the lock barrel

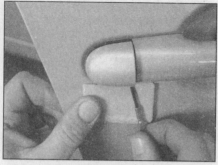

12.6a Prise out the lock barrel, protecting the paint with card or tape . . .

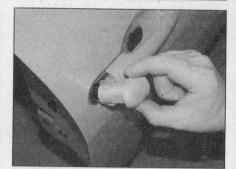

12.6b . . . and withdraw the lock barrel from the door

12.8a Prise out the plastic clips . . .

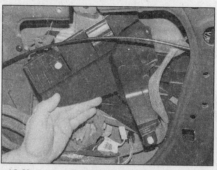

12.8b . . . and withdraw the plastic cover panel from inside the door

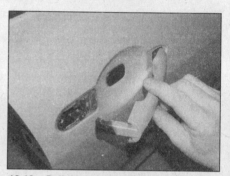

12.10a Pull the handle out at the rear, then unhook it at the front

of the handle. Release the two clips, and withdraw the plastic panel from inside the door **(see illustrations)**. Disconnect the wiring plug from the handle module.

9 Remove the lock barrel or handle rear trim piece as described in paragraphs 4 to 6.

10 Pull the rear end of the handle outwards, and unhook it at the front. On models with 'hands-free' locking, take care not to damage the wiring plug as the handle is withdrawn. Recover the rubber gasket from the door, and check its condition – fit a new one if necessary,

to prevent water getting into the door **(see illustrations)**.

11 Refitting is a reversal of removal. Refit the lock barrel/trim piece as described in paragraph 7. Where applicable, refit the door trim panel as described in Section 13.

Door lock

12 Remove the exterior handle as described previously in this Section.

13 Remove the door inner trim panel as described in Section 13, and unclip the large round cover cap at the rear of the panel Disconnect the door lock wiring plug with the help of a small screwdriver **(see illustrations)**.

14 Unscrew the three lock securing screws from the rear edge of the door **(see illustration)**.

15 From outside, unclip the inner part of the door handle, then unclip the operating cable from the door interior handle, and remove

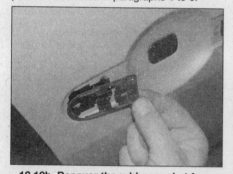

12.10b Recover the rubber gasket from the door

12.13a Prise out the round cover cap from the door . . .

12.13b . . . for access to disconnect the door lock wiring plug

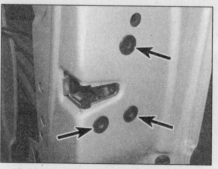

12.14 Remove the three lock securing screws

12.15a Unclip the inner part of the door handle . . .

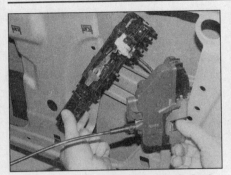

12.15b . . . then remove the handle/lock assembly from the door

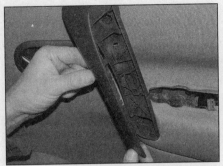

13.3a Prise off the cover from the door pull handle . . .

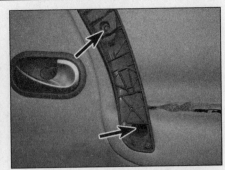

13.3b . . . and remove the two screws inside

the lock/handle assembly from the door **(see illustrations)**.

16 Refitting is a reversal of removal. Refit the exterior handle as described previously. Where applicable, refit the door trim panel as described in Section 13.

Central locking components

17 Refer to Section 16.

13 Door trim panel – removal and refitting

Note: *Removing the complete door trim panel also means removing the door glass. However, to access the door internal components, it may be sufficient to follow this procedure to the point where the fabric-covered section of the trim panel can be swung upwards.*

1 Disconnect the battery negative lead, and move the lead away from the battery (see *Disconnecting the battery*).

Front door

2 Remove the electric window switch and door mirror switch as described in Chapter 12.
3 Prise off the cover from the door pull handle, then remove the two screws inside **(see illustrations)**.
4 Where applicable, open the armrest storage bins, prise out the plastic retaining clip inside, then prise up and lift out the storage bin.
5 Work carefully around the edge of the trimmed upper panel, releasing the clips securing it to the main panel, and fold it down – the panel is secured at the base by two plastic straps **(see illustrations)**.
6 Remove the door interior handle as described in Section 12.

7 Where applicable, prise out and disconnect the footwell illumination light at the base of the door **(see illustrations)**.
8 The trim panel is secured by three screws – one in the centre, and two at the bottom. Remove the screws, then pull the panel outwards and upwards to release it from the door. Disconnect the wiring from the door speaker, then unclip the wiring harness from the back of the trim panel, and it can be removed **(see illustrations)**.
9 Refitting is a reversal of removal.

Rear door

10 Remove the electric window switch panel as described in Chapter 12. On models with manual window winders, note the position of the window winder handle with the window fully open, then pull the handle firmly to release it **(see illustration)**.

13.5a Unclip the trimmed panel . . .

13.5b . . . and fold it down

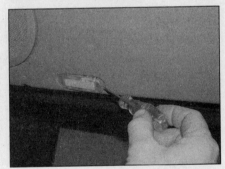

13.7a At the base of the door, prise out . . .

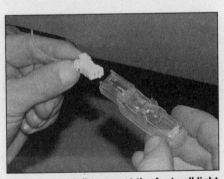

13.7b . . . and disconnect the footwell light

13.8a Remove the trim panel screw in the centre . . .

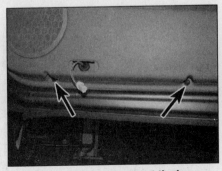

13.8b . . . and two more at the base

13.8c Unclip the panel from the door . . .

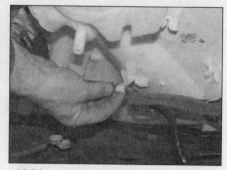

13.8d . . . then unclip the wiring harness from the back . . .

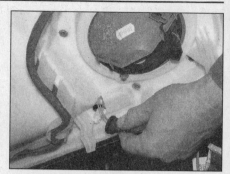

13.8e . . . and pull through the footwell light

13.10 On models with manual rear windows, pull off the handle

13.12a Unclip the trimmed panel, and fold it down . . .

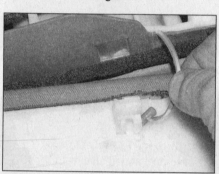

13.12b . . . or unhook the two plastic straps and remove it

11 Remove the door interior handle as described in Section 12.

12 Work carefully around the edge of the trimmed upper panel, releasing the clips securing it to the main panel, and fold it down – the panel is secured at the base by two plastic straps (these straps can be unhooked and the panel removed) **(see illustrations)**.

13 Where applicable, prise out and disconnect the footwell illumination light at the base of the door. Also remove the single trim panel screw at the bottom **(see illustrations)**.

14 Remove the remaining mounting bolt in the centre of the trim panel, then lift the panel off the door. Disconnect the wiring from the door speaker, then unclip the wiring harness from the back of the trim panel, and it can be removed **(see illustrations)**.

13.13a Prise out the footwell light . . .

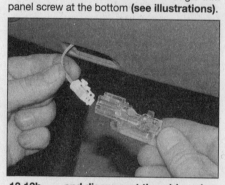

13.13b . . . and disconnect the wiring plug

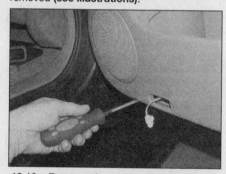

13.13c Remove the trim panel screw from the base of the door

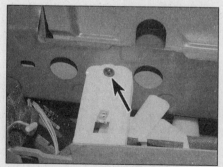

13.14a Remove the trim panel screw in the centre . . .

13.14b . . . then unclip the panel from the door . . .

13.14c . . . and release the wiring harness from the back

14.2 Prise up and remove the weatherstrip from the door

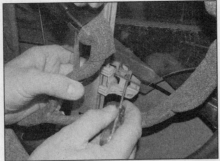

14.4 Release the glass securing clip with a small screwdriver

14.5a Unclip the inner plastic frame trim

14.5b Unclip the metal outer frame

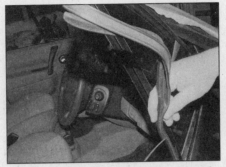

14.5c Pull out the rubber guide channel

14.6 Lift the sliding glass out of the door

15 Refitting is a reversal of removal.

14 Door window glass and motor – removal and refitting

Front door

Door sliding glass

1 Remove the door trim panel, as described in the previous Section.

2 Carefully prise up and remove the weatherstrip from the outside top edge of the door. Make sure the door is fully open, otherwise the strip will hang up on the base of the door mirror (see illustration).

3 Temporarily refit the window switch and battery, and position the window glass so that the green plastic window securing clip

is visible. Disconnect the battery and switch when this is done.

4 Release the glass securing clip by depressing the catch with a small screwdriver, while an assistant pulls gently upwards on the glass (see illustration).

5 Unclip and detach the plastic inner frame trim from the door. Also unclip the metal outer frame – it is not necessary to remove the frame completely. Pull out the rubber guide channel from the front of the frame, noting how it is fitted (see illustrations).

6 With the frame free, lift the glass up and out of the door (see illustration).

7 Refitting is a reversal of removal. Ensure that the glass securing clip is fully engaged.

Door fixed glass

8 Remove the sliding glass as described previously in this Section.

9 Remove the screw at the top securing the

fixed glass inner frame (see illustration).

10 Unclip and remove the fixed glass inner frame (see illustration).

11 Carefully prise up and remove the trim strip from the inside top edge of the door (see illustration).

12 Remove the fixed glass upright bolt from the door panel (approximately 10 cm below the base of the upright) (see illustration).

13 Unclip the window outer frame along its whole length, and remove the frame with the fixed glass – turn the glass through 90° as it is withdrawn from the door, to clear the bracket on the upright (see illustrations). Once removed, the fixed glass can be separated from the frame as required.

14 Refitting is a reversal of removal. Ensure that the anti-rattle foam pads are fitted to the fixed glass on the outer side, between the glass and the door panel.

14.9 Remove the frame screw on the outside . . .

14.10 . . . then unclip and remove the inner frame from the fixed glass

14.11 Unclip the trim strip from the inside

14.12 Remove the fixed glass upright mounting bolt

14.13a Unclip the window outer metal frame completely . . .

14.13b . . . then lift out the fixed glass, turning it through 90°

14.19a Disconnect the motor wiring plug . . .

14.19b . . . then remove the two screws . . .

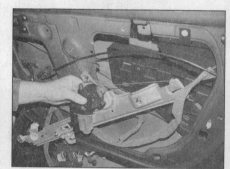

14.19c . . . and withdraw the window motor/regulator from the door

Window motor

15 Remove the door trim panel, as described in the previous Section.

16 Temporarily refit the window switch and battery, and position the window glass so that the green plastic window securing clip is visible. Disconnect the battery and switch when this is done.

17 Release the glass securing clip by depressing the catch with a small screwdriver,

while an assistant pulls gently upwards on the glass (refer to illustration 14.4).

18 Slide the glass to the top of the door frame, and secure it there using tape.

19 Disconnect the window motor wiring plug, then unscrew the two mounting screws and withdraw the motor from the door (see illustrations).

20 Refitting is a reversal of removal. On completion, initialise the motor (to restore the 'one-touch' operation) as follows. Raise the glass, holding the button for two further seconds once it has closed, then lower it fully, again holding the button for two seconds once it has opened.

Rear door

Sliding glass

21 Remove the door trim panel, as described in the previous Section.

22 Carefully prise up and remove the weatherstrip from the outside top edge of the door (see illustration).

23 Position the window glass so that the white plastic window securing clip is visible (see illustration). On models with electric rear windows, temporarily refit the window switch and battery to achieve this - disconnect the battery and switch on completion.

24 Remove the two screws securing the window guide channel at the rear of the door, then depress the upper tab on the guide channel to release and remove it (see illustrations).

25 Release the glass securing clip by depressing the catch with a small screwdriver,

14.22 Unclip the outer weatherstrip from the rear door

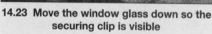

14.23 Move the window glass down so the securing clip is visible

14.24a Remove the screw on the front . . .

14.24b . . . and rear of the door . . .

14.24c ... then depress and release the upper tab ...

14.24d ... and remove the window rear guide channel

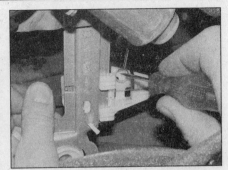

14.25 Depress and release the glass securing clip ...

14.26 ... then withdraw the rear glass from the door

14.29 Disconnect the rear window motor wiring plug

14.30a Remove the lower mounting nut ...

while an assistant pulls gently upwards on the glass **(see illustration)**.

26 Tilt the window glass forwards, and withdraw it upwards from the door **(see illustration)**.

27 Refitting is a reversal of removal.

Window motor

28 Remove the glass as described previously.

29 Disconnect the motor wiring plug **(see illustration)**.

30 Remove the lower mounting nut, then

withdraw the motor/regulator assembly from the door **(see illustrations)**. Note that the upper mounting screw was removed during door trim panel removal.

31 Refitting is a reversal of removal.

15 Tailgate and related components – removal and refitting

Tailgate

1 Disconnect the battery negative lead, and move the lead away from the battery (see *Disconnecting the battery*).

2 Remove the tailgate main trim panel, which is secured by four screws (one inside each tailgate 'handle', one either side at the top) and a number of clips. There is also a cover panel fitted over the lock, which must be unclipped **(see illustrations)**.

14.30b ...then withdraw the motor assembly from the door

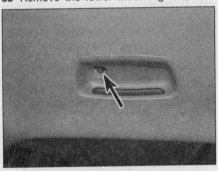

15.2a Remove the tailgate trim panel screw inside each handle ...

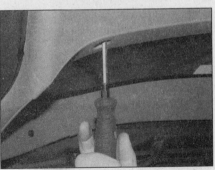

15.2b ... and the one each side, at the top ...

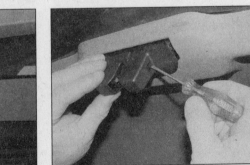

15.2c ... then unclip the lock cover ...

15.2d ... and remove the trim panel

15.3 Unclip the tailgate glass top panel

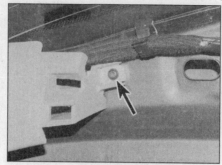

15.5a Remove the upper screw . . .

15.5b . . . then unclip the window side trim panels

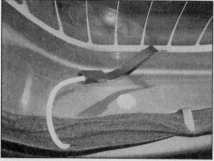

15.7 Disconnect the heated rear window wiring

15.8 Disconnect the number plate light supply wiring plug

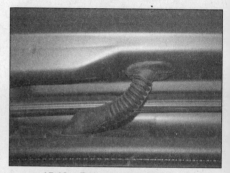

15.10a Release the wiring . . .

3 Prise up and unclip the tailgate window surround top panel **(see illustration)**.
4 On models with the optional opening rear glass, prise out the spring clips from each end of the glass support struts, then pull them from the ball fittings on the tailgate.
5 Remove the screw at the top, and unclip the tailgate glass side trim panels **(see illustrations)**.
6 Remove the high-level brake light as described in Chapter 12. Feed the wiring plug and tailgate washer hose back into the tailgate.
7 Disconnect the wiring from the heated rear window, tailgate wiper motor, central locking motor, and tailgate glass lock (where applicable) referring where necessary to the relevant removal procedures **(see illustration)**. Release the wiring loom from any securing clips.
8 Disconnect the wiring plug from the harness

which supplies the number plate lights **(see illustration)**.
9 Unclip the wiring from its support clips and ties, then feed it up to the top of the tailgate, noting its routing.

> **HAYNES HiNT** *If string is tied to the end of the loom, it can be un-tied once the wiring is pulled through, and left in place to pull the wiring back through on refitting.*

10 Release the wiring and washer tube grommets at the top of the tailgate, and pull the wiring clear **(see illustrations)**.
11 Have an assistant support the tailgate, then prise out the spring clips and pull the top ends of the support struts from the ball fittings.
12 Again with the help of an assistant,

unscrew the hinge bolts and lift the tailgate clear of the car **(see illustration)**.
13 Refitting is a reversal of removal.

Support struts

14 Remove the rear lights as described in Chapter 12.
15 Open the tailgate, and have an assistant support it in the fully-open position.
16 Disconnect the support strut from the tailgate by prising out the securing clip using a small screwdriver, then pull the end of the strut off the ball fitting **(see illustration)**. Repeat the procedure for the clip securing the strut to the body, and withdraw the strut from the car.
17 Refitting is a reversal of removal.

Tailgate outer trim panel

18 Remove the main trim panel as described in paragraph 2.

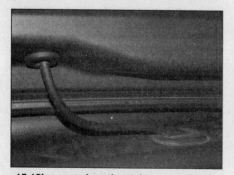

15.10b . . . and washer tube grommets at the top

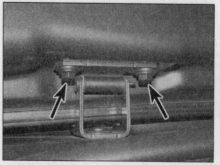

15.12 Unscrew the tailgate hinge bolts

15.16 Prise out the strut spring clip with a small screwdriver

15.23 Remove the tailgate lock mounting screws

15.24 Release the clip, and ease the lock out of the tailgate

15.25 Disconnect the wiring plug from the lock

19 Disconnect the number plate wiring harness plug as described in paragraph 8.
20 The outer trim panel is secured by two screws and a bead of mastic. Remove the two screws from inside, then carefully prise the trim panel off from outside. Prise out the grommets at either end of the number plate wiring harness.
21 Refitting is a reversal of removal. Clean all mastic off the panel and tailgate, then apply a fresh bead before offering the panel into position.

Tailgate lock

22 Remove the main trim panel as described in paragraph 2.
23 Remove the two tailgate lock mounting screws **(see illustration)**.
24 Release the lock retaining clip, and ease the lock out of the tailgate **(see illustration)**.
25 Disconnect the wiring plug from the lock, and remove it completely **(see illustration)**.
26 Refitting is a reversal of removal.

Tailgate release switch

27 Open the tailgate. Protect the paint surrounding the switch using masking tape. Using a screwdriver, carefully prise the switch from its location **(see illustration)**.
28 Disconnect the wiring plug, and remove the switch **(see illustration)**.
29 Refitting is a reversal of removal.

Glass release switch

30 On models with the optional opening tailgate glass, the release switch is next to the tailgate release switch, and can be removed as described in paragraphs 27 and 28.

Opening glass lock

31 Remove the main trim panel as described in paragraph 2.
32 Disconnect the wiring plug from the glass lock motor.
33 Remove the two motor mounting screws, and remove the motor from the tailgate.
34 The glass lock striker may be removed after unscrewing the two mounting bolts – it is advisable to mark its position on the glass before removal.
35 Refitting is a reversal of removal.

Opening glass

36 Open the tailgate and remove the two

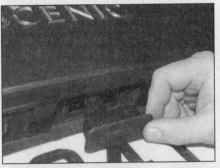

15.27 Prise out the tailgate release switch . . .

15.28 . . . and disconnect the wiring plug

screws securing the side trim panels on either side of the glass.
37 Remove the other tailgate trim panels as described in paragraphs 2 to 5.
38 On the inside of the top corners of the tailgate, remove the two bolts securing the end trim panels. Similarly, remove the two bolts securing these panels to the top corner of the rear bodywork.
39 Unscrew the bolt securing the heated rear window wiring to the top of the tailgate.
40 Have an assistant support the glass, then remove the hinge screw at the top and remove it from the car.
41 Refitting is a reversal of removal.

16 Central locking components – general information

The central locking is operated by radio

17.3 Remove the door mirror inner mounting screw

frequency and is controlled by the interior multiplex unit, which also holds a number of relays. This unit is located under the left-hand side of the facia (as seen from the driver's seat). If there is a fault with this unit, it will require checking with Renault diagnostic equipment.

The door lock motors and switches are an integral part of the lock assemblies – see Sections 12 and 15 of this Chapter.

17 Mirrors – removal, refitting and glass renewal

Door mirror

1 On models with electric mirrors, disconnect the battery negative lead, and move the lead away from the battery (see *Disconnecting the battery*).
2 Remove the mirror shell as described in paragraphs 9 and 10.
3 With the door open, remove the mirror inner mounting screw on the inside of the door **(see illustration)**.
4 Support the mirror, then remove the mirror outer retaining screw and withdraw the mirror from the door. Where applicable, disconnect the wiring plug from it **(see illustrations)**.
5 Refitting is a reversal of removal.

Glass renewal

6 Using a flat-bladed tool, carefully prise behind the top edge of the mirror glass. Support the glass, lever the tool forwards and the mirror glass will unclip from the mirror

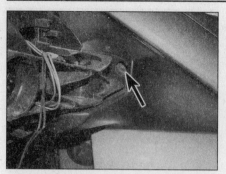

17.4a Remove the mirror outer mounting screw . . .

17.4b . . . then withdraw the mirror from the door . . .

17.4c . . . and disconnect the wiring plug

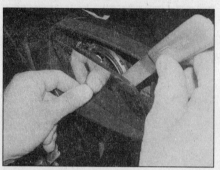

17.6a Prise behind the mirror glass with a flat-bladed tool . . .

17.6b . . . and unclip the glass from the mirror

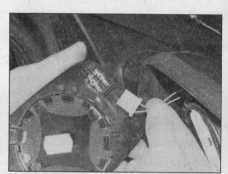

17.7 Disconnect the heating element wiring plug from the glass

assembly **(see illustrations)**. Take care not to drop the mirror glass as the clip is released.

7 Where applicable, disconnect the wiring connectors from the rear of the mirror glass **(see illustration)**.

8 To refit the glass, press the glass into

position until it engages securely, taking care not to damage the glass.

Shell renewal

9 Remove the mirror glass as described previously in this Section.

10 Using a small screwdriver, release the four retaining tabs, then carefully prise the shell from the mirror **(see illustrations)**.

11 Refitting is a reversal of removal.

Interior mirror

12 Using a small screwdriver, unclip the front section of trim surrounding the mirror base **(see illustrations)**.

13 Slide the rear section of trim towards the windscreen, and remove it **(see illustration)**.

14 Disconnect the wiring plugs behind the mirror – the number of these will depend on equipment level **(see illustrations)**.

15 The interior mirror is very firmly attached, but can be removed by sliding it towards the windscreen **(see illustration)**. Note, however, that considerable effort may be required, and care should be taken not to damage the light/rain sensor when the mirror is released.

16 Refitting is a reversal of removal.

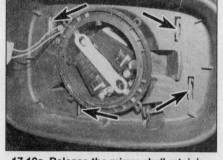

17.10a Release the mirror shell retaining tabs . . .

17.10b . . . then unclip and remove it from the mirror

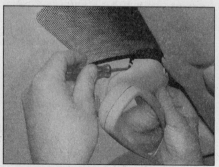

17.12a Using a small screwdriver, unclip . . .

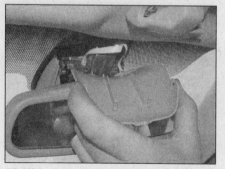

17.12b . . . and remove the front section of trim from the mirror

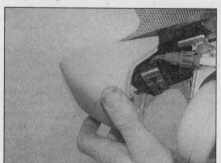

17.13 Slide the rear section of trim towards the windscreen

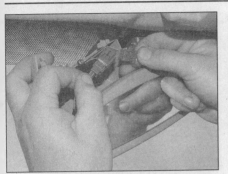

17.14a Disconnect the wiring plugs from the interior temperature sensor . . .

17.14b . . . and from the light/rain sensor

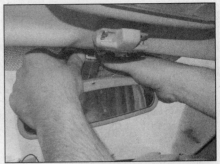

17.15 Slide the mirror towards the screen to remove it

17.17 Unclip the panel from the mirror recess

17.18a Use a screwdriver to unhook the clip, with a finger to depress it . . .

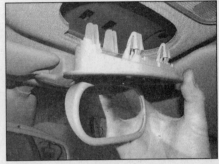

17.18b . . . and remove the mirror from the headlining

Child minder mirror

17 Fold the mirror open, then prise out the panel inside the mirror recess **(see illustration)**.

18 Release the mirror retaining tabs using a small screwdriver and finger, then carefully prise/pull the mirror from the headlining **(see illustrations)**.

19 Refitting is a reversal of removal.

18 Windscreen, tailgate and rear side glass – general information

These areas of glass are secured by the tight fit of the weatherseal in the body aperture, and are bonded in position with a special adhesive. Renewal of such fixed glass is a difficult, messy and time-consuming task, which is considered beyond the scope of the home mechanic. It is difficult, unless one has plenty of practice, to obtain a secure, waterproof fit. Furthermore, the task carries a high risk of breakage; this applies especially to the laminated glass windscreen. In view of this, owners are strongly advised to have this sort of work carried out by one of the many specialist windscreen fitters.

19 Sunroof components – removal and refitting

The sunroof is a complex piece of equipment, consisting of a large number of components. It is strongly recommended that the sunroof mechanism is not disturbed unless absolutely necessary. If the sunroof mechanism is faulty, or requires overhaul, consult a Renault dealer for advice. Even removing the sunroof motor requires that the headlining be taken down, which is not a job to be taken on lightly.

In the event of failure, it may be possible to close the sunroof using a 6 mm Allen key in the hole provided below the motor, after removing the sunroof switch and/or interior light.

Sunroof switch removal and refitting is described in Chapter 12.

The rear glass section of the sunroof is bonded in position, and its renewal should only be attempted by a Renault dealer or windscreen specialist – see Section 18.

20 Body exterior fittings – removal and refitting

Wheel arch liners

1 Various plastic shields may be fitted to the wheel arches and various engine components to protect against road dirt and moisture.

2 The shields are secured by a combination of plastic clips, screws, or flat metal nuts. Removal and refitting should be self-evident **(see illustrations)**. Take particular care not to break plastic clips when removing them – renew where necessary.

Rubbing strips

Note: *Take care not to damage the paintwork when removing the rubbing strips.*

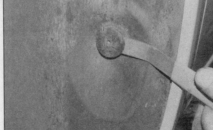

20.2a The wheel arch liners may be secured by plastic clips . . .

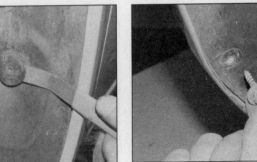

20.2b . . . or screws, which may also secure the bumper

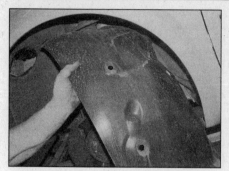

20.2c The front wheel arch liners are removed in two sections – rear . . .

20.2d . . . and front, as required

20.2e The rear wheel arch liners are removed in one piece

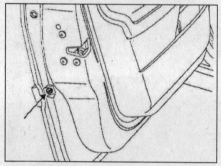

20.3 Remove the cover from the door's back edge to access the securing clip

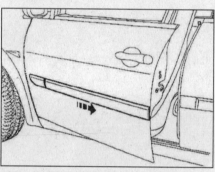

20.4 Slide the rubbing strip rearwards to remove it

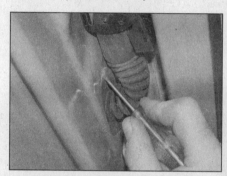

20.6a Unclip the rear door wiring grommet . . .

Front door

3 Open the door, and remove the plastic cover from the rear edge of the door to expose the rubbing strip securing clip **(see illustration)**. Depress the locking clip with a small screwdriver.
4 Working outside the door, unclip the end of the rubbing strip and slide it towards the rear of the door **(see illustration)**.
5 When refitting a rubbing strip, first pull out the locking clip fitted at the rear of the door. Align the clips in the strip with the corresponding holes in the door. Push the strip towards the front of the door to engage the holes. Refit the plastic cover to the door edge on completion.

Rear door

6 Open the front door first, then taking care

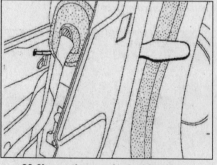

20.6b . . . then probe inside for the securing clip, and release it

Note: Illustration shows door trim panel removed

not to damage the paint, prise the front edge of the strip and slide it forwards to remove **(see illustrations)**.
7 When refitting a rubbing strip, first pull out the locking clips slightly.

Badges

8 The various badges may be secured with adhesives. To remove them, either soften the adhesive using a hot-air gun or hairdryer (taking care to avoid damage to the paintwork), or separate the badge from the body by 'sawing' through the adhesive using a length of nylon cord. **Note:** *Some badges are located by pegs in plastic grommets – these will need to be carefully prised from the bodywork.*
9 Clean off all traces of adhesive using white spirit, then wash the area with warm soapy water to remove all traces of spirit, and allow to dry. Ensure that the surface to which the

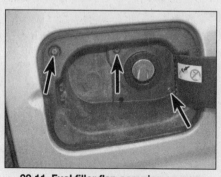

20.11 Fuel filler flap securing screws (arrowed)

new badge is to be fastened is completely clean, and free from grease and dirt.
10 Use the hot-air gun to soften the adhesive on the new badge, then press it firmly into position.

Fuel filler flap

11 Open the filler flap, then remove the three screws inside **(see illustration)**.
12 Unclip the inner section around the edges, and withdraw slightly **(see illustration)**.
13 Reach in behind the inner section, and unclip the guide tube for the lock operating rod. Remove the filler flap from the car **(see illustrations)**.
14 Refitting is a reversal of removal.

Filler flap release solenoid

15 Remove the boot side trim panel as described in Section 23.

20.12 Unclip the flap inner section around the edges

16 Remove the right-hand rear wheel arch liner as described previously in this Section.
17 Remove the single large nut inside the wheel arch which secures the solenoid **(see illustration)**.
18 Remove the fuel filler flap as described previously in this Section. Unclip the rear cover panel from the filler flap, then disconnect the wiring plug and withdraw the solenoid **(see illustration)**.
19 Refitting is a reversal of removal.

21 Seats –
removal and refitting

Front seat

⚠ **Warning: Disconnect the battery negative lead (see Disconnecting the battery), then wait for five minutes before proceeding. If this waiting period is not observed, there is danger of activating the side airbags and seat belt tensioners.**

1 Using a small screwdriver in the hole provided, depress the catch to release the seat belt from the buckle on the outside of the seat **(see illustration)**.
2 Slide the seat forwards, and unscrew the seat mounting bolt at the rear of each runner **(see illustration)**.
3 Slide the seat fully to the rear, and unscrew the seat mounting bolts at the front ends of the runners **(see illustration)**.
4 Lift the front of the seat, then swing the locking lever to the side and disconnect the seat wiring plug **(see illustration)**.
5 The seat is a very heavy assembly – take care when lifting it from the car **(see illustration)**. Also, be careful that the seat runners do not scratch any trim or paintwork as the seat is removed. Remember that the seat contains at least one airbag – handle it gently.
6 Refitting is a reversal of removal, noting the following points:
  a) Reconnect the seat wiring plug securely before reconnecting the battery.
  b) Tighten the mounting bolts to the specified torque, starting with the inner bolts.

20.13a Unclip the solenoid operating rod guide tube . . .

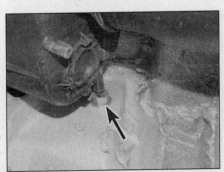

20.17 Remove the nut inside the wheel arch . . .

Rear seats (Scénic)

7 First ensure that the headrest is pushed fully downwards, and unfasten/unclip the seat belt.
8 Lift the handle at the side of the backrest to

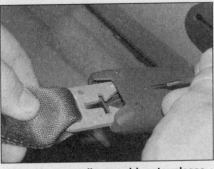

21.1 Use a small screwdriver to release the seat belt buckle

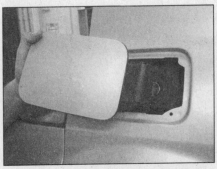

20.13b . . . and withdraw the filler flap

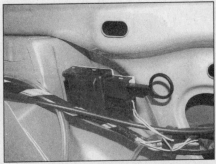

20.18 . . . then disconnect the wiring plug and remove the solenoid

fold the backrest down, then use the handle at the front to slide the seat fully to the rear **(see illustration)**.
9 Release the catch behind the seat at the base, and lift it to the vertical position, where it should lock **(see illustration)**.

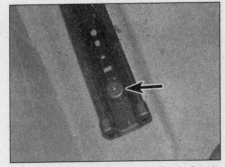

21.2 Unscrew the seat mounting bolts at the rear . . .

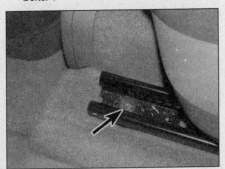

21.3 . . . and at the front

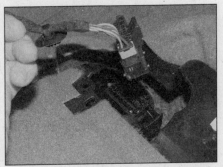

21.4 Disconnect the seat wiring plug underneath

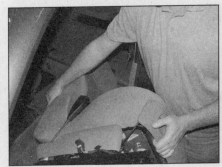

21.5 Lift out the seat

21.8 Lift the side handle and fold the seat

21.9 Release the catch at the base of the seat, and swing it forwards

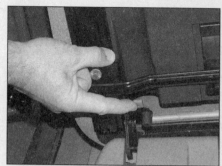

21.10a Release the hinge catch (red tab) . . .

21.10b . . . and lift the seat out

21.13a Fold the seat backrest down . . .

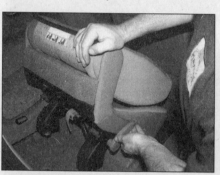

21.13b . . . then use the belt or handle at the seat base to lift it vertical

10 Release the hinge catches at the base of the seat, then lift it out of the car **(see illustrations)**.

11 Refitting is a reversal of removal, noting the following points:

a) With the seat upside-down, check that the front mounting bar is in contact with the end stop in the centre of the seat. If not, operate the seat release handle at the front, and slide the bar up to the stop.

b) Fit the feet at the front of the seat into the recesses in the car floor, and they should lock. Release the hinge catches, lower the seat almost to the floor, then let it go so that it locates under its own weight. Adjust the backrest as required.

c) Ensure that the seat is securely locked in position before anyone uses it.

Centre-row seats (Grand Scénic)

12 First ensure that the headrest is pushed fully downwards, and unfasten/unclip the seat belt.

13 Lift the handle at the side of the backrest to fold the backrest down, then use the belt at the seat base or the handle at the outer side to lift the seat vertical, where it should lock **(see illustrations)**.

14 Pull the bar at the base of the seat to release the catch, then lift it out of the car **(see illustrations)**.

15 Refitting is a reversal of removal, noting the following points:

a) Fit the feet at the front of the seat into the recesses in the car floor, and they should lock. Lower the seat almost to the floor, then let it go so that it locates under its own weight. Adjust the backrest as required.

b) Ensure that the seat is securely locked in position before anyone uses it.

Third-row seats (Grand Scénic)

16 With both seats initially folded flat, first unclip the two panels fitted between the seats **(see illustrations)**.

17 Remove the two front bolts, and three

21.14a Pull the bar at the back to release the seat . . .

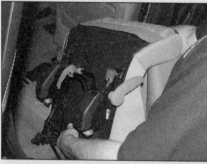

21.14b . . . and lift it from the car

21.16a Unclip and remove the rear panel (over the handbrake release lever) . . .

21.16b . . . and the front panel (over the seat belt buckles)

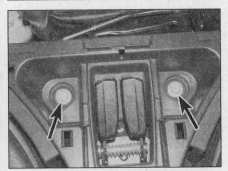

21.17a Remove the two front bolts . . .

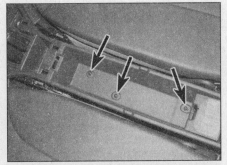

21.17b . . . and three rear screws . . .

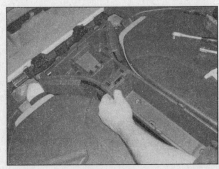

21.17c . . . then lift out the centre 'tray'

21.18a Remove the securing bolt . . .

21.18b . . . and lift out the seat belt buckle
assembly

21.19a Lift out the seat locking bracket . . .

rear screws, then lift out the centre 'tray' **(see
illustrations)**.
18 Remove the seat belt buckle bolt, and lift
out the buckle assembly **(see illustrations)**.
19 Remove the two nuts securing the seat
locking bracket – these also double as

mounting nuts for the seats themselves. Lift
out the bracket, and recover the flat washers
underneath **(see illustrations)**.
20 Remove the four screws securing the
boot rear trim panel, and lift it out **(see
illustrations)**.

21 Remove the four screws from the seat side
trim panels, then raising the seat if necessary,
lift the panels out **(see illustrations)**.
22 Raise the seat fully (note that it will not
lock). Remove the remaining three mounting
nuts from each seat, then lift it off its mounting

21.19b . . . and recover the flat washers
underneath

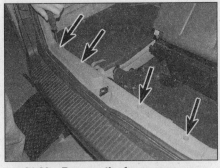

21.20a Remove the four screws . . .

21.20b . . . and lift out the boot rear trim
panel

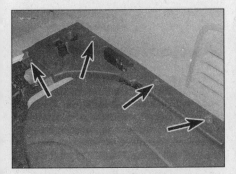

21.21a Remove the four screws . . .

21.21b . . . and lift out the seat side trim
panels

21.22a Remove the remaining three seat
mounting nuts . . .

21.22b . . . and lift out the seat

studs and remove it from the car **(see illustrations)**.

23 Refitting is a reversal of removal. Tighten all nuts and bolts to the specified torque.

Seat tables

24 All models have folding tables built into the backs of the front seats. If required, the tables could presumably be removed by carefully drilling out the four mounting rivets, then the tray surround can be unclipped from the seat back. Check on parts availability before dismantling the seats, however.

---

22 Seat belt components
– removal and refitting

⚠ **Warning: Disconnect the battery negative lead (see Disconnecting the battery), then wait for five minutes before proceeding. If this waiting period is not observed, there is danger of activating the seat belt tensioners.**
Note: If the car has been in an accident, all the affected seat belt components must be renewed.

Seat belt tensioners

Information and precautions

1 Seat belt pretensioners are fitted to remove any slack from the front and outer rear seat belts in the event of a frontal impact. The system is designed to reduce the chances of injury to the driver and front seat passenger in the event of an accident, by pulling your body back into the seat.
2 The system consists of two special seat belt tensioner/stalk assemblies mounted directly on the front seats, or on the outer rear belt inertia reels, connected to the airbag control unit.
3 Each tensioner/stalk assembly consists of a special buckle attached to a cable. The end of the cable is attached to a piston inside the tensioner cylinder.
4 In the event of a sufficiently-severe frontal impact, the seat belt tensioners will be triggered by the airbag control unit (for more information on the airbag system, refer to Chapter 12).
5 When a tensioner ignition module is triggered, a small capsule is energised, which rapidly releases gas into the tensioner cylinder. As the gas is released, the piston is forced along the cylinder, pulling the cable (approximately 70 mm) and hence the seat

belt stalk, which in turn removes any slack from the seat belt, pulling the belt tight against the wearer. The rear belt reels contain similar systems, to spin the reel and retract the belt.
6 Once a seat belt tensioner has been triggered, it must be renewed.
7 Take care, when working on the car, not to expose the pretensioner system components to excess heat, impact, or even magnetic field, as this may cause inadvertent triggering or a malfunction in an accident.

Front belt

8 Using a small screwdriver in the hole provided, depress the catch to release the belt from the buckle on the outside of the seat **(see illustration)**.
9 Remove the B-pillar trim panels as described in Section 23.
10 Unscrew the inertia reel mounting bolt, then unhook and lift out the belt reel **(see illustration)**.
11 Unscrew the upper anchor bolt, and remove the seat belt from the car **(see illustration)**.
12 Refitting is a reversal of removal. Tighten the belt mountings to the specified torque.

Front belt height adjuster

13 Remove the B-pillar trim panel, as described in Section 23.
14 To remove the adjuster completely, unscrew the seat belt upper anchor bolt **(refer to illustration 22.11)**.
15 Unscrew the adjuster upper bolt, then lift the adjuster to unhook the lower mounting, and withdraw the adjuster from the pillar **(see illustrations)**.
16 Refitting is a reversal of removal. Tighten the mountings to the specified torque.

Front belt tensioners

17 Remove the front seat as described in Section 21.
18 Remove the single screw securing the relevant seat side trim panel, then unclip and remove it **(see illustrations)**.
19 Disconnect the wiring plug from the belt tensioner.
20 Unscrew the tensioner mounting bolt, and remove the tensioner from the seat, unclipping the operating cable as required **(see illustration)**.

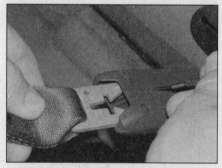

22.8 Use a small screwdriver to release the seat belt buckle from the seat

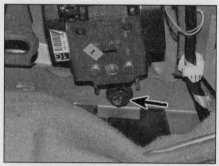

22.10 Remove the inertia reel mounting bolt . . .

22.11 . . . and the seat belt upper anchor bolt

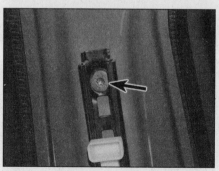

22.15a Remove the adjuster upper bolt . . .

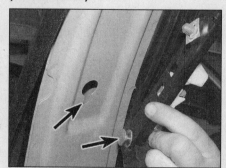

22.15b . . . then lift the adjuster to unhook it from the door pillar

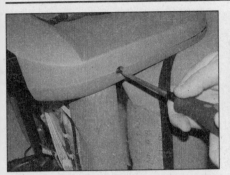

22.18a For the outer tensioner, remove the screw at the rear . . .

22.18b . . . unclip the inner trim panel . . .

22.18c . . . then unclip the outer panel and remove it over the buckle

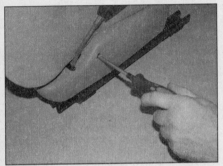

22.18d For the inner tensioner, remove the single screw . . .

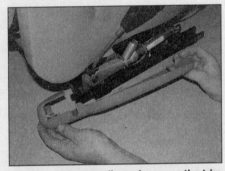

22.18e . . . then unclip and remove the trim panel from the seat

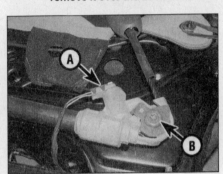

22.20 Disconnect the wiring plug (A), then remove the mounting screw (B)

21 Refitting is a reversal of removal. Ensure the wiring plugs are securely reconnected before refitting the battery lead, and tighten the mounting bolts to the specified torque.

Rear side belt

22 Remove the rear sill and wheel arch trim panels as described in Section 23.

23 Unscrew the seat belt lower anchor bolt (see illustration).

24 Remove the parcel shelf trim panel and the C-pillar trim panel as described in Section 23. Note: If removing the centre-row rear side belt on the Grand Scénic, only the parcel shelf trim panel should be removed.

25 Unscrew the seat belt upper anchor bolt (prise off the cover first, where applicable) and the inertia reel mounting bolt. On the Grand Scénic, if removing the centre-row side belt, unscrew the two screws securing the belt guide, and remove it (see illustrations).

26 Disconnect the belt tensioner wiring plug (see illustration), then unhook and lift out the reel. Remove the seat belt from the car.

27 Refitting is a reversal of removal. Tighten the mountings to the specified torque.

Rear centre belt

28 Unclip the belt trim cover from the

22.23 Unscrew the rear seat belt lower anchor bolt

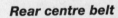

22.25a Prise off the cap and unscrew the upper anchor bolt

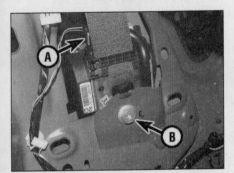

22.25b Inertia reel pretensioner wiring plug (A) and mounting bolt (B) – Scénic

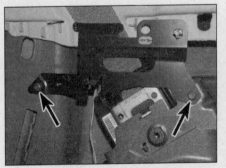

22.25c Remove the two screws . . .

22.25d . . . and remove the belt guide – Grand Scénic

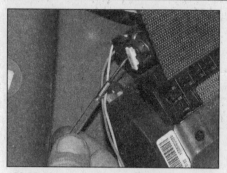

22.26 Use a small screwdriver to release the belt tensioner wiring plug

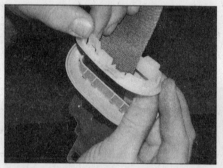

22.28b Before refitting, the inner section's legs must be folded up

headlining. This is in two parts – before refitting, the locating legs for the inner part should be folded up so that it will enter the headlining **(see illustrations)**.

29 Open the tailgate, and prise out the two clips from the rear of the headlining. Prise off the tailgate weatherstrip at the top, to release the headlining at the rear. Remove the rear grab handles and C-pillar trim panels as described in Section 23 to make lowering the headlining easier.

30 Carefully prise down the headlining at the rear, sufficient to gain access to the two seat belt mounting bolts. If access cannot be gained this way, the headlining may have to be removed completely – this is not considered to be a DIY operation, and should be referred to a Renault dealer. Remember that the side curtain airbag units are located above the headlining.

31 Unscrew the seat belt mounting bolts, and withdraw the belt from the car.

23.12a Unclip the facia end panel . . .

22.28a Unclip the belt trim cover from the headlining

22.33 Rear outer seat belt buckle – seen with seat and trim panels removed

32 Refitting is a reversal of removal. Tighten the mountings to the specified torque.

Rear seat belt buckles

33 The belt buckles are bolted to the floor, and removal should be self-evident, once the relevant seats and trim panels have been removed as described elsewhere in this Chapter **(see illustration)**.

34 In some cases, the bolts used to secure the buckles are also used for other brackets – make sure to note their positions as they are removed.

35 The buckles for the third-row seats on the Grand Scénic can be removed as described in the seat removal procedure, in Section 21.

23 Interior trim panels – removal and refitting

General information

1 The interior trim panels are all secured using either plastic clips built into the panel, or screws.

2 Before removing a panel, study it carefully, noting how it is secured. Often, other panels or ancillary components (such as seat belt mountings, grab handles, etc) must be removed before a particular panel can be withdrawn.

3 Once any such components have been removed, check that there are no other panels overlapping the one to be removed. Usually, the sequence to be followed will become obvious on close inspection.

4 Remove all obvious fasteners, such as screws, which may have plastic covers fitted. If the panel cannot be freed, it is probably secured by hidden clips or fasteners on the rear of the panel. Such fasteners are usually situated around the edge of the panel, and can be prised up to release them. Note that plastic clips can break quite easily, so it is advisable to have a few new clips of the correct type available for refitting. Generally, the best way of releasing such clips is to use a wide flat-bladed tool, designed for the purpose – these are available from tool suppliers such as Draper. If this is not available, an old, broad-bladed screwdriver with the edges rounded-off and wrapped in insulating tape will serve as a good substitute.

5 The following Section and the accompanying illustrations describe removal and refitting of all the major trim panels. Note that the type and number of fasteners used often varies during the production run of a particular model, so differences may be found to the procedures provided.

6 When removing a panel, **never** use excessive force, or the panel may be damaged. Always check carefully that all fasteners have been removed or released before attempting to withdraw a panel.

7 When refitting, secure the fasteners by pressing them firmly into place. Ensure that all disturbed components are correctly secured, to prevent rattles.

Driver's lower facia panel

⚠ **Warning: Disconnect the battery negative lead (see Disconnecting the battery), then wait for five minutes before proceeding. If this waiting period is not observed, there is danger of activating the passenger airbag.**

8 On models with the automatic handbrake, remove the facia control as described in Chapter 9, Section 16.

9 Remove the gear lever housing as described later in this Section.

10 Remove the radio/CD player as described in Chapter 12.

11 Remove the heater control surround panel as described in Chapter 3.

12 At the outer side, unclip the facia end cover panel. Disconnect the passenger airbag selector switch wiring plug, then remove the panel completely **(see illustrations)**.

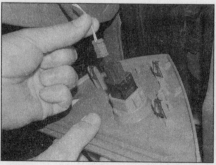

23.12b . . . then disconnect the wiring plug from the airbag switch

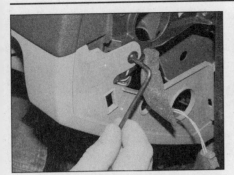

23.13a Remove the screw behind the facia end panel . . .

23.13b . . . one more below that . . .

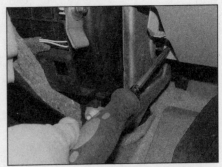

23.13c . . . one at the lower left-hand corner . . .

23.13d . . . one below the heater control panel . . .

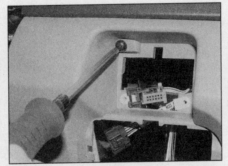

23.13e . . . and one behind the automatic handbrake . . .

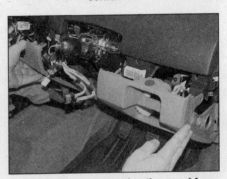

23.13f . . . before removing the panel from the facia

13 Remove the four screws around the lower facia panel, and one more behind the automatic handbrake facia control location (or inside the coin holder), and withdraw it from the facia **(see illustrations)**.
14 Refitting is a reversal of removal.

Glovebox

15 Remove the gear lever housing as described later in this Section.
16 Remove the radio/CD player as described in Chapter 12.
17 Remove the heater control surround panel as described in Chapter 3.
18 Prise off the facia end cover panel from the passenger side, then remove the upper and lower screws behind and below that **(see illustrations)**.
19 Remove the two mounting screws on the right-hand side of the glovebox, and the two inside at the top **(see illustrations)**.

20 Pull down the fusebox access panel from the top of the glovebox. Reach in behind and above the main fuse panel, and release the two clips securing the fusebox, so that the glovebox can be withdrawn **(see illustration)**.

21 Withdraw the glovebox from the facia, disconnecting the glovebox light wiring and air conditioning supply pipe from the back (where applicable) **(see illustrations)**.
22 Refitting is a reversal of removal.

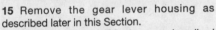
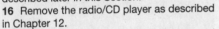
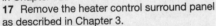

23.18a unclip the facia end panel . . .

23.18b . . . then remove the upper . . .

23.18c . . . and lower screws behind it

23.19a Remove the two mounting screws on the right-hand side . . .

23.19b . . . and one screw either side at the top

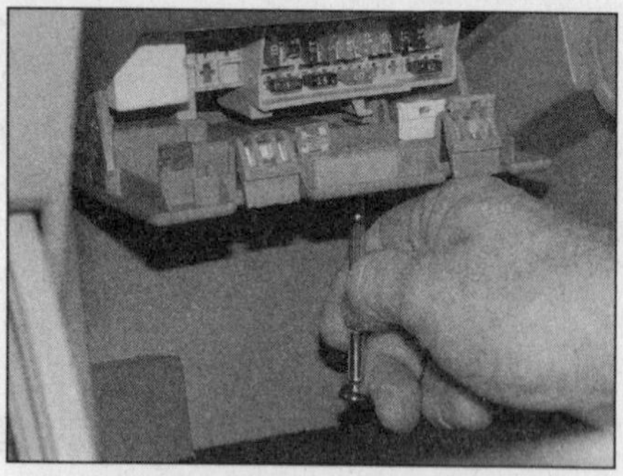

23.20 Use a small screwdriver to release the fusebox clips

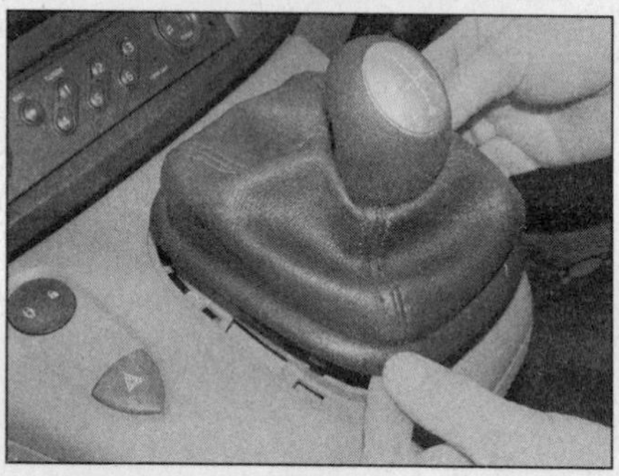

23.23 Unclip the gear lever gaiter

Gear lever housing

23 Unclip the gear/selector gaiter from the housing, and fold it up round the gear/selector lever **(see illustration)**.

24 Unclip the housing top panel, then

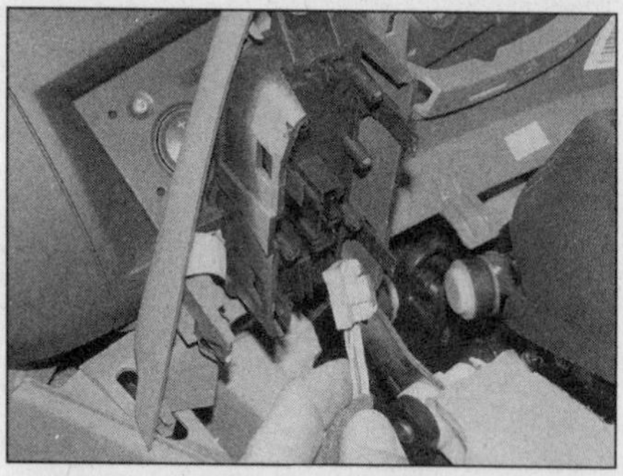

23.24b . . . then disconnect the switch wiring and remove it

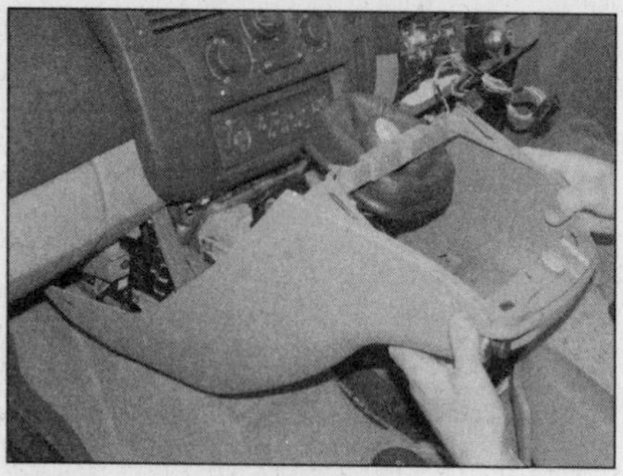

23.26b . . . then unclip the housing at the sides and withdraw it . . .

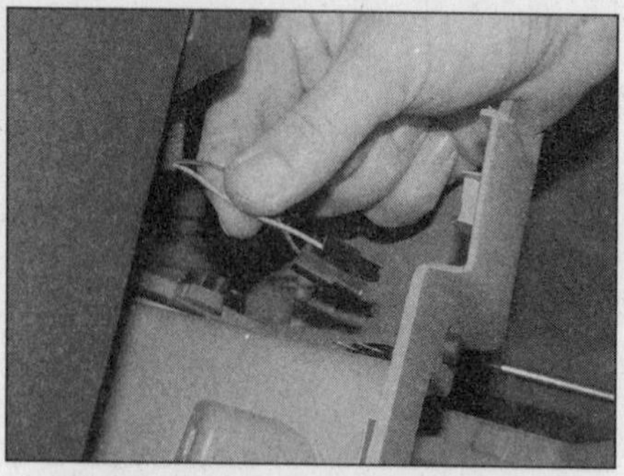

23.21a Pull out the glovebox, then disconnect the glovebox light . . .

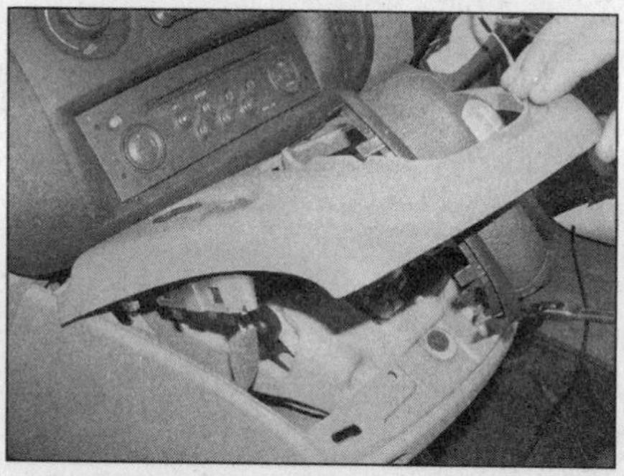

23.24a Unclip the housing top panel . . .

disconnect the wiring connector from the hazard warning light and central locking switch unit **(see illustrations)**. Feed through the gaiter, and remove the top panel.

25 Taking care not to mark the trim, prise out the plastic clip either side which secures

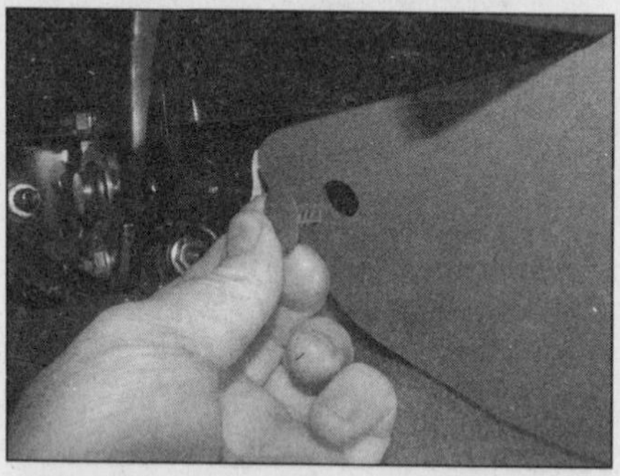

23.25 Prise out the plastic clip either side at the front

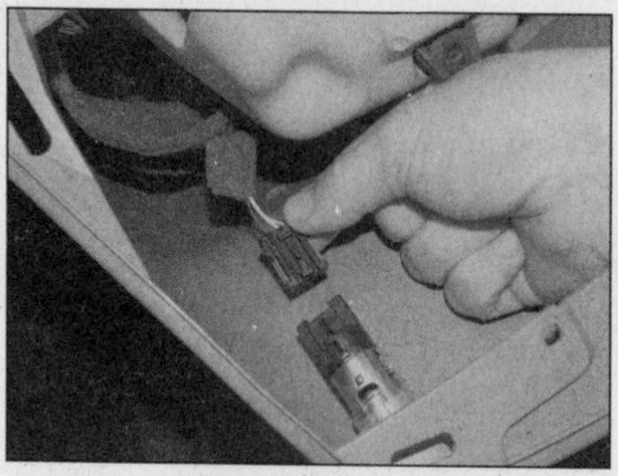

23.26c . . . until the cigar lighter wiring can be disconnected

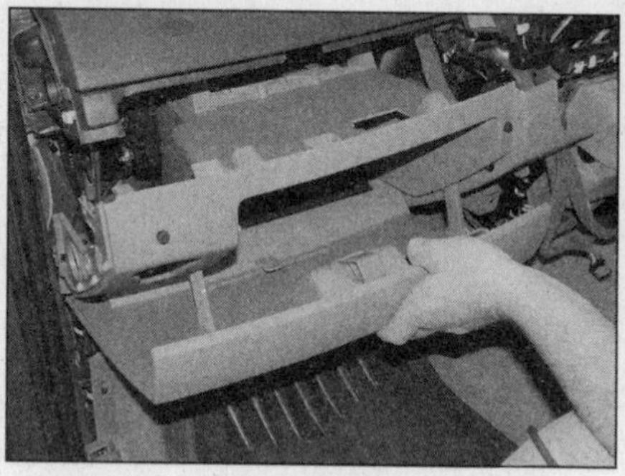

23.21b . . . and remove the glovebox completely

the housing to the main facia panel **(see illustration)**.

26 Remove the three mounting screws (two from the facia, one at the rear of the housing), then release the side clips securing the housing to the facia, sliding it rearwards and upwards to remove it. Disconnect the wiring plug from the cigar lighter as the housing is withdrawn **(see illustrations)**.

27 Refitting is a reversal of removal.

A-pillar trim panel

28 Pull the rubber weatherstrip down from the door aperture, adjacent to the trim panel.

29 Pull the panel inwards slightly at the top to release it there. Taking care not to mark the surface of the facia, carefully prise the panel upwards at the base. By pulling the panel upwards, and inwards at the top, it should come free **(see illustrations)**. Remove the panel from the car.

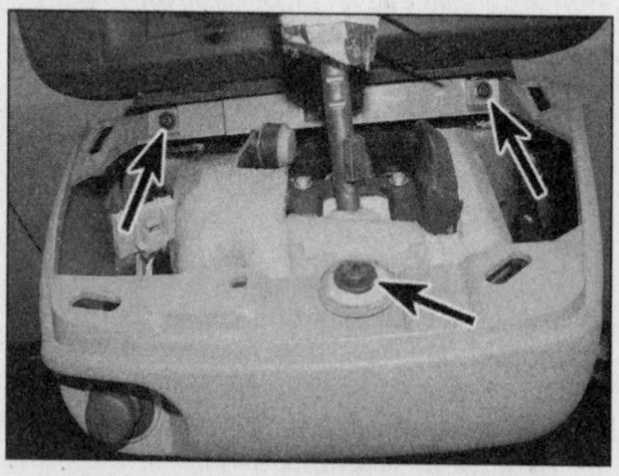

23.26a Remove the three mounting screws . . .

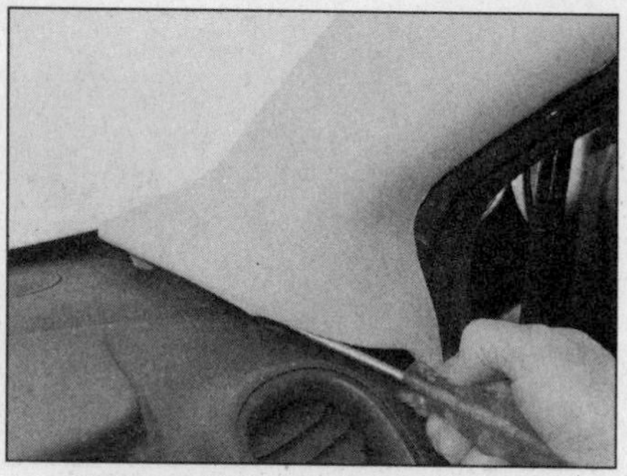

23.29a Prise the A-pillar trim panel upwards at the base . . .

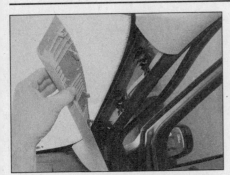

23.29b . . . and out at the top to remove

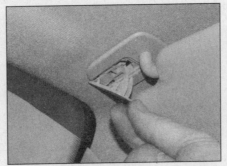

23.31 Prise down the sunvisor mounting cover . . .

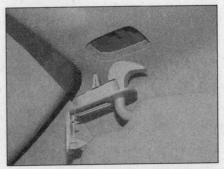

23.32 Release the retaining tab inside, and withdraw the sunvisor

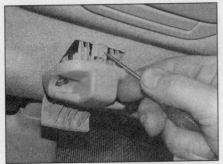

23.33 Releasing the retaining tabs on the sunvisor centre mounting

23.36 Removing the footwell trim panel

23.40 Removing a sill trim panel

30 Refitting is a reversal of removal.

Sunvisors

31 Prise down the cover panel using a small screwdriver (see illustration).
32 Release the retaining tab inside, and withdraw the sunvisor mounting from the headlining (see illustration)..
33 A similar method is used to remove the sunvisor centre mounting (see illustration).
34 Refitting is a reversal of removal.

Footwell trim panel

35 Prise up and unclip the front edge of the sill trim panel.
36 Pull the footwell trim panel outwards at the bottom, then unclip it at the top and remove it from the car (see illustration).
37 Refitting is a reversal of removal.

Sill trim panels

Front

38 Pull up the sill panel at the front edge to release the clips.
39 Unclip the lower section of the B-pillar trim by lifting it first at the base, then out at the top.
40 Unclip the rest of the sill panel, and remove it (see illustration).
41 Refitting is a reversal of removal.

Rear

42 Unclip the lower section of the B-pillar trim by lifting it first at the base, then out at the top.
43 Unclip the sill panel along its length, and remove it.
44 Refitting is a reversal of removal.

B-pillar trim panels

Lower panel

45 Unclip the lower section of the B-pillar trim by lifting it first at the base, then out at the top (see illustration).
46 Refitting is a reversal of removal.

Upper panel

47 Remove the lower B-pillar trim panel as described previously in this Section.
48 Pull back the rubber weatherstrip in front of and behind the panel as necessary, then prise down the retaining flap at the base of the panel (see illustration).
49 Pull the panel out at the base, then downwards to free it from the pillar. Feed the seat belt through the panel, and remove it (see illustrations).
50 Refitting is a reversal of removal.

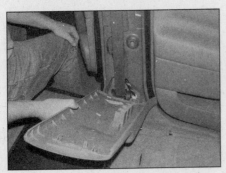

23.45 Removing the B-pillar lower trim panel

23.48 Prise down the retaining flap at the base of the panel

23.49a Unclip the panel at the base . . .

23.49b . . . then pull downwards from the headlining . . .

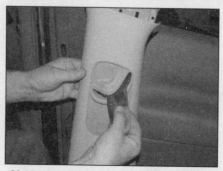

23.49c . . . and feed the seat belt through

23.51 Unclip the end of the door sill trim panel

23.52a Remove the screw at the front of the parcel shelf trim panel . . .

Rear wheel arch trim panel

51 Unclip the rear end of the rear door sill trim panel (see illustration).

52 On the Grand Scénic, remove the screw at the front of the parcel shelf trim panel, and

23.52b . . . then pull the front of the panel out slightly (Grand Scénic)

pull the panel out slightly (see illustrations).

53 Unclip and remove the wheel arch trim panel from the car. On the Grand Scénic, the rear seat belt guide can also be unclipped if required (see illustrations).

54 Refitting is a reversal of removal.

Parcel shelf/boot trim panel

55 Remove the parcel shelf (or luggage cover) itself. Where applicable, prise out and disconnect the boot light from the panel (see illustration).

56 Remove the rear wheel arch trim panel as described previously in this Section.

57 Remove the boot carpet by prising out the two front securing clips or seat guides, as applicable (see illustrations).

58 On the Scénic, there are three screws to remove along the parcel shelf support, then the whole side trim panel is removed (see illustrations).

59 On the Grand Scénic, the parcel shelf support is secured by two screws, and is removed separately before taking out the side trim panel from the boot (see illustrations).

60 Refitting is a reversal of removal.

23.53a Unclip and remove the wheel arch trim panel

23.53b On Grand Scénics, the belt guide panel can also be unclipped

23.55 On the left-hand panel, prise out and disconnect the boot light

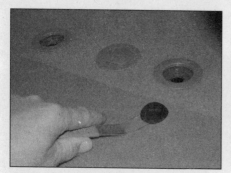

23.57a Prise out the boot carpet securing clips . . .

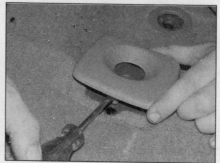

23.57b . . . or seat guides

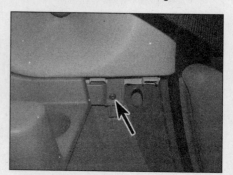

23.58a On the Scénic, remove the front screw . . .

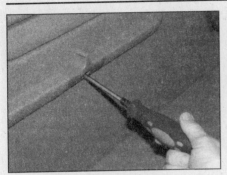

23.58b . . . middle screw . . .

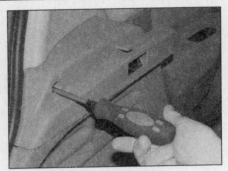

23.58c . . . and rear screw . . .

23.58d . . . and remove the complete panel

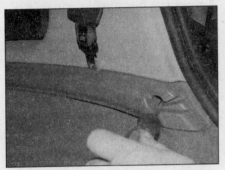

23.59a On the Grand Scénic, remove the front and rear screws . . .

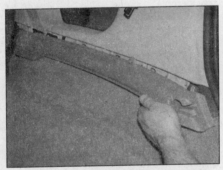

23.59b . . . take off the separate shelf support . . .

23.59c . . . then remove the trim panel from the boot

C-pillar trim panel

61 Open the tailgate, and pull away the rubber weatherstrips from the front and rear of the panel as necessary.

62 Remove the parcel shelf trim panel as described previously in this Section.

Scénic

63 Unclip the panel at the front and rear. The panel is also clipped to the headlining in two places (the clips are visible through the fixed side window), and care must be taken not to damage the headlining when releasing them. Remove the panel, feeding through the seat belt once the panel has been released **(see illustration)**.

64 Refitting is a reversal of removal.

Grand Scénic

65 Unscrew the two bolts securing the centre-row side belt guide, and remove it **(see illustration)**.

66 Prise off the cover, then unscrew the centre-row side belt upper mounting bolt and lower the seat belt away from the panel **(see illustration)**.

67 Unclip the belt guide from the third-row belt at the rear of the panel.

68 Unclip the trim panel first from the headlining, then at the front and rear. Feed through the third-row seat belt as the panel is removed.

69 Refitting is a reversal of removal. Where applicable, tighten the seat belt mounting bolt to the specified torque.

Carpets

70 The carpet is held in position by the sill trim panels, and other surrounding panels and components.

71 Carpet removal and refitting is reasonably straightforward, but very time-consuming, due to the fact that many of the adjoining trim panels must be removed first. It will also be necessary to remove components such as the seats and their mountings, the centre console, etc.

Grab handles

72 Using a small screwdriver, prise out the retaining peg at each end of the grab handle **(see illustrations)**.

73 Lower the grab handle from the headlining and remove it **(see illustration)**.

23.63 Carefully unclip the C-pillar trim panel

23.65 Take off the centre-row side belt guide

23.66 Prise off the cover, and remove the belt upper anchor bolt

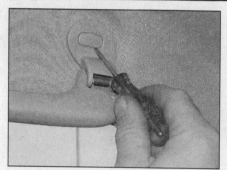

23.72a Using a small screwdriver . . .

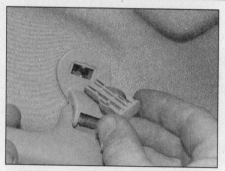

23.72b . . . prise out the grab handle retaining pegs

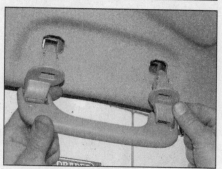

23.73 Lower the handle from the headlining, and remove it

74 Refitting is a reversal of removal.

Headlining

⚠ *Warning: Disconnect the battery negative lead (see Disconnecting the battery), then wait for five minutes before proceeding. If this waiting period is not observed, there is danger of activating the side curtain airbags, which are located in the headlining.*

75 The headlining is held in place by the grab handles, sun visors, sunroof trim, door pillar trim panels, C-pillar trim panels, weatherseals, etc. There are also two plastic clips at the top of the tailgate aperture to prise out. When all the fittings have been removed or prised clear, it can then be withdrawn through the tailgate aperture. Disconnect the wiring plugs for the side curtain airbags as they become accessible.

76 Note that headlining removal requires

considerable skill and patience if it is to be carried out without damage, and is therefore best entrusted to an expert.

24 Centre console – removal and refitting

Manual handbrake models

1 Lift out the rubber mat from the centre console **(see illustration)**.
2 Remove the two front mounting screws and two rear mounting nuts below the mat **(see illustration)**.
3 Lift out the centre console over the handbrake lever **(see illustration)**. This may prove difficult – sliding one of the front seats fully forwards or backwards may provide extra room to manoeuvre the console.
4 Refitting is a reversal of removal.

Automatic handbrake models

Storage tray

5 Lift out the rubber mat from the centre console **(see illustration)**.
6 Remove the two front mounting screws and two rear mounting nuts below the mat **(see illustration)**.
7 Lift out the centre console **(see illustration)**.
8 Refitting is a reversal of removal.

Sliding storage unit

9 Move the front seats fully forwards, and/or slide the console rearwards.
10 Fold the front armrests up past the vertical position, then pull them off to the side.
11 Using a small screwdriver, and taking care not to mark the finish, prise up the small blanking plate below each armrest hinge. Remove the upper mounting screw below each blanking plate **(see illustration)**.

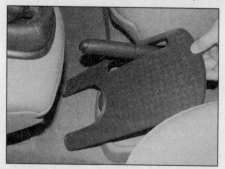

24.1 Lift the rubber mat off the centre console

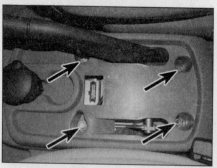

24.2 Remove the front screws and rear nuts . . .

24.3 . . . and lift out the centre console over the handbrake lever

24.5 Lift the rubber mat off the centre console

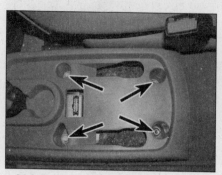

24.6 Remove the front screws and rear nuts . . .

24.7 . . . and lift out the centre console

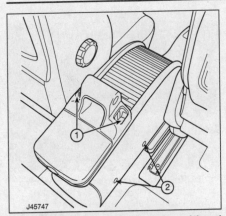

24.11 Centre console upper screws (1) and two of the lower side screws (2)

12 Remove the two screws visible each side at the base of the console, then slide the front seats fully rearwards (and the console fully forwards) to remove the remaining screw each side at the front.

13 Slide the console rearwards again, and remove the trim panel from the console baseplate by sliding it off forwards. Also unclip and remove the side trim pieces from the baseplate, either side of the console **(see illustration)**. Finally, unclip the ashtray/cup holder at the front.

14 Tip the console backwards for access to the two console-to-baseplate bolts, and remove them. Disconnect the wiring connector from the base of the console, then lift it out of the car.

15 If required, the console baseplate itself

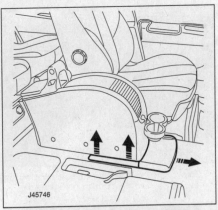

24.13 Unclip the front and side trim panels, and the ashtray/cup holder

can also be removed, after unscrewing the mounting nuts from the floor.

16 Refitting is a reversal of removal. Tighten all mountings securely – observe the tightening torque for the console baseplate nuts.

25 Facia panel and crossmember – removal and refitting

Removal

Note: *This is a difficult procedure, carried out in two stages – removing the plastic facia panel, and then the large metal crossmember underneath it, which requires making up a special tool. Both facia sections have to be*

removed, for example, to gain access to the heater assembly. It is strongly recommended that this Section is read through thoroughly before starting the procedure.

Facia panel

1 Disconnect the battery negative lead (see *Disconnecting the battery*), then wait for five minutes before proceeding. If this waiting period is not observed, there is danger of activating the airbags.

2 Remove the A-pillar and footwell trim panels as described in Section 23.

3 Remove the tweeter speakers, steering column switch assembly and the instrument panel as described in Chapter 12.

4 From below, release the two clips securing the upper trim above the steering column, and remove the trim **(see illustrations)**.

5 On models with automatic air conditioning (climate control), carefully prise out the sun sensor from the top of the facia, then disconnect its wiring plug and remove it. Even on lesser models, there will be a blanking plug with a wiring plug clipped to it **(see illustration)**.

6 Remove the driver's side lower facia panel and the glovebox as described in Section 23.

7 Remove the heater control panel as described in Chapter 3.

8 Unscrew the single bolt securing the multiplex wiring module to the side of the crossmember. Unclip it, and move it sideways as far as possible to gain access to the wiring plugs on the back. Release the locking catches from the module wiring plugs, and remove the module **(see illustrations)**.

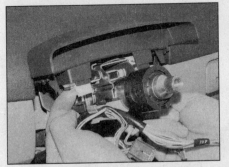

25.4a Release the two clips underneath . . .

25.4b . . . and lift out the steering column upper trim

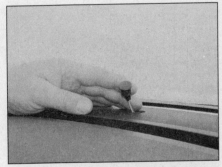

25.5 Prise out and disconnect the sun sensor (or blanking plug)

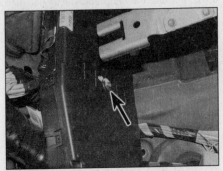

25.8a Unscrew the single central bolt . . .

25.8b . . . then unclip the module and disconnect the wiring plugs on the back . . .

25.8c . . . before withdrawing the module into the footwell

25.9a Disconnect the yellow wiring plug at either end of the passenger airbag . . .

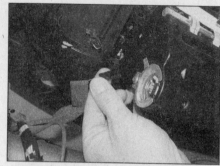

25.9b . . . and pull off the spade connector

25.10a Remove two screws at each end . . .

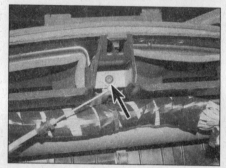

25.10b . . . one screw above . . .

25.10c . . . and two below the heater control panel . . .

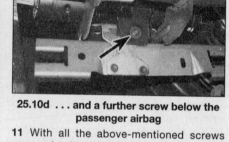

25.10d . . . and a further screw below the passenger airbag

9 Reach up under the facia and disconnect the (yellow) wiring connector at each end of the passenger airbag unit. Also take off the single earth spade connector above one of the airbag's main wiring connectors **(see illustrations)**.

10 The facia panel is now held in place by a number of screws, as follows **(see illustrations)**:
  a) *Two at each end of the facia panel.*
  b) *Three in the centre, behind the heater control location.*
  c) *One underneath the passenger airbag.*

11 With all the above-mentioned screws removed, with the help of an assistant, lift and withdraw the facia panel into the car **(see illustration)**. Check as this is done that the wiring harness behind is not being strained, and release it as necessary.

Crossmember

12 Now the metal crossmember has to be removed – this requires some studying of the wiring harness beforehand, to ensure its correct routing when refitting. If possible, take some digital photos before starting, to use as a guide later.

13 Using the information in Chapter 10, remove the wiring and mounting nuts from the steering column, and lower it into the footwell – it does not have to be removed completely.

14 Ensure that the gear/selector lever is in Neutral. Working as described in Chapter 7A or 7B, unclip the soundproofing material, then unscrew the three mounting nuts on the rear of the gearchange mechanism, and lower the assembly away from the facia.

15 Unclip and remove the ventilation duct from the driver's footwell **(see illustration)**.

16 Work around the crossmember, disconnecting the cable-tied and clipped-on wiring harness as necessary, noting how it is routed. Some of the cable-ties will have to be cut, but several of them can be prised out **(see illustrations)**. Also note the routing of items such as the radio aerial lead.

17 Unbolt the earth straps at either end of the crossmember, and the one in the centre **(see illustration)**.

25.11 Lift the facia, and remove it

25.15 Unclip the driver's side ventilation duct above the footwell

25.16a Ordinary cable-ties must be cut . . .

25.16b . . . but some cable clips are prised out

25.17 Remove the nuts securing the earth straps

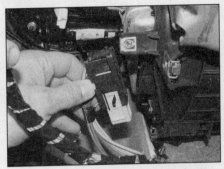

25.18a Unclip the relays from in front of . . .

25.18b . . . and behind the crossmember

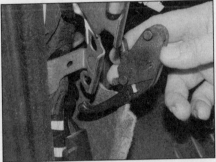

25.18c Unclip the bonnet release lever from the crossmember

18 Unclip the relays from the left-hand end of the crossmember, and the bonnet release lever below that (see illustrations).

19 Where applicable, disconnect the large wiring plug in front of the heater assembly – there may be some additional spare wiring

25.19a Disconnect the large wiring plug in front of the heater assembly . . .

plugs, which should also be unclipped (see illustrations).

20 On the driver's side, a centre support is fitted between the crossmember and the floor. First, remove the two upper bolts and the small front bolt. In the footwell, pull down the carpet to

25.19b . . . and where necessary, unclip any spare wiring plugs

access the two lower bolts – with these removed, take out the centre support (see illustrations).

21 Work around the crossmember, removing the mounting bolts on top of the heater unit, in front of the windscreen, and in the footwell (see illustrations).

25.20a Remove the two centre support upper bolts . . .

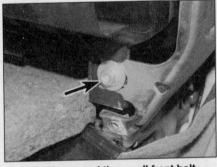

25.20b . . . and the small front bolt

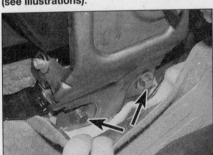

25.20c Pull down the carpet to access the two lower bolts . . .

25.20d . . . then remove the centre support

25.21a Remove the crossmember mounting bolts on top of the heater . . .

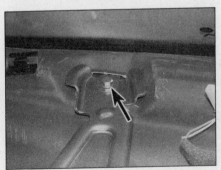

25.21b . . . in front of the windscreen . . .

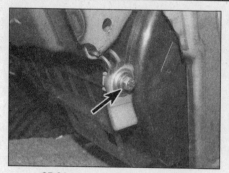

25.21c ... and in the footwell

25.22a Unscrew and remove the two side mounting bolts ...

24 With the doors removed, both end bolts can be unscrewed and removed **(see illustration)**. However, even this does not free the crossmember, which has large left-hand threaded nuts fitted either end inside, which are 'wound out' during assembly to brace the crossmember across the car. To loosen these nuts requires that a special tool be made, as described next. **Note:** *If the Renault tool can be obtained instead, this is tool no Car 1673.*

25 Obtain either a length of M12 threaded rod, or an M12 bolt, approximately 210 mm long, and some M12 nuts to fit it. In addition, a length of strong metal tube will be needed, approximately 150 mm in length, to fit closely over the M12 thread. If a bolt is not used, lock two of the nuts together at one end of the threaded rod. We brazed another nut onto the metal tube, but found this wasn't really necessary – they can be left separate **(see illustration)**.

26 Insert the tool into the hole left by the end bolt just removed, and tighten until it bottoms – only tighten gently. Now tighten the remaining nut to push the metal tube down the threaded rod, and tighten this firmly – this 'clamps' the tube against the surface of the left-hand threaded nut inside. Now unscrew the whole tool by a few turns, which should loosen the inner nut and free the crossmember **(see illustrations)**. Unlock the tool by loosening the metal tube clamp nut, then unscrew and remove the tool.

27 With the inner nuts loosened, the crossmember can be removed – check that there is no wiring still attached or hooked up as this is done **(see illustration)**.

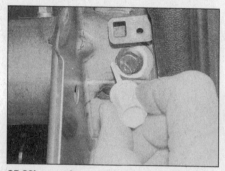

25.22b ... after marking round their heads with paint

25.23 Prise out the large cap fitted over the crossmember end bolts

22 Unscrew and remove the two side mounting bolts at either end of the crossmember – as these are in slotted holes, we marked round the bolt heads first with paint **(see illustrations)**.

23 To access the crossmember end mounting bolts, both front doors have to be removed, as described in Section 11 – the need for this was ably demonstrated after we removed the cover caps from the bolts **(see illustration)**.

25.24 Unscrew the end mounting bolt either side

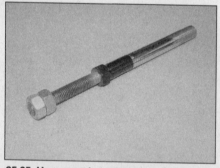

25.25 Home-made tool for unscrewing the crossmember inner nuts

25.26a Insert the tool, tighten gently until it just bottoms ...

25.26b ... then tighten the nut to clamp the metal tube ...

25.26c ... and unscrew the whole tool to release the crossmember inner nut

26.27 Removing the crossmember

Refitting

28 Refitting is a reversal of removal, bearing in mind the following points:

a) If the facia is to be refitted at a later date, ensure that the battery is disconnected before starting. It is dangerous, for example, to reconnect the airbag wiring with the battery connected.

b) Offer in the crossmember, aligning the marks made between the crossmember and the side mounting bolts before continuing. Fit the home-made tool for setting the inner nuts as before (paragraph 26), only this time, tighten the whole tool to wind the inner nuts out until they stop. Remove the tool, and repeat on the other inner nut.

c) Coat the threads of the end bolts generously with thread-locking fluid – as the end bolts are tightened, the 'drag' of the thread-lock also helps to finally tighten the inner nuts.

d) Ensure that the wiring harnesses, aerial lead, etc, are routed as noted before removal.

e) Tighten all bolts securely, or to the specified torque.

Notes

Chapter 12
Body electrical system

Contents

Degrees of difficulty

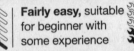

Easy, suitable for novice with little experience	Fairly easy, suitable for beginner with some experience	Fairly difficult, suitable for competent DIY mechanic	Difficult, suitable for experienced DIY mechanic	Very difficult, suitable for expert DIY or professional

Specifications

General
System type .... 12-volt, negative-earth

Bulbs | Wattage

Exterior lights

Headlight with halogen bulbs:
Main beam	55 (H1 type*)
Dipped beam	55 (H7 type*)

Headlight with xenon bulbs:
Main beam	55 (H7 type*)
Dipped beam	37 (D2S type*)
Front foglight	55 (H11 type)
Front sidelight (wedge-base)	5
Direction indicator (orange-coloured)	21
Direction indicator side repeater (wedge-base)	5
Stop/tail	21/5
High-level brake light	LEDs (no bulbs fitted)
Reversing light	21
Rear foglight (driver's side only works)	21
Number plate light (wedge-base)	5

Interior lights
Interior/footwell lights (wedge-base)	5
Boot/glovebox light (festoon)	5

*Note: As the headlights have plastic lenses, anti-UV type bulbs are used (the headlight may be damaged if any other type of bulb is used).

1 General information and precautions

⚠️ **Warning: Before carrying out any work on the electrical system, read through the precautions given in 'Safety first!' at the beginning of this manual, and in Chapter 5A.**

The electrical system is of 12-volt negative-earth type. Power for the lights and all electrical accessories is supplied by a lead-acid type battery, which is charged by the alternator.

This Chapter covers repair and service procedures for the various electrical components not associated with engine. Information on the battery, alternator and starter motor can be found in Chapter 5A.

It should be noted that, prior to working on any component in the electrical system, the battery negative terminal should first be disconnected, to prevent the possibility of electrical short-circuits and/or fires.

Caution: Before disconnecting the battery, refer to the information given in 'Disconnecting the battery' in the Reference Section of this manual.

2 Electrical fault-finding – general information

Note: *Refer to the precautions given in Safety first! and at the beginning of Chapter 5A before starting work.*

⚠️ **Warning: Since this is a multiplex wiring system, every circuit in the car passes through at least one 'ECU'. For this reason, it is inadvisable to use any kind of self-powered test equipment, as this may cause damage to the electronic modules fitted.**

General

1 A typical electrical circuit consists of an electrical component, any switches, relays, motors, fuses, fusible links or circuit breakers related to that component, and the wiring and connectors which link the component to both the battery and the chassis. To help to pinpoint a problem in an electrical circuit, wiring diagrams are included at the end of this Chapter.

2 Before attempting to diagnose an electrical fault, first study the appropriate wiring diagram, to obtain a more complete understanding of the components included in the particular circuit concerned. The possible sources of a fault can be narrowed down by noting whether other components related to the circuit are operating properly. If several components or circuits fail at one time, the problem is likely to be related to a shared fuse or earth connection.

3 Multiplex wiring makes traditional electrical fault-finding more difficult, as inter-related circuits are connected together as required by the multiplex modules. This factor makes tracing faults from one end of the car to the other almost impossible, with the added factor that the multiplex modules may also be at fault, in not switching/connecting the circuits correctly. Once testing has passed beyond the basic stage, it may be more time-efficient to have the fault diagnosed by a Renault dealer.

4 Electrical problems usually stem from simple causes, such as loose or corroded connections, a faulty earth connection, a blown fuse, a melted fusible link, or a faulty relay (refer to Section 3 for details of testing relays). Visually inspect the condition of all fuses, wires and connections in a problem circuit before testing the components. Use the wiring diagrams to determine which terminal connections will need to be checked, in order to pinpoint the trouble-spot.

5 The basic tools required for electrical fault-finding include a voltmeter (a 12-volt bulb with a set of test leads can also be used for certain tests), an ohmmeter (to measure resistance), and a jumper wire, preferably with a circuit breaker or fuse incorporated, which can be used to bypass suspect wires or electrical components. Before attempting to locate a problem with test instruments, use the wiring diagram to determine where to make the connections.

6 To find the source of an intermittent wiring fault (usually due to a poor or dirty connection, or damaged wiring insulation), a 'wiggle' test can be performed on the wiring. This involves wiggling the wiring by hand, to see if the fault occurs as the wiring is moved. It should be possible to narrow down the source of the fault to a particular section of wiring. This method of testing can be used in conjunction with any of the tests described in the following sub-Sections.

7 Apart from problems due to poor connections, two basic types of fault can occur in an electrical circuit – open-circuit, or short-circuit.

8 Open-circuit faults are caused by a break somewhere in the circuit, which prevents current from flowing. An open-circuit fault will prevent a component from working, but will not cause the relevant circuit fuse to blow.

9 Short-circuit faults are caused by a 'short' somewhere in the circuit, which allows the current flowing in the circuit to 'escape' along an alternative route, usually to earth. Short-circuit faults are normally caused by a breakdown in wiring insulation, which allows a feed wire to touch either another wire, or an earthed component such as the bodyshell. A short-circuit fault will normally cause the relevant circuit fuse to blow.

Finding an open-circuit

10 To check for an open-circuit, connect one lead of a test light or voltmeter to either the negative battery terminal or a known good earth.

11 Connect the other lead to a connector in the circuit being tested, preferably nearest to the battery or fuse.

12 Switch on the circuit, bearing in mind that some circuits are live only when the ignition is on (with the keycard in position, and neither brake nor clutch depressed, press the starter button to switch on the ignition).

13 If voltage is present (indicated either by the tester bulb lighting or a voltmeter reading, as applicable), this means that the section of the circuit between the relevant connector and the battery is problem-free.

14 Continue to check the remainder of the circuit in the same fashion.

15 When a point is reached at which no voltage is present, the problem must lie between that point and the previous test point with voltage. Most problems can be traced to a broken, corroded or loose connection.

Finding a short-circuit

16 To check for a short-circuit, first disconnect the load(s) from the circuit (loads are the components which draw current from a circuit, such as bulbs, motors, heating elements, etc).

17 Remove the relevant fuse from the circuit, and connect a test light or voltmeter to the fuse connections.

18 Switch on the circuit, bearing in mind that some circuits are live only when the ignition is on (with the keycard in position, and neither brake nor clutch depressed, press the starter button to switch on the ignition).

19 If voltage is present (indicated either by the test bulb lighting or a voltmeter reading, as applicable), this means that there is a short-circuit.

20 If no voltage is present, but the fuse still blows with the load(s) connected, this indicates an internal fault in the load(s).

Finding an earth fault

21 The battery negative terminal is connected to 'earth' – the metal of the engine/transmission unit and the car body – and most systems are wired so that they only receive a positive feed, the current returning via the metal of the car body. This means that the component mounting and the body form part of that circuit. Loose or corroded mountings can therefore cause a range of electrical faults, ranging from total failure of a circuit, to a puzzling partial fault.

22 In particular, lights may shine dimly (especially when another circuit sharing the same earth point is in operation), motors (eg, wiper motors or the radiator cooling fan motor) may run slowly, and the operation of one circuit may have an apparently-unrelated effect on another.

23 Note that on many vehicles, earth straps are used between certain components, such as the engine/transmission and the body, usually where there is no metal-to-metal contact between components, due to flexible rubber mountings, etc.

24 To check whether a component is properly earthed, disconnect the battery, and connect one lead of an ohmmeter to a known good earth point. Connect the other lead to the wire or earth connection being tested. The resistance reading should be zero; if not, check the connection as follows.

25 If an earth connection is thought to be faulty, dismantle the connection, and clean back to bare metal both the bodyshell and the wire terminal or the component earth connection mating surface. Be careful to remove all traces of dirt and corrosion, then use a knife to trim away any paint, so that a clean metal-to-metal joint is made.

26 On reassembly, tighten the joint fasteners securely; if a wire terminal is being refitted, use serrated washers between the terminal and the bodyshell, to ensure a clean and secure connection.

27 When the connection is remade, prevent the onset of corrosion in the future by applying a coat of petroleum jelly or silicone-based grease, or by spraying on (at regular intervals) a proprietary ignition sealer.

3 Fuses, relays and multiplex modules – general information

Fuses

1 Fuses are designed to break a circuit when a predetermined current is reached, in order to protect the components and wiring which could be damaged by excessive current flow. Any excessive current flow will be due to a fault in the circuit, usually a short-circuit (see Section 2).

2 The main fuses are located inside the glovebox.

3 Open the glovebox, then prise down the fusebox cover panel at the top – the cover has a label inside giving details of the circuits each fuse protects **(see illustration)**.

4 A blown fuse can be recognised from its melted or broken wire.

5 To remove a fuse, first ensure that the relevant circuit is switched off – for maximum safety, disconnect the battery (see *Disconnecting the battery*).

6 Pull the fuse from its location, using the plastic tweezer tool provided **(see illustration)**. Spare fuses are provided in the cover panel.

7 Before renewing a blown fuse, trace and rectify the cause, and always use a fuse of the correct rating. Never substitute a fuse of a higher rating, or make temporary repairs using wire or metal foil; more serious damage, or even fire, could result.

8 Additional fuses are located the engine compartment fusebox. Unclip and lift off the fusebox cover – one of the clips is situated quite low down, next to the battery. This gives access to only about six of the fuses **(see illustrations)** – to reach the rest, remove the engine multiplex module as follows.

9 Remove the battery as described in Chapter 5A.

10 Unclip the large wiring plug from the top of the fusebox, sliding it out sideways without disconnecting it **(see illustration)**.

11 Unscrew the bolt and disconnect the large red fusebox supply lead from the front of the fusebox **(see illustration)**.

12 Slide the engine multiplex module out from its location in the top of the fusebox – this provides access to the rest of the fuses on top **(see illustrations)**. With the module removed

3.3 Unclip the fusebox from inside the top of the glovebox

3.6 Extract the fuse with the tweezer tool

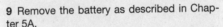

3.8a Unclip and lift out the fusebox lid . . .

3.8b . . . for access to some of the fuses

3.10 Unclip and slide out the main wiring plug

3.11 Disconnect the red supply lead at the front

3.12a Slide out the multiplex module . . .

3.12b . . . for access to the larger fuses below

3.13 The battery positive terminal has built-in fusible links

3.17a Slide out the storage drawer, and press the tabs to remove it . . .

3.17b . . . for access to the relay and fuses inside

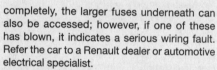

3.23a Unscrew the single central bolt . . .

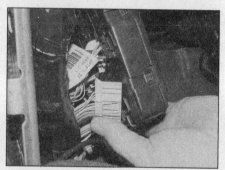

3.23b . . . then unclip the module and disconnect the wiring plugs on the back . . .

3.23c . . . before withdrawing the module into the footwell

completely, the larger fuses underneath can also be accessed; however, if one of these has blown, it indicates a serious wiring fault. Refer the car to a Renault dealer or automotive electrical specialist.

13 Fusible links are incorporated into the battery positive terminal, but again, if these have blown, a serious wiring fault is indicated **(see illustration)**.

14 Some models may have additional fuses in the compartment under the passenger seat, together with some relays – see paragraph 17.

Relays

15 A relay is an electrically-operated switch, which is used for the following reasons:
  a) *A relay can switch a heavy current remotely from the circuit in which the current is flowing, allowing the use of lighter-gauge wiring and switch contacts.*
  b) *A relay can receive more than one control input, unlike a mechanical switch.*
  c) *A relay can have a timer function – for example, the intermittent wiper relay.*

16 As a result of the switching functions contained within the multiplex modules, fewer relays are fitted than normal. Those that are fitted are located adjacent to the two main fuseboxes in the passenger and engine compartments. Refer to the wiring diagrams at the end of this Chapter for more information.

17 Additional relays are fitted on some models in the compartment under the passenger seat. To access these, remove the storage drawer by opening it and depressing the sides to release the tabs. The relays are

inside, together with a small number of fuses **(see illustrations)**.

18 If a circuit or system controlled by a relay develops a fault, and the relay is suspect, operate the system. If the relay is functioning, it should be possible to hear it 'click' as it is energised. If this is the case, the fault lies with the components or wiring of the system. If the relay is not being energised, then either the relay is not receiving a main supply or a switching voltage, or the relay itself is faulty. Testing is by the substitution of a known good unit, but be careful – while some relays are identical in appearance and in operation, others look similar but perform different functions.

Multiplex modules

19 The engine multiplex module (also known as the protection and switching unit) is located in the top of the engine compartment fusebox.

20 Remove the unit from the fusebox as described in paragraphs 8 to 12, then disconnect the wiring plugs and it can be removed completely.

21 The interior multiplex module (also known as the UCH, or Unité de Commande d'Habitacle) is located under the facia panel, on the passenger side.

22 To gain access to the module, remove the glovebox as described in Chapter 11. It will also be useful to unclip and detach the ventilation duct, referring to Chapter 3 if necessary.

23 Unscrew the single bolt securing the

multiplex module, then unclip and lower it into the footwell. Release the locking catches from the module wiring plugs, and remove the module **(see illustrations)**.

24 Any suspected problems with either module are best referred to a Renault dealer, who will have the dedicated diagnostic equipment available to determine the problem. Fitting a module from another car will probably mean reprogramming the module to the car before it will work properly.

4 Switches – removal and refitting

Note: *Before removing any switch, at least make sure the ignition is off (remove the keycard). Ideally, disconnect the battery negative lead, and position the lead away from the battery (also see Disconnecting the battery).*

Ignition keycard reader

1 Remove the radio/CD player as described in Section 19.

2 Remove the gear lever housing as described in Chapter 11, Section 23.

3 Remove the two screws at the base of the surround panel, then unclip the surround panel from the facia (it is secured by two clips either side). Reach in behind and disconnect the wiring connectors from the card reader and starter button **(see illustrations)**.

4 Unclip and remove the card reader from the surround panel **(see illustration)**.

5 Refitting is a reversal of removal.

Starter button

6 Remove the heater control surround panel as described in paragraphs 1 to 3.
7 Using two small screwdrivers, release the switch securing tabs, and remove it from the surround panel (see illustrations).
8 Refitting is a reversal of removal.

Hazard warning light switch

9 Remove the gear lever housing as described in Chapter 11, Section 23.
10 Release the switch securing tabs, and remove it from the gear lever housing top panel. The hazard warning light switch is not available separately.
11 Refitting is a reversal of removal.

Central locking switch

12 Proceed as described for the hazard warning light switch, in paragraphs 9 and 10. The central locking switch is not available separately.

Steering column switches

13 Remove the steering wheel as described in Chapter 10.
14 The steering column switches are mounted on, and connected through, a module fitted behind the steering wheel, which also contains the airbag rotary connector. Remove the switch 'module' as described for the airbag rotary connector, in Section 25.
15 To renew an individual switch, typically remove the two mounting screws, then

4.3a Remove the two screws from the surround panel . . .

4.3c Disconnect the wiring plug from the starter button . . .

release the retaining tabs and withdraw it. Some of the switches have an individual wiring plug which must also be disconnected (see illustrations).
16 Refitting is a reversal of removal.

4.3b . . . then unclip and lift off the panel

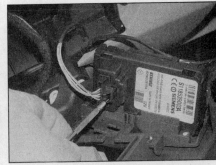
4.3d . . . and from the keycard reader

Radio remote controls

17 Remove the steering column switch module as described for the airbag rotary connector, in Section 25.
18 Remove the mounting screws, then

4.4 Unclip and remove the keycard reader

4.7a Use two screwdrivers to release the tabs on the back . . .

4.7b . . . then withdraw the switch through the front

4.15a Remove the two screws . . .

4.15b . . . disconnect the individual wiring plug (where applicable) . . .

4.15c . . . then release the retaining tabs . . .

4.15d . . . and remove the switch

4.18a Remove the switch mounting screws . . .

4.18b . . . then unclip the switch retaining tabs . . .

4.18c . . . and withdraw the switch

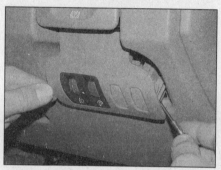

4.21 Carefully prise out the headlight adjuster switch . . .

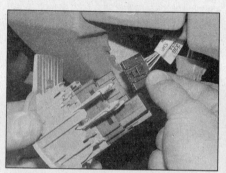

4.22 . . . and disconnect the wiring plug

unclip the switch tabs and withdraw it – finally disconnect the wiring plug **(see illustrations)**.
19 Refitting is a reversal of removal.

Blower and air conditioning switches

20 These switches are built into the heater control panel – remove the panel as described in Chapter 3.

Headlight adjuster switch

21 Taking care not to damage the finish, carefully prise out the switch from the facia **(see illustration)**.
22 Disconnect the switch wiring plug, and remove the switch panel **(see illustration)**.
23 Refitting is a reversal of removal.

Instrument dimmer switch

24 Proceed as described for the headlight

adjuster switch, in paragraphs 21 to 23. The instrument dimmer switch is not available separately.

Passenger airbag selector switch

⚠️ **Warning: Disconnect the battery negative lead (see 'Disconnecting the battery'), then wait for five minutes before proceeding. If this waiting period is not observed, there is danger of activating the passenger airbag.**

25 Unclip the facia end cover panel at the driver's side **(see illustration)**.
26 Disconnect the wiring plug from the switch, then unclip and withdraw it from the 'front' of the panel **(see illustration)**.
27 Refitting is a reversal of removal. Reconnect the switch before reconnecting the battery.

Electric window switches

28 On front door switches, carefully prise up the window switch assembly, and lift it out of the door trim panel **(see illustration)**.
29 The rear door switches have a screw under a trim cap, which must be removed before the switch can be prised out **(see illustrations)**.
30 The window switch wiring plugs are wrapped in self-adhesive foam sheeting, and this takes skill to unwrap without tearing. Peel back the foam, disconnect the wiring plugs, and remove the assembly **(see illustrations)**.
31 Refitting is a reversal of removal.

Electric mirror switch

32 Taking care not to damage the door trim panel, carefully prise the switch body out. Disconnect the wiring plug, and remove the switch **(see illustrations)**.

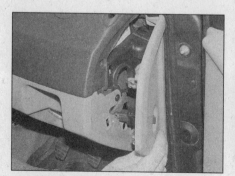

4.25 Unclip the facia end cover panel

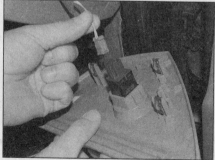

4.26 Disconnect the switch plug, then release and remove it

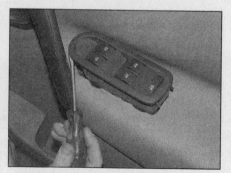

4.28 The front electric window switch panel can be prised out . . .

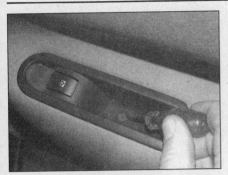

4.29a . . . while the rear window switches have a trim cap . . .

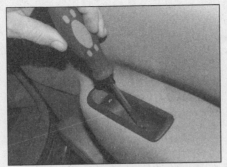

4.29b . . . with a screw underneath to remove . . .

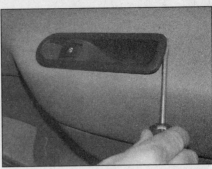

4.29c . . . before the switch can be lifted out

33 Refitting is a reversal of removal.

Interior light switches

34 The interior/courtesy lights are operated by the interior multiplex unit (see Section 3), using information from the central locking system. Conventional switches are therefore not used.

Heated rear window/ mirror switches

35 These switches are built into the heater control panel – remove the panel as described in Chapter 3.

Heated seat switches

36 Taking care not to damage the seat trim, carefully prise the switch body out. Disconnect the wiring plug, and remove the switch.
37 Refitting is a reversal of removal.

4.30a Peel back the foam covering . . .

Sunroof switch

38 Prise the switch panel out of the headlining, and disconnect the wiring plug from it (see illustrations).

4.30b . . . and disconnect the switch wiring plugs

39 Use a small screwdriver, release the tabs around the switch body, and remove it from the panel (see illustrations).
40 Refitting is a reversal of removal.

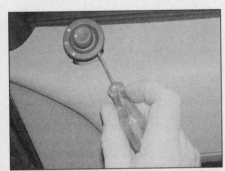

4.32a Prise out the mirror switch . . .

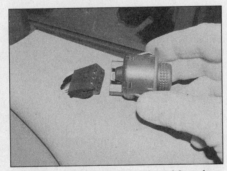

4.32b . . . and disconnect the wiring plug

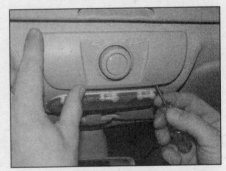

4.38a Prise the sunroof switch from the headlining . . .

4.38b . . . and disconnect the wiring plug

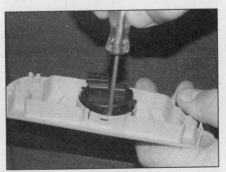

4.39a Release the tabs from the switch . . .

4.39b . . . and remove it from the panel

4.43 Disconnect the handbrake switch wiring plug

Brake light switch

41 The brake light switch is removed as described in Chapter 9.

Handbrake warning light switch

Note: *A separate warning light switch is only fitted to models with a manual handbrake – on models with the automatic handbrake, the facia warning light operates through the facia control and the control unit (see Chapter 9).*

42 Remove the centre console as described in Chapter 11.

43 Disconnect the wiring plug from the warning light switch **(see illustration)**.

44 Pull back the carpet as necessary, then remove the switch securing screw and withdraw the switch from the handbrake lever.

45 Refitting is a reversal of removal. Check the switch operation before refitting the centre console.

5 Bulbs (exterior lights) – renewal

General

1 Whenever a bulb is renewed, note the following points:
  a) *Disconnect the battery negative lead, or at least make sure that the lighting circuit is switched off, before starting work.*
  b) *Remember that if the light has recently been in use, the bulb may be extremely hot.*
  c) *Always check the bulb contacts and/or holder (as applicable). Ensure that there is clean metal-to-metal contact between the bulb contacts and the contacts in the holder, and/or the holder and the wiring plug. Clean off any corrosion or dirt before fitting a new bulb.*
  d) *Ensure that the new bulb is of the correct rating and that it is completely clean before fitting; this applies particularly to headlight bulbs.*

Headlight (halogen)

Note: *The headlight lenses are plastic, and may melt or become discoloured if the correct bulbs are not fitted.*

2 Accessing the headlight bulbs from the engine compartment is not easy. Removing either the battery cover or unclipping the washer reservoir filler neck will make access to the bulbs easier.

3 Realistically, the only way to improve the situation is to remove the headlight as described in Section 7.

4 To access the main and dipped beam bulbs, remove the relevant round cover from the back of the light unit, as follows:
  a) *On halogen headlights, the inner cover is for the dipped beam bulb, with the outer one for the main beam* **(see illustration)**.
  b) *On xenon headlights, the inner cover is for the main beam bulb, with the outer one for the dipped beam xenon bulb – refer to the next sub-Section.*

5 Twist the dipped beam headlight bulbholder anti-clockwise, and withdraw it from the headlight. Disconnect the wiring plug from the bulb, and remove it **(see illustrations)**.

6 On the main beam bulb, pull off the wiring plug, then squeeze together the legs of the wire retaining clip and fold the clip down to release the bulb **(see illustrations)**.

7 When handling the new bulbs, use a tissue or clean cloth to avoid touching the glass with the fingers; moisture and grease from the skin can cause blackening and rapid failure of this type of bulb.

8 Refitting is a reversal of removal.

Headlight (xenon)

Note: *Renewal of the main beam bulb is as described for the halogen light previously in this Section – for renewal of the xenon dipped beam bulb, proceed as follows.*

⚠ *Warning: Before carrying out any operations on xenon headlight units, it is recommended that*

5.4 Unclip the round rubber cover from the back of the headlight

5.5a Twist the dipped beam bulbholder out anti-clockwise . . .

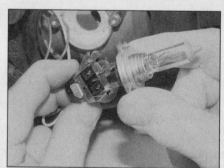

5.5b . . . and disconnect the wiring plug

5.6a Disconnect the main beam bulb wiring plug . . .

5.6b . . . squeeze together the legs of the wire retaining clip . . .

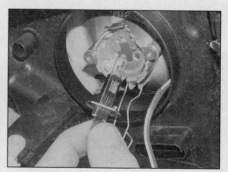

5.6c . . . and pull out the bulb

protective gloves and safety glasses are worn. It is essential that the wiring connectors are disconnected from the rear of the headlight unit, then wait until the bulbs have cooled down before removal. DO NOT switch the headlights on with the bulb removed as it is harmful to the eyes.

9 Remove the headlight unit as described in Section 7.

10 The xenon bulb is located behind the outermost round cover on the rear of the headlight unit – prise out the cover for access. Turn the condenser unit on the rear of the bulb anti-clockwise by 45°, and withdraw it from the bulb (**see illustration**).

11 Release the wire clip retaining the bulb, then turn the bulb anti-clockwise about an eighth of a turn and withdraw it from the light unit. The external conductor of the bulb is fragile, take care not to damage or knock it.

12 When handling the new bulb, use a tissue or clean cloth to avoid touching the glass with the fingers; moisture and grease from the skin can cause blackening and rapid failure of this type of bulb.

13 Refitting is a reversal of removal. According to Renault, the xenon headlight system will need to be re-initialised by a dealer following bulb renewal.

Front sidelight

14 The sidelight bulbholder is located above and between the two headlight bulb rear covers. Gain access to the back of the headlight as described in paragraphs 2 and 3.

15 Twist the bulbholder anti-clockwise from the rear of the headlight assembly (**see illustration**).

16 The bulb is a push-fit (capless) in the bulbholder (**see illustration**).

17 Refitting is a reversal of removal.

Front indicator

18 The indicator bulb is the outermost one in the headlight unit, at the top. Gain access to the back of the headlight as described in paragraphs 2 and 3.

19 The bulbholder has a flat 'handle' on the back, which makes it easier to twist anti-clockwise for removal (**see illustration**).

20 With the bulbholder removed, twist and remove the indicator bulb (**see illustration**).

21 Refitting is a reversal of removal.

Front indicator side repeater

22 The light unit is clipped into the front wing, and in theory can be unclipped at the front edge, after pushing the light unit to the rear. However, we found this carries a high risk of scratching the paint (and maybe damaging the light), so if this method is used, stick masking tape around the light.

23 A much safer method is to carefully prise away the wheel arch liner near the light unit, then reach inside and unclip the light (**see illustrations**).

24 Twist the bulbholder to release it from the

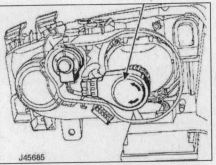

5.10 Twist and remove the high-voltage unit (arrowed) from the headlight

5.16 . . . and pull out the bulb

light, then pull out the wedge-base bulb (**see illustrations**).

25 Refitting is a reversal of removal. Clip the light unit securely back into the wing.

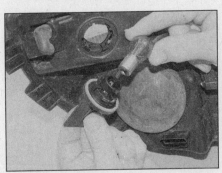

5.20 . . . then twist and remove the bayonet bulb

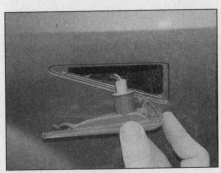

5.23b Showing the sidelight unit front and rear retaining clips

5.15 Twist and remove the bulbholder from the headlight . . .

5.19 Use the flat handle to twist out the indicator bulbholder . . .

Front foglight

26 Reach in under/behind the bumper, and twist the bulbholder anti-clockwise to remove it from the back of the light (**see illustration**).

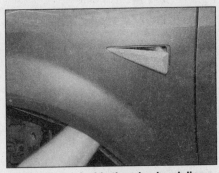

5.23a Reach inside the wheel arch liner and push out the light unit

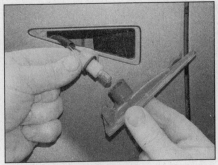

5.24a Twist the bulbholder from the back of the light . . .

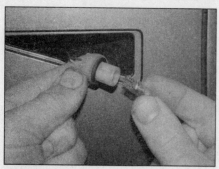

5.24b ... and pull out the wedge-base bulb

5.26 Twist the bulbholder off the back of the foglight

5.27 Disconnect the wiring plug and remove the bulbholder

5.30 Remove the two screws on the inner side of the light unit

5.31 Pull the light unit straight back to release the two locating pegs

5.32 Disconnect the wiring plug from the light cluster

27 Disconnect the wiring plug from the base of the bulbholder – note that the wiring socket, bulb and holder are a complete unit (the bulb cannot be renewed separately) (see illustration).

28 When handling the new bulb, use a tissue or clean cloth to avoid touching the glass with the fingers; moisture and grease from the skin can cause blackening and rapid failure of this type of bulb. If the glass is accidentally touched, wipe it clean using methylated spirit.

29 Refitting is a reversal of removal.

Rear light cluster

30 Open the tailgate, then remove the two screws on the inner side of the rear light unit (see illustration).

31 Withdraw the light unit from the car, noting that it has locating pegs on the back which fit into holes in the car body. These pegs are quite stiff to pull out (see illustration).

Caution: Make sure that the upper peg is released first, as the light unit will suffer damage to the top corner if the lower one releases first – ie do not let the light unit tilt upwards as it is removed.

32 Disconnect the wiring plug from the light unit, and remove from the car completely (see illustration).

33 Unclip the bulbholder from the light unit by releasing the two tabs at the top and bottom, and remove the bayonet-fitting bulb (see illustrations).

34 Refitting is a reversal of removal.

High-level stop-light

35 The 'bulbs' in the high-level stop-light are non-replaceable LEDs. The light unit can be removed as described in Section 7.

Rear number plate light

36 Open the tailgate to improve access, then carefully prise out the light unit. Disconnect the wiring plug and remove the unit completely (see illustrations).

5.33a Unclip the bulbholder from the light unit ...

5.33b ... and remove the relevant bulb

5.36a Prise out the number plate light ...

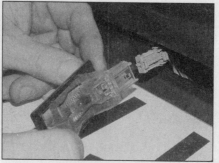

5.36b ... and disconnect the wiring plug

37 Pull out the wedge-base bulb to remove it **(see illustration)**.
38 Refitting is a reversal of removal.

6 Bulbs (interior lights) – renewal

General

1 Refer to Section 5, paragraph 1.

Interior lights

2 Unclip the light unit lens for access to the bulbs. Pull the bulb to remove it **(see illustrations)**.
3 Refitting is a reversal of removal.

Footwell light

4 Prise out the light unit from the base of the door trim panel **(see illustration)**.
5 Pull out the wedge-base bulb, and remove it **(see illustration)**.
6 Refitting is a reversal of removal.

Instrument panel and warning lights

7 The instrument panel is a 'solid-state' type, which means the 'bulbs' are non-replaceable LEDs. The instrument panel is removed as described in Section 10.

Cigar lighter illumination

8 Remove the cigar lighter as described in Section 14.

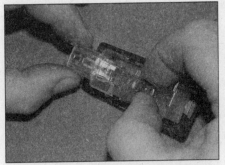

5.37 Pull out the wedge-base bulb to renew it

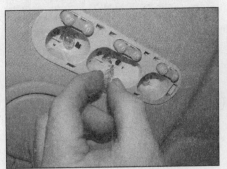

6.2b ... and pull out the bulb

9 The bulb may have to be renewed as part of the holder, check with your Renault dealer for availability.
10 Reassemble and refit the cigar lighter using a reversal of the removal procedure.

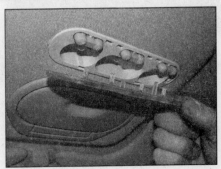

6.2a Unclip the lens ...

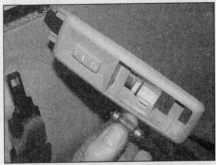

6.2c The rear interior lights may have festoon bulbs

Glovebox light

11 Open the glovebox. Prise down the light unit inside, then take off the light unit lens. Unclip the festoon-type bulb from its contacts **(see illustrations)**.

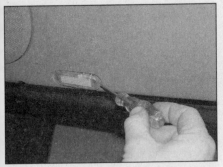

6.4 Prise out the footwell light from the door ...

6.11b ... then unclip the lens ...

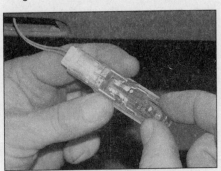

6.5 ... and pull out the bulb

6.11c ... and pull out the festoon bulb

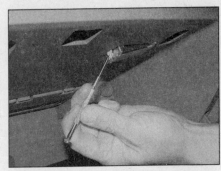

6.11a Prise down the glovebox light ...

6.14 Unclip the boot light, and disconnect it

6.15 Unclip the light lens, and take out the festoon bulb

12 Refitting is a reversal of removal.

Heater control illumination

13 Refer to Chapter 3, Section 11 for heater control panel removal and bulb renewal.

Luggage compartment light

14 Unclip the light from its location in the luggage compartment, then disconnect the wiring plug and remove it **(see illustration)**.
15 Unclip the lens, then unclip and remove the festoon bulb **(see illustration)**.
16 Refitting is a reversal of removal.

| 7 | Exterior light units – removal and refitting | |

Note: *Before removing any light, at least make sure the light concerned is switched off, and that the ignition is also off (remove the keycard). Ideally, disconnect the battery negative lead, and position the lead away from the battery (also see Disconnecting the battery).*

Headlight

⚠ **Warning: Before carrying out any operations on xenon headlight units, it is recommended that protective gloves and safety glasses are worn. It is essential that the wiring connectors are disconnected from the rear of the headlight unit, then wait until the bulbs have cooled down before removal. DO NOT switch the headlights on with the bulb removed, as it is harmful to the eyes.**

1 Remove the front bumper as described in Chapter 11.
2 Remove the four headlight mounting bolts (two above, two below) **(see illustrations)**.
3 Depress the catch on the inside lower corner of the headlight which secures the lower trim piece, and withdraw the trim from under the light **(see illustration)**.
4 Disconnect the wiring plugs from the back of the headlight, and remove it **(see illustrations)**.
5 Refitting is a reversal of removal.
6 On completion, the headlight beam alignment should be checked, ideally using optical setting equipment. This check should be carried out by a Renault dealer or a suitably-equipped garage (see Section 9).

Front foglight

7 Remove the bulb as described in Section 5.
8 Unscrew the two foglight mounting bolts, and remove the light from the bumper **(see illustration)**.

7.2a Remove the headlight lower mounting bolts – one at the front . . .

7.2b . . . with the other further back

7.2c Headlight upper mounting bolts (arrowed)

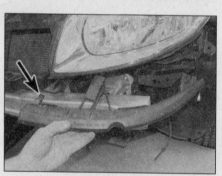

7.3 Release the inner tab and pull out the lower trim piece

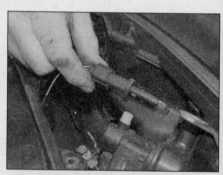

7.4a Disconnect the sidelight bulbholder (or remove it completely) . . .

7.4b . . . then disconnect the headlight adjuster motor . . .

7.4c . . . and the main headlight wiring plug (non-xenon light shown) . . .

7.4d Removing the headlight

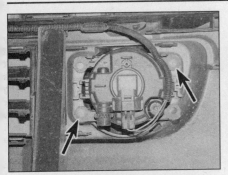

7.8 Front foglight mounting bolts (arrowed)

7.12 Unclip the top section of the tailgate window trim

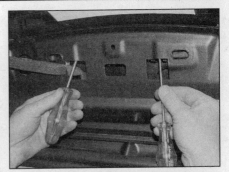

7.13a Using two screwdrivers in the slots provided . . .

7.13b . . . release the metal retaining clips and withdraw the light

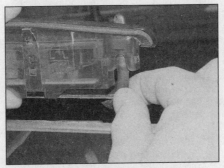

7.14a Disconnect the washer tube . . .

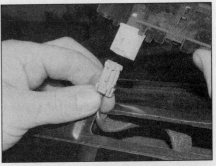

7.14b . . . and the light wiring plug

9 Refitting is a reversal of removal. It is advisable to have the foglight beam alignment checked on completion.

Front indicator side repeater

10 The procedure is described in the bulb renewal sequence, in Section 5.

Rear light cluster

11 The procedure is described in the bulb renewal sequence, in Section 5.

High-level stop-light

12 Unclip the top section of the tailgate window trim panel, immediately below the light unit (see illustration).
13 Using two small screwdrivers, press the retaining lugs at either end of the light unit to release it from the tailgate (see illustrations).

14 Disconnect the washer jet tubing and the wiring plug, and remove the light completely (see illustrations).
15 Other than the washer jet, which can be removed as described in Section 18, the light unit cannot be dismantled further.
16 Refitting is a reversal of removal.

Rear number plate light

17 The procedure is described in the bulb renewal sequence, in Section 5.

8 Interior light units –
removal and refitting

Interior lights

1 Unclip the lens from the light unit, then

release the retaining tab at one end and lower the light from the headlining (see illustrations).
2 Disconnect the wiring plug from the opposite end, and remove the light unit (see illustration).
3 Refitting is a reversal of removal.

Glovebox light

4 The procedure is described in the bulb renewal sequence, in Section 6.

Footwell lights

5 The procedure is described in the bulb renewal sequence, in Section 6.

Luggage compartment light

6 The procedure is described in the bulb renewal sequence, in Section 6.

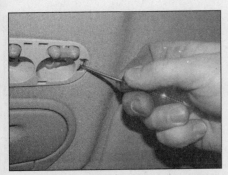

8.1a Release the retaining tab at one end . . .

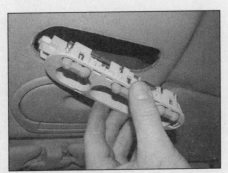

8.1b . . . and lower out the interior light

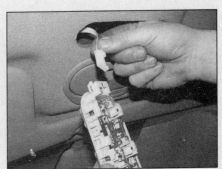

8.2 Disconnect the wiring plug and remove the light

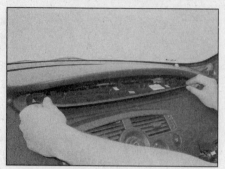

10.2 Unclip the instrument panel top shroud downwards, and remove it

9 Headlight beam alignment
– general information

Accurate adjustment of the headlight beam is only possible using optical beam-setting equipment, and this work should therefore be carried out by a Renault dealer or suitably-equipped workshop.

To make a temporary adjustment of the headlights, position the car on a level surface 10 metres from a wall. The tyres must all be at the correct pressure, and the manual adjustment switch inside the car set at 0. Use the adjuster screws at the rear of the headlight to reset the beams accordingly.

Most models have a headlight beam manual adjustment control, which allows the aim of the headlights to be adjusted to compensate for variation in the car's payload. The aim is

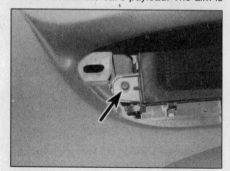

10.4a Remove the screw on the left . . .

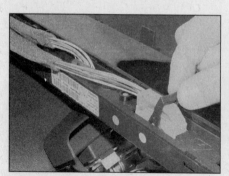

10.5a Hinge the plug locking levers to the side . . .

10.3 Prise up the lower shroud, disconnect it where applicable, and remove

altered by means of facia-mounted switch, which controls electric adjuster motors located in the rear of the headlight assemblies.

Models with xenon headlights have an automatic levelling system. If a fault occurs in the system, a warning light will show up on the instrument panel, and the headlights will be angled down to avoid dazzling oncoming traffic. If this happens, the driving speed must be adjusted accordingly to allow for decreased visibility.

10 Instrument panel –
removal and refitting

Removal

1 Disconnect the battery negative lead, and move the lead away from the battery (see *Disconnecting the battery*).
2 Taking care not to damage the finish, unclip

10.4b . . . and on the right . . .

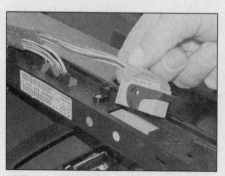

10.5b . . . then disconnect the wiring plugs and remove the panel

the instrument panel upper shroud downwards and remove it **(see illustration)**.
3 Prise up the lower surround, then (where applicable) disconnect the wiring plug and remove it **(see illustration)**.
4 Remove the screw either side, and withdraw the instrument panel **(see illustrations)**.
5 Hinge the wiring plug locking levers to one side, disconnect the plugs, and remove the instrument panel **(see illustrations)**.

Refitting

6 Refitting is a reversal of removal.

11 Outside air temperature sensor
– removal and refitting

Note: *Check with your local Renault dealer for availability of parts, the sensor may only be available as part of the mirror as a complete assembly.*

Removal

1 The sensor is mounted in the bottom of the driver's door mirror, behind the front casing (shell).
2 To dismantle the door mirror for access to the sensor, proceed as described in Chapter 11, Section 17 and remove the mirror front shell.
3 Unclip the sensor from its location **(see illustration)**. As there is no wiring plug, the two sensor wires have to be cut to remove it.
4 Refitting is a reversal of removal. Join the sensor wires together using a reliable connection method, and insulate the joints.

10.4c . . . and withdraw the instrument panel

11.3 Unclip the temperature sensor from the driver's door mirror

12 Rain sensor and automatic headlight sensor – removal and refitting

Note: *This sensor is not really intended for DIY removal and refitting. It works through a clear gel coating on the inside of the windscreen, which if damaged or contaminated in any way will result in faulty operation of the sensor. We felt we had been lucky when we successfully removed and refitted the sensor fitted to our project car. Seek the advice of a Renault dealer before disturbing the sensor.*

General information

1 The sensor used to automatically switch on the headlights and wipers, on models so equipped, consists of several photo-electric cells fitted at the top of the windscreen, detecting the amount of light coming through. If the light is refracted by raindrops on the glass, the sensor signals the interior multiplex module to operate the wipers, independently of the driver. Similarly, if the light level is reduced (as in the evening, or when entering a tunnel, for example), the headlights are automatically switched on (and then off again, if the light level increases).
2 Since the sensor is highly sensitive, it is vital for its correct operation that the windscreen be as clean as possible. Also, any damage to the glass, such as a stone chip in the vicinity of the sensor, will seriously affect it.

Removal

3 Unclip the front section of the interior mirror surround, then slide off the rear section **(see illustrations)**.
4 Use a small screwdriver to release the metal clip from either side of the sensor body, then carefully lower the sensor from the screen – this operation can result in damage to the clear gel in the sensor base, which might require a new base to be fitted. Disconnect the wiring plug from the sensor and remove it **(see illustrations)**.
5 The sensor base (which contains the clear gel) is stuck firmly to the windscreen, and there is a great risk of damage to the screen in removing it. This operation may be better entrusted to a Renault dealer, or possibly to a windscreen

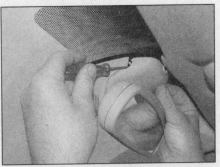

12.3a Unclip the front section of the interior mirror surround . . .

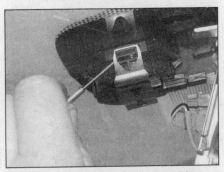

12.4a Release the metal clips either side . . .

replacement specialist. A new base must be fitted in conditions of absolute cleanliness, to avoid the sensor malfunctioning.

Refitting

6 Refitting is a reversal of removal.

13 Cigar lighter – removal and refitting

Removal

1 Remove the gear lever housing as described in Chapter 11, Section 23.
2 Release the clips securing the cigar lighter to the panel, and withdraw it from the front.

Refitting

3 Refitting is a reversal of removal.

14 Horn – removal and refitting

Removal

1 The horn is located at the front of the car, almost directly behind the Renault badge in the centre of the front bumper/grille.
2 Remove the front bumper as described in Chapter 11.
3 Disconnect the wiring plug from the horn **(see illustration)**.
4 Unscrew the mounting bolt, and withdraw the horn from the front crossmember.

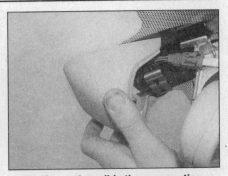

12.3b . . . then slide the rear section towards the screen

12.4b . . . and separate the sensor from the base

Refitting

5 Refitting is a reversal of removal.

15 Wiper arms – removal and refitting

Removal

1 The wiper motor should be in the parked position before removing the wiper arm. Mark the position of the blade on the glass with adhesive tape, as a guide to refitting.

Windscreen wiper arms

2 Lift the hinged cover or unclip the plastic cap, and remove the nut underneath securing the arm to the spindle. In the case of the driver's side windscreen wiper arm, there are two nuts to unscrew **(see illustrations)**.

14.3 Disconnect the horn wiring plug – mounting bolt arrowed

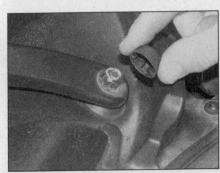

15.2a Unclip the plastic cap . . .

15.2b . . . and unscrew the wiper arm nut

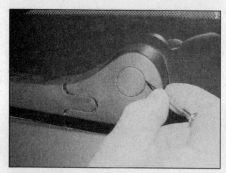

15.4 Prise out the tailgate wiper arm nut cover

3 Pull or prise the arm from the spindle(s), using a puller or screwdriver if necessary **(see illustration)**. Take care not to damage the trim or paintwork.

16.3a Two of the wiper linkage mounting bolts, and the stay bracket

16.3d . . . and lift out the assembly

15.3 Pull the arm from the spindle, and remove it

Tailgate wiper arm

4 Reach behind the arm with your fingertip to unclip and remove the trim cap over the spindle nut. Help the cover out by carefully prising with a small screwdriver (see illustration).
5 Unscrew the nut, and pull the arm from the splines.

Refitting

6 Refitting is a reversal of removal. Position the arms so that the blades align with the tape applied to the glass before removal.

---

16 Windscreen wiper motor and linkage – removal and refitting

Removal

1 Make sure that the wipers are in the parked

16.3b Remove the third wiper linkage mounting bolt

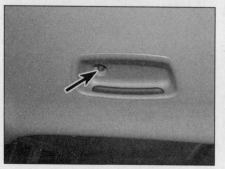

17.2a Remove the tailgate trim panel screw inside each handle . . .

position (switch the wipers on, then off).
2 Remove the plastic windscreen cowl panels, as described in Chapter 11.
3 Remove the three wiper linkage mounting bolts, and the two bolts from the stay bracket. Lift the linkage/motor assembly out **(see illustrations)**.
4 Disconnect the wiring plug from the wiper motor, and remove the assembly.
5 To remove the motor, mark the relative positions of the motor shaft and crank, then unscrew the retaining nut and washer and free the wiper linkage from the motor spindle. Unscrew the three motor retaining bolts and separate the motor from the linkage.

Refitting

6 Refitting is a reversal of removal.

---

17 Tailgate wiper motor – removal and refitting

Removal

Models with fixed tailgate glass

1 Remove the tailgate wiper arm with reference to Section 15. Carefully prise off the wiper spindle rubber seal.
2 Remove the tailgate main trim panel, which is secured by four screws (one inside each tailgate 'handle', one either side at the top) and a number of clips. There is also a cover panel fitted over the lock, which must be unclipped **(see illustrations)**.

16.3c Take off the stay bracket . . .

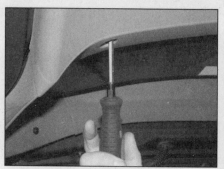

17.2b . . . and the one each side, at the top . . .

3 Disconnect the wiring plug from the motor (**see illustration**).

4 The motor is secured by three bolts – remove these and take off the motor (**see illustration**).

Models with opening tailgate glass

5 On models with the optional opening tailgate glass, there is a tailgate wiper linkage, necessitated by the opening glass, to transfer the motor drive to the wiper arm.

6 With the wiper arm removed as described in Section 15, prise off the nut cover, then unscrew the nut beneath and take off the trim from the outside of the glass.

7 With the glass open, unscrew the bolt securing the linkage to the glass, and remove it.

8 The wiper motor is attached to the tailgate in the same way as that for models with a fixed tailgate glass, and can be removed as described in paragraphs 2 to 4.

Refitting

9 Refitting is a reversal of removal.

---

18 Windscreen/tailgate washer system components – removal and refitting

---

Washer jets

Windscreen

1 Open the bonnet. The windscreen washer jets are located under the rear edge of the bonnet, clipped into rectangular holes – use a small screwdriver to prise them out, taking care not to damage the paint (**see illustration**).

2 Disconnect the washer tube from the jet, and remove it (**see illustration**).

3 The washer supply tubing can be disconnected from the underbonnet T-pieces and released from the mounting clips as required (**see illustrations**).

4 Refitting is a reversal of removal. Ensure that the jets are clipped in and the hoses reconnected securely.

Tailgate

5 Remove the high-level stop-light as described in Section 7.

6 Use a small screwdriver to release the jet

securing tabs, then withdraw it from the light unit (**see illustrations**).

7 Refitting is a reversal of removal. Ensure that the jets are clipped in and the hoses reconnected securely.

8 For information, we discovered that the tailgate washer supply tubing runs along the right-hand side of the car, and there is a connector clipped behind the C-pillar trim panel (**see illustration**).

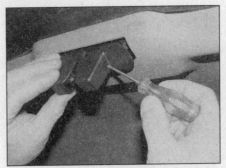

17.2c . . . then unclip the lock cover . . .

17.2d . . . and remove the trim panel

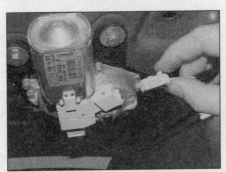

17.3 Disconnecting the tailgate wiper motor wiring plug

17.4 Tailgate wiper motor mounting bolts

18.1 Unclip the washer jet from the underside of the bonnet

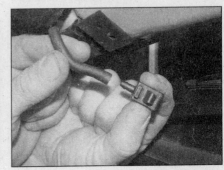

18.2 Pull the washer supply tube off the jet

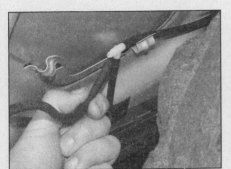

18.3a If required, the supply tube can be pulled off the T-pieces . . .

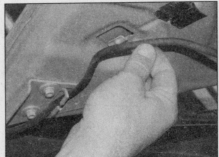

18.3b . . . and released from the bonnet clips

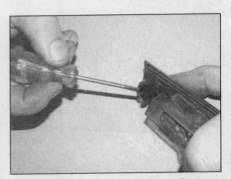

18.6a Release the jet securing tabs . . .

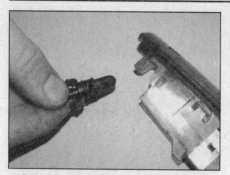

18.6b . . . and withdraw it from the high-level stop-light

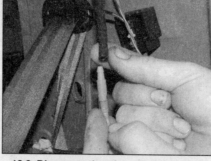

18.8 Disconnecting the tailgate washer supply tube in-line connector

18.10a Disconnect the washer pump wiring plug . . .

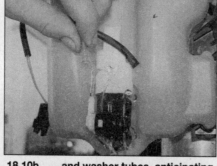

18.10b . . . and washer tubes, anticipating some spillage

Washer reservoir

9 Remove the front bumper as described in Chapter 11.

10 Disconnect the wiring plug and washer tubes from the washer pump – anticipate

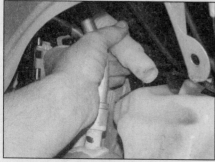

18.11 Pull the filler neck out of the reservoir

losing the entire contents of the reservoir when the tubes are disconnected **(see illustrations)**.

11 At the top of the reservoir, compress the concertina section of the filler neck, and pull it out **(see illustration)**.

18.12 Unclip and remove the reservoir

12 The reservoir is held in position by plastic clips – release these and remove the reservoir from under the front wing **(see illustration)**.

13 Refitting is a reversal of removal. Partially fill the reservoir and check for leaks before refitting the bumper.

Washer pump

14 Remove the front bumper as described in Chapter 11.

15 Disconnect the wiring plug and washer tubes from the washer pump – anticipate losing the entire contents of the reservoir when the tubes are disconnected.

16 Pull the washer pump sideways out of the reservoir – it's likely that the rubber grommet will come with it, in which case this should be refitted to the reservoir before the pump goes back in **(see illustrations)**.

17 Refitting is a reversal of removal. Partially fill the reservoir and check for leaks before refitting the bumper.

19 Radio/cassette/CD player
– removal and refitting

Removal

Radio/cassette or radio/CD player

1 All the radio units fitted to the Scénic range have DIN standard fixings. A pair of removal tools, obtainable from in-car entertainment specialists, will be required for removal – these may have been supplied with the car when new.

2 Disconnect the battery negative lead. **Note:** *If the car has a security-coded radio (such as the one fitted as standard), check that you have a copy of the code number before disconnecting the battery. Refer to your Renault dealer if in doubt.*

3 Insert the tools into the holes at the sides of the unit, and push home until they click. Pull the tools sideways and rearwards to release the unit and pull it from the facia **(see illustration)**.

4 Disconnect the aerial lead and the wiring plugs from the rear of the unit **(see illustrations)**.

18.16a Pull the washer pump out of the reservoir

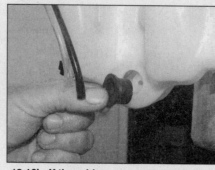

18.16b If the rubber grommet gets pulled out . . .

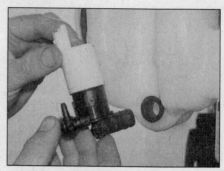

18.16c . . . refit it before fitting the pump

CD changer

5 The facia-mounted changer is removed similarly to the radio unit described previously, except that different, key-type tools are required to release it.

6 The underseat-mounted changer is accessed by opening the underseat storage tray. The changer has its own mounting cage, secured by two bolts – once this is removed, the changer is extracted using DIN tools similar to those for the facia-mounted unit.

Tuner/amplifier

7 Remove the rear seats as described in Chapter 11 (centre row on Grand Scénic) for access to the fuel pump cover.

8 Carefully prise the retaining plugs out to release the carpet, then unbolt the rear seat mountings and move the carpet clear. Detach and remove the soundproofing under the carpet.

9 Remove the screws and take out the floor access plate.

10 Using suitable DIN removal tools in the holes provide in the unit, release the tuner/amplifier from its mounting cage. Disconnect the wiring plugs and remove it from the car.

Refitting

11 Refitting is a reversal of removal. Instructions for re-entering the radio code should be found in the audio booklet which came with the car – if not, a Renault dealer should be able to help.

19.3 Pull the radio out using the special tools

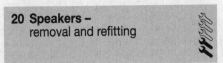

20 Speakers –
removal and refitting

Facia speakers (tweeters)

1 Taking care not to mark the facia, use a small screwdriver to prise out the speaker grille **(see illustration)**.

2 Use the screwdriver to lift out the speaker itself, then disconnect the wiring plug and remove it **(see illustrations)**.

3 Refitting is a reversal of removal.

Door speakers

4 Carefully prise out the speaker grille panel from the door **(see illustration)**.

5 Remove the mounting screws, then

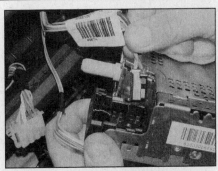

19.4a Disconnect the wiring plugs . . .

19.4b . . . and unclip the aerial lead from the back of the unit

withdraw the speaker from the door trim panel and disconnect the wiring plug from it **(see illustrations)**.

6 Refitting is a reversal of removal.

20.1 Prising out the tweeter grille – note the piece of card protecting the facia

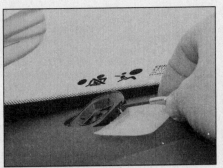

20.2a Lift out the speaker . . .

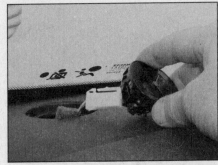

20.2b . . . and disconnect the wiring plug

20.4 Prise out the door speaker grille

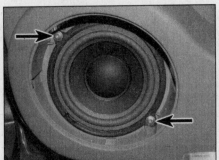

20.5a Remove the two mounting screws . . .

20.5b . . . then withdraw the speaker, and disconnect the wiring

21 Radio aerial – removal and refitting

Aerial

1 The aerial mast can be unscrewed from the base of the aerial if required.
2 Open the tailgate, and prise out the two clips from the rear of the headlining. Prise off the tailgate weatherstrip at the top, to release the headlining at the rear. Remove the rear grab handles and C-pillar trim panels as described in Chapter 11, Section 23 to make lowering the headlining easier.
3 Carefully prise down the headlining at the rear, sufficient to gain access to the aerial mounting nut. If access cannot be gained this way, the headlining may have to be removed completely – this is not considered to be a DIY operation, and should be referred to a Renault dealer. Remember that the side curtain airbag units are located above the headlining.
4 Unscrew the securing nut, and disconnect the aerial lead from the base of the aerial. Lift the aerial from the roof panel.
5 Refitting is a reversal of removal.

Aerial lead

6 With the lead disconnected from the aerial as described previously in this Section, observe the routing of the lead – it appears to run down the right-hand side of the car.
7 Remove the radio unit as described in Section 19, then disconnect the aerial lead from the rear of the unit.
8 The routing of the lead behind the facia can be judged by studying the facia removal procedure in Chapter 11 – to do the job properly would require the facia to be removed.
9 By removing the relevant trim panels as described in Chapter 11, Section 23, it should be possible, with patience, to fit a new lead without necessarily bothering to remove the old one. In routing a new cable, ensure that it will not be kinked or crushed in any way, and that it cannot drop down to interfere with the foot pedals.

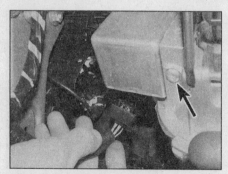

23.3 Disconnect the steering lock wiring plug – mounting bolt arrowed

22 Anti-theft alarm and immobiliser systems – general information

Certain models are fitted with an anti-theft alarm system, which uses various sensing systems and warning sirens, depending on model. No information was available for the alarm systems at the time of writing. Any faults should be referred to a Renault dealer for diagnosis.

All models are fitted with an engine immobiliser device which is activated by the coded ignition keycard. When the immobiliser is armed, the indicator light on the instrument panel will flash continuously. When the keycard is inserted, the code from the card is read by the card reader unit and transmits it to the interior multiplex module (see Section 3). If the multiplex module recognises the code, the engine can be started.

In the event of a non-starting car, remember that the system also relies on the brake or clutch being pressed, and on the transmission being in neutral (manual transmission) or Park (automatics). Therefore, a fault with the clutch pedal switch, brake stop-light switch, manual transmission neutral switch, or automatic transmission multi-function switch, will result in the wrong signal being sent to the multiplex modules. Refer to the relevant Chapters for more details.

23 Steering column lock – removal and refitting

1 The steering column lock is unconventional, in that it is electrically-operated (there is no key on the Scénic) by the interior multiplex module when the keycard is inserted or removed.

Removal

Note: *The steering column lock can only be removed when it is in its unlocked state, meaning that the keycard would have to be in its slot.*
2 Remove the steering column switch 'module' as described for the airbag rotary connector, in Section 25.
3 Disconnect the wiring plug from the base of the steering column lock **(see illustration)**.
4 Remove the single bolt securing the lock, and withdraw it from the column. This bolt has a **left-hand thread** – ie it unscrews **clockwise**. On our project car, it appeared that the bolt was of the shear-head type, as the head was missing – consult a Renault dealer in this instance, as drilling out the bolt may prevent a new one being fitted, and could result in damage to the column itself.

Refitting

5 Refitting is a reversal of removal. New steering column lock units are supplied uncoded, but coding is achieved by inserting

the keycard in its slot and pressing the starter button – if the keycard is then removed, the lock should activate after a few seconds, and the immobiliser light will start to flash.

24 Airbag system – general information and precautions

General information

All Scénic models are equipped with a comprehensive airbag system. In addition to adaptive front airbags for the driver and front passenger, there are side airbags fitted to the front seats, and side curtain airbags which are deployed from modules in the headlining. Rear side airbags are available as an option.

The airbag system is triggered in the event of a heavy frontal or side impact above a predetermined force; depending on the point of impact, not all the airbags will necessarily be fired. The airbags inflate within milliseconds to form a safety cushion which prevents contact with the internal surfaces of the car, greatly reducing the risk of injury. The airbags then deflate almost immediately.

The system is armed only when the ignition is on. However, a reserve power source maintains power to the system in the event of a break in the main electrical supply, for a short period – for this reason, it is essential to wait before disconnecting any of the system wiring.

The system is activated by a 'g' sensor (deceleration sensor), incorporated in the electronic control unit, fitted under the rear of the centre console. Note that the airbag control unit also controls the seat belt tensioners. Impact sensors in the B-pillars detect side impacts, which if severe enough, will cause the side and curtain airbags to be fired on the side concerned.

The airbags are inflated by gas generators, which force the bags out from their locations. Although these are safety items, their deployment is violently rapid, and this may cause injury if they are triggered unintentionally.

Linked to the airbag system are the seat belt tensioners fitted to each seat belt (except the centre belt on the rear seat). All models have two tensioners fitted to the front seats. The seat belt tensioners are fired with the airbags in the event of an accident, to take up the slack in the belts, and hold the occupants in their seats.

Precautions

⚠ *Warning: The following precautions must be observed when working on vehicles equipped with an airbag system, to prevent the possibility of personal injury.*

General precautions

The following precautions **must** be observed when carrying out work on a vehicle equipped with an airbag:

a) Do not disconnect the battery with the engine running.

b) Before carrying out any work in the vicinity of the airbag, removal of any of the airbag components, or any welding work on the car, de-activate the system as described in the following sub-Section.

c) Do not attempt to test any of the airbag system circuits using test meters or any other test equipment.

d) If the airbag warning light comes on, or any fault in the system is suspected, consult a Renault dealer without delay. Do not attempt to carry out fault diagnosis, or any dismantling of the components.

Precautions to be taken when handling an airbag

a) Transport the airbag by itself, bag upward.

b) Do not put your arms around the airbag.

c) Carry the airbag close to the body, bag outward.

d) Do not drop the airbag or expose it to impacts.

e) Do not attempt to dismantle the airbag unit.

f) Do not connect any form of electrical equipment to any part of the airbag circuit.

Precautions to be taken when storing an airbag unit

a) Store the unit in a cupboard with the airbag upward.

b) Do not expose the airbag to temperatures above 80ºC.

c) Do not expose the airbag to flames.

d) Do not attempt to dispose of the airbag – consult a Renault dealer.

e) Never refit an airbag which is known to be faulty or damaged.

De-activation of airbag system

The system must be de-activated as follows, before carrying out any work on the airbag components or surrounding area.

a) Switch off the engine.

b) Remove the ignition keycard – on models with the 'hands-free' system, the keycard should be kept well away from the car.

c) Switch off all electrical equipment.

d) Disconnect the battery negative lead (see Disconnecting the battery).

e) Insulate the battery negative terminal and the end of the battery negative lead to prevent any possibility of contact.

f) Wait for at least five minutes before carrying out any further work.

25 Airbag system components – removal and refitting

Note: Refer to the precautions in Section 24 before carrying out the following operations.

1 Disconnect the battery negative lead and wait for at least five minutes. This will allow the reserve power capacitors in the control unit to discharge and disable the airbag system (see Section 24).

Driver's airbag

Removal

2 Remove the two screws underneath the steering column lower shroud, then unclip it and lower it out (see illustration).

3 Unclip and lift off the column upper shroud (see illustration).

4 Using a thin screwdriver in the hole provided at the back of the wheel, push and prise down the end of the spring clip used to retain the airbag – as this is done, pull gently on the steering wheel centre pad to release it (see illustrations).

5 The airbag is released first by pulling it carefully upwards. Pull the airbag out from the wheel, to access the two airbag wiring plugs. Release the plugs by prising out the yellow locking clip with a small screwdriver, and disconnect them (see illustrations).

6 Remove the airbag from the car, taking care not to knock or drop it, and keeping the front uppermost. Store it somewhere safe while it is removed.

Refitting

7 Ensure that the wiring connectors are securely reconnected and seat the airbag unit centrally in the steering wheel, making sure the wires do not become trapped. Slide the airbag downwards, and press it squarely into place until the retaining clip at the base engages.

8 Ensuring no one is inside the car, reconnect the battery. From the passenger seat, insert the keycard and check the operation of the airbag warning light.

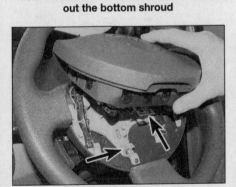

25.2 Remove the two screws and lower out the bottom shroud

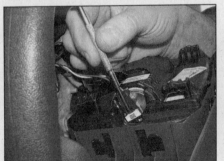

25.3 Unclip and lift off the top shroud

25.4a Use a thin screwdriver in the hole at the base of the wheel . . .

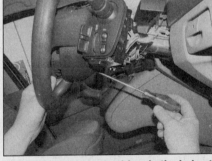

25.4b . . . to unhook the spring clip used to retain the airbag (arrows)

25.5a Prise out the yellow locking clip . . .

25.5b . . . to disconnect the airbag wiring plugs

25.11a Showing the module clamp screw at the top of the assembly

25.11b Loosen the clamp screw by a few turns . . .

25.11c . . . if necessary, remove it and spread the ends of the clamp

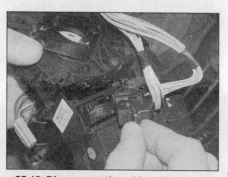

25.12 Disconnect the wiring plugs from the module

Airbag rotary connector (clockspring)

Removal

9 Remove the driver's airbag as described previously in this Section, and the steering wheel as described in Chapter 10.

10 First, check that the '0' mark on the front of the clockspring is uppermost (it should be, by default, if the front wheels were set straight-ahead when the steering wheel was removed, and the steering cannot turn since it will automatically be locked).

11 The airbag rotary connector is an integral part of the steering column switch module, meaning that the whole assembly must be removed. Loosen the clamp screw at the top of the module by a few turns to release the module from the column **(see illustrations)**.

12 Slide the module back off the column for access to the wiring plugs. Slide the locking lever to the side to release the central wiring plug **(see illustration)**. Once all plugs have been disconnected, the module, including the rotary connector, can be removed.

13 While the module is removed, take care that the rotary connector is not turned from its aligned position. A resetting procedure is not given by Renault.

Refitting

14 Check that the '0' mark is still uppermost **(see illustration)**, then refit the module using a reversal of the removal procedure.

15 Refit the steering wheel as described in Chapter 10, and the airbag as described previously in this Section.

Passenger's airbag

Removal

16 Remove the facia panel as described in Chapter 11 – the crossmember does not have to be removed.

17 Turn the facia panel over, and remove the four airbag unit mounting screws from behind **(see illustration)**. Withdraw the airbag unit to the inside of the facia panel.

Refitting

18 Refitting is a reversal of removal.

Front side airbags

19 The side airbags are located internally within the front seat backrest, and no attempt should be made to remove them. Any suspected problems with the side airbag system should be referred to a Renault dealer.

Side curtain airbags

20 The modules for the side curtain airbags are located at the sides of the headlining. It is strongly recommended that any work which requires even just the removal of the headlining, never mind any work on the side curtain airbags, be referred to a Renault dealer.

Airbag control unit

Removal

21 Remove the gear/selector lever assembly as described in Chapter 7A or 7B.

22 Lift the carpet below the gear lever housing, then unclip and remove the soundproofing.

23 Tilt the control unit plastic surround

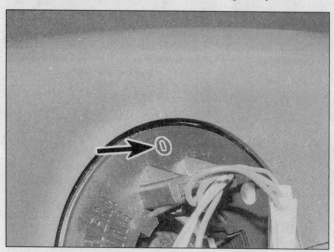

25.14 The circled '0' mark is hard to see, but should be at 12 o'clock

25.17 Airbag unit seen from behind – screws arrowed

rearwards, then unclip it by lifting it at the rear.

24 Disconnect the control unit wiring plug by squeezing together the catches at the front, then slide the locking catch rearwards.

25 Unscrew the three mounting nuts, and remove the unit from the car.

Refitting

26 Refit the control unit, tightening the mounting nuts securely.

27 Reconnect the wiring connector, and secure with the locking catch. Clip on the unit's surround, then refit the soundproofing.

28 Refit the gear/selector lever assembly as described in Chapter 7A or 7B.

29 Ensuring no one is inside the car, reconnect the battery. From the passenger seat, insert the keycard and check the operation of the airbag warning light.

Passenger airbag selector switch

30 Refer to Section 4.

Side impact sensors

Removal

31 Remove the B-pillar lower trim panel as described in Chapter 11, Section 23.

32 Disconnect the wiring plug, then unscrew the mounting bolt and remove the sensor **(see illustration)**.

Refitting

33 Refitting is a reversal of removal. Tighten the sensor mounting bolt securely.

Seat belt tensioners

34 Refer to the seat belt procedures in Chapter 11, Section 23.

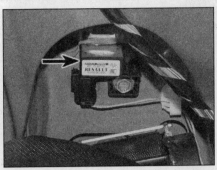

25.32 The side impact sensors are located at the base of the B-pillars

RENAULT SCENIC 2003

Diagram 1

Fuse table

Battery fuse box

Fuses	Rating	Circuit protected
F1	30A	Passenger fuse box, interior multiplex module
F2	350A	Engine fuse box, alternator starter motor (Petrol)
	400A	Engine fuse box, alternator starter motor (Diesel)
F3	30A	Engine multiplex module

Engine fuse box

Fuses	Rating	Circuit protected
F1	40A	Engine cooling
F2	70A	Pre-heating
F3	30A	Diesel filter heater
F4	70A	Passenger fuse box
F5	50A	ABS
F6	70A	Power steering
F7	40A	Additional heater 1000W
	60A	Additional heater 1800W
F8	70A	Passenger fuse box
F9	70A	Additional heater

Passenger fuse box

Fuses	Rating	Circuit protected
F2C	40A	Air conditioning, heater blower
F2D	40A	Electric windows
F2E	20A	Sunroof
F1F	10A	ABS
F1G	15A	Radio, wash/wipe, alarm air conditioning, fuel heater, steering wheel switches
F1H	15A	Brake lights
F1L	25A	Electric windows
F1M	25A	Electric windows
F1N	20A	Radio, instrument panel, electric mirrors, alarm
F1O	15A	Diagnostic socket, horn, headlight washer
F1P	15A	Rear wiper
F1R	20A	Interior multiplex module, air conditioning
F2S	3A	Air conditioning, rain sensor, interior mirror
F2T	15A	Cigarette lighter
F2U	20A	Interior multiplex module
F2W	7.5A	Electric mirrors

Engine multiplex module

Fuses	Rating	Circuit protected
F3	25A	Starter motor
F4	10A	Air conditioning
F5A	15A	Steering column lock, interior multiplex module
F5C	10A	Reversing lights
F5D	5A	Steering column lock, engine control
F5E	5A	Power steering, airbag
F5F	7.5A	Passenger fuse box, switch illumination diagnostic socket, additional heater
F5H	5A	Automatic transmission
F6	30A	Passenger fuse box, heated mirrors, heated rear window
F7A	7.5A	RH side light, switch illumination
F7B	7.5A	LH side light, switch illumination, cigarette lighter, interior multiplex module
F8A	10A	RH main beam
F8B	10A	LH main beam
F8C	10A	RH dipped beam, RH headlight adjustment
F8D	10A	LH dipped beam, LH headlight adjustment
F9	25A	Windscreen wiper
F10	20A	Front fog lights
F11	40A	Cooling fan
F13	25A	ABS
F15	20A	Automatic transmission

Key to circuits

Diagram 1	Information for wiring diagrams
Diagram 2	Starting and charging, engine multiplex module power, interior multiplex module power and radio
Diagram 3	Airbag, horn and cigarette lighter
Diagram 4	Electric windows, sunroof
Diagram 5	Wash/wipe, ABS, power steering and engine cooling with AC
Diagram 6	Engine cooling without AC, central locking and heater blower
Diagram 7	Instrument panel, heated rear window, diesel filter heater, electric and heated mirrors
Diagram 8	Air conditioning, brake lights and fog lights
Diagram 9	Headlights, side lights, tail lights, reversing lights, headlight adjustment steering wheel switches, direction indicators and hazard warning lights
Diagram 10	Interior lights, footwell lights, keyless entry system, card reader, starter button and steering column lock

Earth points

E1	Battery earth
E2	Engine earth
E3	LH dashboard earth
E4	LH dashboard earth
E5	Transmission tunnel
E6	RH dashboard earth
E7	RH of tailgate
E8	LH of tailgate
E9	Above RH rear wheel arch
E10	RH engine bulkhead
E11	On power steering pump

Key to symbols

Bulb	
Switch	
Fuse/fusible link and current rating	F5 10A
Multiple contact switch (ganged)	
Resistor	
Variable resistor	
Heater	
Item no.	2
Pump/motor	M
Earth point and location	E12
Solenoid actuator	
Diode	
Light emitting diode (LED)	
Speaker	
Connecting wires	
Wire joint	
Wire colour (brown with black tracer)	Mr/Nr
Screened cable	
Dashed outline denotes part of a larger item, containing in this case an electronic or solid state device. Pin types:	
2 - Unspecified colour connector, pin 2.	
2Mr 1- Brown two pin connector, pin 1.	2Mr

Please Note

The power supply to the Multiplex units are shown on Diagram 2. Reference should therefore be made to Diagram 2 for power supply details on diagrams including the Multiplex units. These power supply circuits have not been replicated in every circuit due to space considerations.

The prime method of wire identification is by using the terminal pin numbers (moulded into each component or connector and shown in the diagrams) together with the number code printed on each wire. To relate each diagram to the vehicle wiring, locate the relevant component or connector illustrated and find the wire(s) connected to the terminal pin(s) as shown in the diagram.

Caution: Whilst a number (indicating the function of that wire) may be printed on each wire, this is not always the case, and in such instances, this is reflected by the absence of such wire numbering on our diagrams. Similarly, numbering of the connector/component terminal pins is not always available from the manufacturers' source information and may also be missing from our diagrams. In these cases, it may be necessary to refer to your local dealer for further information.

Note that the conventional method of using colour coding does not apply – whilst the wires on the vehicle will be coloured, the wire colour has no relevance.

Wire colours

Nr	Black	Or	Orange
Bj	Beige	Rs	Pink
Be	Blue	Rg	Red
Mr	Brown	Vi	Violet
Gr	Grey	Ba	White
Ve	Green	Jn	Yellow
		Cy	Clear

Key to items

1 Battery
2 Battery fuse box
3 Engine fuse box
4 Passenger fuse box
5 Engine multiplex module
6 Interior multiplex module
7 Alternator
8 Starter motor
9 Accessory relay 1
10 Radio
11 RH front tweeter
12 RH front speaker
13 RH rear speaker
14 LH rear speaker
15 LH front tweeter
16 LH front speaker
17 Aerial
18 Mobile phone connector
19 CD player

Diagram 2

MTS
H33256

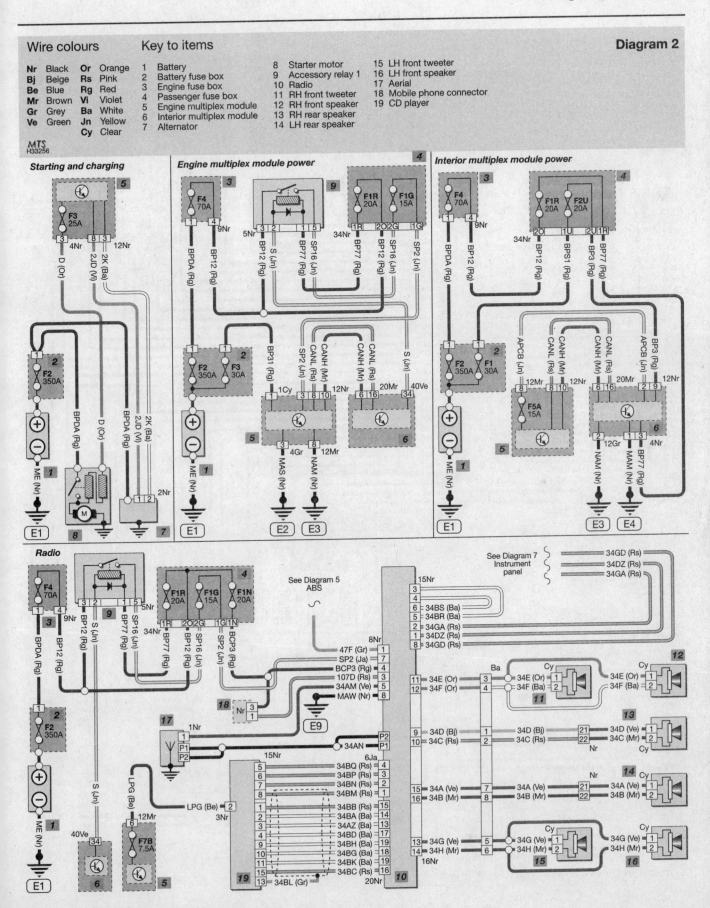

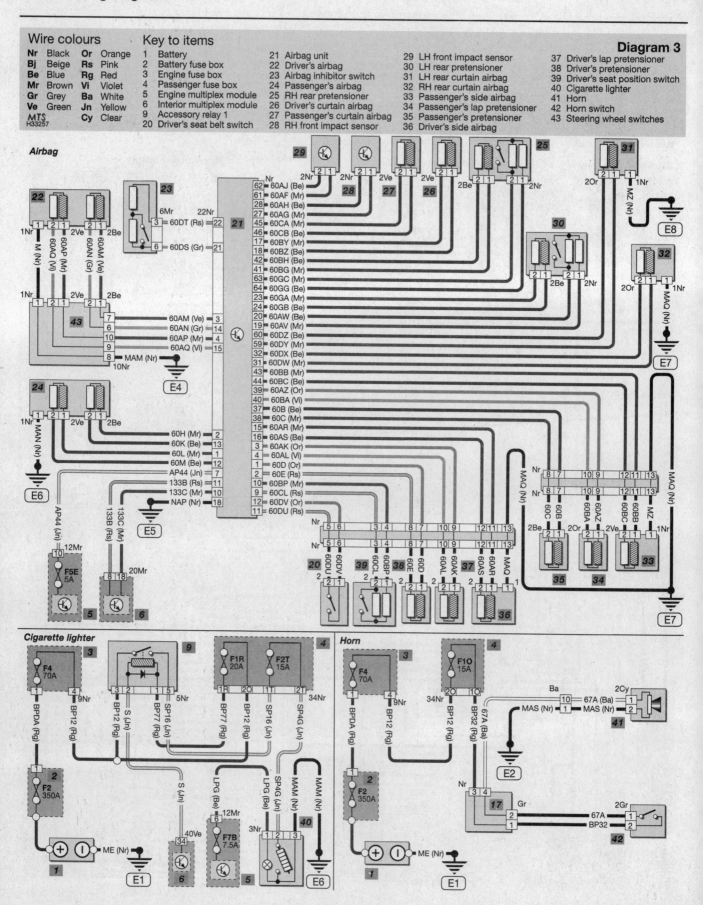

Wire colours

Nr	Black	Or	Orange
Bj	Beige	Rs	Pink
Be	Blue	Rg	Red
Mr	Brown	Vi	Violet
Gr	Grey	Ba	White
Ve	Green	Jn	Yellow
Cy	Clear		

MTS
H33257

Key to items

1 Battery
2 Battery fuse box
3 Engine fuse box
4 Passenger fuse box
5 Engine multiplex module
6 Interior multiplex module
9 Accessory relay 1
20 Driver's seat belt switch
21 Airbag unit
22 Driver's airbag
23 Airbag inhibitor switch
24 Passenger's airbag
25 RH rear pretensioner
26 Driver's curtain airbag
27 Passenger's curtain airbag
28 RH front impact sensor
29 LH front impact sensor
30 LH rear pretensioner
31 LH rear curtain airbag
32 RH rear curtain airbag
33 Passenger's side airbag
34 Passenger's lap pretensioner
35 Passenger's pretensioner
36 Driver's side airbag
37 Driver's lap pretensioner
38 Driver's pretensioner
39 Driver's seat position switch
40 Cigarette lighter
41 Horn
42 Horn switch
43 Steering wheel switches

Diagram 3

Wire colours

Nr	Black	Or	Orange
Bj	Beige	Rs	Pink
Be	Blue	Rg	Red
Mr	Brown	Vi	Violet
Gr	Grey	Ba	White
Ve	Green	Jn	Yellow
		Cy	Clear

Key to items

1. Battery
2. Battery fuse box
3. Engine fuse box
5. Engine multiplex module
6. Interior multiplex module
44. Driver's window switch
45. Driver's window motor
46. Passenger's window switch
47. Passenger's window motor
48. Rear window locking switch
49. RH rear window switch
50. RH rear window motor
51. LH rear window switch
52. LH rear window motor
53. Sunroof switch
54. Sunroof motor
55. ABS unit

Diagram 4

MTS
H33258

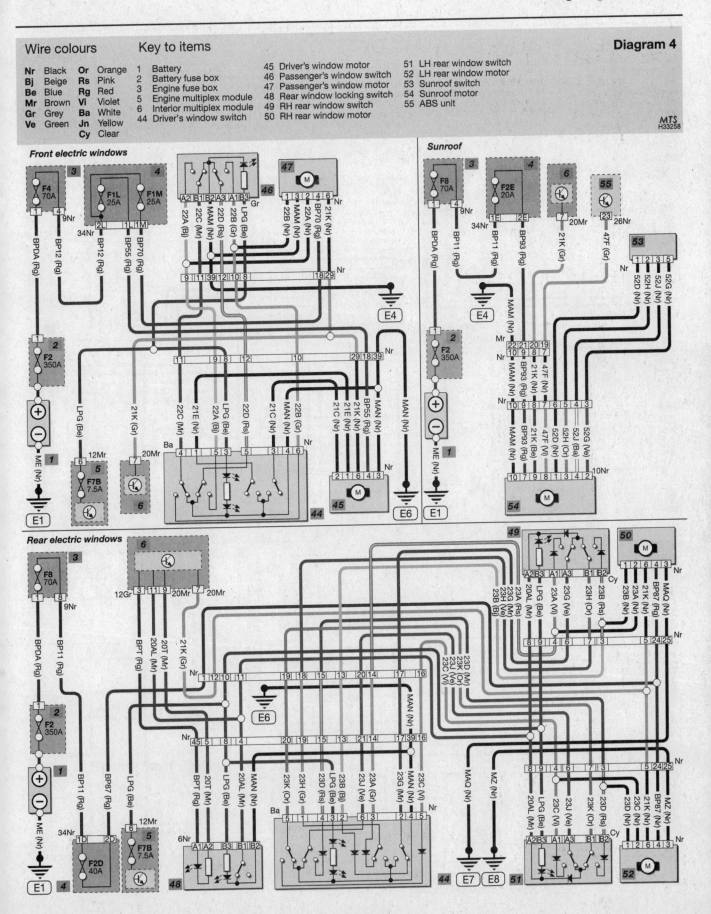

Front electric windows

Sunroof

Rear electric windows

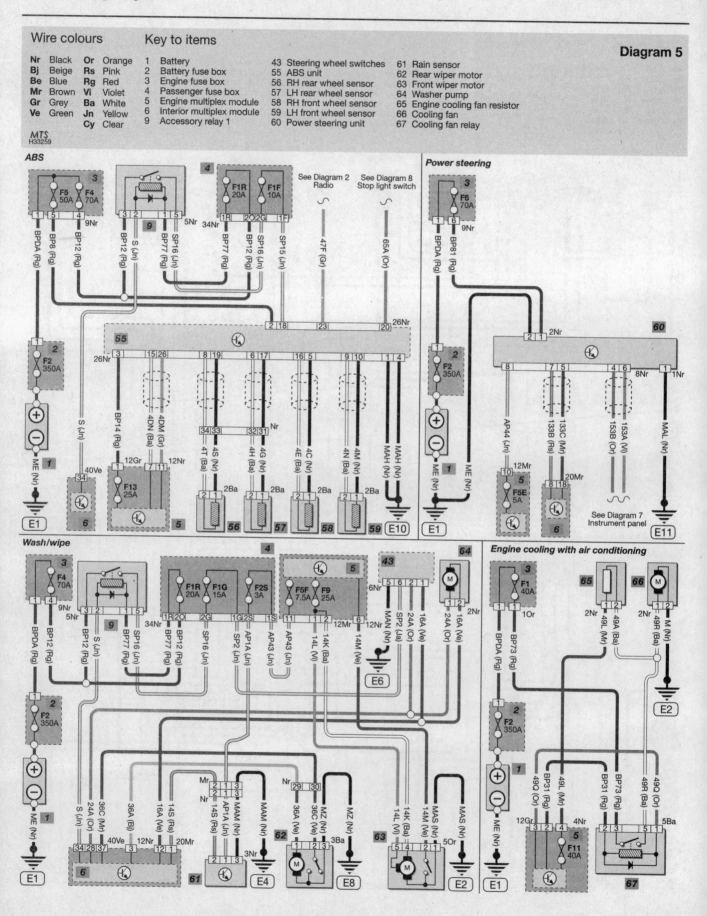

Diagram 5

Wire colours

Nr	Black	Or	Orange
Bj	Beige	Rs	Pink
Be	Blue	Rg	Red
Mr	Brown	Vi	Violet
Gr	Grey	Ba	White
Ve	Green	Jn	Yellow
		Cy	Clear

MTS
H33259

Key to items

1 Battery
2 Battery fuse box
3 Engine fuse box
4 Passenger fuse box
5 Engine multiplex module
6 Interior multiplex module
9 Accessory relay 1

43 Steering wheel switches
55 ABS unit
56 RH rear wheel sensor
57 LH rear wheel sensor
58 RH front wheel sensor
59 LH front wheel sensor
60 Power steering unit

61 Rain sensor
62 Rear wiper motor
63 Front wiper motor
64 Washer pump
65 Engine cooling fan resistor
66 Cooling fan
67 Cooling fan relay

ABS

Power steering

Wash/wipe

Engine cooling with air conditioning

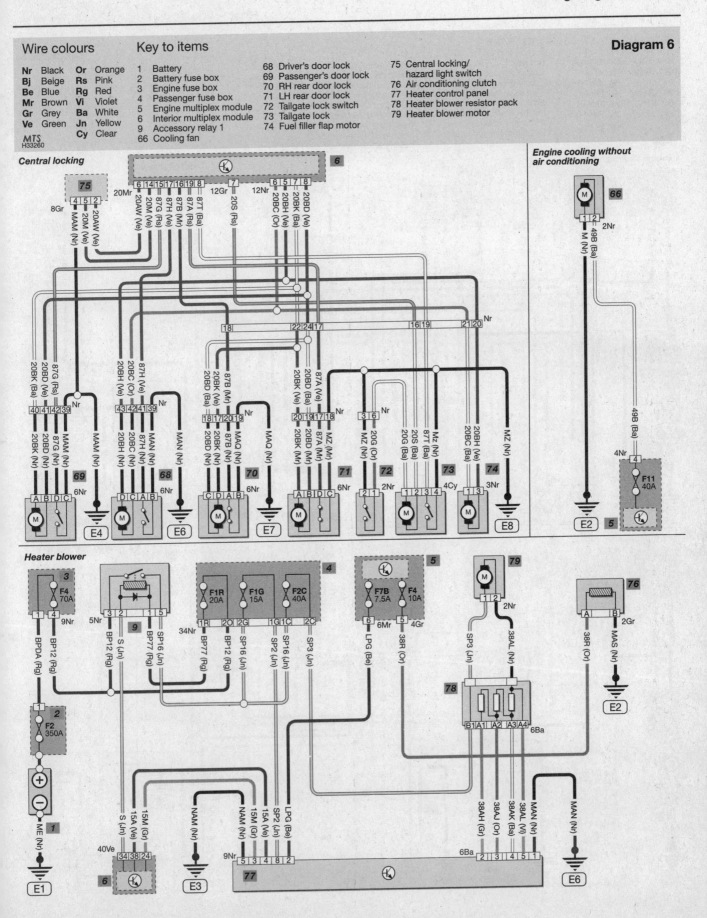

Wire colours

Nr	Black	Or	Orange
Bj	Beige	Rs	Pink
Be	Blue	Rg	Red
Mr	Brown	Vi	Violet
Gr	Grey	Ba	White
Ve	Green	Jn	Yellow
		Cy	Clear

MTS
H33260

Key to items

1 Battery
2 Battery fuse box
3 Engine fuse box
4 Passenger fuse box
5 Engine multiplex module
6 Interior multiplex module
9 Accessory relay 1
66 Cooling fan

68 Driver's door lock
69 Passenger's door lock
70 RH rear door lock
71 LH rear door lock
72 Tailgate lock switch
73 Tailgate lock
74 Fuel filler flap motor

75 Central locking/
   hazard light switch
76 Air conditioning clutch
77 Heater control panel
78 Heater blower resistor pack
79 Heater blower motor

Diagram 6

Central locking

Engine cooling without air conditioning

Heater blower

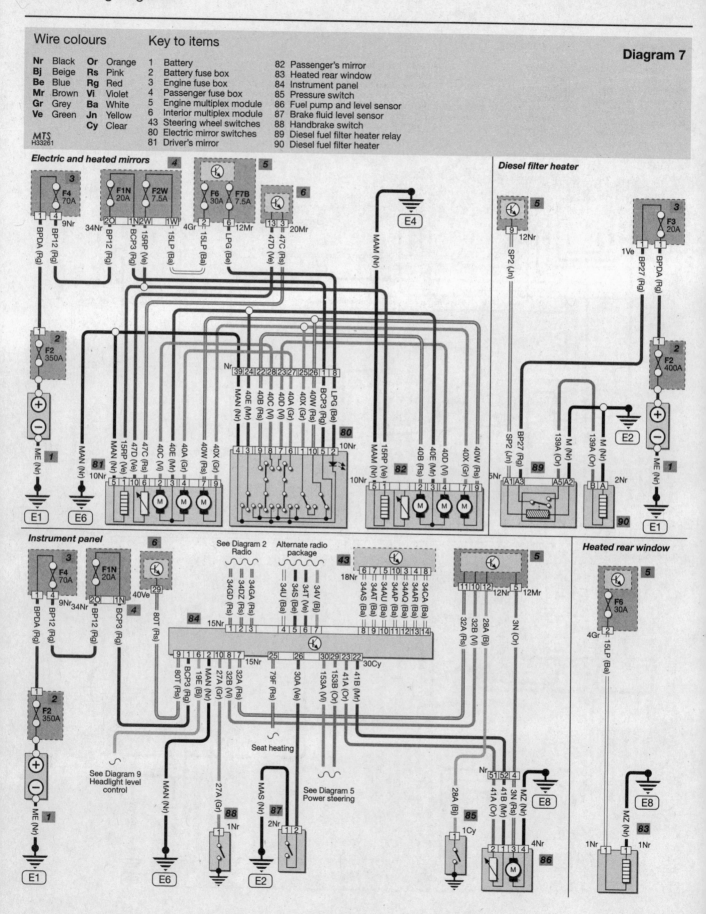

Diagram 7

Wire colours

Nr	Black	Or	Orange
Bj	Beige	Rs	Pink
Be	Blue	Rg	Red
Mr	Brown	Vi	Violet
Gr	Grey	Ba	White
Ve	Green	Jn	Yellow
		Cy	Clear

MTS
H33261

Key to items

1 Battery
2 Battery fuse box
3 Engine fuse box
4 Passenger fuse box
5 Engine multiplex module
6 Interior multiplex module
43 Steering wheel switches
80 Electric mirror switches
81 Driver's mirror
82 Passenger's mirror
83 Heated rear window
84 Instrument panel
85 Pressure switch
86 Fuel pump and level sensor
87 Brake fluid level sensor
88 Handbrake switch
89 Diesel fuel filter heater relay
90 Diesel fuel filter heater

Electric and heated mirrors

Diesel filter heater

Instrument panel

Heated rear window

Wire colours

Nr	Black	Or	Orange
Bj	Beige	Rs	Pink
Be	Blue	Rg	Red
Mr	Brown	Vi	Violet
Gr	Grey	Ba	White
Ve	Green	Jn	Yellow
		Cy	Clear

Key to items

1 Battery
2 Battery fuse box
3 Engine fuse box
4 Passenger fuse box
5 Engine multiplex module
6 Interior multiplex module
9 Accessory relay 1
43 Steering wheel switches
77 Heater control panel
78 Heater blower resistor pack
79 Heater blower motor
76 Air conditioning clutch
91 Brake light switch
92 High level brake light
93 RH tail light
   a) brake light
   b) fog light
94 LH tail light
   (as 93)
95 RH front foglight
96 LH front foglight

Diagram 8

MTS
H33262

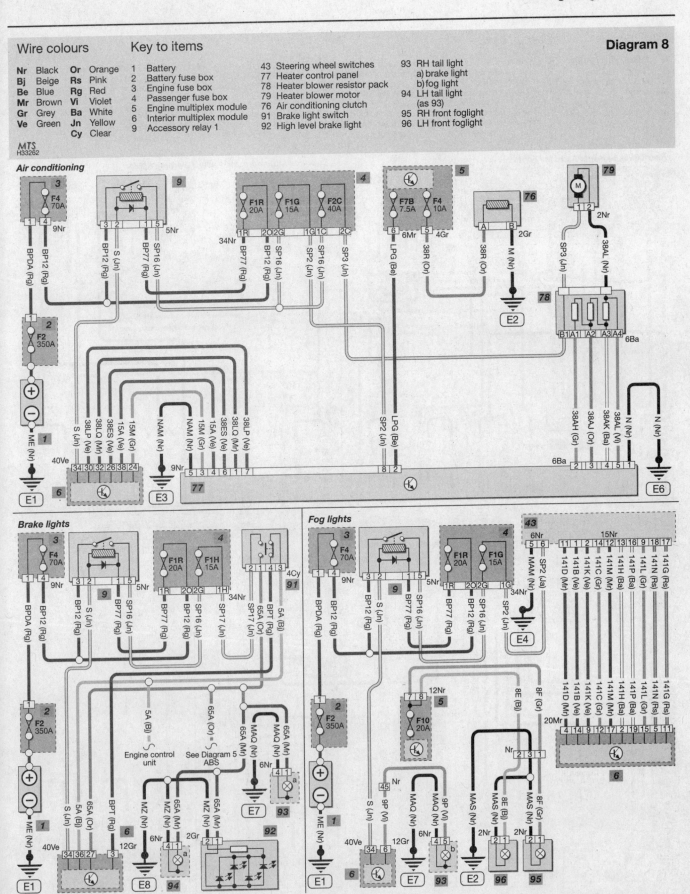

Air conditioning

Brake lights

Fog lights

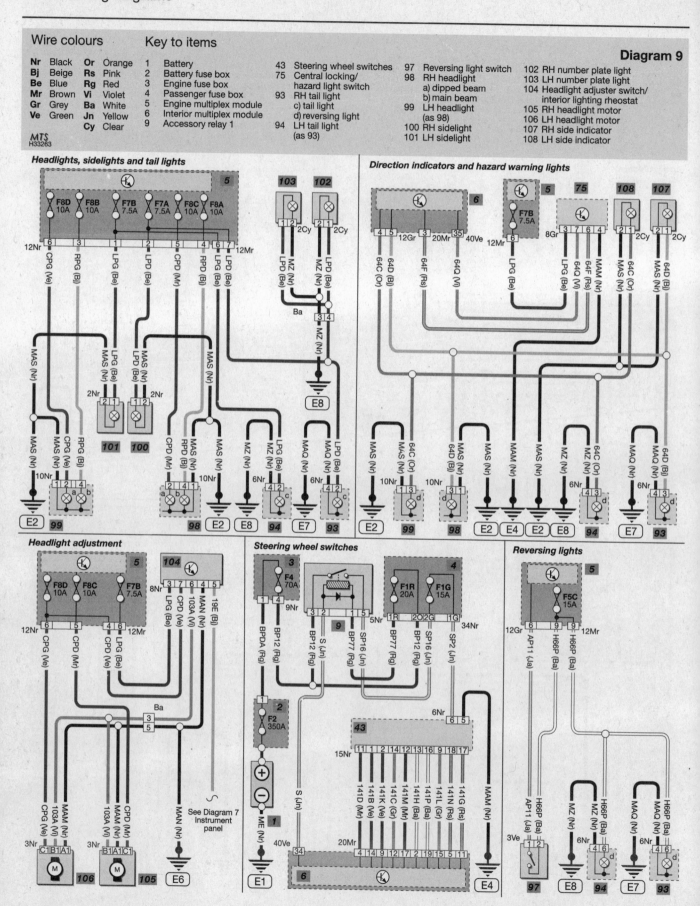

Wire colours

Nr	Black	Or	Orange
Bj	Beige	Rs	Pink
Be	Blue	Rg	Red
Mr	Brown	Vi	Violet
Gr	Grey	Ba	White
Ve	Green	Jn	Yellow
		Cy	Clear

MTS
H33263

Key to items

1 Battery
2 Battery fuse box
3 Engine fuse box
4 Passenger fuse box
5 Engine multiplex module
6 Interior multiplex module
9 Accessory relay 1

43 Steering wheel switches
75 Central locking/
hazard light switch
93 RH tail light
c) tail light
d) reversing light
94 LH tail light
(as 93)

97 Reversing light switch
98 RH headlight
a) dipped beam
b) main beam
99 LH headlight
(as 98)
100 RH sidelight
101 LH sidelight

102 RH number plate light
103 LH number plate light
104 Headlight adjuster switch/
interior lighting rheostat
105 RH headlight motor
106 LH headlight motor
107 RH side indicator
108 LH side indicator

Diagram 9

Headlights, sidelights and tail lights

Direction indicators and hazard warning lights

Headlight adjustment

Steering wheel switches

Reversing lights

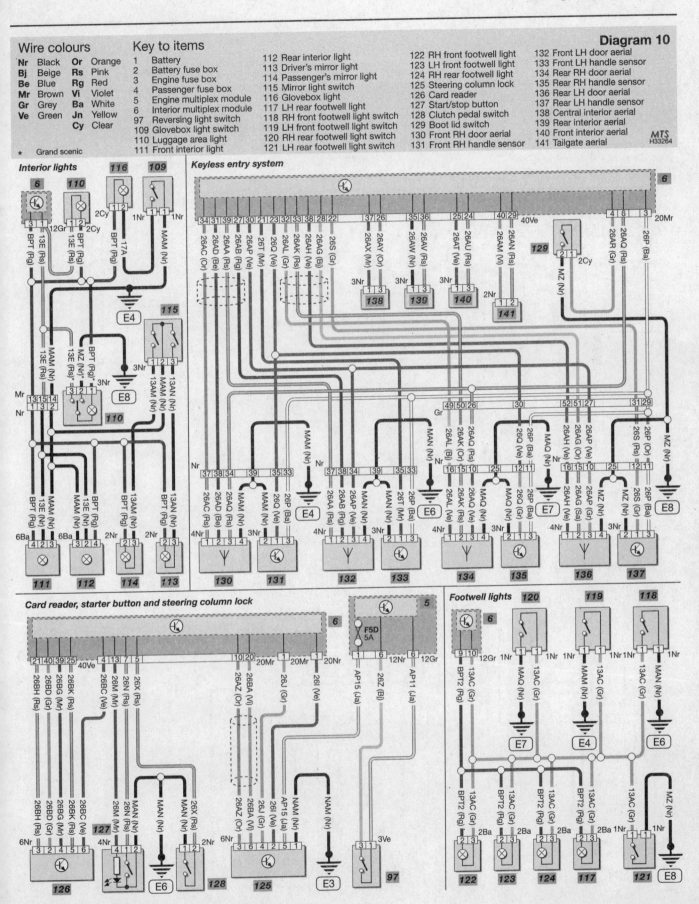

Diagram 10

Wire colours

Nr	Black	**Or**	Orange
Bj	Beige	**Rs**	Pink
Be	Blue	**Rg**	Red
Mr	Brown	**Vi**	Violet
Gr	Grey	**Ba**	White
Ve	Green	**Jn**	Yellow
		Cy	Clear

* Grand scenic

Key to items

1 Battery
2 Battery fuse box
3 Engine fuse box
4 Passenger fuse box
5 Engine multiplex module
6 Interior multiplex module
97 Reversing light switch
109 Glovebox light switch
110 Luggage area light
111 Front interior light
112 Rear interior light
113 Driver's mirror light
114 Passenger's mirror light
115 Mirror light switch
116 Glovebox light
117 LH rear footwell light
118 RH front footwell light switch
119 LH front footwell light switch
120 RH rear footwell light switch
121 LH rear footwell light switch
122 RH front footwell light
123 LH front footwell light
124 RH rear footwell light
125 Steering column lock
126 Card reader
127 Start/stop button
128 Clutch pedal switch
129 Boot lid switch
130 Front RH door aerial
131 Front RH handle sensor
132 Front LH door aerial
133 Front LH handle sensor
134 Rear RH door aerial
135 Rear RH handle sensor
136 Rear LH door aerial
137 Rear LH handle sensor
138 Central interior aerial
139 Rear interior aerial
140 Front interior aerial
141 Tailgate aerial

MTS
H33264

Interior lights

Keyless entry system

Card reader, starter button and steering column lock

Footwell lights

Dimensions and weights

Note: *All figures are approximate, and may vary according to model. Refer to manufacturer's data for exact figures.*

Dimensions

Overall length:
  Scénic . . . . 4259 mm
  Grand Scénic . . . . 4493 mm
Overall width – including mirrors . . . . 1810 mm
Overall height (unladen, according to model):
  Scénic . . . . 1620 mm
  Grand Scénic . . . . 1636 mm
Wheelbase:
  Scénic . . . . 2685 mm
  Grand Scénic . . . . 2736 mm

Weights

Kerb weight*:
  Scénic:
    Petrol models (typical) . . . . 1315 to 1375 kg
    Diesel models (typical) . . . . 1340 to 1390 kg
  Grand Scénic:
    Petrol models (typical) . . . . 1445 to 1490 kg
    Diesel models (typical) . . . . 1465 to 1515 kg
Maximum gross vehicle weight:
  Scénic . . . . 1880 to 2010 kg
  Grand Scénic . . . . 2120 to 2195 kg
Maximum roof rack load . . . . 80 kg
Maximum towing weight . . . . Refer to your Renault dealer
Exact kerb weight varies depending on model – refer to VIN plate.

Conversion factors

Length (distance)

Inches (in)	x 25.4	= Millimetres (mm)	x 0.0394	=	Inches (in)
Feet (ft)	x 0.305	= Metres (m)	x 3.281	=	Feet (ft)
Miles	x 1.609	= Kilometres (km)	x 0.621	=	Miles

Volume (capacity)

Cubic inches (cu in; in³)	x 16.387	= Cubic centimetres (cc; cm³)	x 0.061	=	Cubic inches (cu in; in³)
Imperial pints (Imp pt)	x 0.568	= Litres (l)	x 1.76	=	Imperial pints (Imp pt)
Imperial quarts (Imp qt)	x 1.137	= Litres (l)	x 0.88	=	Imperial quarts (Imp qt)
Imperial quarts (Imp qt)	x 1.201	= US quarts (US qt)	x 0.833	=	Imperial quarts (Imp qt)
US quarts (US qt)	x 0.946	= Litres (l)	x 1.057	=	US quarts (US qt)
Imperial gallons (Imp gal)	x 4.546	= Litres (l)	x 0.22	=	Imperial gallons (Imp gal)
Imperial gallons (Imp gal)	x 1.201	= US gallons (US gal)	x 0.833	=	Imperial gallons (Imp gal)
US gallons (US gal)	x 3.785	= Litres (l)	x 0.264	=	US gallons (US gal)

Mass (weight)

Ounces (oz)	x 28.35	= Grams (g)	x 0.035	=	Ounces (oz)
Pounds (lb)	x 0.454	= Kilograms (kg)	x 2.205	=	Pounds (lb)

Force

Ounces-force (ozf; oz)	x 0.278	= Newtons (N)	x 3.6	=	Ounces-force (ozf; oz)
Pounds-force (lbf; lb)	x 4.448	= Newtons (N)	x 0.225	=	Pounds-force (lbf; lb)
Newtons (N)	x 0.1	= Kilograms-force (kgf; kg)	x 9.81	=	Newtons (N)

Pressure

Pounds-force per square inch (psi; lbf/in²; lb/in²)	x 0.070	= Kilograms-force per square centimetre (kgf/cm²; kg/cm²)	x 14.223	=	Pounds-force per square inch (psi; lbf/in²; lb/in²)
Pounds-force per square inch (psi; lbf/in²; lb/in²)	x 0.068	= Atmospheres (atm)	x 14.696	=	Pounds-force per square inch (psi; lbf/in²; lb/in²)
Pounds-force per square inch (psi; lbf/in²; lb/in²)	x 0.069	= Bars	x 14.5	=	Pounds-force per square inch (psi; lbf/in²; lb/in²)
Pounds-force per square inch (psi; lbf/in²; lb/in²)	x 6.895	= Kilopascals (kPa)	x 0.145	=	Pounds-force per square inch (psi; lbf/in²; lb/in²)
Kilopascals (kPa)	x 0.01	= Kilograms-force per square centimetre (kgf/cm²; kg/cm²)	x 98.1	=	Kilopascals (kPa)
Millibar (mbar)	x 100	= Pascals (Pa)	x 0.01	=	Millibar (mbar)
Millibar (mbar)	x 0.0145	= Pounds-force per square inch (psi; lbf/in²; lb/in²)	x 68.947	=	Millibar (mbar)
Millibar (mbar)	x 0.75	= Millimetres of mercury (mmHg)	x 1.333	=	Millibar (mbar)
Millibar (mbar)	x 0.401	= Inches of water (inH₂O)	x 2.491	=	Millibar (mbar)
Millimetres of mercury (mmHg)	x 0.535	= Inches of water (inH₂O)	x 1.868	=	Millimetres of mercury (mmHg)
Inches of water (inH₂O)	x 0.036	= Pounds-force per square inch (psi; lbf/in²; lb/in²)	x 27.68	=	Inches of water (inH₂O)

Torque (moment of force)

Pounds-force inches (lbf in; lb in)	x 1.152	= Kilograms-force centimetre (kgf cm; kg cm)	x 0.868	=	Pounds-force inches (lbf in; lb in)
Pounds-force inches (lbf in; lb in)	x 0.113	= Newton metres (Nm)	x 8.85	=	Pounds-force inches (lbf in; lb in)
Pounds-force inches (lbf in; lb in)	x 0.083	= Pounds-force feet (lbf ft; lb ft)	x 12	=	Pounds-force inches (lbf in; lb in)
Pounds-force feet (lbf ft; lb ft)	x 0.138	= Kilograms-force metres (kgf m; kg m)	x 7.233	=	Pounds-force feet (lbf ft; lb ft)
Pounds-force feet (lbf ft; lb ft)	x 1.356	= Newton metres (Nm)	x 0.738	=	Pounds-force feet (lbf ft; lb ft)
Newton metres (Nm)	x 0.102	= Kilograms-force metres (kgf m; kg m)	x 9.804	=	Newton metres (Nm)

Power

Horsepower (hp)	x 745.7	= Watts (W)	x 0.0013	=	Horsepower (hp)

Velocity (speed)

Miles per hour (miles/hr; mph)	x 1.609	= Kilometres per hour (km/hr; kph)	x 0.621	=	Miles per hour (miles/hr; mph)

Fuel consumption*

Miles per gallon, Imperial (mpg)	x 0.354	= Kilometres per litre (km/l)	x 2.825	=	Miles per gallon, Imperial (mpg)
Miles per gallon, US (mpg)	x 0.425	= Kilometres per litre (km/l)	x 2.352	=	Miles per gallon, US (mpg)

Temperature

Degrees Fahrenheit = (°C x 1.8) + 32

Degrees Celsius (Degrees Centigrade; °C) = (°F - 32) x 0.56

It is common practice to convert from miles per gallon (mpg) to litres/100 kilometres (l/100km), where mpg x l/100 km = 282

Spare parts are available from many sources, including maker's appointed garages, accessory shops, and motor factors. To be sure of obtaining the correct parts, it will sometimes be necessary to quote the vehicle identification number (see *Vehicle identification*). If possible, it can also be useful to take the old parts along for positive identification. Items such as starter motors and alternators may be available under a service exchange scheme – any parts returned should always be clean.

Our advice regarding spare part sources is as follows.

Officially-appointed garages

This is the best source of parts which are peculiar to your car, and which are not otherwise generally available (eg badges, interior trim, certain body panels, etc). It is also the only place at which you should buy parts if the car is still under warranty.

Accessory shops

These are very good places to buy materials and components needed for the maintenance of your car (oil, air and fuel filters, spark plugs, light bulbs, drivebelts, oils and greases, brake pads, touch-up paint, etc). Components of this nature sold by a reputable shop are of the same standard as those used by the car manufacturer.

Besides components, these shops also sell tools and general accessories, usually have convenient opening hours, charge lower prices, and can often be found not far from home. Some accessory shops have parts counters where the components needed for almost any repair job can be purchased or ordered.

Motor factors

Good factors will stock all the more important components which wear out comparatively quickly, and can sometimes supply individual components needed for the overhaul of a larger assembly (eg brake seals and hydraulic parts, bearing shells, pistons, valves, alternator brushes). They may also handle work such as cylinder block reboring, crankshaft regrinding and balancing, etc.

Tyre and exhaust specialists

These outlets may be independent, or members of a local or national chain. They frequently offer competitive prices when compared with a main dealer or local garage, but it will pay to obtain several quotes before making a decision. When researching prices, also ask what 'extras' may be added – for instance, fitting a new valve and balancing the wheel are both commonly charged on top of the price of a new tyre. **Note:** *Scénics have a tyre pressure monitoring system, which means that new valves should not be fitted when tyres are changed – see Chapter 10.*

Other sources

Beware of parts or materials obtained from market stalls, car boot sales or similar outlets. Such items are not invariably sub-standard, but there is little chance of compensation if they do prove unsatisfactory. In the case of safety-critical components such as brake pads, there is the risk not only of financial loss but also of an accident causing injury or death.

Second-hand components or assemblies obtained from a car breaker can be a good buy in some circumstances, but this sort of purchase is best made by the experienced DIY mechanic.

Jacking and vehicle support

The jack supplied with the car's tool kit should only be used for changing the roadwheels - see *Wheel changing* at the front of this book. When carrying out any other kind of work, raise the car using a hydraulic (or 'trolley') jack, and always supplement the jack with axle stands positioned under the jacking/support points **(see illustration)**. If the roadwheels do not have to be removed, consider using wheel ramps - if wished, these can be placed under the wheels once the car has been raised using a hydraulic jack, and then lowered onto the ramps so that it is resting on its wheels.

Only ever jack the car up on a solid, level surface. If there is even a slight slope, take great care that the car cannot move as the wheels are lifted off the ground. Jacking up on an uneven or gravelled surface is not recommended, as the weight of the car will not be evenly distributed, and the jack may slip as the car is raised.

As far as possible, do not leave the car unattended once it has been raised, particularly if children are playing nearby.

Before jacking up the front of the car, ensure that the handbrake is firmly applied. When jacking up the rear of the car, place wooden chocks in front of the front wheels, and engage first gear.

To raise the front of the car, position the jack head underneath the front subframe, on or near one of the mounting bolts, and use a flat piece of wood to spread the load **(see illustration)**. Always supplement the jack with axle stands under the sill jacking points.

At the rear, provided that work is not being carried out on the rear suspension, if care is taken and a substantial trolley jack is used, the jack can be placed under the rear spring – note, however, that this must only be attempted with the car on solid, level ground **(see illustration)**. Otherwise, place a wide, flat piece of wood centrally under the rear jacking point to spread the load, and position the jack head and axle stand as close together either side of the jacking point as possible.

Do not jack the car under any other part of the sill, sump, floor pan, or (except as described) directly under any of the steering or suspension components.

Never work under, around, or near a raised vehicle, unless it is adequately supported on stands. Do not rely on a jack alone, as even a hydraulic jack could fail under load.

Place axle stands underneath the sill jacking points

Jack underneath the front subframe, with an axle stand

Jack underneath the trailing arm, below the spring seat

Whenever servicing, repair or overhaul work is carried out on the car or its components, observe the following procedures and instructions. This will assist in carrying out the operation efficiently and to a professional standard of workmanship.

Joint mating faces and gaskets

When separating components at their mating faces, never insert screwdrivers or similar implements into the joint between the faces in order to prise them apart. This can cause severe damage which results in oil leaks, coolant leaks, etc upon reassembly. Separation is usually achieved by tapping along the joint with a soft-faced hammer in order to break the seal. However, note that this method may not be suitable where dowels are used for component location.

Where a gasket is used between the mating faces of two components, a new one must be fitted on reassembly; fit it dry unless otherwise stated in the repair procedure. Make sure that the mating faces are clean and dry, with all traces of old gasket removed. When cleaning a joint face, use a tool which is unlikely to score or damage the face, and remove any burrs or nicks with an oilstone or fine file.

Make sure that tapped holes are cleaned with a pipe cleaner, and keep them free of jointing compound, if this is being used, unless specifically instructed otherwise.

Ensure that all orifices, channels or pipes are clear, and blow through them, preferably using compressed air.

Oil seals

Oil seals can be removed by levering them out with a wide flat-bladed screwdriver or similar implement. Alternatively, a number of self-tapping screws may be screwed into the seal, and these used as a purchase for pliers or some similar device in order to pull the seal free.

Whenever an oil seal is removed from its working location, either individually or as part of an assembly, it should be renewed.

The very fine sealing lip of the seal is easily damaged, and will not seal if the surface it contacts is not completely clean and free from scratches, nicks or grooves. If the original sealing surface of the component cannot be restored, and the manufacturer has not made provision for slight relocation of the seal relative to the sealing surface, the component should be renewed.

Protect the lips of the seal from any surface which may damage them in the course of fitting. Use tape or a conical sleeve where possible. Lubricate the seal lips with oil before fitting and, on dual-lipped seals, fill the space between the lips with grease.

Unless otherwise stated, oil seals must be fitted with their sealing lips toward the lubricant to be sealed.

Use a tubular drift or block of wood of the appropriate size to install the seal and, if the seal housing is shouldered, drive the seal down to the shoulder. If the seal housing is unshouldered, the seal should be fitted with its face flush with the housing top face (unless otherwise instructed).

Screw threads and fastenings

Seized nuts, bolts and screws are quite a common occurrence where corrosion has set in, and the use of penetrating oil or releasing fluid will often overcome this problem if the offending item is soaked for a while before attempting to release it. The use of an impact driver may also provide a means of releasing such stubborn fastening devices, when used in conjunction with the appropriate screwdriver bit or socket. If none of these methods works, it may be necessary to resort to the careful application of heat, or the use of a hacksaw or nut splitter device.

Studs are usually removed by locking two nuts together on the threaded part, and then using a spanner on the lower nut to unscrew the stud. Studs or bolts which have broken off below the surface of the component in which they are mounted can sometimes be removed using a stud extractor. Always ensure that a blind tapped hole is completely free from oil, grease, water or other fluid before installing the bolt or stud. Failure to do this could cause the housing to crack due to the hydraulic action of the bolt or stud as it is screwed in.

When tightening a castellated nut to accept a split pin, tighten the nut to the specified torque, where applicable, and then tighten further to the next split pin hole. Never slacken the nut to align the split pin hole, unless stated in the repair procedure.

When checking or retightening a nut or bolt to a specified torque setting, slacken the nut or bolt by a quarter of a turn, and then retighten to the specified setting. However, this should not be attempted where angular tightening has been used.

For some screw fastenings, notably cylinder head bolts or nuts, torque wrench settings are no longer specified for the latter stages of tightening, "angle-tightening" being called up instead. Typically, a fairly low torque wrench setting will be applied to the bolts/nuts in the correct sequence, followed by one or more stages of tightening through specified angles.

Locknuts, locktabs and washers

Any fastening which will rotate against a component or housing during tightening should always have a washer between it and the relevant component or housing.

Spring or split washers should always be renewed when they are used to lock a critical component such as a big-end bearing retaining bolt or nut. Locktabs which are folded over to retain a nut or bolt should always be renewed.

Self-locking nuts can be re-used in non-critical areas, providing resistance can be felt when the locking portion passes over the bolt or stud thread. However, it should be noted that self-locking stiffnuts tend to lose their effectiveness after long periods of use, and should then be renewed as a matter of course.

Split pins must always be replaced with new ones of the correct size for the hole.

When thread-locking compound is found on the threads of a fastener which is to be re-used, it should be cleaned off with a wire brush and solvent, and fresh compound applied on reassembly.

Special tools

Some repair procedures in this manual entail the use of special tools such as a press, two or three-legged pullers, spring compressors, etc. Wherever possible, suitable readily-available alternatives to the manufacturer's special tools are described, and are shown in use. In some instances, where no alternative is possible, it has been necessary to resort to the use of a manufacturer's tool, and this has been done for reasons of safety as well as the efficient completion of the repair operation. Unless you are highly-skilled and have a thorough understanding of the procedures described, never attempt to bypass the use of any special tool when the procedure described specifies its use. Not only is there a very great risk of personal injury, but expensive damage could be caused to the components involved.

Environmental considerations

When disposing of used engine oil, brake fluid, antifreeze, etc, give due consideration to any detrimental environmental effects. Do not, for instance, pour any of the above liquids down drains into the general sewage system, or onto the ground to soak away. Many local council refuse tips provide a facility for waste oil disposal, as do some garages. If none of these facilities are available, consult your local Environmental Health Department, or the National Rivers Authority, for further advice.

With the universal tightening-up of legislation regarding the emission of environmentally-harmful substances from motor vehicles, most vehicles have tamperproof devices fitted to the main adjustment points of the fuel system. These devices are primarily designed to prevent unqualified persons from adjusting the fuel/air mixture, with the chance of a consequent increase in toxic emissions. If such devices are found during servicing or overhaul, they should, wherever possible, be renewed or refitted in accordance with the manufacturer's requirements or current legislation.

OIL CARE
FOLLOW THE CODE
OIL BANK LINE
0800 66 33 66
www.oilbankline.org.uk

Note: It is antisocial and illegal to dump oil down the drain. To find the location of your local oil recycling bank, call this number free.

Several systems fitted to the car require battery power to be available at all times, either to ensure that their continued operation (such as the clock) or to maintain control unit memories (such as that in the engine management system's ECU) which would be wiped if the battery were to be disconnected. Whenever the battery is to be disconnected therefore, first note the following, to ensure that there are no unforeseen consequences of this action:

a) *First, on any vehicle with central locking, it is a wise precaution to remove the keycard, and to keep it with you, so that it does not get locked in, if the central locking should engage accidentally when the battery is reconnected.*

b) *On cars equipped with an engine management system, the system's ECU will lose the information stored in its memory when the battery is disconnected. This includes idling and operating values, and any fault codes detected – in the case of the fault codes, if it is thought likely that the system has developed a fault for which the corresponding code has been logged, the car must be taken to a Renault dealer for the codes to be read, using the special diagnostic equipment necessary for this. Whenever the battery is disconnected, the information relating to idle speed control and other operating values will have to be re-programmed into the unit's memory. The ECU does this by itself, but until then, there may be surging, hesitation, erratic idle and a generally inferior level of performance. To*

allow the ECU to relearn these values, start the engine and run it as close to idle speed as possible until it reaches its normal operating temperature, then run it for approximately two minutes at 1200 rpm. Next, drive the car as far as necessary – approximately 5 miles of varied driving conditions is usually sufficient – to complete the relearning process.

c) *If the battery is disconnected while the alarm system is armed or activated, the alarm will remain in the same state when the battery is reconnected. The same applies to the engine immobiliser system.*

d) *If a Renault audio unit is fitted, and the unit and/or the battery is disconnected, the unit will not function again on reconnection until the correct security code is entered. Details of this procedure, which varies according to the unit and model year, are given in the audio operating guide supplied with the car when new. Ensure you have the correct code before you disconnect the battery. For obvious security reasons, the procedure is not given in this manual. If you do not have the code or details of the correct procedure, but can supply proof of ownership and a legitimate reason for wanting this information, the car's selling dealer may be able to help.*

e) *Where electric windows with 'one-touch' operation are fitted, this function may not work correctly until each window has been reset. This is done by fully opening the window with the button pressed, then*

keeping the button pressed for a few seconds after opening, so the system can 'learn' the fully-open position. Close the window, and again keep the button pressed for a few seconds after closing.

f) *The Scénic is equipped with electric power steering, operated by a motor attached to the steering column. The steering should function normally following battery disconnection, but it may be worth helping it to 're-learn' the full-lock positions, by turning the wheel to each full-lock position and holding it there for a few seconds.*

Devices known as 'memory-savers' (or 'code-savers') can be used to avoid some of the above problems. Precise details vary according to the device used. Typically, it is plugged into the cigarette lighter, and is connected by its own wires to a spare battery; the car's own battery is then disconnected from the electrical system, leaving the 'memory-saver' to pass sufficient current to maintain audio unit security codes and ECU memory values, and also to run permanently-live circuits such as the clock, all the while isolating the battery in the event of a short-circuit occurring while work is carried out.

⚠️ **Warning: Some of these devices allow a considerable amount of current to pass, which can mean that many of the car's systems are still operational when the main battery is disconnected. If a 'memory-saver' is used, ensure that the circuit concerned is actually 'dead' before carrying out any work on it!**

Vehicle identification

Modifications are a continuing and unpublicised process in car manufacture, quite apart from major model changes. Spare parts manuals and lists are compiled upon a numerical basis, the individual vehicle identification numbers being essential to correct identification of the component concerned.

When ordering spare parts, always give as much information as possible. Quote the car model, year of manufacture, body and engine numbers as appropriate.

The *vehicle identification plate* is located at the base of the driver's door B-pillar, and can be viewed with the door open (see illustration). In addition to many other details, it carries the Vehicle Identification Number (VIN), maximum vehicle weight information, and codes for interior trim and body colours.

The *Vehicle Identification Number (VIN)* is given on the vehicle identification plate. It is also stamped on a plate in the engine compartment, next to the coolant expansion tank, and may also be viewed through the base of the windscreen on the passenger's side (see illustrations).

The *body number and paint code numbers* are located on the vehicle identification plate.

The *engine number* is stamped on the front of the engine. Even with the engine top cover removed (where applicable), the number can be hard to see – this is especially true of the diesel engines (see illustration).

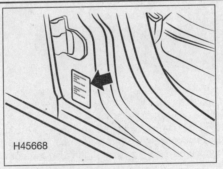

The vehicle identification plate is on the base of the B-pillar

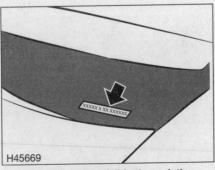

The VIN is also visible through the windscreen

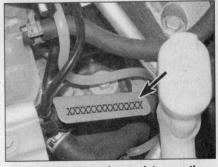

The VIN is stamped on a plate near the expansion tank

The engine number is stamped on the front of the block, and may be hard to see

Introduction

A selection of good tools is a fundamental requirement for anyone contemplating the maintenance and repair of a motor vehicle. For the owner who does not possess any, their purchase will prove a considerable expense, offsetting some of the savings made by doing-it-yourself. However, provided that the tools purchased meet the relevant national safety standards and are of good quality, they will last for many years and prove an extremely worthwhile investment.

To help the average owner to decide which tools are needed to carry out the various tasks detailed in this manual, we have compiled three lists of tools under the following headings: *Maintenance and minor repair, Repair and overhaul*, and *Special*. Newcomers to practical mechanics should start off with the *Maintenance and minor repair* tool kit, and confine themselves to the simpler jobs around the vehicle. Then, as confidence and experience grow, more difficult tasks can be undertaken, with extra tools being purchased as, and when, they are needed. In this way, a *Maintenance and minor repair* tool kit can be built up into a *Repair and overhaul* tool kit over a considerable period of time, without any major cash outlays. The experienced do-it-yourselfer will have a tool kit good enough for most repair and overhaul procedures, and will add tools from the *Special* category when it is felt that the expense is justified by the amount of use to which these tools will be put.

Maintenance and minor repair tool kit

The tools given in this list should be considered as a minimum requirement if routine maintenance, servicing and minor repair operations are to be undertaken. We recommend the purchase of combination spanners (ring one end, open-ended the other); although more expensive than open-ended ones, they do give the advantages of both types of spanner.

☐ *Combination spanners:*
  Metric - 8 to 19 mm inclusive
☐ *Adjustable spanner - 35 mm jaw (approx.)*
☐ *Spark plug spanner (with rubber insert) - petrol models*
☐ *Spark plug gap adjustment tool - petrol models*
☐ *Set of feeler gauges*
☐ *Brake bleed nipple spanner*
☐ *Screwdrivers:*
  Flat blade - 100 mm long x 6 mm dia
  Cross blade - 100 mm long x 6 mm dia
  Torx - various sizes (not all vehicles)
☐ *Combination pliers*
☐ *Hacksaw (junior)*
☐ *Tyre pump*
☐ *Tyre pressure gauge*
☐ *Oil can*
☐ *Oil filter removal tool*
☐ *Fine emery cloth*
☐ *Wire brush (small)*
☐ *Funnel (medium size)*
☐ *Sump drain plug key (not all vehicles)*

Repair and overhaul tool kit

These tools are virtually essential for anyone undertaking any major repairs to a motor vehicle, and are additional to those given in the *Maintenance and minor repair* list. Included in this list is a comprehensive set of sockets. Although these are expensive, they will be found invaluable as they are so versatile - particularly if various drives are included in the set. We recommend the half-inch square-drive type, as this can be used with most proprietary torque wrenches.

The tools in this list will sometimes need to be supplemented by tools from the *Special* list:

☐ *Sockets (or box spanners) to cover range in previous list (including Torx sockets)*
☐ *Reversible ratchet drive (for use with sockets)*
☐ *Extension piece, 250 mm (for use with sockets)*
☐ *Universal joint (for use with sockets)*
☐ *Flexible handle or sliding T "breaker bar" (for use with sockets)*
☐ *Torque wrench (for use with sockets)*
☐ *Self-locking grips*
☐ *Ball pein hammer*
☐ *Soft-faced mallet (plastic or rubber)*
☐ *Screwdrivers:*
  Flat blade - long & sturdy, short (chubby), and narrow (electrician's) types
  Cross blade – long & sturdy, and short (chubby) types
☐ *Pliers:*
  Long-nosed
  Side cutters (electrician's)
  Circlip (internal and external)
☐ *Cold chisel - 25 mm*
☐ *Scriber*
☐ *Scraper*
☐ *Centre-punch*
☐ *Pin punch*
☐ *Hacksaw*
☐ *Brake hose clamp*
☐ *Brake/clutch bleeding kit*
☐ *Selection of twist drills*
☐ *Steel rule/straight-edge*
☐ *Allen keys (inc. splined/Torx type)*
☐ *Selection of files*
☐ *Wire brush*
☐ *Axle stands*
☐ *Jack (strong trolley or hydraulic type)*
☐ *Light with extension lead*
☐ *Universal electrical multi-meter*

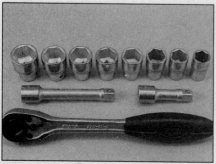

Sockets and reversible ratchet drive

Brake bleeding kit

Torx key, socket and bit

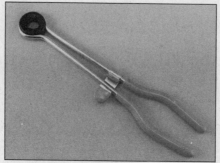

Hose clamp

Angular-tightening gauge

Special tools

The tools in this list are those which are not used regularly, are expensive to buy, or which need to be used in accordance with their manufacturers' instructions. Unless relatively difficult mechanical jobs are undertaken frequently, it will not be economic to buy many of these tools. Where this is the case, you could consider clubbing together with friends (or joining a motorists' club) to make a joint purchase, or borrowing the tools against a deposit from a local garage or tool hire specialist. It is worth noting that many of the larger DIY superstores now carry a large range of special tools for hire at modest rates.

The following list contains only those tools and instruments freely available to the public, and not those special tools produced by the vehicle manufacturer specifically for its dealer network. You will find occasional references to these manufacturers' special tools in the text of this manual. Generally, an alternative method of doing the job without the vehicle manufacturers' special tool is given. However, sometimes there is no alternative to using them. Where this is the case and the relevant tool cannot be bought or borrowed, you will have to entrust the work to a dealer.

- ☐ Angular-tightening gauge
- ☐ Valve spring compressor
- ☐ Valve grinding tool
- ☐ Piston ring compressor
- ☐ Piston ring removal/installation tool
- ☐ Cylinder bore hone
- ☐ Balljoint separator
- ☐ Coil spring compressors (where applicable)
- ☐ Two/three-legged hub and bearing puller
- ☐ Impact screwdriver
- ☐ Micrometer and/or vernier calipers
- ☐ Dial gauge
- ☐ Stroboscopic timing light
- ☐ Dwell angle meter/tachometer
- ☐ Fault code reader
- ☐ Cylinder compression gauge
- ☐ Hand-operated vacuum pump and gauge
- ☐ Clutch plate alignment set
- ☐ Brake shoe steady spring cup removal tool
- ☐ Bush and bearing removal/installation set
- ☐ Stud extractors
- ☐ Tap and die set
- ☐ Lifting tackle
- ☐ Trolley jack

Buying tools

Reputable motor accessory shops and superstores often offer excellent quality tools at discount prices, so it pays to shop around.

Remember, you don't have to buy the most expensive items on the shelf, but it is always advisable to steer clear of the very cheap tools. Beware of 'bargains' offered on market stalls or at car boot sales. There are plenty of good tools around at reasonable prices, but always aim to purchase items which meet the relevant national safety standards. If in doubt, ask the proprietor or manager of the shop for advice before making a purchase.

Care and maintenance of tools

Having purchased a reasonable tool kit, it is necessary to keep the tools in a clean and serviceable condition. After use, always wipe off any dirt, grease and metal particles using a clean, dry cloth, before putting the tools away. Never leave them lying around after they have been used. A simple tool rack on the garage or workshop wall for items such as screwdrivers and pliers is a good idea. Store all normal spanners and sockets in a metal box. Any measuring instruments, gauges, meters, etc, must be carefully stored where they cannot be damaged or become rusty.

Take a little care when tools are used. Hammer heads inevitably become marked, and screwdrivers lose the keen edge on their blades from time to time. A little timely attention with emery cloth or a file will soon restore items like this to a good finish.

Working facilities

Not to be forgotten when discussing tools is the workshop itself. If anything more than routine maintenance is to be carried out, a suitable working area becomes essential.

It is appreciated that many an owner-mechanic is forced by circumstances to remove an engine or similar item without the benefit of a garage or workshop. Having done this, any repairs should always be done under the cover of a roof.

Wherever possible, any dismantling should be done on a clean, flat workbench or table at a suitable working height.

Any workbench needs a vice; one with a jaw opening of 100 mm is suitable for most jobs. As mentioned previously, some clean dry storage space is also required for tools, as well as for any lubricants, cleaning fluids, touch-up paints etc, which become necessary.

Another item which may be required, and which has a much more general usage, is an electric drill with a chuck capacity of at least 8 mm. This, together with a good range of twist drills, is virtually essential for fitting accessories.

Last, but not least, always keep a supply of old newspapers and clean, lint-free rags available, and try to keep any working area as clean as possible.

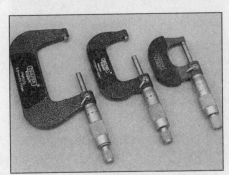

Micrometers

Dial test indicator ("dial gauge")

Strap wrench

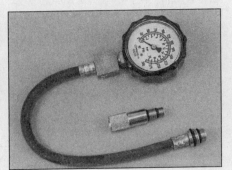

Compression tester

Fault code reader

MOT test checks

This is a guide to getting your vehicle through the MOT test. Obviously it will not be possible to examine the vehicle to the same standard as the professional MOT tester. However, working through the following checks will enable you to identify any problem areas before submitting the vehicle for the test.

Where a testable component is in borderline condition, the tester has discretion in deciding whether to pass or fail it. The basis of such discretion is whether the tester would be happy for a close relative or friend to use the vehicle with the component in that condition. If the vehicle presented is clean and evidently well cared for, the tester may be more inclined to pass a borderline component than if the vehicle is scruffy and apparently neglected.

It has only been possible to summarise the test requirements here, based on the regulations in force at the time of printing. Test standards are becoming increasingly stringent, although there are some exemptions for older vehicles.

An assistant will be needed to help carry out some of these checks.

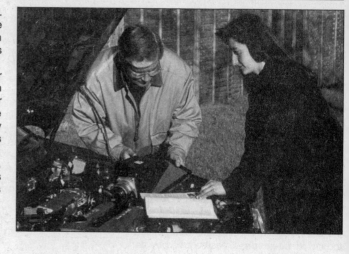

The checks have been sub-divided into four categories, as follows:

1 Checks carried out **FROM THE DRIVER'S SEAT**

2 Checks carried out **WITH THE VEHICLE ON THE GROUND**

3 Checks carried out **WITH THE VEHICLE RAISED AND THE WHEELS FREE TO TURN**

4 Checks carried out on **YOUR VEHICLE'S EXHAUST EMISSION SYSTEM**

1 Checks carried out **FROM THE DRIVER'S SEAT**

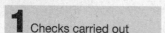

Handbrake

☐ Test the operation of the handbrake. Excessive travel (too many clicks) indicates incorrect brake or cable adjustment.

☐ Check that the handbrake cannot be released by tapping the lever sideways. Check the security of the lever mountings.

Footbrake

☐ Depress the brake pedal and check that it does not creep down to the floor, indicating a master cylinder fault. Release the pedal, wait a few seconds, then depress it again. If the pedal travels nearly to the floor before firm resistance is felt, brake adjustment or repair is necessary. If the pedal feels spongy, there is air in the hydraulic system which must be removed by bleeding.

☐ Check that the brake pedal is secure and in good condition. Check also for signs of fluid leaks on the pedal, floor or carpets, which would indicate failed seals in the brake master cylinder.

☐ Check the servo unit (when applicable) by operating the brake pedal several times, then keeping the pedal depressed and starting the engine. As the engine starts, the pedal will move down slightly. If not, the vacuum hose or the servo itself may be faulty.

Steering wheel and column

☐ Examine the steering wheel for fractures or looseness of the hub, spokes or rim.

☐ Move the steering wheel from side to side and then up and down. Check that the steering wheel is not loose on the column, indicating wear or a loose retaining nut. Continue moving the steering wheel as before, but also turn it slightly from left to right.

☐ Check that the steering wheel is not loose on the column, and that there is no abnormal

movement of the steering wheel, indicating wear in the column support bearings or couplings.

Windscreen, mirrors and sunvisor

☐ The windscreen must be free of cracks or other significant damage within the driver's field of view. (Small stone chips are acceptable.) Rear view mirrors must be secure, intact, and capable of being adjusted.

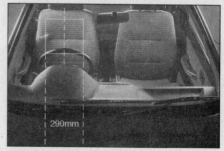

290mm

☐ The driver's sunvisor must be capable of being stored in the "up" position.

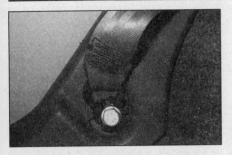

Seat belts and seats

Note: *The following checks are applicable to all seat belts, front and rear.*

☐ Examine the webbing of all the belts (including rear belts if fitted) for cuts, serious fraying or deterioration. Fasten and unfasten each belt to check the buckles. If applicable, check the retracting mechanism. Check the security of all seat belt mountings accessible from inside the vehicle.

☐ Seat belts with pre-tensioners, once activated, have a "flag" or similar showing on the seat belt stalk. This, in itself, is not a reason for test failure.

☐ The front seats themselves must be securely attached and the backrests must lock in the upright position.

Doors

☐ Both front doors must be able to be opened and closed from outside and inside, and must latch securely when closed.

2 Checks carried out WITH THE VEHICLE ON THE GROUND

Vehicle identification

☐ Number plates must be in good condition, secure and legible, with letters and numbers correctly spaced – spacing at (A) should be at least twice that at (B).

☐ The VIN plate and/or homologation plate must be legible.

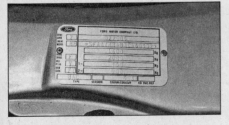

Electrical equipment

☐ Switch on the ignition and check the operation of the horn.

☐ Check the windscreen washers and wipers, examining the wiper blades; renew damaged or perished blades. Also check the operation of the stop-lights.

☐ Check the operation of the sidelights and number plate lights. The lenses and reflectors must be secure, clean and undamaged.

☐ Check the operation and alignment of the headlights. The headlight reflectors must not be tarnished and the lenses must be undamaged.

☐ Switch on the ignition and check the operation of the direction indicators (including the instrument panel tell-tale) and the hazard warning lights. Operation of the sidelights and stop-lights must not affect the indicators - if it does, the cause is usually a bad earth at the rear light cluster.

☐ Check the operation of the rear foglight(s), including the warning light on the instrument panel or in the switch.

☐ The ABS warning light must illuminate in accordance with the manufacturers' design. For most vehicles, the ABS warning light should illuminate when the ignition is switched on, and (if the system is operating properly) extinguish after a few seconds. Refer to the owner's handbook.

Footbrake

☐ Examine the master cylinder, brake pipes and servo unit for leaks, loose mountings, corrosion or other damage.

☐ The fluid reservoir must be secure and the fluid level must be between the upper (A) and lower (B) markings.

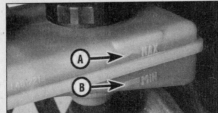

☐ Inspect both front brake flexible hoses for cracks or deterioration of the rubber. Turn the steering from lock to lock, and ensure that the hoses do not contact the wheel, tyre, or any part of the steering or suspension mechanism. With the brake pedal firmly depressed, check the hoses for bulges or leaks under pressure.

Steering and suspension

☐ Have your assistant turn the steering wheel from side to side slightly, up to the point where the steering gear just begins to transmit this movement to the roadwheels. Check for excessive free play between the steering wheel and the steering gear, indicating wear or insecurity of the steering column joints, the column-to-steering gear coupling, or the steering gear itself.

☐ Have your assistant turn the steering wheel more vigorously in each direction, so that the roadwheels just begin to turn. As this is done, examine all the steering joints, linkages, fittings and attachments. Renew any component that shows signs of wear or damage. On vehicles with power steering, check the security and condition of the steering pump, drivebelt and hoses.

☐ Check that the vehicle is standing level, and at approximately the correct ride height.

Shock absorbers

☐ Depress each corner of the vehicle in turn, then release it. The vehicle should rise and then settle in its normal position. If the vehicle continues to rise and fall, the shock absorber is defective. A shock absorber which has seized will also cause the vehicle to fail.

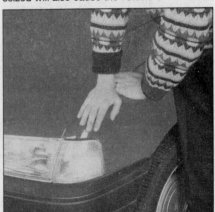

Exhaust system

☐ Start the engine. With your assistant holding a rag over the tailpipe, check the entire system for leaks. Repair or renew leaking sections.

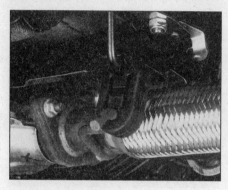

3 Checks carried out
WITH THE VEHICLE RAISED AND THE WHEELS FREE TO TURN

Jack up the front and rear of the vehicle, and securely support it on axle stands. Position the stands clear of the suspension assemblies. Ensure that the wheels are clear of the ground and that the steering can be turned from lock to lock.

Steering mechanism

☐ Have your assistant turn the steering from lock to lock. Check that the steering turns smoothly, and that no part of the steering mechanism, including a wheel or tyre, fouls any brake hose or pipe or any part of the body structure.
☐ Examine the steering rack rubber gaiters for damage or insecurity of the retaining clips. If power steering is fitted, check for signs of damage or leakage of the fluid hoses, pipes or connections. Also check for excessive stiffness or binding of the steering, a missing split pin or locking device, or severe corrosion of the body structure within 30 cm of any steering component attachment point.

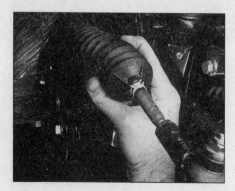

Front and rear suspension and wheel bearings

☐ Starting at the front right-hand side, grasp the roadwheel at the 3 o'clock and 9 o'clock positions and rock gently but firmly. Check for free play or insecurity at the wheel bearings, suspension balljoints, or suspension mountings, pivots and attachments.
☐ Now grasp the wheel at the 12 o'clock and 6 o'clock positions and repeat the previous inspection. Spin the wheel, and check for roughness or tightness of the front wheel bearing.

☐ If excess free play is suspected at a component pivot point, this can be confirmed by using a large screwdriver or similar tool and levering between the mounting and the component attachment. This will confirm whether the wear is in the pivot bush, its retaining bolt, or in the mounting itself (the bolt holes can often become elongated).

☐ Carry out all the above checks at the other front wheel, and then at both rear wheels.

Springs and shock absorbers

☐ Examine the suspension struts (when applicable) for serious fluid leakage, corrosion, or damage to the casing. Also check the security of the mounting points.
☐ If coil springs are fitted, check that the spring ends locate in their seats, and that the spring is not corroded, cracked or broken.
☐ If leaf springs are fitted, check that all leaves are intact, that the axle is securely attached to each spring, and that there is no deterioration of the spring eye mountings, bushes, and shackles.

☐ The same general checks apply to vehicles fitted with other suspension types, such as torsion bars, hydraulic displacer units, etc. Ensure that all mountings and attachments are secure, that there are no signs of excessive wear, corrosion or damage, and (on hydraulic types) that there are no fluid leaks or damaged pipes.
☐ Inspect the shock absorbers for signs of serious fluid leakage. Check for wear of the mounting bushes or attachments, or damage to the body of the unit.

Driveshafts
(fwd vehicles only)

☐ Rotate each front wheel in turn and inspect the constant velocity joint gaiters for splits or damage. Also check that each driveshaft is straight and undamaged.

Braking system

☐ If possible without dismantling, check brake pad wear and disc condition. Ensure that the friction lining material has not worn excessively, (A) and that the discs are not fractured, pitted, scored or badly worn (B).

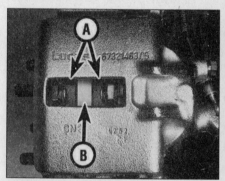

☐ Examine all the rigid brake pipes underneath the vehicle, and the flexible hose(s) at the rear. Look for corrosion, chafing or insecurity of the pipes, and for signs of bulging under pressure, chafing, splits or deterioration of the flexible hoses.
☐ Look for signs of fluid leaks at the brake calipers or on the brake backplates. Repair or renew leaking components.
☐ Slowly spin each wheel, while your assistant depresses and releases the footbrake. Ensure that each brake is operating and does not bind when the pedal is released.

□ Examine the handbrake mechanism, checking for frayed or broken cables, excessive corrosion, or wear or insecurity of the linkage. Check that the mechanism works on each relevant wheel, and releases fully, without binding.

□ It is not possible to test brake efficiency without special equipment, but a road test can be carried out later to check that the vehicle pulls up in a straight line.

Fuel and exhaust systems

□ Inspect the fuel tank (including the filler cap), fuel pipes, hoses and unions. All components must be secure and free from leaks.

□ Examine the exhaust system over its entire length, checking for any damaged, broken or missing mountings, security of the retaining clamps and rust or corrosion.

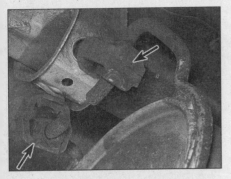

Wheels and tyres

□ Examine the sidewalls and tread area of each tyre in turn. Check for cuts, tears, lumps, bulges, separation of the tread, and exposure of the ply or cord due to wear or damage. Check that the tyre bead is correctly seated on the wheel rim, that the valve is sound and properly seated, and that the wheel is not distorted or damaged.

□ Check that the tyres are of the correct size for the vehicle, that they are of the same size and type on each axle, and that the pressures are correct.

□ Check the tyre tread depth. The legal minimum at the time of writing is 1.6 mm over at least three-quarters of the tread width. Abnormal tread wear may indicate incorrect front wheel alignment.

Body corrosion

□ Check the condition of the entire vehicle structure for signs of corrosion in load-bearing areas. (These include chassis box sections, side sills, cross-members, pillars, and all suspension, steering, braking system and seat belt mountings and anchorages.) Any corrosion which has seriously reduced the thickness of a load-bearing area is likely to cause the vehicle to fail. In this case professional repairs are likely to be needed.

□ Damage or corrosion which causes sharp or otherwise dangerous edges to be exposed will also cause the vehicle to fail.

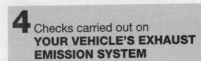

4 Checks carried out on **YOUR VEHICLE'S EXHAUST EMISSION SYSTEM**

Petrol models

□ Have the engine at normal operating temperature, and make sure that it is in good tune (ignition system in good order, air filter element clean, etc).

□ Before any measurements are carried out, raise the engine speed to around 2500 rpm, and hold it at this speed for 20 seconds. Allow the engine speed to return to idle, and watch for smoke emissions from the exhaust tailpipe. If the idle speed is obviously much too high, or if dense blue or clearly-visible black smoke comes from the tailpipe for more than 5 seconds, the vehicle will fail. As a rule of thumb, blue smoke signifies oil being burnt (engine wear) while black smoke signifies unburnt fuel (dirty air cleaner element, or other carburettor or fuel system fault).

□ An exhaust gas analyser capable of measuring carbon monoxide (CO) and hydrocarbons (HC) is now needed. If such an instrument cannot be hired or borrowed, a local garage may agree to perform the check for a small fee.

CO emissions (mixture)

□ At the time of writing, for vehicles first used between 1st August 1975 and 31st July 1986 (P to C registration), the CO level must not exceed 4.5% by volume. For vehicles first used between 1st August 1986 and 31st July 1992 (D to J registration), the CO level must not exceed 3.5% by volume. Vehicles first

used after 1st August 1992 (K registration) must conform to the manufacturer's specification. The MOT tester has access to a DOT database or emissions handbook, which lists the CO and HC limits for each make and model of vehicle. The CO level is measured with the engine at idle speed, and at "fast idle". The following limits are given as a general guide:

At idle speed -
CO level no more than 0.5%
At "fast idle" (2500 to 3000 rpm) -
CO level no more than 0.3%
(Minimum oil temperature 60°C)

□ If the CO level cannot be reduced far enough to pass the test (and the fuel and ignition systems are otherwise in good condition) then the carburettor is badly worn, or there is some problem in the fuel injection system or catalytic converter (as applicable).

HC emissions

□ With the CO within limits, HC emissions for vehicles first used between 1st August 1975 and 31st July 1992 (P to J registration) must not exceed 1200 ppm. Vehicles first used after 1st August 1992 (K registration) must conform to the manufacturer's specification. The MOT tester has access to a DOT database or emissions handbook, which lists the CO and HC limits for each make and model of vehicle. The HC level is measured with the engine at "fast idle". The following is given as a general guide:

At "fast idle" (2500 to 3000 rpm) -
HC level no more than 200 ppm
(Minimum oil temperature 60°C)

□ Excessive HC emissions are caused by incomplete combustion, the causes of which can include oil being burnt, mechanical wear and ignition/fuel system malfunction.

Diesel models

□ The only emission test applicable to Diesel engines is the measuring of exhaust smoke density. The test involves accelerating the engine several times to its maximum unloaded speed.

Note: *It is of the utmost importance that the engine timing belt is in good condition before the test is carried out.*

□ The limits for Diesel engine exhaust smoke, introduced in September 1995 are:
Vehicles first used before 1st August 1979:
Exempt from metered smoke testing, but must not emit "dense blue or clearly visible black smoke for a period of more than 5 seconds at idle" or "dense blue or clearly visible black smoke during acceleration which would obscure the view of other road users".
Non-turbocharged vehicles first used after 1st August 1979: 2.5m-1
Turbocharged vehicles first used after 1st August 1979: 3.0m-1

□ Excessive smoke can be caused by a dirty air cleaner element. Otherwise, professional advice may be needed to find the cause.

Fault finding

Engine

- [ ] Engine fails to rotate when attempting to start
- [ ] Engine rotates, but will not start
- [ ] Engine difficult to start when cold
- [ ] Engine difficult to start when hot
- [ ] Starter motor noisy or excessively-rough in engagement
- [ ] Engine starts, but stops immediately
- [ ] Engine misfires, or idles unevenly
- [ ] Engine stalls, or lacks power
- [ ] Engine backfires
- [ ] Engine noises
- [ ] Oil consumption excessive
- [ ] Oil pressure warning light illuminated with engine running

Cooling system

- [ ] Overheating
- [ ] Overcooling
- [ ] External coolant leakage
- [ ] Internal coolant leakage
- [ ] Corrosion

Fuel and exhaust systems

- [ ] Fuel consumption excessive
- [ ] Fuel leakage and/or fuel odour
- [ ] Black smoke in exhaust
- [ ] Blue or white smoke in exhaust
- [ ] Excessive noise or fumes from exhaust system

Clutch

- [ ] Pedal travels to floor - no pressure or very little resistance
- [ ] Clutch fails to disengage (unable to select gears)
- [ ] Clutch slips (engine speed increases, with no increase in vehicle speed)
- [ ] Judder as clutch is engaged
- [ ] Noise when depressing or releasing clutch pedal

Manual transmission

- [ ] Noisy in neutral with engine running
- [ ] Noisy in one particular gear
- [ ] Difficulty engaging gears
- [ ] Jumps out of gear
- [ ] Vibration
- [ ] Lubricant leaks

Automatic transmission

- [ ] Fluid leakage
- [ ] Transmission fluid brown, or has burned smell
- [ ] General gear selection problems
- [ ] Transmission will not downshift (kickdown) with accelerator fully depressed
- [ ] Engine will not start in any gear, or starts in gears other than Park or Neutral
- [ ] Transmission slips, shifts roughly, is noisy, or has no drive in forward or reverse gears

Driveshafts

- [ ] Vibration when accelerating or decelerating
- [ ] Clicking or knocking noise on turns (at slow speed on full-lock)

Braking system

- [ ] Car pulls to one side under braking
- [ ] Noise (grinding or high-pitched squeal) when brakes applied
- [ ] Excessive brake pedal travel
- [ ] Brake pedal feels spongy when depressed
- [ ] Excessive brake pedal effort required to stop vehicle
- [ ] Judder felt through brake pedal or steering wheel when braking
- [ ] Brakes binding
- [ ] Rear wheels locking under normal braking

Suspension and steering

- [ ] Car pulls to one side
- [ ] Wheel wobble and vibration
- [ ] Excessive pitching and/or rolling around corners, or during braking
- [ ] Wandering or general instability
- [ ] Excessively-stiff steering
- [ ] Excessive play in steering
- [ ] Lack of power assistance
- [ ] Tyre wear excessive

Electrical system

- [ ] Battery will only hold a charge for a few days
- [ ] Ignition (no-charge) warning light remains illuminated with engine running
- [ ] Ignition (no-charge) warning light fails to come on
- [ ] Lights inoperative
- [ ] Instrument readings inaccurate or erratic
- [ ] Horn faults
- [ ] Windscreen/tailgate wiper faults
- [ ] Windscreen/tailgate washer faults
- [ ] Electric window faults
- [ ] Central locking system faults

Intoduction

The car owner who does his or her own maintenance according to the recommended service schedules should not have to use this section of the manual very often. Modern component reliability is such that, provided those items subject to wear or deterioration are inspected or renewed at the specified intervals, sudden failure is comparatively rare. Faults do not usually just happen as a result of sudden failure, but develop over a period of time. Major mechanical failures in particular are usually preceded by characteristic symptoms over hundreds or even thousands of miles. Those components which do occasionally fail without warning are often small and easily carried in the car.

With any fault-finding, the first step is to decide where to begin investigations. Sometimes this is obvious, but on other occasions, a little detective work will be necessary. The owner who makes half a dozen haphazard adjustments or replacements may be successful in curing a fault (or its symptoms), but will be none the wiser if the fault recurs, and ultimately may have spent more time and money than was necessary. A calm and logical approach will be found to be more satisfactory in the long run. Always take into account any warning signs or abnormalities that may have been noticed in the period preceding the fault – power loss, high or low gauge readings, unusual smells,

etc – and remember that failure of components such as fuses may only be pointers to some underlying fault.

The pages which follow provide an easy reference guide to the more common problems which may occur during the operation of the car. These problems and their possible causes are grouped under headings denoting various components or systems, such as Engine, Cooling system, etc. The Chapter and/or Section which deals with the problem is also shown in brackets. Whatever the fault, certain basic principles apply. These are as follows:

Verify the fault. This is simply a matter of being sure that you know what the symptoms are before starting work. This is particularly important if you are investigating a fault for someone else, who may not have described it very accurately.

Don't overlook the obvious. For example, if the car won't start, is there fuel in the tank? (Don't take anyone else's word on this particular point, and don't trust the fuel gauge either!) If an electrical fault is indicated, look for loose or broken wires before using the test gear.

Cure the disease, not the symptom. Substituting a flat battery with a fully-charged one will get you off the hard shoulder, but if the underlying cause is not attended to, the new battery will go the same way.

Don't take anything for granted. Particularly, don't forget that a 'new' component may itself be defective (especially if it's been rattling around in the boot for months), and don't leave components out of a fault diagnosis sequence just because they are new or recently fitted. When you do finally diagnose a difficult fault, you'll probably realise that all the evidence was there from the start.

Consider what work, if any, has recently been carried out. Many faults arise through careless or hurried work. For instance, if any work has been performed under the bonnet, could some of the wiring have been dislodged or incorrectly routed, or a hose trapped? Have all the fasteners been properly tightened? Were new, genuine parts and new gaskets used? There is often a certain amount of detective work to be done in this case, as an apparently-unrelated task can have far-reaching consequences.

Diesel fault diagnosis

The majority of starting problems on small diesel engines are electrical in origin. The mechanic who is familiar with petrol engines but less so with diesel may be inclined to view the diesel's injectors and pump in the same light as the spark plugs and distributor, but this is generally a mistake.

When investigating complaints of difficult starting for someone else, make sure that the correct starting procedure is understood and is being followed. Some drivers are unaware of the significance of the preheating warning light - many modern engines are sufficiently forgiving for this not to matter in mild weather, but with the onset of winter problems begin.

As a rule of thumb, if the engine is difficult to start but runs well when it has finally got going, the problem is electrical (battery, starter motor or preheating system). If poor performance is combined with difficult starting, the problem is likely to be in the fuel system. The low pressure (supply) side of the fuel system should be checked before suspecting the injectors and injection pump. The most common fuel supply problem is air getting into the system, and any pipe from the fuel tank forwards must be scrutinised if air leakage is suspected. Normally the pump is the last item to suspect, since unless it has been tampered with there is no reason for it to be at fault.

Engine

Engine fails to rotate when attempting to start

☐ Battery terminal connections loose or corroded (Weekly checks).
☐ Battery discharged or faulty (Chapter 5A).
☐ Broken, loose or disconnected wiring in the starting circuit (Chapter 5A).
☐ Defective starter solenoid, ignition keycard reader, or starter button (Chapter 5A or 12).
☐ Defective starter motor (Chapter 5A).
☐ Flywheel ring gear or starter pinion teeth loose or broken (Chapter 2A, 2B, 2C or 5A).
☐ Engine earth strap broken or disconnected.
☐ Engine suffering 'hydraulic lock' (eg from water ingested after traversing flooded roads, or from a serious internal coolant leak) - consult a Renault dealer for advice.
☐ Clutch or brake pedal not depressed, or transmission not in neutral.
☐ Clutch pedal switch, transmission neutral switch, or stop-light switch faulty (Chapter 6, 7A or 9).
☐ Automatic transmission not in position N or P, or footbrake not depressed, or faulty stop-light switch (Chapter 7B or 9).

Engine rotates, but will not start

☐ Fuel tank empty.
☐ Battery discharged or inadequate capacity (engine rotates slowly) (Chapter 5A).
☐ Battery terminal connections loose or corroded (Weekly checks).
☐ Ignition components damp or damaged – petrol engines (Chapter 1A or 5B)
☐ Worn, faulty or incorrectly-gapped spark plugs – petrol engines (Chapter 1A)
☐ Incorrect use of diesel preheating system, or preheating system fault (Chapter 5B).
☐ Diesel fuel waxing (in very cold weather).
☐ Immobiliser or anti-theft alarm faulty or incorrectly used, or 'uncoded' ignition keycard being used (Chapter 12).
☐ Crankshaft sensor, or other engine management system sensor, fault (Chapter 4A or 4B)
☐ Air filter element dirty or clogged (Chapter 1A or 1B).
☐ Blockage in exhaust system (Chapter 4A or 4B).
☐ Poor compressions (Chapter 2A, 2B or 2C).

☐ Air in diesel fuel system (Chapter 4B).
☐ Valve timing incorrect, possibly through a poorly-fitted timing belt (Chapter 2A, 2B, or 2C).
☐ Major mechanical failure (eg camshaft drive) (Chapter 2A, 2B, or 2C).

Engine difficult to start when cold

☐ Battery discharged (Chapter 5A).
☐ Battery terminal connections loose or corroded (see Weekly checks).
☐ Worn, faulty or incorrectly-gapped spark plugs – petrol models (Chapter 1A).
☐ Other ignition system fault – petrol models (Chapter 5B).
☐ Fuel system fault (Chapter 4A or 4B).
☐ Diesel glow plug(s) defective (Chapter 5C).
☐ Wrong grade of engine oil used (Weekly checks or Chapter 1A or 1B).
☐ Low cylinder compressions (Chapter 2A, 2B, or 2C)

Engine difficult to start when hot

☐ Air filter element dirty or clogged (Chapter 1A or 1B).
☐ Fuel system fault (Chapter 4A or 4B).
☐ Low cylinder compressions (Chapter 2A, 2B, or 2C).

Starter motor noisy or excessively-rough

☐ Starter pinion or flywheel ring gear teeth loose or broken (Chapter 2A, 2B, 2C or 5A).
☐ Starter motor mounting bolts loose or missing (Chapter 5A).
☐ Starter motor internal components worn or damaged (Chapter 5A).

Engine starts, but stops immediately

☐ Loose or faulty electrical connections in the ignition circuit – petrol models (Chapter 1A or 5B).
☐ Vacuum leak at the throttle body, inlet manifold or associated hoses – petrol models (Chapter 4A).
☐ Blocked injectors/fuel system fault (Chapter 4A or 4B).
☐ Fuel very low in tank.
☐ Restriction in fuel feed or return.
☐ Air in diesel fuel system (Chapter 4B).
☐ Air cleaner dirty or blockage in air intake system (Chapter 1A, 1B, 4A or 4B).
☐ Blockage in exhaust system (Chapter 4A or 4B).

Engine (continued)

Engine misfires, or idles unevenly

☐ Air cleaner dirty or blockage in air intake system (Chapter 1A, 1B, 4A or 4B).
☐ Vacuum leak at the throttle body, inlet manifold or associated hoses – petrol models (Chapter 4A).
☐ Worn, faulty or incorrectly-gapped spark plugs – petrol models (Chapter 1A).
☐ Valve clearances incorrect (Chapter 2A, 2B, or 2C).
☐ Uneven or low cylinder compressions (Chapter 2A, 2B, or 2C)
☐ Camshaft lobes worn (Chapter 2A, 2B, or 2C).
☐ Timing belt incorrectly fitted (Chapter 2A, 2B, or 2C).
☐ Blocked injectors/fuel injection system fault (Chapter 4A or 4B).
☐ Valve(s) sticking, valve spring(s) weak or broken, or poor compressions (Chapter 2A, 2B, or 2C).
☐ Overheating (Chapter 3).
☐ Cylinder head gasket blown (Chapter 2A, 2B, or 2C).

Engine stalls, or lacks power

☐ Fuel filter choked (Chapter 1B or 4A).
☐ Petrol in-tank fuel pump faulty, or delivery pressure low (Chapter 4A).
☐ Diesel lift pump (in injection pump) faulty, or delivery pressure low (Chapter 4B).
☐ Air in diesel fuel system (Chapter 4B).
☐ Valve clearances incorrect (Chapter 2A, 2B, or 2C).
☐ Vacuum leak at the throttle body, inlet manifold or associated hoses – petrol models (Chapter 4A).
☐ Worn, faulty or incorrectly-gapped spark plugs – petrol models (Chapter 1).
☐ Faulty ignition coils – petrol models (Chapter 5B).
☐ Uneven or low cylinder compressions (Chapter 2A, 2B, or 2C).
☐ Blocked injector/fuel system fault (Chapter 4A or 4B).
☐ Blocked catalytic converter (Chapter 4A, 4B or 4C).
☐ Engine overheating (Chapter 3).
☐ Air filter element blocked (Chapter 1).
☐ Throttle position sensor fault (Chapter 4A or 4B).
☐ Engine warning light on (fault code in system) (Chapter 4A or 4B).
☐ Timing belt worn, or incorrectly fitted (Chapter 2A, 2B, or 2C).
☐ Turbo boost pressure inadequate – diesel models (Chapter 4B).
☐ Brakes binding (Chapter 1 or 9).
☐ Clutch slipping (Chapter 6).

Engine backfires

☐ Timing belt incorrectly fitted (Chapter 2A, 2B, or 2C).
☐ Vacuum leak at the throttle body, inlet manifold or associated hoses – petrol models (Chapter 4A).
☐ Blocked catalytic converter (Chapter 4A, 4B or 4C).
☐ Ignition coil faulty – petrol models (Chapter 5B).

Engine noises

Pre-ignition (pinking) or knocking during acceleration or under load

☐ Ignition system fault – petrol models (Chapter 1A or 5B).

☐ Incorrect grade of spark plug – petrol models (Chapter 1A).
☐ Incorrect grade (or type) of fuel used (Chapter 4A or 4B).
☐ Vacuum leak at the throttle body, inlet manifold or associated hoses – petrol models (Chapter 4A).
☐ Excessive carbon build-up in cylinder head/pistons (Chapter 2A, 2B, or 2C).
☐ Blocked injector/fuel injection system fault (Chapter 4A or 4B).

Whistling or wheezing noises

☐ Leaking inlet manifold or throttle body gasket – petrol models (Chapter 4A or 4B).
☐ Leaking exhaust manifold gasket, or pipe-to-manifold joint (Chapter 4A or 4B).
☐ Leaking vacuum hose (Chapter 4 or 9).
☐ Blowing cylinder head gasket (Chapter 2A, 2B, or 2C).
☐ Partially blocked or leaking crankcase ventilation system (Chapter 4C).

Tapping or rattling noises

☐ Valve clearances incorrect (Chapter 2A, 2B, or 2C).
☐ Worn camshaft (Chapter 2A, 2B, or 2C)
☐ Ancillary component fault (coolant pump, alternator, etc) (Chapter 3, 5A, etc).
☐ Air in diesel fuel system (Chapter 4B).

Knocking or thumping noises

☐ Worn big-end bearings (regular heavy knocking, perhaps less under load) (Chapter 2D).
☐ Worn main bearings (rumbling and knocking, perhaps worsening under load) (Chapter 2D).
☐ Piston slap - most noticeable when cold, caused by piston/bore wear (Chapter 2D).
☐ Ancillary component fault (coolant pump, alternator, etc) (Chapter 3, 5A, etc).
☐ Engine mountings worn or defective (Chapter 2A, 2B, or 2C).
☐ Front suspension or steering components worn (Chapter 10).

Oil consumption excessive

☐ External leakage (standing or running) – eg sump gasket, crankshaft oil seals (Chapter 2A, 2B or 2C).
☐ New engine not yet run-in.
☐ Engine oil incorrect grade/poor quality, or oil level too high (Weekly checks).
☐ Crankcase ventilation system obstructed (Chapter 1 or 4C).
☐ Burning oil due to general engine wear - pistons and/or bores, valve stem oil seals, etc (Chapter 2D).

Oil pressure warning light illuminated with engine running

☐ Low oil level or incorrect oil grade (Weekly checks).
☐ Faulty oil pressure warning light switch (Chapter 2A, 2B, or 2C).
☐ Worn engine bearings and/or oil pump (Chapter 2).
☐ High engine operating temperature (Chapter 3).
☐ Oil pick-up strainer clogged – remove sump to check (Chapter 2A, 2B, or 2C).

Cooling system

Overheating

☐ Insufficient coolant in system (Weekly checks).
☐ Thermostat faulty (Chapter 3).
☐ Radiator core blocked or grille restricted (Chapter 3).
☐ Radiator electric cooling fan(s) or coolant temperature sensor faulty (Chapter 3).
☐ Pressure cap faulty (Chapter 3).
☐ Inaccurate coolant temperature gauge sender (Chapter 3).
☐ Airlock in cooling system (Chapter 1A or 1B).
☐ Engine management system fault (Chapter 4A or 4B).
☐ Blockage in exhaust system (Chapter 4A or 4B).
☐ Cylinder head gasket blown (Chapter 2A, 2B, or 2C).

Overcooling

☐ Thermostat faulty (Chapter 3).
☐ Inaccurate coolant temperature gauge sender (Chapter 3).

External coolant leakage

☐ Deteriorated or damaged hoses or hose clips (Chapter 1A or 1B).
☐ Radiator core or heater matrix leaking (Chapter 3).
☐ Pressure cap faulty (Chapter 1A or 1B).
☐ Water pump or thermostat housing leaking (Chapter 3).
☐ Boiling due to overheating (Chapter 3).
☐ Core plug leaking (Chapter 2D).

Internal coolant leakage

☐ Leaking cylinder head gasket (Chapter 2A, 2B, or 2C).
☐ Cracked cylinder head or cylinder bore (Chapter 2D).

Corrosion

☐ Infrequent draining and flushing (Chapter 1A or 1B).
☐ Incorrect antifreeze mixture, or inappropriate antifreeze type (Weekly checks and Chapter 1A or 1B).

Fuel and exhaust systems

Fuel consumption excessive

☐ New engine not yet run-in.
☐ Air cleaner element dirty, or blockage in air intake system. (Chapter 1A, 1B, 4A, or 4B).
☐ Fuel system fault (Chapter 4A or 4B).
☐ Crankcase ventilation system blocked (Chapter 4C).
☐ Unsympathetic driving style, or adverse conditions.
☐ Tyres under-inflated (see Weekly checks).
☐ Brakes binding (Chapter 1 or 9).
☐ Fuel leak, causing apparent high consumption (Chapter 1A, 1B, 4A, or 4B).
☐ Valve timing incorrect, possibly through a poorly-fitted timing belt (Chapter 2A, 2B, or 2C).

Fuel leakage and/or fuel odour

☐ Damaged or corroded fuel tank, pipes or connections (Chapter 1A or 1B).
☐ Evaporative emissions system fault – petrol models (Chapter 4C).

Black smoke in exhaust

☐ Air cleaner element dirty, or blockage in air intake system (Chapter 1A, 1B, 4A, or 4B).
☐ Turbo boost pressure inadequate – diesel models (Chapter 4B).
☐ Exhaust gas recirculation system fault – diesel models (Chapter 4C).
☐ Fuel system fault (Chapter 4A or 4B).

Blue or white smoke in exhaust

☐ Engine oil incorrect grade or poor quality, or fuel passing into sump (worn piston rings/bores).
☐ Diesel glow plug(s) defective (white smoke at start-up only) (Chapter 5C).
☐ Air cleaner element dirty, or blockage in air intake system (Chapter 1A, 1B, 4A, or 4B).
☐ Injector(s) faulty (Chapter 4A or 4B).
☐ Blocked or damaged emissions system hoses or components (Chapter 4C).
☐ General engine wear - pistons and/or bores, valve stem oil seals, etc (Chapter 2D).

Excessive noise or fumes from exhaust system

☐ Leaking exhaust system or manifold joints (Chapter 1A, 1B, 4A, or 4B).
☐ Leaking, corroded or damaged silencers or pipe (Chapter 1A, 1B, 4A, or 4B).
☐ Exhaust gas recirculation system fault – diesel models (Chapter 4C).
☐ Oxygen sensors loose or damaged – petrol models (Chapter 4C).
☐ Broken mountings, causing body or suspension contact (Chapter 1A, 1B, 4A, or 4B).

Clutch

Pedal travels to floor – no pressure or very little resistance

☐ Air in hydraulic system/faulty master or slave cylinder (Chapter 6).
☐ Faulty hydraulic release system (Chapter 6).
☐ Clutch pedal return spring detached or broken (Chapter 6).
☐ Broken clutch release bearing or fork (Chapter 6).
☐ Broken diaphragm spring in clutch pressure plate (Chapter 6).

Clutch fails to disengage (unable to select gears)

☐ Air in hydraulic system/faulty master or slave cylinder (Chapter 6).
☐ Faulty hydraulic release system (Chapter 6).
☐ Clutch disc sticking on transmission input shaft splines (Chapter 6).
☐ Clutch disc sticking to flywheel or pressure plate (Chapter 6).
☐ Faulty pressure plate assembly (Chapter 6).
☐ Clutch release mechanism worn or incorrectly assembled (Chapter 6).

Clutch slips (engine speed increases, with no increase in vehicle speed)

☐ Faulty hydraulic release system (Chapter 6).

☐ Clutch disc linings excessively worn (Chapter 6).
☐ Clutch disc linings contaminated with oil or grease (Chapter 6).
☐ Faulty pressure plate or weak diaphragm spring (Chapter 6).

Judder as clutch is engaged

☐ Clutch disc linings contaminated with oil or grease (Chapter 6).
☐ Clutch disc linings excessively worn (Chapter 6).
☐ Faulty or distorted pressure plate or diaphragm spring (Chapter 6).
☐ Worn or loose engine/transmission mountings (Chapter 2A, 2B, or 2C).
☐ Clutch disc hub or transmission input shaft splines worn (Chapter 6 or 7).

Noise when depressing or releasing clutch pedal

☐ Worn clutch release bearing (Chapter 6).
☐ Worn or dry clutch pedal bushes (Chapter 6).
☐ Worn or dry clutch master cylinder piston (Chapter 6).
☐ Faulty pressure plate assembly (Chapter 6).
☐ Pressure plate diaphragm spring broken (Chapter 6).
☐ Broken clutch disc cushioning springs (Chapter 6).

Manual transmission

Noisy in neutral with engine running

☐ Lack of oil (Chapter 1A or 1B).
☐ Input shaft bearings worn (noise apparent with clutch pedal released, but not when depressed) (Chapter 7A).*
☐ Clutch release bearing worn (noise apparent with clutch pedal depressed, possibly less when released) (Chapter 6).

Noisy in one particular gear

☐ Worn, damaged or chipped gear teeth (Chapter 7A).*

Difficulty engaging gears

☐ Clutch fault (Chapter 6).
☐ Worn or damaged gear cables (Chapter 7A).
☐ Incorrectly-adjusted gear cables (Chapter 7A).
☐ Worn synchroniser assemblies (Chapter 7A).*

Jumps out of gear

☐ Worn or damaged gear cables (Chapter 7A).

☐ Incorrectly-adjusted gear cables (Chapter 7A).
☐ Worn synchroniser assemblies (Chapter 7A).*
☐ Worn selector forks (Chapter 7A).*

Vibration

☐ Lack of oil (Chapter 1).
☐ Worn bearings (Chapter 7A).*

Lubricant leaks

☐ Leaking differential side gear oil seal (Chapter 7A).
☐ Leaking housing joint (Chapter 7A).*
☐ Leaking input shaft oil seal (Chapter 7A).*
☐ Leaking selector shaft oil seal (Chapter 7A).

Although the corrective action necessary to remedy the symptoms described is beyond the scope of the home mechanic, the above information should be helpful in isolating the cause of the condition, so that the owner can communicate clearly with a professional mechanic.

Automatic transmission

Note: *Due to the complexity of the automatic transmission, it is difficult for the home mechanic to properly diagnose and service this unit. For problems other than the following, the car should be taken to a dealer service department or automatic transmission specialist. Do not be too hasty in removing the transmission if a fault is suspected, as most of the testing is carried out with the unit still fitted.*

Fluid leakage

☐ Automatic transmission fluid is usually dark in colour. Fluid leaks should not be confused with engine oil, which can easily be blown onto the transmission by airflow.
☐ To determine the source of a leak, first remove all built-up dirt and grime from the transmission housing and surrounding areas using a degreasing agent, or by steam-cleaning. Drive the car at low speed, so airflow will not blow the leak far from its source. Raise and support the car, and determine where the leak is coming from.

General gear selection problems

☐ Chapter 7B deals with checking and adjusting the selector cable on automatic transmissions. The following are common problems which may be caused by a poorly-adjusted cable:
a) *Engine starting in gears other than Park or Neutral.*
b) *Indicator panel indicating a gear other than the one actually being used.*

c) *Car moves when in Park or Neutral.*
d) *Poor gear shift quality or erratic gear changes.*
☐ Refer to Chapter 7B for the selector cable adjustment procedure.

Transmission will not downshift (kickdown) with accelerator pedal fully depressed

☐ Low transmission fluid level (Chapter 7B).
☐ Incorrect selector cable adjustment (Chapter 7B).

Engine will not start in any gear, or starts in gears other than Park or Neutral

☐ Incorrect selector cable adjustment (Chapter 7B).

Transmission slips, shifts roughly, is noisy, or has no drive in forward or reverse gears

☐ There are many probable causes for the above problems, but unless there is a very obvious reason (such as a loose or corroded wiring plug connection on or near the transmission), the car should be taken to a Renault dealer for the fault to be diagnosed. The transmission control unit incorporates a self-diagnosis facility, and any fault codes can quickly be read and interpreted by a Renault dealer with the proper diagnostic equipment.

Driveshafts

Vibration when accelerating or decelerating

- ☐ Worn inner constant velocity joint (Chapter 1A, 1B, or 8).
- ☐ Bent or distorted driveshaft (Chapter 8).
- ☐ Worn intermediate bearing (Chapter 8).
- ☐ Loose or damaged driveshaft nut (Chapter 1A, 1B, or 8).

Clicking or knocking noise on turns (at slow speed on full-lock)

- ☐ Lack of constant velocity joint lubricant (Chapter 8).
- ☐ Worn outer constant velocity joint (Chapter 1A, 1B, or 8).
- ☐ Worn intermediate bearing (Chapter 8).
- ☐ Loose or damaged driveshaft nut (Chapter 1A, 1B, or 8).

Braking system

Note: *Before assuming that a brake problem exists, make sure that the tyres are in good condition and correctly inflated, that the front wheel alignment is correct, and that the car is not loaded with weight in an unequal manner. Apart from checking the condition of all pipe and hose connections, any faults occurring on the Anti-lock Braking System (ABS) should be referred to a Renault dealer for diagnosis.*

Car pulls to one side under braking

- ☐ Worn, defective, damaged or contaminated front or rear brake pads on one side (Chapter 1A or 1B).
- ☐ Seized or partially-seized caliper piston (Chapter 9).
- ☐ A mixture of brake pad lining materials fitted between sides (Chapter 1A or 1B).
- ☐ Brake caliper mounting bolts loose (Chapter 9).
- ☐ Worn or damaged steering or suspension components (Chapter 10).

Noise (grinding or high-pitched squeal) when brakes applied

- ☐ Brake pad friction lining material worn down to metal backing Chapter 1A or 1B).
- ☐ Excessive corrosion of brake disc (may be apparent after the car has been standing for some time) (Chapter 1A or 1B).

Excessive brake pedal travel

- ☐ Faulty master cylinder (Chapter 9).
- ☐ Air in hydraulic system (Chapter 9).

Brake pedal feels spongy when depressed

- ☐ Air in hydraulic system (Chapter 9).
- ☐ Deteriorated flexible rubber brake hoses (Chapter 9).
- ☐ Master cylinder mounting nuts loose (Chapter 9).
- ☐ Faulty master cylinder (Chapter 9).

Excessive brake pedal effort required to stop car

- ☐ Faulty vacuum servo unit (Chapter 9).
- ☐ Disconnected, damaged or insecure brake servo vacuum hoses (Chapter 9).
- ☐ Brake vacuum pump leaking or faulty – diesel models (Chapter 9).
- ☐ Primary or secondary hydraulic circuit failure (Chapter 9).
- ☐ Seized brake caliper piston (Chapter 9).
- ☐ Brake pads incorrectly fitted (Chapter 9).
- ☐ Incorrect grade of brake pads fitted (Chapter 1A or 1B).
- ☐ Brake pads contaminated (Chapter 1A or 1B).

Judder felt through brake pedal or steering wheel when braking

- ☐ Excessive run-out or distortion of front or rear discs (Chapter 9).
- ☐ Brake pads worn (Chapter 1A or 1B).
- ☐ Brake caliper mounting bolts loose (Chapter 9).
- ☐ Wear in suspension or steering components or mountings (Chapter 10).

Brakes binding

- ☐ Seized brake caliper piston (Chapter 9).
- ☐ Faulty handbrake mechanism (Chapter 9).
- ☐ Faulty master cylinder (Chapter 9).

Rear wheels locking under normal braking

- ☐ Rear brake pads contaminated (Chapter 1A or 1B).
- ☐ Faulty ABS unit (Chapter 9).

Suspension and steering

Note: *Before diagnosing suspension or steering faults, be sure that the trouble is not due to incorrect tyre pressures, mixtures of tyre types, or binding brakes.*

Car pulls to one side

- ☐ Defective tyre (Chapter 1A or 1B).
- ☐ Excessive wear in suspension or steering components (Chapter 10).
- ☐ Incorrect front wheel alignment (Chapter 10).
- ☐ Accident damage to steering or suspension components (Chapter 10).

Wheel wobble and vibration

- ☐ Front roadwheels out of balance (vibration felt mainly through the steering wheel) (Chapter 1A or 1B).
- ☐ Rear roadwheels out of balance (vibration felt throughout the car) (Chapter 1A or 1B).
- ☐ Roadwheels damaged or distorted (Chapter 1A or 1B).
- ☐ Faulty or damaged tyre (Weekly checks).
- ☐ Worn steering or suspension joints, bushes or components (Chapter 10).
- ☐ Roadwheel bolts loose (Chapter 1A or 1B).
- ☐ Wear in driveshaft joint, or loose driveshaft nut (vibration worst when under load) (Chapter 1A, 1B, or 8).

Excessive pitching and/or rolling around corners, or during braking

- ☐ Defective shock absorbers (Chapter 10).
- ☐ Broken or weak coil spring and/or suspension components (Chapter 10).
- ☐ Worn or damaged anti-roll bar or mountings (Chapter 10).

Wandering or general instability

- ☐ Incorrect front wheel alignment (Chapter 10).
- ☐ Worn steering or suspension joints, bushes or components (Chapter 10).
- ☐ Tyres out of balance (Weekly checks).
- ☐ Faulty or damaged tyre (Weekly checks).
- ☐ Roadwheel bolts loose (Chapter 1A or 1B).
- ☐ Defective shock absorbers (Chapter 10).

Excessively-stiff steering

- ☐ Lack of steering gear lubricant (Chapter 10).
- ☐ Seized track-rod end balljoint or suspension balljoint (Chapter 10).
- ☐ Steering motor failure (Chapter 10).
- ☐ Incorrect front wheel alignment (Chapter 10).
- ☐ Steering rack or column bent or damaged (Chapter 10).

Suspension and steering (continued)

Excessive play in steering

- ☐ Worn steering column universal joint (Chapter 10).
- ☐ Worn steering track-rod end balljoints (Chapter 10).
- ☐ Worn rack-and-pinion steering gear (Chapter 10).
- ☐ Worn steering or suspension joints, bushes or components (Chapter 10).

Lack of power assistance

- ☐ Steering motor failure (Chapter 10).

Tyre wear excessive

Tyres worn on inside or outside edges

- ☐ Tyres under-inflated (wear on both edges) (Weekly checks).
- ☐ Incorrect camber or castor angles (wear on one edge only) (Chapter 10).
- ☐ Worn steering or suspension joints, bushes or components (Chapter 10).

- ☐ Excessively-hard cornering.
- ☐ Accident damage.

Tyre treads exhibit feathered edges

- ☐ Incorrect toe setting (Chapter 10).

Tyres worn in centre of tread

- ☐ Tyres over-inflated (Weekly checks).

Tyres worn on inside and outside edges

- ☐ Tyres under-inflated (Weekly checks).

Tyres worn unevenly

- ☐ Tyres out of balance (Weekly checks).
- ☐ Excessive wheel or tyre run-out (Chapter 1A or 1B).
- ☐ Worn shock absorbers (Chapter 10).
- ☐ Faulty tyre (Weekly checks).

Electrical system

Note: *For problems associated with the starting system, refer to the faults listed under Engine earlier in this Section.*

Battery will only hold a charge for a few days

- ☐ Battery defective internally (Chapter 5A).
- ☐ Battery electrolyte level low (Chapter 5A).
- ☐ Battery terminal connections loose or corroded (Weekly checks).
- ☐ Auxiliary drivebelt worn or slipping (Chapter 1A or 1B).
- ☐ Alternator not charging at correct output (Chapter 5A).
- ☐ Alternator or voltage regulator faulty (Chapter 5A).
- ☐ Short-circuit causing continual battery drain (Chapters 5A and 12).

Ignition (no-charge) warning light remains illuminated with engine running

- ☐ Auxiliary drivebelt broken, worn, or slipping (Chapter 1A or 1B).
- ☐ Alternator brushes worn, sticking, or dirty (Chapter 5A).
- ☐ Alternator brush springs weak or broken (Chapter 5A).
- ☐ Internal fault in alternator or voltage regulator (Chapter 5A).
- ☐ Disconnected or loose wiring in charging circuit (Chapter 5A).

Ignition (no-charge) warning light fails to come on

- ☐ Warning light bulb blown (Chapter 12).
- ☐ Broken, disconnected, or loose wiring in warning light circuit (Chapters 5A and 12).
- ☐ Alternator faulty (Chapter 5A).

Lights inoperative

- ☐ Bulb blown (Chapter 12).
- ☐ Corrosion of bulb or bulbholder contacts (Chapter 12).
- ☐ Blown fuse (Chapter 12).
- ☐ Faulty relay (Chapter 12).
- ☐ Broken, loose, or disconnected wiring (Chapter 12).
- ☐ Multiplex module fault (Chapter 12).
- ☐ Faulty switch (Chapter 12).

Instrument readings inaccurate or erratic

Gauges give no reading

- ☐ Faulty gauge sender unit (Chapters 3, 4A or 4B).
- ☐ Wiring open-circuit (Chapter 12).
- ☐ Faulty gauge (Chapter 12).
- ☐ Multiplex module fault (Chapter 12).

Gauges give continuous maximum reading

- ☐ Faulty gauge sender unit (Chapters 3, 4A or 4B).
- ☐ Wiring short-circuit (Chapter 12).
- ☐ Faulty gauge (Chapter 12).
- ☐ Multiplex module fault (Chapter 12).

Horn faults

Horn fails to operate

- ☐ Blown fuse (Chapter 12).
- ☐ Wiring damaged, connections loose or disconnected (Chapter 12).
- ☐ Faulty horn (Chapter 12).

Horn emits intermittent or unsatisfactory sound

- ☐ Wiring connections loose (Chapter 12).
- ☐ Horn mountings loose (Chapter 12).
- ☐ Faulty horn (Chapter 12).

Horn operates all the time

- ☐ Horn push either earthed or stuck down (Chapter 12).
- ☐ Horn wire to horn push earthed (Chapter 12).

Windscreen/tailgate wiper faults

Wipers fail to operate, or operate very slowly

- ☐ Wiper blades stuck to screen, or linkage seized (Chapter 12).
- ☐ Blown fuse (Chapter 12).
- ☐ Wiring damaged, connections loose or disconnected (Chapter 12).
- ☐ Faulty relay (Chapter 12).
- ☐ Faulty wiper motor (Chapter 12).
- ☐ Multiplex module fault (Chapter 12).

Wiper blades sweep over the wrong area of glass

- ☐ Wiper arms incorrectly-positioned on spindles (Chapter 12).
- ☐ Excessive wear of wiper linkage (Chapter 12).
- ☐ Wiper motor or linkage mountings loose or insecure (Chapter 12).

Wiper blades fail to clean the glass effectively

- ☐ Wiper blade rubbers worn or perished (Weekly checks).
- ☐ Wiper arm tension springs broken, or arm pivots seized (Chapter 12).
- ☐ Insufficient windscreen washer additive to adequately remove road film (Weekly checks).

Electrical system (continued)

Windscreen/tailgate washer faults

One or more washer jets inoperative

☐ Blocked washer jet (Weekly checks or Chapter 12).
☐ Disconnected, kinked or restricted fluid hose (Chapter 12).
☐ Insufficient fluid in washer reservoir (Weekly checks).

Washer pump fails to operate

☐ Broken or disconnected wiring or connections (Chapter 12).
☐ Blown fuse (Chapter 12).
☐ Faulty washer switch (Chapter 12).
☐ Faulty washer pump (Chapter 12).

Washer pump runs for some time before fluid is emitted from jets

☐ Faulty one-way valve in fluid supply hose (Chapter 12).

Electric window faults

Window glass will only move in one direction

☐ Faulty switch (Chapter 12).

Window glass slow to move

☐ Regulator seized or damaged, or lack of lubrication (Chapter 11).
☐ Door internal components or trim fouling regulator (Chapter 11).
☐ Faulty motor (Chapter 12).

Window glass fails to move

☐ Blown fuse (Chapter 12).
☐ Faulty relay (Chapter 12).
☐ Broken or disconnected wiring or connections (Chapter 12).
☐ Faulty motor (Chapter 12).

Central locking system faults

Complete system failure

☐ Blown fuse (Chapter 12).
☐ Faulty relay (Chapter 12).
☐ Broken or disconnected wiring or connections (Chapter 12).
☐ Multiplex module fault (Chapter 12).

Latch locks but will not unlock, or unlocks but will not lock

☐ Faulty lock (Chapter 11).

One lock motor fails to operate

☐ Broken or disconnected wiring or connections (Chapter 12).
☐ Faulty lock motor (Chapter 11).
☐ Fault in door latch (Chapter 11).

A

ABS (Anti-lock brake system) A system, usually electronically controlled, that senses incipient wheel lockup during braking and relieves hydraulic pressure at wheels that are about to skid.

Air bag An inflatable bag hidden in the steering wheel (driver's side) or the dash or glovebox (passenger side). In a head-on collision, the bags inflate, preventing the driver and front passenger from being thrown forward into the steering wheel or windscreen.

Air cleaner A metal or plastic housing, containing a filter element, which removes dust and dirt from the air being drawn into the engine.

Air filter element The actual filter in an air cleaner system, usually manufactured from pleated paper and requiring renewal at regular intervals.

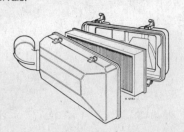

Air filter

Allen key A hexagonal wrench which fits into a recessed hexagonal hole.

Alligator clip A long-nosed spring-loaded metal clip with meshing teeth. Used to make temporary electrical connections.

Alternator A component in the electrical system which converts mechanical energy from a drivebelt into electrical energy to charge the battery and to operate the starting system, ignition system and electrical accessories.

Alternator (exploded view)

Ampere (amp) A unit of measurement for the flow of electric current. One amp is the amount of current produced by one volt acting through a resistance of one ohm.

Anaerobic sealer A substance used to prevent bolts and screws from loosening. Anaerobic means that it does not require oxygen for activation. The Loctite brand is widely used.

Antifreeze A substance (usually ethylene glycol) mixed with water, and added to a vehicle's cooling system, to prevent freezing of the coolant in winter. Antifreeze also contains chemicals to inhibit corrosion and the formation of rust and other deposits that would tend to clog the radiator and coolant passages and reduce cooling efficiency.

Anti-seize compound A coating that reduces the risk of seizing on fasteners that are subjected to high temperatures, such as exhaust manifold bolts and nuts.

Anti-seize compound

Asbestos A natural fibrous mineral with great heat resistance, commonly used in the composition of brake friction materials. Asbestos is a health hazard and the dust created by brake systems should never be inhaled or ingested.

Axle A shaft on which a wheel revolves, or which revolves with a wheel. Also, a solid beam that connects the two wheels at one end of the vehicle. An axle which also transmits power to the wheels is known as a live axle.

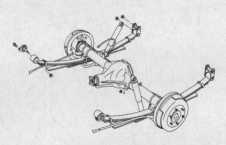

Axle assembly

Axleshaft A single rotating shaft, on either side of the differential, which delivers power from the final drive assembly to the drive wheels. Also called a driveshaft or a halfshaft.

B

Ball bearing An anti-friction bearing consisting of a hardened inner and outer race with hardened steel balls between two races.

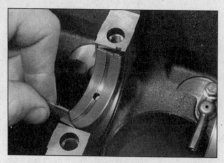

Bearing

Bearing The curved surface on a shaft or in a bore, or the part assembled into either, that permits relative motion between them with minimum wear and friction.

Big-end bearing The bearing in the end of the connecting rod that's attached to the crankshaft.

Bleed nipple A valve on a brake wheel cylinder, caliper or other hydraulic component that is opened to purge the hydraulic system of air. Also called a bleed screw.

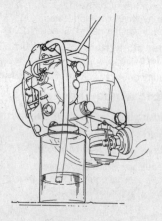

Brake bleeding

Brake bleeding Procedure for removing air from lines of a hydraulic brake system.

Brake disc The component of a disc brake that rotates with the wheels.

Brake drum The component of a drum brake that rotates with the wheels.

Brake linings The friction material which contacts the brake disc or drum to retard the vehicle's speed. The linings are bonded or riveted to the brake pads or shoes.

Brake pads The replaceable friction pads that pinch the brake disc when the brakes are applied. Brake pads consist of a friction material bonded or riveted to a rigid backing plate.

Brake shoe The crescent-shaped carrier to which the brake linings are mounted and which forces the lining against the rotating drum during braking.

Braking systems For more information on braking systems, consult the *Haynes Automotive Brake Manual*.

Breaker bar A long socket wrench handle providing greater leverage.

Bulkhead The insulated partition between the engine and the passenger compartment.

C

Caliper The non-rotating part of a disc-brake assembly that straddles the disc and carries the brake pads. The caliper also contains the hydraulic components that cause the pads to pinch the disc when the brakes are applied. A caliper is also a measuring tool that can be set to measure inside or outside dimensions of an object.

Camshaft A rotating shaft on which a series of cam lobes operate the valve mechanisms. The camshaft may be driven by gears, by sprockets and chain or by sprockets and a belt.

Canister A container in an evaporative emission control system; contains activated charcoal granules to trap vapours from the fuel system.

Canister

Carburettor A device which mixes fuel with air in the proper proportions to provide a desired power output from a spark ignition internal combustion engine.

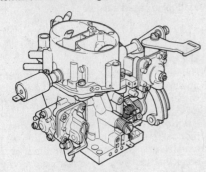

Carburettor

Castellated Resembling the parapets along the top of a castle wall. For example, a castellated balljoint stud nut.

Castellated nut

Castor In wheel alignment, the backward or forward tilt of the steering axis. Castor is positive when the steering axis is inclined rearward at the top.

Catalytic converter A silencer-like device in the exhaust system which converts certain pollutants in the exhaust gases into less harmful substances.

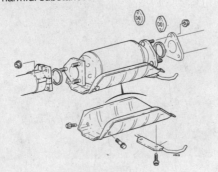

Catalytic converter

Circlip A ring-shaped clip used to prevent endwise movement of cylindrical parts and shafts. An internal circlip is installed in a groove in a housing; an external circlip fits into a groove on the outside of a cylindrical piece such as a shaft.

Clearance The amount of space between two parts. For example, between a piston and a cylinder, between a bearing and a journal, etc.

Coil spring A spiral of elastic steel found in various sizes throughout a vehicle, for example as a springing medium in the suspension and in the valve train.

Compression Reduction in volume, and increase in pressure and temperature, of a gas, caused by squeezing it into a smaller space.

Compression ratio The relationship between cylinder volume when the piston is at top dead centre and cylinder volume when the piston is at bottom dead centre.

Constant velocity (CV) joint A type of universal joint that cancels out vibrations caused by driving power being transmitted through an angle.

Core plug A disc or cup-shaped metal device inserted in a hole in a casting through which core was removed when the casting was formed. Also known as a freeze plug or expansion plug.

Crankcase The lower part of the engine block in which the crankshaft rotates.

Crankshaft The main rotating member, or shaft, running the length of the crankcase, with offset "throws" to which the connecting rods are attached.

Crankshaft assembly

Crocodile clip See Alligator clip

D

Diagnostic code Code numbers obtained by accessing the diagnostic mode of an engine management computer. This code can be used to determine the area in the system where a malfunction may be located.

Disc brake A brake design incorporating a rotating disc onto which brake pads are squeezed. The resulting friction converts the energy of a moving vehicle into heat.

Double-overhead cam (DOHC) An engine that uses two overhead camshafts, usually one for the intake valves and one for the exhaust valves.

Drivebelt(s) The belt(s) used to drive accessories such as the alternator, water pump, power steering pump, air conditioning compressor, etc. off the crankshaft pulley.

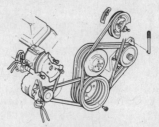

Accessory drivebelts

Driveshaft Any shaft used to transmit motion. Commonly used when referring to the axleshafts on a front wheel drive vehicle.

Driveshaft

Drum brake A type of brake using a drum-shaped metal cylinder attached to the inner surface of the wheel. When the brake pedal is pressed, curved brake shoes with friction linings press against the inside of the drum to slow or stop the vehicle.

Drum brake assembly

E

EGR valve A valve used to introduce exhaust gases into the intake air stream.

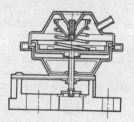

EGR valve

Electronic control unit (ECU) A computer which controls (for instance) ignition and fuel injection systems, or an anti-lock braking system. For more information refer to the *Haynes Automotive Electrical and Electronic Systems Manual.*

Electronic Fuel Injection (EFI) A computer controlled fuel system that distributes fuel through an injector located in each intake port of the engine.

Emergency brake A braking system, independent of the main hydraulic system, that can be used to slow or stop the vehicle if the primary brakes fail, or to hold the vehicle stationary even though the brake pedal isn't depressed. It usually consists of a hand lever that actuates either front or rear brakes mechanically through a series of cables and linkages. Also known as a handbrake or parking brake.

Endfloat The amount of lengthwise movement between two parts. As applied to a crankshaft, the distance that the crankshaft can move forward and back in the cylinder block.

Engine management system (EMS) A computer controlled system which manages the fuel injection and the ignition systems in an integrated fashion.

Exhaust manifold A part with several passages through which exhaust gases leave the engine combustion chambers and enter the exhaust pipe.

Exhaust manifold

F

Fan clutch A viscous (fluid) drive coupling device which permits variable engine fan speeds in relation to engine speeds.

Feeler blade A thin strip or blade of hardened steel, ground to an exact thickness, used to check or measure clearances between parts.

Feeler blade

Firing order The order in which the engine cylinders fire, or deliver their power strokes, beginning with the number one cylinder.

Flywheel A heavy spinning wheel in which energy is absorbed and stored by means of momentum. On cars, the flywheel is attached to the crankshaft to smooth out firing impulses.

Free play The amount of travel before any action takes place. The "looseness" in a linkage, or an assembly of parts, between the initial application of force and actual movement. For example, the distance the brake pedal moves before the pistons in the master cylinder are actuated.

Fuse An electrical device which protects a circuit against accidental overload. The typical fuse contains a soft piece of metal which is calibrated to melt at a predetermined current flow (expressed as amps) and break the circuit.

Fusible link A circuit protection device consisting of a conductor surrounded by heat-resistant insulation. The conductor is smaller than the wire it protects, so it acts as the weakest link in the circuit. Unlike a blown fuse, a failed fusible link must frequently be cut from the wire for replacement.

G

Gap The distance the spark must travel in jumping from the centre electrode to the side

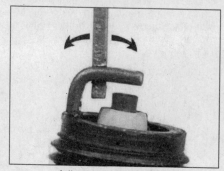

Adjusting spark plug gap

electrode in a spark plug. Also refers to the spacing between the points in a contact breaker assembly in a conventional points-type ignition, or to the distance between the reluctor or rotor and the pickup coil in an electronic ignition.

Gasket Any thin, soft material - usually cork, cardboard, asbestos or soft metal - installed between two metal surfaces to ensure a good seal. For instance, the cylinder head gasket seals the joint between the block and the cylinder head.

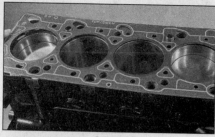

Gasket

Gauge An instrument panel display used to monitor engine conditions. A gauge with a movable pointer on a dial or a fixed scale is an analogue gauge. A gauge with a numerical readout is called a digital gauge.

H

Halfshaft A rotating shaft that transmits power from the final drive unit to a drive wheel, usually when referring to a live rear axle.

Harmonic balancer A device designed to reduce torsion or twisting vibration in the crankshaft. May be incorporated in the crankshaft pulley. Also known as a vibration damper.

Hone An abrasive tool for correcting small irregularities or differences in diameter in an engine cylinder, brake cylinder, etc.

Hydraulic tappet A tappet that utilises hydraulic pressure from the engine's lubrication system to maintain zero clearance (constant contact with both camshaft and valve stem). Automatically adjusts to variation in valve stem length. Hydraulic tappets also reduce valve noise.

I

Ignition timing The moment at which the spark plug fires, usually expressed in the number of crankshaft degrees before the piston reaches the top of its stroke.

Inlet manifold A tube or housing with passages through which flows the air-fuel mixture (carburettor vehicles and vehicles with throttle body injection) or air only (port fuel-injected vehicles) to the port openings in the cylinder head.

J

Jump start Starting the engine of a vehicle with a discharged or weak battery by attaching jump leads from the weak battery to a charged or helper battery.

L

Load Sensing Proportioning Valve (LSPV) A brake hydraulic system control valve that works like a proportioning valve, but also takes into consideration the amount of weight carried by the rear axle.

Locknut A nut used to lock an adjustment nut, or other threaded component, in place. For example, a locknut is employed to keep the adjusting nut on the rocker arm in position.

Lockwasher A form of washer designed to prevent an attaching nut from working loose.

M

MacPherson strut A type of front suspension system devised by Earle MacPherson at Ford of England. In its original form, a simple lateral link with the anti-roll bar creates the lower control arm. A long strut - an integral coil spring and shock absorber - is mounted between the body and the steering knuckle. Many modern so-called MacPherson strut systems use a conventional lower A-arm and don't rely on the anti-roll bar for location.

Multimeter An electrical test instrument with the capability to measure voltage, current and resistance.

N

NOx Oxides of Nitrogen. A common toxic pollutant emitted by petrol and diesel engines at higher temperatures.

O

Ohm The unit of electrical resistance. One volt applied to a resistance of one ohm will produce a current of one amp.

Ohmmeter An instrument for measuring electrical resistance.

O-ring A type of sealing ring made of a special rubber-like material; in use, the O-ring is compressed into a groove to provide the sealing action.

O-ring

Overhead cam (ohc) engine An engine with the camshaft(s) located on top of the cylinder head(s).

Overhead valve (ohv) engine An engine with the valves located in the cylinder head, but with the camshaft located in the engine block.

Oxygen sensor A device installed in the engine exhaust manifold, which senses the oxygen content in the exhaust and converts this information into an electric current. Also called a Lambda sensor.

P

Phillips screw A type of screw head having a cross instead of a slot for a corresponding type of screwdriver.

Plastigage A thin strip of plastic thread, available in different sizes, used for measuring clearances. For example, a strip of Plastigage is laid across a bearing journal. The parts are assembled and dismantled; the width of the crushed strip indicates the clearance between journal and bearing.

Plastigage

Propeller shaft The long hollow tube with universal joints at both ends that carries power from the transmission to the differential on front-engined rear wheel drive vehicles.

Proportioning valve A hydraulic control valve which limits the amount of pressure to the rear brakes during panic stops to prevent wheel lock-up.

R

Rack-and-pinion steering A steering system with a pinion gear on the end of the steering shaft that mates with a rack (think of a geared wheel opened up and laid flat). When the steering wheel is turned, the pinion turns, moving the rack to the left or right. This movement is transmitted through the track rods to the steering arms at the wheels.

Radiator A liquid-to-air heat transfer device designed to reduce the temperature of the coolant in an internal combustion engine cooling system.

Refrigerant Any substance used as a heat transfer agent in an air-conditioning system. R-12 has been the principle refrigerant for many years; recently, however, manufacturers have begun using R-134a, a non-CFC substance that is considered less harmful to the ozone in the upper atmosphere.

Rocker arm A lever arm that rocks on a shaft or pivots on a stud. In an overhead valve engine, the rocker arm converts the upward movement of the pushrod into a downward movement to open a valve.

Rotor In a distributor, the rotating device inside the cap that connects the centre electrode and the outer terminals as it turns, distributing the high voltage from the coil secondary winding to the proper spark plug. Also, that part of an alternator which rotates inside the stator. Also, the rotating assembly of a turbocharger, including the compressor wheel, shaft and turbine wheel.

Runout The amount of wobble (in-and-out movement) of a gear or wheel as it's rotated. The amount a shaft rotates "out-of-true." The out-of-round condition of a rotating part.

S

Sealant A liquid or paste used to prevent leakage at a joint. Sometimes used in conjunction with a gasket.

Sealed beam lamp An older headlight design which integrates the reflector, lens and filaments into a hermetically-sealed one-piece unit. When a filament burns out or the lens cracks, the entire unit is simply replaced.

Serpentine drivebelt A single, long, wide accessory drivebelt that's used on some newer vehicles to drive all the accessories, instead of a series of smaller, shorter belts. Serpentine drivebelts are usually tensioned by an automatic tensioner.

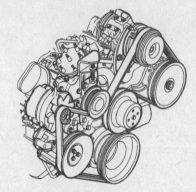

Serpentine drivebelt

Shim Thin spacer, commonly used to adjust the clearance or relative positions between two parts. For example, shims inserted into or under bucket tappets control valve clearances. Clearance is adjusted by changing the thickness of the shim.

Slide hammer A special puller that screws into or hooks onto a component such as a shaft or bearing; a heavy sliding handle on the shaft bottoms against the end of the shaft to knock the component free.

Sprocket A tooth or projection on the periphery of a wheel, shaped to engage with a chain or drivebelt. Commonly used to refer to the sprocket wheel itself.

Starter inhibitor switch On vehicles with an automatic transmission, a switch that prevents starting if the vehicle is not in Neutral or Park.

Strut See MacPherson strut.

T

Tappet A cylindrical component which transmits motion from the cam to the valve stem, either directly or via a pushrod and rocker arm. Also called a cam follower.

Thermostat A heat-controlled valve that regulates the flow of coolant between the cylinder block and the radiator, so maintaining optimum engine operating temperature. A thermostat is also used in some air cleaners in which the temperature is regulated.

Thrust bearing The bearing in the clutch assembly that is moved in to the release levers by clutch pedal action to disengage the clutch. Also referred to as a release bearing.

Timing belt A toothed belt which drives the camshaft. Serious engine damage may result if it breaks in service.

Timing chain A chain which drives the camshaft.

Toe-in The amount the front wheels are closer together at the front than at the rear. On rear wheel drive vehicles, a slight amount of toe-in is usually specified to keep the front wheels running parallel on the road by offsetting other forces that tend to spread the wheels apart.

Toe-out The amount the front wheels are closer together at the rear than at the front. On front wheel drive vehicles, a slight amount of toe-out is usually specified.

Tools For full information on choosing and using tools, refer to the *Haynes Automotive Tools Manual*.

Tracer A stripe of a second colour applied to a wire insulator to distinguish that wire from another one with the same colour insulator.

Tune-up A process of accurate and careful adjustments and parts replacement to obtain the best possible engine performance.

Turbocharger A centrifugal device, driven by exhaust gases, that pressurises the intake air. Normally used to increase the power output from a given engine displacement, but can also be used primarily to reduce exhaust emissions (as on VW's "Umwelt" Diesel engine).

U

Universal joint or U-joint A double-pivoted connection for transmitting power from a driving to a driven shaft through an angle. A U-joint consists of two Y-shaped yokes and a cross-shaped member called the spider.

V

Valve A device through which the flow of liquid, gas, vacuum, or loose material in bulk may be started, stopped, or regulated by a movable part that opens, shuts, or partially obstructs one or more ports or passageways. A valve is also the movable part of such a device.

Valve clearance The clearance between the valve tip (the end of the valve stem) and the rocker arm or tappet. The valve clearance is measured when the valve is closed.

Vernier caliper A precision measuring instrument that measures inside and outside dimensions. Not quite as accurate as a micrometer, but more convenient.

Viscosity The thickness of a liquid or its resistance to flow.

Volt A unit for expressing electrical "pressure" in a circuit. One volt that will produce a current of one ampere through a resistance of one ohm.

W

Welding Various processes used to join metal items by heating the areas to be joined to a molten state and fusing them together. For more information refer to the *Haynes Automotive Welding Manual*.

Wiring diagram A drawing portraying the components and wires in a vehicle's electrical system, using standardised symbols. For more information refer to the *Haynes Automotive Electrical and Electronic Systems Manual*.

Note: *References throughout this index are in the form* **"Chapter number"** • **"Page number"**. *So, for example, 2C•15 refers to page 15 of Chapter 2C.*

Note: *References throughout this index are in the form* "**Chapter number**" • "**Page number**". *So, for example, 2C•15 refers to page 15 of Chapter 2C.*

Note: *References throughout this index are in the form* "**Chapter number**" • "**Page number**". *So, for example, 2C•15 refers to page 15 of Chapter 2C.*

Note: *References throughout this index are in the form* **"Chapter number"** • **"Page number"***. So, for example, 2C•15 refers to page 15 of Chapter 2C.*

Note: *References throughout this index are in the form* "**Chapter number**" • "**Page number**". *So, for example, 2C•15 refers to page 15 of Chapter 2C.*

Haynes Manuals – The Complete UK Car List

Title	Book No.
ALFA ROMEO Alfasud/Sprint (74 - 88) up to F *	0292
Alfa Romeo Alfetta (73 – 87) up to E *	0531
AUDI 80, 90 & Coupe Petrol (79 – Nov 88) up to F	0605
Audi 80, 90 & Coupe Petrol (Oct 86 – 90) D to H	1491
Audi 100 & A6 Petrol & Diesel (May 91 – May 97) H to P	3504
Audi A3 Petrol & Diesel (96 – May 03) P to 03	4253
Audi A3 Petrol & Diesel (June 03 – Mar 08) 03 to 08	4884
Audi A4 Petrol & Diesel (95 – 00) M to X	3575
Audi A4 Petrol & Diesel (01 – 04) X to 54	4609
Audi A4 Petrol & Diesel (Jan 05 – Feb 08) 54 to 57	4885
AUSTIN A35 & A40 (56 – 67) up to F *	0118
Mini (59 – 69) up to H *	0527
Mini (69 – 01) up to X	0646
Austin Healey 100/6 & 3000 (56 – 68) up to G *	0049
BEDFORD/Vauxhall Rascal & Suzuki Supercarry (86 – Oct 94) C to M	3015
BMW 1-Series 4-cyl Petrol & Diesel (04 – Aug 11) 54 to 11	4918
BMW 316, 320 & 320i (4-cyl)(75 – Feb 83) up to Y *	0276
BMW 3- & 5- Series Petrol (81 – 91) up to J	1948
BMW 3-Series Petrol (Apr 91 – 99) H to V	3210
BMW 3-Series Petrol (Sept 98 – 06) S to 56	4067
BMW 3-Series Petrol & Diesel (05 – Sept 08) 54 to 58	4782
BMW 5-Series 6-cyl Petrol (April 96 – Aug 03) N to 03	4151
BMW 5-Series Diesel (Sept 03 – 10) 53 to 10	4901
BMW 1500, 1502, 1600, 1602, 2000 & 2002 (59 – 77) up to S *	0240
CHRYSLER PT Cruiser Petrol (00-09) W to 09	4058
CITROEN 2CV, Ami & Dyane (67 – 90) up to H	0196
Citroen AX Petrol & Diesel (87- 97) D to P	3014
Citroen Berlingo & Peugeot Partner Petrol & Diesel (96 – 10) P to 60	4281
Citroen C1 Petrol (05 – 11) 05 to 11	4922
Citroen C2 Petrol & Diesel (03 – 10) 53 to 60	5635
Citroen C3 Petrol & Diesel (02 – 09) 51 to 59	4890
Citroen C4 Petrol & Diesel (04 – 10) 54 to 60	5576
Citroen C5 Petrol & Diesel (01 – 08) Y to 08	4745
Citroen C15 Van Petrol & Diesel (89 – Oct 98) F to S	3509
Citroen CX Petrol (75 – 88) up to F	0528
Citroen Saxo Petrol & Diesel (96 – 04) N to 54	3506
Citroen Xantia Petrol & Diesel (93 – 01) K to Y	3082
Citroen XM Petrol & Diesel (89 – 00) G to X	3451
Citroen Xsara Petrol & Diesel (97 – Sept 00) R to W	3751
Citroen Xsara Picasso Petrol & Diesel (00 – 02) W to 52	3944
Citroen Xsara Picasso (Mar 04 – 08) 04 to 58	4784
Citroen ZX Diesel (91 – 98) J to S	1922
Citroen ZX Petrol (91 – 98) H to S	1881
FIAT 126 (73 – 87) up to E *	0305
Fiat 500 (57 – 73) up to M *	0090
Fiat 500 & Panda (04 – 12) 53 to 61	5558
Fiat Bravo & Brava Petrol (95 – 00) N to W	3572
Fiat Cinquecento (93 – 98) K to R	3501
Fiat Grande Punto, Punto Evo & Punto Petrol (06 – 15) 55 to 15	5956
Fiat Panda (81 – 95) up to M	0793
Fiat Punto Petrol & Diesel (94 – Oct 99) L to V	3251
Fiat Punto Petrol (Oct 99 – July 03) V to 03	4066
Fiat Punto Petrol (03 – 07) 03 to 07	4746

Title	Book No.
Fiat Punto Petrol (Oct 99 – 07) V to 07	5634
Fiat X1/9 (74 – 89) up to G *	0273
FORD Anglia (59 – 68) up to G *	0001
Ford Capri II (& III) 1.6 & 2.0 (74 – 87) up to E *	0283
Ford Capri II (& III) 2.8 & 3.0 V6 (74 – 87) up to E	1309
Ford C-Max Petrol & Diesel (03 – 10) 53 to 60	4900
Ford Escort Mk I 1100 & 1300 (68 – 74) up to N *	0171
Ford Escort Mk I Mexico, RS 1600 & RS 2000 (70 – 74) up to N *	0139
Ford Escort Mk II Mexico, RS 1800 & RS 2000 (75 – 80) up to W *	0735
Ford Escort (75 – Aug 80) up to V *	0280
Ford Escort Petrol (Sept 80 – Sept 90) up to H	0686
Ford Escort & Orion Petrol (Sept 90 – 00) H to X	1737
Ford Escort & Orion Diesel (Sept 90 – 00) H to X	4081
Ford Fiesta Petrol (Feb 89 – Oct 95) F to N	1595
Ford Fiesta Petrol & Diesel (Oct 95 – Mar 02) N to 02	3397
Ford Fiesta Petrol & Diesel (Apr 02 – 08) 02 to 58	4170
Ford Fiesta Petrol & Diesel (08 – 11) 58 to 11	4907
Ford Focus Petrol & Diesel (98 – 01) S to Y	3759
Ford Focus Petrol & Diesel (Oct 01 – 05) 51 to 05	4167
Ford Focus Petrol (05 – 11) 54 to 61	4785
Ford Focus Diesel (05 – 11) 54 to 61	4807
Ford Focus Petrol & Diesel (11 – 14) 60 to 14	5632
Ford Fusion Petrol & Diesel (02 – 11) 02 to 61	5566
Ford Galaxy Petrol & Diesel (95 – Aug 00) M to W	3984
Ford Galaxy Petrol & Diesel (00 – 06) X to 06	5556
Ford Granada Petrol (Sept 77 – Feb 85) up to B *	0481
Ford Ka (96 – 08) P to 58	5567
Ford Ka Petrol (09 – 14) 58 to 14	5637
Ford Mondeo Petrol (93 – Sept 00) K to X	1923
Ford Mondeo Petrol & Diesel (Oct 00 – Jul 03) X to 03	3990
Ford Mondeo Petrol & Diesel (July 03 – 07) 03 to 56	4619
Ford Mondeo Petrol & Diesel (Apr 07 – 12) 07 to 61	5548
Ford Mondeo Diesel (93 – Sept 00) L to X	3465
Ford Transit Connect Diesel (02 – 11) 02 to 11	4903
Ford Transit Diesel (Feb 86 – 99) C to T	3019
Ford Transit Diesel (00 – Oct 06) X to 56	4775
Ford Transit Diesel (Nov 06 – 13) 56 to 63	5629
Ford 1.6 & 1.8 litre Diesel Engine (84 – 96) A to N	1172
HILLMAN Imp (63 – 76) up to R *	0022
HONDA Civic (Feb 84 – Oct 87) A to E	1226
Honda Civic (Nov 91 – 96) J to N	3199
Honda Civic Petrol (Mar 95 – 00) M to X	4050
Honda Civic Petrol & Diesel (01 – 05) X to 55	4611
Honda CR-V Petrol & Diesel (02 – 06) 51 to 56	4747
Honda Jazz (02 to 08) 51 to 58	4735
JAGUAR E-Type (61 – 72) up to L *	0140
Jaguar Mk I & II, 240 & 340 (55 – 69) up to H *	0098
Jaguar XJ6, XJ & Sovereign, Daimler Sovereign (68 – Oct 86) up to D	0242
Jaguar XJ6 & Sovereign (Oct 86 – Sept 94) D to M	3261
Jaguar XJ12, XJS & Sovereign, Daimler Double Six (72 – 88) up to F	0478
Jaguar X Type Petrol & Diesel (01 – 10) V to 60	5631
JEEP Cherokee Petrol (93 – 96) K to N	1943
LAND ROVER 90, 110 & Defender Diesel (83 – 07) up to 56	3017

Title	Book No.
Land Rover Discovery Petrol & Diesel (89 – 98) G to S	3016
Land Rover Discovery Diesel (Nov 98 – Jul 04) S to 04	4606
Land Rover Discovery Diesel (Aug 04 – Apr 09) 04 to 09	5562
Land Rover Freelander Petrol & Diesel (97 – Sept 03) R to 53	3929
Land Rover Freelander (97 – Oct 06) R to 56	5571
Land Rover Freelander Diesel (Nov 06 – 14) 56 to 64	5636
Land Rover Series II, IIA & III 4-cyl Petrol (58 – 85) up to C	0314
Land Rover Series II, IIA & III Petrol & Diesel (58 – 85) up to C	5568
MAZDA 323 (Mar 81 – Oct 89) up to G	1608
Mazda 323 (Oct 89 – 98) G to R	3455
Mazda B1600, B1800 & B2000 Pick-up Petrol (72 – 88) up to F	0267
Mazda MX-5 (89 – 05) G to 05	5565
Mazda RX-7 (79 – 85) up to C *	0460
MERCEDES-BENZ 190, 190E & 190D Petrol & Diesel (83 – 93) A to L	3450
Mercedes-Benz 200D, 240D, 240TD, 300D & 300TD 123 Series Diesel (Oct 76 – 85) up to C	1114
Mercedes-Benz 250 & 280 (68 – 72) up to L *	0346
Mercedes-Benz 250 & 280 123 Series Petrol (Oct 76 – 84) up to B *	0677
Mercedes-Benz 124 Series Petrol & Diesel (85 – Aug 93) C to K	3253
Mercedes-Benz A-Class Petrol & Diesel (98 – 04) S to 54	4748
Mercedes-Benz C-Class Petrol & Diesel (93 – Aug 00) L to W	3511
Mercedes-Benz C-Class (00 – 07) X to 07	4780
Mercedes-Benz E-Class Diesel (Jun 02 – Feb 10) 02 to 59	5710
Mercedes-Benz Sprinter Diesel (95 – Apr 06) M to 06	4902
MGA (55 – 62)	0475
MGB (62 – 80) up to W	0111
MGB 1962 to 1980 (special edition) *	4894
MG Midget & Austin-Healey Sprite (58 – 80) up to W *	0265
MINI Petrol (July 01 – 06) Y to 56	4273
MINI Petrol & Diesel (Nov 06 – 13) 56 to 13	4904
MITSUBISHI Shogun & L200 Pick-ups Petrol (83 – 94) up to M	1944
MORRIS Minor 1000 (56 – 71) up to K	0024
NISSAN Almera Petrol (95 – Feb 00) N to V	4053
Nissan Almera & Tino Petrol (Feb 00 – 07) V to 56	4612
Nissan Micra (83 – Jan 93) up to K	0931
Nissan Micra (93 – 02) K to 52	3254
Nissan Micra Petrol (03 – Oct 10) 52 to 60	4734
Nissan Primera Petrol (90 - Aug 99) H to T	1851
Nissan Qashqai Petrol & Diesel (07 – 12) 56 to 62	5610
OPEL Ascona & Manta (B-Series) (Sept 75 – 88) up to F *	0316
Opel Ascona Petrol (81 – 88)	3215
Opel Ascona Petrol (Oct 91 – Feb 98)	3156
Opel Corsa Petrol (83 – Mar 93)	3160
Opel Corsa Petrol (Mar 93 – 97)	3159
Opel Kadett Petrol (Oct 84 – Oct 91)	3196
Opel Omega & Senator Petrol (Nov 86 – 94)	3157
Opel Vectra Petrol (Oct 88 – Oct 95)	3158
PEUGEOT 106 Petrol & Diesel (91 – 04) J to 53)	1882
Peugeot 107 Petrol (05 – 11) 05 to 11	4923
Peugeot 205 Petrol (83 – 97) A to P	0932

* Classic reprint

Title	Book No.
Peugeot 206 Petrol & Diesel (98 – 01) S to X	3757
Peugeot 206 Petrol & Diesel (02 – 09) 51 to 59	4613
Peugeot 207 Petrol & Diesel (06 – July 09) 06 to 09	4787
Peugeot 306 Petrol & Diesel (93 – 02) K to 02	3073
Peugeot 307 Petrol & Diesel (01 – 08) Y to 58	4147
Peugeot 308 Petrol & Diesel (07 – 12) 07 to 12	5561
Peugeot 405 Diesel (88 – 97) E to P	3198
Peugeot 406 Petrol & Diesel (96 – Mar 99) N to T	3394
Peugeot 406 Petrol & Diesel (Mar 99 – 02) T to 52	3982
Peugeot 407 Diesel (04 -11) 53 to 11	5550
PORSCHE 911 (65 – 85) up to C	0264
Porsche 924 & 924 Turbo (76 – 85) up to C	0397
RANGE ROVER V8 Petrol (70 – Oct 92) up to K	0606
RELIANT Robin & Kitten (73 – 83) up to A *	0436
RENAULT 4 (61 – 86) up to D *	0072
Renault 5 Petrol (Feb 85 – 96) B to N	1219
Renault 19 Petrol (89 – 96) F to N	1646
Renault Clio Petrol (91 – May 98) H to R	1853
Renault Clio Petrol & Diesel (May 98 – May 01) R to Y	3906
Renault Clio Petrol & Diesel (June 01 – 05) Y to 55	4168
Renault Clio Petrol & Diesel (Oct 05 – May 09) 55 to 09	4788
Renault Espace Petrol & Diesel (85 – 96) C to N	3197
Renault Laguna Petrol & Diesel (94 – 00) L to W	3252
Renault Laguna Petrol & Diesel (Feb 01 – May 07) X to 07	4283
Renault Megane & Scenic Petrol & Diesel (96 – 99) N to T	3395
Renault Megane & Scenic Petrol & Diesel (Apr 99 – 02) T to 52	3916
Renault Megane Petrol & Diesel (Oct 02 – 08) 52 to 58	4284
Renault Megane Petrol & Diesel (Oct 08 – 14) 58 to 64	5955
Renault Scenic Petrol & Diesel (Sept 03 – 06) 53 to 06	4297
Renault Trafic Diesel (01 – 11) Y to 11	5551
ROVER 216 & 416 Petrol (89 – 96) G to N	1830
Rover 211, 214, 216, 218 & 220 Petrol & Diesel (Dec 95 – 99) N to V	3399
Rover 25 & MG ZR Petrol & Diesel (Oct 99 – 06) V to 06	4145
Rover 414, 416 & 420 Petrol & Diesel (May 95 – 99) M to V	3453
Rover 45 / MG ZS Petrol & Diesel (99 – 05) V to 55	4384
Rover 618, 620 & 623 Petrol (93 – 97) K to P	3257
Rover 75 / MG ZT Petrol & Diesel (99 – 06) S to 06	4292
Rover 820, 825 & 827 Petrol (86 – 95) D to N	1380
Rover 3500 (76 – 87) up to E *	0365
SAAB 95 & 96 (66 – 76) up to R *	0198
Saab 90, 99 & 900 (79 – Oct 93) up to L	0765
Saab 900 (Oct 93 – 98) L to R	3512
Saab 9000 4-cyl (85 – 98) C to S	1686
Saab 9-3 Petrol & Diesel (98 – Aug 02) R to 02	4614
Saab 9-3 Petrol & Diesel (92 – 07) 52 to 57	4749
Saab 9-3 Petrol & Diesel (07-on) 57 on	5569
Saab 9-5 4-cyl Petrol (97 – 05) R to 55	4156
Saab 9-5 (Sep 05 – Jun 10) 55 to 10	4891
SEAT Ibiza & Cordoba Petrol & Diesel (Oct 93 – Oct 99) L to V	3571
Seat Ibiza & Malaga Petrol (85 – 92) B to K	1609
Seat Ibiza Petrol & Diesel (May 02 – Apr 08) 02 to 08	4889
SKODA Fabia Petrol & Diesel (00 – 06) W to 06	4376

Title	Book No.
Skoda Felicia Petrol & Diesel (95 – 01) M to X	3505
Skoda Octavia Petrol (98 – April 04) R to 04	4285
Skoda Octavia Diesel (May 04 – 12) 04 to 61	5549
SUBARU 1600 & 1800 (Nov 79 – 90) up to H *	0995
SUNBEAM Alpine, Rapier & H120 (68 – 74) up to N *	0051
SUZUKI SJ Series, Samurai & Vitara 4-cyl Petrol (82 – 97) up to P	1942
Suzuki Supercarry & Bedford/Vauxhall Rascal (86 – Oct 94) C to M	3015
TOYOTA Avensis Petrol (98 – Jan 03) R to 52	4264
Toyota Aygo Petrol (05 – 11) 05 to 11	4921
Toyota Carina E Petrol (May 92 – 97) J to P	3256
Toyota Corolla (Sept 83 – Sept 87) A to E	1024
Toyota Corolla (Sept 87 – Aug 92) E to K	1683
Toyota Corolla Petrol (Aug 92 – 97) K to P	3259
Toyota Corolla Petrol (July 97 0 Feb 02) P to 51	4286
Toyota Corolla Petrol & Diesel (02 – Jan 07) 51 to 56	4791
Toyota Hi-Ace & Hi-Lux Petrol (69 – Oct 83) up to A	0304
Toyota RAV4 Petrol & Diesel (94 – 06) L to 55	4750
Toyota Yaris Petrol (99 – 05) T to 05	4265
TRIUMPH GT6 & Vitesse (62 0 74) up to N *	0112
Triumph Herald (59 – 71) up to K *	0010
Triumph Spitfire (62 – 81) up to X	0113
Triumph Stag (70 – 78) up to T *	0441
Triumph TR2, TR3, TR3A, TR4 & TR4A (52 – 67) up to F *	0028
Triumph TR5 & TR6 (67 – 75) up to P *	0031
Triumph TR7 (75 – 82) up to Y *	0322
VAUXHALL Astra Petrol (Oct 91 – Feb 98) J to R	1832
Vauxhall/Opel Astra & Zafira Petrol (Feb 98 – Apr 04) R to 04	3758
Vauxhall/Opel Astra & Zafira Diesel (Feb 98 – Apr 04) R to 04	3797
Vauxhall/Opel Astra Petrol (04 – 08)	4732
Vauxhall/Opel Astra Diesel (04 – 08)	4733
Vauxhall/Opel Astra Petrol & Diesel (Dec 09 – 13) 59 to 13	5578
Vauxhall/Opel Calibra (90 – 98) G to S	3502
Vauxhall Cavalier Petrol (Oct 88 0 95) F to N	1570
Vauxhall/Opel Corsa Diesel (Mar 93 – Oct 00) K to X	4087
Vauxhall Corsa Petrol (Mar 93 – 97) K to R	1985
Vauxhall/Opel Corsa Petrol (Apr 97 – Oct 00) P to X	3921
Vauxhall/Opel Corsa Petrol & Diesel (Oct 03 – Aug 06) 53 to 06	4617
Vauxhall/Opel Corsa Petrol & Diesel (Sept 06 – 10) 56 to 10	4886
Vauxhall/Opel Corsa Petrol & Diesel (00 – Aug 06) X to 06	5577
Vauxhall/Opel Frontera Petrol & Diesel (91 – Sept 98) J to S	3454
Vauxhall/Opel Insignia Petrol & Diesel (08 – 12) 08 to 61	5563
Vauxhall/Opel Meriva Petrol & Diesel (03 – May 10) 03 to 10	4893
Vauxhall/Opel Omega Petrol (94 – 99) L to T	3510
Vauxhall/Opel Vectra Petrol & Diesel (95 – Feb 99) N to S	3396
Vauxhall/Opel Vectra Petrol & Diesel (Mar 99 – May 02) T to 02	3930
Vauxhall/Opel Vectra Petrol & Diesel (June 02 – Sept 05) 02 to 55	4618

Title	Book No.
Vauxhall/Opel Vectra Petrol & Diesel (Oct 05 – Oct 08) 55 to 58	4887
Vauxhall/Opel Vivaro Diesel (01 – 11) Y to 11	5552
Vauxhall/Opel Zafira Petrol & Diesel (05 -09) 05 to 09	4792
Vauxhall/Opel 1.5, 1.6 & 1.7 litre Diesel Engine (82 – 96) up to N	1222
VW Beetle 1200 (54 – 77) up to S	0036
VW Beetle 1300 & 1500 (65 – 75) up to P	0039
VW 1302 & 1302S (70 – 72) up to L *	0110
VW Beetle 1303, 1303S & GT (72 – 75) up to P	0159
VW Beetle Petrol & Diesel (Apr 99 – 07) T to 57	3798
VW Golf & Jetta Mk 1 Petrol 1.1 & 1.3 (74 – 84) up to A	0716
VW Golf, Jetta & Scirocco Mk 1 Petrol 1.5, 1.6 & 1.8 (74 – 84) up to A	0726
VW Golf & Jetta Mk 1 Diesel (78 – 84) up to A	0451
VW Golf & Jetta Mk 2 Petrol (Mar 84 – Feb 92) A to J	1081
VW Golf & Vento Petrol & Diesel (Feb 92 – Mar 98) J to R	3097
VW Golf & Bora Petrol & Diesel (Apr 98 – 00) R to X	3727
VW Golf & Bora 4-cyl Petrol & Diesel (01 – 03) X to 53	4169
VW Golf & Jetta Petrol & Diesel (04 – 09) 53 to 09	4610
VW Golf Petrol & Diesel (09 – 12) 58 to 62	5633
VW LT Petrol Vans & Light Trucks (76 – 87) up to E	0637
VW Passat 4-cyl Petrol & Diesel (May 88 – 96) E to P	3498
VW Passat 4-cyl Petrol & Diesel (Dec 96 – Nov 00) P to X	3917
VW Passat Petrol & Diesel (Dec 00 – May 05) X to 05	4279
VW Passat Diesel (June 05 – 10) 05 to 60	4888
VW Polo Petrol (Nov 90 – Aug 94) H to L	3245
VW Polo Hatchback Petrol & Diesel (94 – 99) M to S	3500
VW Polo Hatchback Petrol (00 – Jan 02) V to 51	4150
VW Polo Petrol & Diesel (02 – Sep 09) 51 to 59	4608
VW Polo Petrol & Diesel (Oct 09 – Jul 14 (59 to 14)	5638
VW Transporter 1600 (68 – 79) up to V	0082
VW Transporter 1700, 1800 & 2000 (72 – 79) up to V *	0226
VW Transporter (air cooled) Petrol (79 – 82) up to Y *	0638
VW Transporter (water cooled) Petrol (82 – 90) up to H	3452
VW T4 Transporter Diesel (90 – 03) H to 03	5711
VW T5 Transporter Diesel (July 03 – 14) 03 to 64	5743
VW Type 3 (63 – 73) up to M *	0084
VOLVO 120 & 130 Series (& P1800) (61 – 73) up to M *	0203
Volvo 142, 144 & 145 (66 – 74) up to N *	0129
Volvo 240 Series Petrol (74 – 93) up to K	0270
Volvo 440, 460 & 480 Petrol (87 – 97) D to P	1691
Volvo 740 & 760 Petrol (82 – 91) up to J	1258
Volvo 850 Petrol (92 – 96) J to P	3260
Volvo 940 Petrol (90 – 98) H to R	3249
Volvo S40 & V40 Petrol (96 – Mar 04) N to 04	3569
Volvo S40 & V50 Petrol & Diesel (Mar 04 – Jun 07) 04 to 07	4731
Volvo S40 & V50 Diesel (July 07 - 13) 07 to 13	5684
Volvo S60 Petrol & Diesel (01 – 08) X to 09	4793
Volvo S70, V70 & C70 Petrol (96 – 99) P to V	3573
Volvo V70 / S80 Petrol & Diesel (98 – 07) S to 07	4263
Volvo V70 Diesel (June 07 – 12) 07 to 61	5557
Volvo XC60 / 90 Diesel (03 – 12) 52 to 62	5630

* Classic reprint

Preserving Our Motoring Heritage

< The Model J Duesenberg Derham Tourster. Only eight of these magnificent cars were ever built – this is the only example to be found outside the United States of America

Almost every car you've ever loved, loathed or desired is gathered under one roof at the Haynes Motor Museum. Over 300 immaculately presented cars and motorbikes represent every aspect of our motoring heritage, from elegant reminders of bygone days, such as the superb Model J Duesenberg to curiosities like the bug-eyed BMW Isetta. There are also many old friends and flames. Perhaps you remember the 1959 Ford Popular that you did your courting in? The magnificent 'Red Collection' is a spectacle of classic sports cars including AC, Alfa Romeo, Austin Healey, Ferrari, Lamborghini, Maserati, MG, Riley, Porsche and Triumph.

A Perfect Day Out

Each and every vehicle at the Haynes Motor Museum has played its part in the history and culture of Motoring. Today, they make a wonderful spectacle and a great day out for all the family. Bring the kids, bring Mum and Dad, but above all bring your camera to capture those golden memories for ever. You will also find an impressive array of motoring memorabilia, a comfortable 70 seat video cinema and one of the most extensive transport book shops in Britain. The Pit Stop Cafe serves everything from a cup of tea to wholesome, home-made meals or, if you prefer, you can enjoy the large picnic area nestled in the beautiful rural surroundings of Somerset.

> John Haynes O.B.E., Founder and Chairman of the museum at the wheel of a Haynes Light 12.

< Graham Hill's Lola Cosworth Formula 1 car next to a 1934 Riley Sports.

The Museum is situated on the A359 Yeovil to Frome road at Sparkford, just off the A303 in Somerset. It is about 40 miles south of Bristol, and 25 minutes drive from the M5 intersection at Taunton.
Open 9.30am - 5.30pm (10.00am - 4.00pm Winter) 7 days a week, *except Christmas Day, Boxing Day and New Years Day*
Special rates available for schools, coach parties and outings Charitable Trust No. 292048